D0943975

ECSTASIES

ECSTASIES

DECIPHERING THE WITCHES' SABBATH

CARLO GINZBURG

TRANSLATED BY RAYMOND ROSENTHAL

PANTHEON BOOKS　NEW YORK

All rights reserved under International and Pan-American Copyright Conventions. Published in the United States by Pantheon Books, a division of Random House, Inc., New York. Originally published in Italy as *Storia Notturna* by Giulio Einaudi Editore, Turin, in 1989. Copyright © 1989 by Giulio Einaudi Editore. This translation also published in England by Hutchinson Radius, London.

LIBRARY OF CONGRESS CATALOGING-IN-PUBLICATION DATA

Ginzburg, Carlo.
[Storia Notturna. English]
Ecstasies: deciphering the Witches' Sabbath/Carlo Ginzburg.
p. cm.
Translation of: Storia notturna.
Includes bibliographical references and index.
ISBN 0-394-58163-6
1. Sabbat. I. Title.
BF1572.S28G5613 1991
133.4'3'094—dc20   90-52528

Manufactured in the United States of America

First American Edition

In memory of my father
To my mother

But what if oxen (horses and) lions had hands?
Xenophanes, Fragment 15

um sie kein Ort, noch weniger eine Zeit.
(Around them no space and even less time.)
Goethe, *Faust*, Part II,
Scene of the Mothers

CONTENTS

Introduction   1

PART ONE

1. Lepers, Jews, Muslims   33
2. Jews, Heretics, Witches   63

PART TWO

1. Following the Goddess   89
2. Anomalies   122
3. To Combat in Ecstasy   153
4. Disguised as Animals   182

PART THREE

1. Eurasian Conjectures   207
2. Bones and Skin   226

Conclusion   296

Index   315

CONTENTS

ECSTASIES

INTRODUCTION

1. Male and female witches met at night, generally in solitary places, in fields or on mountains. Sometimes, having anointed their bodies, they flew, arriving astride poles or broom sticks; sometimes they arrived on the backs of animals, or transformed into animals themselves. Those who came for the first time had to renounce the Christian faith, desecrate the sacrament and offer homage to the devil, who was present in human or (most often) animal or semi-animal form. There would follow banquets, dancing, sexual orgies. Before returning home the female and male witches received evil ointments made from children's fat and other ingredients.

These are the basic features that recur in most descriptions of the Sabbath. Local variations, especially in the name given to the gatherings, were frequent. Alongside the term *sabbat*, of obscure etymology and late diffusion, we find scholarly expressions such as *sagarum synagoga* or *strigiarum conventus*, which translated a myriad of popular terms such as *striaz, barlòtt, akelarre*, and so on.[1] But this terminological variety is offset by the extraordinary uniformity in the confessions of those who participated in the nocturnal gatherings. From the witchcraft trials held throughout Europe between the beginning of the fifteenth century and the end of the seventeenth, as well as from the demonology treatises directly or indirectly based on them, there emerges an image of the Sabbath which is basically similar to that briefly described above. It indicated to contemporaries the existence of an actual sect of female and male witches, much more dangerous than the isolated figures, familiar for centuries, of sorceresses or enchanters. The uniformity of the confessions was considered proof that the followers of this sect were ubiquitous, and everywhere practised the same horrific rituals.[2]

The stereotype of the witches' Sabbath suggested to the judges the possibility of extracting, by means of physical and psychological pressure on the accused, denunciations which would in turn provoke genuine waves of witch hunting.[3]

How and why did the image of the Sabbath crystallize? What did it conceal? From these two questions (which, as we shall see, have taken me down totally unforeseen paths) my inquiry was born. On the one hand, I wanted to

1

reconstruct the ideological mechanisms that facilitated the persecution of witchcraft in Europe; on the other, the beliefs of the men and women accused of witchcraft. The two themes are intimately linked. But as with *The Night Battles* (1966), of which this is a development that attempts a more profound examination, the second theme places this book in a marginal position as regards the animated discussion on witchcraft underway for more than twenty years among historians. In the pages that follow, I shall try to explain why.

2. What Keith Thomas was fully justified in defining, as late as 1967, as 'a subject that the majority of historians consider peripheral, not to say bizarre',[4] has since become a more than respectable historiographical subject, also cultivated by scholars who have scant love for eccentricity. What are the reasons for this sudden success?

The first impression is that they are both scientific and extra-scientific. On the one hand, the ever-increasing tendency to investigate the behaviour and attitudes of subaltern, or in any case underprivileged groups, such as peasants and women,[5] has led historians to grapple with the themes (and sometimes the methods and interpretative categories) of the anthropologists. As Thomas pointed out in the essay referred to above, in British (but not only British) anthropological research, magic and witchcraft traditionally occupy a central place. On the other hand, the past two decades have seen the emergence not only of the women's movement, but also of a growing impatience with the costs and risks associated with technological progress. New directions in historiography, feminism, the rediscovery of cultures overwhelmed by capitalism, these have contributed – on various levels and to different degrees – to the changed fortune or, if one wishes, the fashion for studies in the history of witchcraft.

Yet if the studies that have appeared in recent years are examined more closely, such connections appear much more tenuous. We are struck above all by the fact that, with very few exceptions, these studies have continued to concentrate almost exclusively on persecution, giving little or no attention to the attitudes and behaviour of the persecuted.

3. The most explicit justification for this focus was offered in a celebrated essay by Hugh Trevor-Roper. How is it possible, he asked, that a cultivated and advanced society like Europe could unleash, contemporaneously with the so-called scientific revolution, a persecution based on a delirious notion of witchcraft – the fruit of the systematic elaboration of a series of popular beliefs, concocted by clerics of the late Middle Ages? These popular beliefs are contemptuously dismissed by Trevor-Roper as 'oddities and superstitions', 'disturbances of a psychotic nature', 'fantasies of mountain peasants', 'mental rubbish of peasant credulity and feminine hysteria'. To those who reproached him for not studying the peasant mentality more sympathetically, Trevor-Roper retorted, in the reprint of his essay, that he

2

had not examined 'witch beliefs that are universal, but the theory of the witch-craze which is limited in space and time'. The latter, he observed, is different from the former, just as 'the myth of the Elders of Zion is different from pure and simple hostility towards the Jews – which in its turn can certainly be investigated sympathetically by those who believe that an error, provided it is shared by the lower classes, is innocent and worthy of respect.'[6]

Previously, Trevor-Roper had suggested that both witches and Jews can be seen as the scapegoats of widespread social tension (an hypothesis to which we shall return). But peasant hostility towards witches can evidently be analyzed from the inside – in the same way as folk anti-Semitism – without thereby implying ideological or moral sympathy for its presuppositions. More significant is the fact that Trevor-Roper should have ignored the attitudes of the individuals accused of witchcraft – comparable, within the analogy proposed by him, to those of persecuted Jews. Belief in nocturnal gatherings, readily recognizable in the 'hallucinations' and 'absurd ideas, born from peasant credulity and female hysteria', only becomes the legitimate object of historical inquiry when 'cultivated men', acting as inquisitors and demonologists, were able to transform the inchoate and 'disorganized peasant credulity' into a 'bizarre but coherent intellectual system'.[7]

4.   Trevor-Roper's essay, published in 1967, is not only debatable,[8] but indeed unrelated – superficially at least – to the focus of subsequent studies of witchcraft. It is a general account that seeks to trace the fundamental lines of the persecution of witchcraft in the European zone, disdainfully rejecting the possibility of utilizing the contribution of anthropologists.

By contrast, a delimitation of the field of inquiry and reference to the social sciences characterize more recent studies such as Alan Macfarlane's *Witchcraft in Tudor and Stuart England* (1970), with a preface by E.E. Evans-Pritchard. Basing himself on the latter's famous book on witchcraft among the Azande, Macfarlane declared that he had not asked, 'why people believed in witchcraft', but rather, 'how witchcraft *functioned*, once the basic assumptions about the nature of evil, the types of causation, and the origins of supernatural "power" were present'. Hence the analysis basically concerned the mechanisms that produced accusations of witchcraft within the community, though Macfarlane (referring to Keith Thomas's forthcoming book) did not question the legitimacy of 'an inquiry into the philosophical basis of witchcraft beliefs and their relation to the religious and scientific ideas of the times'.[9] In fact Macfarlane examined the age and sex of those accused of witchcraft, the motives for the accusation, their relationships with neighbours and the community in general: but he did not dwell on what those men and women believed or claimed to believe. Contact with anthropology did not lead to an intrinsic analysis of the beliefs of the victims of persecution.

This lack of interest emerges strikingly in connection with the trials, rich in descriptions of the Sabbath, held in Essex in 1645. In her well-known book, *The Witch-Cult in Western Europe* (1921), M. Murray, chiefly basing herself on these trials, had maintained that the Sabbath ('ritual withcraft'), as distinct from common spells ('operative witchcraft'), was the central ceremony of an organized cult bound up with a pre-Christian fertility religion diffused throughout Europe. Macfarlane objected: (1) that Murray had mistaken the confessions of the defendants in the witchcraft trials for reports of actual events, rather than beliefs; (2) that the Essex documentation offers no proof whatsoever of the existence of an organized cult such as that described by Murray. In general, Macfarlane concluded, 'the picture of the witchcraft cult' drawn by Murray 'seems far too sophisticated and articulated for the society with which we are concerned'.[10]

This last statement echoes, in more nuanced fashion, the cultural superiority evinced by Trevor-Roper towards those accused of witchcraft. The first (and valid) objection addressed to Murray did not preclude Macfarlane from deciphering, in the descriptions of the Sabbath given by the defendants in the 1645 trials, a historical record of complex *beliefs*, inserted in a symbolic context requiring reconstruction. Beliefs – but whose? The accused? The judges? Or both? It is impossible to give an a priori answer: the accused were not tortured, but they were certainly subjected to strong cultural and psychological pressure by the judges. According to Macfarlane, these trials were 'exceptional', 'abnormal', full of 'strange', 'bizarre' elements that can be traced back to the 'influence [on the judges, evidently] of ideas from the Continent'.[11] This is a highly plausible hypothesis, given the rarity of testimonies on the Sabbath in England – though it does not necessarily follow that all the details reported by the accused were suggested by the judges. In any event, in a book whose subtitle presents it as a 'regional and comparative' study, we would at this point expect an analytical comparison between the descriptions of the Sabbath that recur in these Essex trials and those contained in the demonology treatises and trials of continental Europe. But the comparison, to which Macfarlane devotes an entire section of his book, is based solely on non-European, chiefly African data. It is not clear how a comparison with the Azandes' witchcraft, for example, could possibly be a substitute in this instance for a comparison with European witchcraft: after all, the presumed influence of continental demonological doctrines coincided, as Macfarlane himself demonstrates, with the sudden upsurge in witchcraft trials and sentences in Essex.[12] At any rate, the 'strange' or 'bizarre' details reported by the accused in the 1645 trials were considered 'anomalies', negligible curiosities to anyone who viewed matters from an authentically scientific perspective.

5. The orientation, and limitations, of Macfarlane's study are typical of a historiography strongly influenced by anthropological functionalism, and hence not really interested – until recently – in the symbolic dimension of beliefs.[13] Keith Thomas' imposing study, *Religion and The Decline of Magic* (1971), does not fundamentally diverge from this tendency. The discussion, or lack of discussion, of particular aspects of witchcraft – first of all, the Sabbath – once again proves revealing.

As with all the phenomena he investigated, Thomas has collected a vast documentation on beliefs in witchcraft in England in the sixteenth and seventeenth centuries. He has examined it from three points of view: (a) psychological ('explanation . . . of the motives of the participants in the drama of witchcraft accusation'); (b) sociological ('analysis of the situation in which such accusations tended to occur'); (c) intellectual ('explanation . . . of the concepts which made such accusations plausible').[14] This list lacks any examination of what the belief in witchcraft meant, not for the accusers and the judges, but for the accused. In their confessions (when they did confess) we often encounter a symbolic richness that does not seem reducible to the psychological need for reassurance, to regional tensions, or to the general notions about causality current in England at the time. Certainly, the more the confessions coincided with the doctrines of demonologists on the continent, the more likely it is (Thomas observes) that they were elicited by the judges. But immediately after this he recognizes that one occasionally encounters elements in the trials which are too 'unconventional' to be attributed to prompting.[15] Might not a systematic analysis of these elements shed some light upon the beliefs in witchcraft held by the female and male witches (real or alleged)?

A rigorous critique of the psychological reductionism and sociological functionalism of *Religion and the Decline of Magic* has been formulated by Geertz.[16] In his reply Thomas conceded that he had been insufficiently sensitive 'to the symbolic or poetic meanings of these magical rituals' (a similar objection had been addressed to him by E.P. Thompson),[17] pointing out, in partial self-justification, that historians have a certain familiarity with the notion of 'deep social structure', but are much less accustomed to investigating the 'invisible mental structures . . . underlying inchoate and ill-recorded systems of thought, which are only articulated in a fragmentary way'. He added: 'At a rather less inaccessible level, however, I would fully agree that more justice needs to be done to the symbolism of popular magic. Just as the mythology of witchcraft – the night flying, blackness, animal metamorphosis, female sexuality – tells us something about the standards of the societies which believed in it – the boundaries they were concerned to maintain, the impulsive behaviour that they thought it necessary to repress.'[18]

With these words Thomas, impelled by Geertz's critique, has indicated a path that avoids the rigidly functionalist image of witchcraft proposed in *Religion and the Decline of Magic*.[19] That his choice should have been the Sabbath is significant. Equally significant is the fact that the possibility of attaining, at least partially, the 'invisible mental structures' of popular magic through the Sabbath has been tacitly discarded. Indeed, the Sabbath is revelatory – but of a 'less inaccessible' cultural stratum: that of the surrounding society. Via the symbolism of the Sabbath it formulated its own values in the negative. The darkness enveloping the gatherings of male and female witches expressed an exaltation of light; the explosion of female

5

sexuality and the diabolical orgies, an exhortation to chastity; the animal metamorphosis, a sharply defined border between the feral and the human.

This interpretation of the Sabbath in terms of symbolic reversal is certainly plausible;[20] by Thomas' own admission, however, it remains at a relatively superficial level. It is easy, but somewhat a priori, to maintain that the world view expressed by popular magic cannot be compared, in its coherence, to that of the theologians:[21] in truth, the ultimate meaning of the confessions made by male and female witches remains shrouded in darkness.

6.   As we have seen, all these studies set out from a by now generally accepted observation: namely, that in the evidence on European witchcraft heterogeneous cultural strata – learned and popular – were superimposed. An attempt to distinguish analytically between the two has been made by R. Kieckhefer (*European Witch-Trials, Their Foundations in Popular and Learned Culture, 1300–1500*, 1976). He has classified the documentation preceding the sixteenth century according to its, so to speak, degree of scholarly pollution: the greatest occurs in the demonological treatises and the inquisitorial trials; the least in trials presided over by lay judges, mainly in England, where coercion was less; while, finally, it is almost non-existent in the depositions of accusers and in the trials for defamation initiated by persons who considered themselves unjustly accused of witchcraft.[22] However, he ignored the documentation after 1500, declaring that in it the scholarly and popular elements were by now inextricably merged. All this led him to conclude that, unlike evil spells and the invocation of the devil, the Sabbath (*diabolism*) was not rooted in popular culture.[23]

This conclusion is contradicted by the widespread existence in folklore of beliefs which later partially flowed into the Sabbath. There exists, for example, a rich series of testimonies concerning night flying in which a number of women claimed they participated in ecstasy, in the retinue of a mysterious female divinity who had several names depending on the place (Diana, Perchta, Holda, Abundia, etc). According to Kieckhefer, when recorded in high medieval penitentials or canonical collections, this testimony must be considered extraneous to witchcraft, unless the latter is understood in an 'unusually broad' sense; when contained in literary texts, it is irrelevant because it provides no indication of the real diffusion of such beliefs; when transmitted by folkloric tradition, it represents mere vestiges, which do not enable us to reconstruct the previous situation.[24] But despite this screening of the sources, Kieckhefer occasionally comes across a document such as the sentences handed down at the end of fourteenth century on two women from Milan who had confessed to their periodical meetings with a mysterious 'lady': 'Madonna Oriente'. Here it is a matter neither of late folkloric tradition, nor of a literary text, nor of beliefs considered alien to witchcraft (the two women were in fact sentenced as witches). Kieckhefer wriggles out of it by stating, with obvious embarrassment, that the two cases cannot be categorized as sorcery or the Sabbath ('typical diabolism'): in a fleeting fit of 'Murrayism' he interprets the gatherings of 'Madonna Oriente' as descriptions of popular rituals or festivals, without sensing the obvious kinship, immediately grasped by the inquisitors, between this figure and the multi-form female divinities (Diana, Holda, Perchta . . .) populating the visions of the women mentioned by the canonical tradition.[25] Such records manifestly contradict the thesis, still common today, according to which the Sabbath was an image elaborated exclusively or almost exclusively by the persecutors.

7.   This thesis has again been advanced with somewhat different arguments by Norman Cohn (*Europe's Inner Demons*, 1975). The image of the Sabbath, according to Cohn, harked back to an ancient negative stereotype, composed of sexual orgies, ritual cannibalism, and the worship of a divinity in animal form. These accusations supposedly expressed extremely ancient, largely unconscious obsessions and fears. After having been hurled against the Jews, the first Christians, the medieval heretics, they finally focused around female and male witches.

In my opinion the sequence that led to the crystallization of the image of the Sabbath elaborated by judges and inquisitors is different. As I shall try to prove below (Part One, chapters 1 and 2) the actors, times and places were to a great extent different.[26] Here I wish simply to point out that that image involves the irruption of elements of folkloric origin evidently alien to the stereotype analyzed by Cohn. He mentions them almost by the way, in connection with the witchcraft trials held in the Dauphiné around 1430, in which descriptions of the Sabbath supposedly first emerged. (I say 'supposedly' because, as we shall see, I intend to propose an alternative chronology.) The ecclesiastical and secular authorities, engaged in the persecution of the Waldensian heretics, 'repeatedly came across people – chiefly women – who believed things about themselves which fitted in perfectly with the tales about heretical sects that had been circulating for centuries. The notion of cannibalistic infanticide provided the common factor. It was widely believed that babies or small children were commonly devoured at the nocturnal meetings of heretics. It was likewise widely believed that certain women killed and devoured babies or small children, also at night: and some women even believed this of themselves.' The 'extraordinary congruence' between these two sets of beliefs supposedly provided the judges with the proof that the iniquities traditionally attributed to heretics were true; while the confirmation of the ancient stereotype laid the basis for the subsequent elaboration of the Sabbath's image.[27] According to Cohn's reconstruction, this was a decisive historical event. But the comment is obviously inadequate, as is the reference which immediately follows to the 'deluded' women, who for some unknown reason thought they roamed through the night devouring new-born babies. The chapter that Cohn devotes to 'The Nocturnal Witch in the Folk Imagination' is no more enlightening. Asserting that the explanation for these fantasies is to be sought not, as many scholars maintain, in pharmacology – i.e., the use of mind-altering substances by the witches – but instead in anthropology,[28] amounts to posing the problem without solving it. The confession of an African witch who accuses herself of nocturnal cannibalism is used by Cohn solely to underline his view that we are dealing with events that are purely oneiric and not – as Murray has claimed – real.

The refutation of Murray's old thesis occupies not just one chapter,[29] but in a sense the whole book, which endeavours to prove the non-existence in Europe of an organized sect of female witches. Here we have a polemic conducted with arguments which, while effective, are by now taken for granted. Their persistence is a symptom (and, in part, a cause) of the unilateralism that characterizes many studies of the history of witchcraft. Let us see why.

8.   In her book *The Witch-Cult in Western Europe* Murray, an Egyptologist with a keen interest in anthropology in the wake of Frazer, maintained: (1) that the descriptions of the Sabbath contained in witch trials were neither nonsense extorted by the judges, nor accounts of inner experiences of a more or less hallucinatory character, but rather, exact descriptions of rituals that had actually taken place; (2) that these rituals, deformed by the judges' diabolizing interpretation, were in reality connected with a pre-Christian fertility cult, which possibly dated back to pre-history and which has survived in Europe until the modern age. Although immediately lambasted by several reviewers for its lack of rigour and its incredibility, *The Witch-Cult* nevertheless gained wide support. Murray (who reformulated her theses in increasingly dogmatic fashion) was entrusted with writing the article on 'Witchcraft' for the *Encyclopedia Britannica*, subsequently reprinted without revision for almost half a century.[30] But the republication of *The Witch-Cult* in 1962 coincided with the appearance of a systematic critique (E. Rose, *A Razor for a Goat*), followed by a series of ever harsher polemics against Murray and her followers, real or presumed. Today almost all historians of witchcraft concur in considering Murray's book (as had its first critics) amateurish, absurd, bereft of any scientific merit.[31] Yet this polemic, however justified in itself, has had the regrettable effect of implicitly discouraging all research into the symbolic elements of the witches' Sabbath which are alien to the scholarly stereotypes. As we have seen, such an inquiry was also neglected by historians such as Thomas and Macfarlane on the grounds of the non-existence (or at least the absence of proof) of an organized witchcraft cult.[32] Paradoxically, the confusion between behaviour and belief with which Murray has rightly been reproached has now been thrown back at her critics.

In my preface to *The Night Battles* I made a statement to which I still fully subscribe, even though it earned me ex-officio enrolment in the phantom (but discredited) sect of 'Murrayists': viz., that Murray's thesis, although 'formulated in a totally uncritical manner', contained 'a core of truth'.[33] Clearly, this core is not to be sought in the first of the two points which, as we have seen, the thesis comprises. It is symptomatic that, in seeking to validate the reality of the events mentioned in descriptions of the witches' Sabbath, Murray was obliged to neglect the most embarrassing elements – night flying, animal metamorphosis – having recourse to cuts which amounted to veritable textual manipulation.[34] Of course, we cannot altogether exclude the possibility that in some instances men and women devoted to magical practices assembled to celebrate rituals that included, e.g., sexual orgies; but virtually none of the descriptions of the Sabbath furnishes any proof of such events. This does not mean that they are lacking in documentary value: they simply document myths and not rituals.

Once again we must ask ourselves: whose beliefs and myths? As mentioned before, a long tradition, harking back to Enlightenment polemics against witchcraft trials and still very much alive, has seen in the witches' confessions the projection of the judges' superstitions and obsessions, extorted from the accused by means of torture and psychological pressure. The 'religion of Diana' – the pre-Christian fertility cult that Murray identified, without probing it more deeply, in descriptions of the Sabbath – suggests a different and more complex interpretation.[35]

The 'core of truth' in Murray's thesis is to be found here. More generally, it consists in the decision, contrary to all rationalistic reduction, to accept the witches' confessions – as much more illustrious (but, paradoxically, neglected) predecessors had done, beginning with Jakob Grimm. Yet the equally rationalistic desire to find in those confessions accurate descriptions of the rituals led Murray into a blind alley. To this was added an inability to discount, in evidence on the Sabbath, the incrustations built up over the centuries by the practical and doctrinal interventions of judges, inquisitors and demonologists.[36] Instead of trying to distinguish the oldest strata from subsequent superimpositions, Murray (apart from the textual manipulations already referred to) uncritically accepted the by now consolidated stereotype of the Sabbath as a basis for her own interpretation, rendering it wholly unreliable.

9. What induced me to recognize a correct intuition in Murray's totally discredited thesis (or rather in one of its components) was the discovery of an agrarian cult of an ecstatic character throughout the Friuli between the sixteenth and seventeenth century. It is documented by about fifty inquisitorial trials, which are late (c. 1575–1675), untypical in crucial ways, and originate from a culturally marginal area: elements that contradict all the external criteria established by Kieckhefer to isolate the lineaments of folk witchcraft from all learned superimpositions. And yet, from this documentation elements emerge which are quite distinct from the stereotypes of the demonologists. Men and women who defined themselves as '*benandanti*' affirmed that, having been born 'with a caul' (that is, enveloped in amnion)

they were compelled to go four times a year, at night, to battle 'in spirit', armed with bundles of fennel, against male and female witches armed with stalks of sorghum: at stake in these night battles was the fertility of the fields. Visibly astonished, the inquisitors tried to fit these tales into the pattern of the diabolical Sabbath: but, despite their solicitations, almost fifty years were to pass before the *benandanti*, hesitantly and with changes of heart, decided to modify their confessions in the requisite direction.

The physical reality of witches' assemblies receives no confirmation whatever, even by analogy, from the trials of the *benandanti*. They unanimously declared that they went out by night 'invisibly, in spirit', leaving behind their lifeless bodies. Only in one instance did the mysterious swoons offer a glimpse of the existence of real, everyday relationships, perhaps of a sectarian type.[37] The possibility that the *benandanti* would gather periodically before undergoing individual hallucinatory experiences, as described in their confessions, cannot be definitively proven. It is precisely here that, owing to a curious misunderstanding, some scholars have identified the essence of my research. The *benandanti* have been defined by J.B. Russell as 'the most solid proof that was ever furnished regarding the existence of witchcraft'; and by H.C.E. Midelfort as 'the single witch cult documented to this day in Europe during the first centuries of the modern age'. Expressions such as 'existence of witchcraft' and 'documented witch cults' (not very appropriate because they assume the inquisitors' deforming perspective) betray, as attested by the context in which they are formulated, the confusion already cited between myths and rituals, between a coherent, widespread set of beliefs and an *organized* group of persons who presumably practised them. This is particularly apparent in the case of Russell, who speaks of the night battles with 'members of the local witch cult', overlooking the fact that the *benandanti* declared that they participated in them 'invisibly in spirit'; more ambiguously, after following the tracks of the *benandanti*, Midelfort mentions the difficulty of finding other cases of 'group ritual'.[38] The objection raised against me by Cohn – i.e., that 'the experiences of the *benandanti* ... were all trance experiences' and constituted 'a local variant of what, for centuries before, had been the stock experience of the followers of Diana, Herodias or Holda' – must in fact be raised against Russell and, in part, Midelfort. To me it seems wholly valid and it coincides almost to the word with what I had written in my book.[39]

In my opinion, the value of the Friuli documentation lies elsewhere altogether. On witchcraft (this is quite obvious, but it does not hurt to repeat it) we possess only hostile testimonies, originating from or filtered by the demonologists, inquisitors and judges. The voices of the accused reach us strangled, altered, distorted; in many cases, they haven't reached us at all. Hence – for anyone unresigned to writing history for the nth time from the standpoint of the victors – the importance of the anomalies, the cracks that occasionally (albeit very rarely) appear in the documentation, undermining its coherence.[40] From the disparity between the accounts of the *benandanti* and the stereotypes of the inquisitors there emerges a deep stratum of peasant myths lived with extraordinary intensity. Little by little, by the gradual introjection of a hostile cultural model, it was transformed into the Sabbath. Did analogous events take place elsewhere? To what extent was it possible to generalize the case – exceptional in the documents – of the *benandanti?* At the time I was not in a position to answer these questions. But they seemed to me to imply a 'largely novel formulation of the problem of the folk origins of witchcraft'.[41]

10.   Today I would instead speak of 'the folkloric roots of the Sabbath'. Yet the judgment about the novelty of the formulation still seems valid to me. With a few exceptions, research on witchcraft has in fact followed paths very different from the one I then envisaged. Undoubtedly, in many instances sexual and class prejudice (not always unconscious) have contributed to directing the attention of scholars primarily towards the history of the persecution of witchcraft.[42] Terms such as 'oddities and superstitions', 'peasant credulity', 'female hysteria', 'eccentricities', 'extravagances', which recur again and again in some of the most authoritative studies, reflect a preliminary choice of ideological character. But even a scholar like Larner, who starts out from entirely different presuppositions, ends up concentrating on the history of persecution.[43] The attitude of posthumous solidarity with the victims is certainly quite distinct from superiority towards their cultural crudity: but even in the first instance the intellectual and moral scandal constituted by witch hunts has almost invariably monopolized attention. The confessions of the persecuted, women and men – especially if associated with the Sabbath – have, depending on the particular case, appeared irrelevant by definition, or contaminated by the violence of the persecutors. Anyone who has tried to read them literally, as the document of a separate female culture, has ended up ignoring their dense mythical content.[44] Extremely rare, in truth, have been the attempts to approach these documents with the analytical instruments supplied by the history of religions and by folklore – disciplines which even the most serious among the historians of witchcraft have usually given a wide berth, as if they were minefields.[45] The fear of yielding to sensationalism; incredulity regarding magical powers; bewilderment when faced by the 'almost universal' character of beliefs such as animal metamorphosis (as well as, naturally, the non-existence of an organized witch sect) – these are some of the reasons adduced to justify a drastic, and ultimately sterile, restriction of the field of inquiry.[46]

By contrast, the persecutors as well as the persecuted are at the centre of the study I am now presenting. In the stereotype of the Sabbath I think it is possible to see a 'cultural compromise formation'[47]: the hybrid result of a conflict between folk culture and learned culture.

11.   The heterogeneity of the subject explains the book's structure. It comprises three parts and an epilogue. In the first, I reconstruct the

emergence of the inquisitorial image of the Sabbath; in the second, the very deep mythical and ritual stratum whence sprung the folk belief that was later forcibly channelled into the Sabbath; in the third, the possible explanations of this dispersion of myths and rituals; in the epilogue, I reconstruct the consolidation of the crystallized stereotype of the Sabbath, as a compromise between elements of a learned origin and elements of folk origin. The first part possesses a linear narrative movement; the chronological period and geographical space under examination are circumscribed; the documentary network is relatively dense. The central section of the book frequently drops the narrative thread, and even ignores chronological succession and spatial contiguities, in an attempt to reconstruct through affinities certain mythical and ritual configurations, documented over millennia, sometimes at a distance of many thousands of kilometres. In the concluding pages history and morphology, narrative and (hopefully) synoptic presentation will alternate and overlap.

12.   We begin with the brief, feverish tempo, beat out along the thread of days, of political action, indeed conspiracy. In the long run, it set in motion unforeseeable mechanisms. The plot which, in the course of half a century, led to the persecution of lepers and Jews and to the first trials hinging on the diabolical Sabbath, is in certain respects analogous to that reconstructed by Marc Bloch in his splendid book *The Royal Touch*. By sheer machination the belief, advantageous to the French and English monarchies, was spread, attributing to the legitimate sovereigns of those two countries the power to heal those affected by scrofula by the royal touch. But it could become permanently established because it was underpinned by attitudes that were profoundly implanted in pre-industrial Europe: the widespread need for protection, the attribution of magical powers to sovereigns.[48] The underlying reasons which, from the beginning of the fourteenth century, ensured the success of the conspiracy against Jews and lepers were different: insecurity born out of a deep economic, social, political and religious crisis; growing hostility toward marginal groups; the frenzied search for a scapegoat. But the undoubted analogy between the two phenomena poses a general problem.

Explanations of social movements in a conspiratorial register are simplistic, if not grotesque – beginning with that launched toward the end of the eighteenth century by Abbé Barruel, which characterized the French Revolution as a Masonic conspiracy.[49] But conspiracies do exist: they are, especially today, a daily reality. Conspiracies of secret services, of terrorists, or of both: what is their actual weight? Which succeed, which fail in their various objectives, and why? Reflection on these phenomena and their implications seems curiously inadequate. After all, conspiracy is only an extreme, almost caricatural instance of a much more complex phenomenon: the attempt to transform (or manipulate) society. Growing scepticism about the efficacy and results of both revolutionary and technocratic projects obliges us to rethink the manner in which political action intervenes in deep social structures, and its real capacity to modify them. Various signs suggest that historians attentive to the long-term effects of the economy, of social movements, or mentalities, have begun to reflect upon the significance of the punctual event (including political events).[50] The analysis of a phenomenon such as the genesis of the inquisitorial image of the Sabbath conforms to this tendency.

13.   But in the stereotype of the Sabbath which emerged around the middle of the fourteenth century in the Western Alps, folkloric elements appear which are foreign to the inquisitorial image that was diffused over a much vaster area. As we have seen, the historians of witchcraft have generally ignored them. For the most part, they have implicitly or explicitly derived the subject of their research from the interpretative categories of the demonologists, the judges or witnesses against the accused. When Larner, for instance, identifies witchcraft with the 'power to do evil . . . of a supernatural origin',[51] she offers anything but a neutral definition. In a society riven by conflicts (presumably, any society), what is evil for one individual can be considered good by his enemy: Who decides what is 'evil'? Who *did* decide, when witches were being hunted in Europe, that particular individuals were witches? Their identification was always the result of the balance of forces, all the more efficacious the more its results were diffused in capillary fashion. By means of the introjection (partial or total, gradual or immediate, violent or apparently spontaneous) of the hostile stereotype promoted by the persecutors, the victims ultimately lost their cultural identity. Anyone declining to restrict himself to recording the results of this historical violence must find a lever in those rare cases where the documentation possesses something other than a formal dialogical character: where, that is, one can find fragments, relatively immune from distortions, of the culture that the persecution set out to eradicate.[52]

I have already indicated why the trials in the Friuli seem to me a fissure in the thick and seemingly indecipherable crust of the Sabbath. Two themes emerge from them: the processions of the dead and the battles for fertility. Those who declare that they participated in them in a state of ecstasy were, in the case of the processions, predominantly women: in the battles, chiefly men. Both called themselves *benandanti*. The uniqueness of the term suggests a background of shared beliefs: but whereas the processions of the dead are clearly connected with myths commonplace over a large part of Europe (the followers of Diana, the 'wild hunt'), the battles for fertility initially seemed to me a phenomenon confined to the Friuli. But with one extraordinary exception: an old Livonian werewolf,[53] who around the end of the seventeenth century confessed that he periodically went with his companions to fight the male witches, in order to recover the shoots of the fruits of the earth that they had carried off. The hypothesis I advanced to explain this unexpected juxtaposition – a common, possibly Slavic, substratum – was, as we shall see, only partially accurate. It already involved a considerable extension of the scope of the inquiry. But the inevitable recognition of the underlying unity to the two versions of the *benandanti*'s myth – the agrarian and the funerary – dictated an enormously expanded field of comparison. In fact, in both cases, the exit of the soul from body – to join night battles or the processions of wandering souls – was preceded by a cataleptic state which irresistibly suggests comparison with a shamanistic ecstasy. More generally, the tasks the *benandanti* assigned themselves (contact with the world of the dead; magical control of the powers of nature to ensure the material survival of the community) seem to amount to a social function very similar to that performed by the shamans.

I suggested this connection (later confirmed by M. Eliade) many years ago, defining it as 'not analogical but real';[54] however, I did not dare to confront it. When considering the long trail of research it involved, I remember experiencing a sensation vaguely resembling vertigo. I naively asked myself whether I would one day have the necessary competence to tackle so vast and complex a theme. Today I know that I never will. But the Friuli documents that came to my attention by chance pose questions that demand an answer, however inadequate and provisional. I have tried to offer an answer in this book.

14.   In it the most contentious parts (the second and third) are also, I believe, the most original. I must explain what prompted me to employ an analytical and explanatory strategy rare for a work of historiography.

An inquiry into the roots of the Sabbath in folk culture must obviously be conducted from a comparative perspective. For example, only by shying away from comparison with continental Europe (Macfarlane) or from comparison *tout court* (Thomas) has it been possible to avoid asking whether traces of beliefs analogous to those of the followers of Diana can likewise be found in the English context.[55] But the analogy between the confessions of the *benandanti* and those of the Livonian werewolf, and a fortiori the analogy of both with evidence regarding Eurasian shamans, proved that the comparison must be extended to include regions and periods other than those in which the persecution of witchcraft occurred. To make the beliefs which abruptly surface in the nets of documentation (those about the ecstatic female followers of Oriente, the *benandanti*, the werewolf Thiess, etc.) coincide with 1384, 1575, 1692 – i.e., the times at which they were recorded by inquisitors and judges – would undoubtedly have been an undue simplification. Very recent testimony might preserve traces of much earlier phenomena; conversely, remote testimonies could cast light upon much later phenomena.[56] Naturally, this hypothesis did not authorize an automatic projection of the contents of folk culture onto a very remote antiquity; but it made it impossible to use chronological succession as a connecting thread. A similar consideration applied to geographical contiguity: the discovery of analogous phenomena in very distant areas could be explained by cultural contacts dating back to a much more distant time. The reconstruction of a culture extremely viscous, on the one hand, while documented in a fragmentary and casual manner on the other, necessitated, at least temporarily, renunciation of several postulates basic to historical research: foremost among them, that of a unilinear and uniform time.[57] In the trials it was not only cultures that clashed, but two radically heterogeneous temporalities as well.

For years, starting out from the documentation on the *benandanti*, I tried on the basis of purely formal affinities to correlate testimonies concerning myths, beliefs and rituals, without bothering to insert it into a plausible historical framework. The very nature of the affinities for which I was groping became clear to me only after the event. Pursuing this path I encountered, besides Jakob Grimm's splendid pages, the studies by W.H. Roscher, M. P. Nilsson, S. Luria, Vladimir Propp, K. Meuli, and R. Bleichsteiner – to mention only a few names from a long list. In the end studies often conducted independently of one another converged. Little by little a constellation of phenomena took shape, very compact morphologically, very heterogeneous chronologically, geographically and culturally. It seemed to me that the myths and rituals I had collected traced a symbolic context within which the folkloric elements encrusted in the stereotype of the Sabbath proved less indecipherable. But periodically I was struck by the possibility that I was accumulating meaningless data, pursuing irrelevant analogies.

Only when the study was quite advanced did I discover the theoretical justification for what I'd been doing for years. It is contained in a number of very dense reflections by Wittgenstein in the margins of Frazer's *Golden Bough*: 'Historical explanation, explanation as a hypothesis of development is only *one* way of gathering data – their synopsis. It is equally possible to see the data in their mutual relationships and sum them up in a general image that does not have the form of a chronological development.' This 'perspicuous representation (*übersichtliche Darstellung*)', Wittgenstein observed, 'mediates understanding, which precisely consists in "seeing the connections". Hence the importance of finding the *intermediary links*.'[58]

15.   Without realizing it, this was the path I had followed. Certainly, no historical hypothesis (relating to a religious, institutional, or ethnic context) would have permitted me to bring together the unanticipated documentary constellations presented in the second part of this book. But would an enormously extended, a-historical exposition of the results attained suffice? Wittgenstein's answer was clear: the 'all-encompassing representation' was not simply an alternative way of presenting the data, but, implicitly, superior to an historical exposition because (a) less arbitrary and (b) immune to undemonstrated developmental hypotheses. 'An inner relationship between circle and ellipse,' he observed, is illustrated 'by gradually transforming the ellipse into a circle, but not in order to affirm that the particular ellipse has actually, historically, sprung from a circle (developmental hypothesis) but only to make our eye sensitive to a formal connection.'[59]

This example seemed *too* convincing. I was dealing not with circles and ellipses (entities which are by definition divorced from a temporal context), but with men and women: for instance, *benandanti* from the Friuli. Were I to restrict myself to describing their gradual transformation into witches in purely formal terms, I would end up neglecting a decisive element: the cultural and psychological violence exercised by the inquisitors. The entire story would have proved to be absolutely transparent, but also absolutely incomprehensible. If in a study of human events we bracket the temporal dimension, we obtain a datum which is inevitably distorted because it has been cleansed of all power relationships. Human history does not unfold in the world of ideas, but in the sub-lunar world in which individuals are irreversibly born, inflict or endure suffering and die.[60]

Accordingly, it seemed to me that the morphological inquiry could not (for simultaneously intellectual and moral reasons) be a substitute for historical reconstruction. It could, however, encourage it – above all, in little and badly documented areas or periods. Of the historical character of the connections that I had reconstructed I had no doubt. I had used the morphological inquiries as a probe, to explore a deep, otherwise unattainable stratum.[61] Wittgenstein's thesis must therefore be inverted: in the sphere of history (as opposed to geometry) the formal connection can be considered a developmental or rather a genetic hypothesis, formulated in a different manner. By means of comparison, it was necessary to try to translate into historical terms the distribution of data hitherto presented on the basis of inner, formal affinities. Following Propp's example, it would thus be morphology that, although achronic, established diachrony.[62]

16. The conjectural character of this attempt – acknowledged in the title of Part Three, chapter 1 – was unavoidable given the scant documentation. However, the convergence of testimonies enabled me to delineate several historical connections: a very ancient circulation of myths and rituals linked to ecstasy, and originating from the Asiatic steppes, though not proven in every respect, appeared more than likely. A generally neglected phenomenon was rising to the surface. But this result was obviously inadequate, besides being provisional. The enormous dispersion, and above all the persistence, of those myths and rituals in such diverse cultural contexts remained inexplicable. Could the reappearance of analogous symbolic forms at a distance of millennia, in utterly heterogeneous spatial and cultural environments, be analyzed in purely historical terms? Or were these rather extreme cases that formed an atemporal weft in the fabric of history?

I thrashed about for a long time in this dismaying dilemma.[63] Apparently, only a prior decision of an ideological nature could resolve it in one direction or the other. In the end I tried to elude the blackmail by setting up a sort of experiment (Part Three, chapter 2). Beginning with an enigmatic detail, I assembled a collection – of myths, legends, fables, rituals – that was certainly incomplete, often attesting to vast chronological and spatial spread, and in any case characterized by a high degree of 'family resemblances'.[64] With some partial exceptions (O. Gruppe, S. Luria and A. Brelich) the individual components of the series had been analyzed as separate entities. Later I shall explain the thread that unites – just to give a few examples – Oedipus, Achilles, Cinderella, mythical monosandalism and the ritual gathering of the bones of slain animals. Here it will suffice to say that as a whole the analysis of the series has partially helped me to overcome the initial dilemma, by reaching perhaps not irrelevant conclusions (including a theoretical stand-point).

17. The potential fertility of the experiment derived above all from the extraordinary distribution in time and space that, as we have seen, characterizes virtually all the single units of the series. So far as I know, none of the scholars who has dealt with the subject has dismissed this characteristic as fortuitous; many have confined themselves to recording it as a given fact; others have tried to explain it. The chief hypotheses formulated – invariably independently – are the following.

(a) The persistence and diffusion of similar phenomena supposedly constitutes proof of a semi-cancelled historical continuity, that apparently left behind a sediment of primordial, psychological reactions: hence, according to Meuli, the analogies between the rituals of Paleolithic hunters (partially reconstructible through testimony about the shamans of northern Asia) and Greek sacrifice. Accentuating the element of psychological continuity, W. Burkert has indicated atemporal archetypes, traceable to Jung's theories. The same has been done by Rodney Needham with regard to the myth of the unilateral or split man to be found in extremely hetero-geneous cultural contexts.

(b) Meuli's hypothesis, above all in Burkert's formulation, has been rejected by Jean-Pierre Vernant and Marcel Detienne, because it is necessarily based on 'a psychic archetype or some static structure'. Consequently, they have felt that it was also impossible to offer a comparison with cultures different from, and more ancient than, the Greek. In this polemical context they have emphasized, on one hand, the rejection of 'vertical history' (Detienne), and, on the other, a 'wager in favour of synchronicity' (Vernant),[65] which has also inspired a number of essays on a myth included in the series presented here: that of Oedipus.

(c) One scholar (Claude Lévi-Strauss) has dwelt on the theme of mythical and ritual lameness, observing that its enormous geographical distribution seems to imply an extremely remote, and hence unverifiable, genesis (the Paleolithic age) – whence, as we shall see, a proposal for explanations in formal terms, based on a summary but very broad comparison.

(d) The pre- or proto-historic genesis of some of the phenomena I have examined has frequently been conjectured, but rarely deduced: among the exceptions is L. Schmidt, who sought to define the precise historical and geographical framework within which the myth of the resurrection of animals from their bones, and related myths, were propagated.

These are very different formulations – in their general presuppositions, the criteria used to identify the object of the inquiry, and in their implications. Any assessment must distinguish between these elements, without relying on facile ideological labels whereby the first interpretation would be identified as archetypal, the second and third as structuralist, the fourth as diffusionist.

Archetypes are often referred to in a vague fashion, without making any explanatory claims. Yet when the term more or less explicitly denotes an hereditary transmission of acquired cultural traits, which is entirely un-demonstrated (*a*), its explanatory claims appear wholly unfounded and even potentially racist. And yet, to reject a problem because the proposed solutions are unsatisfactory (*b*) seems to me unacceptable. After all, to speak of the 'heritage of the Paleolithic age', as does Detienne, means arbitrarily to circumscribe, by disqualification, the possible solutions. Hypothesis (*c*), according to which the reappearance of similar phenomena in dissimilar cultures is linked to immutable structures of the human mind, does in fact imply innate formal constraints, not heritage or archetype – even if, as we shall see, the solution proposed in a specific case is unsatisfactory from every theoretical and factual angle. Option (*d*) elicits an objection in principle, applicable to any diffusionist theory: contact or continuity are external events, insufficient to explain the transmission of cultural phenomena in space and time – especially if, as in the cases under examination, they assume macroscopic proportions.

Let us now consider the criteria adopted in each case to identify the object of research. In studies of myth or ritual inspired by structuralism, the object is constructed (and reconstructed) first by disassembling the superficial data, and then by elaborating a series based on a network of deep isomorphisms.[66] The polemical target of this procedure is the positivist habit of commencing with isolated units in search of analogies that imply transmission or filiation. It is of course true that structuralist theoreticians do not always put their principles into practice; conversely, scholars of a positivist orientation have demonstrated that they know how to grasp the profound affinity that binds apparently distinct myths or rituals. But all labels aside, the route to be followed seems clear to me: isomorphism establishes identity, not vice versa. This involves a radical divergence, not only in method but also in premises, from those who assert their intuitive grasp of the immutable symbols – the archetypes – in which the epiphanies of the collective unconscious (Jung) or the primordial manifestations of the sacred (Eliade) are supposedly expressed.[67]

In conclusion, studies based on ample diachronicity and vast comparison answer the question posed by the continuity and dispersion of similar myths and rituals by formulating flimsy (archetypes) or simplifying (mechanical diffusion) hypotheses; hypotheses based on synchronic postulates elude not only the comparison, but also the problem. On the other hand, the intermediate solution, briefly sketched by Lévi-Strauss – conjoint synchronic and comparative analysis of trans-cultural phenomena – raises, as we shall see, objections of principle and of fact. But is a choice between alternatives which involve, respectively, unacceptable responses and inadequate questions genuinely unavoidable? Are diachronic perspective and methodical rigour really incompatible?

18. These questions will make it easier to understand why this book, especially in its more theoretical section (Part Three, chapter 2), contains a dialogue, implicit and explicit, with the scholars who have in recent years revived, from only partially congruent viewpoints, research into myth (Lévi-Strauss) and, in particular, the Greek myths (Vernant and Detienne). I will begin by indicating the terms of my discussion with the latter.

As mentioned previously, Vernant has spoken of 'a wager in favour of synchronicity' against 'a retrospective comparativism' which supposedly tries to retrace the 'stages of a hypothetical genesis'. With equal clarity, Detienne has rejected 'a vertical history' projected back towards the 'mists of the Paleolithic'. The documents examined by Vernant and Detienne are certainly much more circumscribed in time and space, running (to mention only the texts) from Homer to the Hellenistic mythographers. What makes it possible to speak of a 'synchronic' approach is the unitary consideration of this almost millennial textual *corpus*.[68] A reassertion of the originality of Greek civilization and the intention to study its religion and myths as an 'organized system' are two facets of the same project.[69] In this perspective, as Vernant has clearly seen, the relationship between synchronicity and diachronicity represents an unresolved aporia.[70]

Of course, originality is not synonymous with autochthony. In the past, Vernant had seriously considered the hypothesis – sketched out by Rohde and later developed by Meuli and other scholars – that Greek religious phenomena linked to ecstasy constituted a re-elaboration of themes present in Eurasian shamanism.[71] The series I have reconstructed on morphological bases inserts this connection into an even wider chronological perspective, including for example, the followers of Oriente, the *benandanti* of the Friuli and the Livonian werewolf. Consideration of the reappearance of certain specific phenomena within completely unattested historical relationships involves straying from the rigorously synchronic option pursued, in the Greek context, by Vernant and Detienne. It is certainly true that their polemic against 'retrospective comparativism' permits of some exceptions, since both have repeatedly drawn inspiration from the studies of Georges Dumézil and, to a lesser degree, Émile Benveniste.[72] But the Indo-European languages had furnished Dumézil and Benveniste with indubitable proof of a framework of historical filiations. In the case of relations between Uralic and Indo-European languages, such proof is lacking. Had I confined myself to translating into historical terms – albeit conjectural ones (Part Three, chapter 1) – the data I had previously presented on the basis of internal analogies (Part Two), I would have been open to the accusation of implicitly advancing an old diffusionist interpretation, based on genetic filiations and relationships.[73] But the ensuing experiment (Part Three, chapter 2) isolates two themes with the aim of re-examining the whole question from a more complex perspective, which takes account of the compelling point about the 'wager in favour of synchronicity' made by Vernant: systematic formulation.

The indissoluble nexus between 'synchronicity' and 'system' obviously derives, beyond the formulations of Lévi-Strauss, from Ferdinand de Saussure.[74] It is certainly true that the analogical use of the term 'system' in extra-linguistic contexts ('cultural system', 'social system', 'mythical-religious system', and so on) involves risks: in fact, in such cases the constituent units are not rigorously separable. A comparison between the notion of 'mytheme', as introduced by Lévi-Strauss, and that of 'phoneme' on which it was patterned, clearly indicates that derivation of conceptual models from linguistics is insufficient to attain its rigour.[75] Both the phonological system of a dead language (or the declining phase of a living language) and the 'latent system' of a myth[76] must be reconstructed on the basis of an inherently limited, although potentially expanding (through archaeological, papyrological, etc. discoveries) documentary archive. But the often casual, indirect or fragmentary nature of the documentation of myth implies the possibility – less frequent in the linguistic sphere – that elements crucial for their interpretation have either not yet been discovered or have been lost forever.[77] An oversight of Lévi-Strauss' (followed by a happy afterthought) will illustrate the selective mechanisms of the transmission process, and their consequences.[78]

These considerations suggest caution in adopting the notion of a mythical-religious system. Insistence on a purely synchronic approach leads to more serious problems. The risk of thus impoverishing the complexity of phenomena has been stressed not only by historians, professionally, if not inevitably, interested in temporal succession.[79] Similar concerns have been formulated by semioticians like Lotman and his collaborators, who propose a study of culture based on a notion of 'text' so broad as to include myths, rituals, icons, artefacts, and so on:

> in the real existence of culture, alongside the new texts there always function texts transmitted by a given cultural tradition or introduced from without. This confers the characteristics of cultural multilingualism upon each synchronic stage of the culture. Once the speed of cultural development is unequal at different social levels, a synchronic stratum of culture can include its diachrony and the active reproduction of 'old texts'.[80]

In these words we detect the echo of Roman Jakobson's polemic against the extreme antithesis between synchrony and diachrony formulated by

Saussure.[81] It was indeed Jakobson, reflecting on his own youthful experience as a folklorist, who observed that 'when the acts and magical beliefs of present-day folkloric groups are subjected to a systematic-synchronic interpretation . . . the prehistoric antiquity of a great part of what is concealed in the elements that have come down to us appears convincingly attested to. We then realize . . . that folkloric testimonies have their roots in a much more remote time and are much more widely diffused than we thought. If such conclusions could not be more persuasively advanced previously, it is because the mechanistic procedures of prior studies have not allowed for the structural analysis of the diffusion of the folkloric patrimony'.[82]

When the description and explanation of conflicting situations is involved this perspective appears much more appropriate than the both monolithic and static postulate of a 'single system' underlying 'the field of cultural representations'.[83] In the cross-section of any present are also encrusted many pasts, of varying temporal thickness, which (above all in the case of folkloric evidence) can refer us to a much larger spatial context.

19.   As is well known, at the beginning of the 1940s Lévi-Strauss derived a method of analyzing social phenomena (primarily structures of kinship) from Jakobson's phonological studies. It is unquestionably significant that then and subsequently he ignored the need indicated by Jakobson to supersede the antithesis between synchrony and diachrony. But the current interpretation, according to which Lévi-Strauss' synchronic focus implies an aggressively anti-historical attitude, is superficial. Initially, echoing a famous sentence of Marx's, Lévi-Strauss had assigned to the historian the sphere of consciousness ('Men make history') and to the anthropologist that of the unconscious ('but they don't know they're making it'): a division of labour that admitted the possibility of fruitful cross-collaboration, such as Lucien Febvre's studies on the obscure or ignored phenomena of mentalities.[84] Subsequently, Lévi-Strauss formulated the relationship between anthropology and history in mutually exclusive terms: repeated comparison between homologous myths from cultures not connected historically (at least not in a documented fashion) invariably concluded by tracing the analogies back to formal constraints, rather than to cultural borrowings.[85] Recently, however, reviewing in detail an essay written over thirty years ago, Lévi-Strauss has insisted – as he did then – on the possibility of collaboration between historians and anthropologists:

> Diffusionism, and a fortiori any historical research, are of essential importance to structural analysis: by different paths and with distinct means these perspectives tend to the same end – that is to say, rendering superficially heterogeneous phenomena intelligible by shedding light on their unity. Indeed, structural analysis converges with history when, beyond the empirical data, it grasps deep structures which, insofar as they are deep, may in the past have possessed a common patrimony (*des structures profondes qui, parce que profondes, peuvent aussi avoir été communes dans le passé*).[86]

Such considerations introduce some dense reflections, suggested by the system of biological classification known as cladistics. Whereas traditional classification arranged the species along an evolutionary scale in accordance with their more or less complex characteristics, cladistics establishes a plurality of orders (or cladograms) based on homologies that do not necessarily refer to genealogical relationships. Thus, Lévi-Strauss observes, cladistics has opened up 'an intermediary path between the level of the structure and that of the event,' which can also be followed by those who deal with the human species: homologies between phenomena pertaining to different societies, identified via structural analysis, must then be subjected to the historian's appraisal so as to isolate those which correspond to real – and not merely potential – connections.

The convergences between the research programme outlined by Lévi-Strauss and the book I have written would appear to be very strong. But the divergences are equally important. The first consists in rejection of the limited and marginal function accorded historiography by Lévi-Strauss: viz., answering, by assessment of a series of factual data, the questions posed by anthropology. For anyone who, unlike Lévi-Strauss, works with dated or datable documents, the inverse can also occur and not only when (as with the material presented here) morphology and history, the identification of formal homologies and the reconstruction of spatial-temporal contexts, constitute aspects of the research conducted by a single individual. From this intertwining springs a second divergence. The isomorphic series analyzed in the second and third parts of this book belong to a sphere situated between the abstract depth of the structure (favoured by Lévi-Strauss) and the superficial concreteness of the event.[87] In this intermediary space, amid convergences and contrasts, the real contest between anthropology and history is probably played out.

20.   A long time ago I seriously set myself the task of experimentally demonstrating, from an historical standpoint, the non-existence of human nature; twenty-five years later I find myself supporting a diametrically opposed theory. As we shall see, at a certain point my research was transformed into a reflection on the limits of historical knowledge, developed through the examination of what is perhaps an extreme case.

But above all I am well aware of the limits of *my* knowledge. The decision to operate in a perspective at once diachronic and comparative has helped to deepen that awareness. It obviously made it impossible to broaden the inquiry from 'the field of mythology to the corpus of information concerning all the registers of the social, spiritual and material life of the human group under consideration'.[88] The price to be paid in terms of precise knowledge became part of the experiment. A greater cause for regret has been the necessary exclusion (save for a few exceptions) of a dimension often neglected either because it is difficult to document or because it is, mistakenly, considered irrelevant: the subjective dimension. The great majority of testimonies that I have found are fragmentary and, above all, indirect – often third- or fourth-hand. The meanings attributed by the actors to the myths they relived in ecstasy, as well as to the rituals in which they participated, generally escape us. In this connection too the documentation of the *benandanti* is precious. In their accounts we see different individuals articulate, in a distinct manner, each with his own accent, a core of common beliefs. This wealth of lived experience is almost never to be found in the concise summaries elaborated by the Hellenistic mythographers, the authors of the early medieval penitentials, or by the nineteenth-century folklorists. But although they can be described through formal, abstract oppositions, myths are embodied, transmitted and enacted in concrete social situations, by flesh and blood individuals.

However, they also act independently of the individuals' consciousness of them. Here the analogy with language, by definition imperfect, irresistibly comes into play. One is tempted to compare the individual variants of the myth to particular linguistic acts: and the Lap or Siberian shamans, the Baltic werewolves, the *armiers* of the Pyrenean Ariège, the *benandanti* of Friuli, the Dalmatian *kresniki*, the Romanian *călușari*, the Hungarian *táltos*, the Caucasian *burkudzäutä*, with a diverse population dispersed in time and space, speaking different mythical languages, but linked by intimate relationships. In order to reconstruct the meaning of their myths and rituals at a supra-individual level, it is necessary to follow the path traced in the linguistic sphere by Benveniste: 'It is a matter of adducing a meaning by comparison and by means of diachronic analysis where, at the outset, we only have a designation. The temporal dimension thus becomes an explanatory one.'[89] Beyond the synchronically reconstructible use (*désignation*) tied to local conditions, there emerges, via 'retrospective comparativism', a meaning that Benveniste calls 'primary' (*signification première*) – in the purely relative sense of being the oldest attainable.[90] In the case of the phenomena considered here, the primary nucleus consists in the journey of the living into the world of the dead.

21. To this mythical nucleus are also linked folkloric themes such as night flying and animal metamorphoses. From their fusion with the image of a hostile sect, projected in turn onto lepers, Jews, male and female witches, there sprang a cultural formation: the Sabbath. Its diffusion outside the Western Alpine arc, where it had first crystallized, began during the early decades of the fifteenth century. Thanks to the preachings of San Bernardino of Siena, a sect hitherto considered peripheral was discovered in Rome at the very heart of Christianity. Analogous discoveries were destined to be made for more than two centuries throughout Europe. Local and supra-local circumstances explain the intensification of the witch hunts on each occasion: without any doubt the stereotype of the witches' Sabbath, invariant except for certain superficial variations, powerfully contributed to their intensification.

With the end of the persecutions, the Sabbath dissolved. Denied as a real event, relegated to a no longer threatening past, it fed the imagination of painters, poets and philologists. But for a period which was ultimately quite brief (three centuries), the very ancient myths merged into that composite stereotype and have survived its disappearance. They are still active. The unfathomable experience that humanity has symbolically expressed for millennia through myths, fables, rituals and ecstasies, remains one of the hidden centres of our culture, of the way we exist in this world. The attempt to attain knowledge of the past is also a journey into the world of the dead.[91]

Notes

The idea for this research dates back to 1964 or 1965; the actual work began in 1975. Since then it has continued in intermittent fashion, with long pauses and digressions. I have presented some provisional results at the seminars directed by Jacques Le Goff (at the École Pratique des Hautes Études), by Jean-Pierre Vernant (at the Centre de Recherches Comparées sur les Sociétés Anciennes), and by Keith Thomas (at Oxford University); in two series of lectures delivered, respectively, at the Van Leer Foundation of Jerusalem, at the invitation of Yehuda Elkana, and at the Collège de France, at the invitation of André Chastel and Emmanuel Le Roy Ladurie; at Edinburgh in an Antiquary Lecture; in the History Department of Princeton; in the course of my seminars with students at Yale (1983) and Bologna (1975–6, 1979–80, 1986–7). I have learnt a great deal from these encounters and discussions. But without the periods spent, on various occasions, at the Centre de Recherches Historiques (Paris), at the Whitney Humanities Center of Yale University in the autumn of 1983, at the Institute of Advanced Study (Princeton) in the winter of 1986, at the Getty Center for the History of Art and Humanities (Santa Monica) in the spring of that same year, the present book would never have been written.

I have discussed this research at length, first with Stefano Levi Della Torre and Jean Lévi, then with Simona Cerutti and Giovanni Levi: their criticisms and suggestions have been precious for me. Salvatore Settis agreed to improve the text while it was still in proof. In the notes I thank those who, over so many years, have helped me with advice and suggestions. Here I would especially like to remember with affection and gratitude, Italo Calvino and Arnaldo Momigliano.

1. See J. Hansen, *Quellen und Untersuchungen zur Geschichte des Hexenwahns und des Hexenverfolgung im Mittelalter*, Bonn 1901, Index (the entry for 'Hexensabbat'). On the *sabbat* see P.-F. Fournier, *Étymologie de sabbat 'réunion rituelle de sorciers'*, in *Bibliothèque de l'École des Chartes*, CXXXIX (1981), pp. 247–9 (pointed out to me by Alfredo Stussi), which hypothesizes a link with the Jews' day of rest, thus reviving a connection with *ensabatés*, i.e., the Waldensians. (In this regard one should add the entry in S.J. Honnorat, *Vocabulaire français-provençal*, Digne 1846–47, for 'Sabbatatz, ensabatz'). The reconstruction proposed later (Part One, chapter 2) suggests that the two elements may have reinforced each other. One of the first demonological writings in which the term appears, in the plural (*sabbatha*), is L. Daneau's dialogue frequently reprinted and translated into French, German and English (*De veneficis, quos vulgo sortiarios vocant* ... Frankfurt-am-Main, 1581, p. 242). The term 'synagogue', also used contemporaneously to describe gatherings of heretics, proves to have been quite widely used by judges and inquisitors until the late sixteenth century (see, for example, E. W. Monter, *Witchcraft in France and*

Switzerland, Ithaca and London 1976, pp. 56–7). In the German we find 'Hexentanz': see H. C. E. Midelfort, *Witch-Hunting in Southwestern Germany, 1562–1584*, Stanford 1972, p. 246 n. 92. 'Striaz', Italianized as 'striazzo' or 'stregozzo' (this last the title of a famous etching by Agostino Veneziano), shows up in the trials at Modena. On 'barlòtt' see the entry under that term in *Vocabolario dei dialetti della Svizzera italiana*, II, pp. 205–9 – very accurate, but debatable in its conclusions (see below, pp. 78–79). 'Akelarre' is a Basque term, from 'akerra', billy goat (the form assumed by the devil at witches' gatherings): see J. Caro Baroja, *Brujeria Vasca*, 'Estudios Vascos', V, San Sebastian 1980, p. 79. However, in some Basque regions it was completely unknown to those under inquisition: cf. G. Henningsen, *The Witches' Advocate. Basque Witchcraft and the Spanish Inquisition*, Reno (Nevada) 1980, p. 128.

2. See, for example, the passages by M. Del Rio quoted in *The Night Battles* by the author: pp. 8, n. 2, 34, n. 3.
3. See A. Macfarlane, *Witchcraft in Tudor and Stuart England*, London 1970, pp. 58, 130.
4. See K. Thomas, in *Witchcraft, Confessions and Accusations*, M. Douglas, ed London 1970.
5. See A. Momigliano, 'Linee per una valutazione della storiografia del quindicennio 1961–1975', in *Rivista storica italiana* LXXXXIX (1977), p. 596.
6. See H. R. Trevor-Roper, *Religion, The Reformation and Social Change*, London; *idem*, *The European Witch Craze of the 16th and 17th Centuries*, London 1969, p. 9.
7. Ibid.
8. Cf. Lawrence Stone, 'Magic, Religion and Reason' in *The Past and the Present*, London 1981, especially pp. 165–7.
9. Cf. Macfarlane, op. cit., p. 11.
10. Ibid., p. 10.
11. Ibid., p. 139.
12. Ibid., pp. 26–27 and 58. For an anthropological comparison, see pp. 11–12 and 211 ff.
13. See J. Obelkevich, ' "Past and Present". Marxisme et histoire en Grande Bretagne depuis la guerre', in *Le Débat*, 17 December, 1981, pp. 101–02.
14. Cf. Keith Thomas, *Religion and the Decline of Magic*, London 1971, p. 469.
15. Cf. ibid., p. 518.
16. Cf. H. Geertz, 'An Anthropology of Religion and Magic. II', *The Journal of Interdisciplinary History*, VI (1975), pp. 71–89.
17. Cf. E. P. Thompson, *Anthropology and the Discipline of Historical Context*, "Midland History", I, 3, 1972, pp. 41–45.
18. Cf. Keith Thomas, 'An Anthropology of Religion and Magic. II,' *The Journal of Interdisciplinary History* VI (1974), pp. 91–109, especially p. 106.
19. Ibid., p.108.
20. Cf. S. Clark, 'Inversion, Misrule and the Meaning of Witchcraft', *Past and Present* 87 (May 1980), pp. 98–127.
21. Cf. Thomas, art. cit., pp. 103–04.
22. Cf. Kieckhefer, *European Witch-Trials, Their Foundations in Popular and Learned Culture, 1300–1500*, Berkeley 1976, pp. 8, 27 ff.
23. The term 'diabolism' is a not altogether happy one since, as we shall see, the devil constitutes one of the elements imposed by judges on a stratum of pre-existing beliefs.
24. Ibid., pp. 39–40.
25. Ibid., pp. 21–2.
26. The absence of Jews in the medieval part of Cohn's reconstruction (aside from a cross-reference in the introduction to J. Trachtenberg's *The Devil and the Jews* [New

25

York 1943] and another mention in the notes on p. 261) is striking, above all because, in a preceding book, he had momentarily come upon the trajectory which I am trying to trace: see *Warrant for Genocide*. Perhaps Cohn has been induced to foreground the heretic-witch connection (which I consider secondary in the final analysis) by his polemic with J. B. Russell. The latter had read the polemical sources, even the most stereotyped, as objective descriptions of an alleged transformation, over the centuries, of heretics into witches: Cohn has rightly rejected this interpretation, but has become entangled in the same documentary series. See J. B. Russell, *Witchcraft in the Middle Ages*, Ithaca 1972, pp. 86 ff., especially pp. 93, 140–2, etc.; Cohn, *Europe's Inner Demons*, pp. 121–3.

27. Ibid., p. 228.
28. Ibid., pp. 220 ff.
29. Ibid., pp. 107 ff.
30. Ibid., pp. 107–08.
31. Cf., for example, ibid., pp. 108 ff; Henningsen, op. cit., pp. 70 ff; C. Larner, *Witchcraft and Religion. The Politics of Popular Belief*, Oxford 1985, pp. 47–8.
32. Cf. Thomas, op. cit., pp. 514–17.
33. Cf. *The Night Battles*, London 1983 pp. XIX-XX; and see Henningsen, op. cit., p. 440, n. 14, which distinguishes from the flock of adherents to Murray's fantastic theories some 'more serious' scholars, among them the present author. On the objections addressed to me by Norman Cohn, see n. 39. My evaluation of Murray's research has the support of Emmanuel Le Roy Ladurie; see *La Sorcière de Jasmin*, Paris 1983, p. ff.
34. Cf. the exhaustive demonstration in Cohn, op. cit., pp. 111-15.
35. Cf. M. A. Murray, *The Witch-Cult in Western Europe*, Oxford 1962, p. 12.
36. Cf. *The Night Battles*, pp. XIX-XX.
37. Ibid., pp. 129–34.
38. Cf. Russell, op. cit., pp. 41–2; H. C. E. Midelfort, 'Were There Really Witches?' in *Transition and Revolution: Problems and Issues of European Renaissance and Reformation History*, edited by R. M. Kingdon, Minneapolis 1974, p. 204. See also Midelfort, op. cit., pp. I, 231, n. 2. (Midelfort has told me in the course of a conversation that he has changed his opinion on this point.)
39. Cf. Cohn, op. cit., pp. 223–4 (on pp. 123–4, however, criticism is exclusively, and contradictorily, directed at Russell, for having misunderstood the point of view of the present author).
40. I have tried to justify this postulate from a general point of view in *Myths, Emblems, Clues* (London 1989), but see also Thompson, art. cit.
41. *The Night Battles*, p. XXI
42. Albeit in an attenuated form, I think that I too am guilty of the first: overlooking the ecstatic specializations that distinguished male and female *benandanti* seems to me in retrospect a case of sex-blindness (see the discussion in the appendix to *Les Batailles nocturnes*, Lagrasse 1980, p. 231).
43. Cf. C. Larner, *Enemies of God. The Witch-Hunt in Scotland* (London 1981) and *Witchcraft and Religion* (These are studies of great value; it should be noted that the subtitle of the second, which appeared posthumously – *The Politics of Popular Belief* – refers almost exclusively to beliefs *about* witches, not *of* witches.)
44. L. Muraro, *La signora del gioco*, Milan 1976 (concerning which see below, p. 115).
45. Even an historian and folklorist like Henningsen, having dedicated several pages to the usual refutation of Murray's thesis (op. cit., pp. 69–94), limits himself to stating the need for a comparison between Basque folklore on both sides of the Pyrenees and the demonological treatises of the period, in order fully to account for the congruence

between the defendants' confessions. In the conclusion (p. 390) these similarities are attributed to an epidemic of stereotyped dreams – which re-poses the problem of the witches' Sabbath in all its unexplored complexity. (But see now, for a different perspective, the precious essay by Henningsen cited in Part Two, chapter 2, n.1.) The need to confront the problem of European witchcraft from an historical-religious perspective is stated by J. L. Pearl, 'Folklore and Witchcraft in the Sixteenth and Seventeenth Century', in *Studies in Religion*, 5 (1975–76), p. 386, which is based on the essay of M. Eliade, 'Some Observations on European Witchcraft', in *History of Religions*, 14 (1975), pp. 149–72. For an excellent contribution of this type see M. Bertolotti, 'Le ossa e la pelle dei buoi. Un mito popolare tra agiografia e stregoneria', *Quaderni storici*, 41 (May–August 1979), pp. 470–99 (on which see p. 51, n. 77). Much material, analyzed in a different perspective from that adopted here, can be found in H. P. Duerr, *Traumzeit*, Frankfurt-am-Main 1978.

46. Cf. Midelfort, op. cit., p. 1; Monter, op. cit., p. 145. Trevor-Roper has also insisted on the 'universality' of witchcraft beliefs at the folk level (see above, p. 3).

47. See Carlo Ginzburg, 'Présomptions sur le sabbat', in *Annales E.S.C.*, 39 (1984), p. 341 (an article which anticipates some of the results of this research). The implicit reference to Freud has a purely analogical value.

48. See Jacques Le Goff's excellent introduction to the new French edition of Marc Bloch, *Les Rois thaumaturges* (Paris 1981).

49. See J. R. von Bieberstein, *Die These von der Verschwörung*, Bern 1976, and the introductory pages of L. Poliakov, *La Causalité diabolique. Essai sur l'origine des persécutions*, Paris 1980 (a debatable book in many respects). An illuminating instance is the successful history of the *Protocols of the Elders of Zion*, subjected to a profound analysis by Norman Cohn in *Warrant for Genocide*. In general, see C. F. Graumann and S. Moscovici (eds), *Changing Conceptions of Conspiracy*, New York 1987.

50. From a substantially similar point of view Jacques Le Goff considers Bloch's *Royal Touch* the model for a renovated historical and political anthropology (introduction cit., p. XXXVIIII). See also the observations of F. Hartog in 'Marshall Sahlins et l'anthropologie de l'histoire', *Annales E.S.C.*, 38 (1983), pp. 1256–63. The essays collected in Graumann and Moscovici (eds), op. cit., are dedicated to the demystification of the notion of a plot: a necessary but limited goal, and to some extent common ground.

51. See Larner, op. cit., p. 7 (examples of this kind could be multiplied ad infinitum).

52. The term 'dialogical' is used here in the sense introduced by M. M. Bakhtin.

53. Cf. *The Night Battles* pp. 28 ff.

54. Cf. ibid., pp. XXI, 32; Eliade, art. cit., especially pp. 153–8, where an affinity between the *benandanti* and the Rumanian *calusari* is proposed (on whom see pp. 189 ff.) The juxtaposition of *benandanti* and shamans is criticized by Marc Augé, *Génie du paganisme*, Paris 1982, p. 253, who suggests, however, an analogy between the *benandanti* and anti-witchcraft Ashanti. Yet immediately thereafter he concedes that the latter are comparable, 'from a structural point of view', to the shamans. As we shall see, the connection between *benandanti* and shamans is at once structural (or, if one prefers, morphological) and historical.

55. Cf. Thomas, op. cit., p. x. The limitations of the comparison conducted by Macfarlane have already been described.

56. Insofar as it relates to the 'wild hunt', this possibility is denied by Kieckhefer, op. cit., p. 161, n. 45; but see below, pp. 101 ff.

57. On this point see Jacques Le Goff, *Pour un autre Moyen Age*, Paris 1978, p. 314 n. 12.

58. Cf. Ludwig Wittgenstein, 'Bemerkungen uber Frazer's *Golden Bough*', *Synthese*, 17 (1967) pp. 233–53. These reflections should be compared with the studies, inspired

by Goethe's morphological writings, which emerged, in diverse disciplines and cultural spheres at the end of the 1920s: see the present author's 'Datazione assoluta e datazione relative: sul metodo di Roberto Longhi', in *Paragone*, 386 (April 1982), p. 9 (where I mention also *Morphology of the Folktale* by Vladimir Propp and *Forme semplici* by A. Jolles); and, above all, J. Schulte, 'Coro e legge. II "metodo morfologico" in Goethe e Wittgenstein', *Intersezioni* II (1982), pp. 99–124.

59. See Wittgenstein, art. cit., p. 30.
60. See A. Momigliano, 'Historicism Revisited', in *Sesto contributo alla storia degli studi classici e del mondo antico*, Rome 1980, I, p. 27. 'We study change because we are changeable. This gives us a direct experience of change: what we call memory...' (see the entire page).
61. On the same lines see the Overture to Claude Lévi-Strauss, *The Raw and the Cooked*, Harmondsworth 1986.
62. 'Morphology of the Folk-Tale' (1928) in *Theory and History of Folk-Lore*, Minneapolis, 1984, edited by A. Liberman. See present author's 'Présomptions', art. cit., pp. 347–8. Analogous problems have been independently confronted, in another disciplinary sphere, by A. Leroi-Gourhan; see *Documents pour l'art comparé de l'Eurasie septentrionale*, Paris 1943 (e.g., p. 90), based on studies already published in 1937–42.
63. Cf. the Preface to *Clues*.
64. On this notion see the very important essay by Rodney Needham, 'Polythetic Classification', in *Man*, n.s. 10 (1975), pp. 349–69.
65. Cf. Marcel Detienne, *Dioniso e la pantera profumata*, It. tr. Bari 1983, pp. 49–50; J.-P. Vernant, *Religione greca, religioni antiche* (Vernant's inaugural lecture at the Collège de France in 1975), in *Myth and Society in Ancient Greece*, Brighton 1980, p. 265. And see also, by the same author, the objections to G. S. Kirk (which, however, seem more applicable to Burkert's position) in B. Gentili and G. Paione (eds), *Il Mito greco....*, Rome 1977, p. 400. The discussion with Burkert is taken up more fully in Detienne and Vernant, *La Cuisine du sacrifice en pays grec*, Paris 1979, *passim*.
66. In a very fine page Roman Jakobson (*Selected Writings*, I, The Hague 1971, pp. 632) has quoted a sentence of Braque: 'I do not believe in things, I believe in their relationships.' In similar fashion, Lévi-Strauss has spoken of the 'Copernican revolution' brought about in the human sciences by structural linguistics (see *le regard éloigné*), Paris 1983, p. 12).
67. On the interpretation of myth proposed by Jung, see the unexceptionable critical observations of Vernant, op. cit., pp. 229–30. Eliade dissociates himself from the Jungian notion of the archetype only in the preface to the English translation of his *Le mythe de l'éternel retour (Cosmos and History*, New York 1959, pp. VIII-IX). Previously, he had used this idea quite lavishly: see, for example, *Trattato di storia delle religioni*, trad. It., Turin 1954, pp. 39, 41, 408, 422, etc. (and see also the critical observations of E. De Martino, Introduction p. IX).
68. Cf. Vernant, op. cit., p. 265; Detienne, op. cit., p. XI: 'Such an interpretation must not only be economic and coherent, but it must also possess a heuristic value, making evident relations between elements which were previously extraneous or providing a new approach to information explicitly stated, but inscribed elsewhere, in other places, *in the same system of thought and within the same culture*' (my italics).
69. See Vernant, op. cit., pp. 223–4; Detienne, op. cit., p. XI, which refers to 'systematic deduction'.
70. See Vernant, op. cit., pp. 249–50. The solution cautiously envisaged ('The response would probably consist in showing that neither in historical research nor in synchronic analysis does one encounter isolated elements, but always structures,

more or less tightly intertwined . . .') converges with the position of Roman Jakobson, which has also inspired this study.

71. Cf. J.-P. Vernant, *Mito e pensiero presso i Greci* It. tr. Turin 1970 (especially p. 261 ff).
72. The inspiration of Dumézil is particularly evident in the essay *Il mito esiodeo delle razze* (see *Myth and Thought*, especially p. 34). For an overall evaluation of Dumézil's contribution, see Vernant, *Ragioni del mito* (in *Myth and Society*, pp. 235–37) and Detienne, op. cit., pp. 8–9. In the introduction to the Italian edition of *Myth and Thought (Mito e pensiero presso i Greci,* Turin 1970) B. Bravo emphasizes (p. XVI) that Vernant's attitude 'is always implicitly, and sometimes explicitly', 'comparative'. On this point see now 'Greek Religion', in *Myth and Society*.
73. Cf. Detienne, op. cit., pp. 8–9.
74. Jean Starobinski has interestingly proposed that Saussure's selection of synchronicity was provoked by the 'difficulties encountered in the exploration of the long diachronicity of the legend and the brief one of the anagrammatic composition.' *Words upon Words: The Anagrams of Ferdinand Saussure*, New Haven, Italian trans. (*Le parole sotto le parole. Gli anagrammi di Ferdinand de Saussure.* It. tr. Genoa 1982, pp. 6–7).
75. See Georges Mounin, 'Lévi-Strauss' Use of Linguistics' in I. Rossi (ed) *The Unconscious as Culture*, New York 1974, pp. 31–52; C. Calame, 'Philologie et anthropologie structurale. À propos d'un livre récent d'Angelo Brelich', *Quaderni Urbinati*, II (1971), pp. 7–47.
76. Detienne, op. cit., p. II.
77. Lévi-Strauss holds a different opinion (*The Raw and the Cooked*). It is true that elsewhere (*Structural Anthropology*, Harmondsworth 1977, Chapter 11) he has maintained that all the versions of a myth belong to the myth: but that at best eliminates the problem of authenticity, not that of completeness.
78. See, in addition, Part Three, chapter 2.
79. In an essay published in 1975 M. I. Finley polemicized in the name of diachrony with anthropologists ('Anthropology and the Classics', in *The Use and Abuse of History*, London 1975. The growing relations between history and anthropology have complicated the picture: alongside historians who uphold the superiority of synchronic analysis, we find anthropologists who vindicate the utility of a diachronic perspective for their own research (see B. S. Cohn, 'Toward a Rapproachment', in A. Rabb and R. J. Rothberg (eds), *The New History. The 1980s and Beyond*, Princeton 1982, pp. 227–52). On the compatibility between historical and synchronic perspectives, see G. C. Lepschy, *Mutamenti di prospettiva nella linguistica*, Bologna 1981, pp. 10–11.
80. See Ivanov, Lotman and others, *Tesi sullo studio semiotico della cultura*, Parma 1980, pp. 50–1 (and cf. pp. 51–2: 'a broad typological approach eliminates the absolutism of the opposition between synchrony and diachrony').
81. Cf., for example, Roman Jakobson, 'Results of a Joint Conference of Anthropologists and Linguists' (1953), in *Selected Writings*, II, The Hague-Paris 1971, p. 632; idem, *Magia della parola*, K. Pomorska ed., It. tr. Bari 1980, pp. 56–7. The presence of Jakobson's categories in Lotman's work is emphasized by D. S. Avalle (1953) in, ed. K. Pomorska. The repetition of Jakobson's categories by Lotman is underlined by D. S. Avalle in the introduction to a collection of essays edited by him, *La cultura nella tradizione russa del XIX e XX secolo*, Turin 1982, pp. 11–12.
82. Jakobson, *Magia*, pp. 13–14, with a reference to P. G. Bogatyrëv's study on Ukrainian folklore. The sentence that follows immediately after – 'In short, I discover a striking rehabilitation of the romantic conception of folklore as a collective creation' – alludes to the essay by Jakobson co-authored with Bogatyrëv, 'Il folklore

come forma di creazione autonoma' (1929) (translated in *Strumenti critici*, I, 1967, pp. 223–40). Bogatyrëv, 'Die Folklore als eine besondere Form des Schaffens' (1929), in R. Jakobson, *Selected Writings*, IV, The Hague-Paris 1966, pp. 1–15.

83. Cf. J.-C. Schmitt, 'Les traditions folkloriques dans la culture médiévale. Quelques refléxions de methode', in *Archives de sciences sociales des religions*, 52 (1981), pp. 5–20, especially pp. 7–10 regarding Bertolotti, art. cit. (see above, n. 45), who is criticized for his diachronic excesses.

84. Cf. C. Lévi-Strauss, 'History and Anthropology' (1949), in *Structural Anthropology*, pp. 1–27 (the quotation from Marx and the reference to Febvre's *The Problem of Unbelief in the Sixteenth Century* are both to be found on p. 23).

85. Cf. Claude Lévi-Strauss, 'The Scope of Anthropology' (1960), in *Structural Anthropology 2*, Harmondsworth 1978, pp. 3–32; idem, 'De Chrétien de Troyes à Richard Wagner' (1975), in *le regard éloigné*, cit., pp. 301 ff; idem, 'Le Graal en Amérique' (1973–74), in *Paroles données*, Paris 1984, pp. 129 ff.; idem, 'Hérodote en mer de Chine', in *Poikilia. Études offerts à Jean-Pierre Vernant*, Paris, 1987, pp. 25–32.

86. Idem, 'Histoire et ethnologie', *Annales E.S.C.*, 38 (1983), pp. 1217–31 (the passage cited is on p. 1227). For a survey of the discussions under way on cladistics see D.L. Hill, 'Cladistic Theory: Hypotheses that Blur and Grow', in T. Duncan and T.F. Stuessy (eds), *Cladistics: Perspectives on the Reconstruction of Evolutionary History*, New York 1984, pp. 5–23 (with bibliography).

87. This point has been clarified for me by Richard Trexler during a conversation some years ago (autumn 1982): I thank him here.

88. Cf. Detienne, op. cit., p. 13.

89. Cf. E. Benveniste, *Indo-European Language and Society* London 1973; It. trans. *Il vocabolario delle istituzioni indoeuropee*. It. trans. Turin 1976, I, p. 7. The editor of the Italian edition, M. Liborio, identifies (pp. XIII-XIV) the implicit polemic contained in the final sentence against 'Saussurean Manichaeanism'. This passage includes the sentence, also taken from the preface to the same work ('Diachrony is then re-established in its true legitimacy insofar as it is the succession of synchrony'), cited by Vernant, who extends it to an extra-linguistic sphere (see *Nascita di immagini*, Milan 1982, p. 110, n. 1).

90. Cf. Benveniste, op. cit., p. 31.

91. Emmanuel Le Roy Ladurie, *Montaillou, village occitan de 1294 à 1314*, Paris 1975, p. 602; and see also A. Prosperi, 'Premessa a I vivi e i morti', *Quaderni storici*, 50 (August 1982), pp. 391–410.

PART ONE

I

LEPERS, JEWS, MUSLIMS

1. In 1321, we read in the chronicle of the monastery of St Stephen of Condom, a great deal of snow fell during the month of February. The lepers were exterminated. There was another great snowfall before the middle of Lent; then came a great rain.[1]

The anonymous chronicler devotes to the extermination of the lepers the same detached attention given to normal meteorological events. Other chronicles of the same period refer to the event with greater emotion. The lepers, one of them says, 'were burnt in almost all of France, because they had prepared poisons to kill the entire population'.[2] Another, the chronicle of the monastery of St Catherine *de monte Rotomagi*, writes:

> In the entire kingdom of France the lepers were imprisoned and condemned by the Pope; many were sent to the stake; the survivors were confined to their dwellings. Some confessed that they had conspired to kill all the healthy Christians, noble or not noble, and to obtain power over the entire world (*ut delerent omnes sanos christianos, tam nobiles quam ignobiles, et ut haberent dominium mundi*).[3]

Even more expansive is the account of the Dominican inquisitor Bernard Gui. The lepers, 'diseased in body and soul', had strewn poisonous powders in the fountains, wells and rivers, so as to transmit leprosy to the healthy and cause them to fall ill or die. It seems incredible, Gui observes, but they aspired to gain power over the towns and the countryside; they had already divided the power and posts of counts and barons among themselves. After being imprisoned, many of them confessed to having participated in secret gatherings or chapters, which their leaders had held for two successive years for the purpose of furthering the conspiracy. But God took pity on his people; and in many towns and villages the guilty were discovered and burnt. Elsewhere the horrified population, without waiting for a full and proper trial, boarded up the houses of the lepers and set them on fire, along with their inhabitants. Afterwards, however, it was decided to proceed less precipitately: and henceforth the surviving lepers, proven innocent, were by providential decision confined to secluded places, wasting away without prospect of release. And in order that they should not be able to inflict harm or reproduce, the men and women were strictly separated.[4]

Both the extermination and confinement of the lepers had been authorized by Philip the Fifth, the Long One, King of France, in an edict issued at Poitiers on 21 June 1321. Since the lepers – not only in the kingdom of France but throughout the kingdoms of Christianity – had tried to kill the healthy by poisoning waters, fountains and wells, Philip had given orders to incarcerate and burn those culprits who confessed. Some of them, however, went unpunished: hence the measures against them. All surviving lepers who had confessed to the crime were to be burnt. Those who refused to confess were to be subjected to torture – and, once they had confessed the truth, to be burnt. Leprous women who had confessed to the crime spontaneously, or as a result of torture, were to be burnt, unless pregnant; in that eventuality, they must be kept segregated until their confinement and the weaning of their offspring – and then burnt. Those lepers who, despite everything, refused to admit their participation in the crime were to be segregated in their places of origin; men and women must be rigorously separated. The same fate would befall their offspring should any be born in the future. Children under fourteen were to be segregated, and once again, separated by sex; those over fourteen who had confessed to the crime were to be burnt. Furthermore, since the lepers had committed *lèse-majesté* against the State, all their goods were confiscated until further notice: friars, nuns, and all those who benefited in any way from these goods were to be given whatever was necessary for subsistence. All judicial proceedings against the lepers were the purview of the crown.

These provisions were partly modified by two edicts that followed shortly after, issued respectively on 16 and 18 August of the same year. Having met with protests from prelates, barons, noblemen, and communities claiming the right to administer the possessions of the lepers placed under their custody, in the first edict Philip the Fifth gave orders to suspend the confiscations. In the second, he awarded the bishops and the judges of the lower courts permission to judge the lepers, leaving moot the issue (on which opinions differed) as to whether or not a crime of *lèse majesté* had occurred. This waiving of crown prerogatives was explicitly motivated by the need to punish the guilty as speedily as possible. The trials therefore continued, and with them the segregation of the lepers. A year later Philip the Fifth's successor, Charles the Handsome, confirmed that they were to be confined (*renfermés*).[5]

This is the first time in the history of Europe that such a huge programme of segregation was undertaken. In succeeding centuries other protagonists would take the lepers' place: the mad, the poor, criminals and Jews.[6] But the lepers led the way. Despite the fear of contagion, which inspired complex rituals of separation (*De Leproso amovendo*), they had hitherto lived in hospital-like institutions, almost always administered by religious orders, largely open to the outside world, and entered voluntarily. Henceforth in France they were locked up for life in enclosed places.[7]

2.   The pretext for this dramatic turn had, as we have seen, been offered by the providential discovery of the conspiracy. But other chronicles offer a different version.

An anonymous chronicler of those years (his account ends in 1328) reported the same rumour, whose origin he claimed not to know, about the lepers' attempt to poison fountains and wells; he added new details concerning the division of powers they had planned (one was to become King of France, another King of England, a third the Count of Blois); but he also introduced a novel element.

> It was rumoured [he wrote] that Jews were accomplices of the lepers (*consentans aux méseaux*) in this crime: and therefore many of them were burnt together with the lepers. The populace took justice into its hands, without calling provost or bailiff: they locked the people inside the houses together with their animals and chattels and set them on fire.

Jews and lepers are here represented as equally responsible for the conspiracy. But this is an almost isolated voice:[8] indeed, a group of chroniclers presents a third version of the facts, more complex than those mentioned hitherto. They are the anonymous continuators of the chronicles of Guillaume de Nangis and of Girard de Frachet; Jean de Saint-Victor; the author of the chronicle of Saint Denis; Jean d'Outremeuse; the author of the *Genealogia comitum Flandriae*.[9] Except for the last, all of them make explicit reference to a confession delivered to Philip the Fifth by Jean Larchevêque, Lord of Parthenay. In it one of the lepers had declared that he had been corrupted by money from a Jew, who had given him poison to scatter in the fountains and wells. The ingredients were human blood, urine, three unspecified herbs and a consecrated host – all of this dried, reduced to powder and placed in small bags weighted down so as to sink to the bottom more easily. More money had been promised to involve other lepers in this plot. But about it, and its nature, opinions diverged. The most common and reliable opinion (*verior*), according to the chronicles we are considering, fixed responsibility on the King of Granada. Unable to defeat the Christians by force, he had decided to dispose of them by cunning. He had then turned to the Jews, offering them an enormous amount of money to hatch a criminal scheme to destroy Christianity. The Jews had accepted, but had stated that they could not act directly because they were under too much suspicion: it would be better to entrust the execution of the scheme to the lepers, who, being in continuous contact with the Christians, would be able to poison the waters without difficulty. The Jews had then assembled a number of the lepers' leaders and, with the devil's help, had induced them to abjure their faith and grind the consecrated host into the pestilential potions. Then the lepers' leaders had summoned four councils in which the representatives of all the leper colonies (except for two in England) had participated. To the assembled lepers, at the instigation of the Jews, who were in turn inspired by the devil, they had addressed the following speech: the Christians treat you like vile and abject people; we should bring about their deaths or infect them with leprosy; if all were equal (*uniformes*) no-one would despise his fellow.

This criminal plan had been received with great approval and relayed to the lepers in the various provinces, together with the promise of kingdoms, principalities and counties that would become vacant after the death or infection of the healthy. The Jews, says Jean d'Outremeuse, had reserved the lands of certain princes for themselves; the lepers, says the continuator of Guillaume de Nangis' chronicle, had laid claim to the titles they believed to be within reach (one leper burnt in Tours toward the end of June called himself the abbot of the largest monastery). But the conspiracy had been discovered; the guilty lepers burnt; the others jailed in accordance with the prescriptions of the royal edict. In various parts of France, above all in Aquitaine, the Jews had been sent to the stake indiscriminately. In Chinon, near Tours, a large ditch had been dug into which 160 Jews, men and women, had been thrown and burnt. Many, the chronicler says, hurled themselves into the ditch, singing, as though they were going to a wedding feast. Some widows had their own children thrown into the fire so that they would not be baptized and taken away by the noblemen who witnessed the scene. Near Vitry-Le-François forty Jews who had been jailed decided to cut each others' throats so as not to fall into the Christians' hands; the last survivor, a youth, tried to escape with a bundle containing money taken from the dead, but he broke a leg, was caught and put to death. In Paris the guilty Jews were burnt and the others exiled in perpetuity; the richest were forced to turn over their wealth to the treasury, to the tune of 150,000 *livres*.[10] In Flanders the lepers (and possibly the Jews as well) were initially incarcerated and then freed – 'to the great displeasure of many', the chronicler notes.[11]

3. So there are three versions: the lepers instigated by the Jews, in turn instigated by the Muslim king of Granada; or, the lepers and the Jews; or the lepers alone. Why this disaccord between the chronicles? In order to answer this question, it is necessary to go back over the chronology and geography of the discovery of the conspiracy. The entire episode will then appear to us in a clearer light.

The first rumours about the poisoning of the water, immediately followed by accusations, imprisonments and burnings at the stake, had begun in Périgord on Holy Thursday (16 April) of 1321.[12] They had rapidly spread throughout Aquitaine. The previous year the region had been infested by bands of so-called *Pastoureaux*, who originated in Paris: troops of boys and girls about fifteen years old, barefoot and in rags, who marched along bearing a banner marked with the cross. They said they wanted to embark for the Holy Land. They had neither leaders, nor weapons, nor money. Many people received them benevolently and fed them for the love of God. When they reached Aquitaine, in order 'to gain popular favour', Bernard Gui states, the *Pastoureaux* began to try to baptize the Jews by force. Those who refused were robbed or killed. The authorities were concerned. At Carcassonne, for example, they intervened in defence of the Jews inasmuch as they were 'servants of the king'. Many people, however, (this is Jean de Saint-Victor writing) approved of the *Pastoureaux*'s violent actions, saying that 'one mustn't oppose the faithful in the name of the heathen'. [13]

It was precisely from Carcassonne, probably towards the end of 1320 (and at any rate before February 1321), that the consuls of the seneschal had sent a protest to the king. Abuses and excesses of various kinds were disturbing the life of the cities under their rule. Royal officials' violation of the prerogatives of the local courts forced the parties in dispute to go to Paris, at great inconvenience and expense, for the trials; what's more, they forced the merchants to pay heavy fines, unjustly accusing them of usury. Not content with making usurious loans, the Jews prostituted and violated the wives of the poor Christians who were unable to pay the interest; they reviled the consecrated host, which they received from the hands of the lepers and other Christians; they were guilty of every kind of monstrosity in defiance of God and the faith. The consuls pleaded that the Jews be driven from the kingdom, so that faithful Christians would not be punished for their nefarious sins. Moreover, they denounced the vile intentions of the lepers, who were preparing to spread the disease by which they were afflicted 'with poisons, pestilential potions, and sorceries'. In order to prevent the spread of the contagion, the consuls suggested that the king segregate the lepers in buildings set aside for the purpose, separating males from females. They declared themselves ready to provide for the maintenance of those secluded and the administration of the revenues, the alms and pious inheritances that they would receive now or in the future. In this fashion, they concluded, the lepers would at last cease to multiply.[14]

4.   To get rid of the credit monopoly exercised by the Jews once and for all; to administer the rich revenues enjoyed by the leper asylums – these aims, set out by the Carcassonne consuls, were declared with brutal clarity in their protest to the king. Only a few months before the same consuls had tried to defend the Jewish communities against the plunder and massacres perpetrated by the bands of *Pastoureaux*. This had probably not been a gesture of disinterested humanity. For behind the list of complaints sent to the King of France, we perceive the clear determination of an aggressive mercantile class, anxious to sweep away competition – that of the Jews – now deemed intolerable. It is possible that the (doomed) plans for administrative centralization implemented by Philip the Fifth precisely during those months, helped to exacerbate the tensions. The centre's attempt to weaken local identities fed hostility in the periphery toward the least protected groups.[15]

The population of Aquitaine would most likely support anti-Jewish measures. We have seen the sympathy with which they had received the 'disorderly and rustic multitude' of the *Pastoureaux*.[16] The terrible famine of 1315–18 had certainly intensified hostility towards Jewish money lenders.[17] And elsewhere the tensions provoked at all social levels by the establishment of a monetary economy had for some time tended to find an outlet in anti-Semitic hatred.[18] In many parts of Europe the Jews were accused of poisoning wells, of practising ritual murders, of profaning the consecrated host.[19]

This last accusation recurs, as we have seen, in the protest launched by the consuls of Carcassonne and the surrounding cities. In it, however, the lepers – immediately afterwards presented as poisoners – were linked to the Jews as their accomplices. We have here an association dense with symbolic implications, which accordingly cannot be reduced to the authorities' declared intentions regarding the lepers.

5.   The association between Jews and lepers is an ancient one. Since the first century AD, in his apologetic text *Against Apion*, the Jewish historian Flavius Josephus polemicized with the Egyptian known as Manetho, who had maintained that among the ancestors of the Jews was a group of lepers driven out of Egypt. Anti-Jewish traditions, possibly of Egyptian provenance, had undoubtedly found their way into Manetho's apparently intricate and contradictory lost account. The diffusion of *Against Apion* in the Middle Ages circulated this damaging legend in the West, together with others (donkey worship, ritual murder) likewise refuted by Josephus, that were destined to become more or less enduring items of anti-Jewish propaganda.[20]

The influence exercised by this tradition on learned culture was unquestionably considerable. But much more important for the common people was the converging tendency between the thirteenth and fourteenth centuries which made the Jews and lepers two groups that were relegated to the margins of society. The Lateran Council of 1215 had ordered the Jews to carry on their clothes a disk, usually yellow, red or green. For their part the lepers had to wear special clothes: a grey or (more rarely) black cloak, a scarlet cap and hood, and sometimes a wooden rattle (*cliquette*).[21] These identification marks had been extended to *cagots* or 'white lepers' (assimilated to the Jews in Brittany), who were otherwise commonly distinguished from the healthy only by the absence of ear lobes and bad breath: the Council of Nogaret (1290) decreed that they must carry a red badge on the chest or on a shoulder.[22] The imposition of identifying marks on Jews and lepers so that they could be immediately recognized, decided upon by the Council of Marciac (1330), indicates the extent to which a common stigma of infamy now attached to both groups. 'Beware of the friendship of a lunatic, of a Jew or of a leper', read an inscription placed over the door of the Parisian cemetery of the Holy Innocents.[23]

The stigma sewn on garments expressed a profound, above all physical, alienation. The lepers are 'fetid'; the Jews stink. The lepers spread contagion; the Jews contaminate foodstuffs.[24] And yet the revulsion inspired by both, which led people to keep them at a distance, was grafted onto a more complex and contradictory attitude. The tendency to turn them into pariahs struck at precisely these groups, because their condition was ambiguous, borderline.[25] Lepers are an object of horror because the disease, regarded as a bodily sign of sin, disfigures their features, almost wiping out their human appearance: but the love evinced for them by Francis of Assisi or by Louis IX is presented as a sublime testimonial of sanctity.[26] The Jews are the deicide race, to whom, however, God has chosen to reveal himself; their holy book is indissolubly linked with that of the Christians.

All this put lepers and Jews in a position which is at once inside and outside Christian society. But toward the end of the thirteenth and the beginning of the fourteenth century, their position as marginal beings was transformed into segregation. The ghettos rose little by little throughout Europe, initially opted for by the Jewish communities themselves to ward off hostile incursions.[27] And in 1321, with striking parallelism, the lepers were also confined.

6. After the event, the association of lepers and Jews in the portrait of the conspiracy seems almost inevitable. And yet it was slow to crystallize. True enough, in the protests from Carcassonne the lepers were accused, in conjunction with other unidentified Christians, of giving hosts to the Jews for them to profane; but not a word was uttered about the Jews' participation in the lepers' schemes to spread their disease by poison and spell. The silence is all the more surprising given that, for a century and a half, the accusation of poisoning the water had been made several times precisely against the Jews, slowly migrating from the East to the West.[28] The very date of the discovery of the conspiracy – Holy Week, a traditional time for Jewish massacres – seemed to invite the incrimination of the Jews as its authors. Instead, the anger of the population and repression by the authorities focused elsewhere.

On 16 April 1321, the day of Holy Thursday, the mayor of Périgueux ordered the lepers previously sheltered in the leper asylums in the vicinity to assemble in one place, separating males from females. The first rumours concerning the poisoning of wells and fountains – spread anonymously – were evidently already circulating. The lepers were interrogated, doubtless tortured. The trials concluded with general executions at the stake (27 April). The representatives of the city of Périgueux left for Tours on 3 May to inform the king of what had happened.[29] But meanwhile, since Easter Day, an investigation into the poisoners had also begun at Isle-sur-Tarn. The interrogations were conducted by a group of citizens from Toulouse, Montauban and Albi. The lepers and *cagots* of the leper asylums of Isle-sur-Tarn, Castelnau de Montmirail, Gaillac, Montauban, and so on, were accused of having scattered poisons and spells (*fachilas*), were interrogated, and tortured.[30] In this instance we do not know the conclusion of the trials. But we do know, from the registrar at Caen, that between May and June the lepers of the dioceses of Toulouse, Albi, Rodez, Cahors, Agen, Périgueux and Limoges, as well as those from various other parts of France, were all sent to the stake, 'except for a few pregnant women and children incapable of

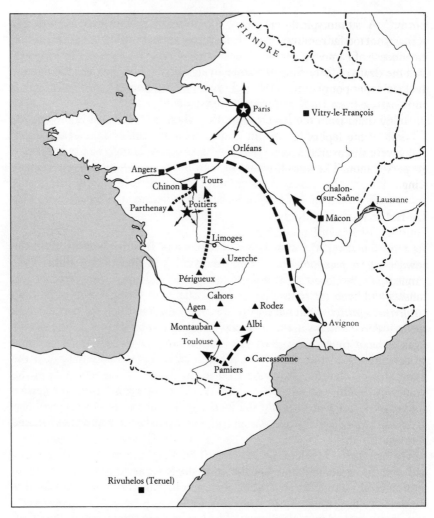

▲ Locality in which responsibility for the plot was attributed to the lepers

■ Locality in which responsibility for the plot was attributed to the Jews

★ Edict of Philip V against the lepers (Poitiers, June 21, 1321)

✪ Edict of Philip V against the Jews (Paris, July 26, 1321)

▪▪▪▶ Attempts to direct the repression against the lepers

▬▶ Attempts to direct the repression against the Jews

Map 1

1321. The conspiracy of lepers and Jews.

harm'.[31] A stereotypical and emphatic declaration, certainly – and yet perhaps not too far removed from the truth, to judge by the case of Uzerche in the diocese of Limoges. Here the trials, begun on 13 May, ended on 16 June with the death of forty-four people, men and women – i.e., three-quarters of the local leper population. The mothers, a chronicler writes, tore their new-born babies from their cribs and carried them with them on to the fire, shielding them from the flames with their bodies.[32]

News of the lepers' imminent plot had spread from Carcassonne. The guilty were discovered and punished everywhere. Their confessions fuelled the persecution. The news burnt like a fuse, crossing France all the way to the King.

7. But it was not only the secular authorities that began to act. Jacques Fournier, Bishop of Pamiers (later Pope Benedict XII), charges Marc Rivel, his representative, with the task of finding out about the poisons and evil powder (*super pocionibus sive factilliis*) scattered by the Provençal lepers. Pamiers is very close to Carcassonne, the epicentre of the initiative, whose consuls had been the first to sound the alarm about the *venenis et potionibus pestiferis et sortilegiis* with which the lepers were preparing to spread the evil spell. And in Pamiers on 4 June, before Rivel appears the accused Guillaume Agassa, head (*commendator*) of the nearby leper asylum of Lestang. The proceedings against him, which have come down to us in their entirety, give some idea of what the hundreds of trials of lepers conducted throughout France during that summer of 1321, the records of which have been lost or not yet retrieved, were like.[33]

Agassa immediately shows that he is repentant; he declares that he wants to help punish the guilty; he begins to confess. The previous year, on 25 November 1320, two lepers, Guillaume Normanh and Fertand Spanhol, had with his agreement gone to Toulouse to obtain certain poisons. Having returned to Lestang, they had told him that they had poured the poisons into Pamiers' wells, fountains and streams in order to spread leprosy and death. Elsewhere, he had been told, the lepers had done the same.

A week passes, and the trial resumes. This time the confessions are much more detailed. 'Spontaneously and not because threatened with torture' (the notary's words), Agassa says that the year before an unknown young man had come to him with a letter from the director of another lepers' asylum, the asylum of Porte Arnaud-Bernard in Toulouse. This man asked Agassa to come to Toulouse on the following Sunday to discuss matters that would bring him advantages and honours. On the agreed date, approximately forty people, both lepers and people in charge of the leper asylums of Toulouse and its vicinity, had assembled. All of them had received letters like the one delivered to Agassa. The person who had organized the assembly (Agassa did not know his name) had said: 'You see how the healthy Christians despise us sick people, how they keep us at a distance, deride us, hate us and curse us.' The heads of the leper hospitals throughout Christendom, he had continued,

41

should convince the patients to administer poisons, incantations and harmful potions to the healthy Christians so as to bring about their deaths or infect them with leprosy. In this way, the diseased and their leaders would eventually rule and administer, or even own, the lands of the healthy. In order to achieve all this they would have to accept the King of Granada as their protector and defender – a role he had promised to perform after a meeting with several of the lepers' leaders. Following this speech, with the help of certain doctors, poisons had been prepared that were to be scattered in the waters of wells, fountains and rivers throughout Christendom. Each of those present had received a small leather or cloth bag which contained the poison he was to spread in his region. The discussion lasted for two consecutive days, Sunday and Monday. At the end they had all declared themselves in agreement and had sworn to carry out the mission assigned to them. Then the assembly came to an end.

At this point Agassa, who during the first interrogation had denied having himself spread the poison, lists the places where he had scattered it; he minutely describes how he had attached the small bag to stones so that the water would not wash it away; he gives the names of other accomplices who had participated in the meeting with him. A few days later he is again brought before the judges. Among them is Jacques Fournier, Bishop of Pamiers. With his appearance in the role of inquisitor, the trial ceases to be an ordinary criminal trial, as it had been up until then. Agassa states that he made his first confession 'immediately after having been released from torture' (in the preceding documents there is no indication of this kind) and that he had repeated it without being tortured. He confirms the truth of everything he has said hitherto. Then, in the course of a new interrogation, he repeats his account of the Toulouse meeting, adding a range of new details. In the interim he has remembered the name – Jourdain – of the person who had called the meeting. In the speech this man had supposedly given there appears, along with the King of Granada, the Sultan of Babylon. Meanwhile their promises have become more precise: the head of each leper asylum was to become the master of the surrounding locality it served. In return, the Saracen sovereign has set a condition not referred to in the preceding confession, and which was sufficient to justify the trial's transfer to a tribunal of the Inquisition. The heads of the leper asylums were expected to 'abjure Christ's faith and its law, and would be given a powder contained in a pot in which there was some consecrated host mixed with serpents, toads, lizards, geckoes, bats, human excrement and other things', which had been prepared in Bordeaux on the orders of the King of Granada and the Sultan of Babylon. Anyone refusing to abjure Christ's faith would have been decapitated by 'a tall dark man wearing a cuirass and a helmet on his head, armed with a scimitar', who was present at the meeting. Jourdain had said that at a future meeting, besides heads of all the leper asylums of Christendom, the King of Granada and the Sultan of Babylon would also attend. In their presence all would be required to spit on the host and cross and trample the latter underfoot: this was the commitment made by the head of the Bordeaux leper asylum, who kept in contact with the Saracens to obtain their support. A number of the Saracens present at the meeting had promised to relay everything to their respective sovereigns. Jourdain had said that the King of Granada and the Sultan of Babylon intended to take over all the domains of the Christians, after they had been killed or infected by leprosy.

In great detail Agassa describes the poison, the pot that contained it, the method used to scatter it in the fountains and the wells, the localities in which he had scattered it. This time he maintains that he acted on his own. He exonerates Guillaume Normanh and Fertand Spanhol, who were mentioned during the first interrogation, saying that he had falsely accused them. Similarly, he exonerates the head of the Savardun asylum, 'already burnt', and the head of the Unzent and Pujols asylums, mentioned as participants at the Toulouse meeting, declaring them innocent. As for himself, in replying to one of the judges' questions, he says that he abjured Christ's faith and his law, thinking 'that it was worth nothing'. He held to this opinion for three months.

On 20 May, before Bishop Fournier and several other Dominican friars, Agassa confirms that he has told the truth. He declares himself generally repentant of the crimes committed and ready to perform the penances that will be imposed upon him. As was to be expected in a trial of the Inquisition, he abjures only the crimes committed against the faith: his apostasy, the outrage to the host and the cross, every heresy and every curse. The poisoning of the water is no longer mentioned. A year later, on 8 July 1322, he is sentenced to be immured for life, in the most rigid form (*in muro stricto in vincolis seu conpedibus*), together with a group of followers of the heretical doctrines of the Beguines.[34]

8. It is clear that in his trial torture and threats played a decisive role. Agassa was subjected to torture even prior to the interrogations.[35] But the initial results were disappointing. Agassa denounces a couple of accomplices, sketches the general outlines of the conspiracy, but does not show much imagination. Then, obviously under pressure from the judges, new details gradually emerge: the meeting of the lepers, the promises of the King of Granada and the Sultan of Babylon. Finally, with the third interrogation, the picture is complete. Agassa admits that he has abjured the faith, trampled on the cross, profaned the consecrated host under the threatening gaze of the Moor brandishing his scimitar. In order to convince him to make these confessions, the judges had probably promised to save his life. Therefore, before the end of the trial, Agassa retracts his initial admissions, which involved innocent people, or at least their memory (one of them has already perished at the stake).

So, during the course of the trial, little by little Agassa's version is made to coincide with the judges' prior version. If we compare it with the versions circulated by the contemporary chronicles, we see that it is a compromise between the simpler one, which attributed the plot solely to the lepers, and the more complex one, according to which the lepers had been recruited by the Jews, who had in turn acted at the instigation of the King of Granada. In Agassa's confessions we find the latter, accompanied by the Sultan of Babylon; we find the lepers; but the Jews are once again absent.

Their presence or absence in the various versions of the conspiracy was decisive on a practical level. Like the lepers, the Jews could be identified to the populace as guilty, tried and sent to the stake, or massacred without a trial. The Saracen kings, remote, indeed unreachable, were a decorative element, which functioned only at a symbolic level. In this regard we should note that among the judges who on 8 July 1322 pronounced sentence against Agassa, was the inquisitor Bernard Gui. It is likely that on this occasion he examined the trial documents. We do not know whether he had already written the account of the 1321 conspiracy with which, in one part of the manuscript tradition, his *Flores chronicarum* ends. At any rate, neither at the time nor subsequently did he feel the need to include reference to the Saracen kings mentioned by Agassa, though he followed his confessions in several essential respects: the secret gatherings of the leper leaders, which lasted two years; the projected division of the ruler over cities and land; the poisoning of the water. Like Agassa, Bernard Gui said not a word about the participation of the Jews.[36]

9. In the ferocious royal edict issued on 21 June in Poitiers, the lepers were once again named as solely responsible for the conspiracy. At first sight this is surprising, because on 11 June riots had broken out in Tours against the Jews, followed by arrests, since they were thought to be accomplices of the leper poisoners.[37] Not far from Tours, at Chinon, perhaps during the same days, there occurred the massacre mentioned in the chronicles of 160 Jews, burnt and then buried in a common grave. With methods presumably similar to those employed in Agassa's case, the authorities had hastened to extort proof of the Jews' guilt. As has already been mentioned, the guilt was to be revealed by the confession of one of the lepers' leaders, incarcerated and tried in the domains of Jean Larchevêque, Lord of Parthenay.[38] He sent the document, duly sealed, to the King who was in the nearby town of Poitiers. Here, on 14 June, a meeting was held of representatives of towns in the central part of Southern France to discuss a vast programme of administrative reforms. It seems that the meeting lasted nine days; on 19 June, so the Parisian chronicle informs us, the involvement of the Jews was communicated to the King.[39] If this information is correct, why did the King, in the edict issued two days later, accuse only the lepers?

An explanation for this silence must in all probability be sought in an event that immediately preceded it. On 14 or 15 June, the Jewish communities of the kingdom of France had been sentenced to pay an exorbitant fine for crimes of usury: 150,000 *livres tournois*, to be divided up according to each community's ability to pay.[40] Faced with an outburst of popular anger (orchestrated from above) the representatives of the communities had tried to ward off the worst by yielding to Philip the Fifth's demands for money.[41] This is obviously a conjectural reconstruction since there exists no direct documentary proof of such bargaining; but there is an indirect clue.

10.   It is a long missive sent by Philippe de Valois, Count of Anjou (and later King of France under the name Philip the Sixth) to Pope John XXII. Having asked that it be read by the cardinals assembled in consistory at Avignon – at the time part of the feudal domains of Anjou – the Pope included it in a pontifical letter exhorting Christians to the Crusade.[42] This is how the missive has come down to us.

Here is what Philippe de Valois had written. On the Friday after the feast of St John the Baptist (i.e., 26 June) there had been a solar eclipse in the counties of Anjou and of Touraine.[43] During the day, for a period of four hours, the sun had appeared enflamed and red as blood; during the night the moon had been seen covered with spots and black as sackcloth. Such observations (implicit in the text was a reference to *Apocalypse* 6. 12–13) led people to believe that the end of the world was imminent. There had been earthquakes; fiery spheres had fallen from the heavens, setting fire to the thatched roofs of the houses a dreadful dragon had appeared in the sky, murdering many people with its fetid breath. The next day people began to attack the Jews because of their evil deeds against the Christians. During the search of the house of a Jew named Bananias, in a room that was set apart, inside the casket containing his money and secrets, was found a skin of a ram inscribed with Hebrew characters and sealed. The cord of the seal was crimson-coloured silk. The seal, of purest gold and weighing the equivalent of nineteen Florentine florins, was a most skilfully carved crucifix that represented a monstrous Jew or Saracen atop a ladder leaning against the cross, in the act of defecating on the sweet face of the Saviour. This had focused attention on the writing: two baptized Jews had revealed its content. At this point Bananias, together with six other co-religionists able to read Hebrew fairly well, had been imprisoned and subjected to torture. Their interpretations of the writing had more or less coincided (*satis sufficienter unum et idem dicebant, vel quasi similia loquebantur*). Three Christian theologians had translated it from Hebrew into Latin with all possible diligence. Philip of Anjou conveyed the entire text of this translation.

It was a letter addressed to the most glorious and most powerful Amicedich, King of thirty-one kingdoms (Jericho, Jerusalem, Hebron, etc.), to Zabin, Sultan of Azor, to His Magnificence Jodab of Abdon and Semeren, and to their viceroys and coadjutants. Prostrating himself before all of them, Bananias, together with the entire people of Israel, declared his subjection and obedience. Several times, since the year 6294 after the creation of the world, his Majesty the King of Jerusalem had, through his intermediary the Viceroy of Granada, deigned to conclude a pact in perpetuity with the Jewish people, sending it a message. Therein it was recounted that Enoch and Elijah had appeared to the Saracens on Mount Tabor, to teach them the Jewish law;

in a ditch in the Sinai valley the Old Testament's lost ark had been discovered and subsequently escorted with great jubilation by foot soldiers and knights to the city of Ay; inside the ark had been found the manna sent by God in the desert, still unspoiled, together with the rods of Moses and Aaron and the tablets of the Law carved by God's very finger; confronted with this miracle, all the Saracens had declared a wish to be circumcised, converting to the faith of the God of the Jews. They wished to return Jerusalem, Jericho and Ay, the seat of the ark, to them; in exchange however, the Jews must deliver to the Saracens the kingdom of France and the illustrious city of Paris. Having learned of this wish of the Viceroy of Granada, Bananias continued, we Jews devised a clever stratagem: with the help of the lepers, whom we had corrupted with large sums of money, we poured powders prepared with bitter herbs and the blood of poisonous reptiles into the wells, fountains, cisterns, and rivers to exterminate the Christians. But the poor, unfortunate lepers behaved naively (*se simplices habuerunt*): at first they accused us Jews; then, deceived by other Christians, they confessed everything. We exult over the massacre of the lepers and the poisoning of the Christians because the division of kingdoms leads to their destruction. As for the martyrdom that we suffer on account of the lepers' accusations, we endure it with patience for the love of God, who will repay us a hundred-fold in the future. We would doubtless have been exterminated, had not our great wealth made the Christians greedy enough to demand ransom, as you certainly must have heard from the Viceroy of Granada (*et procul dubio credimus depopulati fuisse, nisi grandis noster thesaurus corda eorum in avaritia obdurasset: unde aurum et argentum nostrum et vestrum nos redemit, prout valetis scire ista omnia per praedictum subregem vestrum de Granada*). Now send us gold and silver: the poisons have not had full effect, but we hope to do better on another occasion, after some time has gone by. Thus you will be able to cross the sea, disembark at the port of Granada, expand your rule over the lands of the Christians and install yourself on the throne of Paris: and we shall gain possession of the land of our fathers that has been promised to us by God, and we shall all live together under one Law and one God. And there will no longer be sorrows, and there will be no oppression for eternity, in accordance with the words of Solomon and David. And for the Christians the prophecy of Hosea will come true: 'their heart is divided, and therefore they shall perish' (*Hosea, 10*). Bananias concluded by stating that in order for it to reach the East the document would be entrusted to Sadoch, High Priest of the Jews, and to Leo, expert of the Law, who would be better able to explain it in person.

11.   According to the Hebrew calendar we were then in the year 5081. Was the date mentioned in Bananias' letter – the year 6294 since the creation of the world – due to an actual oversight? Or was it instead a deliberate error introduced by the Jews forcibly involved in the letter's composition with the aim of signalling the falseness of the document to their co-religionists?[44] We shall never know. Philip of Anjou delivered Bananias' letter to the Pope,

communicating his intention (later put in effect) of leaving for the Crusades.[45] To him and all those who were to accompany him, John XXII imparted the ritual absolution. At that moment, his past lack of enthusiasm for the Crusade had ended in the face of the Muslim advance that threatened Cyprus and Armenia.[46] Hence, in all likelihood, his decision not only to give credence to, but also to circulate, a document that proved how the Muslims, with the complicity of the Jews, aimed at nothing less than the French throne. John XXII had displayed benevolence towards the Jewish communities even in the recent past, taking up their defence against the gangs of *Pastoureaux*: but the proof of their complicity with the lepers, transmitted by Philippe de Valois, must have seemed irrefutable to him. It is impossible to calculate the extent to which this was influenced by the Pope's debt of gratitude to Philippe, who a year earlier had led an unsuccessful expedition against the Ghibellines in Italy.[47] The fact is that, in a sudden (and hitherto unexplained) volte-face, in 1322 John XXII expelled the Jews from his domain.[48]

We do not know the provenance of so complex and elaborate a forgery as Bananias' letter. It is a document that reflects preoccupations very different from those that can be deciphered in the confession extorted from Agassa during the trial initiated approximately a month earlier in Pamiers. The lengthening of the chain evoked to explain the conspiracy (lepers-Jews-Viceroy of Granada-King of Jerusalem, etc.) served to focus attention on the closest intermediaries. The guilt of the lepers was by now taken for granted, regarded as of secondary importance given the unfolding events. An attempt was being made to kindle a new wave of persecutions against the Jews, and involved turning to the Pope in order to circumvent the King's hesitation. The latter was indirectly criticized in the reference made by Bananias (or rather the person writing on his behalf) to the greed of the Christians, who had preferred to extort ransom from the Jews instead of exterminating them.

12.   To those same days can probably be traced the fabrication of other proofs of the Jews' participation in the plot: two letters on parchment penned by the same hand, accompanied by seals, both in French, followed by an appendix in Latin.[49] The first, by the King of Granada, is addressed to 'Samson the Jew, son of Elias'; the second, by the King of Tunis, 'to my brothers and their sons'. The King of Granada stated that he had been informed that Samson had paid the lepers with the money sent him; he recommended that they should be paid well, considering that 115 of them had sworn to play their part. He enjoined them to take the poisons that had already been sent and have them placed in the cisterns, wells and fountains. If the powders were not sufficient, he would send more. 'We have promised to return the Promised Land to you,' he wrote, 'and in that regard we shall keep you up to date.' He was sending 'something else, for you to throw into the water the king drinks and uses'. He insisted that they mustn't worry about expenses – for those who had committed themselves to the enterprise: but it

47

was necessary to act quickly. The letter was to be shown to the Jew Aaron, the King of Granada concluded, recommending that they remain united in the undertaking.

The King of Tunis quickly came to the point.

> Try to take proper care of the matter of which you know, because I will let you have sufficient gold and silver for the expenses: if you wish to entrust your children to me, I shall take care of them as if they were flesh of my flesh. As you know, the agreement between us, the Jew and the diseased, was concluded a short while ago, on the day of Palm Sunday. Ensure to poison the Christians in the shortest possible time, without worrying about what it costs. As you know, seventy-five people, both Jews and diseased, were present at the oath. We greet you and your brothers, because we are brothers in the same law. We greet the young and the old.

As mentioned, the two letters were accompanied by a statement in Latin, dated Mâcon, 2 July 1321, in which the physician Pierre *de Aura* swore in the presence of the local bailiff François *de Aveneriis*, the judge Pierre Majorel, and various clerics and notaries, that he had faithfully translated the text from Arabic into French. There followed the signatures of the notaries, accompanied by the notary's office, profession and cipher which guaranteed the authenticity of the document.

The authenticated original of this dual forgery is not to be found in Mâcon but Paris: in the middle of the seventeenth century it was kept in the Chartes Treasury; today it figures among the treasures of the Archives Nationales.[50] It is very likely that Paris was its original destination: the menacing request addressed by the King of Granada to the Jew Samson – that he pour an unspecified substance 'into the water the king drinks and uses' had to be brought to the King's attention. In short, pressure was exerted on Philip the Fifth from many sides to take a position, publicly denouncing the Jews' participation in the plot.

13. At last the denunciation arrived. Philip sent to the seneschals and bailiffs a letter in which he stated that he had ordered 'the capture of all the Jews in our kingdom' because of the horrendous crimes committed by them, and especially their

> participation and complicity in meetings and conspiracies conducted long since by lepers in order to place deadly poisons in wells and fountains and other places. . . to bring about the death of the people and subjects of our kingdom.

For this purpose the Jews had obtained the aforementioned poisons, paying out considerable sums of money. It was therefore obligatory for them to be interrogated without delay, men and women, in order to identify those responsible for the misdeed and punish them in accordance with the law. Torture should be inflicted only on the most serious suspects and those who had been denounced by other Jews or lepers; those who declared themselves innocent must be spared. But it was absolutely necessary to requisition all the wealth the Jews were hiding, guarding against the fraud which had been committed against previous kings of France: those condemned to death would therefore be approached by four upright citizens (*bourgeois prud-hommes*) who would try by all possible means to recover this wealth.[51]

The letter was dated Paris, 26 July; on 6 August it was sent to the seneschal of Carcassonne – the man who, in conjunction with his colleagues from the neighbouring cities, had lit the spark that would set off the conspiracy with his message to the King a few months earlier. Thus the circle was complete. Further copies of the royal letter were sent, inter alia, to the seneschals of Poitou, Limoges, and Toulouse, to the bailiffs of Normandy, Amiens, Orleans, Tours, Mâcon, and the Provost of Paris.

14. So, the sum of 150,000 *livres tournois*, extorted from the Jews by Philip the Fifth in the middle of June as the price for his silence, served only to delay the persecution for a few weeks. At best it led to the inclusion of the request in the King's letter to the authorities, not to employ torture indiscriminately. A tragic trick, destined to be repeated many times (even in recent times). The trials, followed by the burning, of Jews who had confessed to complicity with the lepers continued for two more years, in tandem with the exaction of the enormous fine (later reduced to 100,000 *livres*). In the spring or summer of 1323 (in any case before 27 August) Philip the Fifth's successor, Charles the Fourth, expelled the Jews from the kingdom of France.[52]

15. The seneschal of Carcassonne and the nearby cities had requested the segregation of the lepers and the expulsion of the Jews in the message sent to Philip the Fifth between the end of 1320 and the beginning of 1321. After a little more than two years both had been obtained, thanks to the intervention of the King, the Pope, Philip of Valois (future King of France), Jacques Fournier (future pontiff), Jean Larchevêque, Lord of Parthenay, of the inquisitors, judges, notaries, local political authorities – and, of course, the anonymous mobs that massacred lepers and Jews, 'without waiting', as the chronicler wrote, 'for either provost or bailiff'. Everyone had played his part: some had fabricated the forged proofs of the conspiracy and some had spread them abroad; some had instigated and some had been incited; some had judged, some had tortured, some had killed (according to the rituals prescribed by law or outside them). Given the coincidence between the starting point and the destination of this very rapid series of events, there is little alternative but to conclude that not one, but two conspiracies occurred in France between the spring and summer of 1321. The wave of violence against lepers unleashed by the first conspiracy spread throughout the south and south-west, with an outbreak toward the east, in the area of Lausanne.[53] But the wave that followed very shortly after, fuelled by the conspiracy against the Jews, predominantly struck the north and the north-east.[54] It is probable that in some places the persecution fell indiscriminately upon both.[55]

In referring to conspiracy it is not our wish to simplify unduly a plot whose origins were complex. It may very well be that the first accusations arose spontaneously from below. But the rapidity with which the repression spread in an age when news travelled on foot, on muleback, at most on horseback; and the geographical diffusion from the likely epicentre of Carcassonne (see map 1) – the combination of these reveals the presence of deliberate and co-ordinated actions, intended to guide a series of pre-existing tensions in a predetermined direction.[56] Conspiracy means this, and this alone. To assume the existence of a single co-ordinating centre, composed of one or more persons, would obviously be absurd and in any case refuted by the delayed and contested emergence of the accusation against the Jews. It would be just as absurd to maintain that all the participants in the episode (victims excluded) acted in bad faith. In fact, in this context bad faith is irrelevant – besides being unverifiable. The use of torture in the trials to extract an already fabricated version, or the manufacture of forgeries for more or less worthy purposes, are (then as today) operations that it is possible to perform in perfect good faith, in the conviction of certifying a truth for which the proof is regrettably lacking. Those who ordered, solicited, or manufactured the proofs of the supposed conspiracy – from the small bags full of poisonous herbs, to the false confessions, to the apocryphal letters – may even have been convinced of the guilt of the lepers and Jews. That the great majority of the population was convinced of it seems more than probable. As for the authorities (the King of France, the Pope, etc), we shall never know to what extent they believed in the innocence of those they were persecuting. But their intervention was decisive. To characterize the whole episode as an obscure convulsion of the collective mentality which swept up all layers of society is a mystification. Beneath the apparent uniformity of behaviour we detect a field of forces, of varying intensity, now converging, now con-flicting.[57]

16.   In at least one case – beyond the borders of the kingdom of France, on the other side of the Pyrenees – we know that the accusation against the alleged poisoners met with immediate resistance. On 29 July, at Rivuhelos, not far from Teruel, a man was discovered throwing poisonous powders into fountains. Subjected to torture 'to attain knowledge of the truth', this man (his name was Diego Perez) at first confessed that he had received the poisonous powders and herbs from a Breton; then later, correcting his previous statements, he accused two rich Jews, Simuel Fatos and Yaco Alfayti, who lived in the nearby village of Serrion. The judge and the *alcaldes* of Teruel had them immediately arrested, provoking a reaction from the bailiff, who less than a month later sent a report on the entire affair to the King of Aragon. Suspecting that Perez's accusations were unfounded, the bailiff had insisted that Fatos and Alfayti be handed over to him, on the basis of a law that reserved proceedings against Jews to him or to the King. The city council had balked at this: Simuel Fatos had been tortured several times, but had confessed to nothing. (What became of Alfayti is not known.) Since Perez continued to repeat his own version, he had been sent a man disguised

as a priest who had pretended to take his confession. Perez had fallen into the trap, and admitted that the Jew was innocent; if he continued to accuse him it was only 'for fear of the great torment that he had undergone', and because in exchange release had been promised him. The bailiff had tried in vain to have Fatos delivered to him: 'there were people on the council who were lusting to kill a Jew, even if there were neither confessions nor proofs against him.' The judges had condemned Diego Perez to death; but Simuel Fatos had been delivered to the mob which had mutilated, dismembered and burnt him. And yet, the bailiff repeated, the Jew 'had died unjustly'.[58]

17. The authorities and judges who exert pressure so that the accusation will fall upon those who are already candidates for the role of scapegoat; the accused who yields, terrorized by torture; the mob unleashed against those presumed guilty: all of this seems predictable, almost obvious – even if documented, in this instance, with an unusual wealth of detail thanks to the discord between the authorities in Teruel. The resistance put up by the bailiff throws into stark relief the general readiness to accept rumours about the conspiracy automatically. In France, as we have seen, things unfolded in similar fashion. The authorities' version could spread and take root because at all levels of the population there was a willingness to accept, indeed to anticipate, the guilt of the lepers and Jews.

Such accusations were not new. We find them already formulated in the chronicles of the preceding century. Vincent of Beauvais attributed the children's crusade of 1212 to a diabolical plan of the Old Man of the Mountain, leader of the mysterious sect of Assassins, who had promised freedom to two imprisoned clerics provided they bring him all the young boys of France.[59] According to the chronicles of Saint-Denis, the crusade of the *Pastoureaux* in 1251 was the result of a pact between the Sultan of Babylon and a Hungarian master of magical arts. The latter, having promised, through the power of spells, to bring the Sultan all the young men of France, at the price of four gold *bisanti* each, had gone to Picardy where he had made a sacrifice to the devil by casting a powder into the air: all the *Pastoureaux* had followed him, leaving their animals in the fields. On the person of another leader of the same crusade (Matthew Paris added) had been found poisonous powders and letters from the Sultan, written in Arabic and Chaldean, which promised large sums of money in the event of the undertaking being crowned with success.[60] Perhaps someone had interpreted the 1320 crusade of the *Pastoureaux* in the same way; what is not in doubt is that the following year, the same pattern reappears not only in the chronicles, but in the forged letters and the forced confessions extracted from lepers and Jews alike.

In all these accounts we encounter the fear aroused by the unknown and menacing world that loomed beyond the confines of Christianity.[61] Every disquieting or incomprehensible event was attributed to the infidels' machinations. There is almost always a Muslim sovereign behind it, generally inspired by the devil: the Old Man of the Mountain (Vincent of Beauvais); the Sultan of Babylon (Matthew Paris, Chronicle of Saint-Denis, Agassa's trial); the King of Jerusalem (Bananias' letter); the Kings of Tunis and Granada (Agassa's trial, the apocryphal letters of Mâcon, the continuator of Guillaume of Nangis and his imitators). Directly or indirectly, these characters conspire with isolated figures or with groups, marginal from a geographical or ethnic-religious point of view (the Hungarian master, the Jews), promising them money in exchange for the execution of the plot. The plot is materially executed by other groups, who, because of their age (the children), their social inferiority (the lepers), or both of these reasons (the *Pastoureaux*) are readily susceptible to false promises of wealth and power. The causal chain can be long or short – in Teruel, for instance, the search for those responsible stops at the Jews (in the first version a Breton filled the role). Certain stages are occasionally omitted (in Agassa's confession the Muslim kings conclude an agreement with the lepers, ignoring the Jews). Others may be repeated (in his letter to Bananias, the King of Jerusalem corrupts the Jews through the King of Granada). In general, however, the chain we have described implies a gradual series of stages that leads from the enemy without to the enemy within, who is his accomplice and, as it were, a manifestation of him – the latter a figure destined for a long and successful career.[62] And if the first was by definition beyond the reach of justice, the second was within reach, waiting to be massacred, imprisoned, tortured, burnt.

A series of sensational cases in France during the first decades of the fourteenth century helped to spread this fear of conspiracies. Among the many accusations circulated against the order of the Templars was that of having made secret agreements with the Saracens.[63] Guichard, Bishop of Troyes, and Hugues Geraud, Bishop of Cahors, were tried in 1308 and in 1317 on respective charges of having attempted to kill Queen Joan of Navarre and Pope John XXII by magical means.[64] These are cases that seem to anticipate on a minor scale the conspiracy attributed some years later to the lepers and Jews. Here for the first time the tremendous potentialities for social purification contained in the conspiratorial schema (every phantasmic plot tends to generate a real one of an inverse nature) were fully exploited. Amidst the fear of a physical and metaphorical contagion, the ghettos, the infamous badges on clothes, were no longer sufficient.[65]

18.   The first wave of the persecution, against the lepers, had reached its peak during the summer of 1321. On 27 August, in conformity with the royal edict, fifteen men and women, who had escaped the fires that had exterminated three-quarters of the lepers of Uzerche in the diocese of Limoges, were branded on the neck with red-hot irons so that they could be recognized in the event of their escape, and were locked up in a house owned by the leper asylum. Theirs was to have been a permanent confinement; but after a month they were suddenly released.[66] It is not clear how this is to be

reconciled with the information about the confinement of lepers during subsequent years. It does, however, indicate that the accusations formulated at the beginning of the summer were no longer considered valid. Yet the second wave of persecution which crashed down upon the Jews lasted longer, as we have seen: but gradually the references to the poisoning of waters included in the Treasury records began to be accompanied by a cautionary formula: 'It is said that (*ut dicitur*).'[67] Evidently, not even the authorities were now prepared to underwrite the official version of the conspiracy without qualifications.

It is unlikely that the accusations against the Jews were formally withdrawn; in any event, this did not prevent their expulsion from France. In the case of the lepers, things developed differently. We do not know whether the innocence of the lepers had already been officially recognized in 1325, when the visionary béguine Prous Boneta, tried at Carcassonne as a heretic, compared the béguines and lepers sent to the stake by Pope John XXII to the children murdered by Herod.[68] But at some stage this did occur, as we can see from a Bull issued on 31 October 1338 by Pope Benedict XII to the Archbishop of Toulouse. The lepers of the diocese had asked the Pope to support their attempt to recover the goods (rents, houses, fields, vineyards, sacred utensils) confiscated by the secular authorities. The Pope supported their request and invited the Archbishop to do the same, pointing out that the lepers had been recognized in court as 'innocent and guiltless' of the crimes of which they had stood accused, to the point of formal restitution (evidently not carried out) of the confiscated goods.[69] The Pope who wrote these words was the same Jacques Fournier who, less than twenty years earlier, in his capacity as Bishop and inquisitor of the diocese of Pamiers, had been present at the interrogation during which Agassa docilely described the plot against Christianity hatched by the assembled lepers.

Thus a parenthesis was closed: living and dead lepers were given retrospective absolution by their persecutors. For the Jews, by contrast, everything was about to begin all over again.

Notes

1. Dom M. Bouquet, *Recueil de historiens de la Gaule...*, new edn., Paris 1877–1904, XXIII, p. 413 (a note of the editors on p. 491 reminds us that this passage, together with others, was written in 1336: the temporal distance from the events explains the mistaken placing of the extermination of the lepers during the winter, rather than in the spring-summer, of 1321).
2. Ibid., p. 483. See also *Annales Uticenses* in Ordericus Vitalis, *Historiae ecclesiasticae libri tredecim*, A. Le Prevost ed., V, Parisiis 1855, pp. 169–70.
3. Bouquet, op. cit., pp. 409–10 (compiled in 1345; cf. p. 397).
4. Cf. E. Baluze, *Vitae paparum Avenionensium*, G. Mollet ed, I, Paris 1916, pp. 163–4. Similar accounts have been furnished by Peter di Herenthals and Amalricus Auger (ibid., pp. 179–80, 193–4). As can be seen from the manuscript tradition, the

passage from Bernard Gui's chronicle referred to was written immediately after the events it narrates: see L. Delisle, *Notice sur les manuscripts de Bernard Gui*, Paris 1879, pp. 188, 207 ff.

5. Cf. H. Duplès-Augier, 'Ordonnance de Philippe Le Long contre les lepreux', in *Bibliothéque de l'Ecole des Chartes*, 4ᵉ s., III (1857) pp. 6–7 of the extract; *Ordonnance des rois de France. . .* , XI, Paris 1769, pp. 481–2.

6. On the mad and criminals see, of course, Michel Foucault, *Madness and Civilization: A History of Insanity in the Age of Reason*, London 1965 and *Discipline and Punish: The Birth of the Prison*, Harmondsworth 1977. It is strange that in the first of these the lepers are mentioned but not the events leading to their imprisonment.

7. The most recent study of this event, very useful although based on incomplete documentation, is by M. Barber 'The Plot to Overthrow Christendom in 1321', *History*, vol. 66, no. 216 (February 1981), pp. 1–17. Its conclusions differ from mine (see below, n. 57). The dossier promised by B. Blumenkranz, 'A propos des Juifs en France sous Charles le Bel', *Archives juives*, 6 (1969–70), p. 36, has not, so far as I know, appeared. Less recent studies of the subject will be mentioned as we proceed. An analogy between the 'conspiracy' of 1321 and the persecution of witchcraft has been pointed out by G. Miccoli, 'La storia religiosa' *Storia d'Italia*, II, 1, Turin 1974, p. 820. See now F. Bériac, *Histoire des lépreux au Moyen Age*, Paris 1988, pp. 140–8 which ignores the present author's article, ('Présomptions', cit.).

8. Bouquet, op. cit., XXI, p. 152. See also *Chronique parisienne anonyme de 1316 a 1339. . .* , A. Hellot ed, in *Mémoires de la société de l'histoire de Paris. . .* , XI (1884), pp. 57–9. A marginal addition to the third sequel to *Gestorum abbatum Monasterii Sancti Trudonis . . . libri* (MGH, *Scriptorum*, X, Hannoverae 1852, p. 416), introduced by the words 'sequenti anno', speak of lepers 'a Judaeis corrupti' burnt as poisoners in France and Hanover. By an apparent oversight the editor has identified the passage with 1319: the reference to Hanover, however, remains obscure.

9. See respectively, Bouquet, op. cit., XX, pp. 628 ff.; XXI, pp. 55–7; Baluze, op. cit., I, pp. 132–4; Bouquet, op. cit., XX, pp. 704–5; Jean de Preis dit d'Outremeuse, *Ly Myreur des Histors*, S. Bormans ed, VI, Brussels 1880, pp. 264–5; *Genealogia comitum Flandriae*, in Martène-Durand, *Thesaurus novus anecdotorum*, III, Lutetiae Parisiorum 1717, col. 414. And see also Bibliothéque Nationale, *ms fr.* 10132, c.403v.

10. In this account I almost exclusively follow the continuator of Guillaume de Nangis, from whom derives, more or less strictly, the chronicle of Saint-Denis, Jean de Saint-Victor and the continuator of the chronicle of Gérard de Frachet. See also the introduction by H. Géraud and G. de Nangis to *Chronique latine*, Paris 1843, I, pp. XVI ff. On the Chinon episode see also H. Gross, *Gallia Judaica*, Paris 1897, pp. 577–8, 584–5.

11. *Genealogia comitum Flandriae*.

12. See G. Lavergne, 'La persécution et la spoliation des lépreux à Perigueux en 1321' in *Recueil de travaux offerts à M. Clovis Brunel. . .* , II, Paris 1955, pp. 107–13.

13. Cf. Baluze, op. cit., I, pp. 161–3 (B. Gui); ibid., pp. 128–30 (Jean de Saint Victor). In general, see M. Barber, 'The Pastoureaux of 1320', *Journal of Ecclesiastical History*, 32 (1981), pp. 143–66. P. Alphandery, 'Les croisades des enfants' in *Revue de l'histoire de religions*, 73 (1916), pp. 259–82 is still useful on some problems. Idyllically apologetic, by contrast, are the pages devoted to the two 'crusades' of the *Pastoureaux* in P. Alphandéry, and A. Dupront, *La Chretienté et l'esprit de Croisade*, II, Paris 1959, which seem to me on stylistic grounds attributable to the second of the two authors. An important document – the deposition of the Jew Baruch before the Pamiers Inquisition – has been translated and analyzed several times: see the text in J. Duvernoy, *Le registre d'Inquisition de Jacques Fournier*, I, Paris 1965, pp. 177–90 (and,

most recently, A. Pales-Gobilliard, 'L'Inquisition et les Juifs: le cas de Jacques Fournier', in *Cahiers de Fanjeaux*, 12, 1977, pp. 97–114).

14. This text, which eluded Barber ('The Plot' art. cit.), can be found in C. Compayré, *Études historiques et documents inédits sur l'Albigeois, le Castrais et l'ancien diocése de Lavaur*, Albi 1841, pp. 255–7. Its importance was first noticed by A. Molinier (see C. Devic and Dom J. Vaissete, *Histoire générale de Languedoc . . .* IX, Toulouse 1885, p. 410, n. 6). More recently, it has been analyzed by V. R. Rivière-Chalan, *La marque infâme des lepreux et des christians, sous l'Ancien Régime*, Paris 1978, pp. 51 ff. (a precious book, despite its gaps), which has clarified on the basis of new material the conjectural dating proposed by Compayré. The document, as the Director of the Departmental Archives of Tarn courteously informs me in a letter of 2/2/1983, is no longer to be found in the communal archives of Albi, and cannot at present be located.

15. Cf. below n. 39. In general see R. I. Moore, *The Formation of a Persecuting Society. Power and Defiance in Western Europe, 950–1250*, Oxford 1987, which also mentions the events of 1321 (pp. 60, 64). Some stimulating reflections can be found in Ernest Gellner, *Nations and Nationalism*, Oxford 1983.

16. 'Incomposita et agrestis illa multitudo' (Paolino Veneto o.f.m., in Baluze op. cit., I, p. 171).

17. For an example of the reactions of contemporaries, see Jean de Saint-Victor in Baluze, op. cit., I, pp. 112–15, 117–18 and 123. Still useful is H. S. Lucas, 'The Great European Famine of 1315–17', *Speculum*, V (1930), pp. 343–77; see, in addition, J. Kershaw, 'The Great Famine and Agrarian Crisis in England 1315–1322', *Past and Present*, 59 (May 1973), pp. 3–50, which emphasizes, however, on the basis of M.-J. Larenaudie, 'Les famines en Languedoc aux XIVe et XVe siècles' (*Annales du Midi*, LXIV (1952), p. 37), that the documents for these years do not allude to a famine in the Languedoc. In this Guy Bois has detected the symptom of a profound crisis of the feudal system: cf. *The Crisis of Feudalism*, Cambridge 1984, pp. 261 ff.

18. Cf. L. K. Little, *Religious Poverty and the Profit Economy in Medieval Europe*, London 1978.

19. Cf. Trachtenberg, *The Devil and the Jews*, New York 1943, pp. 97 ff.; and the general picture drawn by G. I. Langmuir, 'Qu'est-ce que "les Juifs" signifiaient pour le société médiévale?' in L. Poliakov ed, *Ni juif ni grec. Entretiens sur le racisme*, Paris-La Haye 1978 pp. 178–90. Especially, on the accusation of ritual homicide see Langmuir's excellent essay, 'The Knight's Tale of Young Hugh of Lincoln', *Speculum*, XLVII (1972), pp. 459–82.

20. Cf. Flavius Josephus, *Against Apion*, I, 26 ff.; on which see A. Momigliano, *Quinto contributo alla storia degli studi classici e del mondo antico*, I, Rome, 1975, pp. 179–84; and the same author's *Sagezza straniera*, Turin 1980, pp. 78–9. See also J. Y. Yoyotte, 'L'Égypte ancienne et les origines de l'antijudaïsme', *Revue de l'histoire de religions*, 163 (1963), pp. 133–43; L. Troiani, *Commento storico al 'Contro Apione' di Giuseppe*, Pisa 1977, pp. 46–8. On the fortunes of Flavius Josephus, see H. Schreckenberg, *Bibliographie zu Flavius Josephus*, Leiden 1968 and 1979; idem, *Die Flavius-Josephus -Tradition in Antike und Mittelalter*, Leiden 1972; idem, *Rezeptionsgeschichtliche und textkritische Untersuchungen zu Flavius Josephus*, Leiden 1977.

21. See U. Robert, *Les signes d'infâmie au Moyen Age*, Paris 1889, pp. 11, 90–1, 148.

22. Cf. ibid., p. 174; C. Malet, *Histoire de la lèpre et son influence sur la littérature et les arts*, thesis presented at the Faculty of Medicine of Paris, 1967 (BN: 4° . Th. Paris. 4430; typewritten). pp. 168–9. On *cagots*, see F. Michel, *Histoire des races maudites de la France et de l'Espagne*, Paris 1847, 2 vols; V. de Rochas, *Les parias de France et de*

l'Espagne. Cagots et Bohemiens, Paris 1876; H.M. Fay, *Histoire de la lèpre en France. Lépreux et Cagots du Sud-Ouest*, Paris 1910.

23. See Robert, op. cit., p. 91; Malet, op. cit., pp. 158–9.
24. Cf. M. Kriegel, 'Un trait de psychologie sociale', in *Annales E.S.C.*, 31 (1976), pp. 326–30; J. Shatzmiller, *Recherches sur la communauté juive de Monosque au Moyen Age (1241–1329)*, Paris – La Haye 1973, pp. 131 ff.; Little, op. cit., pp. 52–3.
25. Cf. Mary Douglas, *Purity and Danger* Harmondsworth 1970; and, in general, the anthropological literature (from V. Turner to Edmund Leach) that draws its inspiration from the well-known book by A. Van Gennep, *Les rites de passage* (1909) – in its turn deriving from the fundamental essay by Robert Hertz, 'Contribution à une étude sur la représentation collective de la mort' *L'Année sociologique*, 1907). See Carlo Ginzburg ed, 'Saccheggi rituali', *Quaderni storici*, n.s. 65 (August 1987), p. 626.
26. Cf. J. C. Schmitt, 'L'histoire des marginaux', in ed. Jacques Le Goff, *La nouvelle histoire*, Paris 1978, p. 355.
27. Cf. M. Kriegel, *Les Juifs à la fin du Moyen Age dans l'Europe méditerranéenne*, Paris 1979, pp. 20 ff. Suggestive indications can be found in A. Boureau, 'L'inceste de Judas. Essai sur la génèse de la haine antisemite au XIIe siecle', *Nouvelle Revue de Psychanalyse*, XXXIII (spring 1986), *L'amour de la haine*, pp. 25–41. In general cf. Moore, op. cit.
28. Cf. Trachtenberg, op. cit., pp. 101, 238 n. 14, in which is recorded accusations of this kind – one from the twelfth century (Troppau in Bohemia, 1163); two from the thirteenth (Breslavia, 1226 and Vienna, 1267); and three from the fourteenth (the Vaud 1308, the region of Eulenberg, 1316, and Franconia 1319) prior to the events of 1321.
29. Cf. Lavergne, op. cit.; E. A. R. Brown 'Subsidy and Reform in 1321: the Accounts of Najac and the Policies of Philip V', *Traditio*, XXVII (1971), p. 402 n. 9.
30. Cf. Rivière-Chalan, op. cit., pp. 47 ff.
31. Cited from L. Guibert, 'Les lépreux et les léproseries de Limoges', *Bulletin de la société archéologique et historique du Limousin*, LV (1905), p. 35 n. 3. The same observation occurs in the municipal register of Cahors: see E. Albe, *Les lépreux en Quercy*, Paris 1908 (extract from 'Le Moyen Âge'), p. 14. Thanks to the author's courtesy, on Rodez I have been able to consult the accurate study, as yet unpublished, of S.F. Roberts (*The Leper Scare of 1321 and the Growth of Consular Power*).
32. Cf. G. de Manteyer, 'La suite de la chronique d'Uzerche (1320–1373)', in *Mélanges Paul Fabre*, Paris 1902, pp. 403–15 (utilized also by Guibert, art. cit., pp. 36 ff.) It should be noted that on p. 410 de Manteyer speaks of 'judicial execution' of sixty lepers, lumping together the prisoners (fifteen) with the victims of the stake (forty-four).
33. The document was discovered and analyzed by J.-M. Vidal: see 'La poursuite des lépreux en 1321 d'aprés des documents nouveaux', *Annales de Saint-Louis-des-Francais*, IV (1900), pp. 419–78 (a first version, with significant variations, can be consulted in *Melanges de littérature et d'histoire religieuses publiées á l'occasion du jubilée episcopal de Ms^r de Cabrières...*, I, Paris 1899, pp. 483–518). The complete text occurs in Duvernoy, op. cit., II, pp. 135–47. I am grateful to Lella Comaschi who in the course of a seminar at Bologna (1975–6) first pointed out to me the importance of this document.
34. Cf. The *Liber sententiarum Inquisitionis Tholosanae* published in the appendix (with separate numbering) in P. á Limborch, *Historia Inquisitionis*, Amstelodami 1692, pp. 295–7. Among a group of people whose sentence of confinement was remitted after several years there figures (p. 294) a 'Bartholomeus Amilhati presbyter de Ladros dyocesis Urgelensis' – quite likely the head of a leper's asylum like Agassa ('ladres' means lepers).

35. On the use of torture in the inquisitional trials of this period, see J.-L. Biget, 'Un procès d'Inquisition à Albi', *Cahiers de Fanjeaux*, 6 (1971), pp. 288–91, which also records the prescriptions contained in the *Practica* by Bernard Gui (one of the judges who handed down the sentence against Agassa: see above, p. 44).
36. This omission is rightly emphasized by Barber, art. cit., p. 10.
37. See L. Lazard, 'Les Juifs de Touraine' in *Revue des études juives*, XVI (1888), pp. 210–34.
38. Subsequently (at the end of 1322 or the beginning of 1323), he was accused of idolatrous practices by the inquisitor of Tours and taken to Paris; there he was acquitted, after the intervention of Pope John XXII. See J.-M. Vidal, 'Le messire de Parthenay et l'Inquisition (1323–1325)' *Bulletin historique et philologique*, 1913, pp. 414–34; N. Valois, 'Jacques Duèse, pape sous le nom de Jean XXII', *Histoire littéraire de la France*, XXXIV (1915), p. 426.
39. See C. H. Taylor, 'French Assemblies and Subsidy in 1321', *Speculum*, XLIII (1968), pp. 217–44; Brown, 'Subsidy and Reform', art. cit., pp. 399–400. The anonymous Parisian chronicler, having described the conspiracy as the responsibility of the lepers instigated by the Jews, concluded:

    Et la verité sceue et ainssi descouverte et à Philippe le roy de France et de Navarre rapportée en la deliberacion de son grant conseil, le vendredi devant la feste de la Nativité saint Jehan-Baptiste, furent tous les Juifz par le royaulme de France pris et emprisonnez, et leurs bien saisis et inventories (*Chronique parisienne anonyme*, p. 59).

    The parenthetical clause 'le vendredi . . .' evidently refers to the preceding clauses – i.e., to the moment when the news was reported to the King – and not (as is mistakenly assumed by Brown, art. cit., p. 426) to the incarceration of the Jews, which was decreed only a month later.
40. I follow here Lazard's interpretation in *Les juifs* cit., p. 220.
41. In his *Histoire de Philippe le Long* (I, Paris 1897, p. 425) P. Lehugeur, advanced an interpretation which was in certain respects analogous, even though he was unaware of the document published by Langlois (see below, n. 51) which attests to the king's subsequent volte-face concerning the Jews.
42. See G. D. Mansi, *Sacrorum Conciliorum nova, et amplissima collectio*, XXV, Venetiis 1782, coll. 569–72. Although published in such an obvious location, the document has (so far as I know) been explicitly mentioned only twice: by the anti-Semitic polemicist L. Rupert (*L'Eglise et la synagogue*, Paris 1859, pp. 172 ff.), which does not cast the least doubt on its contents; and by H. Chrétien (*Le prétendu complot des Juifs et des lépreux en 1321*, Châteauroux 1887, p. 17), which assumes the falsity of Bananias' letter reproduced in it. This, incidentally, is mentioned, without any indication of the source, by Trachtenberg (op. cit., p. 101) who confuses it, however, with the lost trial records sent to the king by the Lord of Parthenay. The hypothesis that the entire document (including the letter from Philippe d'Anjou and even the Pope's favourable reaction to it) is the result of a late falsification seems to me absolutely untenable, for internal and external reasons. On one hand, the references (not merely chrono-logical) to contemporary events are very precise; while on the other, the document explains, as we shall see, the Pope's sudden change of mind regarding the Jews. On the relations of Anjou with Avignon, see L. Bardinet, 'Condition civile des Juifs du Comtat Venaissin pendant le séjour des papes à Avignon', in *Revue historique*, vol. 12 (1880), p. 11.
43. See T. von Oppolzer, *Canon of Eclipses*, New York 1962 (reprint of the 1886 edition): the eclipse of 26 June 1321 was visible throughout France; its characteristics varied between those of an annular and a total eclipse.
44. As is well known, Bukharin resorted to a similar expedient during the Moscow trials

of the 1930s, so as to let it be understood that his supposed confession was a pack of lies.

45. The project of an expedition to the East, warmly supported by Philip in July 1322, was taken up again in 1329: see A. de B[oislisle], 'Projet de croisade du premier duc de Bourbon (1316–1333)', in *Annuaire-Bulletin de la société de l'histoire de France*, 1872, p. 236, n.; J. Viard, 'Les projets de croisade de Philippe VI de Valois', in *Bibliothéque de l'École des Chartes*, 97 (1936), pp. 305–16.

46. See G. Duerrholder, *Die Kreuzzugspolitik unter Papst Johann XXII (1316–1334)*, Strassburg 1913, pp. 27 ff.; Valois, art. cit., pp. 498 ff.; Taylor art. cit., pp. 220 ff. We do not know precisely when the Pope circulated the letter: probably at the beginning of July, when the cardinals met in Avignon to discuss the crusade (but the date of 5 July indicated by Duerrholder is arbitrarily deduced from the date of a letter from the Pope to the King of France on the same subject).

47. See J. Viard, 'Philippe de Valois avant son avénement au trône', in *Bibliothèque de l'École des Chartes*, 91 (1930), pp. 315 ff.

48. Cf. Bardinet, art. cit., pp. 16–17; A. Prudhomme, 'Les Juifs en Dauphiné aux XIVe et XVe siècles', in *Bulletin de l'Académie Delphinale*, 3e s., 17 (1881–2), p. 141; J. Loeb, 'Notes sur l'histoire des Juifs, IV: Deux livres de commerce du commencement du XIVe siècle', in *Revue des Ètudes juives*, 10 (1885), p. 239; idem, 'Les Juifs de Carpentras sous le gouvernement pontifical,' ibid., 12 (1886), pp. 47–9; idem, 'Les expulsions des Juifs en France au XIVe siècle', in *Jubelschrift zum siebzigsten Geburtstage des Prof. Dr. H. Graetz*, Breslau 1887, pp. 49–50; R. Moulinas, *Les Juifs du pape en France. Les communautés d'Avignon et du Comtat Venaissin aux 17e et 18e siècles*, Paris 1981, p. 24. Strangely, Baron does not mention the expulsion: he wonders why John XXII, having intervened in favour of the Jews against the *Pastoureaux*, had remained silent when confronted by the accusation of conspiracy with the lepers (see S. W. Baron, *A Social and Religious History of the Jews*, X, New York 1965, p. 221). In reality, as we can see, John XXII did not keep silent at all. His intervention is ignored also by S. Grayzel, 'References to the Jews in the Correspondence of John XXII' *Hebrew Union College Annual*, vol. XXIII, part II (1950–1), pp. 60 ff., which brings back the date of the expulsion of the Jews from Avignon, proposing February 1321 – i.e., before the discovery of the alleged leper conspiracy. But this dating (already proposed by Valois, art. cit., pp. 421 ff.) is based on an erroneously interpreted document. The papal letter in which is announced the foundation on 22 February 1321 of a chapel *in castro Bidaride 'in loco sinagoga ubi extitit hactenus Judeorum* – cannot (as Grayzel thinks) imply the expulsion, because the chapel was erected on lands *acquired* from the Jews, who are specifically mentioned (*'a quibusdam de prefatis Judeis specialiter emi fecimus et acquiri'*: Archivio Segreto Vaticano, *Reg. Vat.* 71, cc. 56V–57r, n. 159; see also G. Mollat, *Jean XXII (1316–1334). Lettres communes*, III, Paris 1906, p. 363).

49. Cf. *Musée des Archives Nationales*, Paris 1872, p. 182. They have been published on three occasions, each time as new material: by Chrétien, op. cit., pp. 15–16; by Vidal, art. cit., pp. 459–61 (the most accurate edition; it should be noted that in the first version of the essay, which appeared in the *Mélanges Cabrières*, Vidal tended to accept the authenticity of the two letters); by Rivière-Chalan, op. cit., pp. 41–2. Barber (art. cit., p. 9) mistakenly links their confection to the trial of Agassa and the desire to inculpate the Muslims (rather than the Jews).

50. Cf. H. Sauval, *Histoire et recherches des antiquités de la ville de Paris*, II, Paris 1724, pp. 517–18, who was scandalized that such forgeries had been preserved; *Musée des Archives*, p. 182.

51. Cf. C. V. Langlois, 'Registres perdus des Archives de la Chambre des Compte de

Paris', *Notices et extraits des manuscrits de la Bibliothèque Nationale. . .* , XI (1917), pp. 252–6. This document, which eluded M. Barber (art. cit.) has been used by R. Anchel, *Les Juifs de France*, Paris 1946, pp. 86 ff., who is primarily concerned to prove that Philipe V reacted sceptically to the rumours of a conspiracy by the lepers and Jews.

52. Cf. Langlois, art. cit., pp. 264–5, 277–8; Blumenkranz, art. cit., p. 38, which on the basis of new documents sets the time of expulsion, traditionally fixed at 1321, later. According to some scholars (among them S.W. Baron) the expulsion of the Jews from France occurred only in 1348: a thesis that is hard to accept (see, however, R. Kohn, 'Les Juifs de la France du Nord à travers les archives du Parlement de Paris (1359?– 1394)' *Revue des études juives*, 141, 1982, p. 17).

53. Cf. N. Morard, 'A propos d'une charte inédite de l'évêque Pierre d'Oron: lépreux brûlés à Lausanne en 1321', *Zeitschrift für schweizerische Kirchengeschichte*, 75 (1981), pp. 231–8: a document of 3 September 1321 complained that the burning of leper poisoners had led to the suspension of alms and annuities to innocent lepers.

54. I. Langmuir insists upon the absence of the accusation of ritual homicide in southern France, where the Jews were more integrated into the social life, in 'L'absence d'accusation de meurtre rituel à l'Ouest du Rhône', *Cahiers de Fanjeaux*, 12 (1977), pp. 235–49, especially p. 247.

55. There is information on the sentencing of lepers as poisoners in the Artois (cf. A. Bourgeois, *Lépreux et maladreries du Pas-de-Calais (Xe-XVIIIe siècles)*, Arras 1972, pp. 68, 256 and 258) in Metz (cf. C. Buvignier, *Les Maladreries de la Cité de Verdun*, 1882, p. 15), and beyond the borders of France, in Flanders (see above, p. 36). A Parisian chronicle mentions persecution of the Jews in Burgundy, Provence and Carcassonne for the same reason (*Chronique*, p. 59). This information should be rounded out by the kind of analytical study of the entire episode which regrettably has yet to be attempted. Evidence as to the atmosphere produced during the months of persecution is offered by the confession of a friar, Gaufridus de Dimegneyo, who presented himself at the Cistercian monastery of Chalon-sur-Saône asking to be given absolution for a sin he had committed ten years before, when lepers and Jews were sent to the stake by the secular authorities 'for their sins, as was commonly believed'. Gaufridus had seen a man with a bag full of seeds enter his father's tavern and had denounced him as a poisoner. Tortured, the man had said that he was a thief and that he had with him a sleeping potion; accordingly he had been hung (cf. Grayzel, art. cit., pp. 79–80).

56. At Rodez, for example, as can be seen from the study of S. F. Roberts (see n. 31), the seignorical tribunal intervened in the conflict between the bishop and the councillors over the administration of the lepers, siding with the latter. On the diffusion of news, cf. B. Guenée, 'Espace et État dans la France du Bas Moyen Age,' *Annales E.S.C.*,, 31 (1968), pp. 744–58 (with bibliography). In exceptional cases the king could despatch couriers at a speed of 150 kilometres a day; on average, however, they covered much smaller distances (50–75 kilometres).

57. This conclusion can hardly be taken for granted, as is shown by any review of succeeding interpretations up to the present. For a jurist like Sauval (op. cit.) the documents accusing the Jews and lepers were a crude fraud, and that was that; of the same opinion, as regards the lepers, was B. de Montfaucon (*Les Monuments de la monarchie françoise*, II, Paris 1730, pp. 227–8). More than a century later, for L. Rupert the entire dossier constituted irrefutable proof of eternal Jewish perfidy, while the lepers took a back seat (*L'Égliseat*) However, Michelet, to whose pages can be traced back mention of the episode in treatises of a general character, had considered the King of Granada's vengeance absurd, but did not feel inclined to

exonerate the lepers completely: 'in the minds of those sad solitaries such culpable insanities could very well have taken shape . . .' *Histoire de France (livres V–IX)*, P. Viallaneix ed, Paris 1975, pp. 155–7). A few decades later, the events of 1321 will suddenly become topical. The doctor H. Chrétien (most likely a pseudonym) refers in the introduction to his pamphlet *Le prétendu complot des Juifs et des lépreux en 1321* to the new crusade which 'for some years' – we are in 1887 and the Dreyfus *affaire* had already begun – people had been preaching against the Jews, and to the enemies who 'seemed to be waiting impatiently for a repetition of the atrocious scenes of St. Bartholomew's Night'. At the turn of the century, during the years in which *The Protocols of The Elders of Zion* were fabricated and the *affaire* came to a climax (see Cohn, *Licenza*, pp. 72 ff.; P. Nora, '1898. Le thème du complot et la définition de l'identité juive', in M. Olender ed *Pour Léon Poliakov: le racisme, mythes et sciences*, Brussels 1981, pp. 157 ff.) J.-M. Vidal exhumed the subject, concluding that Agassa's confessions, which he had discovered, were too detailed, too obviously imbued with sincerity, not to be considered, despite the torture, 'spontaneous, sincere, truthful'. Certainly, Vidal believed that the letters of the kings of Granada and Tunis were forgeries (even if, as has been noted, he had at first judged them differently): but to attribute their fabrication to the Mâcon magistrates seemed to him morally absurd, because it implied that 'respectable persons who were present during the translation were nothing more than vulgar forgers'. He therefore had to deduce that those who had forged the documents were the lepers' leaders, who wanted to convince their followers of the existence of outside support for the plot against the authorities. Vidal concluded that the extermination of the lepers and Jews – unquestionably excessive – had been provoked by a genuine (albeit ineffective) conspiracy by the lepers, probably nipped in the bud: however, the participation of the Saracen kings and the Jews was 'hard to prove'. Despite discovering a papal document from which it became clear (see n. 69) that some time after the persecution the innocence of the lepers had been recognized by the authorities themselves, Vidal did not change his mind, at the time or subsequently (see Vidal, op. cit.; idem, *Le Tribunal d'Inquisition de Pamiers*, Toulouse 1906, pp. 34, 127). It should be noted that in an older case, in which by sheer coincidence another Agassa (Bernard) had been implicated, Vidal recognized that the plot attributed by the Carcassonne inquisitor to a group of defendants – seeking to destroy the archives of the ecclesiastical court – had actually been organized by the inquisitor himself (*Un inquisiteur jugé par ses 'victimes': Jean Galand et les Carcassonnais (1285–1286)*, Paris 1903). On this occasion, basing himself on a charge of irregularity in the trial later brought by Jacques Fournier, Vidal did not hesitate to acknowledge the determinant role played by torture in extracting false confessions from the defendants – even if he ultimately tried to save the good faith of the Carcassonne inquisitor in defiance of the factual evidence. But contemporary echoes of the supposed conspiracy of 1321 were so strong as to overwhelm Vidal's philological prudence: how could he accuse the political authorities of some six centuries ago of fraud at the very moment when senior officers of the French General Staff were being accused of protecting M. Esterhazy, the author of the false proof which incriminated the Jewish Captain Dreyfus? (Besides the scholarly essays listed by L. Blazy, *Monseigneur J.-M. Vidal (1872–1940)*, Castillon-en-Couserans 1941, pp. 10–17, Vidal also wrote an account of an autobiographical character, *À Moscou durant le premier triennat soviétique (1917–1920)*, Paris 1933, which goes back to 1921 and illuminates his personality and political orientation.) Ch. Molinier reacted harshly to the immediate political implications of Vidal's essay (polemicizing with P. Dognon's favourable review), calling its conclusions 'absurd' and the publication of the letters of the Saracen kings 'superfluous at the very least'. As for the legend of the poisoning of the waters, its implications (anti-semitic obviously) were too topical to be recalled with such nonchalance: 'the slightest jar,' Molinier wrote, in words that seem retrospectively prophetic, 'can revive it and give it a semblance of truth.' (cf. *Annales du Midi*, XIII (1901), pp. 405–7; P. Dognon's review is in ibid., pp. 260–61. It should be noted that Albe, op. cit., pp. 16–17, reiterated Vidal's conclusions exonerating the lepers and insisting on the probable guilt of the Jews and Saracens.) But the judgment on the events of 1321 continues, even today, to be a matter for discussion. Publishing the records of the trial of Agassa for the first time in 1965, Duvernoy asked rhetorically whether Vidal had really considered the confessions truthful: their stereotyped form, he observed, was clear proof of the fact that they had been extorted by the judges. A very just observation, to which, however, Duvernoy replied with a manifestly unfounded hypothesis – namely, that the inquisitor Jacques Fournier had deliberately extorted a series of incredible admissions from Agassa to save his life, since if he freed him he would in fact have handed him over to the mob, enraged against the lepers; and what is more he would have transgressed the prescriptions of Philippe V's edict (op. cit., II, p. 135 n.). But the edict was issued only *after* Agassa's interrogation: as for the solicitude of the inquisitor for the defendant, frankly it seems less than plausible (Le Roy Ladurie, *Montaillou*, Paris 1975, pp. 17, 583 n. 1, takes it for granted that in this case Fournier acted at the instigation of the royal officials). Finally, for Barber the persecution of 1321 was a collective phenomenon that involved the entire social hierarchy, from the King downwards, (art. cit., p. 11): explicit renunciation of a detailed examination of the diffusion of the accusations, considered impossible (p. 6 n. 24), suggests that the hypothesis of a conspiracy by the authorities was not even considered. This hypothesis is not new (see, for example, the title of the superficial essay by Vincent, 'Le complot de 1320 [dated according to the old style] contre les lépreux et ses répercussions en Poitou', *Bulletin de la société des antiquaires de l'Ouest*, 3e s., VII (1927), pp. 325–44): but it does not seem to me ever to have been illustrated in all its complexity. In formulating it I have kept in mind as a model of research, besides Lefebvre's *The Great Fear* (mentioned by Barber, p. 12, n. 40), Bloch's *The Royal Touch*, for the reasons given in the introduction.

58. See F. Baer, *Die Juden im christliche Spanien*, I, Berlin 1929, pp. 224 ff.; and see also Baron, op. cit., XI, New York 1967, p. 160.
59. See Alphandéry, art. cit., p. 269.
60. See Bouquet, op. cit., XXI, pp. 115–16; M. Paris, *Chronica majora*, H. R. Luard ed, V, London 1880, p. 252.
61. The observations of Le Goff (*Pour un autre Moyen Âge*, pp. 280 ff.) as regards the image of the world that gravitated around the Indian Ocean can be extended.
62. On all this, see Barber, art. cit., p. 17.
63. See M. Barber, *The Trial of the Templars*, Cambridge 1978, p. 182, which refers to *Les Grandes Chronicques de la France*, 8, J. Viard ed, 1934, pp. 274–6.
64. On the first case, see Barber, op. cit., p. 179. On the second (which ended at the stake), see Valois, art. cit., pp. 408 ff., which expresses doubts about the guilt of the defendant; and E. Albe, *Autour de Jean XXII. Hugues Géraud évêque de Cahors. L'affaire des Poisons et des Envoutements en 1317*, Cahors 1904, who, on the contrary, is certain of it. On Albe's position (lacking in critical sense: see above, n. 57), see also G. Mollat, *Les papes d'Avignon (1305–1378)*, Paris 1950, pp. 42–44. Since this is a conspiracy that involves a small group, the accusations, though unverifiable, are less absurd than those directed at Jews and lepers; but given the predictably stereotyped confessions (solicited by torture) one cannot share Valois' attitude.
65. Cf. R. I. Moore, 'Heresy as Disease', in *The Concept of Heresy in the Middle Ages*

(11th–13th C.), Louvain 1976, pp. 1–11, especially pp. 6 ff. (drawn to my attention by J.-C. Schmitt, whom I thank here). Of limited use is S. N. Brody, *The Disease of the Soul. Leprosy in Medieval Literature*, Ithaca 1974.

66. See de Manteyer, art. cit., p. 413.
67. See Blumenkranz, art. cit., p. 37.
68. See W. H. May, 'The Confessions of Prous Boneta Heretic and Heresiarch', in *Essays in Medieval Life and Thought Presented in Honour of Austin Patterson Evans*, New York 1955, p. 242. On Prous Boneta (who in her confession alternately identified John XXII with Herod and the devil), see also R. Manselli, *Spiritual e Beghini in Provenza*, Rome 1959, pp. 239–49. Mention of the condemnation of the lepers by John XXII also occurs in the chronicle of the monastery of Saint Catherine *de monte Rotomagi* (see above p. 33).
69. See Vidal, 'La poursuite', pp. 473–78 (the appendix is missing from the previous version, which appeared in *Mélanges Cabrières*).

2

JEWS, HERETICS, WITCHES

1. In 1347, at the end of September, twelve Genoan galleys en route from Constantinople disembarked at Messina. Among the merchandise piled up in the holds there were rats, carriers of the plague bacillus. After almost six centuries, the scourge was returning to the West. From Sicily, the epidemic rapidly spread until it overran almost the entire continent.[1] Few events have so profoundly convulsed European society.

That an attempt was widely made to attribute the responsibility for the epidemic to the Jews is well known. Equally familiar is the analogy between these accusations and those made against lepers and Jews less than thirty years before.[2] But once again only an analytical reconstruction of the geography and chronology of the persecution can illuminate the intrication of impulses from below and interventions from above which led to the identification of the Jews as the culprits of the plague.

2. The first outburst of hostility against the Jews occurred, as was customary, at the beginning of Holy Week: on the night of 13/14 April 1348, Palm Sunday, the Toulon ghetto was invaded; the houses were plundered; approximately forty people – men, women and children – were massacred in their sleep. The plague was already raging in the city. Three years later those responsible for the slaughter were amnestied: amidst the depopulation that followed the epidemic, the authorities were chiefly concerned with maintaining the labour force by cancelling the trials that were underway.[3]

The events at Toulon were soon repeated elsewhere. In nearby Hyères, and later in various localities of Provence – Riez, Digne, Manosque, Forcalquier – between April and May, a series of plunderings and attacks against the Jewish communities took place, some more bloody than others. The wave reached its crest on the 16 May at La Baume, where all the Jews were exterminated, with the exception of a single one – Dayas Quinoni who, by chance happened to be in Avignon.[4] At the same time (17 May) a banal incident in Barcelona transformed the funeral of a plague victim into a massacre of Jews. Similar episodes occurred during the subsequent months in other towns in Catalonia.[5]

On both sides of the Pyrenees we find similar phenomena: sudden outbursts of popular fury, followed by condemnation on the part of the authorities. The sovereigns (Queen Joan in Provence, Peter III in Catalonia) and their local representatives are at one in condemning the violence.[6] Obviously, the plague is the backdrop to this wave of anti-Jewish persecutions: but in the localities that we have listed, the spread of the epidemic is not attributed to the Jews.

3.   Elsewhere, however, the fear of a plot had already emerged, with predictable consequences. As early as March, probably, when the plague had already penetrated Provence but had not yet reached Catalonia,[7] the authorities at Gerona had written to their colleagues in Narbonne requesting information: was the disease spreading because someone scattered powders and potions, or due to other causes? The letter containing these questions is lost: but we have the answer, forwarded, on 17 April, by André Benezeit, vicar of the Viscount Aymeric, Lord of Narbonne. Up until Lent the plague had raged at Narbonne, Carcassonne, Grasse and in the surrounding localities, killing approximately a quarter of the inhabitants. At Narbonne and elsewhere they had arrested paupers and beggars of various origins, carrying powders that they strewed in the water, food, houses and churches so as to spread disease and death. Some had confessed spontaneously, others under torture. They stated that they had received the powders, together with sums of money, from individuals whose names they did not know: this had given rise to the suspicion that the instigators were enemies of the kingdom of France. At Narbonne four of the accused, having confessed, were tortured with red-hot irons, quartered, mutilated and finally burnt. At Carcassonne five of the accused had been executed, at Grasse two; many more had been imprisoned. Some learned men maintain (the letter continued) that the plague is due to natural causes, i.e., to the current conjunction of two dominant planets:[8] but we believe that both planets and powders are responsible for the advent of the plague. You must know (it concluded) that the disease is contagious: the servants, acquaintances and relatives of the victims die in turn, usually within the space of three or four days.[9]

This conclusion may today appear paradoxical: it would seem to us that recognition of the contagiousness of the pestilence implies exclusion of the intervention of the planets or human agents. In reality, we learn from other testimonies by contemporary physicians or chroniclers that the three interpretations seemed, in principle, perfectly reconcilable, involving a possible distinction between the cause of the disease and the cause of its propagation. The first was attributed to the stars, to the corruption of the air or the waters, or to both; the second to physical contact.[10] But identification of contaminated water as a contributory factor in the origin of the plague inevitably meant referring back to the rumours spread in 1321. Indeed, the thesis of conspiracy reappeared in Carcassonne and the surrounding cities – sources, thirty years earlier, of the first nebulous accusations against lepers and Jews. The pattern was familiar: individuals belonging to suspect social groups confessed to having been corrupted by money from external enemies, so that they would scatter poisonous powders designed to spread contagion. But the identity of the individuals had changed. The lepers had disappeared from the scene (besides, leprosy was now disappearing, and not only from France);[11] the Muslim kings had been replaced by anonymous enemies – probably English, given the war then raging (later called the Hundred Years' War); the Jews had been replaced by other marginal groups – paupers and beggars.

This version of the conspiracy immediately spread eastwards. On 27 April, precisely ten days after André Benezeit's message from Narbonne, an anonymous person wrote from Avignon, where the plague had begun in January, declaring that certain powders had been found on the persons of several paupers (*homines ... miseri*). They had been accused of having scattered them in the waters, and had been condemned to death. More stakes were being prepared. Whether the accusations are just or unjust, the anonymous writer remarked, only God knows.[12] There had been no epidemics in 1321 (the only evidence on this point came too late to be taken into account)[13]; the fear of infection by leprosy was sufficient to unleash the persecution, duly guided by the authorities. By 1348 the plague was spreading unchecked, and people were dropping like flies. Identification of the human culprits offered the illusion of it being possible to do something to halt the epidemic. But the reality of the disease did not lend itself to being moulded in accordance with pre-existing schemas. Conspiracy theories prosper best in the soil of the imagination.

4. Like a chemical reaction, the various widely dispersed elements that had appeared during the first stage – the massacres of the Jewish communities of Provence carried out by the enraged mob, the notion of the beggars' conspiracy advanced by the authorities of Narbonne and Carcassonne and taken up in Avignon – fused and exploded. This took place still further east, in the Dauphiné, probably during the second half of June. We know that at the beginning of July two judges and a notary, bearing the Dauphiné's special letters, conducted an investigation at Vizille, not far from Grenoble, against a group of Jews – seven men and a woman – publicly accused (*publice diffamati*) of having scattered poisonous powders in the fountains, wells and food.[14] We do not know the outcome of this investigation, but can easily imagine it. In various localities of the Dauphiné, other Jews were sent to the stake as a result of the usual accusations, to which were added, in at least one case, the further charge (likewise recurrent) of ritual murder.[15]

The fusion of tensions originating from below and the intervention of the political authorities was, as in 1321, decisive. Henceforth it is possible to track the extremely rapid diffusion, as if by contagion, of persecution of presumed Jewish poisoners, which sometimes follows and sometimes anticipates the spread of the plague, presumably with the intention of

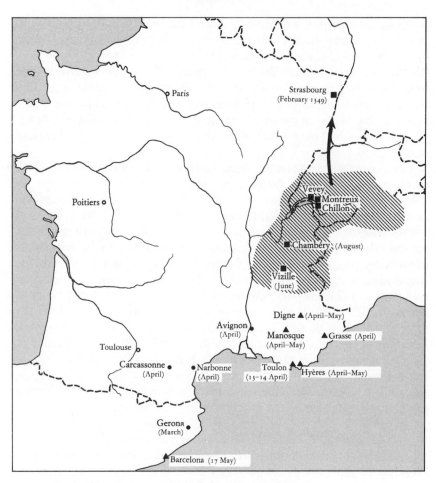

- Locality in which non-Jews were accused of spreading the plague
- ▲ Locality that saw riots against the Jews
- ■ Places in which Jews were accused of spreading plague
- ▨ Zone inside which the first trials involving the sabbath took place (second half of the fourteenth century)
- → Attempts to spread the persecution of the presumed plague-bearers

Map 2

1348. Identification of those held responsible for the Black Death.

preventing or blocking it.[16] The confessions obtained in the Dauphiné, doubtless thanks to torture, served as a model: a copy of the trial records was acquired by a notary for the price of one gold florin, by order of Amadeus VI of Savoy, after a mob in Chambéry had set upon the Jews with the intention of massacring them.[17] On 10 August Amadeus VI and Ludwig, Lord of the Pays de Vaud, each ordered an investigation in his domain against the Jews, whom public opinion avowed to be poisoners.[18]

But as early as 6 July Pope Clement VI had issued a Bull from Avignon which promptly and with great clarity condemned the conspiracy thesis. Too many innocent Jews and Christians had been put to death: the plague, the Pope declared, is not the result of human actions but of astral conjunctions or divine vengeance. So ineffectual was the Bull that a few months later, on 16 October, Clement VI issued another, even sharper one with the sole purpose of proclaiming the innocence of the Jews unjustly put to death by impious and rash Christians. Confronted by the growing wave of accusations against the Jews of having spread the plague by scattering poisons, Pope Clement VI pointed out that the Jews were themselves dying of the plague just like the Christians; and that the epidemic had spread in regions where there wasn't the least trace of a Jew.[19]

5.   However, in the Dauphiné and Savoy where the wave of persecution had begun, a large number of Jews expelled from France in 1322–23 had concentrated.[20] It is likely that in the upsurge of popular violence[21] hostility towards a comparatively recent immigration compounded traditional anti-Jewish feeling. As we have seen, the authorities had underwritten that violence, supplying legal justification and proof: the confessions of the guilty.

In at least one instance, these have come down to us. What we have are not the complete records of a trial, such as that of Guillaume Agassa analyzed above, but the summary, prepared at the behest of the Lord of Chillon, of the confessions made between the middle of September and the beginning of October 1348 by a group of Jews: eleven men and a woman. All of the accused lived at Villeneuve, or in other towns situated on the shores or in the vicinity of Lake Leman. All of them had been subjected to torture; and after greater or lesser resistance, they had all ended by admitting their guilt, describing the conspiracy in which they had participated with a great wealth of detail. Once again the inspiration for the plot came from afar: the surgeon Balavigny, domiciled in Thonon, had been given the poison by a Jew from Toledo, together with a letter of instruction issued in the name of the teachers of Hebrew law. Similar letters had been forwarded to other Jews in Avignon, Montreux, Vevey, and St Moritz. The silk merchant Agimet had been assigned the task of spreading the poison in Venice, where he had gone on business, and in Calabria and Apulia. The accused described the poisons (black or red powders), the wrappings that contained them (small leather or canvas bags, paper twists), the quantity used (one egg, one nut), the places where they had been scattered. Mamson of Villeneuve declared that all Jews over the age of six participated in this criminal enterprise. But in the letter that accompanied the confessions sent to the Strasbourg authorities, the Lord of Chillon advised that a number of Christians had also been detected and punished for the same reason.[22]

Henceforth, the spread of the accusations against the Jews and the attendant confessions coincides with the history of the spread of the plague (see map 2). In dozens of cities located along the Rhine (from Basel to Strasbourg and Mannheim), or in central and eastern Germany (from Frankfurt to Erfurt and Breslau), there were burnings at the stake or massacres of Jews.[23] In Strasbourg opposition to the persecution by a section of the authorities provoked very violent clashes. In vain did Burgomaster Chonrad von Winterthur write to the Strasbourg magistrates, exhorting them to conduct themselves with 'reason and discretion' and not put their faith in popular rumours. Two thousand Jews were killed.[24]

6. In 1321 as in 1348 the rumours about a plot had branched out from Carcassonne to the surrounding towns. In both cases the ultimate target of the persecution – the Jews – had emerged during the second phase, replacing the original target (lepers in 1321, paupers and beggars in 1348). The change of target had coincided with a geographical displacement of the persecution, northward and eastward in 1321, eastward in 1348. The analogies between the two waves of violence are manifest, but they conceal some very real differences. In 1321 the political and religious authorities, even though partially in conflict with others, had directed the latent hostilities of the populace against precise targets – first the lepers, then the Jews. In 1348–9 those who wielded power had taken very different positions toward the supposed conspiracy: some had been opposed, some had yielded to the pressures of the mob, some had possibly anticipated them. But this time the pressure from below carried much greater weight. One gets the impression that in the space of thirty years, in a generation, the obsession with conspiracy had formed a thick sediment in the popular mentality. The outbreak or, more often, the mere imminence of the plague had brought it to the surface.[25] It was precisely from the western Alps, where the charge against the Jews of having spread the pestilence had first appeared, that approximately half a century later a new persecutory wave commenced. But this time the role of victim, having briefly touched the Jews, fell to others.

7. In June 1409, at the height of the schism that lacerated the western Church, a council gathered in Pisa to resolve the conflict between the two popes up for election by selecting a third, the Franciscan Pietro Filargis, Archbishop of Milan, who took the name of Alexander V. On 4 September, the new pontiff issued from Pisa a Bull addressed to the Franciscan Ponce Fougeyron, who performed the duties of Inquisitor General over a very wide area encompassing the dioceses of Geneva, Aosta, Tarantasia, the Dauphiné, the Venaissin countryside, the town and diocese of Avignon. The

Bull, evidently compiled on the basis of information received from the Inquisitor, complained that in the aforementioned regions some Christians, together with perfidious Jews, had established and clandestinely spread new sects and forbidden rituals contrary to the Christian religion (*nonnulli Christiani et perfidi Iudaei, infra eosdem terminos constituti, novas sectas et prohibitos ritus, eidem fidei repugnantes, inveniunt, quos saltem in occulto dogmatizant, docent, praedicant et affirmant*). Furthermore, the Bull went on, in the same regions there are many Christians and Jews who practise witchcraft, soothsaying, invocations to the devil, magical spells, superstition, forbidden and pernicious arts, with which they pervert and corrupt many true Christians; there are Jewish converts who more or less covertly revert to their old erroneous ways and, what is more, try to spread among the Christians the Talmud and other books of their law; finally, there are Christians and Jews who contend that usury is not sinful. The pontiff concluded that vigilance was necessary with regard to the Christians and Jews guilty of these errors. One month later Ponce Fougeyron received the three hundred gold florins required for him to perform his inquisitorial duties in a more adequate manner.[26]

In this extremely diverse catalogue are included familiar and less familiar charges: beliefs and practices of a magical nature, attempts at underground propaganda on behalf of Judaism, attempts to justify lending money at interest. A dense fabric of cultural and social exchanges between different religious communities can be perceived, in an area where many of the Jews expelled from France and Avignon had collected. The pontiff was seeking to restrict this excessive proximity with its potential for syncretistic deviations. But the phenomenon condemned at the beginning of the Bull (and hence with particular emphasis) evidently possessed a different character. The unspecified secret sects were defined on the one hand as 'new', on the other as alien to the Christian religion. How should we interpret this dark hint?

8. Among the incunabula of demonological literature there is a text hitherto more quoted than analyzed: the *Formicarius*.[27] The German Dominican Johannes Nider wrote it between 1435 and 1437 in Basel, where he had gone for the ecumenical council; it appears that he read parts of it to the assembled fathers during breaks in their sessions.[28] It takes the form of a dialogue: to the insistent questions of a 'lazy' man, a theologian replies, tracing very detailed parallels, in the tradition of the medieval bestiaries, between the virtues and vices of men and the customs of ants. The fifth book is wholly devoted to superstition, magic and witchcraft. Besides making use of the advice of theologians in the order to which he belonged, in compiling it Nider also availed himself of material received in the course of long and numerous conversations with informants: Judge Peter von Greyerz, the Castelan of Blankenburg in the Bernese Simmenthal, and the Dominican Inquisitor of Evian, reformer of the convent of Lyons.[29] Both had presided over numerous trials of male and female witches, sending not a few to the

stake. These oral sources, always scrupulously identified, imbue the picture painted by Nider with an unusual freshness. Alongside the accounts of evil spells, derived from Gregorius Magnus or Vincent of Beauvais, appear precise testimonies, which can be geographically and chronologically circumscribed because they derive from the concrete experiences of the two judges.

As was to be expected, Nider insists on the diffusion of the so-called traditional spells: ranging from those designed to induce disease or death to those used to procure love. But there also emerges from his pages the as yet unfamiliar image of a sect of male and female witches quite distinct from the isolated figures, whether casters of spells or enchanters, mentioned in penitential literature or medieval homiletics. This is an image still in the process of being elaborated: Nider transcribes its partial, uncertain and contradictory elements in haphazard fashion.

From the inquisitor of Evian and from the judge Peter von Greyerz he has learned that in the Bernese there exist 'casters of spells' of both sexes who, more like wolves than men, devour infants. In particular, from the inquisitor he has learned that in the region of Lausanne several of these witches had cooked and eaten their own children; furthermore, they had assembled and summoned up a demon, which appeared in the shape of a man. Anyone wishing to become his follower must swear to renounce the Christian faith, cease venerating the consecrated host, and trample on the cross in secret and at every possible opportunity. Not long before, Peter von Greyerz had tried and sent to the stake a number of witches who had devoured thirteen infants: from one of these 'parricides' he had learned that it was their custom to attack the children, provided they were not yet baptized or protected by prayers and crucifixes, in their cribs or when in bed with their parents. (The aggressions were thus also directed against the children of strangers.) The corpses of the children, killed with magical ceremonies, were removed from the graves in which they had been buried: the witches put them in a pot to cook until the flesh turned to pulp and fell off the bones. The more solid part was used as an ointment for magical practices and metamorphoses (*nostris voluntatibus et artibus et transmutationibus*); the more liquid part was poured into a flask or a leather bottle and, in conjunction with certain ceremonies, given to those wishing to become teachers of the sect to drink. This last detail had been revealed to Judge Peter von Greyerz by a young repentant male witch shortly before he died at the stake. The initiation ceremony of new members took place in church, on Sunday, before the consecration of the holy water. Before the masters, the future disciple repudiated Christ and the faith, baptism, the Catholic Church; then he paid homage to the *magisterulus*, i.e., the little master, the term by which members of the sect referred to the devil; finally, he drank the liquid described above.[30]

Several key elements of what will become the stereotype of the witches' Sabbath are already present: homage to the devil, abjuration of Christ and the faith, profanation of the cross, the magical ointment, and the devoured children. However, other, no less important, components are lacking or are only present in embryonic form: the metamorphoses are barely hinted at, without specifying whether it is animal metamorphosis; magical flying is not mentioned at all, and nor are the nocturnal gatherings, with their attendant feasts and sexual orgies. But the decisive step in the direction of the witches' Sabbath was taken with the emergence of the notion of a menacing sect of male and female witches.

9. According to Judge Peter von Greyerz (we are informed by Nider) these evil spells had been performed by many in the Bernese and its adjacent territories for approximately sixty years. The person who had begun them was a certain Scavius, who boasted to his companions that he knew how to change himself into a mouse (here we have a more specific trace of the theme of animal metamorphosis).[31] Nider wrote the *Formicarius* in 1435–7: Peter von Greyerz's remark therefore refers us back to c. 1375. So precise a reference is presumably based on an examination of trial records, rather than oral traditions.[32] At the beginning of 1500, having examined the trial records preserved in the archives of the Inquisition in Como, the Inquisitor Bernardo Rategno concluded, in his *Tractatus de Strigibus*, that the witches' sect had begun to expand rapidly 150 years before.[33] The convergence of the two chronologies leads us to conclude that the image of the new witchcraft practised by groups of men and women, rather than by isolated individuals, emerged on both slopes of the western Alps more or less during the same period: that is, shortly after the middle of the fourteenth century.

It is sorely tempting to connect this phenomenon with the *novas sectas et prohibitos ritus* identified in the western Alps by the Inquisitor Ponce Fougeyron at the beginning of the fifteenth century.[34] In that event we would possess documentation which is highly compact from a chronological, geographical and thematic point of view. Chronological: accusations against lepers and Jews (1321); accusations against Jews (1348); the formation of a sect of male and female witches around 1375; accusations against Jews and Christians for having spawned, we don't know how long ago, 'new sects and proscribed rituals' contrary to the faith of Christ (1409); testimony recorded by Nider regarding a sect of male and female witches which can be joined by precise initiation ceremonies (1435–7). Geographic: the persecution which had developed in 1321 against lepers and Jews in the southwest and northwest of France, respectively, is concentrated in 1348 on the Jews, migrating with them toward the Dauphiné, the Savoy and Lake Leman – precisely where the emergence of new sects, in which Jews and Christians mingle, is denounced and the persecution against the new sect of male and female witches commences (see map 2). Thematic: the unifying element of these persecutory waves, as the target alters (lepers-Jews; Jews; Jews-witches), consists in the obsessional image of a plot directed against society.

10. Clearly, this is a partially conjectural reconstruction: one of the

intermediary links of the chain – that represented by the fusion of Jews and witches in the Western Alps (the Dauphiné, Savoy, Valais) – has no direct evidence, due to the disappearance of the records of the first trials against the sect of witches. We can only surmise it on the basis of the remark contained in Alexander V's Bull or even later documents. During an investigation conducted in 1466 against a group of Jews of Chambéry, the traditional accusation of murdering Christians (adults and especially children) for ritual purposes is accompanied by that of practising magic and casting spells. In these documents there is no talk of the Sabbath, although an obscure allusion is made to a mysterious ritual glimpsed by a witness: in a barred room two Jewish men and two Jewish women had placed a girl on a heap of burning straw in the presence of an unspecified 'monster' and two toads.[35] Very vague descriptions, which were obviously destined to remain such in the absence of more precise evidence. Perhaps we shall never know how the confessions extracted from the Jews by torture in 1348 gave way to those extracted, in all likelihood by similar means, from the witches a few years later, according to the chronology provided by Nider in his *Formicarius*. But even if the details of this phase escape us, the overall significance of the documentary series seems clear. From a relatively restricted social group (the lepers) one passes to a larger, but ethnically and religiously delimited group (the Jews), finally reaching a potentially boundless sect (male and female witches). Like the lepers and Jews, male and female witches are located at the margins of the community; their conspiracy is once again inspired by an external enemy – the enemy par excellence, the devil. Inquisitors and lay judges will search for physical proof of the pact sealed with the devil on the bodies of the male and female witches: the stigma that lepers and Jews carried sewn onto their clothing.

In retrospect, this succession of events seems to be dictated by an implacable logic. But developments that were potentially equally logical did not occur, or were suppressed at their inception. In Strasbourg, in 1348, among the Christians charged along with the Jews with having scattered the poisons that spread the plague, there was a beguine.[36] Now, the beguines – women who lived communally in an ambiguous condition, semi-lay, semi-religious, between artisanship and beggary, and suspected of heresy – were perfectly qualified to be included in the affair which, in less than a century, had led from the persecution of lepers to the persecution of witches. But the Strasbourg case did not have a sequel. And when the trials hinging on the image of the Sabbath began, the beguine sodality was already in decline. Witches and beguines remained distinct social categories.[37]

11. We have seen that in the descriptions collected by Nider in 1435–7, animal metamorphosis was barely mentioned, and night flying and nocturnal gatherings did not feature at all. But during these years, in the Dauphiné and the Valais, the same ingredients had already become part of the image of the witches' sect. This is clear from the report compiled in 1438 by a Lucerne

chronicler, Jüstinger von Königshofen, who repeated almost word for word the chronicle written ten years before by Johann Fründ.[38] The trials, begun in the valleys of Henniviers and Hérens, had continued at Sion, ending with the burning at the stake of more than one hundred people, both men and women. Subjected to torture, the accused had confessed that they had been members of a diabolical sect or society (*gesellschaft*). The devil appeared to them in the shape of a black animal – sometimes a bear, sometimes a ram.[39] After having renounced God, faith, baptism and the Church, members of the sect learned how to induce the illness and death of adults and children by magical means. Some said they knew how to transform themselves temporarily into wolves so as to devour the cattle; others said that they could become invisible by eating special herbs indicated to them by the devil. They went to the gatherings flying on sticks and brooms: then they stopped in the cellars, drank the best wine and shat into barrels. The sect, formed fifty years previously (an indication that once again takes us back to c. 1375) by now numbered 700 followers, according to the accused. One more year, they said, and they would have become lords and masters of the country, with their own king.

At this point the stereotype was almost complete; it would not change for approximately 250 years. The same elements reappeared in two small treatises compiled in the Savoy around 1435: one by the jurist Claude Tholosan, based on more than a hundred witchcraft trials held in the valleys surrounding Briançon, and the anonymous *Errores Gazariorum*.[40] All except the last: of the extraordinary political conspiracy confessed to by members of the witches' sect in the Valais there is not a trace in the Dauphiné, nor in the innumerable witchcraft trials held throughout much of Europe in subsequent centuries. This is an exceptional fact, but it is not incomprehensible in the light of the documentary series that we have reconstructed. We should remember that in 1321 the lepers had confessed that they had already divided the positions of counts and barons among themselves on the eve of the conspiracy planned against the society of the healthy.[41]

12.   Thus, through successive reincarnations, in the space of less than half a century, the image of the conspiracy had become established in the western Alps. In the process, as we have seen, the hostile group had, at least potentially, been enlarged. Parallel with this the scope of its aggression against the community had widened: the accused in the Valais had confessed that they had caused blindness, madness, abortions, and sexual impotence; that they devoured children; dried up cows' milk; destroyed the harvests. The image of the sect had gradually become more specific: the apostasy from the faith, already imposed on the lepers, according to Agassa's account, had become enriched with new, macabre details; the devil, hidden inspirer of the lepers' and Jews' plot, had leapt into the foreground, in frightful bestial forms. The sinister ubiquity of the plot, at first represented by the flow of contaminated waters, had finally been symbolically translated into the witches' aerial journey to the Sabbath.

In the meantime, however, something had changed. In 1321 and 1348 the accused, duly solicited by torture, had said exactly what the judges expected of them. The confessions of the leper Agassa or, some thirty years later, of the Jewish doctor Balavigny, were the projection, largely uncontaminated by extraneous facts, of an image proposed by the representatives of the lay and ecclesiastical authorities. In the trials of followers of the witches' sect the relationship between judges and accused is much more complicated.

13.   Before analyzing it, we must make a digression. It has been maintained that the Sabbath is the final destination of a hostile stereotype, successively projected along the arc of 1500 years onto Jews, Christians, medieval heretics and witches.[42] This is an interpretation which is in part complementary to the one delineated here; in part, however, sharply divergent.

As is well known, very soon, and with greater intensity as the second century AD proceeded, Christians were accused of horrible crimes: bestial cults, cannibalism, incest.[43] Those who joined the sect (so the rumour went at the time) were forced to cut a child's throat; after devouring its flesh or drinking its blood, they doused the lanterns and staged an incestuous orgy. In his second *Apology*, written soon after 150, the converted Greek Justin rejected these infamous rumours, attributing them to the Jews' hostility toward the new religion. For that matter, similar insinuations had been directed against the Jews themselves: at Alexandria, in the first century before Christ, it was said that they worshipped a donkey's head and practised ritual murders followed by acts of cannibalism.[44] This last is a recurrent accusation: we find it ascribed, inter alia, to Catiline and his followers. To reinforce it, where Christians were involved, other elements were added, foremost among them a more or less deliberate misinterpretation of the eucharist: the accusation of ritual cannibalism of children or infants was itself perhaps a distortion of John 6.54 ('who so eateth my flesh and drinketh my blood, hath eternal life').[45] It has been assumed that echoes of the rituals actually practised at the time by a number of sects contributed to the elaboration of this aggressive stereotype. A shocking description of initiatory cannibalism, followed by a sexual orgy, is contained in the fragment of a Greek novel (*Phoinikika*) set in Egypt: but there is no reason to believe that the text, probably written in the second century AD by a certain Lollianos, refers to an actual event.[46] At any rate, for some fifty years, from Minucius Felix to Tertullian, Christian writers attempted to refute the criminal rumours spread by the pagans. From Lyons to Carthage, martyrs responded with scorn to executioners who taunted them with them. In the middle of the fifth century, in his *De gubernatione Dei*, Salvianus mentioned all this as an ignominy attached to a long distant past.[47]

As regards the Christians, Salvianus was undoubtedly right. But by now, beginning with St Augustine, they were hurling the old accusations of ritual cannibalism at the Cataphrygians, Marcionites, Carpocratians, Borborians, and other heretical sects spread throughout Africa and Asia Minor.[48] The targets changed, not the content. In a sermon delivered around 720, John IV of Ojun, head of the Armenian Church, wrote that the Paulicians, followers of Paul of Samosata, gathered at night to commit incest with their own mothers; practised idolatry and, foaming at the mouth, knelt to worship the devil; mixed the host with the blood of a child and ate it, surpassing in gluttony the swine who devour their own offspring; placed the bodies of the dead on the roofs and invoked the sun, the demons of the air. It was their custom to pass a newly born infant from hand to hand, assigning the supreme honour of the sect to the one in whose hands the victim exhaled its last breath. Stereotyped elements such as idolatry, incest and cannibalism mingled with distorted echoes of rites that may actually have been performed.[49]

After 1000 AD the hostile stereotype re-surfaced in the West. At first (according to the interpretation we are discussing) it was related to the heretics burnt at Orléans in 1022; then, in turn, to Cathars, Waldensians, and Fraticelli. Similar rituals were attributed to the Bogomils of Thrace in a treatise *On the Operations of the Demons*, for a long time considered the work of the Byzantine writer Michael Psellus (in fact compiled by someone who lived two centuries later, c. 1250, if not later).[50] But only in the West did the stereotype assume a new form: the image of the nocturnal ceremony in which male and female anthropophagous witches engaged in sexual orgies, devoured children and worshipped the devil in the shape of an animal.[51]

14. This reconstruction becomes shakier as it approaches the phenomenon it seeks to explain: the witches' Sabbath. The continuity between anti-heretical and anti-witchcraft stereotypes is only a secondary element in a much more complex phenomenon. This is corroborated by the varying degrees of success of the accusations of sexual promiscuity as opposed to those hinging on ritual homicide and cannibalism. While the former were monotonously applied to heretics of all types, the latter were at first modified, and then totally forgotten for several centuries.

According to Adhemar de Chabannes, the canons burnt as 'Manicheans' at Orléans in 1022 had been deceived by a peasant who claimed to possess extraordinary powers, most likely of a magical character. This man carried with him the ashes of a dead child: whoever ate of them immediately became a member of the sect.[52] In this account, evidently based on hearsay, neither orgies nor ritual murders were mentioned – even though Adhemar obscurely hinted at abominations better left unmentioned. The comparison between the sect's cannibalistic rituals and the eucharist, implicit in the verb used by Adhemar to describe the ingestion of the macabre powder (*communicare*), followed the pattern of similar accusations many centuries earlier in anti-heretical literature.[53] Around 1090, the Benedictine monk Paul de Saint-Père de Chartres returned to the same themes. Commenting on the account of an eyewitness, he stated that the Orléans heretics, having, in the manner of ancient pagans, committed the children born of their incestuous orgies to the flames, would gather their ashes and religiously preserve them as do Christians with eucharistic particles. The power of these ashes was so great that anyone who tasted them was unable to leave the sect.[54] The ancient stereotype reappeared, but with a far from insignificant variant: rather than preceding the orgy, the ritual murder followed it, eliminating its sinful fruits.[55] Since the cannibalistic rituals were performed exclusively within the sect, the heretics appeared as a separate group that attacked society in a symbolic, indirect manner – denying the very laws of nature. Some years later Guibert of Nogent made similar accusations against the dualistic heretics tried at Soissons in 1114, with the addition of another detail originating, who knows by what paths, from the sermon of John of Ojun: the members of the sect would sit around a fire and throw to each other through the flames one of the children born from the orgy, until they killed it.[56] But thereafter the charge of ritual murder was for centuries reserved for the Jews. It virtually never appeared in the furious polemics against heretical groups.[57] We must wait 350 years for another description, in one of the confessions extracted from the Fraticelli of the Marches, tried in Rome in 1456, of the infanticide that followed an incestuous orgy nine months later. In the possibly further reworked versions which circulated immediately afterwards, an element mentioned in John of Ojun's sermon against the Paulicians reappeared: the leader of the sect became the person in whose hands the child hurled through the flames expired.[58] But this reappearance postdates the crystallization of the Sabbath and therefore cannot explain it. For almost a century trials had been held against the sect of anthropophagous male and female witches: a cannibalism mainly directed outwards, and not restricted to children of the sect's members.

To detect in this persecution the last link in a chain of accusations stretching over a millennium and a half is tantamount to denying the discontinuity introduced by the image of the witches' sect. The distinctly aggressive characteristics attributed to it by inquisitors and lay judges fused ancient traits with new elements, linked to a quite specific chronological, geographical and cultural context. All this implies a complex phenomenon of interaction which cannot be reduced to the pure and simple projection of very ancient and recurrent obsessions onto the accused.

15. Up to this point we have only dwelt on one of these elements: the image of the conspiracy. We have followed its trajectory from France to the Western Alps. It was precisely here, during the second half of the fourteenth century, that the inquisitors were conducting a full-fledged offensive against groups of heretics. The name by which they were known – 'Waldensians' – identified them as belated followers of the religious teachings of Valdo (or Valdes), two centuries old. But the fragmentary documentation we possess sketches a different, more colourful and contradictory physiognomy.

These are trials held by the Inquisition around 1380 and involving artisans and small trades people (tailors, shoemakers, innkeepers), a few peasants and several women, living in the valleys situated on the Italian slopes of the Western Alps or in the Piedmontese area, i.e., at the foot of those mountains.[59] The confessions of these individuals attest to beliefs and attitudes current among heterodox groups, now intensified by the schism that sundered the Church in two: the polemic against the corrupt ecclesiastical hierarchy, rejection of the sacrament and the cult of the saints, the denial of Purgatory. Secondly, they reveal positions which were more properly Catharist, frequent above all in the Chieri area, where one of the heads of the community came 'from Sclavonia'; some members of the sect had in fact gone to Bosnia to make contact with the Bogomils.[60]

More than at any other time, during this period the Alps joined rather than divided. Men and ideas travelled the roads which, via the Large and Small San Bernardo, Monginevro and Moncenisio passes, connected Piedmont and Lombardy with the Valais, Savoy, Dauphiné, and Provence.[61] Amid the disintegration of the old sectarian divisions these exchanges, due to actual itinerant preachers such as the former Franciscan Tertiary Antonio Galosna or Giovanni Bech from Chieri (both burnt at the stake as heretics) brought different experiences into contact. Bech, for instance, had initially joined the group of Apostolics in Florence; then he had left them to go to Perugia and to Rome; he had returned to Chieri; had vainly tried to reach the Serbian Bogomils; had gone into the Dauphiné, joining the group of the 'poor of Lyons'. These episodes of heretical syncretism, the fruit of a restlessness that mingled heteroclite doctrines, are not in doubt.[62] On the other hand, very little credence can be given to the admissions of sexual promiscuity scattered throughout the trials of the Waldensians of Piedmont. It is obviously impossible to check on the veracity of statements such as the one made by Antonio Galosna and others, according to which, once they had eaten and drunk, the members of the sect would douse the oil lamps and commence an orgy with the words 'Whoever has should keep'. But the stereotyped nature of the description, and its coincidence with the pre-existing and documented expectations of the judges, suggest the intervention of physical or psychological pressure on their part.[63]

The reverse hypothesis is equally legitimate: the more a detail strays from the stereotype, the greater is the likelihood that it brings to the surface a cultural stratum immune from the judges' projections.[64] But it is not always easy to isolate this stratum in the documents under discussion. A few examples will suffice. Antonio Galosna said that twenty-two years earlier, in 1365, at Andezeno near Chieri, he had participated in an orgy with other members of the sect. Before the orgy a certain Billia la Castagna had given all the participants a repulsive-looking liquid: those who drank it were thenceforth incapable of leaving the sect. It was said that the liquid had been made from the excrement of a large toad which Billia kept under her bed, feeding it meat, bread and cheese. Another woman, Alasia de Garzo, had been accused of mixing into the potion the ashes of hair and pubic hair. The head of the heretical communities of Val di Lanzo, Martino da Presbitero, said that he kept a black cat in his house: it was 'as big as a lamb', 'the best friend he had in the world'.[65] Behind these seemingly bizarre or insignificant

77

details, we can perceive ancient commonplaces of anti-heretical propaganda. Of the Manicheans burnt at the stake in Orléans in 1022 it was said, we remember, that by eating the ashes of a dead child they irrevocably entered the sect; to the Cathars (whose name was said to derive from *Cattus*) was attributed the worship of the devil in the form of a cat, or the celebration of orgiastic ceremonies in the presence of a gigantic cat.[66] But when presented in the words of Antonio Galosna and Martino da Presbitero these stereotypes seem filtered and reworked by a different culture, a folkloristic culture.

The inquisitor Antonio da Settimo confined himself to recording this admixture of beliefs, categorizing the accused as 'Waldensians'. Our knowledge, so much more indirect and fragmentary than his, is, however, more extended in space and time. We know that during those years in both Berne and Como the persecution of the witches' sect had already begun or was about to begin. We know that half a century later Judge Peter von Greyerz was to collect (and then pass on to Nider) the description of the ritual to which the new followers were subjected: after having drunk a liquid made of mashed children's flesh they acquired knowledge of the sect's mysteries. We know that the cat as a diabolical animal would become a permanent feature of the witches' confessions. Thus the confessions of the 'Waldensians' of the Piedmontese valleys appear as a moment in the interaction between inquisitorial stereotypes and folkloric culture that would lead to the Sabbath.

16. In so fluid a situation the perception of the new witches' sect slowly became accepted among those – the inquisitors – who actively contributed to its crystallization. Exceptional for its precociousness is a passage contained in *Errores haereticorum Waldensium* preserved in a single Munich manuscript, compiled during the very last years of the fourteenth century.[67] This dating is based on an allusion at the very beginning of the text to the conversion of 600 Waldensians carried out in the course of a single year by a 'Friar Peter', recognized as the Celestinian Friar Peter Zwicker, the persecutor of 'Luciferian' heretics in the Brandenburg marches and in Pomerania between 1392 and 1394, and later (with much greater ferocity) of the Waldensians in Styria between 1395 and 1398.[68] Besides the errors of the Waldensians, the anonymous author listed those of the followers of another unnamed sect: dualistic conceptions ('they worship Lucifer and consider him the brother of God unjustly exiled from heaven and destined to reign'); rejection of the sacrament and of Mary's virginity; ritualistic sacrifice of their own children (*pueros eorum ei* – i.e., Lucifer – *immolant*); and sexual orgies. The latter were performed in underground places usually called *Buskeller* – a term which the anonymous author claimed not to understand. This is a Swiss dialectal expression, which literally means 'full cellar'.[69] Thus the author of the *Errores*, which was probably written not far from Styria, where persecution of the Waldensians was under way, possessed not only distorted but also hearsay information about the unnamed sect. It largely coincides with the

themes which surfaced in a more or less reliable manner in the confessions of the Piedmontese 'Waldensians': vague heterodoxy, dualism of a Cathar origin, sexual promiscuity. But the presence of two further elements leads us to identify the still nameless sect active in the Western Alps with the new witchcraft sect. The accusation of killing one's own children for a ritualistic purpose, which had long since disappeared from anti-heretical propaganda, anticipates the rumours about the 'parricidal' male witches reported by Nider in his *Formicarius*. The obscure term *Buskeller* is most likely a derisory allusion to the macabre initiatic ceremony, based on the ingestion of powders or liquids made from the flesh of murdered children contained in a bottle or leather flask. Some years later, on the Italian slope, the leather flask was to become a keg, and those of the 'full cellar' would become 'those of the small keg' or barrel.[70]

Usually, however, old names were preferred when it came to defining the new sect. Distinctions, such as the one outlined by the anonymous author of *Errores* between Waldensians and heretics of the 'other pernicious sect', remained isolated cases; new terms such as *scobaces* (those who ride brooms) were not very successful.[71] Within a few decades 'Waldensians', 'Cathars', or, more generically, 'heretics' became synonymous with 'participants in diabolical assemblies'. It is possible to follow the traces of this progressive terminological assimilation: from *Errores Gazariorum* (Errors of the Cathars), compiled in Savoy before 1437, to the sentence handed down in 1453 against the theologian Guillaume Adeline, who confessed to being a member of the 'secte des Vaudois', which assembled at night in the mountains near Clairvaux, at a trial held in Fribourg in 1498 which demonstrates that insults such as '*herejoz, vaudey*' were currently used to describe anyone who was suspected of attending the *chète* (the Sabbath).[72] The identification made by the inquisitors had spread so widely as to become part of common parlance. But as we have seen it did not spring out of a vacuum. An admixture of heterodox, dualistic and folkloric motifs had emerged among the 'Waldensians' of Piedmont in the second half of the fourteenth century.[73]

17. This last piece of information leads us cautiously to raise the possibility, today generally rejected, that a tradition of belief linked to Cathar dualism contributed to the crystallization of the image of the Sabbath.[74] Antonio Galosna told the inquisitor that Lorenzo Lormea, who had introduced him to the Waldensian sect, preached that God the Father had only created the sky; that the earth had been created by the dragon; and that on the earth the dragon was more powerful than God. Another fellow in the sect had told Galosna that the Dragon must be worshipped.[75] Naturally, this was the dragon of the *Apocalypse* (12,9): *Draco ille magnus, serpens antiquus qui vocatur diabolus et Satanas* (the great dragon, the ancient serpent whose name is the devil and Satan). The role of torture and of psychological pressure must have been great during the trials, whose records are now lost, and which first furnished proof of the existence of a witches' sect. But the presence of

dualistic beliefs in the Western Alps was probably not irrelevant to the formulation by the inquisitors of the charge of worshipping the devil in animal form, just as the introjection of the same accusation on the part of the defendants themselves seems quite in place.

18.   In conclusion, the ancient hostile image based on incest, cannibalism, worship of a bestial divinity, does not explain why the Sabbath emerged precisely in that period, in that area, and with those characteristics – which cannot be fully traced back to the stereotype. However, the sequence proposed here – lepers, Jews, witches – allows us to answer the first question (why at that time?): the emergence of the Sabbath presupposes the crisis of European society in the fourteenth century and the famines, plague, confinement or expulsion of marginal groups that accompanied it. The same sequence offers an answer to the second question (why there?): the region in which the first trials based on the Sabbath occurred coincides with that whence emerged proof of the supposed Jewish plot of 1348, which in turn was patterned on the alleged plot hatched by lepers and Jews in 1321.

The presence in the dialects of the Dauphiné and the Savoy of terms such as *gafa*, 'witch', etymologically linked to the Spanish *gafo*, 'leper' (in the area of Briançon) or *Snagoga*, 'nocturnal dance of unspecified mythical beings', from *synagogue*, in the sense of 'gatherings of heretics' (in the Vaux-en-Bugey) recapitulate, together with the already cited assimilation of the *vaudois* to male witches, the complex chain of events that we have reconstructed.[76] On the other hand, the interaction between the expectations of the judges and the attitudes of the accused supplies a preliminary answer to the question about the specific shape assumed by the image of the Sabbath (why like this?). It will be remembered that as early as 1321 the passing of the trial of Guillaume Agassa into the hands of Jacques Fournier, the inquisitor of Pamiers, had caused two crimes traditionally attributed to heretical sects to surface in the description of the lepers' conspiracy: apostasy of the faith and desecration of the cross.[77] Decades of inquisitorial activity in the Western Alps completed the convergence between heretics and followers of the witches' sect: worship of the devil in animal form, sexual orgies and infanticides became invariant components of the stereotype of the witches' Sabbath.

But in this list of ingredients something is missing: animal metamorphosis, flying to the nocturnal gatherings. With these elements, added belatedly, the heterogeneous mixture reached the temperature of fusion. They derived from a cultural layer much deeper and more remote than anything analyzed up to this point.

Notes

1. See J.-N. Biraben, *Les Hommes et la peste en France et dans les pays européens et*

mediterranéens, Paris and La Haye 1975, p. 54 (and see the very extensive, albeit flawed bibliography at the end of volume II). In general see Emmanuel Le Roy Ladurie's fine essay, 'Un concept: l'unification microbienne du monde (XIVe – XVIIIe siécles)', in *Le territoire de l'historien*, II, Paris 1978, pp. 37–97.

2. See Biraben, op. cit., I, pp. 57 ff., and S. W. Baron, *A Social and Religious History of the Jews*, XI, New York 1965, pp. 160 ff.; Léon Poliakov, *Storia dell'antisemitismo*, I, Florence 1974, p. 118. The most analytical study, although contentious in its conclusions, remains the essay by E. Wickersheimer, *Les Accusations d'empoisonnement portées pendant la première moitié du XIVe siècle contre les lepreux et les Juifs; leur relations avec les épidémies de peste*, Anvers 1923 (communication presented to the 4th International Congress of the History of Medicine, Brussels 1923). On this see also notes 16 and 19.

3. See A. Crémieux, 'Les Juifs de Toulon au Moyen Âge et le massacre du 13 avril 1348', *Revue des études juives*, 89 (1930), pp. 33–72, and 90 (1931), pp. 43–64. Cf. J. Shatzmiller, 'Le Juifs de Provence pendant la Peste Noire', ibid. 133 (1974), pp. 457 ff.

4. On all this see the fine essay by Shatzmiller, art. cit.

5. See A. Lopes de Meneses, 'Una consequencia de la Peste Negra en Cataluña: el pogrom de 1348', *Sefarad*, 19 (1959), pp. 92–131 and 322–64, especially pp. 99 ff.

6. For Catalonia, see ibid., pp. 322 ff.; for Provence, Shatzmiller, art. cit., p. 460.

7. Cf. Biraben, op. cit., I, pp. 74–5.

8. Jupiter and Mars: see S. Guerchberg, 'La controverse sur les prètendus semeurs de la 'Peste Noire' d'après les traités de peste de l'epoque', *Revue des études juives*, 108 (1948), p. 10.

9. See J. Villanueva, *Viaje literario a las iglesias de España*, vol. XIV, Madrid 1850, pp. 270–71.

10. On all this see the learned essay by Guerchberg, art. cit.

11. The reasons remain obscure: see the hypotheses discussed by Malet, *Histoire de la lèpre et son influence sur la littérature et les arts*, thesis presented at the Faculty of Medicine of Paris, 1967, pp. 155 ff.

12. See *Breve chronicon clerici anonymi*, in J.-J. de Smet ed, *Recueil des chroniques de Flandre*, III, Brussels 1856, pp. 17–18.

13. See S. Usque, *Consolaçam as tribulaçoens de Israel*, III, M. dos Remedios ed, Coimbra 1908 (*Subsídios para o estudo da Historia da Litteratura Portuguesa*, X), pp. XIXv–XXv. The book was published for the first time in Ferrara in 1553; of the author, who probably lived between the end of the fifteenth century and the beginning of the sixteenth, we know hardly anything.

14. See Prudhomme, 'Les Juifs en Dauphiné aux XIVe et XVe Siècles', *Bulletin de l'Académie Delphinale . . .*, 3^{e}s., 17 (1881–82), pp. 216–17.

15. See [J.-P. Valbonnais], *Histoire du Dauphiné . . .*, II, Geneva 1721, pp. 584–85.

16. Wickersheimer (op. cit.) has insisted, on the basis of a study by R. Hoeniger (*Der Schwarze Tod in Deutschland*, Berlin 1882, especially pp. 40 ff.), on the fact that in 1348 the accusations of poisoning against Jews generally do not mention the plague; according to him, the connection between the two phenomena was only made during the following year. This thesis has been rightly rejected by S. Guerchberg (art. cit., p. 4, n. 3) who, however, postponed her own position to a succeeding essay, which so far as I know has never been published. The reconstruction presented here attempts to analyze the roots of what Wickersheimer too simplistically defines as 'confusion' between Jews as poisoners and Jews as spreaders of the plague (op. cit., p. 3).

17. See C. A. M. Costa de Beauregard, 'Notes et documents sur la condition des Juifs en Savoie dans les siècles du Moyen Âge', *Memoires de l'Académie Royale de Savoie*, 2e s., II (1854), p. 101.

18. See A. Nordmann, 'Documents relatifs à l'histoire des Juifs à Genève, dans le Pays de Vaud et en Savoie', *Revue des études juives*, 83 (1927), p. 71.
19. See O. Raynaldus, *Annales ecclesiastici*, VI, Lucae 1750, p. 476. According to Wickersheimer (op. cit., p. 3) the Pope, terrified by the plague then raging in Avignon, had misunderstood the charges against the Jewish poisoners, interpreting them as accusations of having induced and spread the plague; this misunderstanding was supposedly behind the anti-Jewish legend already mentioned. This dual hypothesis seems to me far-fetched and utterly unconvincing. It is much more plausible that the connection between the Jews and the plague, which was slowly emerging in these months, was made in the proceedings (today lost or unobtainable) that took place in the Dauphiné, and that Clement VI's Bull, which was couched in very precise terms, was a response to these charges.
20. See Prudhomme, art. cit., p. 141.
21. See Costa de Beauregard, art. cit., pp. 101–4.
22. See Jacob Twinges von Königshoven, *Die alteste Teutsche so wol Allgemeine als insonderheit Elsassische und Strassburgische Chronicke* ..., Strassburg 1698, pp. 1029–48. For a rapid review of these trials, see W.-F. de Mulinen. 'Persécutions des Juifs au bord du Léman au XIVe siècle' *Revue historique vaudoise*, 7 (1899), pp. 33–6; A. Steinberg, *Studien zur Geschichte der Juden während des Mittelalters*, Zurich, 1903, pp. 127 ff. They are, however, ignored in the very detailed essay by A. Haverkamp, 'Die Judenverfolgungen zur Zeit des Schwarzen Todes in Gesellschaftsgefüge deutscher Städte' in idem, ed, *Zur Geschichte der Juden im Deutschland des späten Mittelalters und der frühen Neuzeit*, Stuttgart, 1981, pp. 27–94 (a summary chronology can be found on pp. 35–9). It should be remembered that Guillaume de Machaut, in condemning the infamous conspiracy master-minded by the Jews, stated that many Christians were also implicated (*Le Jugement du Roy de Navarre*, in *Oeuvres*, E. Hoepffner, ed, I, Paris 1908, pp. 144–5 – a thesis repeated, with an irrelevant comment, by René Girard, *Il capro espiatorio*, It. trans., Milan 1987, pp. 13–14.
23. See Haverkamp, art. cit.; F. Graus, 'Judenpogrome im 14. Jahrhundert: der schwarze Tod', in B. Martin and E. Schulin eds, *Die Juden als Minderheit in der Geschichte*, Munich 1981, pp. 68-84.
24. Cf. Twinges von Königshoven, op. cit., pp. 1021 ff. and 1052–3; *Urkundenbuch der Stadt Strassburg*, V, H. Witte and G. Wolfram eds, Strassburg 1896, pp. 162–79; M. Ephraïm, 'Histoire des Juifs d'Alsace et particulièrement de Strasbourg . . .,' *Revue des études juives*, 77 (1923), pp. 149 ff.
25. The Jews were killed before the arrival of the plague, as is observed by F. Graus (art. cit., p. 75), repeating an observation of Hoeniger's (op. cit.).
26. See L. Wadding, *Annales Minorum*, IX, Romae 1734, pp. 327–9. Alexander V's Bull is indicated and summarized by J.-B. Bertrand, 'Notes sur les procès d'hérésie et de sorcellerie en Valais', *Annales Valaisannes* III (August 1921), pp. 153–4. For another campaign conducted by Ponce Fougeyron against the Talmud and other Jewish books in 1426, see I. Loeb, 'Un épisode de l'histoire des Juifs en Savoie', *Revue des études juives*, 10 (1885), p. 31.
27. I have consulted an edition without typographical notes and unpaginated (Bibliothèque Nationale: Rés.D. 463). For easy reference the quotations from the fifth book are taken from *Malleorum quorundam maleficarum . . . tomi duo*, I, Frankfurt-am-Main 1582, where Nider's text occupies pp. 694–806. On the *Formicarius* see now: A. Borst, 'Anfänge des Hexenwahns in den Alpen', in *Barbaren, Ketzer und Artisten*, Munich 1988, pp. 262–86 (kindly sent me by the author).
28. See in general K. Schieler, *Magister Johannes Nider aus dem Orden der Prediger-Brüder. Ein Beitrag zur Kirchengeschichte des fünfzehnten Jahrhunderts*, Mainz 1885. On the

dating of the *Formicarius*, see ibid., p. 379, n. 5; Hansen, *Quellen und Unter-suchungen*..., Bonn 1901, p. 89.

29. Cf. J. Nider in *Malleorum*, I, pp. 714–15.
30. Ibid., pp. 716–18.
31. Ibid., p. 722.
32. The biographical facts collected by Hansen about von Greyerz (op. cit., p. 91 n. 2) are as follows: member of the consul of Berne council from 1385 to 1392; castelan of Blankenburg from 1392 to 1406 (with six months interruption in 1397); and then again member of the Berne council. Date of death is unknown.
33. The *Tractatus*, written around 1508, was reprinted with another work of Rategno's by the jurist Francesco Pegna: see Bernardo da Como, *Lucerna inquisitorum haereticae pravitatis*, Venetiis 1596. According to Norman Cohn the chronology suggested by Rategno is not confirmed by other documents, Italian or French (*Europe's Inner Demons*, p. 145). But the coincidence with Nider's indications, emphasized by Hansen, op. cit., p. 282, permits us to circumvent the loss or inaccessibility of the oldest records of witchcraft trials.
34. The allusion to witchcraft has already been hypothesized by P. Paravy, 'A propos de la genèse médiévale des chasses aux sorcières: le traité de Claude Tholosan (vers 1436)', *Mélanges de l'Ecole Française de Rome. Temps Modernes*, 91 (1979), p. 339, who, however, does not dwell on the importance of the presence of Jews in this context. By contrast, the significance of the passage in the Bull was misunderstood by J. Chevalier, *Mémoire historique sur les hérésies en Dauphiné*..., Valence 1890, pp. 29–30.
35. Cf. Costa de Beauregard, art. cit., pp. 106–7, 119–22.
36. See Haverkamp, art. cit.
37. See J.-C. Schmitt, *Mort d'une hérésie*, Paris and La Haye 1978, pp. 195 ff.
38. See T. von Liebenau, 'Von den Hexen, so in Wallis verbrannt wurdent in den Tagen, do Christofel von Silinen herr und richter was', *Anzeiger für Shweizerische Geschichte*, N.F.IX (1902–1905), pp. 135–8. Cf Bertrand, art. cit., pp. 173–6.
39. In the trials held in 1457 in Val Leventina the devil is also called *Ber* (bear) or appears in the form of a bear (as well as that of a cat, a ram, etc.): see P. Rocco da Bedano, 'Documenti leventinesi del Quattrocento. Processi alle streghe', *Archivio storico ticinese*, 76 (1978), pp. 284, 291 and 295 (I owe this reference to J. G. Kral).
40. Claude Tholosan's essay was discovered, edited and thoroughly analyzed by Paravy, art. cit., pp. 354–79. On pp. 334–5 she convincingly proposes a dating of the *Errores Gazariorum* before 1437 (whereas Hansen had supposed a date around 1450).
41. See above, p. 33.
42. See Cohn, *Europe's Inner Demons* and cf. the Introduction above, pp. 7–8.
43. On this theme one should also keep in mind two studies that eluded Cohn: W. Speyer, 'Zu den Vorwürfen der Heiden gegen die Christen', *Jahrbuch für Antike und Christentum*, 6, (1963), pp. 126–36; and A. Henrichs' important 'Pagan Ritual and the Alleged Crimes of the Early Christians', in *Kyriakon. Festschrift Johannes Quasten*, P. Granfield and J. A. Jungmann eds, I, Münster 1973, pp. 18–35.
44. See E. Bickermann, 'Ritualmord und Eselskult. Ein Beitrag zur Geschichte antiker Publizistik', *Monatsschrift für Geschichte und Wissenschaft des Judentums*, 71 (1927), pp. 171–87 and 255–64; Henrichs, art. cit.
45. See F. J. Dölger, 'Sacramentum infanticidii', *Antike und Christentum*, IV (1934), pp. 188–228, especially pp. 223–4.
46. Henrichs (art. cit.) is of a cautiously different opinion, and has published the text of the papyrus fragment, with an extended commentary (*Die Phoinikika des Lollianos. Fragmente eines neuen griechischen Romans*, Bonn 1972). But see T. Szepessy, 'Zur

Interpretation eines neu entdeckten griechischen Romans', *Acta Antiqua Academiae Scientiarum Hungaricae*, XXVI (1978), pp. 29–36; G.N. Sandy, 'Notes on Lollianus' "Phoenicica" ' *American Journal of Philology*, 100 (1979), pp. 367–76.

47. On all this see J.-P. Waltzing, 'Le crime rituel reproché aux chrétiens du IIe siècle', *Bulletin de l'Académie Royale de Belgique*, 1925, pp. 205–39; and, above all, Dölger, art. cit.

48. Cf. ibid., p. 218 (which quotes a passage from chapter 26 of Augustine's *De haeresibus*); Speyer, art. cit.

49. See *Domini Johannis Philosophi Ozniensis Armeniorum Catholici Opera*, J.-B. Aucher ed, Venice 1834, pp. 85 ff. (Armenian text with Latin translations on facing pages); and the analysis of N. Garsoian, *The Paulician Heresy*, The Hague and Paris 1967, pp. 94-5.

50. Cf. P. Gautier, 'Le *De Daemonibus* du Pseudo-Psellos', *Revue des études byzantines*, 38 (1980), pp. 105–94 (for the date, see p. 131; the passage of the orgies is on pp. 140–1). In the text mention is made of the 'Euchitians', a heretical sect which disappeared centuries ago. The reference to the Bogomils has been suggested by Puech, in H.-Ch. Puech-A. Vaillant, *Le traité contre les Bogomiles de Cosmas le Prêtre*, Paris 1945, pp. 326–7, followed by Cohn, *Europe's Inner Demons*, p. 18 (who naturally preserves the old attribution to Psellus). It had already been seen by Boissonade (*M. Psellus*, De operatione daemonum, *cum notis Gulmini curante Jo.Fr. Boissonade*, Norimbergae 1838, p. 181).

51. Cf. Cohn, *Europe's Inner Demons*, pp. 20–1 and 266 n. 10. The themes of night flying and animal metamorphoses are absent from the lives of the Byzantine saints written between 800 and 1000 AD, as noted by D. de F. Abrahamse, 'Magic and Sorcery in the Hagiography of the Middle Byzantine Period', *Byzantinische Forschungen* VIII (1982), pp. 3–17; but in the West too they were included much later.

52. Cf. Adhemar de Chabannes, *Chronique*, J. Chavanon ed, Paris 1897, pp. 184–5. On the Orléans episode see especially R. H. Bautier, 'L'hérésie d'Orléans et le mouvement intellectuel du début du XIe siècle', in *Actes du 95e congrès national des Sociétés Savantes. Reims 1970. Section de Philologie et d'Histoire jusqu'à 1610*, I, Paris 1975, pp. 63–88; see also M. Lambert, *Medieval Heresy*, New York 1977, pp. 26–7, 343–7 (which includes discussion of the sources).

53. The probable source is a passage in St. Augustine, *De haeresibus*, in Migne, *Patrologia latina*, XLVI, col.30, on the Cataphrigian heretics. Similar accusations circulated in Asia Minor: besides the already cited sermon by John of Ojun, on the use for ritual purposes (attributed to the Paulicians) of incinerating and mixing with food the umbilical cords of new-born infants, one should consult C. Astruc et al., *Les sources grecques pour l'histoire des Pauliciens de l'Asie Mineure*, extract from *Travaux et mémoires du Centre de Recherche d'histoire et civilization byzantines*, 4 (1970), pp. 188–9, 92–3, 130–1, 200–01 and 204–5 (texts edited by J. Gouillard). I warmly thank Evelyne Patlagean for having pointed these out to me. It should be noted that in an anathema dated somewhere between the ninth and the middle of the tenth century (pp. 200, 204) it is stated that orgies took place on 1 January, taking advantage of the holiday.

54. See Paul de Saint-Père de Chartres, in *Cartulaire de l'Abbaye de Saint-Père de Chartres*, B. E. C. Guérard ed, Paris 1840, 2 vols, pp. 109–15. Lambert (op. cit., p. 26 n. 11) believes that the entire digression is the result of an interpolation. But a reference to the powders reappears in the final description of the burning of heretics (*Cartulaire* , p. 115).

55. Epiphanius of Salamis had accused the heretical Borborians and Coddianis of devouring, with appropriate condiments, not new-born infants, but foetuses: *Adversus haereses*, in Migne, *Patrologia Graeca*, XLI, coll. 337 ff.

56. See Guibert de Nogent, *Histoire de sa vie (1053–1124)*, G. Bourgin ed, Paris 1907, pp. 212–13.

57. A feeble echo occurs in a fourteenth century manuscript published by Döllinger (*Beiträge zur Sektengeschichte des Mittelalters*, II, Munich 1890, p. 295): the Manicheans *de semine virginis vel de sanguine pueri conficiunt cum farina panem*. See in addition p. 78–9.

58. See F. Ehrle, 'Die Spiritualen, ihr Verhältniss zum Franziskanerorden und zu Fraticellen', *Archiv für Literatur- und Kirchengeschichte des Mittelalters*, IV (1888), p. 117, interrogation of Francesco Maiolati: '*interrogatus de pulveribus respondit, quod de illis natis in sacrificio capiunt infantulum et facto igne in medio, faciunt circulum et puerulum ducunt de manu ad manum taliter, quod desiccatur, et postea faciunt pulveres*'. Cf. also pp. 123 ff. and Cohn, *Europe's Inner Demons*, pp. 42 ff., which points out (pp. 49, 53 n.) the convergence with the texts of Guibert de Nogent and of John of Ojun. See also F. Biondo, *Italia illustrata*, Veronae 1482, cc. Er–v: '*sive vero ex huiusmodi coitu conceperit mulier, infans genitus ad conventiculum illud in spelunca delatus per singulorum manus traditum tamdiu totienesque baiulandus quousque animam exhalaverit. Isque in cuius manibus infans exspiraverit maximus pontifex divino ut aiunt spiritu creatus habetur . . .*' whence evidently derives F. Panfilo, *Picenum*, Macerata 1575, p. 49.

59. See the excellent book by G. G. Merlo, *Eretici e inquisitori nella societá piemontese del Trecento*, Turin 1977.

60. Ibid., p. 93.

61. Ibid., pp. 75 ff. And see in general, although referring to a period immediately prior to this, G. Sergi, *Potere e territorio lungo la strada di Francia*, Naples 1981.

62. See Merlo, op. cit., pp. 93–4; see also G. Gonnet, 'Casi di sincretismo ereticale in Piemonte nei secoli XIV e XV', *Bollettino della Societá di Studi Valdesi*, 108 (1960), pp. 3–36. It is not clear to me why Lambert (op. cit., p. 161, n. 46) considers Bech's stories unreliable, calling him 'a verbal exhibitionist'.

63. See G. Amati, 'Processus contra Valdenses in Lombardia Superiori, anno 1387', *Archivio storico italiano*, s. III, t. II, part I (1865), p. 12 (and see ibid., pp. 16–40). Merlo (op. cit., p. 72) conjectures the deformed echo of two passages of the *Apocalypse* (2,25: *Id quod habetis, tenete dum veniam*; 3,11: *Ecce venio cito: tene quod habes, ut nemo accipiat coronam tuam*), which invite perseverance in faith in the imminence of the end of the world. On the question of reliability, see Merlo, op. cit., pp. 71 ff., and Russell, *Witchcraft in the Middle Ages*, Ithaca 1972, p. 221. The hypothesis of G. Audisio (see *Les vaudois du Luberon. Une minorité en Provence (1460–1560)*, Gap 1984, pp. 261-4), that the Waldensians preserved a tradition of sexual promiscuity already widespread in the countryside, does not take account either of the stereotyped form of the confessions or of their alleged ritual implications.

64. See above, Introduction, pp. 10–11

65. See Amati, art. cit., pp. 12–13; Merlo, op. cit., pp. 68–70 (see below, p. 307).

66. Cf. Cohn. *Europe's Inner Demons*, p. 22.

67. Cf. von Döllinger, op. cit., II, pp. 335 f. (this is the Bavarian Munich codex 329, pp. 215 ff).

68. See D. Kurze, 'Zur Ketzergeschichte der Mark Brandenburg und Pommerns vornehmlich im 14. Jahrhundert', *Jahrbuch für die Geschichte Mittel- und Ostedeutschlands*, 16–17 (1968), pp. 50–94, especially pp. 58 ff., which inserts the passage on the 'other sect' in the context (not specified geographically) of the phenomena of heretical syncretism, which were gradually assimilated in the witches' Sabbath. On the biography of Peter Zwicker see ibid., pp. 71–2.

69. Cf. F. Staub and L. Tobler, *Schweizerisches Idiotikon*, IV, 1901, 1744–45, under the

heading *Bus* ('in great quantity', referring above all to the beer), with a reference to Grimm, *Deutsches Wörterbuch*, I, 1198 (*bausbacke, pausback, pfausback*: 'with swollen cheeks'). The old eighteenth-century etymology conjectured by Kurze (*Kusskeller*, from *küssen*, to kiss) seems to me unacceptable (see Kurze, art. cit., p. 65 n. 50; pp. 63–5 contain further information on the story of the *Putzkeller* in Pomerania).

70. See the heading *barlòtt* in *Vocabolario dei dialetti della Svizzera italiana*, II, pp. 205 ff; see also pp. 278–88.

71. See Hansen, op. cit., p. 240.

72. The *Errores Gazariorum* have been published by Hansen, ibid., pp. 118–22 (for the dating see above, n. 40); the sentence against Adeline is from J. Friedrich, 'La Vauderye (Valdesia). Ein Beitrag zur Geschichte der Valdesier', *Sitzungsberichte der Akademie der Wissenschaften zu München*, phil. und hist. Classe, I (1898), pp. 199–200 (but see the whole essay in ibid., pp. 163 ff.) On the Fribourg trials see M. Reymond, 'Cas de sorcellerie en pays fribourgeois au quinzième siècle', *Schweizerisches Archiv für Volkskunde*, XIII (1909), pp. 81–94, in particular p. 92. On the spread of the term *vaudey* as a synonym for a participant in the Sabbath, see the same author's 'La sorcellerie au pays de Vaud au XVᵉ siècle', ibid., XII (1908), pp. 1–14. As late as 1574 we learn of 'some sorcerers and Vaudois folk' who cause the sterility of the fields (*Arrest memorable de la cour du Parlement de Dole contre Gilles Garnier, Lyonnois, pour avoir en forme de Loup-garou devoré plusieurs enfans . . .*, at Angers 1598, reprint of the Sens edition of 1574, p. 14; I am grateful to Natalie Davis for telling me about this pamphlet).

73. This point is also underlined by Merlo, op. cit., p. 70.

74. In the past this hypothesis was proposed (including by the present writer: see *The Night Battles*, pp. 46–7) on the basis of some trials held in Toulouse in 1335. In reality, as Cohn has brilliantly demonstrated (*Europe's Inner Demons*) they are a forgery concocted by Lamothe-Langon, the nineteenth-century polygraph who published them. But it seems problematic to attribute, as Cohn does, the traces of Cathar beliefs found in the trials of the Piedmontese 'Waldensians' in the second half of the fourteenth-century to the inquisitors' solicitation. In the light of these documents, which Lamothe-Langon did not know, the non-existent trials at Toulouse appear like a singularly penetrating 'critical forgery'.

75. See Amati, art. cit., pp. 15, 23 and 25.

76. For *gafa* see J.-A. Chabrand and A. de Rochas d'Aiglun, *Patois des Alpes Cottiennes (Briançonnais et Vallées Vaudoises) et en particulier du Queyras*, Grenoble and Paris 1877, p. 137; and J. Corominas, *Diccionario crítico etimológico castellano e hispánico* (under the heading *gafo*). For *snagoga*, cf. A. Duraffour, *Lexique patois-français du parler de Vaux-en-Bugey (Ain)*, Grenoble 1941, p. 285; see also P. Brachat, *Dictionnaire du patois savoyard tel qu'il est parlé dans le canton d'Albertville*, Albertville 1883, p. 129 (*sandegôga*, in the sense of 'dance of sprites, a noisy festival').

77. See above, pp. 42–43.

PART TWO

I

FOLLOWING THE GODDESS

1. Returning from the nocturnal assemblies (so said the mountaineers of the Valais tried for witchcraft in 1428) we stopped in the cellars to drink the best wine; then we shat into the barrels.[1] One hundred and fifty years later, in 1575, at the opposite end of the Alpine arc, a nobleman of Friuli, Troiano de Attimis, reported to the Inquisitor Friar Giulio d'Assisi and to the Vicar-General Jacopo Marocco that he had heard the town crier Battista Moduco say in the piazza of Cividale,

> that he is a *benandante* and that at night, especially on Thursdays, he goes with the others, and they repair to certain locations to perform marriages, to dance and eat and drink; and on the way home they go into cellars to drink and then urinate in the casks. If the *benandanti* did not go along, the wine would be spilt. And he told other tall tales like these. . . .[2]

Let us go back 250 years. In 1319 the sacristan in a small village of the Pyrenees, Arnaud Gélis called Botheler, told Jacques Fournier, Bishop and Inquisitor of Pamiers, that he was an *armier*: someone who had the power of seeing souls and talking to them.

> Even if the souls of the dead do not eat [he had explained], they still drink good wine and warm themselves at the hearth whenever they find a house with a great deal of wood; but the wine does not diminish or grow less because it is the dead who drink it.[3]

Three testimonies dispersed in time and space. Is there a link between them?

2. To answer this we shall begin with a very well-known text, included around 906 by Regino of Prüm in a collection of instructions for bishops and their representatives (*De synodalibus causis et disciplinis ecclesiasticis libri duo*). Half way through a list of beliefs and superstitious practices to be eradicated from the parishes, there appears a passage probably derived from an older Frankish capitular:

> *Illud etiam non est omittendum, quod quaedam sceleratae mulieres, retro post Satanam conversae (I Tim. 5,15), daemonum illusionibus et phantasmatibus seductae, credunt se et profitentur nocturnis horis cum Diana paganorum dea et innumera multitudine mulierum equitare super quasdam bestias, et multa terrarum spatia intempestae noctis silentio pertransire, eiusque iussionibus velut dominae obedire, et certis noctibus ad eius servitium*

89

evocari ('One mustn't be silent about certain wicked women who become followers of Satan (I *Tim*. 5,15), seduced by the fantastic illusion of the demons, and insist that they ride at night on certain beasts together with Diana, goddess of the pagans, and a great multitude of women; that they cover great distances in the silence of the deepest night; that they obey the orders of the goddess as though she were their mistress; that on particular nights they are called to wait on her').[4]

One hundred years later, in his *Decretum*, Burchard, Bishop of Worms, resumed this canon with very slight changes, attributing it in error to the Council of Ancyra (314) and adding to the name of Diana that of Herodias (*cum Diana paganorum dea vel Herodiate*). Generally referred to as the *Canon episcopi*, from the title that preceded it (*Ut episcopi de parochiis suis sortilegos et maleficus expellent*, 'So that the bishops shall expel witches and enchanters from their parishes'), the text had wide circulation in canonic literature.[5]

This was not an isolated text. In the nineteenth book of the *Decretum* entitled *Corrector* we find a group of passages that explicitly or implicitly refer to the passage on the followers of Diana in Regino's version, or are connected to the same beliefs.[6] Some women stated that on certain nights they were forced to accompany a swarm of demons transformed into women, which the foolish populace calls *holda* (XXIX. 60). Others said that they went out through closed doors in the silence of the night, leaving their sleeping husbands behind: after having journeyed through boundless spaces with the other women victims of the same error, they killed, cooked and devoured baptized men to whom they restored an appearance of life by stuffing them with straw or wood (XIX. 158). Yet others maintained that after having passed through closed doors, they flew, together with other followers of the devil, fighting amongst the clouds, sustaining and inflicting injury (XIX. 159).[7] To these passages of the *Corrector* we must add a canon erroneously attributed by Burkhardt to the Council of Agde in 508: the women participating in the imaginary nocturnal ride asserted that they knew how to prepare enchantments capable of transforming people from a state of hatred to one of love and vice versa.[8] All these texts refer to women, occasionally described as 'wicked'. All of them feature, in identical form or with minor variations, expressions used in the *Canon episcopi*: *retro post Satanam conversae* (XIX. 158); *certis noctibus equitare super quasdam bestias* (X. 29; XIX. 60); *terrarum spatia . . . pertransire* (XIX. 159); *noctis silentio* (XIX. 159). These formal parallels underscore an indisputable unity of content. The target is not isolated superstitions, but an imaginary society in which the followers of the goddess consider themselves participants (*et in eorum consortio [credidisti] annoveratam esse* (XIX. 60) and for which they tried to gain new followers. Through this daytime proselytizing activity a multitude of women have in the end shared the same illusion (X. 29). They say that they do not join of their own free will but because they are coerced (*necessario et ex praecepto*, XIX. 60). Flights, battles, murders, followed by acts of cannibalism and by resurrection of the victims: these are the imaginary rituals that the goddess demands from her followers on certain nights.

In the eyes of Regino and of Burchard, the author of the *Corrector*, these were all diabolical fantasies. The punishments prescribed for the women who shared such illusions were relatively mild: forty days, a year, two years of penances. Great severity (expulsion from the parish) was reserved for those who boasted of procuring love or hatred and was probably due to the presence, in this instance, of rituals – albeit ineffective – as opposed to mere beliefs. But during the first decades of the fifteenth century, confronted by the confessions of followers of the witches' sect, theologians and inquisitors assumed a wholly different attitude: the Sabbath was a real event – a crime punishable by being burnt at the stake. A need was felt to come to terms with the *Canon episcopi*, which since the middle of the twelfth century had merged with Gratian's great canonistic systematization. There were those who denied the identification between Diana's followers and modern witches; others, referring to the authority of the canon, maintained that the Sabbath was a mere delusion, possibly inspired by the devil.[9]

3. Let us temporarily turn aside from this discussion (even if we shall ultimately have to return to the problem of the Sabbath's reality). We shall confine ourselves to observing that the reference to the *Canon episcopi* suggested by the demonologists is anything but absurd. In fact, the beliefs described in that text (and in others connected with it) present limited but evident analogies with the image of the Sabbath that crystallized many centuries later: suffice it to think of night flying and ritual cannibalism. But to accept these analogies as proof of a continuity of beliefs would obviously be premature. The canonistic collections offer us stereotyped descriptions filtered through the eyes of outsiders. It is not easy to disentangle the attitudes of those anonymous women from the possible distortions introduced by the clerics. Many features seem enigmatic; the name of the goddess who led the throng of 'wicked' women is uncertain.

In the documents of a Diocesan council held in 1280 at Conserans in the Ariège region, she is called Bensozia (probably a corruption of *Bona Socia*, good partner).[10] The Council of Trier in 1310, however, set Herodiana alongside Diana.[11] In other instances we find figures belonging to folkloric culture (Bensozia, Perchta or Holda – this last term referred in the *Corrector* to the entire retinue of women);[12] to pagan mythology (Diana); and to scriptural tradition (Herodias).[13] The presence of these variants indicates that similar traditions, or what were at least perceived as such, were found in different times and places. This could confirm the propagation of such beliefs; the doubt persists, however, that canonists and bishops (and, later, inquisitors) forced the beliefs that they encountered into pre-established moulds. For example, the reference to Diana 'goddess of the pagans' immediately leads us to suspect the presence of an *interpretatio romana*, of a gradual deformation derived from ancient religion.[14]

4. Such scepticism is perfectly legitimate. In 1390 the Milanese Inquisitor Friar Beltramino da Cernuscullo recorded in his dossiers that a woman

called Sibillia (possibly a nickname)[15] had confessed to his predecessor that she periodically attended the 'game of Diana whom they called (*quam appellant*) Herodias'. Also in 1390 the Friar Beltramino inserted in the sentence that concluded the trial of another woman, Pierina, who had confessed to the same crime, an allusion to the 'game of Diana whom you call (*quam appellatis*) Herodias'.[16] In reality, in the trial records that have come down to us, Sibillia and Pierina only speak of 'Madona Horiente'; her identification with Diana had probably been suggested to Sibillia by the first inquisitor and then, without further ado, attributed to Pierina by the second, together with the gloss (*quam appellant Herodiadem*) which referred back to the text of the *Canon episcopi*. But the records of these two trials (or rather, what is left of them) yield a more complex picture.

Sibillia, wife of Lombardo de Fraguliati from Vicomercato, and Pierina, wife of Pietro de Bripio, appeared in 1384, separately, before the Dominican Friar Ruggero da Casale, Inquisitor of Upper Lombardy. We do not know whether the two women knew each other. Having interrogated them, Friar Ruggero, confronted by the 'enormous crimes' confessed to, in particular, by Sibillia, requested the assistance of the Archbishop of Milan, Antonio da Saluzzo, and two other inquisitors. Then both women were sentenced to various penances as heretics (Sibillia as a 'manifest heretic'). In 1390 the new inquisitor, Friar Beltramino da Cernuscullo, likewise a Dominican, tried them again, sentencing them to death because they were recidivists (*relapsae*). Of these four trials only the two sentences of 1390 have survived: however, that against Sibillia reproduces the sentence pronounced six years before; the other, against Pierina, only cites a number of passages from the previous trial. These are therefore documentary fragments that were originally part of more extensive dossiers.

The crimes to which Sibillia confessed were as follows. Already when young, every week, on Thursday night, she had joined Oriente and her 'society'. She had paid homage to Oriente, not thinking that this was a sin. In the subsequent trial she specified that she would bow her head as a sign of reverence, saying 'Be well, Madona Horiente'; Oriente would answer, 'Welcome, my daughters (*Bene veniatis, filie mee*)'. Sibillia had believed that every kind of animal communed with the society, at least two of each species, with the exception of asses, because they had carried the cross; should one of them have been missing, the entire world would have been destroyed. Oriente answered the questions of the society's members, predicting future and occult events. To her, Sibillia, she had always spoken the truth: and this had in turn enabled her to answer the questions of many people, providing information and instruction. Of all this she had said nothing to her confessor. During the 1390 trial she pointed out that over the last six years she had attended the society only twice: the second time she had by chance thrown a stone into a certain stretch of water from which she was walking away; as a result she had no longer been able to go there. In answer to a question from the inquisitor, she said that in the presence of Oriente the name of God is never uttered.

The passages of Pierina's confessions that we possess are essentially in accord with those of Sibillia, but they supply new details. Pierina attended the society from the time she was sixteen, every Thursday night. Oriente answered her greeting by saying 'Be well, good people (*Bene stetis, bona gens*)'. In addition to asses, foxes were excluded from the society; hanged and decapitated persons attended, but since they were ashamed they dared not raise their heads. Oriente (Pierina recounted), together with her society, roamed through the various houses, above all those of the wealthy.[17] There they eat and drink: when the houses are well swept and tidy they rejoice and are pleased and Oriente blesses them. To the members of the society Oriente teaches the virtues of herbs (*virtutes herbarum*), remedies to cure diseases, how to find things that have been stolen and how to dissolve spells. But all of this must be kept secret. Pierina thought that Oriente was the mistress of the 'society', just as Christ is the master of the world. For the rest, Oriente was capable of restoring life to dead creatures (but not to human beings). In fact, her followers sometimes slaughtered oxen and ate their meat; then they gathered the bones and put them inside the skin of the dead animals. Oriente would then strike the skin with the pommel of her wand, and the oxen were instantly revived: but they were no longer capable of working.

5.   As has been noted, for the *Canon episcopi* Diana's followers were the victims of dreams and diabolical illusions. Guided by this text, the Inquisitor Friar Ruggero of Casale had sentenced Sibillia for having believed that she had gone (*credidisti . . . quod . . . ivisti*) 'to join the game of Diana whom they call Herodias' – that is, to Oriente's society. His successor, the Inquisitor Friar Beltramino of Cernuscullo, wrote that Pierina, as revealed by the trial held six years previously, had been (*fuisti*) 'in the game of Diana, whom you call Herodias'. This implicit relinquishment by the judge of the *Canon episcopi*'s position coincided with a change in the confessions of the accused. Alongside the image of Oriente's society there now surfaced the image of the Sabbath, which had begun to crystallize several decades before, not far from there, in the diocese of Como.[18] Pierina – perhaps subjected to torture – confessed to having given herself to a spirit named Lucifello, to having donated him a bit of her blood so that he could draw up a pact of devotion, to having let him lead her to the 'game'. Like Sibillia at first she had declared that being a member of Oriente's society was not a sin: now she implored the inquisitor to save her soul.

6.   Women (1) who believe and state (2) that they go out at night (3) following Diana (4) on the backs of animals (5) travelling great distances (6) obeying the orders of the goddess like those of a mistress (7) and serving her on particular nights (8): all these elements recur in Sibillia's and Pierina's confessions, with the exception of two (4, 5). The name of the goddess is different and the animals, though present (they almost all attend Oriente's society), are not used as mounts. But the partial divergence between the

93

accounts of the two women and the text of the *Canon episcopi* is, from an interpretative angle, much more precious than total accordance would be, because it excludes the possibility of a forced adjustment to a pre-existing scheme. And so the priest Giovanni de Matociis, mansionary of the Veronese Church, was correct to affirm in a passage of his *Historiae Imperiales* (1313) that 'many lay persons' believed in a nocturnal society headed by a queen: Diana or Herodias.[19] In northern Italy the beliefs schematically recorded by Regino of Prüm were, four hundred years later, still very much alive.

At this point the attempts by priests, canonists and inquisitors to translate the multifarious names of the nocturnal goddess appear to us in a different light. Interpretative efforts and interpretative excesses were two sides of the same coin. Diana and Herodias offered the clerics a thread with which to trace their way through the labyrinth of local beliefs. As a result a feeble and modified echo of those women's voices has come down to us.

7.   In no instance, probably, was the cultural distance between judge and accused so great as in the trial held in Bressanone in 1457. The trial record is lost: we can reconstruct it in part, thanks to the Latin version of a sermon delivered by the bishop, Nicholas of Cusa, during Lent of the same year.[20] The theme of the sermon (certainly reworked by the author in translating it) was the words addressed by Satan to Christ to tempt him: 'If thou therefore wilt worship me, all shall be thine' (Luke 4.7). Nicholas illustrated them for the faithful with a very recent case. Three old women from Val di Fassa had been brought to him: two had confessed that they belonged to the 'society of Diana'. This, however, was Nicholas's interpretation. The two old women had simply spoken of a 'good mistress (*bona domina*)'. But this identification offered Nicholas the pretext for a dense series of references, which permit us to reconstruct the complex cultural prism through which the words of the two old women were perceived. The reference to Diana – the divinity worshipped at Ephesus, of which mention is made in *Acts of the Apostles* (19.27 ff.) – was of course suggested by the *Canon episcopi*, cited in a version which declared that the followers of the goddess 'venerate her as though she were Fortune (*quasi Fortunam*) and in common parlance are called *Hulden* from Hulda'.[21] There followed an allusion to the treatise compiled on the basis of information provided by Peter of Bern (i.e., Nider's *Formicarius*), in which there is talk of a 'little master' who is Satan. Finally, a passage from the life of St Germanus (probably read in Jacopo da Varazze's *Legenda Aurea*), about certain spirits called 'good women who wander about at night', whose diabolical nature the saint had unmasked.

In a passing phrase, Nicholas pronounced the name the devil had assumed in Val di Fassa. 'That Diana who they say is Fortune' was called by the two old women 'in the Italian language Richella, that is, the mother of riches and good fortune'. And *Richella*, he continued with inexhaustible erudition, was nothing other than a translation of *Abundia* or *Satia* (a figure mentioned by

William of Auvergne and by Vincent of Beauvais). 'Of the homage rendered her and of the foolish ceremonies of this sect', Nicholas preferred not to speak. But at the end of the sermon he could not restrain himself. He said that he had interrogated the two old women, and had concluded that they were half mad (*semideliras*); they did not even know the *Credo* properly. They had said that the 'good mistress', i.e., Richella, had come to them at night, on a cart. She had the appearance of a well-dressed woman: but they had not seen her face (we shall say why later). She had touched them, and from that moment on they had renounced the Christian faith. Then they had arrived at a place crowded with people who danced and made merry: a number of men covered with hair had devoured men and children who had not been properly baptized. They had gone to this place for several years, during the four Ember weeks, until they had thoroughly made the sign of the cross; then they had stopped.

For Nicholas all of this was nonsense, madness, fantasies inspired by the devil. He tried to convince the two old women that they had been dreaming: but in vain. So, he sentenced them to public penance and to jail. Later on he would decide on how to deal with such people. In the sermon he explained the reasons for his tolerant attitude. Those who believe in the efficacy of spells fuel the idea that the devil is more powerful than God: persecution spreads widely and the devil achieves his purpose, because of the risk of executing as a witch some old fool who is completely innocent. Therefore, one must proceed with caution, rather than with force, so as not to increase evil in the process of attempting to eradicate it.

This exhortation to tolerance was prefaced by a bitter rhetorical question. Is it not perhaps true (Nicholas had inquired of the faithful gathered to listen to him) that in these mountains Christ and the saints are worshipped and celebrated almost exclusively for the purpose of obtaining more material goods, better harvests, more cattle? In a not dissimilar spirit – he gave them to understand – the two old women of Val di Fassa had turned to Richella rather than to Christ and the saints. For Nicholas, to pray to God with an impure heart already meant to sacrifice to the devil.

But Nicholas's erudition, his will to understand, his Christian compassion could not bridge the abyss that separated him from the two old women. Finally, their obscure religion was destined to remain incomprehensible to him.

8. The case we have just presented confronts us with a difficulty which recurs in our research. Despite the emotional solidarity that we feel for the victims of the persecution, intellectually we tend to identify with the inquisitors and the bishops – even when they were not like Nicholas of Cusa. Our aims are different, but our questions largely coincide with the ones they asked. Unlike them, we are not in a position to address them directly to the accused. Instead of producing the documentation, we have it here before us as a datum. All we can do is use the notebooks that record the fieldwork conducted by ethnographers who have been dead for centuries.[22]

Naturally, the comparison is not to be taken literally. Very often the accused, conveniently guided by suggestion or torture, confessed the truth that the judges did not bother to seek, since they already possessed it. The forced convergence between the answers and the questions and expectations render many of these documents monotonous and all too predictable. Only in exceptional cases do we find a discrepancy between questions and answers that brings to the surface a cultural stratum substantially uncontaminated by the judges' stereotypes. The lack of communication between the inter-locutors then underscores (only by an apparent paradox) the dialogical nature of the documents, not to mention their ethnographic richness.[23] The trials of the followers of the nocturnal goddess figure as an intermediate instance between these two extremes. The embarrassing proximity between today's interpreter and the artificers of repression here reveals its contradictory implications. The cognitive categories of the judges have subtly contami-nated the documentation; but we cannot do without them. We try to make a distinction between Oriente or Richella and the more or less prevaricating translations suggested by the Milanese inquisitors or by Nicholas of Cusa; but like them (and also thanks to them) we believe that the comparison with Diana or Habonde is based on an illuminating analogy. Our interpretations in part derive from the knowledge and the experience of those men. As we know, neither was innocent.

9.   The diabolistic incrustations that emerge at the end of the accounts of the two women from Val di Fassa echo the pact with Lucifello made half a century previously by Pierina, Oriente's follower. A forced glissade of the old beliefs towards the Sabbath stereotype occurs between the middle of the fifteenth and the beginning of the sixteenth century at both ends of the Alpine arc and in the Po valley. In the Canovese, in Val di Fiemme, in Ferrara and the outskirts of Modena, the 'women of the good game', the 'wise Sibilla', and other analogous female figures gradually assume diabolical traits.[24] In the area of Como too the Sabbath was superimposed upon a layer of similar beliefs: the nocturnal gatherings, as the inquisitor Bernardo da Como recorded, were there called 'the game of the good society (*ludum bonae societatis*)'.[25]

An analogous phenomenon occurred much later, in a completely different part of Europe: Scotland, between the end of the sixteenth and the end of the seventeenth century. Various women tried as witches described going in spirit to visit the fairies – the 'good people', the 'good neighbours' – and their queen, sometimes flanked by a king. 'I was in the Downie-hills', said one of these women, Isabel Gowdie, 'and got meat ther from the Qwein of Fearrie, mor than I could eat. The Qwein of Fearrie is brawlie clothed in whyt linens, and in whyt and browne cloathes, etc.; and the King of Fearrie is a braw man, weill favoured, and broad faced. . . .' The ellipses mark the points at which the transcriber, doubtless at the request of the judges (the pastor and the sheriff of Auldern, a village on the bank of the Moray Firth), considered it useless to record such fantasies. The year was 1662. We shall never know the sequel to this story. The judges wanted to hear about the witches, the devil; and Isabel Gowdie satisfied them unprompted, restoring the momentarily interrupted communication.[26]

Sometimes (but more rarely) this admixture of old and new beliefs appears in the trials of men. In 1597 Andrew Man told the judges at Aberdeen that he had paid homage to the Queen of the Elves and to the devil, who had appeared to him in the guise of a stag, emerging from the snow on a summer's day during the harvest. His name was Christsonday (the Sunday of Christ). Andrew Man had kissed its behind. He thought it was an angel, God's godchild, and that 'it had all the power under God'. The Queen of the Elves was inferior to the devil, but 'has a grip of all the craft'. The Elves had set the tables with food, played music and danced. They were shadows, but with the appearance and clothes of human beings. Their queen was very beautiful; and Andrew Man had coupled with her carnally.[27]

The judges at Aberdeen considered these accounts 'plane witchcraft and devilrie'. We recognize in them a more complex stratification. The thin diabolical crust that covers them is easily explained by the Europe-wide circulation of treatises on demonology. Based on the stereotypes that had crystallized in the Western Alps between the end of the fourteenth and the first half of the fifteenth century, it was probably the Aberdeen judges who, with questions and torture in the course of interrogation (unfortunately not preserved), elicited details such as the homage to the devil. But the Christian elements that contradictorily emerge in Andrew Man's confessions (the devil Christsonday, God's angel and godson) cannot be traced back to the circulation of texts. In the confessions of a number of *benandanti* in the Friuli or those of a werewolf in Livonia we find similar assertions: we fight, they said, 'for the faith of Christ', we are 'God's dogs'. Attributing these coinciding statements to spontaneous defensive expedients, concocted in the course of the trials, is implausible: it was probably a more profound and unconscious reaction, which spread a Christian veil over a more ancient stratum of beliefs, subjected to a frontal attack which distorted its meaning in a diabolistic direction.[28] In the case of Andrew Man it was a matter of beliefs revolving around the 'good neighbours' – elves and fairies. Over this world of shadows, where there is banqueting, music, dancing, rules the Queen of the Elves, by now relegated (like the 'woman of the good game' in the trials at Trento in the early sixteenth century) to a subordinate position vis-à-vis the devil.

10. The judges at Rouen had also asked Joan of Arc (it was 18 March 1430) whether she knew anything about those who 'went or travelled through the air with the fairies'. She rejected the insinuation: she had never done anything of the kind, but she had heard of it; she knew that it took place on Thursdays, and that it was simply 'a spell (*sorcerie*)'.[29] This is only one of innumerable testimonies to the gradual, centuries-long diabolization of a stratum of beliefs that has only reached us in a fragmentary manner, through texts

Ecstatic journeys in search of predominantly female divinities

Fairies (Scotland); Diana, Habonde,
the 'badessa' of the benandanti,
Matres, fairies etc. (France, North-
Central Italy, the Rhineland); 'spirit
women' (Sicily).
Part II, Chapters 1 and 2

Battles fought in ecstasy, mainly to
encourage fertility.

Benandanti (Friuli); *mazzeri* (Corsica); *kresniki* (Istria, Slovenia, Dalmatia, Bosnia-Herzegovina, Montenegro; *taltos* (Hungary); *burkudzauta*
(Ossetia); werewolves (Livonia);
shamans (Lappland).
(Part II, Chapter 3)

Semi-animal apparitions during the
twelve days.
Kallikantzoroi (Greece).
(Part II, Chapter 3)

Groups of young men masquerading
as animals, mainly during the
twelve days.
Regos (Hungary); *eskari* (Macedonian
Bulgaria); *surovaskari* (Eastern Bul-
garia); *calusari* (Romania); *koljadanti*
(Ukraine).
(Part II, Chapter 4)

Ritual battles for fertility.
Punchiadurs (Grisons,
Switzerland)

Apparitions of the dead to predestined individuals
Benandanti (Friuli); *armiers* (Ariege);
mesultane (Georgia).
(Part II, Chapters 1 and 4)

Map 3

Cults, Myths and Rituals
of Shamanic Origin in
Europe.

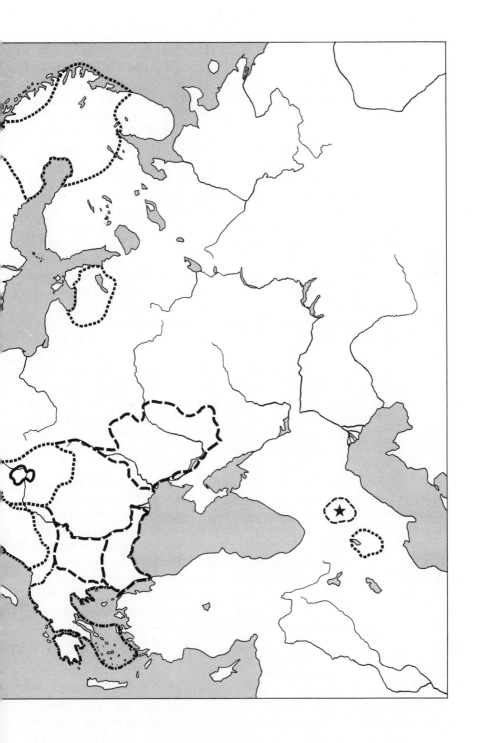

produced by canonists, inquisitors and judges. The key fossil that makes it possible for us to identify this stratum is composed of allusions to mysterious female figures, venerated above all by the women.

In the middle of the thirteenth century Vincent of Beauvais quoted the *Canon episcopi* in his *Speculum morale*, adding to Diana and Herodias 'other persons' whom the deluded women call 'good things (*bonae res*)'. The *Roman de la Rose* spoke of the 'bonnes dames' who waited upon the lady Habonde.[30] In his previously cited life of St Germanus, Jacopo da Varazze mentioned the 'good women who go about at night'.[31] A canon of the council of Conserans in the Ariège region, patterned on the *Canon episcopi*, included, as we have already seen, a reference to Bensozia (*Bona Socia*). Still in the Ariège, one of the customers of the *armier* Arnaud Gélis explained to the inquisitor who questioned her that the 'bonnes dames' had on earth been rich and powerful women, who now wandered about on carts dragged through mountains and valleys by demons.[32] Madonna Oriente addressed her followers as the 'good people (*bona gens*)'. The old women of Val di Fassa addressed Richella as 'Good Mistress'. In Val di Fiemme, the nocturnal goddess was called 'the woman of the good game'. In Scotland and in Ireland 'good people' or 'good neighbours' were the fairies. To this company we can add the *benandanti* of the Friuli: one of them, Maria Panzona, tried by the inquisition at the beginning of the seventeenth century, had paid homage, 'bowing her head' (like Sibillia and Pierina), to 'a certain woman, called the abbess, who sat in majesty on a stool'.[33] In this recurrent adjective – 'good' – we detect an ambiguous nuance of a propitiatory character. Such epithets as *bona dea* or *placida*, respectively associated with Hecate – the funereal goddess closely linked to Artemis – and a divinity identified with Hecate, worshipped at Novae in lower Moesia (third century AD), spring to mind.[34]

Behind the women (and the few men) linked to the 'good' nocturnal goddesses we glimpse a cult of an ecstatic nature. The *benandanti* women declared that they fell into ecstasy during the four Ember weeks, the same time of the year that the old women of Val di Fassa visited their goddess. The alleged Scottish witches periodically plunged into 'ecstasies and transis', abandoning their lifeless bodies in the form of an invisible spirit or animal (a crow).[35] Of the followers of the lady Habonde it was said that they fell into catalepsy before undertaking their journeys as spirits, passing through doors and walls.[36] The *Corrector* had already stated that barred doors were no barrier to night flying. An ecstatic experience can also be inferred where it is not explicitly mentioned, as, for example, in the case of Richella and Oriente. Via a temporary death one accedes to the world of beneficent female figures who bestow prosperity, wealth, knowledge. Their world is the realm of the dead.[37]

This identity is confirmed by a series of convergences. The custom, recorded until recent times over a vast geographical area, of leaving water for the dead on certain days that they may quench their thirst, harks back to the custom already condemned and derided by William of Auvergne and by

Vincent of Beauvais of leaving propitiatory offerings to the *bonae res* or to Abundia. Moreover, Abundia, like Oriente, imparts blessings on the houses in which she has banqueted with her invisible retinue.[38] In Arnaud Gelis' confessions these blessings are reserved, as in the case of Oriente, for well-swept houses: 'the dead gladly frequent clean places and enter clean houses, whereas they do not like to enter sordid places or filthy houses.'[39] The meaning of the analogy with which we began suddenly becomes clear. We can relate the male and female witches of the Valais to the *benandanti*, as well as to the throngs of souls in the Ariège, because the night flights to the diabolical gatherings echoed, in a distorted and unrecognizable form, a very ancient theme: the ecstatic journey of the living into the realm of the dead. The folkloric nucleus of the stereotype of the Sabbath is here.

11.   In the *Sermones* of the Dominican preacher Johannes Herolt, compiled in 1418 or shortly before, and then reprinted many times during the second half of the fifteenth century, there appears a long list of the superstitious. In the nineteenth position, in the edition which was published in Cologne in 1474, are listed those who believe that 'Diana, commonly called in the vernacular Unholde, that is, *die selige Frawn* (the beatific woman), goes about at night with her army, travelling over great distances (*cum exercitu suo de nocte ambulet per multa spacia*).' Other, slightly later editions of the same collection (Strasbourg after 1478 and Strasbourg 1484), added synonyms of Diana to the list, first *Fraw Berthe* and then *Fraw Helt* (in place of *Unholde*).[40] This was evidently a variation on the text of the *Canon episcopi*. Certain elements were skipped (animals used as mounts, the obedience to the goddess, and the journey on particular nights). Others were added, like the synonyms. But what about the army? From the eleventh century onwards, a series of literary texts in Latin and the vulgate, originating throughout the European continent – France, Spain, Italy, Germany, England and Scandinavia – speak of the apparition of the 'furious army' (*Wütischend Heer, Mesnie furieuse, Mesnie Hellequin, exercitus antiquus*), also called 'wild hunt' (*Wilde Jagd, Chasse sauvage, Chasse Arthur*). In them the throng of the dead is recognized; sometimes, more precisely, the throng of those dead before their time – soldiers killed in battle, unbaptized children. They are led by various personages, mythical (Herlechinus, Wotan, Odin, Arthur and so on) or mythicized (Dietrich von Bern).[41] As is evident even in the earliest testimonies, a theme identifiable in cultures which are quite distant from each other – the menacing apparition of the unplaced dead – is reinterpreted in a Christian and moralizing sense closely related to the image of Purgatory, which was then being elaborated.[42] But the intimately folkloric characteristics of the belief are apparent in the figures that lead the 'wild hunt'.

Herolt's reference to Diana's army mixed these traditions with those condemned by the *Canon episcopi*. It is not clear whether he recorded a belief encountered during his activity as an itinerant preacher, or whether he was proposing a personal interpretation of some of the superstitions he was trying to eradicate. Certainly, the instances in which mythical female figures

(Berchtholda, Perchta) appear at the head of a 'furious army' are very few, and all of them come a century and a half or more after Herolt's text, or even later.[43] But to my mind the words 'Diana with her army' are important, because they implicitly identify the deluded women of the *Canon episcopi* with the throng of the dead. This confirms the interpretation of the Sabbath's folkloric nucleus as a journey to the beyond:[44] but it simultaneously suggests the possibility of extending our research to testimony on apparitions of the dead.

12.   The dilemma that faces us at this point has not only intellectual implications. The traditions concerning the 'furious army' have been interpreted as a coherent mythical and ritual configuration, in which, through implicit or explicit reference to the figure of Wotan, a remote and persistent warrior vocation of German men is expressed.[45] The Milanese trials of Oriente's two followers, Sibillia and Pierina, have been construed as testimony of a female aspiration to a separate world composed only of women and governed by a maternal, wise goddess.[46] Herolt's passage seems to suggest that these images, superficially so different, were in fact perceived (by himself or by others) as aspects of a single mythical image. A comparison between the two documentary series is therefore necessary.[47]

13.   We shall set out from the literary texts. They are a diverse set covering a chronological span that runs from the tenth to the eighteenth century: demonological treatises, verse romances, sermons, canons and so on.[48] But the juxtaposition that emerges from them is very clear-cut. The throng of the dead, composed of men and women and, as has been noted, usually led by mythical or mythicized male figures, appeared almost exclusively to men (hunters, pilgrims, wayfarers) through occasional apparitions, which were especially frequent during the period between Christmas and Epiphany. The cortège of ecstatic women, led by female figures, almost always manifested itself to women,[49] by means of ecstasies that were regularly repeated on definite dates.

An examination of the non-literary documentation – mainly trial records – complicates the picture. In some cases we find men who in ecstasy visited the Queen of the Elves (in whom we have recognized a variant of the nocturnal goddess); women who, like the *benandanti* of Friuli, watch the processions of the dead in ecstasy; men who, as we shall see, participated in ecstasy in the battles for the fertility of the fields. The connection between (a) men, apparitions and throngs of the dead led by male personages and (b) women, ecstasies and cortèges following female divinities, becomes flawed in part, without, however, altering the sexual division of the roles that seems to regulate these relationships with the beyond. The apparitions of the dead are almost invariably defined as 'hunt' (*Jagd, chasse*), 'army' (*Heer, mesnie, exercitus*) 'society' (*societas*), 'following' (*familia*); and the encounters between the goddess and her followers, at least in testimony originating in northern

Italy, are 'society' (*societas*), 'game (*ludus*), 'game of the good society' (*ludus bonae societatis*).[50] Aside from the promiscuous use of a neutral term such as 'society' (*societas*), we see a juxtaposition emerging between activities reserved for men (war, the hunt) and activities to which women were also admitted (games).

Herolt's allusion to Diana's army, identified with the 'beatific women', may therefore be considered an isolated variation. It reminds us that apparitions and ecstasies, different ways of communicating between the living and the world of the dead, sprang from a background of commonly held beliefs. But the ecstatic cult of the nocturnal female divinities, practised overwhelmingly by women, stands out as a specific and relatively more delimited phenomenon. The geographical distribution of the testimony confirms this.

14. It refers to the Rhineland, where the penitential books and synods mentioned above originate, with the exception of the Toulouse area (synod of Conserans); to continental France; to the Alpine arc and the Po valley and Scotland. To this list we must add Rumania, where, as we shall see, semi-ecstatic rituals were performed under the protection of *Doamna Zînelor*, also called *Irodiada* or *Arada* – that is, respectively Diana and Herodias, two names which attest to the at least verbal introjection of the interpretations suggested by the clerics.[51] These are only apparently heterogeneous areas: what they have in common is that for hundreds of years (in some instances since the fifth century BC) they have been inhabited by Celts.[52] In the Germanic world, immune from Celtic infiltrations, the ecstatic cult of the nocturnal goddess seems to be absent. Hence it should apparently be traced back to a substratum, surfacing at a distance of more than a millennium in the Milanese trials at the end of fourteenth century and the Scottish trials three centuries later. Only in this way can we explain, for example, the astonishing analogies between the boasting of the *benandanti* in the Friuli and those of the 'boy of the fairies' who, so a report of the late seventeenth century informs us, went every Thursday to beat the drum beneath the hill between Edinburgh and Leith: men and women went through invisible doors into sumptuous rooms, and after banqueting amid music and merriment, they flew to distant lands such as France and Holland.[53]

Up until now – not unlike the inquisitors – we have used the so-called *Canon episcopi* as a key to decipher testimonies that are closer and closer to us. But if we try to decipher the *Canon* itself (in origin, as we have said, a Frankish capitular), we discover that it is the terminus of a documentary series that involves, over and above a substratum, an actual continuity with Celtic religious phenomena.

At the beginning of the fifth century, in a sermon against pagan cults, Maximus of Turin described a drunken peasant ready to mutilate himself in honour of an unnamed goddess (perhaps Cybele), comparing him to a *dianaticus* or soothsayer. The term *dianaticus*, introduced by the qualification 'as people say' (*sicut dicunt*), was, it would seem, a word in common use: just as its synonym *lunaticus* probably meant 'possessed', 'obsessed', prey to a religious frenzy.[54] Gregory of Tours speaks of a statue of Diana worshipped in the vicinity of Trier; moreover, as late as the end of the seventh century, according to a life of St Cilianus, the populations of the Franconia demonstrated their hostility to certain Christian missionaries by paying homage to the 'great Diana' – the hagiographer's reference to the passage from the *Acts of the Apostles* on the great goddess of Ephesus, also mentioned by Nicholas of Cusa. But undoubtedly the same Roman divinity Diana had been superimposed on one or more Celtic divinities: their names and their physiognomies surface only rarely.[55] In a grave of the end of the fourth or the beginning of the fifth century AD, discovered at Roussas in the Dauphiné, there was found a square roof tile: on its surface is a crude graffito representing a person mounted on a long-horned animal, accompanied by the inscription FERA COMHERA, 'with cruel Hera' (fig. 1).[56] Inscriptions of the same period dedicated to Hera or Haerecura have been found in Istria, in Switzerland, and in Cisalpine Gaul.[57] As late as the beginning of the fifteenth century the peasants of the Palatinate believed that a divinity named Hera, harbinger of abundance, roamed about in flight during the twelve days between Christmas and Epiphany, the period consecrated to the return of the dead.[58] Amid testimonies so chronologically distant the female figure scratched on the tile found in the Roussas grave inserts itself as an intermediary link. On the one hand, it confirms the old hypothesis which explained the presence of 'Herodiana' (later normalized to read Herodias) among the synonyms of the nocturnal goddess as a misreading of 'Hera Diana'.[59] On the other, it confirms the interpretation in a funerary key of the belief concerning the 'deluded women', who rode 'certain animals' following 'Diana goddess of the pagans'.

Thus the Roman rind enclosed a Celtic pulp. At any rate, the image of the nocturnal cavalcade is basically alien to Greek and Roman mythology.[60] For example, neither the Homeric gods nor heroes rode on horseback: they used horses almost solely in order to yoke to their chariots. The images of Diana (or Artemis) on horseback are extremely rare.[61] It has been thought that they could have inspired the, by contrast, very numerous images of a Celtic divinity almost always associated with horses: Epona. Now, the most ancient testimonies on Diana's cavalcade originate from Prüm, Worms and Trier – that is to say, from a region in which a large number of images of Epona on horseback, or standing alongside one or more horses, have been found (fig. 2). In the *Diana paganorum dea* of the Frankish capitular taken up by Regino, we shall therefore probably have to recognize an *interpretatio romana* of Epona or some local equivalent.[62] Like the Hera of Roussas, Epona was a mortuary divinity, often represented with a cornucopia, the symbol of abundance.[63] As we have seen, both these elements reappear in the names and characteristic features of figures such as Abundia, Satia, and Richella. Thus the representation of Epona, possibly patterned after that of Diana, fed local cults subsequently interpreted as cults of Diana. The mirror play between the interpretations and re-elaborations of the hegemonic culture, and their reception by the subaltern culture, continued for a long time. Halfway through the thirteenth century a word like *genes* (derived from Diana) still designated an ambiguous entity, a sort of fairy. Two hundred years thence *ianatica* was synonymous with witch.[64]

15. But Epona, patroness of horses and stables, is only one of the divinities that fed into the beliefs which later merged in the stereotyped description of Diana's cavalcade. In fact, to Epona were linked other figures of the enigmatic Celtic religious world, by now dissolving under the offensive of Christianity.[65] At the height of the thirteenth century they reappear in a passage by William of Auvergne, which immediately precedes the page about the 'nocturnal mistresses' led by Abundia. They are spirits who appear in the form of young girls or matrons dressed in white, in the woods or in the stable, where they let the wax from their candles drip on the horses' manes, which are deftly braided by them: a detail, this, that recurs in the description of Queen Mab – another nocturnal divinity – supplied by Mercutio in *Romeo and Juliet* (1.4).[66] These *matronae* dressed in white are a late echo of the *Matrae*, *Matres* or *Matronae*, to whom are dedicated a great number of inscriptions, often commissioned by women, found in the lower Rhineland, in France, in England, and in northern Italy (fig.3).[67] In one instance – an inscription found in the area between Novara and Vercelli – these divinities are associated with Diana.[68] The bas-reliefs that often accompany the epigraphs represent the *Matronae* in the form of three seated women (more rarely two, sometimes only one). They too, like Epona, display the symbols of prosperity and fertility: a cornucopia, a basket full of fruit, a swaddled child. The ecstatic nature of these cults is attested by the frequency with which, in the inscriptions dedicated to the *Matres* or *Matronae*, there appear expressions that allude to a direct contact with the divinity, both visual (*ex visu*) and auditory (*ex imperio, ex iussu*).[69]

Most probably, with these divinities we should associate the expression *modranicht* (night of the mothers) which, according to the Venerable Bede, in pagan Britannia designated the night of vigil – consecrated, perhaps, also to Epona – and corresponding in the Christian calendar to Christmas Eve.[70] Now, in the Celtic calendar the nights between 24 December and 6 January had an intercalary function comparable to that of the *Zwölften*, the twelve days during which, in the Germanic world, it was thought that the dead roamed abroad.[71] Like Epona, besides protecting women in childbirth, the *Matres* too were most likely connected to the world of the dead: a Britannic inscription, and several monuments from the first centuries AD originating in the Rhineland, associated them with the Parcae. Shortly after the year 1000, Burkhardt of Worms identified with the pagan Parcae the three divinities (certainly the *Matres*) for whom, on particular nights, the people left food with three knives.[72]

The *Fatae* to whom was dedicated an altar recovered at Cologne, Claudia

Savaria (today Szombathely), a region inhabited by the Gallic Boi, have been identified with a local variant of the *Matres*.[73] For a long time – centuries, indeed millennia – matrons, fairies, and other beneficent and mortuary divinities invisibly inhabited Celtified Europe.[74]

16.   All of this casts unexpected light on a page of the Byzantine historian Procopius of Caesarea probably written around 552 or 553. It is perhaps the most famous page of the *Gothic Wars*. Procopius is talking about an island which he calls Brittia. Suddenly his account breaks off to make way for a digression, introduced by wary and solemn words:

> Having reached this point of the story, I must inevitably report an event that is related rather to superstition and that to me seems wholly incredible, even though it is constantly mentioned by very many people, who affirm that they have carried out what I am about to recount with their own hands and that they have heard the words with their own ears. . . .

It concerns the inhabitants of certain fishing villages, located opposite Brittia, on the ocean's shore. They are subjects of the Franks, but they have long since not had to pay any sort of tribute, as a reward for the service that they perform. This is what the service consists in. All the souls of the dead end up on the island of Brittia. The inhabitants of the coastal villages are charged in turn with ferrying them across:

> The men who know that they must go and do this work during the night, relieving those who did it before them, as soon as darkness falls withdraw to their houses and go to sleep, waiting for someone who will come and call them for that task. In fact, late at night they hear knocks at the door and a muffled voice that calls them to work; without hesitation they jump out of bed and go to the edge of the sea, without understanding what mysterious power drives them to act in this manner, but feeling nevertheless impelled to do so.

On the shore they find special empty boats. But when they climb into them, the boats sink almost to the surface of the water, as though they were heavily laden. They begin to row; within approximately one hour they arrive at Brittia (whereas normally the voyage lasts a night and a day). After disembarking their passengers, they depart again with light ships. They haven't seen anyone, save for a voice that informs the boatmen of the social rank of the passengers, the names of their fathers, and in the case of the women the name of the husband.[75]

We do not know from what informants Procopius learned of this local tradition.[76] The identification of Brittia with Britannia seems very probable, although alternative hypotheses have been advanced (Jutland, Helgoland). The villages of the fishermen-ferryers of souls, which under normal circumstances lay at a distance of a day and a night's rowing, must have been situated on the coasts of Armorica (today's Brittany).[77] Since antiquity these lands have been enveloped in a nebulous halo of legend. At the beginning of the fifth century, Claudian was writing that Armorica, on the shores of the ocean, was indicated as the place where Ulysses had met the people of shadows: there 'the peasants see the pallid shadows of the dead wander about.'[78] Plutarch (who was perhaps elaborating on Celtic traditions) had already reported a myth according to which, on an island situated beyond Britannia, the god Kronos lay sleeping.[79] In the twelfth century the Byzantine scholar Tzetzes still believed, on the basis of Procopius' passage which he summarized, that the Fortunate Islands – i.e., the Islands of the Blessed – were located beyond the ocean.[80]

But the discussions provoked by Procopius' vague and partly fabulous geographic indications have overshadowed the truly singular element of the entire story: the night voyages periodically made by the ferryers of souls.[81] When inserted in the evidential series that we are analyzing, this detail appears less exceptional:

> Late in the night . . . there are knocks at the door and they hear a muffled voice that calls them to work [Procopius says]. A certain invisible thing appeared to me in my sleep, which had the semblance of a man, and it seemed to me I was sleeping and not sleeping . . . and it seemed to me that the thing said: 'You must come with me. . . .' Without hesitation they jump out of bed and go to the edge of the sea, without understanding what mysterious power drives them to act in this manner, but feeling nevertheless impelled to do so [Procopius continues]. We need to go. . . ; and so I said that if I had to go I would go. . . .

The contrapuntal voices are those of two *benandanti* of Friuli tried at the end of the sixteenth century.[82] Procopius' anonymous informants, who stated that they had personally participated in the ferrying of souls, may perhaps have used words analogous to theirs to describe the unknown power that compelled them. The tasks performed in spirit by the *benandanti* were, as we shall see, different. Neither account mentions female divinities (in Procopius' account the voice that pronounces the names of the dead on the dark beach is sexless). But in both resounds the more or less reworked, but unmistakable echo of an ecstatic experience. A thousand years separate these testimonies. One is tempted to compare them, assuming in both cases the presence of a Celtic substratum which, in Brittany as in Friuli, in conjunction with different traditions, continued for a long time to nourish a popular religion of the dead.[83]

17. But in the course of the Middle Ages this mythical nucleus also nourished a tradition of a totally different kind, not oral but written (albeit vernacular); not popular but courtly; tied to a literary and not an ecstatic experience. These are the romances of the Arthurian cycle. In them, as already noted, Arthur sometimes appears as the genuine king of the dead. His depiction mounted on a sort of ram (*super quandam bestiam*, we might say paraphrasing the *Canon episcopi*) in the great floor mosaic at Otranto dated 1163–5 (fig. 4), like his appearance one hundred years later at the head of the 'wild hunt', attests to the proximity between literary reworking and folkloric belief revolving around communication with the beyond.[84] A journey to the

world of the dead has been recognized in the odysseys of heroes such as Eric, Percival, Lancelot, to mysterious castles, separated from the world of men by a bridge, a meadow, a heath or the sea. At times the very toponyms (Limors, Schastel le mort) declare this identity.[85] These are places in which existence is abstracted from the flow of time. The traveller must beware of the food eaten there – the food of the dead, which a very ancient tradition forbids to the living.[86] The literary precedents of these narratives have been recognized in certain Irish texts (*echtrai*, or adventures).[87] But the analogies with the ecstatic tradition which concerns us refer us back to a common stock of Celtic myths. Arthur's sister, Morgan le Fay, *fata Morgana*, is a latter incarnation (albeit enriched by new elements) of two Celtic goddesses: the Irish Morrigan, linked to Epona, and the Welsh Modron.[88] The latter is none other than one of the *Matronae* worshipped from the first centuries of the Christian era.[89] The affinity between the fairies whom we meet in the confessions of Scottish witches of the sixteenth and seventeenth centuries, and the fairies who populate the Arthurian romances, is extremely close.

All this confirms the importance of the elements of Celtic folklore which, blending with Christian themes, flowed into the '*matière de Bretagne*'.[90] The theme of the hero's journey into the realm of the dead, which occurs on several occasions in the Arthurian romances, must be traced back to this tradition.[91] But the mythical juxtaposition between Arthur's court and the surrounding universe, inhabited by magical and hostile presences, also lent itself to the expression of a precise historical situation in atemporal form: the entrenchment of the knights into a closed caste, when confronted by a rapidly changing society.[92]

18.   The old peasant women of Val di Fassa were undoubtedly unaware of this courtly literary tradition. But a man sentenced as a witch at the beginning of the sixteenth century in Val di Fiemme, Zuan delle Piatte, constitutes a more complicated instance of hybridization.[93] He confessed to the judges that he had gone with a friar to the Sibilla's mountain near Norcia, also known as 'mount of Venus where lived Donna Herodias', to be initiated into the society of witches. Upon arriving at a lake the two had met 'a huge friar dressed in black and he was a black', who, before allowing them to cross, had induced them to renounce the Christian faith and give themselves to the devil. Then they had gone into the mountain, passing through a door barred by a serpent: here an old man, 'the faithful Ekhart', had warned them that if they remained there for longer than a year they would never return. Among the people shut up in the mountain they had seen an old sleeping man, 'the Tonhauser' and 'Donna Venus'. Together with her Zuan delle Piatte had gone to the Sabbath, where he had also found the 'woman of the good game'. The diabolical elements which punctuate these confessions can be attributed to the use of torture during the trial: but the Sibilla 'Donna Venus', 'the faithful Ekhart' and 'the Tonhauser' have more distant origins. Almost one hundred years previously local Umbrian traditions about the Sibilla's

mountain, re-elaborated in a very successful popular novel like Andrea da Barberino's *Guerin Meschino*, had fused with German legends based on the figure of Tannhäuser.[94] But in Zuan delle Piatte's story echoes of a possible reading of *Guerin Meschino* mingled with elements pertaining to a clearly folkloric oral culture. Zuan declared that he had gone 'with that woman (Venus) and her company on a Thursday night of the Ember week of Christmas riding black horses through the air and in five hours they had circled the entire world'.[95] Once again we find the cavalcade of Diana (or her synonyms), the ecstatic journey through the four Embers of Richella's followers or the *benandanti* of Friuli. A century later, in 1630, an enchanter from Hesse, Diel Breull, confessed that for several years he had gone in spirit, during the Ember weeks, to the Venusberg, where 'fraw Holt' (Holda or Holle, another of the goddess's personifications) had shown him the dead and their sufferings, reflected in a basin full of water: splendid horses, men engaged in banqueting or sitting among the flames.[96] Some time earlier, in 1614, Heinrich Kornmann had published his *Mons Veneris*, in which he recounted the legend of Tannhäuser.[97] Like Breull, Kornmann came from Hesse: but as we have seen, such traditions cannot be tied to a particular region. And even if Breull had read the *Mons Veneris*, this would not have sufficed to explain the lethargy into which he had sunk, at a moment of intense unhappiness (his wife and son had died), then to find himself on the Venusberg. Nevertheless, it is significant that on the rare occasions when the theme of the ecstatic journey seems to mingle with elements derivative from the written tradition, they refer to men, who are more likely to have been literate, than to women. Similarly, in the confessions made by Arnaud Gélis at the beginning of the fourteenth century the descriptions of the throngs of souls are accompanied by assertions that echo Irish hagiographic texts (they too interwoven with folkloric elements) on St Patrick's journey to Purgatory.[98]

19. The confluence of Celtic traditions concerning elves and fairies in the image of witchcraft elaborated by the demonologists was long ago recognized (and then basically forgotten).[99] The geographical and chronological context which we have reconstructed permits us to make this intertwining more precise and complex. To the more or less recent elements that contributed to the crystallization of the Sabbath stereotype in the Western Alps, between the Dauphiné, Suisse Romande, Lombardy and Piedmont – the presence of heretical groups in a state of disintegration, the diffusion of the fear of conspiracy – we can now add another, far more ancient: the sedimentation of Celtic culture. It is a material sedimentation (the archaeological deposits of La Tène, in the vicinity of Lake Neuchâtel, have given the oldest nucleus of Celtic civilization its name) and a metaphorical one. In the night flying described by the male and female witches of the Valais tried at the beginning of the fifteenth century – foreign, as we said, to the inquisitorial stereotype – we can now recognize the distorted echo of an ecstatic cult of Celtic tradition.

The localization in time and space of the first trials based on the image of the Sabbath appears (in retrospect) inevitable. Not only that, but a striking coincidence of linguistic and geographical data has prompted the hypothesis that the great majority of the proper names and place names that recur in the Arthurian cycle must be referred back to toponyms concentrated in the region of Lake Leman.[100] It could be said that the literary and inquisitorial re-elaborations of the ancient Celtic myth of the journey into the world of the dead were diffused, at different times and in different ways, from the same area and from similar folkloric materials. All the accounts seem to balance.

Notes

1. Cf. above, p. 101.
2. See *The Night Battles*, p. 3.
3. Duvernoy, *Le registre d'Inquisition de Jacques Fournier*, Paris 1965, I, p. 139. See also ibid., pp. 128–43, 533–52; J.-M. Vidal, 'Une secte de spirites à Pamiers en 1320', extract from *Annales de Saint-Louis-Des-Français*, III (1899); Emmanuel Le Roy Ladurie, *Montaillou*, Paris 1978, pp. 592–611; M. P. Piniès, *Figures de la sorcellerie languedocienne*, Paris 1983, pp. 241 ff.
4. *Reginonis abbatis Prumiensis libris duo de synodalibus causis et disciplinis ecclesiasticis...*, F. W. H. Wasserschleben ed, Lipsiae 1840, p. 355. There also exists a briefer version: cf. Russell, *Witchcraft in the Middle Ages*, Ithaca 1972, pp. 291 ff. On the penitential literature in general, see now A. J. Gurevič, *Contadini e santi*, Turin 1986, pp. 125–72.
5. See Migne, *Patrologia latina*, CXL, coll. 831 ff. And cf. E. Friedberg, *Aus deutschen Busbüchern*, Halles 1868, pp. 67 ff.
6. The attribution of *Corrector* to Burchard by P. Fournier, ('Etudes critiques sur le décret de Burchard évêque de Worms', *Nouvelle revue historique du droit français et étranger*, XXXIV (1910), pp. 41–112, 289–331 and 563–84, especially pp. 100–06) is today commonly accepted: cf. C. Vogel, 'Pratiques superstitieuses au début du XIe siècle d'après le *Corrector sive medicus* du Burchard, évêque de Worms (965–1025)', in *Mélanges offerts à E. R. Labande*, Poitiers 1976, pp. 751 ff. (pointed out to me by Martina Kempter).
7. Cf. F. W. H. Wasserschleben, *Die Bussordnungen der abendländischen Kirche*, rist. anast. Graz 1958, pp. 645 and 660–1.
8. Cf. Migne, *Patrologia latina*, CXL, coll. 837 (and see Friedberg, op. cit., p. 71).
9. For some initial bearings, see the documentation collected by G. Bonomo, *Caccia alle streghe*, Palermo 1959 (new edn. 1986): but the analysis is superficial.
10. Cf. ibid., pp. 22–3 (where *Bensoria* is written by mistake. Another variant: *Bezezia* (see Du Cange, *Glossarium mediae et infimae Latinitatis*, under the heading 'Bensozia'). See also A. Wesselofsky, 'Alichino e Aredodesa', *Giornale storico della letteratura italiana*, XI (1888), pp. 325–43, especially p. 342 (but the etymology is not convincing). In presenting the statutes of the diocese of Conserans (or Couserans), written by his ancestor, Bishop Auger (d. 1304), Montfaucon immediately recognized the relation between the beliefs based on Diana and the witches' Sabbath: see B. de Montfaucon, *Supplément au livre de l' antiquité expliquée et présentée en figures...*, I, Paris 1724, pp.111–16. These pages of Montfaucon's (referred to in Du Cange's 1733 edition, under the heading 'Diana') were drawn

Following the Goddess

upon by Dom***[Jacques Martin], *Le religion des Gaulots*, Paris 1727, II, pp. 59–67.

11. See E. Martène and U. Durand, *Thesaurus novus anecdotorum*, IV, Lutetiae Parisiorum 1717, col. 257 (see also Wesselofsky, art. cit., pp. 332–3).

12. To the bibliography contained in *The Night Battles* (p. 187 n. 21) should be added: on Perchta, R. Bleichsteiner, 'Iranische Entsprechungen zu Frau Holle und Baba Jaga', *Mitra*, I (1914), 65–71; M. Bartels and O. Ebermann, 'Zur Aberglaubensliste in Vintlers Pluemen der Tugent', *Zeitschrift für Volkskunde*, 23 (1913), p. 5; F. Kauffmann, 'Altgermanische Religion', *Archiv für Religionswissenschaft*, 20 (1920–21), pp. 221–2; A. Dönner, *Tiroler Fasnacht*, Vienna 1949, pp. 338 ff. (especially rich in suggestions); J. Hanika, 'Bercht schlitzt den Bauch auf – Rest eines Initiationsritus?', *Stifter – Jahrbuch*, II (1951), pp. 39–53; idem, 'Peruchta-Sperechta-Žber', *Boehmen und Maehren, Archiv für Völkerkunde*, VIII (1953), pp. 58–75; F. Prodinger, 'Beiträge zur Perchtenforschung', *Mitteilungen der Gesellschaft für Salzburger Landeskunde*, 100 (1960), pp. 545–63; N. Kuret, 'Die Mittwinterfrau der Slovenen Pehtra Baba und Torka)', *Alpes Orientales, V. Acta quinti conventus. . .*, Ljubljana 1969, pp. 209 ff. On Holda, see A. Franz, 'Des Frater Rudolphus Buch "De Officio Cherubyn" ', *Theologische Quartalschrift*, III (1906), pp. 411–36; J. Klapper, 'Deutscher Volksglaube in Schlesien in ältester Zeit', *Mitteilungen der schlesischen Gesellschaft für Volkskunde*, 17 (1915–16), pp. 19 ff., above all pp. 42–52 (a very useful collection of testimonies); A. H. Krappe, *Études de mythologie et de folklore germaniques*, Paris 1928, pp. 101–14 (very contentious); K. Helm, *Altgermanische Religionsgeschichte* II, 2, Heidelberg 1953, pp. 49–50; F. Raphael, 'Rites de naissance et médecine populaire dans le judaïsme rural d'Alsace', *Ethnologie française*, n.s. I (1971), nos. 3–4, pp. 83–94 (traces of beliefs linked to Holda in the Jewish folklore of Alsace and the Low Countries etc.); Gurevič, op. cit., pp. 134–6.

13. See Wesselofsky, art. cit., pp. 332–3 (and see above pp. 104).

14. See G. Wissowa, 'Interpretatio Romana. Römische Götter in Barbarenlande', *Archiv für Religionswissenschaft*, XIX (1916–1919), pp. 1–49.

15. Cf. Bonomo, op. cit., p. 71.

16. The sentences have been published in the appendix to L. Muraro, *La signora del gioco*, Milan 1976, pp. 240–5; see especially pp. 242–3. The old essay by E. Verga, 'Intorno a due inediti documenti di stregheria milanese del secolo XIV', *Rendiconti del R. Istituto lombardo di scienze e lettere*, s. II, 32 (1899), pp. 165–88, remains fundamental. On the material conditions of the ms, see G. Giorgetta, 'Un Pestalozzi accusato di stregoneria', *Clavenna*, 20 (1981), p. 66 n. 35 (I thank Ottavia Niccoli for alerting me to this essay).

17. I complete the word 'divitum', not deciphered in the transcription in the appendix to Muraro, op. cit., p. 243. On the basis of this I correct my previous reading error ('veniatis' not 'veivatis': cf. *The Night Battles*, p. 198 n. 2).

18. See above, p. 71.

19. Cf. G. Mansionario, *Historiarum imperialium liber*: *'adhuc multi laycorum tali errore tenentur credentes predictam societatem de nocte ire et Dianam paganorum deam sive Herodiadem credunt hujus societatis reginam . . .'* (Vallicelliana Library, Rome, ms. D. 13, c. 179 r). The passage is cited, à propos of the nocturnal miracle of St. Germanus, by G. Tartarotti, *Del congresso notturno del lammie*, Rovereto 1749, p. 29; and see also, by the same author, *Relazione d'un manoscritto dell'Istoria manoscritta di Giovanni Diacono Veronese*, in Calogierà, *Raccolta d'opuscoli. . .*, 18, Venice 1738, pp. 135–93, especially pp. 165–7, where the reference to the magistrates who 'furiously' condemn the witches to decapitation possibly contains the germ of the future *Congresso notturno*.

111

20. The sermon, without the introductory section, can be found in *Nicolai Cusae Cardinalis Opera*, II, Parisiis 1514, (Frankfurt-am-Main 1962), cc. CLXXv-CLXXIIr ('Ex Sermone: Haec omnia tibi dabo'). The complete text is contained in *Vat. lat.* 1245, cc. 227r-229r. On the history of the manuscript sermon and its dating (Bressanone, 6 March 1457), see J. Koch, *Cusanus-Texte, I: Predigten*, 7, *Untersuchungen über Datierung, Form, Sprache und Quellen. Kristisches Verzeichnis sämtlicher Predigten*, Heidelberg 1942 ('Sitzungsberichte der Heidelberger Akademie der Wissenschaften', Phil.-hist. Kl., Jahrgang 1941–42, I. Abh.), pp. 182–3, n.CCLXVIII. A translation and commentary (both quite inadequate) can be found in C. Binz, 'Zur Charakteristik des Cusanus', *Archiv für Kulturgeschichte*, VII (1909), pp. 145–53. There are brief mentions in E. Vasteenberghe, *Le cardinal Nicolas de Cues*, Paris 1920, p. 159; H. Liermann, *Nikolaus von Cues und das deutsche Recht*, in *Cusanus-Gedächtnisschrift*, N. Grass ed, Munich 1970, p. 217; W. Zeigeler, *Möglichkeiten der Kritik am Hexeb-und Zauberwesen im ausgehenden Mittelalter*, Köln u. Vienna 1973, pp. 99–100. G. J. Strangfeld, *Die Stellung des Nikolaus von Kues in der literarischen und geistigen Entwicklung des österreichischen Spätmittelalters*, Phil. Diss. Vienna 1948, pp. 230–7, deals exclusively with Nicholas of Cusa's attitude. (This last text was very kindly pointed out and sent to me by Dr Hermann Hallauer, who is preparing the critical edition of Nicholas of Cusa's sermons. He informs me that he has not succeeded in tracking down the records of the trials against the old women of Val di Fassa. The research which I conducted in the Archive of the Curia of Bressanone also proved fruitless.)
21. On this term see Helm, op. cit., II, 2, pp. 49–50.
22. I am developing here – albeit in a different direction – the analogy discussed by R. Rosaldo: cf. 'From the door of His Tent: The Fieldworker and the Inquisitor', in J. Clifford and G. F. Marcus eds, *Writing Culture*, Berkeley and Los Angeles 1986, pp. 77–97.
23. On all this see above, Introduction, p. 11.
24. Cf. Bertolotti, 'Le ossa e la pelle dei buoi. . .', *Quaderni storici* 41 (May-August 1979), pp. 487 ff.
25. See Bernardo da Como, *Lucerna inquisitorum . . . et Tractatus de strigibus*, with notes by F. Pegna, Romae 1584, pp. 141–2.
26. On these trials see J. A. Macculloch, 'The Mingling of Fairy and Witch Beliefs in Sixteenth and Seventeenth Century Scotland', *Folklore*, XXXII (1921) , pp. 229–44. For the trial of Isabel Gowdie, see R. Pitcairn, *Ancient Criminal Trials in Scotland*, III, 2, Edinburgh 1833, pp. 602 ff., especially p. 604. The editor comments: 'The above details are perhaps, in all respects, the most extraordinary in the history of witchcraft of this or any other country', complaining that the judges had eliminated them from the records on the grounds of irrelevance. The fortunes of this passage are instructive. Murray quoted it, on the basis of the Pitcairn edition, as regards the means of locomotion used by the witches to travel to meetings which she considered completely real (*The Witch-Cult in Western Europe*, Oxford 1962, pp. 105–6; see also pp. 244–5). Cohn (*Europe's Inner Demons*, pp. 113–14) observed that the passage was not interpretable in a realistic sense: the defendant evidently drew on vague 'local fairy lore'. Larner, who checked the passage in the manuscript, making some small corrections but inadvertently conflating two different segments of the same trial (cf. *Enemies of God*, London 1981, p. 152 and *Ancient Criminal Trials*, III. 2, pp. 604 and 608), remarked that, as Cohn had rightly seen, it was a matter of 'incidents which can only relate to dreams, nightmares and collective fantasies'. These are obviously absurd (Murray) or inadequate (Cohn, Larner) interpretations.

27. See the records published in *The Miscellany of the Spalding Group*, I (1841), pp. 117 ff., above all pp. 119–22. The passage is reproduced by Murray in an appendix to her op. cit., p. 242, like the other passages from the Scottish trials discussed here (cf. the headings 'Aberdeen', 'Auldearne' and 'Orkney' in the index).

28. See *The Night Battles*, p. 31. The inner tensions provoked by diabolization of the 'fairy folk' emerge clearly in several Scottish trials of 1623 held in the Burg of Perth: See *Extracts from the Presbitery Book of Struthbogie*, Aberdeen 1843, pp. X-XIII.

29. *Procès de condemnation de Jeanne d'Arc. . . . I*, P. Tissot and Y. Lanhers eds, Paris 1960, p. 178.

30. Cf. *The Night Battles*, pp. 40 ff.

31. Cf. Bonomo, op. cit., p. 23.

32. Cf. Duvernoy, op. cit., I, p. 544 (interrogation of Mengarde, wife of Arnaud de Pomeriis). The mythic implications of the reference to the 'bonae dominae' eluded Le Roy Ladurie (see op. cit., pp. 592, 603).

33. For Ireland see [J. Aubrey], *Fairy Legends and Traditions of the South of Ireland*, London 1825, pp. 193 ff. For Scotland, see Pitcairn, op. cit., I. 3, p. 162 and *passim* (and cf. ibid., III. 2, p. 604. n.3 for the attribution to Aubrey of the preceding work). In the Orkney islands a woman, Jonet Drever, was permanently banished in 1615 for maintaining over twenty-six years relations (also carnal) with 'the fairy folk, callit of hir our guid nichtbouris [the fairies, that she called our good neighbours]' (*The Court Books of Orkney and Shetland 1614–1615*, R. S. Barclay ed, Edinburgh 1967, p. 19). On the fairies, besides R. Kirk, *The Secret Commonwealth (Il regno segreto*, It.tr. Milan, edited by M. M. Rossi, whose essay 'Il Cappellano delle fate' is reprinted in the appendix), see the texts collected by [W. C. Hazlitt], *Fairy Mythology of Shakespeare*, London 1875, and the essays of M. W. Latham, *The Elizabethan Fairies*, New York 1930, and K. M. Briggs, *The Anatomy of Puck*, London 1959. On the Friuli see *The Night Battles*, p. 54.

34. See J. Kolendo, 'Dea Placida à Novae et le culte d'Hécate, la bonne déesse', *Archaeologia* (Warsaw), XX (1969), pp. 77–83. The identification between the subterranean Hecate and *Bona dea* is in Macrobius, *Saturnalia*, 1, 12, 23. On this point see also H. H. J. Brouwer, *Bona Dea*, Leiden 1989 (pointed out to me by Jan Bremmer).

35. See J. G. Dalyell, *The Darker Superstitions of Scotland, Illustrated from Theory and Practice*, Edinburgh 1834, pp. 470, 534 ff. and 590–1 (a book that remains precious, since based on judicial sources for the islands of Orkney and Shetland: see p. 5 n.).

36. Cf. G. de Lorris, *Le Roman de la Rose*, E. Langlois ed., IV, Paris 1922, pp. 229–30, vv. 18425–60.

37. I develop here an interpretation already formulated in *The Night Battles*, pp. 58 ff. on the basis of substantially different documentation. Quite independently, K. M. Briggs, 'The Fairies and the Realm of the Dead', *Folk-Lore*, 81 (1970), pp. 81–96, reaches similar conclusions. (Previously, the same scholar had rejected a summary connection between belief in the fairies and the cult of the dead: see 'The English Fairies', ibid., 68, 1957, pp. 270–87).

38. See *The Night Battles*, p. 41. In general see R. Parrot, 'Le 'Refrigerium' dans l'au-delà', *Revue de l'histoire de religions*, t. CXIII (1936), p. 149 ff.; t. CXIV (1936), p. 69 ff, and 158 ff.; t. CXV (1937), pp. 53 ff.; more specifically, see W. Deonna 'Croyances Funeraires. La soif des morts. . . .', ibid., t. CXIX (1939), pp. 53–77.

39. Cf. Duvernoy, op. cit., I, p. 137: *Item dixit quod mortui libenter veniunt ad loca munda et intrabant domos mundas, et nolunt venire ad loca sordida, nec intrare domos immundas.*

Oriente's mortuary connotations have been well emphasized by G. Scalera McClintock, 'Sogno e realtà in due processi per eresia', in F. Lazzari and G. Scalera McClintock, *Due arti della lontananza*, Naples 1979, pp. 69–70.

40. The passages are included in the collection *Sermones de tempore* (sermon 41). I have checked the following editions: Köln 1474; Strassburg *post* 1478 (Haln 8473); Nürnberg 1480 and 1481; Strassburg 1484; Nürnberg 1496; Strassburg 1499 and 1503; Rouen 1513 (which mentions only Diana). Other indications on Herolt (who was born around 1390) can be found in Klapper, art. cit., pp. 48–50, which lists the different lessons of the cited passage (and of another passage, similar but briefer, taken from sermon 11) to be found in the mss of the *Sermones de tempore* kept in the Universitätsbibliothek of Breslau.

41. Besides *The Night Battles*, pp. 40 ff., see the documentation collected and analyzed by A. Endter, *Die Sage vom wilden Jäger und von der wilden Jagd*, Frankfurt-am-Main 1933; K. Meisen, *Die Sagen vom Wütenden Heer und wilden Jäger*, Munster 1935. The old meteorological interpretation of the myth proposed by W. Mannhardt and by his school was rejected by A. Endter on the basis of the fundamental work of L. Weiser (later Weiser-Aall) quoted below in notes 2 and 26 to Part Two, chapter 3. On Dietrich von Bern (who in the Italian translations becomes Teodorico of Verona), cf. A. Veselovskij, in Veselovskij and Sade, *La fanciulla perseguitata*, D. S. Avalle ed. Milan 1977, pp. 62 ff.; F. Sieber, 'Dietrich von Bern als Führer der wilden Jagd', *Mitteilungen der schlesischen Gesellschaft für Volkskunde*, 31–32 (1931), pp. 85–124; A. H. Krappe, 'Dietrich von Bern als Führer der wilden Jagd', ibid., XXXIII (1933), pp. 129–36; J. de Vries, 'Theoderich der Grosse', in *Kleine Schriften*, Berlin 1965, pp. 77–88. On the sixteenth-century re-elaboration of these themes, see O. Niccoli, *Profeti e popolo nell' Italia del Rinascimento*, Bari 1987, pp. 89–121.

42. See Jacques Le Goff, *La naissance du Purgatoire*, Paris 1981 (on which see also the review of F. Génicot in *Revue d'histoire ecclésiastique*, LXXVIII, 1982, pp. 421–6, and C. Carozzi, in *Cahiers de civilisation médiévale*, XXXVIII, 1985, pp. 264–6). A detailed investigation of the connection between folkloric beliefs regarding the realm of the dead and theological elaborations of Purgatory would be very useful: see, meanwhile, the general observations of A. J. Gurevič, 'Popular and Scholarly Medieval Cultural Traditions: Notes in the margin of Jacques Le Goff's Book', *Journal of Medieval History*, 9 (1983), pp. 71–90.

43. See Meisen, op. cit., p. 103 (Berchtholda, in a folksy German ditty published in 1557 or 1558); p. 124 (Holda, in a sixteenth-century description of the carnival at Nuremberg); p. 132 n. 1('the old Berchta', cited together with *Frau Herodias* and *Frau Hulda* and other diabolical spirits by J. Mathesius, *Auslegung der Fest-Evangelien*, 1571). That the reference to Herolt in Diana's army is utterly unusual can be inferred, albeit indirectly, from Endter, op. cit.

44. The souls of the 'ecstatics' who had not returned to their own bodies became part of the 'furious army', passing from a condition of temporary death to death proper: thus affirmed a group of *clerici vagantes* (wandering clerics) who, in the middle of the sixteenth century, roamed through the fields of Hessen extorting gifts and money from the peasants (See *The Night Battles*, pp. 55–6).

45. All this is not contradicted by the presence, in the realm of myth, of the Walkyrie in the retinue of Wotan. This line of interpretation was first proposed by O. Höfler, *Kultische Geheimbünde der Germanen*, I (sole volume published), Frankfurt-am-Main 1934 (see below Part Two, chapter 3, n. 2). More recently, see J. de Vries, 'Wodan und die wilde Jagd', *Die Nachbarn*, 3 (1962), pp. 31–59, which repeats in a more nuanced fashion some of Höfler's conclusions. On the ideological orientation

of de Vries, see the observations of W. Baetke, *Kleine Schriften*, K. Rudolph and E. Walter eds, Weimer 1973, pp. 37 ff.

46. Cf. Muraro, *La signora del gioco*, Milan 1976, pp. 152–5.

47. Höfler on the one hand emphasized the fact that the insertion of Perchta in the traditions related to the army of the dead is a late phenomenon; on the other, that in the ritual processions (on which see below, pp. 193 ff.) the 'Perchten' were impersonated by masked boys and not by women (op. cit., pp. 15, 89–90, 277–8). Both elements confirmed for him the distinction between a bellicose nucleus (properly Germanic) and marginal elements linked to fertility and the eroticism engaged in by the witches. The presence of male and female figures (both as animals and human beings, of the living and dead) in the descriptions of the 'wild hunt' is recorded by A. Endter (op. cit., p. 32) and above all by Dönner, (op. cit., p. 142). De Vries has insisted on the marginal or geographically circumscribed function of Perchta and Holda in this set of beliefs (art. cit., p. 45). The problem of the 'wild hunt' is completely ignored by Muraro.

48. For the 'wild hunt' I use for convenience sake the collection edited by Meisen, op. cit., even though, for the post-medieval period, it is scarcely exhaustive. I skip the texts from Graeco-Romano antiquity, as well as the few nineteenth-century texts: the former because they are clearly extraneous to the theme, the second because chosen in a casual manner. For the ecstatic women I recommend the bibliography indicated in this chapter. On both phenomena I have tried to identify a tendency; the existence of exceptions is taken for granted. On the apparition of dead individuals see Schmitt, 'Gli spettri nella società feudale', in *Religione, folklore e società nell' Occidente medievale*, Bari 1988, pp. 182–205.

49. The *Roman de la Rose* (vv. 18425–60) speaks of the followers of Dame Habonde and of the 'good ladies' without identifying their sex.

50. The Aristotelian philosopher Vincenzo Maggi, born in Brescia, and later professor in the Studios of Padua and Ferrara, where he died in 1564, wrote a '*delightful dialogue* in which he introduces the god Pan worshipped by those crazy pagans, as responsible for the rumours that the silly women of the region around Brescia attribute to that Apparition which they call the "Lady of the Game" '. (see L. Cozzando, *Libraria bresciana*, Brescia 1694, p. I, p. 203). The dialogue is apparently lost; but one of its initials (figs. 5 and 6) is used in the edict of Camillo Campeggio of Pavia, an inquisitor in Ferrara, dated January 1564 (Archive of the State of Modena, *S. Uffizio*. b. I). The printer, Francesco de' Rossi of Valenza, had already published the inaugural lecture by Maggi entitled *De cognitionis praestantia oratio* (1557) (cf. P. Guerrini, *Due amici bresciani di Erasmo*, extract from *Archivio storico lombardo*, 1923, pp. 6 ff.). In this exceptional portrayal of the 'lady of the game' 'F' would stand for 'Fantasima' (ghost, apparition) ; the *Piacevole dialogo [Delightful dialogue]* (which is not mentioned in the *Annali della tipografia ferrarese de' secoli XV e XVI* by Girolamo Baruffaldi jr., Biblioteca Communale Ariostea, ms CI. I, 589) must have been printed at Ferrara by Francesco de' Rossi of Valenza in 1564 or just before. Unfortunately, I have not succeeded in tracking it down. The anonymous engraver is obviously inspired by the iconography of Cybele.

51. See below, pp. 168–9.

52. For a complete picture see J. de Vries, *I Celti*, Italian trans., Milan 1982, pp. 21ff. On the Celtification of the Trentino region, see C. Battisti , *Sostrati e parastrati nell'Italia preistorica*, Florence 1959, pp. 236 ff.; and especially W. T. Elwert, *Die Mundart des Fassa-Tals*, (Wörter und Sachen', N. F., Beiheft 2.), Heidelberg 1943, pp. 215 ff.

53. See R. Bovet, *Pandaemonium, or the Devil's Cloyster, being a further blow to modern*

Sadduceism, proving the existence of witches and spirits, London 1684, pp. 172 ff. ('A remarkable passage of one named the Fairy-Boy of Leith in Scotland...': this is an account signed by Captain George Burton).

54. See *Maximi episcopi Taurinensis Sermones*, A. Mutzenbecher ed, Turholti 1962 ('Corpus Christianorum', Latin series, vol. XXIII), pp. 420–1: the sermon is a little later than 403–405 (see Introduction, p. XXXIV). For the interpretation, see F. J. Dölger, 'Christliche Grundbesitzer und heidnische Landarbeiter', *Antike und Christentum*, 6 (1950), Munster 1976, pp. 306 ff. Du Cange, on the other hand (*Glossarium, sub voce*), construes 'dianaticus' as 'follower of Diana'. The young men castrated in honour of Berecinzia (i.e., Cybele), in the city of Autun are mentioned in the *Passio Sancti Symphoriani:* see T. Ruinart, *Acta martyrum*... Veronae 1731, pp. 68–71, cited by F. J. Dölger, 'Teufels Grossmutter', *Antike und Christentum*, 3 (1932), p. 175.

55. See in general A. K. Michels, under heading *Diana* in *Reallexikon für Antike und Christentum*, III, Stuttgart 1957, pp. 970–2. See in addition E. Krüger, 'Diana Arduinna', *Germania*, I (1917). pp. 4–12, which refers to Gregory of Tours, *Historia Francorum*, VIII. 15; S. Reinach, 'La religion des Galates', in *Cultes, mythes et religions*, I, Paris 1922, p. 276 (and see also idem, 'Clelia et Epona', in ibid., pp. 60–1).

56. F. Benoît, *L'héroïsation équestre*, Gap 1954, pp. 27–30 and plate I, 2, supposes that the animal portrayed is a horned peacock. According to A. Ross, *Pagan Celtic Britain*, London 1967, p. 225 (which reproduces the tile as the image of Epona) it instead portrays a goose. Neither of the two identifications seems convincing. Cf. also C. B. Pascal, *The Cults of Cisalpine Gaul*, Brussels-Berchem 1964, pp. 102–5.

57. See H. Gaidoz, 'Dis Pater et Aere-Cura', *Revue Archéologique* XXX (1892), pp. 198–214; E. Thevenot, 'Le culte des déeses mères à la station gallo-romaine des Bolards', *Revue Archéologique de l'Est et du Centre-Est*, II (1951), p. 23 n. 2; R. Egger, *Eine Fluchtafel aus Carnuntum*, now in *Römische Antike und frühes Christentum*, I, Klagenfurt 1962, pp. 81 ff., especially pp. 84–5.

58. Cf. Jakob Grimm, *Deutsche Mythologie*, 4th edition, E. H. Meyer ed, I, Berlin 1875, p. 218.

59. Cf. Wesselofsky, art. cit., pp. 332–3; but see also Du Cange, op. cit., the heading for 'Hera' (2). Of a different opinion is Friedberg, op. cit., p. 72.

60. For a different opinion see K. Dilthey, 'Die Artemis von Apelles und die wilde Jagd', *Rheinisches Museum*, 25 (1870), pp. 321–36 (but the arguments do not seem convincing).

61. Cf. Reinach, 'Clelia et Epona', pp.54–68. On Selene on horseback, see I. Chirassi-Colombo, *Miti e culti arcaici di Artemis nel Peloponneso e Grecia centrale*, Trieste 1964, p. 34 n. 96. In the goddess on horseback, depicted on some coins from Pherai, T. Kraus (*Hekate*, Heidelberg 1960, pp. 80 ff.) recognizes not (as had previously been thought) Artemis, but a divinity of Thessaly: Enodia. L. Robert, *Hellenica*, XI-XII, pp.588–95, has come independently to the same conclusions.

62. That the Diana of the *Canon episcopi* (mistakenly said to derive from the non-existent council of Ancyra) was in reality a Celtic divinity had already been realized by Reinach, 'La religion des Galates', p. 262.

63. Cf. H. Hubert, 'Le mythe d'Epona', in *Mélanges linguistiques offerts à M. J. Vendryes*, Paris 1925, pp. 187–98. A review of iconographic evidence on Epona has been furnished by E. Thevenot, in the appendix to R. Magnen, *Epona déesse gauloise des chevaux protectrice des chevaliers*, Bordeaux 1953. Cf. also de Vries, op. cit., pp. 158–61; K. M. Linduff, 'Epona: a Celt among the Romans', *Latomus*, 38 (1979), pp. 817–37 (on p. 835 the funerary connotations are emphasized); L. S. Oaks,

'The Goddess Epona : Concepts of Sovereignty in a Changing Landscape', in *Pagan Gods and Shrines of the Roman Empire*, M. Henig and A. King eds, Oxford 1986, pp. 77–83.

64. In the middle of the fifteenth century St. Antonino alluded to the women condemned in the *Canon episcopi*, comparing them to *streghe (witches)* or *ianatiche* (see *Summa moralis*, II, Florentiae 1756, col. 1548, also cited by Bonomo, op. cit., p. 70; I correct the erroneous transcription *ianutiche*). Cf. in general the excellent essay by D. Lesourd, 'Diane et les sorciers. Étude sur les survivances de Diana dans les langues romanes', *Anagrom*, 1972, pp. 55–74 (pointed out to me by Daniel Fabre, whom I thank here). The popular reception of the schemas constructed by the dominant culture was very widespread (see the Rumanian *Doamna Zînelor*) and not confined to areas of Celtic civilization (as is shown by the Neapolitan *janara*, the word for a witch). Naturally, the linguistic continuity does not necessarily imply a continuity of beliefs, which has to be demonstrated case by case.

65. On the close connections between Haerecura, Epona and *Matres*, cf. G. Faider-Feytmans, 'La "Mater" de Bavai', *Gallia*, 6 (1948), pp. 185–94; and especially p. 390.

66. See William of Auvergne, *Opera*, Parisiis 1674, p. 1066 (this passage had already received the attention of Grimm, op. cit., II, p. 885). And see William Shakespeare, *Romeo and Juliet*, R. Gibbons ed, London and New York 1980, p. 109 (for I. 4. 53).

67. The oldest discussion known to me is that of G. Keysler, *Dissertato de mulieribus fatidicis veterum Celtarum gentiumque Septentrionalium; speciatim de Matribus et Matronis...*, in idem, *Antiquitates selectae Septentrionales et Celticae*, Hanover 1720, pp. 369–510. Still fundamental is M. Ihm, 'Der Mütter- oder Matronenkultus und seine Denkmäler', *Jahrbuch des Vereins von Alterhumsfreunden im Rheinlande* (then *Bonner Jahrbücher*), LXXXIII (1887), pp. 1–200, which reviews the results of previous studies (the most conspicuous being H. Schreiber, *Die Feen in Europa. Eine historisch-archëologische Monographie*, Freiburg i. Breisgau 1842, reprint Allmendingen 1981). See in addition H. Güntert, *Kalypso. Bedeutungsgeschichtliche Untersuchungen auf dem Gebiet der indogermanischen Sprachen*, Halle a. S. 1919, p. 241 ff; W. Heiligendorff, *Der keltischen Matronenkultus und seine 'Fortentwickelung' im deutschen Mythos*, Leipzig 1934, which underlines the analogy between *Matronae, Parcae, Felices Dominae* (in the Tyrol and Carinthia, *salige Fräulein*) and fairies, but insists on distinguishing them a trifle artificially; E. A. Philippson, 'Der germanische Mütter- und Matronenkult am Niderrhein', *The Germanic Review*, 19 (1944). pp. 116 ff.; Pascal, op. cit., pp. 116 ff.; G. Webster, *The British Celts and Their Gods Under Rome*, London 1986, pp. 64 ff. The filiation of Habonde and the 'ladies of the night' from *Matronae* was recognized by M. P. Nilsson, *Studien zur Vorgeschichte des Weinachtsfestes* (1916–19) in *Opuscula selecta*, Lund 1951, I. pp. 298 ff. But see also Dom*** [J. Martin], op. cit., II, pp. 170–1. The book by J. Harf-Lancner, *Les fées au Moyen Âge*, Paris 1984, predominantly analyzes the fairies as a literary theme.

68. Cf. F. Landucci Gattinoni, *Un culto celtico nella Gallia Cisalpina. Le Matronae-Iunones a sud delle Alpi*, Milan 1986, p. 51, which identifies Celtic influence in an inscription in Vicenza that has a dedication to the goddesses called *Dianae*.

69. Cf. A. C. M. Beck, 'Die lateinischen Offenbarungsinschriften des römischen Germaniens', *Mainzer Zeitschrift*, XXXI (1936), pp. 23–32: the expression *ex iussu* would be typical of Cisalpine Gaul, while *ex imperio* (and, to a lesser degree, *ex insu*) would be more frequent in the area of the lower Rhine (p. 24). In general on these formulas, see M. Leglay, *Saturne Africain. Histoire*, Paris 1966, p. 342 n. 1.

70. See E. Maass, 'Heilige Nacht', *Germania*, XII (1928), pp. 59–69 (originally published in 1910).

117

71. See J. Loth, 'Les douze jours supplémentaires ('gourdeziou') des Bretons et les Douze Jours des Germains et des Indous', *Revue Celtique*, 24 (1903), pp. 310–12; S. de Ricci, 'Un passage remarquable du calendrier de Coligny', ibid. pp. 313–16; Loth, 'L'année celtique d'après les textes irlandais. . .', ibid., 25 (1904), pp. 118–25.

72. Cf. CIL, VII, 927: *Matribus Parcis*; Pascal, op. cit., p. 118; Thevenot, art. cit.; Nilsson, op. cit., pp. 289 ff.

73. Cf. G. Alföldi, 'Zur keltischen Religion in Pannonien', *Germania*, 42 (1964), pp. 54–59 (but see also Landucci Gattinoni, op. cit., p. 77); *Die römischen Steindenkmäler von Savaria*, A. Mócsy and T. Szentléleky eds, 1971, n. 46, fig. 36. And see R. Noll, '*Fatis:* Zu einem goldenen Fingerring aus Lauriacum', in *Römische Geschichte, Altertumskunde und Epigraphik. Festschrift für A. Betz*, Vienna 1985, pp. 445–50.

74. The continuity with the Celtic fairies is also underlined by someone like E. A. Philippson, who sees in the *Matronae* a Celto-Germanic and not exclusively Celtic phenomenon (cf. art. cit., pp. 125–35).

75. Procopius of Caesarea *History of the Wars*, VIII, XX (tr. H. B. Dewing. The Loeb Classical Library, Cambridge, Mass. 1954). On the detail of the boat weighed down by an invisible cargo which transports the dead, cf. A. Freixas, 'El peso de las almas', *Anales de Historia Antigua y Medieval*, Buenos Aires, 1956, pp. 15–22; other material can be found in B. Lincoln, 'The Ferryman of the Dead', *The Journal of Indo-European Studies*, 8 (1980), pp. 41–59. On the theme of the boat of the dead, diffused over the most varied cultures, see also M. Ebert, 'Die Bootsfahrt ins Jenseits', *Prähistorische Zeitschrift*, XI-XII (1919–20), pp. 179 ff.

76. J. B. Bury supposed, on flimsy grounds, that these were Erules mercenaries in the pay of Narses (cf. 'The Homeric and the Historic Kimmerians', *Klio*, VI (1906), pp. 79 ff.), successively attributed the function of intermediaries to the Angles who formed part of the Frankish embassy sent to Justinian (cf. E. A. Thompson, 'Procopius on Brittia and Britannia', *The Classical Quarterly*, n.s., XXX (1980), p. 501). The identification of the Homeric Kimmerians and the Cimbrians, proposed by Bury, had already been made (together with that, even more surprising, of Ulysses and Odin) by Jonas Ramus, in a curious pamphlet based on comparison between the *Odyssey* and the *Edda* (*Tractatus historico-geographicus, quo Ulyssem et Outinum eundemque esse ostenditur. . .* , Hafniae 1713), which should be included in the 'Gothicizing' current inaugurated by the *Atlantica* of O. Rudbeck (see below, p. 224 n. 48).

77. Cf. the note of D. Comparetti to *La guerra gotica*, III, Rome 1898, p. 317; and see now Thompson, art. cit., pp. 498 ff. See also E. Brugger, 'Beiträge zur Erklärung der arthurischen Geographie, II. Gorre', *Zeitschrift für französische Sprache*, XXVII (1905), pp. 66–9, which ends by connecting to Brittany the traditions gathered by Procopius.

78. Cf. Claudian, *In Rufinum*, vv. 123 ff. : *est locus extremum plandit qua Gallia litus. . . .* A. Graf, *Miti, leggende e superstizioni del Medio Evo*, I, Turin 1892, reckons that the allusion refers to Cornwall rather than Brittany.

79. Cf. Plutarch, *De facie quae in orbe lunae apparet*, 941–42, translated with a commentary by H. Cherniss, London 1957 (*Plutarch's Moralia*, XII, The Loeb Classical Library), pp. 188–9. Cf. also F. Le Roux, 'Les îles au Nord du Monde', in *Hommages à Albert Grenier*, II, Brussels 1962, pp. 1051–62.

80. Cf. *Lycophronis Alexandra*, rec. E. Scheer, II, Berolini 1908, pp. 345–46 (scholium gloss at v. 1204).

81. Cf. A. R. Burn, 'Procopius and the Island of Ghosts', *The English Historical Review*

70 (1955), pp. 258–61; Thompson, art. cit.; A. Cameron, *Procopius and the Sixth Century*, Berkeley and Los Angeles 1985, p. 215.

82. Cf. *The Night Battles*, p. 160.

83. On Friuli cf. the linguistic observations of G. Francescato in G. Francescato and F. Salimbeni, *Storia, lingua e società in Friuli*, Udine 1976, pp. 24–8 and 243–4. On Brittany cf. the folkloric documentation collected by A. Le Braz, *La légende de la mort chez les Bretons Armoricains*, new edition edited by G. Dottin, Paris 1902, II, pp. 68 ff. The traditions recounted by Procopius are referred to a Celtic context by A. C. L. Brown, *The Origin of the Grail Legend*, Cambridge, Mass. 1943, p. 134 n. 36; M. Dillon and N. K. Chadwick, *The Celtic Realms*, London 1972, p. 130; in the same vein see Grimm, op. cit., II, pp. 694 ff. However, reference to the Nordic beliefs about the ship of the dead had been made by F. G. Welcker in *Die Homerische Phäaken und die Inseln der Seligen* (1832) and later in *Kleine Schriften*, II, Bonn 1845, pp. 17–20. See also T. Wright, *Essays on Subjects Connected with the Literature, Popular Superstitions and History of England in the Middle Ages*, I, London 1846, pp. 302–3 (but the passage from Tzetzes does not contain a fragment of Plutarch's lost commentary on Hesiod, but rather Procopius' passage : cf. H. Patzig, *Questiones Plutarcheae*, Berlin 1876, p. 21. Similar traditions, spread along the coast of eastern Frisia, were re-elaborated by Heine (who certainly knew Procopius' page) in the description of the Dutch ferrymen of the dead: cf. *Gli dei in esilio*. It. tr. Milan 1978, pp. 78 ff. According to G. Mücke, *Heinrich Heines Beziehungen zum deutschen Mittelalters*, Berlin 1908, p. 101, Heine had drawn upon oral testimony. The recent book by A. I. Sandor, *The Exile of Gods. Interpretation of a Theme, a Theory and a Technique in the Work of Heinrich Heine*, The Hague and Paris 1967, neglects the problem of Heine's sources and does not mention Mucke's very accurate research.

84. I follow the interpretation proposed by R. S. Loomis and L. Hibbard Loomis, *Arthurian Legends in Medieval Art*, New York 1938, p. 36; in the same vein see also C. Settis Frugoni, 'Per una lettura del mosaico pavimentale della cattedrale di Otranto', *Bullettino dell'Istituto storico italiano per il Medio Evo*, 80 (1968), pp.237–41. Of a different opinion are M. A. Klenke, 'Some Medieval Concepts of King Arthur', *Kentucky Foreign Language Quarterly*, 5 (1958), pp. 195–7, and W. Haug, 'Artussage und Heilgeschichte Zum Programm des Fussbodenmosaiks von Otranto', *Deutsche Vierteljahrschrift für Literaturwissenschaft und Geistesgeschichte*, 49 (1975), pp. 577 ff., in particular p. 580 (repeated, in a more nuanced form, in *Das Mosaik von Otranto*, Wiesbaden 1977, p. 31). Both interpret King Arthur as a positive figure, but do not succeed in explaining why he is portrayed on the back of billy goat. Cf. also H. Birkhan, 'Altgermanistiche Miszellen...', in idem ed., *Festgabe für O. Höfler*, Vienna 1976, pp. 62–6 and 82; M. Wierschin, 'Artus und Alexander im Mosaik der Kathedrale von Otranto', *Colloquia Germanica*, 13 (1980), pp. 1-34, especially pp. 16–17.

85. Cf. G. Paris, 'Études sur les romans de la Table Ronde – Lancelot du Lac', *Romania*, XII (1883), pp. 508 ff., developed by G. Ehrismann, 'Märchen im hofischen Epos', *Beiträge zur Geschichte der deutschen Sprache und Literatur* 30 (1905), pp. 14-54. (For a different, but less convincing, interpretation of *Limors* see F. Lot, 'Celtica', *Romania*, 24, 1895, p. 335.) This interpretative line has been developed by S. Singer: cf. 'Lanzelet', in idem *Aufsätze und Vortäge*, Tübingen 1912, pp. 144 ff., above all 156 ff.; idem, *Die Artus-sage*, Bern and Leipzig 1920; idem, 'Erec', in *Vom Werden des deutschen Geistes. Festgabe Gustav Ehrismann*, P. Merker and W. Stammler eds, Berlin and Leipzig 1925, pp. 61–5. See also K. Varty, 'On Birds and Beasts, "Death" and "Resurrection", Renewal and Reunion

in Chrétien's Romances', P. B. Grout ed., in *The Legend of Arthur in the Middle Ages. Studies Presented to A. H. Diverres*, Cambridge 1983, pp. 194 ff., especially pp. 200–12 (which however, overlooks Singer's studies). In general see the heading 'Artustradition' by K. O. Brogsitter, in *Enzyklopädie des Märchens*, I, Berlin and New York 1977, coll. 828– 49. In line with the interpretation proposed here, cf. C. Corradi Musi, 'Sciamanesimo ugro-finnico e magia europea. Proposte per una ricerca comparata', *Quaderni di Filologia Germanica della Facoltà di Lettere e filosofia dell'Università di Bologna*, III (1984), pp. 57–69.

86. Cf. O. Jodogne, 'L'Autre Monde celtique dans la littérature française du XIIe siècle', *Bulletin de l'Académie Royale de Belgique*, 5e s., XLVI (1960), pp. 584 ff.; J. de Caluwé, 'L'Autre Monde celtique et l'élément chrétien dans les lais anonymes', in P. B. Grout ed, op. cit., pp. 56–66.

87. Cf. M. Dillon, 'Les sources irlandais des romans Arthuriens', *Lettres Romanes*, IX (1955), pp. 143 ff.

88. See R. S. Loomis, '*Morgain la Fée and the Celtic Goddesses*', now in *Wales and the Arthurian Legend*, Cardiff 1956, pp. 105–30.

89. Ibid., pp. 127–8.

90. This interpretation, developed above all by R. S. Loomis, has stirred up bitter debate: cf. R. S. Loomis, 'Objections to the Celtic Origin of the "Matière de Bretagne" ', *Romania*, 79 (1958), pp. 47–77; F. L. Utley, 'Arthurian Romance and International Folk Method', *Romance Philology*, 17 (1963–64), pp. 596–607; R. Bromwich, 'The Celtic Inheritance of Medieval Literature', *Modern Language Quarterly*, 26 (1965), pp. 203–27; I. Lovecy, 'Exploding the Myth of the Celtic Myth: a New Appraisal of the Celtic Background of Arthurian Romance', *Reading Medieval Studies*, 7 (1981), pp. 3–18; R. Bromwich, 'Celtic Elements in Arthurian Romance : a General Survey', in P. B. Grout ed, op. cit., pp. 41–55. It must be obvious that the identification of the mythical materials of Celtic provenance does not preclude (indeed favours) an analysis of their literary re-elaboration. On the folkloric irruption into profane literature during the eleventh and twelfth centuries, cf. Le Goff, op. cit., p. 244, which refers us back to the studies of Köhler, cited in n. 92.

91. Cf., besides Ehrismann, art. cit., M. Volker, *Märchenhafte Elemente bei Chrétien de Troyes*, Bonn 1972; H. D. Mauritz, *Der Ritter im magischen Reich. Märchenelemente im französischen Abenteuerroman des 12 und 13. Jahrhunderts*, Bern and Frankfurt-am-Main 1974 (vitiated by a dogmatically Jungian approach). The observations of A. Guerreau-Jalabert, 'Romans de Chrétien de Troyes et contes folkloriques. Rapprochements thématiques et observations de méthode', *Romania*, 104 (1983), pp. 1–48 should be borne in mind. Cf. in addition I. Nolting-Hauff, 'Märchen und Märchenroman, Zur Beziehung zwischen einfacher Form und narrativer Gross-form in der Literatur, *Poetica*, 6 (1974), pp. 129–78, which, unlike the aforementioned writers, takes account of Propp's researches. In fact, at the end of *Morphology of the Folk Tale* he had laconically observed that 'this same structure [of the magical fable] appears, for example, in several novels of Chivalry' (p. 107).

92. Cf. E. Köhler, *L'avventura cavalleresca. Ideale e realtà nei poemi della Tavola Rotonda*, (1956)., It. tr., Bologna 1985, p. 105 ff., 130 ff. and 139 ff; Georges Duby, 'Au XIIe siècle : les "jeunes" dans la société aristocratique', *Annales E. S. C.*, 19 (1964), pp. 835–96; Jacques Le Goff and Pierre Vidal-Naquet, *Lévi Strauss en Brocéliande* (1973).

93. Cf. Bonomo, op. cit., pp. 78–84. This is one of the trials in the Trentino at the beginning of the sixteenth century already published in a mutilated and inaccurate form by A. Panizza (see below, p. 146). Giovanni Kral is preparing a new edition.

94. Cf. W. Søderhjelm, 'Antoine de la Sale et la légende de Tannhäuser', *Mémoires de la société néo-philologique*, 2 (1897), pp. 101–67; in general see O. Löhmann's last essay, 'Die Entstehung der Tannhäusersage', *Fabula*, III (1959–60), pp. 224–53.

95. Venus is an *interpretatio romana* of Holda: cf. Klapper, art. cit., pp. 36, 46, which compares a passage from the *Summa de confessionis discretione* by Friar Rudolph de Bibraco, written before 1250 (*'In nocte nativitatis Christi ponunt regine celi, quam dominam Holdam vulgus appellat, ut eas ipsa adiuvet'*), with a passage two centuries later, from a sermon of Friar Thomas Wunschilburg, which prescribes banning from communion anyone who believes *in dictam Venus, quod personaliter visitat mulieres insane mentis. . . . in noctibus Christi*. It should be noted that both texts specifically refer to women.

96. See *The Night Battles*, pp. 56–7. An analogous case: in 1623 Hans Hauser, a poor wandering cleric, had bragged in an inn that he knew how to predict the future and cure the sick. To the magistrates who interrogated him he said that he had been taken by a friend on the Venusberg: here he had remained for nine years, among extraordinary people, (including a woman) who had instructed him in the magical art. Later, in the course of the trial, he denied everthing (cf. E. W. M. Bever's as yet unpublished thesis, *Witchcraft in Early Modern Württemberg*, Princeton 1983; I am very grateful to the author for permission to consult and quote from this work).

97. See Löhmann, art. cit., p. 246.

98. See Duvernoy, op. cit., I, p. 133 n. 61.

99. Cf. Jakob Grimm, *Irische Elfenmärchen*, Leipzig 1826, pp. CXXII–CXXVI, introduction.

100. Cf. C. Musès, ('Celtic Origins and the Arthurian Cycle: Geographic-Linguistic Evidence', *Journal of Indo-European Studies*, 7 (1979), pp. 31–48, which develops in a more convincing manner some of the results of a study which had already appeared ('Celtic Origins. . .', *Ogam*, no. 98, 1965, pp. 359–84). Neither essay figures in E. Reiss et al. eds *Arthurian Legend and Literature: An Annotated Bibliography*, I, New York and London 1984. Musès seems unaware that in certain respects his conclusions repeat those of Singer, *Die Artussage* (for example, on the Arthur-Artio connection: see below, pp. 109). It should be noted that E. Freymond had already asked (without receiving a convincing answer) how on earth the saga based on the struggle between Arthur and the 'Cath Paluc' was localized in south-western Switzerland and in the Savoy: see 'Artus' Kampf mit dem Katzenungetüm. Eine Episode der Vulgata des Livre d'Artus, die Sage und ihre Lokalisierung in Savoyen', *Beiträge zur romanischen Philologie. Festgabe für G. Gröber* (1899), especially pp. 369 ff. Even Bromwich, art. cit., p. 43, cannot answer this question.

2

ANOMALIES

1. Evidence originating from one end of Europe to the other, in the course of one thousand years, has led us to identify the features of a primarily female ecstatic religion, dominated by a nocturnal goddess with many names. In this figure we have recognized a hybrid, belated descendant of the Celtic divinities. This conjecture is possibly contentious, because based on chronologically and geographically dispersed documentation; and certainly insufficient, since it is incapable of explaining the reasons for such dogged continuity. Not only this: it seems to be disproven by other documents to which we have not hitherto referred.

These are a series of trials held by the Holy Office in Sicily beginning in the second half of the sixteenth century, against women (occasionally even little girls) who stated that they periodically met with mysterious female beings: 'women from outside'. They went with them, flying through the night, to banquet in remote castles or on meadows. They were richly dressed, but had cats' paws or equine hooves. At the centre of their 'companies' (from Rome, Palermo, Ragusa, etc.) was a female divinity who had many names: the Matron, the Teacher, the Greek Mistress, the Wise Sibilla, the Queen of the Fairies – at times accompanied by a king. She taught her followers how to cure the spellbound.[1] These accounts, so similar to those given by the women in ecstasy who visited the nocturnal goddess, sprung from specifically Sicilian traditions. As early as the middle of the fifteenth century a popularization of a manual for confessors compiled on the island referred to the 'women from outside who travel at night'.[2] Despite the hostile attitude of the clergy, the belief survived for a long time. In 1640 a woman from Palermo, Caterina Buní, 'who went at night *with the women from outside* and who promised to take people with her and wanted them to ride on castrated sheep, as she herself did', was tried and sentenced by the Holy Office. As late as the middle of the nineteenth century, *Donni di fuora* (Women from Outside), *Donni di locu* (Local Women), *Donni di notti* (Night Women), *Donni di casa*, *Belli Signuri* (Beautiful Ladies) and *Patruni di casa* (Mistresses of the House) continued to reveal themselves to men and women: ambiguous figures, generally beneficent but ready to cause trouble for those who did not pay them due reverence. A detail, such as the preference displayed by 'the women from outside' for well-swept houses, underlines the analogy with the 'good mistresses', the fairies, the followers of Oriente. We are tempted to recognize the characteristic head-dress of the Celtic *Matronae* (fig. 3) in the 'three young girls dressed in white, and wearing on their head a sort of red turban' who appeared in the mid-nineteenth century to an old woman of Modica, Emanuela Santaéra, inviting her to dance.[3] But we are in Sicily. The presence on the island of Celtic mercenary troops, engaged by Greeks and Carthaginians in the fourth century BC, was an exceptional event which cannot have created the basis for so tenacious a cultural continuity.[4] In the 'women from outside' we are forced to recognize an anomalous phenomenon, definitely incompatible with the historical hypothesis advanced here.

We could try to circumvent the obstacle by utilizing, in analogical manner, another tradition, whose Celtic physiognomy (albeit re-elaborated) by contrast seems obvious. I refer to the legendary accounts, documented in Sicily since the thirteenth century, according to which King Arthur, wounded in battle, lay asleep in a cave on the slope of Etna. These legends have been traced back to the diffusion (undocumented but plausible) of the themes of the Arthurian epic, which were supposedly brought to Sicily at the end of the eleventh century by Breton knights, who had landed together with the Norman invaders. Moreover, the later epithet, 'fata Morgana', which refers to the mirages seen in the Strait of Messina, seems to corroborate this cultural circulation.[5] At any rate, the association of Morgana with Sicily and, in particular, Etna is already recorded in certain French and Provençal poems.[6] Might not the fairies who appear in the accounts of the women and the young girls tried by the Holy Office of Palermo be traced back to the importation into the island of the themes of the *matière de Bretagne*? If this were so, we should once more find a Celtic substratum – though much more recent and much more profoundly modified than that hitherto identified. The ecstasies of the followers of 'women from outside' would have brought to the surface the folkloric content latent in the orally transmitted literary tradition which underlay them.

This supposition is difficult to accept. But the surprising presence in Sicily of traditions linked to Morgana has raised a further hypothesis that refers us to a much more distant past. Both the Celtic Morrigan and the Sicilian Morgana should be inserted in a tradition harking back to a great pre-Greek Mediterranean goddess, who would have inspired the figures of such sorceresses as Circe and Medea. This cultural filiation would explain the presence of similar names and toponyms (also of the *morg*-type) in Mediterranean and Celtic contexts.[7] Obviously, these are vague and fragile conjectures, which resolve the documentary difficulties by projecting them into a nebulous past. The 'great goddess' herself is an abstraction, which arbitrarily homogenizes heterogeneous cults.[8] And yet this hypothesis, though formulated in an unacceptable manner, indirectly suggests a path of research quite different from any pursued up to this point.

2. From Posidonius of Apamea – probably from his great historical and ethnographical work, now lost – Plutarch, as he explicitly pointed out, drew chapter 20 of the *Life of Marcellus*.[9] The events described therein date back to the year 212 BC; Posidonius wrote around 80 BC, Plutarch between the first and second century AD. The chapter tells of the expedient used by Nicias, first citizen of Engyon (a city of eastern Sicily, identified with today's Troina)[10] to escape from Marcellus, the Roman general who had invaded the island with his army. Engyon was famous for the apparitions of certain goddesses, called Mothers; a famous sanctuary was dedicated to them. Nicias makes hostile speeches against the Mothers, saying that their apparitions are nonsense. During a public assembly he suddenly lets himself fall to the ground as though dead. Shortly after, pretending to regain consciousness, in a feeble and broken voice he says that the Mothers are tormenting him. He tears his clothes like a madman and, exploiting the general dismay, he flees towards the Roman encampment. His wife in turn pretends she is going to the temple of the Mothers to ask for forgiveness and she joins Nicias at Marcellus' palace.

Other information about the cult of the Mothers appears on a page of Diodorus' based on local traditions (possibly derived from Timaeus) and on first-hand information, as well as on his probable knowledge of the work of Posidonius.[11] The renown of the Engyon sanctuary was great: various Sicilian cities, at the suggestion of oracles inspired by Apollo, celebrated it with sacrifices, honours, golden and silver votive offerings to the Mother goddesses, providers of prosperity to private citizens and the State. Agyrion (where Diodorus was born) had helped in the construction of the great Engyon temple, sending carts loaded with stones, even though it was located at a distance of one hundred stadia. No expense had been spared, because the sanctuary of the Mothers was extremely rich: up until a short time before (Diodorus affirms) it possessed three thousand sacred oxen and a great expanse of land, from which it drew considerable revenues.[12]

In the temple of Engyon (Plutarch informs us, repeating Posidonius) were preserved the weapons of the Cretan hero Meriones, the mythical colonizer of Sicily. Diodorus specifies that the founders of Engyon – Cretans – had brought the cult of the Mothers from their land of origin. Cicero, by contrast, states (*Verr.*, IV.97; V. 186) that Engyon was famous for the temple dedicated to the Great Mother, Cybele. But the same oscillation between plural and singular appears in archaeological evidence from eastern Sicily. On two missile acorns dating back to the Second Slave War and found at Syracuse and at Leontini, we read, respectively, the words 'victory of the Mothers (*nike meteron*)', 'victory of the Mother (*nike materos*)'.[13] The duplication or triplication of single divinities are widely documented phenomena in the Mediterranean area.[14] And Cybele was worshipped not only in eastern Sicily, but also in Crete (under the name Rhea), with tumultuous rituals which have been compared to the behaviour mimed by Nicias. The divergences between Posidonius and Diodorus, on the one hand, and Cicero, on the other, would in the last analysis seem to be negligible.[15]

It has been supposed that this cult, presumably Cretan in origin, was grafted onto a pre-existing, indigenous cult: on the basis of a statement by Protagoras, reported by Timaeus, which assimilated the Mothers to the Nymphs and to Kore, the goddesses of Engyon have been identified in triads of nymphs portrayed in reliefs or Siciliot coins.[16] But the pages of Posidonius and Diodorus appear to refer to specific divinities. An attempt has been made to identify them in the three small female figures, wrapped in a mantle, which were found in a tomb on Cyprus, or with those of much larger dimensions that can be seen in a bas-relief (52 by 42 by 37 cm) found at Camàro near Messina (fig. 7).[17] More recently, the Mothers of Engyon have been mentioned in connection with the nymphs portrayed in a number of ex-votos, discovered in the Thracian sanctuary of Saladinovo.[18]

3. It is popularly referred to as the 'cemetery of the fairies'; the triads of nymphs wear turban-shaped head-dresses, similar to those of the Celtic *Matronae* (fig. 3) – or to those of the 'women from outside' who, in the mid-nineteenth century, appeared to the old woman at Modica. As for Saladinovo, it is not a cause for surprise: the presence of Celtic settlements in Thrace is documented in the fourth and third century BC.[19] But this explanation, as we have seen, does not hold for Sicily.

The analogy between the enigmatic Mother goddesses of Engyon and the Celtic *Matronae*, already pointed out by an eighteenth-century antiquarian, has been interpreted in the most diverse ways. Sometimes it has been seen as a derivation from vaguely defined Indo-European female divinities; at other times it is considered a mere coincidence; alternatively, it is proof of the presence in the Celtic as well as the Siceliot sphere of manifold maternal divinities, not identifiable with Mother Earth or the Mother of the gods worshipped in Asia Minor.[20] That the latter hypothesis is the correct one is proven by a datum neglected until now. In a votive inscription possibly dating back to the first century BC, preserved in a shrine near Allan (a locality in the Dauphiné), a certain Niger – probably a slave – steward of the cellar of a large estate, addressed the 'victorious mothers' (*Matris V[ic]tricibus*) in crude Latin.[21] It is impossible not to think of the expressions carved on the missile acorns used by the Sicilian blow-pipe soldiers during the slave wars: 'victory of the Mothers' (or 'of the Mother'). This convergence, though difficult to interpret, confirms the conjectures, formulated independently, on the simultaneously Celtic and Sicilian roots of figures such as Morgan le Fay or the 'women from outside'.[22]

4. At this point the hypothesis of a subterranean continuity, in the Sicilian sphere, between the Mothers of Engyon and the 'women from outside' seems irresistible. Of course, continuity does not mean identity. Unlike 'the women from outside', the Mothers were at the centre of a public cult, not private ecstatic experiences. But the fainting followed by frenetic exaltation, mimed by Nicias, as well as the reference to the apparitions of the Mothers, indicate

125

that these divinities habitually revealed themselves to individuals in a state of ecstasy. And the tortures that the Mothers inflicted on those who, like Nicia, denied their apparitions, remind us of the hostile reaction of the 'women from outside' to anyone who failed to be respectful of them. Nevertheless, the physiognomy of the Mothers of Engyon remains obscure. The converging information as to their Cretan provenance complicates the picture further. According to the myth, Rhea had sought shelter on Crete in order to escape Kronos, who wanted to devour their new-born son Zeus, in conformity with his previous practice. Two female bears (or, according to other evidence, two nymphs), Helike and Kynosura, had raised the infant, hiding him in a cave on Mount Ida. As a token of his gratitude, Zeus had transformed them into constellations: Ursa Major and the Ursa Minor.[23] Quoting a passage from *Phaenomena* (vv. 30–35), the poem of astrological popularization written by Aratus around 275 BC, Diodorus identified the Mothers of Engyon with the two bears.

According to other versions, it was a nymph (or a goat) named Amaltheia who reared Zeus, and was later transformed into a constellation; a bitch; a sow; a swarm of bees.[24] The infant god reared by animals (later anthropomorphized) is a very different figure from the lord of Olympus, a celestial divinity that is definitely Indo-European: the Cretan myths would thus derive from a more ancient cultural stratum.[25] It is indeed the case that they were not only to be found in Crete. Near Cyzicus on the Propontis (today's Sea of Marmora), there was a mountain which, so we are told by a scholium gloss to the *Argonautica* by Apollonius of Rhodes (I.936), was called mountain 'of the bears' in memory of Zeus' nurses.[26] In a mountainous and isolated region of the Peloponnese such as Arcadia these myths became interwoven with local traditions, recorded by Pausanias in the second century BC. They proclaim that Zeus had not been born in Crete, but in a region of Arcadia called Creteia; that one of the nurses, Helice, was the daughter of the Arcadian King, Lycaon – while other versions identify her with Phoenix, a nymph transformed into a bird by Artemis because she was guilty of having been seduced by Zeus.[27] We glimpse here a contamination, already pointed out by Callimachus, between the myths of the Cretan birth of Zeus and the myths of Callisto, the daughter (at least in certain versions) of Lycaon, King of Arcadia, who was mistress of Zeus; mother of the eponymous hero Arcas; transformed into a bear and then killed by Artemis; elevated to the heavens to form the constellation of the Ursa.[28] Among Greek dialects, the Arcadian-Cypriot is the most similar to the language used by the population that conquered Crete around the middle of the second millennium BC: Mycenaean (more precisely, the variant referred to as Linear B, in which are rendered the administrative documents found at Pylos and at Knossos).[29] The convergence, possibly belated in part, between the two groups of myths – the Cretan and Arcadian – was therefore grafted onto very ancient cultural relationships. The elements are approximately the same (female bears-nymphs-Zeus-constellation): their combinations and their immediate functions are different. Instead of two nursing female bears, a mistress transformed into a bear; instead of a god's fabulous infancy, the declaration of Arcas' divine origin. The link between the descendants of Arcas and the son of the founder of the Pelargic lineage, Lycaon, whom Zeus had transformed into a wolf because he performed human sacrifices, was weakened to make room for a new mythical genealogy. Through the myth of Callisto – an authentic myth of re-establishment – the Pelasgians, as Pausanias observed (VIII. 3. 7), had become Arcadians: a name which popular etymology traced back to that of the (bear) Urso (*arktos, arkos*).[30]

There is no doubt that the Siceliot cult of the Mother goddesses presupposes the Cretan myths based on the nursing-bears; by contrast, the relation between Cretan myths and Arcadian myths on the Mother-nymph transformed into a bear appears less clear, even if the anteriority of the first seems likely.[31] But the Arcadian re-elaboration poses new difficulties. Callisto has long been considered a projection or hypostasis of Artemis: and her metamorphosis has been interpreted as indicative of the extremely ancient ursine nature of the goddess, a totemic nucleus later semi-erased by the superimposition of elements of a completely different character. The use of contentious categories such as 'hypostasis' or 'totemism' has recently led to the total rejection of any such interpretation.[32] Despite the dubious theoretical postulates, however, it rests on incontestable documentary data, such as the remains of an Athenian sanctuary dedicated to Artemis 'Kalliste';[33] or the famous and debated passage in Aristophanes (*Lysistrata*, vv. 641–7) from which it appears that Artemis was worshipped in the sanctuary of Brauron by little girls called 'bears', who wore saffron-coloured robes.[34] It is impossible a priori to exclude the possibility that such evidence of a close connection between Artemis and the bear expressed, in an attenuated form, a more ancient identification.[35] Precisely in the region of Arcadia, strongly conservative from a cultural standpoint, there existed substantial traces, as late as the second century BC, of cults linked to partial or total animal divinities.[36] Futhermore, as in the case of other religious (or linguistic) phenomena, the Arcadian data are clarified by their comparison with Crete. It would appear that on the northwestern coast of the island there existed a Mycenaean city called Kynosura – the name of one of Zeus' nurses. The same name also designated the peninsula on which the city was located: present-day Akrotiri. Here one can still see a 'cave of the bear' (*Arkoudia*), so-called because of an imposing stalagmite suggestive of the animal. In the cave fragments of images of Artemis and Apollo that date back to the classical and Hellenistic period have been found. Today the 'Virgin of the bear's cave' (*Panaghia arkoudiotissa*) is worshipped here: according to a local legend, the Madonna entered the cave to find some shade and came face to face with a female bear who turned her into stone. Behind the Christian re-elaborations we catch a glimpse of the cult which was perhaps already alive in the second millennium BC, in the Minoan age, of a nursing goddess of ursine appearance: a remote ancestor of the Mothers of Engyon.[37]

In all probability the name of this goddess will forever remain unknown to us. We do, however, know that the name of another of Zeus' nurses – Adrasteia – designated a Thraco-Phrygian divinity worshipped in Athens together with the Thracian goddess Bendis. That Herodotus (V.7) identified Bendis with Artemis is quite probable; that Pausanias (X. 27.8) assimilated Adrasteia to Artemis is certain.[38] In the eyes of Greek observers, disparate figures of foreign female divinities irresistibly summon up the name of Artemis. Perhaps they are not far wrong. In the *Iliad* Artemis is the 'mistress of the animals' (*potnia thērōn*, XXI. 470) – an epithet that evokes the representation, derived from the Mediterranean and from Asia Minor, of a goddess flanked by animals, often in pairs (horses, lions, deer, etc.).[39] Onto this archaic pre-Greek nucleus were grafted cults and properties that have been traced back to a common motif: the relationship with marginal, intermediary, transient realities. The virgin huntress Artemis, on the border between the city and the formless wilderness, the human and the bestial, was also worshipped as the nurse of children (*kourotrophos*) and the protectress of young girls.[40] Pregnant women also turned to her: ex-votos representing breasts and vulvas have been found in the sanctuary of Artemis Kalliste. From Euripides (*Iphigenia in Tauris*, 1462 ff.), we learn that to Iphigenia, priestess in the sanctuary of Artemis Brauronia, were dedicated the garments of women who died in childbirth – whereas, presumably, the goddess was entitled to the garments of those who had brought their labours to a happy conclusion.[41] In both cases, as we have seen, Artemis, virgin and nurse – two elements obstinately interwoven in Mediterranean religious imagery – was closely associated with the female bear. The female bear's solicitude for her children was proverbial among the Greeks.[42] Moreover, the humanoid appearance of the bear, a plantigrade animal, probably made her suitable to symbolize, like Artemis, intermediary and liminal situations.

5. In the second or third century AD, a woman called Licinia Sabinilla dedicated a bronze sculpture group to the goddess Artio. Rediscovered in fragments at Muri near Berne in 1832, it was reassembled only in 1899. In its present form at the Historical Museum in Berne it shows a seated female divinity holding a bowl in her right hand and with her lap full of fruit (height 15.6 cm); next to her, to the left, more fruit fills a basket resting on a pilaster; in front of her, a female bear (height 12 cm) stands with a tree behind it (height 19 cm). The pedestal (height 5.6 cm width 28.6 cm depth 5.2 cm) bears the inscription DEAE ARTIONI LICINIA SABINILLA (fig. 8). Epigraphs with dedications to the goddess Artio have been found in the Rhinish Palatinate (near Bitburg), in northern Germany (Stockstadt, Heddernheim), perhaps in Spain (Sigüenza or Huerta). The distribution of the evidence and the name point to a Celtic divinity, whose name summons up the bear (in Gallic *artos*, in ancient Irish *art*).[43] From a more thorough examination it has become clear that originally the group was made up only of the bear – Artio – crouching in front of the tree. The goddess in human form

is a later, though still ancient, addition. Her image reproduces that of the Celtic *Matronae* or *Matres*, as well as (more vaguely) that of Demeter seated.[44]

The present physiognomy is thus the outcome of a twofold stratification, to which corresponds a splitting of Artio, represented first in animal and then in human form. Here again we find the nexus ursine goddess – nursing goddess, which had already emerged in the cult of Engyon and in the Cretan myths that inspired it, as in the cults of Artemis Kalliste and Artemis Brauronia. For those reluctant to recognize in the bear a symbol independent of cultural contexts, this convergence between Celtic and Greek evidence initially appears disconcerting. The possibility of a linguistic (and therefore historical) relationship between *Artio* and *Artemis* even further complicates the picture. It has been supposed that the Celtic divinity is a filiation of the Greek, inasmuch as * *artos* is supposed to derive from *arktos*, by way of the Latin *arctus* ('bear').[45] But that *artos* constitutes a borrowing seems unlikely, for reasons that are both linguistic and cultural.[46] On the other hand, the meaning of the name *Artemis* is obscure (the connection with *arktos* is a popular, linguistically inadmissible etymology).[47] So a hypothesis was advanced which overturns the preceding one: the Greek goddess supposedly derives from a Celto- (or Dacio-) Illyric goddess, introduced into the Peloponnese by the presumed Doric invasion (1200 BC).[48] However, anterior evidence – i.e., the names *A-te-mi-to* and *A-ti-mi-te* written in linear B on tables from a Mycenean city, Pylos – would also seem to refute this hypothesis. But the meaning of those names is obscure; their identification with Artemis is contested.[49] The relation between Artio and Artemis remains unresolved.

6.   The attempt to explain the anomalous presence of 'the women from outside' in Sicily has dictated a long digression. In the course of it we have met the Celtic Matrons, closely linked to the Mothers transplanted from Crete to Sicily; we have met the Cretan myths and cults linked to nurturing goddesses of ursine appearance; the cults of Artemis Kalliste and Artemis Brauronia, where the goddess with the nursing function appears closely associated with the bear; and finally Artio, represented as bear and as Matron. The circle is suddenly completed. We are back where we started. We not only rediscover the roots of the ecstatic cult that we are reconstructing, but also, perhaps, its literary re-elaborations – if the name *Arthur*, through *Artoviros*, derives (as it has been supposed) from Artio.[50] But the anomaly of the Sicilian evidence has caused a deeper, more ancient stratum to emerge, in which are commingled Celtic, Greek, possibly Mediterranean elements. Fragments of this stratum are encrusted in the confessions of the nocturnal goddesses' followers.

7.   They seem to me decrepit and mad, Nicholas of Cusa said in his sermon to the faithful at Bressanone, referring to the two old women from Val di Fassa. They had made offerings to Richella, he added; they had touched her

hand, as if sealing a contract. They say her hand is hairy. She had stroked their cheeks with hairy hands.[51]

8. This detail has reached us by tortuous paths: the Latin translation of the sermon delivered by Nicholas of Cusa in the vernacular, based on the lost trial records (also possibly in Latin) in which the notary must have summarily recorded the confessions that the two old women, intimidated and frightened, probably mumbled in the dialect of their valley, perhaps in the presence of a cleric who acted as interpreter, trying to describe in words the mysterious experience that had visited them – the manifestation of the nocturnal goddess with many names.

For the two old women she was simply Richella. Despite the insistence of the Bishop of Bressanone, so erudite and powerful, they had obstinately refused to deny her. To her they had made offerings; from her they had received affectionate caresses and promises of wealth; with her, over many years, they had periodically forgotten the toil and the monotony of everyday life. An *exemplum* inserted in a fifteenth-century manuscript in the Breslau library tells of an old woman who in a swoon dreamt she was being transported in flight by 'Herodiana': with an impulse of joy ('leta') she had thrown open her arms, spilled the vase of water meant for the goddess and found herself stretched out on the ground.[52] An adjective which escaped the narrator (who, with ironic detachment, displayed his cultural superiority) communicates for an instant the emotional intensity that must have accompanied the ecstasies of Richella's two followers.

In his sermon Nicholas of Cusa had spoken of Diana, or rather Artemis, the great goddess of Ephesus. Only now do we begin to understand how much truth, despite everything, this identification contains. Behind Diana-Artemis we have seen loom the figure of Richella, the goddess dispenser of prosperity, richly dressed, who with a hairy paw touched the wrinkled cheeks of the two ecstatic old women of Val di Fassa. We perceive in Richella a goddess similar to Artio, depicted on the far slope of the Alps, more than a thousand years earlier, in the twofold shape of bear and Matron, dispensing prosperity with her lap overflowing with fruit. Behind Artio there opens up a dizzy temporal chasm, at the bottom of which Artemis reappears, the 'mistress of the animals', perhaps; or perhaps once again a bear.

9. Only a daily, verbal mediation could perpetuate a religion bereft of institutional structures and cult sites, composed of silent nocturnal enlightenment, for such a long time. Regino of Prüm had already complained that the followers of the goddess, by speaking their visions, gained new followers for the 'society of Diana'. Behind the descriptions of these ecstatic experiences we must imagine a very long chain comprising tales, confidences, gossip, capable of travel over enormous chronological and geographical distances.

An example can illustrate the complexity (only reconstructible to a minimal extent) of this transmission process. In a Mantuan trial at the end of the fifteenth century we read of a weaver, Giuliano Verdena, who performed magic with the help of some children. After getting them to look into a vase full of water (a witness recounted), Giuliano made them tell him what they saw. A crowd of people had appeared: some on foot, others on horseback, yet others without hands. Then on the surface of the water there had appeared an isolated figure who, through the mouths of the questioned children, had said that it could reveal to Giuliano the 'power of the herbs and the nature of animals (*potentiam herbarum et naturam animalium*)'. Giuliano had recognized her as the 'mistress of the game (*domina ludi*)', 'dressed in black clothes, with her head lowered (*cum mento ad stomacum*)'.[53] In certain respects the evidence is anomalous: there is no mention of female ecstasy, but rather of male divination, conducted via young children (who as such are sexually neuter). But the details we have cited are not altogether new. The Mantuan 'mistress of the game' calls to mind Oriente, the mysterious nocturnal lady whom the Milanese trials at the end of the fourteenth century describe as surrounded by animals, intent on teaching her followers 'the virtues of the earth'. The proximity to animals characteristic of these figures becomes, in the case of Richella or the 'women from outside', a semi-bestial nature, revealed by hirsute limbs, equine hooves, feline paws. Moreover, when they are leading a throng of souls, the protagonists of the nocturnal ecstasies appear to us as variations on an identical mythical theme: that of the 'mistress of the animals'.

That this undeniable resemblance also implies an actual historical connection is for the moment a conjecture. It should, at any rate, be noted that it offers a plausible explanation for the detail of the lowered head of 'the mistress of the game'. The attribution of an often lethal power to the glance of the divinity (and to her gaze in general) recurs in the most disparate cultures.[54] A common power is possessed by the Gorgon, Artemis and the goddess from whom, in a certain sense, they derive: the 'mistress of the animals'.[55] The Gorgon petrified humans with her awesome gaze; threatening legends surround the statues of Artemis. The statue in Pallene, concealed throughout the entire year, was only displayed in public for a very few days, but no one could look at it: it was said that the eyes of the goddess turned fruits dry on the trees, making them sterile forever.

The authenticity of Artemis Orthia's image was demonstrated, according to Pausanias (III. 16.7), by the madness that had struck its discoverers.[56] In the temple at Ephesus there was a statue of Hecate (the funereal goddess associated with Artemis) which was so resplendent as to force those who looked at it to cover their eyes: a mode of behaviour in all probability connected to a prohibition of a religious nature.[57] Now, a number of testimonies from the first years of the sixteenth century, originating in an area between the Po valley and the Eastern Alps, showed that the lowered head of the 'Mantuan mistress of the game' had analogous implications to those recorded in ancient Greece. In Ferrara a number of presumed witches described how, in order to escape death, they had been forced to avoid the

131

face of the 'wise Sibilla' (whose followers they were), infuriated by the immense effort to reach the waters of the River Jordan.[58] In Val di Fiemme, another woman tried as a witch, Margherita called Tessadrella, declared that the 'mistress of the good game' had two stones around her eyes, 'that is, one on each side, which open and close continually at her wish'. 'She had a black band around her head with patches before her ears and eyes so that she should not see or hear anything', as was confirmed by Caterina della Libra of Carano: 'and everything she hears and sees she makes hers, if she can.'[59]

> She always journeys through the air and she has two patches around her eyes, one on each side, so that she cannot see anything: and if she were able to see everything [explained Margherita dell 'Agnola called Tommasina] she would do great harm to the world.[60]

The partial inability to see, on the part of 'the mistress of the good game' and her Mantuan namesake, brings us back to the 'mistress of the animals'. In fables the sorceress who guards the entrance to the kingdom of the animals and of the dead is often blind, not only in an active but also in a passive sense: invisible to the living, besides being unable to see them.[61] In any case, the substantial identity of the various local versions cannot be attributed to an intervention by the judges. From the canonical tradition, they could learn, as in Val di Fiemme, the name of the 'mistress of the good game' – Herodias; but not her appearance. The witches of Val di Fiemme described it with a wealth of detail: 'a large ugly woman . . . [who] had a huge head' (Margherita called Tessadrella); 'an ugly black woman with a black smock and a black kerchief, tied around her head in a strange way' (Margherita called the Vanzina); 'an ugly brazen black woman, with a black kerchief wrapped around her head, in the German manner' (Bartolomea del Papo).[62] This concordance, accompanied by marginal variants, is typical of oral transmission, as is the likely misunderstanding (of the accused, the judges, the notaries?) whereby the 'two patches' 'around the eyes', in the case of the 'mistress of the good game' in Val di Fiemme, become, a short distance away (Fié allo Sciliar) and in the same years (1506–10), 'eyes as large as two plates'.[63] But the oral tradition was periodically nourished by a very vivid, direct experience of an ecstatic nature.

According to Caterina della Libra from Carano, the eyes and the ears of the goddess were covered by two stones or 'patches'. This rather vague description is clarified by testimony from the adjacent valley. Fifty years earlier, in the middle of the fifteenth century, the two old women of Val di Fassa interrogated by Nicholas of Cusa had said that Richella hid her face: they had not been able to see her in profile 'because of certain protuberances of a semicircular ornament attached to her ears' (*propter quasdam protensiones cuiusdam semicircularis ornamenti ad aures applicati*).[64] Words of visionary precision. The ornament must have been very large. If we were to imagine it shaped like a circle, instead of a semicircle, we would have before us an image like this (fig. 9).

10. There exist no direct historical links between the so-called *Dama* of Elche (fig. 10) and the ecstatic visions of a group of women who lived in the valleys of the Trentino two thousand years later.[65] Certainly, the *Dama* provokes a number of questions which arise in part from the lack of archaeological documentation on the circumstances surrounding her re-discovery.[66] It is not clear whether she was originally, as today, a bust or, as seems more likely, a whole figure: seated like the so-called *Dama* of Baza, or standing like the statue of a woman found in the Cerro de los Santos.[67] The chronology is disputed, although the majority of scholars favour a date between the middle of the fifth and the beginning of the fourth century BC.[68] Even more contentious is the provenance of the statue: Iberian, according to some; Ionic (perhaps Rhodian) according to others.[69] Though fashioned in the local manner, from a typological point of view the *Dama* at Baza has been compared to certain small statues from Magna Graecia (above all Sicilian) portraying a seated goddess, sometimes holding a child in her lap.[70] To extend this conjecture to the *Dama* of Elche would be risky, since her original physiognomy is uncertain. In any event, the presence of cavities in the back, probably used to hold ashes, seems to indicate a funerary purpose.[71]

The identity of the *Dama* of Elche (goddess, priestess, celebrant?) remains obscure. However, there is nothing mysterious about the two huge wheels, fastened by a band, that flank her temples. This is an ornament that appears in various small female votive figures found in the sanctuary of Castellar; an analogous object, made of silver, has been found in Estremadura.[72] The wheels, of larger or smaller dimensions, were made to contain braids, either natural or artificial. The extravagance of Iberian hairstyles was renowned in antiquity, as is attested by a passage in Strabo (III. 4. 17) based on testimony by Artemidorus.[73] But similar hairstyles can also be seen on Greek statuary, from Sicily to Boeotia.[74] The coincidence between the hairstyle of the *Dama* of Elche and that of the nocturnal goddess in Val di Fiemme – 'a black band around the head with two wheels at the side' – possibly conceals a historical nexus which eludes us. A further unexpected convergence emerges to suggest a possible solution (we shall see it emerge little by little): the temples of the *Dama* of Elche are adorned with pendants placed inside two wheels, similar to those which accompany a number of gold temporal discs of Graeco-Scythian craftsmanship (fourth century BC), found both in Crimea and in what is today the region of Dnepropetrovsk (figs. 11–12).[74 bis.]

11. The explanations proposed up to this point are in part conjectural; the facts to which they refer are much less so. The existence of actual ecstatic continuities seems undeniable. Unwittingly, men and women – above all, women, possibly living in forlorn mountain villages – relive, during their nocturnal swoons, myths that have reached them from the most remote places and periods. Through the reconstruction of this deep context incomprehensible details suddenly reveal their significance. In one of the Milanese sentences handed down at the end of the fourteenth century –

against Pierina – it is said that Oriente brought back to life the oxen (which had been killed and devoured by her followers) by touching their bones, wrapped in the skins, with her wand. Now, according to the *Historia Brittonum* by Nennius (c. 826), repeated in Jacopo da Varazze's *Legenda Aurea* (compiled at the end of the thirteenth century), an analogous miracle, based on the resurrection of certain slaughtered oxen, had been performed by St Germanus d'Auxerre in Britain, during the conversion of the Celts. It has been demonstrated that Nennius' narrative derives from a more ancient source.[75] The reappearance in Ireland, or in an area evangelized by Irish monks such as Flanders and Brabant, of the same hagiographic theme – the resurrection of deer or geese from their bones – once again attests to the presence of a Celtic substratum.[76] Up to this point, nothing very surprising. But in Snorri Sturlusson's *Edda* (first half of the thirteenth century) the feat is attributed to the Germanic god Thor, who resuscitates several rams (animals sacred to him) by striking their bones with the weapon he traditionally carries: the hammer. The relationship between these versions – the Christianized Celtic and pre-Christian Germanic – is not clear. Does the second derive from the first? Or vice versa? Or do both derive from a yet more ancient version?[77]

What induces us to favour the last hypothesis is the geographical distribution of myths and rituals revolving around the collection of the bones (as intact as possible) of slaughtered animals for the purpose of bringing them back to life.[78] Such myths are documented in the Alpine region where the feat is accomplished by the procession of the dead or by the nocturnal goddess who leads it.[79] Among the many names attributed to the goddess was that of Pharaildis, the patron saint of Gand who, according to a legend, resuscitated a goose by collecting its bones.[80] In a totally different cultural sphere, among the Abkhaz of the Caucasus, it is a male divinity of the hunt and forest who restores life to the game that has been killed (rather than working animals such as oxen).[81] These beliefs, documented in the most diverse cultures (including continental Africa), inspire certain rituals performed by the hunting population which lives in the boundless Arctic band between Lapland and the northern islands of the Japanese archipelago inhabited by the Ainu. The bones of the larger game (bears, elks, deer) are amassed in piles, gathered in baskets or placed on platforms; sometimes the skins are stuffed with straw and wood shavings.[82] In the middle of the eighteenth century the Laplandic shamans (*no'aidi*), entrusted with the preparation of the victims for the ritual, explained to the Danish missionaries that the bones must be gathered and arranged with great care, because the god to whom the sacrifice was made would then restore life to the animals, making them even fatter than before.[83] Testimonies of this kind are very numerous. The Yukagir of eastern Siberia, for example, collect the bones of bears, elks or deer so that they may be resuscitated: then they place them on a platform, together with skulls filled with wood shavings ('now let's give you a brain', they say) with a piece of wood inserted in place of the tongue.[84] From these ephemeral ritual constructions derive the mysterious wooden sculptures to be found in Ch'angsha (province of Hunan, China, fourth or third century BC), which portray a human face with a protruding tongue and a head mounted by deer antlers (fig. 11).[85]

12. Later we shall see whether these convergences can be attributed to hazard, to the independent effect of similar circumstances, or to other factors. Let us provisionally take it as agreed that the idea (expressed in myths or ceremonies) of resuscitating animals by gathering their bones intact is a specific cultural trait – so specific as to imply, given its presence in the most diverse times and places, either contact or a substratum. At this point we are confronted by the difficulty that we had already glimpsed when comparing the miracle of St Germanus to the feat performed by Thor. The absolute chronology of the evidence does not necessarily coincide with the relative chronology of the beliefs or the myths that it documents. How can we translate the spatial dispersion of the data into a historical succession?

The Laplanders worship a god of lightning, armed with a hammer or cudgel. The analogy with the Germanic Thor is evident, beginning with the name: Horagalles. We are therefore faced with a loan, resulting from contacts with the Scandinavian populations.[86] But it may be that the linguistic borrowing conceals a more complex reality.[87] Like Ruto, the Laplandic goddess who personifies the plague, Horagalles also possibly came from northern Eurasia.[88] Both these divinities are mentioned in the above-cited report by the Danish missionaries who evangelized Lapland in the middle of the eighteenth century: the basket of birch twigs in which the bones of the sacrificed animals were collected was surmounted by a carved tree-trunk portraying Horagalles with his hammer, the weapon with which the 'idol [*deaster*] terrified witches and sorcerers'.[89] Thus Horagalles too was associated with the resurrection of animals. To suppose that the echo of Thor's feat was propagated throughout the sub-Arctic band, all the way to the Japanese archipelago, is obviously absurd; just as absurd is the inverse hypothesis – that is, that the myth spread in the European sphere thanks to the mediation of the Laplanders. We are irresistibly led to recognize in Horagalles, Thor, St Germanus d'Auxerre and Oriente so many variants of the same myth whose roots lie in a remote Eurasian past: a divinity, sometimes male, but more often female, the generator and resuscitator of animals.[90] The presence of a corresponding ritual in the Eurasian sphere, like its absence in the Celtic and Germanic spheres, seems to confirm this derivation. That the belief in the resurrection of slain animals should have been born in a culture of hunters is, after all, quite plausible.

13. The spatial and temporal reach of our research has been further extended. The testimonies about the nocturnal goddess seem like a palimpsest in which semi-cancelled fragments of different writing are superimposed: Diana, 'divinity of the pagans', mentioned by canonists and

135

inquisitors; Habonde, Oriente, Richella, and their namesakes; the Matrons and the fairies; the Mother Goddesses; Artemis; the 'mistress of the animals'; the Eurasian divinities of hunting and the forest.

We have attained this last and probably more profound cultural stratum by an almost exclusively morphological route, based, however, on the identification of specific traits rather than on vague convergences of a typological order. The possibility of inserting Artemis (in certain respects), as well as the divinities of the Eurasian hunters, in a category called 'masters of the animals' is evidently insufficient to prove the existence of a historical connection between these figures.[91] More significant, even if hypothetical, seems to be the etymological nexus between *Artemis* (in Doric, *Artamis*) and *artamos*: the 'butcher' or, more precisely, 'the one who severs the joints'. The term, less common than its synonym *mageiros*, was used both in the vocabulary of the kitchen and in that of sacrifice.[92] The name of Artemis would then preserve a trace of the prohibition, widespread in the Eurasian sphere (we also see it surface in the Old Testament), against breaking the bones of the sacrificial victim.[93] A prohibition of this kind was possibly associated with Despoina (that is, the Lady): the most venerated among the goddesses of Arcadia, similar in certain ways to Artemis, even though belatedly assimilated to Kore, the daughter of Demeter. According to Pausanias (VIII. 35.8), sacrifices in honour of Despoina adhered to a totally unusual ritual. The victim's throat was not cut: its limbs were severed, 'at random', that is in no fixed order, but taking account of the joints.[94] This type of sacrifice has been associated with a number of Minoan gems and an archaic Theban amphora, in which a female divinity is portrayed surrounded by the severed limbs of animals.[95] The Eurasian divinities who resuscitated animals from gathered bones are perhaps not far removed from these images. At any rate, the theme of resurrection from the bones was also present in Greek culture: we shall see this later when analyzing the myth of Pelops.

14.   In the evidence on the nocturnal goddess originating from much of the European continent, the presence of features that recall the myths and rituals of Siberian hunters is a disconcerting but not isolated datum. Moreover, the ecstasies of the followers of the goddess irresistibly call to mind those of the shamans – men and women – of Siberia or of Lapland.[96] In both we find the same elements: the flight of the soul to the realm of the dead, in the shape of an animal, on the back of animals or other magical vehicles. The *gandus* or wand of the shamans of Lapland resembles, on the one hand, the horseshoe-shaped wand used by the Buryat shaman and, on the other, the broomstick on which the witches claim they rode to the Sabbath.[97] The folkloric nucleus of the Sabbath – magic flight and metamorphosis – seems to derive from a remote Eurasian substratum.

15.   A connection of this order had been dimly perceived by one of the most ferocious persecutors of witches: the judge, Pierre de Lancre. At the

beginning of the seventeenth century, reflecting on the trials he had presided over in the Labourd, on the French slope of the Pyrenees, de Lancre compared the followers of Diana mentioned in the *Canon episcopi* to werewolves, on the one hand, and 'magi', on the other – i.e., to the shamans of Lapland described by Olaus Magnus and by Peucer. In them de Lancre detected a common characteristic: the ability to fall into a diabolical ecstasy, erroneously interpreted by some as a separation of the soul from the body. An understandable mistake, de Lancre remarked:

> One must admit that in the past witch doctors were much less numerous than they are today. They lived apart in the mountains and in the deserts, or in the countries of the north, such as Norway, Denmark, Sweden, Gothia, Ireland, and Livonia: therefore their idolatries and evil spells were largely unknown, and were often thought to be fables or old wives' tales.

Among the incredulous in the past had been St Augustine: but for more than a hundred years (de Lancre observed) inquisitors and lay judges have been casting light upon these subjects.[99]

This proud tone was in some ways justified. With an eye sharpened by hatred, de Lancre observed the object of his persecution with a penetration often absent in the more detached observers of the subsequent century.[100] Unimportant events in small Basque communities were suddenly inserted in a vast geographical frame, the theatre of the offensive launched by Satan against humanity. De Lancre was convinced that the werewolves were able to abandon their human guises to assume animal shapes, just as the witches were physically able to go to the Sabbath: but he did admit the possibility that sometimes metamorphoses and flights might occur only in dreams. These, however, were not innocent dreams: it was the devil in person who evoked them in the corrupt minds of witches, sorcerers and werewolves. For a scientist like Della Porta, ecstasy represented a natural phenomenon, induced by the – scrupulously listed – ingredients of the witch's ointments.[101] For de Lancre, it was the element that unified the various idolatrous cults inspired by the devil: foremost among them, the Sabbath.

De Lancre's reflections passed completely unobserved. But when, half a century later, the persecution of witchcraft began to wane amidst growing cultural discredit, the extraordinary variety of beliefs that had previously been branded diabolical were gradually considered in a new light. Precisely in Germany, where the witch hunts had reached a peak of ferocity, curiosity of an antiquarian character developed about these phenomena. In 1668 J. Praetorius printed in Leipzig a book in which he collected, from previous writings and oral traditions, information on the witches' flights and on the Sabbath of St Walpurgis Night, to which a mountain in Thuringia, the Blocksberg, owed its fame. In this context too the legend of the faithful Eckhart as leader of the demonic cohort was recorded. The title of the book (*Blockes-Berges Verrichtung oder ausfürlicher geographischer Bericht*, 'The effects of the Blockesberg or a detailed geographical report') intimated an intention of scientific detachment, which was particularly evident in the geographical appendix, based on a survey made fifteen years previously by a team of fifteen people and twelve horses. Some time later, in a work dedicated to ancient and recent beliefs connected with the beginning of the year (*Saturnalia*), Praetorius included sections on the werewolves of Livonia and Lapland, on the army of Diana, on Holda.[102] P.C. Hilscher, a Lutheran pastor and professor, drew on these for a learned dissertation (*De exercitu furioso, vulgo Wuetenden Heer*) which was discussed in Leipzig under his guidance in 1688, and later translated into German.[103] Here antiquarian erudition was put at the service of an anti-Catholic polemic in which the echo of the writings of an Illuminist like Thomasius can be detected. From courtrooms, where, in some parts of Europe, they continued to be the object of judicial repression, beliefs connected with witchcraft had migrated to the lecture rooms. Hilscher compared the processions of souls to the fictitious entities imagined by the Scholastics and to the invention of Purgatory, which the reformers, guided by the Scriptures, had buried. Half a century later, a moderate Illuminist influenced by Muratori, Girolamo Tartarotti of Rovereto, emphasized how in the past beliefs about the 'brigade of Diana', defined by him as 'medieval witchcraft', had been derided and not persecuted.[104] From both confessional sides learned polemic brought about the emergence of traditions which the stereotype of the diabolical Sabbath had distorted and erased for centuries. It is no accident that the most ancient study of the Celtic *Matronae* – the *Dissertatio de mulieribus fatidicis veterum Celtarum* of the antiquarian J.G. Keysler – included a harsh attack on the persecution of witchcraft.[105]

The great poetry and philology of German Romanticism made of the Sabbath a theme that was destined enduringly to nourish the imagination of scholars and poets. Goethe drew on Praetorius' *Blockes-Berges Verrichtung* for the scene on St Walpurgis Night in his *Faust*.[106] In his *Deutsche Mythologie* (1835) Jakob Grimm traced the inventory of a mythical tradition largely hinging on the 'wild hunt' and the figures who led it. One of the threads offered the reader to orient himself in the enormous accumulation of material was the hypothesis of continuity between pagan beliefs and diabolical witchcraft. At the end of the section devoted to cannibalistic witches, this hypothesis was formulated in an especially dense, almost cryptic fashion.[107] With an abrupt leap, Grimm proceeded to refer to that other belief, equally ancient and recurrent in a large number of legends, according to which the soul can abandon the body of a sleeping person in the form of a butterfly. The Longobard historian Paul the Deacon, who lived in the eighth century, tells how one day while he was sleeping, watched over by his squire, an animal, a sort of tiny serpent, suddenly came out of the mouth of the Burgundian King Guntram. It moved toward a nearby brook which it vainly tried to cross. The squire then placed his sword across its banks. The serpent crossed to the other side and disappeared behind a small hill; after a while it retraced its route, slipping back into the mouth of the sleeping man. The King awoke and said that he had dreamt that he had crossed an iron bridge, and then had gone into a mountain where a treasure was kept (which was in fact found). In more recent versions of the same legend, the animal changes: instead of a serpent, we find a weasel, a cat or a mouse. Might not all this be linked, Grimm asked, on the one hand to the metamorphoses of witches into mice, on the other to the bridge, narrow as a thread, which the soul must cross to reach the other world?

With this question, which seems addressed to himself rather than to the reader, Grimm identified, in the flash of a fading bolt of lightning, the same overwhelming connection that had come to Pierre de Lancre, persecutor of witches in Labourd, two centuries earlier. In all probability the latter was an unconscious convergence.[108] De Lancre had apparently been speaking of something else entirely: of werewolves, of Diana's followers, of Laplandic magicians. But the unifying element of the two analogical series was the same: ecstasy. Immediately after formulating his question, Grimm had in fact returned to the catalepsis of witches in Serbia: the soul exits in the guise of a butterfly or a hen from the inanimate body, which, when in this condition, must not be turned over. And in turn the ecstasy or *trance* brought to mind the example, most sublime of all, of Odin, who, according to a famous passage of Snorri's *Ynglingasaga*, was able to assume different shapes: leaving his sleeping body in the blink of an eye, he travelled to distant lands, transmuted into a bird, a fish or a serpent.

16.   Innumerable paths branch out from this crucial and neglected page: shamanistic components of the figure of Odin or of the Legend of King Guntram;[109] the diffusion in the Arthurian romances of the Celtic theme of the sword as a bridge to the world of the dead and, more generally, the presence of shamanistic themes in Celtic literary texts;[110] the *benandanti* of Friuli who, before falling into catalepsis, begged their wives not to turn them over, lest the soul, having issued forth in the shape of a tiny *sorzetto* (mouse), be unable to re-enter the body and reawaken it;[111] the Laplandic shamans watched over during the ecstasy so that their inanimate bodies would not be touched by flies or mosquitoes (as reported by Olaus Magnus) or attacked by the demons (as Peucer affirmed);[112] the journey of the soul in ecstasy in the shape of an animal, and the transformation of witches and sorcerers into animals, etc. Figures and themes echo each other, bounce back off each other, until they compose, not merely a chain, but a sort of magnetic field – which explains how, starting from diverse viewpoints and proceeding independently, it has been possible to arrive at analogous conjectures.[113] But the question formulated by Grimm has yet to receive a genuine answer. Subsequent research has been dispersed in disparate streams, losing sight of the unitary nexus that Grimm had glimpsed. Ecstasies, animal metamorphoses, mythical journeys to the beyond, rituals and beliefs connected

with the processions of the dead – and, naturally, the Sabbath – have been analyzed separately.[114] We must reknit the many threads that bound them.

Notes

1. See the important essay by G. Henningsen, 'Sicilien: ett arkaiskt mönster för sabbaten', in A. Ankarloo and G. Henningsen eds, *Häxooras Europa (1400–1700)*, Lund 1987, pp. 170–90, which I have read in the English version ('The Ladies from Outside': Fairies, Witches and Poverty in Early Modern Europe') presented to the conference on witchcraft at Stockholm in September 1985.
2. Cf. G. Bonomo, *Caccia alle streghe*, Palermo 1959, p. 65: the popularization, dated between 1450 and 1470, was by Giovanni Vassallo.
3. On all this see G. Pitré, *Usi e costumi credenze e pregiudizi del popolo siciliano*, IV, Palermo 1889, pp. 153–77: Emanuela Santaéra's story is on p. 165 n. 2. On p. 177 Pitré suggests some possible parallels with the 'women from outside' (fairies, Etruscan and Latin *Lares*), concluding with a tentative reference to the 'Latin *Deae Matres*, about whom we know so little'. The head covering of the *Matronae* has been linked with the local costumes; cf. Ihm, *Der Mütter- oder Matronenkultus*, pp. 38–9, and above all L. Hahl, 'Zur Matronenverehrung in Niedergermanien', *Germania*, 21 (1937). pp. 253–64, in particular pp. 254 ff.
4. Cf. Diodorus Siculus, *Biblioteca storica*, XV, 70 (369 BC); XVI, 73 (342 BC).
5. Cf. A. Graf, 'Artú nell'Etna', in *Miti, leggende e superstizioni del Medio Evo*, I, Turin 1892. According to A.H. Krappe, 'Die Sage vom König im Berge', *Mitteilungen der schlesische Gesellschaft für Volkskunde*, XXXV (1935), pp. 76–102 (especially p. 92), the saga was never truly popular in Sicily: but Gervase of Tilbury in his *Otia imperialia* attributed to the 'indigenae' the stories about the apparitions of Arthur. On the Breton knights as possible mediators, cf. R.S. Loomis, 'Morgain la Fée in Oral Tradition', in *Studies in Medieval Literature*, New York 1970, p. 6. On Etna as the entry point to Purgatory, cf. Jacques Le Goff, *La naissance du Purgatoire*, Paris 1981, pp. 273 ff. On Arthur's presence in the Otranto mosaics (1163–65) cf. above, pp. 119, n. 84.
6. See W. Fauth, 'Fata Morgana', in K. Baldinger, ed, *Beiträge zur romanischen Mittelalter*, Tübingen 1977, pp. 417–54, in particular pp. 436 ff.
7. Cf. M. Marconi, 'Da Circe a Morgana', *Rendiconti del R. Istituto Lombardo di Scienze e Lettere*, Cl. di Lettere, 74 (1940–41), pp. 533–73, against which one should consult the objections of Fauth, art. cit., pp. 439 ff.
8. Cf. I. Chirassi-Colombo, *La religione in Grecia*, Bari 1983, pp. 9–10.
9. Cf. M. Mühl, *Poseidonius und der plutarchische Marcellus*, Berlin 1925, pp. 8 ff. (on which cf. F. Münzer, in *Gnomon*, I (1925), pp. 96–100); cf. also the comment of R. Flacelière and E. Chambry on the *Life of Marcellos* ('Belles Lettres', Paris 1966). The possibility that the passage forms part of Posidonius' book on divination is cautiously advanced by J. Malitz, *Die Historien des Poseidonios*, Munich 1983, p. 363 n. 33. Together with another of Plutarch's writings (*On the destruction of the oracles*), chapter 20 of the *Life of Marcellus* gave Goethe the idea for his scene of the Mothers in *Faust* (II, 6213 ff.): cf. *Goethes Gespräche*, F. von Biedermann ed, IV, Leipzig 1910, pp. 187–8 (dialogue with Eckermann, 10 January 1830) in combination with J. Zeitler, *Goethe-Handbuch*, II, Stuttgart 1917, pp. 641–2 (heading 'Mütter'). The reading of Plutarch dates back to 1820–21: cf. F. Koch, 'Fausts Gang zu den Müttern', in *Festschrift der Nationalbibliothek in Wien*, [Vienna]

1926, pp. 509–28; C. Enders, *Faust-Studien. Müttermythus und Homunkulis-Allegorie, in Goethes* Faust, Bonn 1948, pp. 26–7.

10. See M.I. Finley, *Storia della Sicilia antica*, It. trans., Bari 1970, p. 125. For other identifications, cf. G. Sfameni Gasparro, *I culti orientali in Sicilia*, Leiden 1973, p. 153.

11. On the reliance of Posidonius on Diodorus' pages on the slave wars cf. A. Momigliano, *Saggezza Straniera*, Turin 1980, pp. 36 ff.

12. Cf. Diodorus Siculus, *Biblioteca storica*, IV, 79–80.

13. Cf. G. Alessi, *Lettera su di un ghianda di piombo inscritta col nome di Acheo condottiero degli schiavi rubelli in Sicilia*, Palermo 1829, pp. 11, 13; G. de Minicis, *Sulle antiche ghiande missili e sulle loro iscrizioni*, Rome 1844, p. 60.

14. Cf. in general H. Usener, 'Dreiheit', *Rheinisches Museum*, 58 (1903), pp. 1–47, 161–208 and 321–362; on the Mothers of Engyon, pp. 192–93. Sfameni Gasparro, op. cit., pp. 153 ff., came to similar conclusions, independently. The identification of the Mothers with images of multiple female divinities discovered in Crete is regarded as intriguing but unverifiable by L. Banti, 'Divinità femminili a Creta nel tardo Minoico III', *Studi e materiali di storia delle religioni*, XVII (1941), p. 30 (which does not cite Usener).

15. This is the opinion of A. Boeckh: cf. the article 'Meteres' in Pauly-Wissowa, *Real-Encyclopädie der Classischen Altertumswissenschaft*, XV, 1373–75 (Pfister). On the rock sculptures of Palazzolo Acreide (the so-called 'holy men') linked to the cult of Cybele, cf. Gasparro, op. cit., pp. 126 ff.

16. Cf. E. Ciaceri, *Culti e miti nella storia dell'antica Sicilia*, Catania 1911, p. 241; see also pp. 5 ff., 120 ff., 239 ff. and 306 ff.; P. E. Arias, 'Sul culto delle ninfe a Siracusa', *Rendiconti dell'Accademia dei Lincei*, Classe di scienze morali etc., s. VI, XI (1935), pp. 605–8; B. Pace, *Arte e civiltà della Sicilia, III: Cultura e vita religiosa*, Città di Castello 1945, pp. 486 ff. The attempt of these scholars to find in Sicily an indigenous, pre-Greek religious stratum, has been decisively rejected (without referring particularly to the Mothers) by A. Brelich, 'La religione greca in Sicilia', *Kokalos*, X-XI (1964–65), pp. 35–54. According to G. Pugliese-Carratelli, 'Minos e Cocalos', ibid. II (1956), p. 101, the cult of Engyon was actually 'extraneous to the Sicelot religious milieu'.

17. Cf. respectively: F. Welcker, 'Drei Göttinnen, vielleicht die Mütter', in *Alte Denkmaler*, II, Göttingen 1850, pp. 154–57, which tries to make more precise the vague conjectures (three sisters? a mother with two daughters?) proposed by L. Ross, 'Kyprische Grabrelief', *Archäologische Zeitung*, N.F., VI (1848), coll. 289–92; U. Wilamowitz-Moellendorff, *Der Glaube der Hellenen*, I, Darmstadt 1959, p. 199 n. 3, and, independently, N. Putortí, 'Rilievo di Camàro con rappresentazione delle "Meteres"', *Archivio storico per la Sicilia Orientale*, XIX (1922–23), pp. 203–10.

18. Cf. G. Zuntz, *Persephone*, Oxford 1971, p. 69, which utilizes material published by V. Dobrusky, 'Inscriptions et monuments figurés de la Thrace. Trouvailles de Saladinovo', *Bulletin de correspondance hellénique*, 21 (1897), pp. 119–40 (which, however, does not mention the *Matronae*).

19. Cf. R. F. Hoddinott, *The Thracians*, London 1981, pp. 89 ff., especially p. 162. On the fairies in the Balkan sphere, see now the ample and penetrating study by E. Pócs about to be published in the FF Communications of Helsinki. I am grateful to the author for having given me the chance to read her work.

20. Cf. Dom*** [Jacques Martin], *La religion des Gaulois* II, Paris 1727, pp. 195 ff.; A. de Boissieu, *Inscriptions antiques de Lyon*, Lyon 1846–54, pp. 55–6 (which also cites Morgana); J. Becker, 'Die inschriftlichen Ueberreste der keltischen Sprache', *Beiträge zur vergleichenden Sprachforschung*, IV (1885), p. 146; idem, in *Neue*

Jahrbücher für Philologie, 77 (1858), pp. 581–2. Ihm takes a sharply negative attitude in art. cit., pp. 58–9; see also idem, 'Griechische Matres', *Jahrbücher des Vereins von Alterthumsfreunden im Rheinlande*, 90 (1891), pp. 189–90. (A sheer coincidence had been already suggested by Welcker in art. cit., p. 157.) In favour of an identification between these divinities, see Wilamowitz-Moellendorff, op. cit., I, p. 199 and Zuntz, op. cit., p. 62. The convergence is explained in racist terms by E. Bickel, 'Die Vates der Kelten und die 'Interpretatio Graeca' des südgallischen Matronenkultes im Eumenidenkult', *Rheinisches Museum*, N.F., LXXXVII (1938), pp. 193–241.

21. Cf. R. Vallentin du Cheylard, 'Sacellum consacré aux Mères victorieuses à Allan (Drôme)', *Cahiers Rhodaniens*, IV (1957), pp. 67–72. On Allan's inscriptions, cf. E. Espérandieu, in *Revue épigraphique*, V (1903–1908), pp. 179–83, which also furnishes a summary description of the three damaged statues (now lost) of the Mothers. Finding no precedents for the epithet 'victorious' in connection with the Mothers, Espérandieu referred to the coins of Diocletian and Maximian portraying three women with cornucopias, encircled by the inscription *Fatis victricibus*.

22. Cf. above, p. 123.

23. Cf. Diodorus Siculus, *Biblioteca Storica*, IV, 80. See also Avienus, *Les Phénomènes d'Aratus*, J. Soubiran ed, 'Les Belles Lettres', Paris 1981, verses 99 ff. (where there is an allusion to the Arcadian myth of Callisto – on whom see below) p. 185 n. 8.

24. See E. Neustadt, *De Iove Cretico*, Berlin 1906, pp. 18 ff.

25. Cf. M. P. Nilsson, *The Minoan-Mycenean Religion and its Survival in Greek Religion*, Lund 1950, pp. 533 ff.; idem, *Geschichte der i griechi schen Religion*, I, Munich 1967, pp. 319 ff.; W. Aly, 'Ursprung und Entwicklung der kretischen Zeusreligion', *Philologus*, LXXI (1912), pp. 457 ff.; P. Chantraine, 'Réflexions sur les noms des dieux helléniques', *L'antiquité classique*, 22 (1953), pp. 65–6.

26. *Scholia in Apollonium Rhodium*, rec. C. Wendel, Berolini 1935, p. 81.

27. Cf. S. Reinach, 'L'Artémis arcadienne et la déesse aux serpents de Cnossos' (1906), in *Cultes, Mythes et Religions*, III, Paris 1922, pp. 210–22; see, in addition, the heading *Helike* (by Gundel) in Pauly-Wissowa, op. cit., VII, 2860–61.

28. Cf. R. Franz, 'De Callistus fabula', *Leipziger Studien zur classischen Philologie*, XII (1890), pp. 235–365; P. Lévêque, 'Sur quelques cultes d'Arcadie: princesse-ourse, hommes-loups et dieux-chevaux', *L'Information historique*, XXIII (1961), pp. 93–108; W. Sale, 'Callisto and the Virginity of Artemis', *Rheinisches Museum*, N.F., 108 (1965), pp. 11–35; G. Maggiulli, 'Artemide-Callisto', in *Mythos, Scripta in honorem Marii Untersteiner*, [Genoa] 1970, pp. 179–85; P. Borgeaud, *Recherches sur le dieu Pan*, Geneva 1979, pp. 41 ff.; W. Burkert, *Homo necans*, It. trans., Turin 1981, p. 69; A. Henrichs, 'Three Approaches to Greek Mythology', in J. Bremmer ed, *Interpretations of Greek Mythology*, London and Sydney 1987, pp. 242–77, in particular pp. 254 ff.

29. Bibliographic indications in Borgeaud, op. cit., p. 10; cf. also L. R. Palmer, *Minoici e micenei*, It. trans. Turin 1969, pp. 111–12.

30. According to V. J. Georgiev, *Introduzione alla storia delle lingue indoeuropee* It. trans. Rome 1966, p. 15 (which refers back to W. Merlingen, in *Mnémés Kharin. Gedenkschrift P. Kretschmer*, II, Vienna 1957, p. 53), *arkos* is the most archaic form. W. Sale's conjecture of the extra-Arcadian origin of Callisto's transformation into a bear seems hard to sustain. The structural analogy between the Arcadian and Cretan myths is emphasized, in a slightly different perspective, by Borgeaud, op. cit., pp. 44 and 66–9 (while Henrichs, art. cit., pp. 261–2, considers it irrelevant).

31. On the dependence of Arcadian on Cretan myths, already stated by Reinach, art. cit., especially p. 221, cf. J. Laager, *Geburt und Kindheit des Gottes in der griechischen*

Anomalies

Mythologie, Winterthur 1957, pp. 174 ff.; R. Stiglitz, *Die grossen Göttinen Arkadiens*, Baden bei Wien 1967, p. 64 n. 218. The opposite hypothesis has been maintained by S. Marinatos, in *Archäologischer Anzeiger*, 1962, coll. 903–16. The Cretan element is strongly emphasized by Nilsson, *Geschichte*, I, p. 320.

32. Cf. Giampiera Arrigoni, 'Il maestro del maestro e i loro continuatori: mitologia e simbolismo animale in Karl Wilhelm Ferdinand Solger, Karl Ottfried Müller e dopo', *Annali della Scuola Normale Superiore di Pisa*, s. III, XIV (1984), pp. 937–1029, especially pp. 975 ff. Points of disagreement with this important essay will be formulated as we proceed.

33. The epithet is also recorded by Pausanias who mentions the 'wooden statues of Aristaeus and Callisto; as I believe, and the verses of Pamphos confirm, these last are attributes of Artemis; I leave aside, though knowing it, another interpretation given to me' (Pausanias, *Guida della Grecia*, I. 29. 2, D. Musti and L. Beschi eds, Milan 1982). It does not seem to me that the reference back to Panphos, instead of Sappho (today unanimously accepted, as Arrigoni observes in art. cit., p. 978 n. 80) negates the value of the evidence. See, meanwhile, A. Philadelpheus, 'Le Sanctuaire d'Artémis Kallistè et l'ancienne rue de l'Académie', *Bulletin de correspondance hellénique*, LI (1927), pp. 158–63 (to which Arrigoni refers).

34. Cf. L.G. Kahil, 'Autour de l'Artémis attique', *Antike Kunst*, 8 (1965), pp. 20 ff.; A. Brelich, *Paides e Parthenoi*, I, Rome 1969, pp. 229–311; C. Sourvinou (later Sourvinou-Inwood), 'Aristophanes, "Lysistrata", 641–647', *The Classical Quarterly*, n.s. XXI (1971), pp. 339–42; T. C. W. Stinton, 'Iphigeneia and the Bears of Brauron', ibid., XXVI (1976), pp. 11–13; L. Kahil, 'L'Artémis de Brauron: rites et mystères', *Antike Kunst*, 20 (1977), pp. 86–98; C. Montepaone, 'L'arkteia a Brauron', *Studi storico-religiosi*, III, (1979), pp. 343 ff.; M. B. Walbank, 'Artemis Bear-Leader', *Classical Quarterly*, 31 (1981), pp. 276-81; S. Angiolillo, 'Pisistrato e Artemide Brauronia', *La parola del passato*, XXXVIII (1983), pp. 351–54; Hugh Lloyd-Jones,'Artemis and Iphigenia', *Journal of Hellenic Studies*, CIII (1983), pp. 91 ff.; L. G. Kahil, 'Mythological Repertoire of Brauron', in *Ancient Greek Art and Iconography*, W.G. Moon ed, Madison 1983, pp. 231–44. Another bibliography can be found in Arrigoni, art. cit., p. 1019.

35. Cf. the texts discussed by Arrigoni, art. cit.

36. See, for example the description, indirect but very precise, written by Pausanias (VIII, 41, 4 ff.) of the ancient image of Demeter of Phigalia: and in general cf. Lévêque, art. cit. The statements here (as well as those that follow) presuppose the analysis of the classic image of Arcadia offered by Borgeaud (op. cit.), without, however, accepting its sceptical implications (p. 10). The essential verisimilitude of that image, based on exclusively literary evidence, is in any event confirmed by the simultaneous reference of Borgeaud himself to the archaism of the Arcadian dialect.

37. Cf. P. Faure, 'Nouvelles recherches de spéléologie et de topographie crétoises', *Bulletin de correspondance hellénique*, LXXIV (1960), pp. 209–15; idem, *Fonctions des cavernes crétoises*, Paris 1964, pp. 144 ff.; R. F. Willets, *Cretan Cults and Festivals*, London 1962, pp. 275–77; A. Antoniou, 'Minoische Elemente im Kult der Artemis von Brauron', *Philologus*, 125 (1981), pp. 291–96; Lloyd-Jones, art. cit., p. 97 n. 72. See, in addition, the article 'Kynosura' in Pauly-Wissowa, op. cit. On the possibility of tracing a continuity between the Mycenaean religion and the Greek religion, cf. W. K. C. Guthrie, 'Early Greek Religion in the Light of the Decipherment of Linear B', *Bulletin of the Institute of Classical Studies of the University of London*, 6 (1959), pp. 35–46.

38. Cf. Neustadt, op. cit., which develops the observations of A. Claus, *De Dianae*

143

antiquissima apud Graecos natura, Breslau 1881, pp. 87 ff.; H. Posnansky, 'Nemesis und Adrasteia', *Breslauer Philologische Abhandlungen*, V, 2, Breslau 1890, pp. 68 ff. On Bendis, see R. Pettazzoni, 'The Religion of Thrace', in *Essays in the History of Religion*, Leiden 1954, pp. 81 ff.; I. Chirassi-Colombo, 'The Role of Thrace in Greek Religion', in *Thracia II*, Serdicae 1974, pp. 71 ff., in particular pp. 77–8; Z. Gočeva, 'Le culte de la déesse thrace Bendis à Athènes', in ibid., pp. 81 ff.; D. Popov, 'Artemis Brauro (déesse thraco-pélasgique), in *Interaction and Acculturation in the Mediterranean*, I, Amsterdam 1980, pp. 203–21.

39. In general see C. Christou, *Potnia Thērōn*, Thessaloniki 1968; L. Kahil, 'Artemis', in *Lexicon Iconographicum Mythologiae Classicae*, II, 1 and 2, Zurich and Munich 1984, pp. 618–753 (and see besides, p. 135). For a Cretan example, cf. L. Pernier, 'Templi arcaici di Priniàs. Contributo allo studio dell'arte dedalica', *Annuario della R. Scuola archeologica di Atene . . .*, I, (1914), pp. 68 ff., figs. 37–8.

40. J.-P. Vernant, *La mort dans les yeux*, Paris 1985, insists on these borderline characteristics.

41. Cf. Philadelpheus, art. cit.; and see Claus, cit., pp. 64 ff. and Neustadt, art. cit., p. 49. On Artemis *Kourotrophos*, cf. M. P. Nilsson, *The Minoan-Mycenean Religion*, p. 503.

42. This and other aspects were emphasized by J.J. Bachofen in his famous essay, *Der Bär in den Religionen des Alterthums* (Basel 1863). On this cf. T. Gelzer, 'Bachofen, Bern und der Bär', in *Jagen und Sammeln. Festschrift für Hans-Georg Bandi zum 65. Geburtstag*, Bern 1985, pp. 97–120 (I owe knowledge of this essay to the kindness of Giampiera Arrigoni, who sent me a xerox copy). W. Sale's observations (art. cit.) on the absence of truly maternal characteristics in the figure of Artemis should be borne in mind.

43. Cf. Bachofen, op. cit., to which can also be traced back the first intuition of the unity of the group. An epigraph discovered at Zurich in 1868 suggested further reflections to Bachofen on the theme of the bear (*Gesammelte Werke*, X, Basel u. Stuttgart 1967, pp. 409–11). On the group of Muri, cf. S. Reinach, 'Les survivances du totémisme chez les anciens Celtes', in *Cultes*, I, pp. 30 ff.; F. Stähelin, 'Aus der Religion des römischen Helvetien', *Anzeiger für schweizerische Altertumskunde*, XXIII (1921), pp. 17 ff.; A. Leibundgut, *Die römischen Bronzen der Schweiz, III, Westschweiz Bern und Wallis*, Mainz am Rhine 1980, pp. 66–70 n. 60, tavv. 88–94, with an additional bibliography (fundamental); *Lexicon Iconographicum*, II, 1, 1984, p. 856. It would seem that the pamphlet of the *Dissertationes Bernenses* dedicated to the *Dea Artio* never appeared. In it was to be featured an essay by A. Alföldi (cf. by this author 'Die Geburt der kaiserlichen Bildsymbolik . . .', *Museum Helveticum*, 8, 1951, p. 197 n. 22). On the evidence about Artius, see also M. L. Albertos, 'Neuvas divinidades de la antiqua Hispania', *Zephyras*, III (1952), pp. 49 ff. On the names of the bear, cf. Antoine Meillet, *Linguistique historique et linguistique générale*, Paris 1948, I, pp. 282 ff.

44. Cf. Leibundgut, op. cit., pp. 69–70; on the iconography of the seated goddess, already identified by Bachofen (*Der Bär*, p. 34), cf. Faider-Feytmans, cit., H. Möbius, *Studia varia*, W. Schiering ed, Wiesbaden 1967, pp. 140–5 ('Bronze-statuette einer niederrheinischen Matrone in Kassel'); pp. 239–42 ('Statue einer Muttergöttin aus der Normandie'). The conclusion, a trifle definitive, of Arrigoni's essay – 'The goddess Orsa, whether she be called Artemis or Artio, has definitively seen her sun set' (art. cit., p. 1019) – is refuted in the case of Artio by the perfect accord between the etymology (on which, however, Arrigoni pp. 1004–5, does not pronounce) and the most ancient version of the Muri group. In a note added to take account of Leibundgut's results, Arrigoni admits that her own interpretation of an

" 'ursine' goddess as a protector of bears' 'could in any event at most be traced back to the second arrangement of the Muri bronzes' (p. 1005 and n. 137 bis), thus excluding the first. The identification of the two strata of the group certainly simplifies the task of the interpreter, as Arrigoni acknowledges, but in a contrary direction to the one she asserts.

45. See V. Pisani, 'Ellēnokeltikai', *Revue des études anciennes*, XXVII (1935), pp. 148–50: but cf. P. Kretschmer, *Glotta*, 27 (1939), pp. 33–4.

46. Cf. Antoine Meillet, *Mémoires de la Société Linguistique de Paris*, XI (1900), pp. 316–17; E. Zupitza, 'Miscellen', *Zeitschrift für vergleichende Sprachforschung*, XXXVII (1904), p. 393 n., followed by G. Bonfante, *I dialetti indoeuropei* (1931), Brescia 1976, pp. 123 ff.

47. Cf. P. Chantraine, *Dictionnaire étymologique de la langue grecque*, Paris 1968, pp. 110, 117; W. Burkert, *Greek Religion*, expanded English trans., Cambridge (Mass.) 1985, p. 149.

48. Cf. M. Sánchez Ruipérez, 'El nombre de Artemis, dacio-ilirio . . .', *Emerita*, XV (1947), pp. 1–60 idem 'La "Dea Artio" celta y la "Artemis" griega. Un aspecto religioso de la afinidad celto-iliria', *Zephyrus*, II (1951), pp. 89–95. On the identification (now contentious) of the invaders with the Dorians cf. M. I. Finley, pp. 85 n. 3, 98–9. Scepticism as regards Sánchez Ruipérez's hypothesis (insufficiently distinct from that of V. Pisani in Arrigoni, art. cit., p. 1004 n. 136) is displayed by H. Krahe, *Die Sprache der Illyrier*, I, Wiesbaden 1955, p. 81, despite the presence of Illyrian names like *Artemo, Artemia* (Messapician *Artemes*). To these should be added the Messapician *Artos* (C. De Simone, in Krahe, op. cit., II. Wiesbaden 1964, p. 113) which R. S. Conway (in R. S. Conway, J. Whatmough and S. E. Johnson, *The Pre-Italic Dialects of Italy*, III, Cambridge, Mass., 1933, p. 6) juxtaposes to the Illyrian *Artus* and the Celtic *Artobriga*. The Illyrian parallels have already been recorded by G. Bonfante, 'Di alcune isoglosse indoeuropee "centrali"', *Rivista Greco-Indo-Italica*, XVIII (1934), pp. 223–25, vis-à-vis *arktos* (not Artemis). In the same author's communication on 'Les éléments illyriens dans la mythologie grecque' at the *Vme Congrès International des Linguistes, Bruxelles 28 août-2 septembre 1939*, reprinted 1973 (*Résumés des communications*, pp. 11–12), Artemis is not mentioned. See also A. J. van Windekens, 'Sur les noms de quelques figures divines ou mythiques grecques', *Beiträge zur Namenforschung*, 9 (1958), pp. 163–7.

49. On the debated statements in Linear B, cf. E. L. Bennett, *The Pylos Tablets*, Princeton 1955, pp. 208–09. Against the identification with Artemis, see M. Gérard-Rousseau, *Les mentions religieuses dans les tablettes mycéniennes*, Rome 1968, pp. 46–7, and above all C. Sourvinou, *Kadmos*, 9 (1970), pp. 42–7 (which adheres cautiously to Ruipérez's hypothesis); for it, A. Heubeck, *Gnomon*, 42 (1970), pp. 811–12 and T. Christidis, *Kadmos*, II, (1972), pp. 125–8.

50. Cf. Singer, *Die Artussage*, Bern and Leipzig, pp. 9 ff.; idem, 'Keltischer Mythos und französische Dichtung', in *Germanisch-romanisches-Mittelalter*, Zurich u. Leipzig 1935, pp. 170–1.

51. *'Dicunt eam habere irsutas manus, quia tetigerit eas ad maxillas, et sentiebant esse irsutam'* (*Vat. lat.* 1245, c. 299r). C. Binz (*Zur Charakteristik* pp. 150–1), disconcerted by all this 'confusion', strives to get to the bottom of it by supposing that the goddess' hands were 'coarse' (*rauhe*), 'bare' (*bloss*), and that the 'irsuti homines' (hairy men) mentioned just before by the two old women were 'naked'.

52. *'Nam pro tunc vetula sine motu locali dormire cepit, et cum se iam sompniaret versus Herodianam vehi et manus leta proiceret, versum est ex motu vas et vetulam cum confusione ad terram proiecit'* (Klapper, *Deutscher Volksglaube* p. 45).

53. See *The Night Battles*, pp. 49–51

54. See W. Deonna, *Le symbolisme de l'oeil*, Paris 1965, especially pp. 159 ff.; idem, in *Latomus*, XVI (1957), p. 205.

55. Cf. Christou, op. cit., pp. 136 ff.; Vernant, op. cit., pp. 29, 35–6.

56. See Deonna, op. cit., pp. 162–3, a propos Plutarch, *Vita Arat.* 32; cf. also W. Hertz, *Die Sage von Giftmädchen*, in *Gesammelte Abhandlungen*, F. von der Leyen ed, Stuttgart and Berlin 1905, pp. 181 ff.; S. Seligmann, *Der böse Blick und Verwandtes*, I, 1910, pp. 164 ff.; E. S. McCartney, 'The Blinding Radiance of the Divine Visage', *The Classical Journal*, XXXVI (1940–41), pp. 485–8.

57. Cf. S. Reinach, 'L'Hécate de Ménestrate', in *Cultes, mythes et religions*, II, Paris 1922, pp. 307 ff. (in regard to Pliny, *Naturalis Historia*, 36, 32); the placing of the Hecate statue in the temple of Ephesus is now discussed by Kraus, *Hekate*, Heidelberg 1960, pp. 39–40. Reinach also records (referring to Plutarch, *Parall.*, 17) the palladium of the temple of Athena at Ilion, which no man must see: Ilos, having tried to save it during a fire, was blinded by the goddess.

58. Cf. B. Spina, *Quaestio de strigibus*, in *Tractatus universi iuris*, t. XI, part 2, J. Menochio, G. Panciroli and F. Ziletti eds, Venetis 1584, p. 356v. One of these women was possibly the Agnesina burnt at the stake as a sorceress on 6 August 1523 (the first edition of the *Quaestio* dates from the same year): see the list of persons sentenced transcribed by the Ferrarese Confraternity of Death (Biblioteca Communale Ariostea, ms C1. I, n. 160 c. 16v).

59. Cf. A. Panizza, 'I processi contro le streghe del Trentino', *Archivio Trentino*, VIII (1889) p. 239; IX (1890), p. 99.

60. Ibid., p. 236.

61. Cf. Propp, *Le radici storiche* cit., pp. 114 ff., recalled very acutely vis-à-vis the hairstyle of the 'woman of the good game' by Scalera McClintock, in *Due arti della lontananza*, Naples 1979, pp. 95–6 n. 35.

62. Cf. Panizza, art. cit., pp. 244 and *passim*. The detail of the old kerchiefs that cover the head of Sprecht (Perchta) is preserved in the Austrian Alps to this day: cf. Hanika, *Bercht schlitz den Bauch auf* cit., p. 40.

63. See L. Rapp, *Die Hexenprozesse und ihre Gegner aus Tirol. Ein Beitrag zur Kulturgeschichte*, Innsbruck 1874, p. 168: Juliane Winklerin tells how Anna Jobstin, elected Queen of England (the king was the devil), came 'dressed in a beautiful golden mantle and sat down on a stone. Her face had two great eyes large as two plates (*wie zwei Teller*), and had a terrible look' (cf. the description of the 'abbess' on the throne in *The Night Battles*, p. 54). Also Katherina Haselriederin speaks of 'two eyes large as a plate' (p. 153). On Rapp's work (as Giovanni Kral pointed out to me) rests P. Di Gesaro, *Streghe nel Tirolo*, Bolzano 1983, chapter 5 (pages unnumbered).

64. Cf. *Vat lat.* 1245, c. 229v: '*cuius faciem non viderunt quia eam occultat ita quod laterali videri nequeunt, propter quasdam etc.*'

65. The possibility of comparing the *Dama de Elche* to the descriptions of the 'woman of the good game' in the trials at Val di Fiemme was first suggested to me, many years ago, by Ippolito Marmai (who subsequently informed me of his change of mind). I later discussed this problem at length with Xavier Arce, who with patience and wisdom dismantled the fanciful conjectures I proposed to him. I thank both of them; the responsibility for what follows is of course mine alone.

66. In '*La Dame d'Elche*: questions d'authenticité', *Bulletin de la Société nationale des Antiquaires de France*, 1974 (published in 1976), pp. 60–72, G. Nicolini responds, in an offhand manner, to some of these questions. But see the analysis on a piece of sculpture which is in certain respects typologically akin: F. Presedo Velo 'La Dama de Baza', *Trabajos de Prehistoria*, n.s., 30 (1973), pp. 151–203.

67. That this is a bust has been maintained by E. Kukahn, 'Busto femenino de terracotta de origen rhodio en el ajuar de una tumba ibicenca', *Archivo Español de Arqueologia*, XXX (1957), pp. 3 ff., in particular p. 13 n. 38. More cautious is A. Blanco Freijeiro, 'Die klassischen Wurzeln der iberischen Kunst'; *Madrider Mitteilungen*, I (1960), p. 116. According to Presedo Velo, art. cit., p. 192, on the base of the *Dama de Elche* the marks of an axe blow should be visible.

68. For the beginning of the fourth century as *terminus ante quem*, cf. E. Kukahn, art. cit., p. 14. According to A. García y Bellido – '¿Es la "Dama de Elche" una creación de época augústea' *Archeologia classica*, X (1958), pp. 129–32 and 'De nuevo la "Dama de Elche"' *Revista de Occidente*, 15 (June 1964), pp. 358-67 (German trans. in *Iberische Kunst in Spanien*, Mainz 1971, pp. 36–42) – the *Dama* is a pseudo- archaic work of the second century or even the first century BC: a hypothesis ignored by more recent research.

69. See, on one hand, Nicolini, art. cit.; on the other, E. Langlotz, 'Ein Artemis-Kopf', in *Studies Presented to David M. Robinson*, I, Saint Louis 1951, p. 646 and plate 65c (compared with the metope of the temple of Hera at Selinunte); Blanco Freijeiro, art. cit., p. 117, who compares the *Dama* to a fragment, possibly from Syracuse, preserved at the Vatican Museum; Kukahn, art. cit.

70. Cf. Presedo Velo, art. cit., pp. 196 ff. and Zuntz, op. cit., pp. 110-14.

71. On the funerary destination see T. Reinach, 'La Tête d'Elche au Musée du Louvre', *Revue des Études Grecques*, II (1898), p. 51 n.; independently, S. Ferri, 'Supplemento ai busti fittili di Magna Grecia (La Dama di Elche)', *Klearchos*, 19 (1963), pp. 53-61; García y Bellido, *De nuevo la 'Dama de Elche'*.

72. Cf. Blanco Freijeiro, art. cit., p. 114 and plate 24b; G. Nicolini, *Les bronzes figurés des sanctuaires ibériques*, Paris 1969, pp. 228–9; idem, *Bronces ibéricos*, Barcelona 1977, figs. 48, 49 and 51.

73. The text has already been singled out by Reinach, art. cit., p. 52.

74. See the ample documentation gathered by P. Jacobsthal, 'Zum Kopfschmuck des Frauenkopfes von Elche', *Athenische Mitteilungen*, 57 (1932), pp. 67–73 (in particular, see table X, where the Kore 666 of the Museum of the Acropolis is reproduced).

74. (bis). Cf. *L'art seythe*, B. Piotrovski ed, N. Golamina, N. Gratch, Leningrad 1986, pp. 90–1 and fig. 134, 252–53.

75. Cf. Bertolotti *Le ossa* cit., pp. 477–80.

76. Cf. J. W. Wolf, 'Irische Heiligenleben', *Zeitschrift für deutsche Mythologie*, I (1853), pp. 203 ff., on the stag resuscitated by St. Mochua Cuanus. On the miracle of the goose attributed to Saint Pharaildis, cf. *Acta Sanctorum*, I, Antverpïae 1643, pp. 170–3; L. van der Essen, 'Étude critique et littéraire sur les 'Vitae' des saints mérovingiens de l'ancienne Belgique', Louvain 1907, pp. 303–7; *Bibliotheca Sanctorum*, V, Rome 1964, coll. 457–63; on the miracle of the ox attributed to the Abbot William de Villers, in the Brabant, cf. Thomas of Cantimpré, *Miraculorum, et exemplorum memorabilium sui temporis, libri duo*, Duaci 1597, pp. 201–2. And see also W. Mannhardt, *Germanische Mythen*, Berlin 1858, p. 60.

77. These questions were formulated for the first time by Mannhardt, op. cit., p. 60 n. 1. At the end of his study 'Tors färd till utgård', *Danske Studier*, I (1910), pp. 65 ff., C. W. von Sydow inclined in favour of the Celtic hypothesis (which could be confirmed by the analogy between Thor and the Celtic god Taranis: cf. H. Gaidoz, 'Le dieu gaulois au maillet sur les autels à quatre faces', *Revue Archéologique*, XV, 1890, p. 176). The derivation from a pre-Celtic and pre-Germanic version has been advanced by L. Schmidt (cf. below p. 285, n. 154). Along the same lines, but independently, cf. also Bertolotti, op. cit.

78. For a review of the discussions of this theme, see the excellent essay by J. Henninger, 'Neuere Forschungen zum Verbot des Knochenzerbrechens', in *Studia Ethnographica et Folkloristica in Honorem Béla Gunda*, Debrecen 1971, pp. 673–702; H. J. Paproth, *Studien über das Bärenzeremoniell*, I, Uppsala 1976, pp. 25 ff. Further references will be cited as we proceed.

79. See L. Röhrich, 'Le monde surnaturel dans les légendes alpines', *Le monde alpin et rhodanien*, 10 (1982), pp. 25 ff.

80. In the *Ysengrimus*, a Latin poem of the mid-twelfth century, Saint Pharaildis is explicitly identified with Herodias, the 'sad mistress' of the night whom a third of the human species obeys (*'pars hominum meste tertia servit here'*. See *Ysengrimus*, text, translation and commentary by J. Mann, Leiden 1987, Book. II, vv. 71–94; *The Night Battles*, p. 187 n., should be corrected in regard to the interpretation of an analogous passage in the *Roman de la Rose*). In these words Jakob Grimm quite rightly sees an allusion to the beliefs in the throng of souls guided by Diana Herodias or Holda, even if he does not succeed in finding in the life of St. Pharaildis elements to justify their probable derivation from Verelde (the middle-Dutch equivalent of Frau Hilde or Holda) (*Deutsche Mythologie*, I, pp. 236–7, followed by Wesselofsky, *Alichino*, pp. 235–36). The reference to the saint was clarified by the discovery that the presumed author of *Ysengrimus*, Nivardus, probably held a position in the church of Saint Pharaildis at Gand (cf. *Ysengrimus*, E. Voigt ed, Halle a.S. 1884, I, pp. CXIX-CXX): but the identification of Pharaildis with Herodias, in the role of a nocturnal guide of souls, remains unexplained. According to the most recent editor of *Ysengrimus* (J. Mann, ed. cit., pp. 89–97) this is an invention by the poem's author, not an element derived from folkloric culture: Voigt (and hence also Grimm) supposedly misunderstood the meaning of the episode. In reality, the beginning of Book II of *Ysengrimus* suggests the opposite conclusion. In it an old peasant woman, Aldrada, is described, who kills a wolf, cuts it to pieces, walks three times around the dismembered cadaver to ensure that it does not come to life again, and finally offers a prayer to a group of saints (in part non-existent). The invocation to Pharaildis, which closes the series, jokingly alludes to the miracle of the goose: obviously, Aldrada prays to the saint so that it will not resuscitate the wolf from the bones. The same miracle provides the key, sought in vain by Grimm, to the identification (certainly predating *Ysengrimus*) of Pharaildis with Herodias.

81. See A. Dirr, 'Der kaukasische Wild-und Jagdgott', *Anthropos*, 20 (1925), pp. 139–47.

82. Cf. the documentation collected by A. Gahs in 'Kopf, Schadel-und Langknochenopfer bei Rentiervölkern', in *Festschrift . . . P.W. Schmidt*, W. Koppers ed, Vienna 1928, pp. 231–68. Gahs' attempt to interpret these rituals (along the lines of his teacher Schmidt), as sacrifices to a cosmic god or Supreme Being, has been rightly criticized by Henninger, op. cit.

83. Cf. E. J. Jessen, in the appendix (with separate pagination) to K. Leem, *Beskrivelse over Finmarkens Lapper . . . De Lapponibus Finmarchiae . . . commentatio . . . una cum . . . E. J. Jessen . . . Tractatu singulari de Finnorum Lapponumque Norvegic, religione pagana*, Kiøbenhavn 1767, pp. 52–3. This and other passages were singled out by A. Thomsen, 'Der Trug des Prometheus', *Archiv für Religionswissenschaft*, XII (1909), pp. 460–90.

84. Cf. A. I. Hallowell, 'Bear Ceremonialism in the Northern Hemisphere', *American Anthropologist*, 28 (1926), p. 142 n. 617, cited by Gahs, art. cit., p. 251.

85. See A. Salmony, *Antler and Tongue* (1954): but on the derivation of the motif from India, see the reservations of R. Heine-Geldern in *Artibus Asiae* 18 (1955), pp. 85–90. Besides M. Badner, 'The Protruding Tongue and Related Motifs in the Art

Styles of the American Northwest Coast, New Zealand and China', see the related essay by Heine-Geldern, 'A Note on Relations Between the Art Styles of the Maori and Ancient China' (the two essays are printed together under the title *Two Studies of Art in the Pacific Area*, in *Wiener Beiträge zur Kulturgeschichte und Linguistik*, XII, 1966). Heine-Geldern suggests that both Ch'angsha art and the art of the northwestern American coast derived from a neolithic style of wood carving, which towards 2500 BC had united eastern Russia, Siberia and China in a common style. The artistic links, Heine-Geldern observes (p. 60), like the linguistic ones, constitute proof: but see, on the same question, Lévi-Strauss's essay cited on p. 225 n. 54.

86. Cf. J. de Vries, *Altergermanische Religionsgeschichte*, Berlin 1957 (2nd revised edition), II, p. 115, which is based on a study by ä. Olrik.

87. The doubt is expressed by R. Karsten, *The Religion of the Samek*, Leiden 1955, pp. 24–5.

88. Cf. G. Ränk, *Der mystische Ruto in der samischen Mythologie*, Stockholm 1981, idem, 'The North-Eurasian Background of the Ruto-cult', in *Saami Pre-Christian Religion. Studies on the Oldest Traces of Religion Among the Saamis*, L. Bäckman and Å. Hultkrantz eds, Stockholm 1985, pp. 169–78; O. Pettersson, 'The god Ruto', in ibid., pp. 157–68.

89. Cf. Jessen, op. cit., p. 47.

90. On this last see Burkert, *Homo necans*, p. 235 n. 296. The hypothesis formulated here is given as demonstrated by K. Beitl, 'Die Sagen vom Nachtvolk', in *Laographia*, XXII (1965), p. 19 (as regards Thor and St. Germanus).

91. See further on, p. 220–1.

92. See C. Robert, in L. Preller, *Griechische Mythologie*, I, Berlin 1894, p. 296 n. 2 (but the reference to H. Bazin, *Revue Archéologique*, 1886, pp. 257 ff., must be dropped: cf. R. Fleischer, *Artemis von Ephesos*, Leiden 1973, pp. 329, 415). Cf. also U. Wilamowitz-Moellendorff, 'Isyllos von Epidauros', *Philologische Untersuchungen*, 9 (1886) p. 68; idem, *Hellenistische Dichtung in der Zeit des Kallimachos*, 1924, II, p. 50 and P. Kretschmer, in *Glotta*, XV (1927), pp. 177–8 (by the same author cf. also ibid., XXVIII (1939), pp. 33–4); and see also Chantraine, op. cit., I, pp. 116–17. On *artamos*, cf. J. - L. Durand, 'Bêtes greques', in M. Detienne and J.-P. Vernant, *La cuisine du sacrifice en pays grec*, Paris 1979, p. 151; in general, G. Berthiaume, *Les rôles du mágeiros*, Leiden 1982 (neither of the two mention the possible link with *Artemis*).

93. Cf. *John*, 19. 31–36 (used by Bertolotti as the epigraph of his essay 'Le ossa e la pelle dei buoi', which refers to *Exodus*, 12, 46 and *Numbers* 8, 12, implicitly assimilating Christ to the Easter lamb. On the question see below, p. 247

94. This interpretation is suggested by the verb *apokopto*, used by Pausanias: it is a synonym of *kopto*, *katakopto*, which in sacrificial language signifies precisely 'cut according to the joints' (cf. Berthiaume, *Les rôles* cit., pp. 49 and 5). See also M. Jost, 'Les grandes déesses d'Arcadie' *Revue des études anciennes*, LXII (1970), pp. 138 ff., especially pp. 150–1, which discusses the relations between this ritual and the Dionysian *diasparagmos*; and now *Sanctuaries et cultes d'Arcadie*, Paris 1985, pp. 297 ff. (on p. 335 occurs a reference to the Despoina-Artemis connection). The analogy between these figures had already been pointed out by Claus, *De Dianae antiquissima natura* cit., p. 28. But see also B. C. Dietrich, 'Demeter, Erinys, Artemis', *Hermes*, 90 (1962), pp. 129–48. The mysterious procession (animals disguised as men? men disguised as animals?) portrayed on Despoina's mantle discovered at Lykosura (today in the archaeological museum at Athens) may be connected to the issues we are discussing: cf. Kahil, *L'Artémis de Brauron* cit., pp.

94 ff., with bibliography. In general see E. Lévy and J. Marcadé, in *Bulletin de corréspondance hellénique*, 96 (1972), pp. 967–1004.

95. See Nilsson, *The Minoan-Mycenean Religion*, pp. 508–9 (and see also pp. 232–5), which refers to P. Wolters, 'Eph. Arch.' 1892, pp. 213 ff. plate 10, 1; R. Stiglitz, *Die grossen Göttinnen* cit., pp. 34–5.

96. On the existence of a female shamanism, cf. R. Hamayon, 'Is There a Typically Female Exercise of Shamanism in Patrilinear Societies such as the Buryat?', in M. Hoppál ed, *Shamanism in Eurasia* 2 vols., with continuous pagination, Göttingen 1984, pp. 307–18. According to U. Harva (Holmberg), *Les représentations religieuses des peuples altaïques*, Paris 1959, p. 309, the woman shaman was always in a subordinate position; Lot-Falck, 'Le chamanisme en Sibérie . . .', *Asie du Sud-Est et Monde insulindien. Bulletin du Centre de documentation et de recherche (CEDRASEMI)*, IV (1973), n.3, pp. 1 ff., denies it, admitting, however, that they are less numerous than men. Another subject to be considered is the question of the frequency of homosexuals and (male) transvestites among the shamans, raised by M. Z. Czaplicka, *Aboriginal Siberia*, Oxford 1914, pp. 242 ff.

97. Cf. L. Weiser (later Weiser-Aall), 'Zum Hexenritt auf dem Stabe', in *Festschrift für Maria Andree-Eysn*, 1928, pp. 64–69; idem, 'Hexe', in *Handwörterbuch des deutschen Aberglaubens*, III, Berlin u. Leipzig 1930–31, coll. 1849–51. And cf. J. Fritzner, 'Lappernes Hedenskab og Trolddomskunst . . .', *Historisk Tidsskrift* (Kristiania), IV, (1877), pp. 159 ff. In general see *Studies in Lapp Shamanism*, L. Bäckman and Å. Hultkrantz eds, Stockholm 1978. The term *gandreidh* ('magical cavalcade') appears in the Icelandic saga of Thorstein (which I have read in the Latin translation: *Vita Thorsteinis Domo-Majoris*, in *Scripta Historica Islandorum de rebus gestis veterum borealium, latine reddita. . . .*, III, Hafniae 1829, pp. 176–8). The hero, following a small boy, straddles a staff directing himself towards a subterranean beyond, whence he returns with a ring and a lid studded with jewels stolen from the sovereign of the nether world. The narrative is impregnated with Celtic motifs: cf. J. Simpson, 'Otherworld Adventures in an Icelandic Saga', *Folk-Lore*, 77 (1966), pp. 11 ff. On the shamanistic characteristics of the theme of the theft from the beyond, see below, pp. 171–2.

98. Besides *The Night Battles*, p. XXI (and see above, Introduction, p. 14) cf., from a different point of view, H. Biedermann, *Hexen. Auf den Spuren eines Phänomens*, Graz 1974, pp. 35 ff.

99. Cf. P. de Lancre, *Tableau de l'inconstance des mauvais anges et démons*, Paris 1613, pp. 253 ff., in particular p. 268. It is quite unlikely that Lancre would have read a small treatise by S. Fridrich, native of Lindau, devoted to the various forms of the temporary loss of the senses: *Von wunderlicher Verzückung etlicher Menschen welche bissweilen allein mit der Seele ohne den Leib an diesem und jenen Orth verzückt werden und wohin?* ('Of the extraordinary ecstasies of some men who sometimes go into ecstasy in this or that place with the soul and without the body'), s.1. 1592, pp. not numbered (I have consulted a copy owned by the Carolina Rediviva of Uppsala). Fridrich distinguished between the ecstasy of the prophets; that of men and pious women (for example, his mother and his grandmother); that due to natural causes (discussed in Cardano's *De varietate rerum*); that of witches, obtained by salves (recorded in Della Porta's *De magia naturali*, on which see n. 101). As regards animal metamorphosis it mentions the *Canon episcopi* and, in a marginal note, the ecstasies of Lapp enchanters. These are, however, associated with the werewolves by an author whom de Lancre knew well, C. Peucer, in a chapter devoted to ecstasy (*Commentarius de praecipuis generibus divinationum*, Francofurti ad Moenum 1607, pp. 279 ff.)

100. Michelet emphasizes de Lancre's 'lucidity', and also the elegance of his style (*La sorcierè*, Paris 1966, p. 168. A recent essay insists in a superficial manner on his prolixity and credulity (M. M. McGowan, 'Pierre de Lancre's "Tableau de l'inconstance des mauvais anges et démons": The Sabbat Sensationalised', in S. Anglo ed, *The Damned Art. Essays in the Literature of Witchcraft*, London 1977, pp. 182–201); the long section on lycanthropy is described as 'irrelevant and extraordinary'.

101. See G. B. Della Porta, *Magiae naturalis sive de miraculis rerum naturalium libri IIII*, Neapoli 1558, p. 102. In subsequent editions Della Porta replied violently to the accusations of necromancy directed at him by Bodin, quietly suppressing the passage: cf. *Magiae naturalis libri XX*, Neapoli 1589, introduction, pp. not numbered. Cf. also Tartarotti, *Del congresso notturno*, pp. 141–2, 146–7 (and Bonomo, op. cit., p. 394).

102. Cf. J. Praetorius, *Saturnalia*, Leipzig s.a., pp. 65 ff., 395 ff. and 403 ff.

103. Cf. P. C. Hilscher, *Curiöse Gedancken von Wütenden Heere, aus dem Lateinischen ins Teutsche übersetzt*, Dresden u. Leipzig 1702, p. Br. The scientific value of this small book is mistakenly denied by Meisen, *Die Sagen* cit., p. 12 n. The earliness of its date is pointed out in L. Röhrich, *Sage*, Stuttgart 1966, p. 24. Hilscher (1666–1730: see the article on him in the *Allgemeine Deutsche Biographie*) is a figure who deserves to be better studied.

104. Cf. Tartarotti, op. cit., in particular pp. 50 ff.; idem, *Apologia del congresso notturno delle lammie*, Venezia 1751, p. 159. The second piece of writing is a reply to Scipione Maffei, who had considered the *Congresso notturno* excessively timid. On the polemic (which involved other personalities), cf. F. Venturi, *Settecento riformatore*, I, Turin 1969, pp. 353 ff.

105. Cf. Keysler, *Antiquitates selectae* cit., in particular pp. 491 ff. The identification between the *Matronae* and the druidess, supported by Keysler, has been correctly refuted by Martin (*La religion des Gaulois* cit., II, p. 154). In general see S. Piggott, *The Druids*, New York 1985, pp. 123 ff.

106. Cf. A. Schöne, *Götterzeichen, Liebeszauber, Satanskult*, Munich 1982, p. 134, which refers to G. Witkowski, *Die Walpurgisnacht im ersten Teile von Goethes Faust*, Leipzig 1894, pp. 23 ff. (which I have not seen).

107. Cf. Grimm, *Deutsche Mythologie*, II, p. 906. The core of this page dates back to precisely twenty years previously: cf. 'Das Märlein von der ausschleichenden Maus', in *Kleinere Schriften*, VI, Berlin 1882, pp. 192–6. For later additions by the author, see Grimm op. cit., III, pp. 312–13.

108. De Lancre was, however, known to Heine: cf. Mücke, *Heinrich Heines Beziehungen* cit., p. 116.

109. On Odin, cf. in general de Vries, op. cit., II, pp. 27 ff. In a polemic with D. Strömbäck, *Sejd*, Lund 1935, Georges Dumézil has tried to minimize the presence of shamanistic features in the figure of Odin: cf. *Gli dèi dei Germani*, It. trans. Milan 1979, pp. 53 ff. and *Du mythe au roman*, Paris 1970, pp. 69 ff.; see, however, the revision implicit in *Gli dei sovrani degli indoeuropei* (Italian translation 1985), pp. 174 ff., where reference is made to 'shamanistic practices and claims' and to texts in which 'an almost Siberian shamanism is predominant'. Of a different opinion is J. Fleck, 'Odinn's Self-Sacrifice – A New Interpretation', *Scandinavian Studies*, 43 (1971), pp. 119–42 and 385–413; idem, 'The "Knowledge-Criterion" in the Grimnismál: The Case against "Shamanism"', *Arkiv för nordisk filologi*, 86 (1971), pp. 49–65. On Guntram, fundamental is H. Lixfeld, 'Die Guntramsage (AT 1645 A). Volkserzählungen vom Alter Ego und ihre schamanistiche Herkunft', *Fabula*, 13 (1972), pp. 60–107, with a rich bibliography; see also R. Grambo, 'Sleep as a

Means of Ecstasy and Divination', in *Acta Ethnographica Academiae Scientiarum Hungaricae*, 22 (1973), pp. 417–25. Both overlook L. Hibbard Loomis 'The Sword-Bridge of Chrétien de Troyes and its Celtic Original', in *Adventures in the Middle Ages*, New York 1962 (the essay dates from 1913), pp. 19–40, above all pp. 39–40. The legend's shamanistic components are denied by J. Bremmer, *The Early Greek Concept of the Soul*, Princeton 1983, pp. 132–5, which refers to other studies, among which cf. in particular A. Meyer-Matheis, *Die Vorstellung eines Alter Ego in Volkserzählungen*, Freiburg 1973 (diss.). pp. 65–86. A comparison with Odin's shamanistic metamorphoses had been proposed by F. von der Leyen: cf. 'Zur Entstehung des Märchens', *Archiv für das Studium der neueren Sprachen und Literaturen* 113, N.F. 13 (1904), pp. 252 ff. A version of the Guntram legend circulated in the Ariège at the beginning of the fourteenth century, in the form of an *exemplum*: cf. Le Roy Ladurie, *Montaillou*, pp. 608–9.

110. Cf. Hibbard Loomis, art. cit.; B. Beneš, 'Spuren von Schamanismus in der Sage "Buile Suibhne"', *Zeitschrift für celtische Philologie*, 28 (1961), pp. 309–34 (other studies of the same theme are less reliable). The analogy between druids and shamans is rejected as irrelevant by de Vries, *I Celti* cit., p. 268; of a contrary opinion is Piggott, op. cit., pp. 184–5.

111. Cf. *The Night Battles*, pp. 19–20; and see also de Lorris and de Meun, *Le Roman de la Rose*, IV, p. 229, vv. 18445–48, regarding the followers of 'Lady Habonde'.

112. Cf. Olaus Magnus, *Historia de gentibus septentrionalibus*, Romae 1555, pp. 115–16; Peucer, op. cit., p. 143ʳ. Both the passages are quoted, together with some more recent evidence, by J. Scheffer, *Lapponia*, Francofurti and Lipsiae 1674, pp. 119 ff. (chapter XI: *De sacris magicis et magis Lapponum*).

113. I should have cited Grimm's page mentioned above in connection with what I wrote in *The Night Battles*, pp. 58–61.

114. See the present author's 'Présomptions', pp. 352 ff. for an overall synthetic picture of the various currents of research. It will be set forth in detail, as we proceed, in the pages that follow. However, I must correct an inaccurate statement, to the effect that Propp did not know L. Radermacher's *Das Jenseits im Mythos der Hellenen*.

3

To Combat in Ecstacy

1. In 1692 at Jürgensburg in Livonia an eighty-year-old man named Thiess, whom the townsmen considered an idolater, confessed to the judges interrogating him that he was a werewolf. Three times a year, he said, on St Lucy's night before Christmas, the night of St John, and of the Pentecost, the werewolves of Livonia go into hell, 'at the end of the sea' (he later corrected himself: 'underground'), to fight with the devil and the sorcerers. Women also fight with the werewolves: but not young girls. The German werewolves go to a separate hell. Similar to dogs (they are the dogs of God, Thiess said), and armed with iron whips, the werewolves pursue the devil and sorcerers, who are armed with broomsticks wrapped in horse tails. Many years before, Thiess explained, a sorcerer (a peasant named Skeistan, now dead) had broken his nose. At stake in the battles was the fertility of the fields: the sorcerers steal the shoots of the grain, and if they cannot be wrested from them there will be famine. However, that year the Livonian and the Russian werewolves had both won. The harvest of barley and of rye was going to be abundant. There was also going to be enough fish for everyone.

In vain the judges tried to induce the old man to admit that he had made a pact with the devil. Thiess obstinately continued to repeat that the worst enemies of the devil and the sorcerers were werewolves like himself: after death, they would go to paradise. Since he refused to repent he was sentenced to ten whiplashes.[1]

We can imagine the judges' bewilderment at finding themselves confronted by a werewolf who protected the cross instead of attacking the cattle. Several modern scholars have reacted in a similar way. In fact, old Thiess's stories were not confined to disrupting an ancient stereotype. They also wrought havoc with a relatively recent interpretative schema, which included the werewolves in a wider mythical complex, substantially Germanic, intrinsically bellicose, hinging on the theme of 'the army of the dead' (*Totenheer*). Testimonies concerning this mythical complex have been accepted for centuries as proof of the existence of rituals performed by groups of men consumed by demonic fury, convinced they impersonated the army of the dead.[2] Now, Thiess's reference to the battles for fertility, also

153

fought by women, seemed to contradict the first point; the extravagance of details, such as the battle fought against the witches 'at the end of the sea', seemed to contradict the second. Hence, the impulse more or less subtly to undermine the testimony. The confessions of the old werewolf were judged to be echoes of real events, mingled with fragments of myths, lies, boasting; or a disorderly jumble of superstitions and rituals; or, again, some mixture of elements from sagas and remote memories of actual life experiences.[3] Confronted by this eccentric and incoherent Baltic variation, an attempt was made to reassert the original purity of the Germanic warrior myth revolving around the 'army of the dead'.[4]

2.   As early as the fifth century BC, Herodotus alluded to men capable of periodically transforming themselves into wolves. In Africa, in Asia, on the American continent analogous beliefs have been found, concerning temporary metamorphoses of human beings into leopards, hyenas, tigers, and jaguars.[5] It has been supposed that in these parallel myths, dispersed over so vast a spatial and temporal area, an aggressive archetype profoundly rooted in the human psyche is expressed, transmitted by heredity, in the form of psychological disposition, from the Paleolithic age on down.[6] Obviously, this is a totally undemonstrated hypothesis. But the general perplexity that it provokes is accompanied by other, more specific queries. In the case that we are discussing, for example, the image of werewolves as protectors of fertility blatantly contradicts the putative aggressive nucleus of the myth. What value should be attributed to this isolated, apparently typical testimony?

The verse and prose romances, the sagas, the penitential books, the theological and demonological treatises, the philosophical and medical dissertations that speak of *loup-garous, werwölfen, lupi-mannari,* werewolves, *lobis-homem* and so on, are numerous and well known. But in the medieval texts – especially in the literary ones – werewolves are portrayed as innocent victims of fate, if not indeed as beneficent figures. Only towards the middle of the fifteenth century is the contradictory aura surrounding these ambiguous beings obliterated by the superimposition of a ferocious stereotype – that of the werewolf, devourer of flocks of sheep and infants.[7]

Approximately during this same period the hostile image of the witch crystallized. This is not a mere coincidence. In his *Formicarius* Nider speaks of male witches who transform themselves into wolves; in the Valais trials, at the beginning of the fifteenth century, the defendants confessed that they had temporarily assumed the shape of wolves when attacking the cattle. From the very first evidence about the Sabbath, the connection between witches and werewolves therefore appears to be quite intimate. But here too anomalous, perhaps even late confessions, such as that of Thiess, allow us to scratch the surface of the stereotype, bringing a deeper stratum to light.

3.   The interpretative difficulties raised by Thiess's confessions disappear as soon as we compare the battles against male and female witches described

by him with those fought in their ecstasies by the *benandanti*. As we have seen, this term designated in the Friuli, between the sixteenth and seventeenth centuries, those (primarily women) who maintained that they periodically participated in processions of the dead. But the same name was also given to other individuals (predominantly men) who declared that, armed with bunches of fennel stalks, they periodically fought for the fertility of the fields, against male and female witches armed with canes of sorghum. The name, the sign that materially identified both types of *benandanti* (having been born with a caul); the period (the four Ember days), during which they performed the feats for which they were destined; the state of lethargy or catalepsis that preceded them – in both cases, these were identical. The spirits of the *benandanti* (men or women) left the inanimate body for a space of time, sometimes in the shape of a mouse or a butterfly, sometimes astride hares, cats or other animals, to journey in ecstasy to the procession of the dead or the battle against male and female witches. In both cases, the journey of the soul was compared by the *benandanti* themselves to a temporary death. At the end of the journey there was the encounter with the dead. In the processions they appeared in a Christianized form, as purging souls; in the battles, in an aggressive and probably more archaic guise as *malandanti* – enemies of fertility assimilated to male and female witches.[8]

But the battles for fertility are not the only point of contact between the werewolf Thiess and the *benandanti*. In the Slavic world (from Russia to Serbia) it was believed that anyone born with a caul was destined to become a werewolf. A contemporary chronicle recounts that a magician begged the mother of Prince Vseslav of Polock, who died in 1101 after having briefly been the King of Kiev, to tie to the child the membrane in which he had been wrapped at birth, so that he might always have it on his person. That is why, the chronicler comments, Vseslav was so ruthlessly bloodthirsty. In *Igor's Tale* he is portrayed as an actual werewolf. Similar characteristics are attributed to the protagonist of another *bylina* (probably one of the most ancient): Volch Vseslav' evič, who was able to transform himself not only into a wolf, but also a falcon and an ant.[9]

The Friulian *benandanti*, at their mothers' wish, wore around their neck the caul in which they had been born.[10] But their future as peasants did not promise glorious, princely enterprises: only the obscure, irresistible impulse to fight periodically 'in spirit' for the harvest, astride or in the guise of animals, wielding bundles of fennel against male and female witches. It is to this sort of battle that old Thiess insisted he had gone armed with an iron whip and transformed into a wolf. True enough, he did not say he had fought them 'in spirit'; of ecstasy or catalepsis he said not a word (we don't even know whether he had been born with a caul). But his stories must certainly be related to a mythical, not a ritual dimension – not unlike the declaration made by the *benandante* Maria Panzona, who stated that she had gone to paradise and to hell *in soul and body*, accompanied by her uncle in the shape of a butterfly.[11] In both cases we sense the attempt to describe an ecstatic experience perceived as absolutely real.

4.   The trial against Thiess is an extraordinary document; however, it is not unique. Other testimonies confirm partially its contents.

In a treatise entitled *Christlich Bedencken und Erinnerung von Zauberey* ('Christian consideration and memory on magic') which appeared in Heidelberg in 1585, the author, who concealed his real name – Hermann Witekind – under the pseudonym of Augustin Lercheimer, discussed in a chapter devoted to this 'whether witches and magicians transformed themselves into cats, dogs, wolves, donkeys, etc.' The answer he gave – that it was a matter of diabolical delusion – was not particularly original, although even among the erudite the contrary thesis was widespread: that the transformation of witches and werewolves into animals was an incontrovertible physical phenomenon. The singularity of the *Christlich Bedencken* is to be sought elsewhere. It was based in part on a conversation that Witekind, Livonian by birth and a professor at the University of Riga (subsequently at Heidelberg), had had with a werewolf from his region. (Old Thiess, as we are bound to remember, had also been born in Livonia, the land of the werewolves.) In fact, some time before, Witekind had visited the governor of the province, who had arranged for him to meet an incarcerated werewolf. 'The man,' Witekind remembered, 'behaved like a crazy person, he laughed, skipped about, as if he were from a place of pleasure and not a prison.' The night before Easter (he told his astonished interlocutor) he had transformed himself into a wolf: after freeing himself from his shackles, he had escaped through the window, heading for an immense river. But why had he returned to prison? they had asked him. 'I had to do it, the master wishes it.' About this master (Witekind noted retrospectively) he spoke with great emphasis. 'An evil master', they had objected. 'If you know how to give me a better one, I will follow him,' the man had answered. In the eyes of Professor Witekind, author of books on history and astronomy, the nameless werewolf appeared an incomprehensible being: 'he knew about God as a wolf might. To see him and listen to him was painful.'[12] Perhaps the werewolf thought that about his own mysterious master, Witekind knew just as much as a professor. Certainly, the prisoner's merry insolence brings to mind the assurance, full of sarcasm, with which the *benandanti* sometimes held their own against inquisitors.[13]

An echo of this conversation can be found in a fleeting reference by Caspar Peucer to the dialogue between a 'homo sapiens' (certainly Witekind) and a werewolf, eruditely defined as a 'rustic Lycaon' from the mythic King of Arcadia transformed into a wolf by Zeus because of his cannibalism.[14] The reference appears in the expanded reprint of Peucer's *Commentarius de praecipuis generibus divinationum*, which was published in 1560, i.e., five years *before* the *Christlich Bedencken*. This apparent chronological oddity is easily explained: around 1550 Witekind, then a student, had spent some time at Wittenberg, where he had evidently told Peucer about his encounter with the anonymous werewolf.[15] Peucer's Latin text is far removed from the almost ethnographic freshness of the conversation reported, at the distance of so many years, by Witekind. The brashness of that peasant werewolf, a precious index of psychological and cultural estrangement, has vanished into thin air in the *Commentarius*. But despite the pedantic allusion to Lycaon, Peucer's treatise transmits a series of details (only partially reproduced in Witekind's work) which contradict the current image of werewolves. They boast of deterring witches and of fighting them when they have changed themselves into butterflies; they assume (or at least believe they assume) the guise of a wolf during the twelve days between Christmas and Epiphany, compelled so to do by the apparition of a lame child; they are driven in their thousands by a tall man armed with an iron whip towards the bank of an enormous river, which they cross without getting wet, because the man separates its waters with a lash of his whip; they attack cattle but cannot do any harm to human beings.[16] Another professor at the University of Wittenberg lectured on these topics: Philip Melanchthon (who was Peucer's father-in-law). From one of his listeners we learn that as a source he had quoted a letter received from 'Hermannus Livonus', a 'man most respectable' and totally reliable.[17] In compiling his *Commentarius* Peucer in all likelihood also had before him the letter written to Melanchthon by the Livonian Hermann Witekind.[18] Through this precious informant, close, by birth and language, to Baltic folk traditions, we have therefore received a piece of information – the hostility of the werewolves towards witches – which substantially coincides with the confessions of Thiess, attenuating the anomaly. We discern a background of beliefs that are far removed from the negative stereotype of the werewolf.

5.   From the Scythians and the Greeks living in Scythia, Herodotus had picked up a rumour (which he repeated without giving it credence) concerning a population that he knew only indirectly: the Neuroi. For a number of days each year they changed into wolves. Who the Neuroi were and where they lived, we do not know with certainty. In the sixteenth century, it was thought that they had lived in a region corresponding to Livonia; today, some scholars consider them a proto-Baltic population.[19] But this supposed ethnic continuity, as yet undemonstrated, does not explain why analogous beliefs in werewolves are found in heterogeneous cultural milieux – Mediterranean, Celtic, Germanic, and Slavic – over a very long span of time.

We might ask ourselves whether these really are analogous beliefs. Certainly, the ability to transform oneself into a wolf is periodically attributed to groups of very different sizes. To entire populations, such as the Neuroi, according to Herodotus; to the inhabitants of a region, like Ossory in Ireland, according to Giraldus Cambrensis; to specific families, such as the Anthi in Arcadia, according to Pliny; to individuals fated to this by the Parcae (identifiable with the *Matres*),[20] as Burchard of Worms wrote at the beginning of the eleventh century, condemning the belief as superstitious. However, this variety is accompanied by a number of recurrent elements.

First of all, the transformation is always temporary, though of varying duration; nine years in Arcadia, according to Pausanias and Pliny; seven years, or for a specific period every seven years, in medieval Ireland; twelve days in the Germanic and Baltic countries. Secondly, it is preceded by gestures of a ritual character: the werewolf undresses and hangs his clothes on the branches of an oak (Pliny) or sets them on the ground, urinating all around them (Petronius); then he crosses a pond (in Arcadia, according to Pliny) or a river (in Livonia, according to Witekind).[21]

In this crossing and the attendant gestures a rite of passage has been identified: more precisely, an initiatory ceremony, or the equivalent of the crossing of the infernal river that separates the world of the living from that of the dead.[22] The two interpretations are not mutually contradictory, provided we recognize that death is the passage par excellence and that every ritual of initiation hinges on a symbolic death.[23] It is well known that in the ancient world the wolf was associated with the world of the dead: for example, in the Etruscan tomb at Orvieto, Hades is depicted with the head of a wolf covering his head.[24] Various features lead us to extend this connection beyond the spatial, chronological and cultural confines of the ancient Mediterranean world. The time favoured by the werewolves for their forays in the Germanic, Baltic and Slavic countries – the twelve nights between Christmas and Epiphany – corresponds to that in which the souls of the dead went roaming.[25] In ancient Germanic law the proscribed – expelled from the community and considered symbolically dead – were referred to by the term *wargr* or *wargus*, i.e. 'wolf'.[26] A symbolic death – the ecstasy – can be detected behind the stories of the old werewolf Thiess, so similar to those of the *benandanti* of the Friuli. Animal transformation or the cavalcade astride animals represented the temporary departure of the soul from the inanimate body.[27]

6. In his *Historia de gentibus septentrionalibus* (1555) Olaus Magnus, Bishop of Uppsala, after having described the bloody attacks on men and beasts perpetrated during the night of Christmas by the werewolves in Prussia, Livonia and Lithuania, added: 'they enter into the rooms where beer is stored, empty the barrels of wine and mead, and then they place the empty vessels one on top of the other in the middle of the cellar.'[28] In this sort of behaviour he saw a characteristic trait distinguishing men transformed into wolves from actual wolves. As to the physical reality of their metamorphosis, he entertained not the slightest doubt, and reconfirmed it against Pliny's authority. A century later, the dissertations on werewolves discussed at the Universities of Leipzig and Wittenberg advanced, on the basis of information collected in the Baltic countries, a thesis that concurred with Witekind's: the metamorphosis was preceded by a profound sleep or ecstasy and hence must always, or almost always, be considered purely imaginary (natural or diabolical, depending on the interpreters).[29] Several modern scholars have chosen to follow the opinion of Olaus Magnus, and have used his account to

bolster the interpretation already mentioned in connection with old Thiess's stories: the alleged werewolves were, in reality, young followers of sectarian associations, formed by enchanters or by individuals disguised as wolves, who identified with the army of the dead in their rituals.[30] This last connection is incontrovertible, but it must be understood in a purely symbolic sense. The incursions of Baltic werewolves into the cellars will have to be set alongside those performed in 'spirit' by the *benandanti* of the Friuli, who 'climbed astride the barrels, drank with a pipe' – wine, naturally, rather than the beer and mead their colleagues drank in the north. In both we perceive the echo of a myth – the myth of the unquenchable thirst of the dead.[31]

7.   We set out from the thirst of the sorcerers in the Valais, of the *benandanti* of the Friuli, of the dead of the Ariège in order to reconstruct a layer of beliefs which later, in partial and distorted form, merged in the Sabbath. We have returned to the same point, following a different route. Through the evidence about the nocturnal battles fought by werewolves and *benandanti* against male and female witches, we begin to glimpse a symmetrical, primarily male version of the predominantly female ecstatic cult analyzed up to this point.

In the Friuli the goddess who led the cohorts of the dead appears in a single testimony:[32] but both versions were present. The subterranean analogy linking them was underscored by the uniqueness of the term – *benandanti* – which designated those who behaved ecstatically. This is an almost unique instance (only that of the Rumanian *călusari*, as we shall see, is comparable). The evidence about the followers of the nocturnal divinities came from a Celto-Mediterranean environment, which inscribed the theme of the resurrection of animals from their bones in a much vaster framework. As we shall see, testimony on the night battles sketches a different geography: more fragmentary and, at least at first sight, incoherent. The Friuli will then have to be considered as a sort of border country in which the two, habitually severed versions of the ecstatic cult were superimposed and merged (see map 3).

Hitherto it has been the inquisitors, preachers and bishops who have guided our research; the analogies that their usually infallible eyes had detected by following the thread of Diana, 'goddess of the pagans', suggested a preliminary organization of the material. Yet the ecstatic battles have left very faint traces in canonistic as well as demonological literature.[33] In the only region in which they were confronted by these beliefs – the Friuli – the inquisitors considered them an incomprehensible local variant of the Sabbath. The impossibility of recourse to the comparative efforts of the persecutors has hindered not only the interpretation, but the very reconstitution, of the documentary series. The morphological strategy, which momentarily flashed before us the possibility of a Eurasian substratum beneath the ecstatic cult of the nocturnal goddess, was the only one available.

Recognizing a formal resemblance is never a clear-cut operation. The dates on which Thiess and the *benandanti* fought their ecstatic battles were different, as were the weapons used by either side against the male and female witches. But behind these superficial divergences we recognize a profound similarity, because both cases involve (a) periodic battles, (b) fought in ecstasy, (c) for the purposes of fertility, (d) against male and female witches. The bundles of fennel wielded by the *benandanti*, and the iron whips brandished by the werewolves, must be understood not as different but as isomorphic elements. The connection, documented in the sphere of Slavic folklore, between being born with a caul and becoming werewolves, then appears as an unanticipated intermediary link of a formal character.[34] In this case it is reinforced by a historical datum: the presence of a Slavic component in the Friuli's ethnic background and culture.

8. A series of beliefs tracked down in Istria, Slovenia, Croatia, and all along the Dalmatian coast down to Montenegro, analogous to those about the *benandanti* as protectors of the harvest, accords perfectly well with this configuration.[35] As early as the seventeenth century, Monsignor G. F. Tommasini remarked, in a somewhat confused manner, that in Istria people believe

and cannot escape the fantasy, that there are some men, born under certain constellations, and in particular those who are born closed in a certain membrane (they call these *chresnichi*, and those others *vucodlachi* [i.e., vampires], who go by night in spirit on the crossroads and also into the houses to inspire fear or do damage, and that they are accustomed to congregating together at some of the most famous crossroads, particularly at the time of the four Ember weeks, and there fight against one another for the abundance or scarcity of all sorts of products. . . .[36]

No mention is made of women here. The *kresnik* (or *krestnik*) in Istria and Slovenia, called *krsnik* in Croatia, corresponds in northern Croatia to the *mogut*, in Southern Dalmatia to the *negromanat*, in Bosnia, Herzegovina and, above all, Montenegro to the *zduhač*. He is almost invariably a man.[37] Generally, he is marked by some peculiarity connected with his birth. The *kresnik* and the *zduhač* are born with the caul; the *negromanat* has a tail; the *mogut* is the son of a woman who has died giving birth to him or has given birth to him after an unusually long pregnancy. They are all destined to fight, sometimes for fixed periods such as the Ember weeks or Christmas night, against sorcerers and vampires, chasing away evil spells or protecting the cross. These combats are savage collisions between animals, boars, dogs, oxen, horses, often of contrasting colours (the witches black, their adversaries white or dappled). The animals are the spirits of the contenders. At times small animals are involved: of the *kresniki* it is said that, while they sleep, their spirit issues from their mouth in the shape of a black fly.

It is also said that the male witches (*strigoi*) are born with a caul: but the envelope in which they are wrapped is black or red, whereas that of the *kresniki* is white. In Istria the midwives sew this envelope around the little *kresniki*, under their armpits; in the island of Krk (Veglia) it is dried and then mixed with food for the future *kresnik* to eat. Then, at the age of seven (more rarely at eighteen or twenty-one), the nocturnal battles commence. But about them the *kresniki* (like the *benandanti*) must preserve secrecy.

At Krk it is said that every people, every stock is protected by a *kresnik* and threatened by a *kudlak* (vampire). Elsewhere the hostile witches are aliens: in the Dalmatian island of Dugi Otok they are the Italians, near Dubrovnik the Venetians, in Montenegro the Turks or those who come from across the sea. More generally, they are what is most unmitigatedly hostile: the unplacated dead, jealous of the living – the vampire (*vukodlak*), whose terrifying features are confused with those of the witch among the western Slavs.[38] For that matter, in the Friuli male and female witches, men and women of flesh and blood, are obscurely assimilated to the *malandanti*, that is, the vagrant souls of the restless dead.[39]

9. In the case of *benandanti* and *kresniki* formal analogies and historical connections converge. But evidence from different sources complicates the picture. In the throng of witches and enchanters who populate Hungarian folklore there stand out, owing to their singularity, a number of figures who have been linked to Oriental, and probably extremely ancient, traditions. The most important is the *táltos*. This name, possibly of Turkish origin, designated the men and women tried for witchcraft as early as the end of the sixteenth century.[40] But the *táltos* strenuously denied the accusations levelled at them. A woman, András Bartha, tried at Debrecen in 1725, declared that she had been named leader of the *táltos* by God himself: because God forms the *táltos* when they are still in their mother's womb, then he takes them under his wing and makes them fly through the sky like birds to fight against male and female witches 'for the dominion of the sky'.[41] A number of later testimonies, collected almost down to the present day, confirm and enrich this fundamental juxtaposition. They also modify it: women *táltos* become increasingly rare. The *táltos* are chiefly men, marked since birth by some physical peculiarity, such as being born with teeth, with six fingers on one hand, or, more rarely, with the caul.[42] When very young they are silent, melancholy, extremely strong, greedy for milk (then, as adults, for cheese and eggs). At a certain age (usually seven, sometimes thirteen) they have a vision: an older *táltos*, in the shape of an animal – invariably a stallion or bull. A struggle begins between the two: if the youngster succumbs, he remains half a *táltos*; if he prevails, he becomes a full *táltos*. In other localities it is said that the male *táltos* initiate the girls (provided they are virgins) and vice versa. As a rule, the initiation is preceded by a 'sleep' that lasts three days; during this time the future *táltos* 'hides himself'. At times he dreams that he is being chopped to pieces, or he passes extraordinary tests (climbing very tall trees, for example). The *táltos* go into combat periodically (three times a year, or once every seven years, etc.) in the shape of stallions, bulls or flames. Usually,

they engage each other, more rarely male and female witches, sometimes enemies of alien origin, for example Turks or Germans, who are likewise transformed into animals or flames, but of a different colour. Before changing into an animal, the *táltos* is overcome by a sort of heat and babbles disconnected words, entering into contact with the world of the spirits. Often the battle takes place among the clouds and to the accompaniment of storms; whoever wins ensures abundant harvests for seven years or for the following year for his side. As a result, when there is a drought, the peasants bring money and gifts to the *táltos* so that they may cause rain to fall. For their part, the *táltos* extort milk and cheese from the peasants, threatening to unleash a storm or boasting of their feats: discovering hidden treasures, healing those struck by evil spells, identifying the witches in the village by banging a drum (or, alternately, a sifter). But theirs is a vocation they have not elected: they cannot resist the call. After a while (at the age of fifteen, but often much later) they cease their activities.

From this schematic account the analogy between the *táltos* and *benandanti* clearly emerges. In both cases we find the initiation or the call to work by an older follower, the animal metamorphoses, the struggles for fertility, the ability to discover witches and cure the victims of evil spells, the conscious-ness of the ineluctability of their extraordinary mission and its justification, sometimes cast in religious terms.[43] Even though they pertain to this analogy, the *kresniki* seem to figure, not only formally but also geographically, as an intermediate term: for example, they are born with a caul like the *benandanti* but, like the *táltos*, they fight in animal form against other *kresniki*, likewise transformed into animals.[44] But the undeniable formal compactness of the series contrasts with the heterogeneity of the phenomena it includes; the Hungarian *táltos* evidently carry us outside the Indo-European linguistic milieu.

10.   Fully part of it, by contrast, are the Ossetians, as the Orientalist Julius Klaproth recognized at the beginning of the nineteenth century, while travelling through the mountains of the northern Caucasus. Klaproth especially studied the language of these very remote descendants from the Scythians of antiquity, the Alans and Roxolans of the Middle Ages, identifying it as having an Iranian origin: but he also took an interest in the religion, which he defined as 'a bizarre mixture of Christianity and ancient superstition'.[45] He described their intense devotion to the prophet Elijah, whom they consider their supreme protector.[46] Goats are sacrificed to him in caves, and they eat their meat: then they spread the skins under a large tree and worship them, particularly during the prophet's feast day, that he may deign to ward off hail and grant a rich harvest. The Ossetians often visit these caves to intoxicate themselves with the smoke from the *rhododendron caucasicum* which plunges them into sleep: the dreams that ensue are considered to be omens. However, they also have professional soothsayers

who live on the sacred cliffs and predict the future in exchange for gifts. 'Among them,' Klaproth observed,

> there are also some old men and women who, on the eve of St Sylvester, fall into a sort of ecstasy, remaining motionless on the ground as though asleep. When they awake, they say they've seen the souls of the dead, sometimes in a great swamp, alternatively, astride pigs, dogs or rams. If they see a soul gathering wheat in the fields and bringing it to the village, they detect the omen of an abundant harvest.[47]

The research conducted towards the end of the nineteenth century by Russian folklorists has confirmed and enriched this evidence. In the period between Christmas and New Year, the Ossetians affirm, some individuals, leaving their body fast asleep, go in spirit to the land of the dead. This land is a great meadow, called *burku* in Digor dialect and *kurys* in the Iron dialect; those who have the ability to visit it are called, respectively, *burkudzäutä* and *kurysdzäutä*. To reach the meadow of the dead they use the most varied mounts: doves, horses, cows, dogs, children, scythes, brooms, benches and bowls. The souls who have undertaken this journey many times already possess the requisite vehicles; the inexperienced steal them from their neighbours. In consequence, with the approach of Christmas, the Ossetians address solemn prayers to Uazilla (i.e., Elijah) to protect children, horses, dogs and household objects from the thieving incursions of 'astute and impure people', against whom they invoke the prophet's curse. When they arrive at the great meadow, the inexperienced souls allow themselves to be attracted by the perfume of the flowers and fruits scattered upon it: and so they incautiously pluck a red rose that causes a cough, a white rose that causes a cold, a large red apple that causes a fever, and so on. By contrast, the more experienced souls catch the seeds of the wheat and of other fruits of the earth, as promise of a rich harvest. As they flee with their booty, the souls are pursued by the dead, who try to shoot them with arrows: the hunt ends only on the threshold of the village. The arrows do not cause wounds, but black spots which are incurable; some of the *burkudzäutä* heal by themselves; some die after long suffering. Those who bring the seeds of the earth's fruits back from the world of the dead describe their feats to their fellow villagers, who then express their gratitude. The souls who bring back illnesses endure the curses of those who catch the fever or cough.[48]

11. Other neighbouring populations appear to have shared analogous beliefs. In 1666, on the twentieth day of the tenth month (according to the Gregorian calendar 28 April), the Turkish geographer and traveller, Evliyâ Celebi, happened to be in a Circassian village. From its inhabitants he learned that that was 'the night of the *Kara-Kondjolos* (vampires)'. As he later recounted the story, he had left his encampment with eighty people. Suddenly, he had seen the sorcerers of the Abkhaz appear: they crossed the

sky astride uprooted trees, terracotta vases, axes, mats, cart wheels, oven shovels, and so on. From the opposite side, hundreds of Circassian sorcerers (*Uyuz*) had immediately risen in flight, with dishevelled hair and gnashing teeth, emitting fiery rays from their eyes, nose, ears and mouth. They rode on fishing boats, horse or oxen carcasses, enormous camels; they brandished serpents, dragons, the heads of bears, horses and camels. The battle had lasted six hours. At a certain stage pieces of their mounts had begun to rain down from the sky, frightening the horses. Seven Circassians and seven Abkhaz witches had plunged to the ground, fighting and trying to suck each other's blood. The village's inhabitants had come to the aid of their champions, setting fire to their opponents. At cock crow the contenders had dissolved, becoming invisible. The ground was strewn with corpses, objects and the carcasses of animals. In the past Evliyâ had not believed such stories. Now he was obliged to change his mind: the battle had really taken place, as the thousands of soldiers who had witnessed the scene could confirm. The Circassians swore that they had seen nothing of the kind for forty or fifty years. Usually the combatants were five or ten in number: after engaging each other on the ground, they took flight.[49]

It will be remembered that the Balkan *kresniki* and the Livonian werewolves periodically fought against alien witches. And the aerial cavalries which Evliyâ, in his grandiloquent and fantastic account, attributes to the Abkhaz witches, are more or less identical to those of the Ossetian *burkudzäutä* (and not those of their opponents, as we would expect).[50] However, it is not proven that among the Circassians, the issue of the battle between witches was the abundance of the harvest. For the sake of prudence, let us restrict ourselves to the Ossetian documentation: the resemblances with the phenomena we are investigating leap to the eye. Ecstasy; the flight to the realm of the dead astride an animal (to which are added here children and domestic utensils); the struggle with the dead (elsewhere identified with the witches) to wrest away the seeds of fertility: all this clearly connects the Ossetian *burkudzäutä* to the *benandanti* of the Friuli, the Baltic werewolves like Thiess, to the Balkan *kresniki*, the Hungarian *táltos*. In one case at least the structural analogy even contains superficial coincidences. A young Friulian cowherd, Menichino da Latisana, tried in 1591, recounted that some years before, on a winter night during the Ember weeks, he had dreamt that he was accompanying the *benandanti* (a dream that was destined to be repeated three times every year thereafter):

And I was afraid and it seemed to me I was in a wide meadow, large and beautiful, and it smelled oily, that is, it gave off a good smell, and it seemed to me that in it were many flowers and roses. . . .

There, amidst the perfume of roses – he was unable to see them, everything was enveloped in smoke – he had fought the witches and won, wresting a good harvest from them.

This meadow was the 'meadow of Josafat', Menichino said: the meadow of the dead overflowing with roses, which the souls of the *burkudzäutä* visited in ecstasy. Still according to Menichino, it was possible to reach it only in a state of temporary death: 'if anyone had turned over our bodies while we were outside . . . we would have died.'[51]

12. The ecstatic experiences of these *burkudzäutä* are echoed in the Ossetian epic of the Narts. Soslan, one of the heroes of this cycle of legends, visits the country of the dead. It is a plain where all the cereals of the world grow and all the animals of the world, domesticated or wild, roam. Along the river are young girls who dance the dance of the Narts. Before them are tables laden with exquisite foods. Soslan barely manages to escape from this place of delights: the devils (who here replace the dead), instigated by his antagonist, Syrdon, pursue him, hurling flaming arrows at him.[52] Thus, in the Caucasus as in the West, the theme of the journey to the world of the dead also nourished the ecstasies of a number of predestined individuals and a series of poetic compositions.[53] Perhaps this is not a coincidence. It has been suggested that the singular parallelisms between the Ossetian epic and the Celtic epic (re-elaborated in the romances of the Arthurian cycle) presuppose precise historical relationships.[54]

But more about all this later. First we must examine more closely the series we have constructed.

13. The single element which all the components of this series have in common is the capacity to enter into periodic ecstasies. It seems reasonable to postulate an ecstatic experience behind the accounts of old Thiess (an experience that during the seventeenth century, at any rate, was less and less often attributed to werewolves).[55] During the ecstasy, all the figures whom we have considered fight for the fertility of the fields: only among the *táltos* does this theme enjoy less prominence.[56] All of them, except for the *burkudzäutä*, are predestined for ecstasy by some physical sign (being born with a caul, with teeth, with six fingers on one hand, with a tail); or by some circumstance linked to their birth (the mother dead in childbirth, an exceptionally long pregnancy). Among all of them (here too except for the *burkudzäutä*) the men seem to predominate. For the *benandanti*, *kresniki* and *táltos*, the vocation commences at a variable age, between seven and twenty-eight. To *benandanti* and *táltos* the announcement of vocation is given by another member of the sect, in spirit or animal shape, respectively. The ecstasy is accompanied by egress from the soul in the shape of small animals (mice or flies for *benandanti* and *kresniki*); or by transformation into larger animals (boars, dogs, oxen, horses for *kresniki*; birds, bulls, stallions for *táltos*; wolves, or, exceptionally, dogs, donkeys, horses for werewolves[57]); by a journey astride animals (dogs, hares, pigs, cocks for the *benandanti*; dogs, doves, horses, cows for the *burkudzäutä*); by a journey riding children or various objects (benches, mortars, scythes, brooms for the *burkudzäutä*); by a

transformation into flame (*táltos*) or smoke (*benandanti*). The ecstatic sleep coincides with calendar dates – sometimes precise, such as the four Ember weeks (*benandanti, kresniki*) or twelve days (werewolves, *burkudzäutä*); at other times vaguer, such as three times a year or once every seven years (*táltos*).[58] For the *kresniki* and *táltos*, the enemies of the fertility of the fields against whom the battles are fought are the *kresniki* and *táltos* of other communities, or, indeed, other peoples; for the *benandanti, kresniki* and werewolves (the latter specify that their opponents are transformed into butterflies), they are the male and female witches; for the *burkudzäutä*, they are the dead.

All this information more or less directly derives from the very protagonists of these ecstatic cults: *benandanti*, werewolves, *kresniki*, *táltos* and *burkudzäutä*. As we have seen, they present themselves as beneficent figures, possessors of an extraordinary power. But in the eyes of the surrounding community this power was inherently ambiguous, apt to be transformed into its opposite. The belief that the *burkudzäutä* could, out of negligence, bring back illnesses instead of prosperity from their nocturnal journeys, highlights a symbolic ambivalence that probably also characterized the diurnal behaviour of these figures. The *benandanti* attracted resentment and hostility with their claim that they could identify the witches in the neighbourhood; the *táltos* practised blackmail vis-à-vis the peasants, threatening to unleash storms.

14. The series of which we are speaking might be compared to an accumulation of energy distributed in an uneven manner, rather than to an object with well-defined contours. It is indeed true that every component of the series is characterized by the simultaneous presence of several distinctive elements or traits: (a) the periodic battles, (b) fought in ecstacy, (c) for the sake of fertility, (d) against male and female witches (or their stand-ins, the dead).[59] Around this solid nucleus rotate other elements, whose presence is fluctuating, contingent: they are sometimes absent, sometimes present in an attenuated form. Their superimposition and intersection impart to the figures constitutive of the series (*benandanti, táltos*, etc.) a family likeness.[60] Hence the almost irresistible temptation to integrate analogically a record which in other respects seems full of lacunae. In Romania, for example, it is said that *strigoi* are born with the caul (or, alternatively, with a tail); when they become adult, they don it and become invisible. Transformed into animals or astride horses, brooms, or barrels, they move in spirit to the meadow at the end of the world (at the end of the sea, said old Thiess) where no grass grows. Here they resume human form and fight with cudgels, axes, and sickles. Having warred all night, they become reconciled. Despite the absence of references to the battle for fertility, the approximation to the series that we are discussing seems extremely close.[61]

At other times we glimpse a more complex relationship of morphological proximity. In various parts of Corsica (the Sartenais and the surrounding mountains, the Niolo) it is said that specific persons called *mazzeri* or *lanceri*, *culpatori*, *culpamorti*, *accacciatori*, *tumbatori*, are in the habit, of roaming in spirit during sleep, alone or in groups through the countryside – especially near streams of water, of which they are, however, afraid. They may be either men or women; but the men have greater power. Driven by an irresistible force, they attack animals (wild boars, pigs, but also dogs, etc.), killing them: the men with rifle shots or a cudgel or knife; the women by tearing them to pieces with their teeth. By turning its muzzle, the *mazzeri* momentarily recognize in the killed animal a human face – the face of a fellow villager, sometimes even that of a relative. This person is destined to die within a short time. The *mazzeri* (usually they are imperfectly baptized persons) are the messengers of death: the innocent instruments of fate. Some play their role joyfully; others with resignation; yet others seek forgiveness from the priests for the killings perpetrated in their dreams. However, these killings do not exhaust the dream-activities of the *mazzeri*. In certain localities it is believed that once a year, generally during the night of 31 July/1 August, the *mazzeri* of neighbouring villages fight each other. These are usually communities separated by geographical obstacles (for example, a hill) or by ethnic differences. In the battles normal weapons are used; only in one village (Soccia) do the contenders employ branches of asphodel, the plant which, according to the ancients, grew in the meadows of the nether world. The community to which the defeated *mazzeri* belong will, in the course of the following year, suffer the greater number of deaths.[62]

This last motif is possibly also traceable in an obscure passage of the confessions of Florida Basili, a *benandante* interrogated in 1599 by the Inquisitor of Aquileia and Concordia:

> I pretended [she said, lying] that I had been born with the caul, that I am compelled to go out every Thursday night, and that we fight the witches on St Christopher's square, and that wherever the banner dips, there someone dies.[63]

Certainly the *mazzeri*, like the *benandanti*, go out at night 'in spirit'; and like them, at least in one case, they brandish plants as weapons, though stalks of asphodel, and not bunches of fennel. Instead of male and female witches, their opponents are (as with the *kresniki* and the *táltos*) other *mazzeri*. But rather than being pursued by the dead, like the *burkudzäutä*, the *mazzeri* pursue those who are about to die.

Faced by this partially contradictory tangle, we might be tempted to doubt that the *mazzeri* belong to the series outlined. And yet, it does not seem forced to assimilate the recurrent dreams of the *mazzeri* to ecstatic swoons, and to consider the stake of their dream battles – inflicting on the antagonist the maximum number of dead in the coming year – a formal variant of the combat for the fertility of the fields. The simultaneous presence of the two elements identified as pertinent features of the series would then allow us positively to resolve the classificatory question that we have formulated.

15.   At this point we could conclude that at least the cases lacking any reference to ecstasies and battles for fertility should be excluded from the analysis. But sometimes, as the account of the Turkish traveller, Evliyâ Celebi, suggests, this decision does not follow automatically.

In 1587 a midwife from Monfalcone, Caterina Domenatta,

> having delivered a woman whose child came out feet-first . . . persuaded the mother that if she did not want the child to become a *benandante* or a witch she should put it on a spit and turn it I don't know how many times over the fire.

For this advice, picked up from the 'old wives', the Domenatta woman earned denunciation to the Inquisitor of Aquileia and Concordia by the parish priest, who accused her of being 'a guilty sorceress'. Thus, in the same region it was believed that being born feet-first was similar to being born with a caul – a peculiarity that predestined the new-born to venture out at night with male and female witches.[64] To follow or to fight them? 'So that they will not fall into witchery' (i.e., the witches' Sabbath), Domenatta said, echoing the denunciation's ambiguous formulation. It is not impossible that her words represent a comparatively early record of the forced assimilation of the *benandanti* to the witches, their adversaries. But certain customs alive until not long ago in Istria refer to an initially undifferentiated vocation of those whose fate it is to be born clothed: at Momiano the midwife comes to the window shouting 'A *kresnik* has been born, a *kresnik*, a *kresnik*!', to prevent the child becoming a witch (*štrjdlak*).[65]

On the other hand, the ritual of 'piercing with the spit' and turning around the fire ('three times', the Domenatta woman specified) the child born feet-first, is apparently unknown in Istria and the Friuli alike.[66] However, we find evidence of it in the middle of the seventeenth century on the island of Chios. It is described, in words of harsh condemnation for such superstitions, by the celebrated scholar Leone Allacci, who was born in Chios and spent his childhood there. Children born on Christmas Day (but Allacci had first referred to the period between Christmas Eve and the last day of the year) are predestined to become *kallikantzaroi*: bestial beings, subject to periodical furies that precisely coincide with the last week in December, during which they run around dishevelled and unable to find peace. They pounce on anyone they see, overwhelm them and with their nails (which are clawlike and very long because they never cut them) scratch their face and chest, asking: 'Hemp or lead'? If the victim answers 'hemp', he or she is released; if the answer is 'lead', the victim is savaged and left on the ground half-dead. To prevent a child becoming a *kallikantzaros*, Allacci continues, he must be held over a fire by the heels, so as to scorch the soles of his feet. The child howls and cries because of the burns (immediately after they will be soothed with a bit of oil): but the people believe that in this way the nails are shortened, thus rendering the future *kallikantzaros* inoffensive.[67]

This conclusion – whether shared by the inhabitants of Chios or suggested by Allacci, we don't know – seems dictated by a desire to explain a custom already perceived as incomprehensible.[68] In the meantime all traces of it have been lost. The figure of the *kallikantzaros*, by contrast, is very much alive in the folklore of the Peloponnese and the Greek islands.[69] The *kallikantzaroi* are monstrous beings, black, hairy, sometimes gigantic, sometimes very small, usually equipped with animal-like limbs: donkeys' ears, goatish paws, equine hooves. They are often blind or lame; they are invariably males, provided with enormous sexual organs. They appear during the twelve nights between Christmas and Epiphany, having remained underground throughout the year, intent on sawing the tree that supports the world; but they never manage to bring this enterprise to completion. They roam about frightening people; enter houses, eating the food and sometimes pissing on it; they wander through the villages guided by a lame leader, the 'great *kallikantzaros*', riding roosters or horses. Their ability to transform themselves into all sorts of animals is renowned. In short, they are supernatural beings: but it is also said (according to a tradition previously recorded in a slightly different form by Allacci) that the children born between Christmas and Epiphany become *kallikantzaroi*. Similar notoriety surrounds (or did) the inhabitants of southern Euboea.

According to one etymological conjecture that has met with many objections, the term *kallikantzaros* derives from *kalos-kentauros* (beautiful centaur). In antiquity, the centaurs, portrayed as half-men and half-horses were in fact only an equine variation – the *hippokentauroi* – of a larger mythological family that also included centaurs in the shape of donkeys (*onokentauroi*) and, in all probability, in the shape of wolves (*lykokentauroi*). There is no evidence of this last term: however there is evidence (in Messenia, in southern Laconia and Crete) for the term *lykokantzaroi*, as a synonym of *kallikantzaroi*. Thus, like the centaurs from whom they derive, the latter are figures born from the remote belief that certain individuals are capable of periodic metamorphosis into animals.[70] To this interpretation has been counterposed others, sometimes based on more or less plausible etymological conjectures. For instance, a derivation from *kantharoi* (cockroaches) has been suggested, or an identification with the souls of the dead, since the *kallikantzaroi* are offered food during the twelve nights for which they roam abroad.[71] This last element, together with the physical peculiarity linked to their birth, and their capacity to transform themselves into animals, seems to indicate assimilation of the *kallikantzaroi* – simultaneously human and mythical beings – to the series we have constructed. We should then have to revise the criteria we have established (a posteriori), given that the *kallikantzaroi* are not known to be associated with either ecstasy or the battle for fertility.

16. The Circassian witches, the Romanian *strigoi*, the Corsican *mazzeri*, and especially the Greek *kallikantzaroi* thus bring us to a fork in the road. If we exclude them from the analysis, we have a series defined by the presence of two elements: ecstasy and the battle for fertility. By including them, we have a series characterized by the superimposition and intrication of a network of resemblances which, at various times, contains some of the phenomena we have considered (but never all of them). The first type of classification, called monothetic, will appear more rigorous to those who (also on aesthetic grounds) prefer research into phenomena with clearly defined contours. The second, called polythetic, broadens the research in an arguably indeterminate manner, at any rate, in directions difficult to predict.[72]

This is the criterion that we have decided to adopt, for reasons which will become clearer during the course of the study. Certainly, any classification contains an arbitrary element: the criteria that guide it are not given. But it does not seem inconsistent to combine this nominalistic awareness with the realistic claim to uncover, through purely formal connections, factual relations which have left scant or non-existent documentary traces.[73]

17. The presence of the *táltos* (like the more contentious presence of the Circassian witches) demonstrates, as has already been suggested, that the battles fought in ecstasy for the sake of fertility are not a cultural trait confined to the Indo-European linguistic milieu. If we try to follow this morphological thread we once again arrive at the shamans. For that matter, at various times in the past the *benandanti*, the werewolves, the *táltos* (and, through these, the *kresniki*), the *burkudzäutä*, the *mazzeri* have all been compared to them: never, however, the entire series constructed here.[74] It will be remembered that a shamanic substratum emerged from our analysis of beliefs linked to the nocturnal goddess. This convergence confirms the extremely intimate links between the two versions of the ecstatic cult that we are reconstructing.

Ecstasy, in fact, has for some time been identified as a characteristic trait of the Eurasian shamans.[75] In the middle of the sixteenth century, Peucer described the Laplandic 'magicians' emerging from catalepsy in these words: 'Twenty-four hours having passed, with the return of the spirit, as though from a deep sleep, the inanimate body awakens with a moan, almost as though called back to life from the death into which it had fallen.'[76] Thirty years later, the author of an anonymous testimony about the *benandanti*, Toffolo di Buri, 'herdsman' from a village near Monfalcone, used overwhelmingly similar terms: 'When he is forced to go into combat he is overcome by a very deep sleep, and sleeping belly up as the spirit issues forth, one hears him emit three moans, as oftentimes do those who are dying.'[77] In both cases sleep, lethargy, catalepsy, explicitly compared to a state of temporary death, destined, however, to become definitive should the spirit delay re-entering the body.[78]

Onto this analogy are grafted others, which become more specific as we proceed. The ecstasies of the Eurasian shamans (Lapp, Samoyed, Tungus) are replete with battles. Sunk deep in catalepsy, men fight men, and women fight women: their souls collide in animal form (usually reindeers) until one of them succumbs, bringing about the infirmity and death of the defeated shaman.[79] In the *Historia Norwegiae* written in the thirteenth century, it is recounted that the spirit (*gandus*, literally 'cudgel') of a Laplandic shaman, fallen into ecstasy and transformed into a whale, was mortally wounded by the *gandus* of a hostile shaman, which had assumed the shape of sharply pointed poles.[80] Still in Lapland a number of sagas collected during the present age describe two shamans (*no'aidi*) who fight a duel after having fallen into ecstasy, seeking to attract to their side the greatest possible number of reindeer.[81] How can we fail to be reminded of the battles for the prosperity of the harvest waged in animal form by *kresniki* and *táltos*, by the old werewolf Thiess – or, astride animals, by *benandanti* and *burkudzäutä*? We are bound to conclude that one and the same mythical pattern has been adopted and adapted by societies very different from one another in ecological, economic and social respects. In communities of nomadic shepherds the shamans fall into ecstasy in order to procure reindeer. In agricultural communities their colleagues do the same to procure – depending on climate and latitude – rye, wheat, grapes.

But in one crucial respect these analogies prove to be imperfect. The catalepsy of the Eurasian shaman is public; that of the *benandanti*, the *kresniki*, the *táltos*, the *burkudzäutä*, the *mazzeri*, is always private. Occasionally, it is witnessed by the wives; more rarely by the husbands; but these are exceptional cases. Not one of these protagonists makes his ecstasy the centre of a spectacular ceremony such as the shamanic session.[82] Almost as a kind of compensation, during their public catalepsies the Eurasian shamans fight isolated duels: during their private catalepsies, their European counterparts participate in veritable battles.

18. This divergence stands out starkly against a homogeneous background. In fact, amongst the shamans we rediscover many of the characteristics we encountered in the protagonists of the battles fought in ecstasy.[83] Sometimes the analogy becomes an identity. In certain parts of Siberia one becomes a shaman by heredity; but among the Yurak Samoyeds the future shaman is marked out by a physical peculiarity – being born with a caul, like a *benandante* or a Slavic werewolf.[84] More often we find isomorphisms or family resemblances. For the shamans too their vocation commences at a variable age: generally, it coincides with sexual maturity, but sometimes it is much later.[85] The revelation of vocation is often accompanied by psychological disorders: a complex phenomenon which some European observers previously simplified in a pathological direction, speaking of 'arctic hysteria'.[86] In the European sphere, individual reactions seem more varied, ranging from the despair of the unknown woman in Friuli, who had turned to a witch to be freed from the compulsion to 'see the dead', to the pride of

171

benandante Gasparo, who showed the inquisitor his hatred for witches, to the joy or guilt experienced, depending on the case, by the *mazzeri*, murderers in their dreams.[87] In a Christian society the position of these individuals was necessarily more problematic. But precisely because the cultural contexts are so profoundly different, the resemblances between the ecstasies of the Eurasian shamans and those of their European counterparts are striking. The soul of the shaman, transformed into a wolf, bear, reindeer, fish, or astride an animal (horse or camel), which in the ritual is symbolized by the drum, abandons the inanimate body. After a period of time, now longer now shorter, the shaman comes out of the catalepsy to report to the spectators what he has seen, what he has learnt, what he has done in the other world: the Laplandic 'magicians', Olaus Magnus recounted, even brought back a ring or knife as tangible proof of the journey they made (fig. 12).[88] In many cases a representation of the realm of the dead has been recognized on the shamans' drums.[89] But the protagonists of the ecstatic cult sparsely recorded on the European continent likewise considered themselves – and were considered – mediators between the living and the dead. In both cases the animal metamorphoses and the cavalcades astride animals symbolically express ecstasy: the temporary death indicated by the egress of the soul from the body in animal form.

19.   These last features recur, albeit in distorted form, in the trial held in the Valais at the beginning of the fifteenth century and then in innumerable confessions by witches and sorcerers from one end of Europe to the other. By contrast, with the exceptions we have already noted, the theme of battles for fertility disappears, or almost. We occasionally detect its distorted echo in the minutest details. In 1532 three women – Agnes Callate, Ita Lichtermutt, and Dilge Glaserin – were tried for witchcraft. They lived in Pfeffingen, a locality then in the domain of the Bishop of Basel. One after the other, apparently 'without being subjected to duress or torture', they related in almost identical terms the following story. On a spring day, while they sat with another woman under a peach tree, they saw some ravens who asked them what they wanted to eat. Cherries, said one; birds, said another; wine, said the third. Accordingly, they explained in the course of the trial, that year there would be lots of cherries, lots of birds, lots of wine. Three devils – their lovers – arrived bearing food and wine; they feasted and made love together; then the women returned home on foot. The trial records have evidently reached us in abbreviated and impoverished form.[90] Nevertheless, the incongruous connection between the requests made of the ravens and the prosperity of the crops and game, seems to echo ancient themes, grafted onto a diabolical pattern which is by now consolidated. Thus, when we learn that in a completely different time and place (1727, at Nosovki near Kiev) a certain Semyon Kalleničenko confessed that he was born a vampire; that he knew how to recognize which women were witches and which were not; that as a vampire he had been immune to the attacks of witches until the age of twelve;

that he had then gone to the Sabbath in which the witches participated, organized militarily – we recognize in this Ukranian vampire a relative of the Hungarian *táltos*, the Dalmatian *kresniki*, the *benandanti* of the Friuli.[91] Fragmentary testimonies, separated in time and space, which once again demonstrate the depth of the cultural stratum that we have sought to uncover.

Notes

1. The trial records have been published by H. von Bruiningk, 'Der Verwolf in Livland und das letzte im Wendeschen Landgericht und Döptschen Hofgericht i.J. 1692 deshalb stattgehabte Strafverfahren', in *Mitteilungen aus der livländischen Geschichte*, 22 (1924), pp. 163–220. I develop here the interpretation sketched in *The Night Battles*, pp. 28–32. I had missed the declarations (irrelevant) of J. Hanika, 'Kultische Vorstufen des Pflanzenanbaues', *Zeitschrift für Volkskunde*, 50 (1953), pp. 49–65, and H. Kügler, 'Zum "Livländischen Fruchtbarkeitskult"', ibid. 52 (1955), pp. 279–81. An earlier testimony on Baltic werewolves occurs in Birkhan, 'Altgermanistische Miszellen. . .', in *Festgabe für O. Höfler*, Vienna 1976. pp. 36–7. For some folkoric connections cf. A. Johansons, 'Kultverbände und Verwandlungskulte', *Arv*, 29–30 (1973–74), pp. 149–57 (courteously pointed out to me by Erik af Edholm, whom I thank here).

2. See especially O. Höfler, *Kultische Geheimbünde der Germanen*, Frankfurt a. Main 1934. On the ideological matrix (Nazi) and the widespread fortune of this book among scholars such as S. Wikander, K. Meuli (who subsequently took a more critical attitude) and Georges Dumézil, see the present author's 'Germanic Mythology and Nazism. . .', in *Clues, Myths*. cit., pp. 126–45. Against the prevailing tendency to accept or reject Höfler's thesis en bloc, it should be emphasized that in reality it is divided into three points. The sagas and the general evidence on the 'wild hunt' (*Wilde Jagd*) or 'the army of the dead' (*Totenheer*) had (a) a mythico-religious content; (b) expressed a heroic or bellicose myth, substantially Germanic, (c) must be interpreted as rites practised by organizations or secret groups of generally masked young men, pervaded by ecstatic fervour, who felt that they were impersonating the spirits of the dead. In my opinion only point (a), which goes back at least to Grimm, has good grounds: the objections of an anti-Nazi folklorist like F. Ranke ('Das wilde Heer und die Kultbünde der Germanen. . .', 1940; now in *Kleine Schriften*, H. Rupp and E. Studer eds, Bern 1971, pp. 380–408) which considers the testimonies on the 'wild hunt' as hallucinations, pure and simple, are completely unacceptable. Point (b), inspired by the philo-Nazi orientation of Höfler, interprets the documentation in unilateral fashion, isolating the bellicose themes from a wider context which also includes themes related to fertility. Point (c) exaggerates, also for obvious ideological reasons, the suggestive hypotheses formulated by L. Weiser in *Altgermanische Jünglingsweihen* (Bühl [Baden] 1927), reaching, as pointed out by W. Krogmann (in *Archiv für das Studium des neueren Sprache*, 168, Band, 90, 1935, pp. 95–102) completely absurd conclusions, dictated by the preconceived notion of systematically interpreting the descriptions of the processions of the dead and the forays of the werewolves as testimonies of real events. On this current of research see the timely critical observations of E. A. Philippson, 'Die Volkskunde als Hilfswissenschaft der germanischen Religionsgeschichte', *The Germanic Review*, XIII (1938), pp. 273–51. Höfler's influence is evident in F. Cardini, *Alle radici della cavalleria medievale*, Florence 1981.

3. Cf. respectively, Höfler, op. cit., pp. 345 ff.; W. E. Peuckert, *Geheimkulte*, Heidelberg 1951, pp. 109–17; L. Kretzenbacher, *Kynokephale Dämonen südosteuropäischer Volksdichtung*, Munich 1968, pp. 91–5. In polemic with my essay, 'Freud, l'umo dei lupi e i lupi mannari' (in *Miti emblemi spie* pp. 239–51), in which I anticipate some themes of this book, see.R. Schenda, 'Ein Benandante, ein Wolf, oder Wer?', *Zeitschrift für Volkskunde*, 82 (1986), pp. 200–2 (other interventions appear in the same booklet).

4. Though from different viewpoints, the interpretation of Thiess' confessions in the ritual key is shared by Hanika, art. cit., and H. Rosenfeld, 'Name und Kult der Istrionen (Istwäonen), zugleich Beitrag zu Wodankult und Germanenfrage', *Zeitschrift für deutsches Altertum und deutsche Literatur*, 90 (1960–61), p. 178.

5. Dated, but still useful, is the body of studies by W. Hertz, *Der Werwolf*, Stuttgart 1862; R. Andree, *Ethnographische Parallelen...*, I, Stuttgart 1878, pp. 62–80; C. T. Stewart, 'The Origin of the Werewolf Superstition', *University of Missouri Studies, Social Science Series*, II, 3, 1909. A systematic bibliography that improves on the attempt of F. Black, 'A List of Books relating to Lycanthropy', *New York Public Library Bulletin*, 23 (1919), pp. 811–15, is lacking. Studies of specific characters will be cited as we proceed. Among those devoted to extra-European phenomena, see, for example, B. Lindskog, *African Leopard Men*, Stockholm 1954.

6. See the book (very erudite but utterly unconvincing) by R. Eisler, *Man into Wolf*, London 1951; on the author, cf. the ferocious portrait drawn by Gershom Scholem, *From Berlin to Jerusalem*, New York 1980, pp. 126–132. In a perspective analogous to that of Eisler (still substantially Jungian), see also Burkert, *Homo necans*, pp. 31, 37, 42 etc. (but on p. 77 Thiess' confessions are understood, as usual, as testimony to ritual behaviour).

7. Cf. L. Harf-Lancner, 'La métamorphose illusoire: des théories chrétiennes de la métamorphose aux images médiévales du loup-garou', *Annales E.S.C.*, 40 (1985), pp. 208–26; to the studies on *Bisclavret* add W. Sayers, 'Bisclavret' in Marie de France: a Reply', *Cambridge Medieval Celtic Studies*, 4 (Winter 1982), pp. 77–82 (with a rich bibliography). According to L. Harf-Lancner, the contradictory physiognomy of werewolves in medieval texts would seem to be inspired by the attempt to temper a metamorphosis unacceptable to Christian thought: the folklore tradition, by contrast, insisted on the 'bestial and inhuman behaviour of the werewolf' (art. cit., pp. 200–21). But this same folkloric tradition should be regarded as the result of a historical process, not as an immutable datum.

8. Cf. on all this *The Night Battles*.

9. Cf. The splendid essay by Roman Jakobson and M. Szeftel, 'The Vseslav Epos', *Memoirs of the American Folklore Society*, 42 (1947), pp. 13–86, in particular pp. 56–70; to be combined with Jakobson and G. Ružičić, 'The Serbian Zmaj Ognjeni Vuk and the Russian Vseslav Epos,' *Annuaire de l'Institut de philologie et d'histoire orientales et slaves*, X (1950), pp. 343–55. Both essays are taken into account by the very useful book by N. Belmont, *Les signes de la naissance*, Paris 1971, pp. 57–60. In Italian see the *Cantare della gesta di Igor*, R. Poggioli ed, Turin 1954, and the collection *Le byline*, by B. Meriggi ed, Milan 1974, pp. 41–9 ('Volch Vselav' evič').

10. Cf.*The Night Battles*, pp. 15–16. The custom is also documented in Lapland: cf. T. I. Itkonen, *Heidnische Religion und späterer Aberglaube bei den Finnischen Lappen*, Helsinki 1946, pp. 194–5.

11. Ibid., p. 103.

12. Cf. *Augustin Lercheimer (Professor H. Witekind in Heidelberg) und seine Schrift wider den Hexenwahn*, C. Binz ed, Strassburg 1888, pp. 55 ff. Elsewhere the same person is called Wilken.

174

13. See *The Night Battles*, p. 5.
14. See above, p. 127.
15. See O. Clemen, 'Zum Werwolfsglauben in Nordwestrussland', *Zeitschrift des Vereins für Volkskunde*, 30–32 (1920–22), pp. 141–4.
16. Cf. C. Peucer, *Commentarius de praecipuis generibus divinationum*, Witebergae 1560, pp. 140ᵛ-45ʳ (these pages are missing in the first edition, and printed in 1553).
17. Cf. *Corpus Reformatorum*, XX, Brunsvigae 1854, col. 552. The identification (missed by Binz) of the author of the letter with Witekind is made by Clemen, art. cit. Both this essay and the *Christlich Bedencken* by Lercheimer have been generally neglected by scholars of this subject: among the exceptions are von Bruiningk, art. cit., and K. Straubergs, 'Om varulvarna i Baltikum,' *Studier och Oeversikter Tillägrade Erik Nylander...*, 'Liv och Folkkultur', s.B. 1 (1951), pp. 107–29, especially pp. 114–16. But see now, from another point of view, F. Baron, 'The Faust Book's Indebtedness to Augustin Lercheimer and Wittenberg Sources', *Daphnis*, 14 (1985), pp. 517–45 (with further bibliography).
18. The detail of the lame child who guides the werewolves, lacking in *Christlich Bedencken*, is also missing in the account of Melanchton's lesson (cf. *Corpus Reformatorum*, XX, cit.): Peucer will have taken it from Witekind's letter or directly from him in conversation. On it, see below p. 239 ff.
19. Besides Herodotus, *Histories* (IV, 105), cf. Peucer, op. cit., p. 141r. Bodin affirmed that a letter in his possession from a German to the High Constable of France described similar phenomena: 'Posterity has in the meanwhile verified many things written by Herodotus, which appeared incredible to the ancients' (*Demonomania de gli stregoni*, It. trans., Venice 1597, p. 176). M. Gimbutas, *Bronze Age Cultures in Central and Eastern Europe*, The Hague 1965, p. 443, refers to Herodotus and to linguistic and archaeological evidence not further identified.
20. See above, p. 105.
21. The passages of Herodotus (IV. 105), Pausanias (VIII. 2,6) and of Pliny (VIII. 81) are commented upon, in what is to my mind a reductionist perspective, by G. Piccaluga, *Lykaon*, Rome 1968. On Petronius cf. the fine essay by M. Schuster, 'Der Werwolf und die Hexen. Zwei Schauermärchen bei Petronius', *Wiener Studien*, XLVIII (1930), pp. 149–78, which escaped R. O. James, 'Two Examples of Latin Legends from the Satyricon', *Arv*, 35 (1979), pp. 122–5 (sketchy but useful for its mention of parallel themes in the Scandinavian ambit). For Ireland, cf. Hertz, op. cit., p. 133, which refers to Giraldus Cambrensis, *Topographia Hibernica*, II, 19 (*Opera*, V, London 1887, by J. F. Dimock ed, pp. 101 ff.), published not later than 1188, in which is related the encounter that took place five or six years before between a priest with a man and a woman transformed into wolves; Eisler, op. cit., pp. 138–9 n. 111. For Burchard of Worms, cf. Migne, *Patrologia Latina*, CXL, 971. On Witekind, see above, pp. 156–7.
22. See respectively R. Buxton, 'Wolves and Werewolves in Greek Thought', in *Interpretations of Greek Mythology*, pp. 60–79, and Schuster, art. cit., p. 153 n. 14 (not mentioned in the preceding essay).
23. On the first point, it seems symptomatic that the discovery of 'rites of passage' occurred in the researches of Robert Hertz on double burial (see below, p. 56, n. 25). As to the second, it will suffice to consult Propp, *Le radici storiche*.
24. Cf. the fundamental essay of W. H. Roscher, 'Das von der "Kynanthropie" handelnde Fragment des Marcellus von Side', *Abhandlungen der philologisch-historischen Classe der königlich Sächsischen Gesellschaft der Wissenschaften*, 17 (1897), in particular pp. 44–5, 57; on p. 4 the overall debt to Rohde's *Psyche* is recognized. The latter replied with an important review, which appeared posthumously in the

Berliner Philologische Wochenschrift, 18 (1898), coll. 270–76 (included in *Kleine Schriften*, Tübingen and Leipzig 1901, II, pp. 216–23). Roscher's indications were developed by L. Gernet, '*Dolon le loup*', now in *Anthropologie de la Grèce antique*, Paris 1968, pp. 154–71. On Hades' head covering, cf. S. Reinach, article on 'Galea', in C. Daremberg and E. Saglio, *Dictionnaire des antiquités grecques et romaines*, II, 2, Paris 1896, p. 1430; other bibliographic indications can be found in A. Alvino, 'L'invisibilità di Ades', *Studi storico-religiosi*, V (1981), pp. 45–51, which seems, however, to ignore Gernet's essay. There is copious documentation on the link between the wolf (and the dog) and the world of the dead in Kretschmar *Hundestammvater und Kerberos*, 2 vols., Stuttgart 1938.

25. Cf. W. E. Peuckert, in *Handwörterbuch des deutschen Aberglaubens*, 9, Berlin 1938–41, coll. 783–84; and Höfler, op. cit., pp. 16–18. It should be noted that on the island of Guernsey the *varou* is a nocturnal spirit, identifiable with the dead (*varw* in Breton): cf. E. MacCulloch, *Guernsey Folk Lore*, London 1903, pp. 230–1.

26. See the important essay by L. Weiser-Aall, 'Zur Geschichte der altergermanischen Todesstrafe und Friedlosigkeit', *Archiv für Religionwissenschaft*, 30 (1933), pp. 209–27. Cf. besides: A. Erler, 'Friedlosigkeit und Werwolfsglaube', *Paideuma*, I (1938–40) pp. 303–17 (strongly influenced by Höfler); G. C. von Unruh, 'Wargus, Friedlosigkeit und magisch-kultische Vorstellungen bei den Germanen', *Zeitschrift für Rechtsgeschichte*, Germ. Abt., 74 (1957), pp. 1–40; T. Bühler, 'Wargus-friedlos-Wolf', in *Festschrift für Robert Wildhaber*, Basel 1973, pp. 43–8. Against this interpretative line, cf. H. Siuts, *Bann und Acht und ihre Grundlagen im Totenglauben*, Berlin 1959, pp. 62–7; M. Jacoby, *Wargus, vargr, 'Verbrecher', 'Wolf'. Eine sprach- und rechtsgeschichtliche Untersuchung*, Uppsala 1974 (which seeks, unconvincingly, to demonstrate that the medieval and post-medieval testimonies on werewolves have no link with the folkloric culture because they were heavily influenced by classical and Christian notions; see also the astringent review by J. E. Knirk in *Scandinavian Studies*, 49, 1977, pp. 100–03). On the roots of the connection between wolves and outlaws in ancient Greece and Roman antiquity, cf. J. Bremmer, 'The "suodales" of Poplios Valesios', *Zeitschrift für Papyrologie und Epigraphik*, 47 (1982), pp. 133–47; and see now J. Bremmer and H. M. Horsfall, *Roman Myth and Mythography*, London 1987 (University of London, Institute of Classical Studies, Bulletin Supplement 52), pp. 25 ff.

27. In a penetrating review of Kretzenbacher, op. cit., R. Grambo proposes to link the complex beliefs in werewolves 'to an ecstatic technique widespread in the Eurasian ambit' (*Fabula*, 13, 1972, pp. 202–4).

28. Cf. Olaus Magnus, *Historia de gentibus septentrionalibus*, Romae 1555, pp. 442 ff.

29. Cf. E. Strauch, *Discursus physicus lykanthropiam quam nonnulli in Livonia circa Natalem Domini vere fieri narrant, falsissimam esse demonstrans . . . praeses M. Michael Mej Riga Livonus*, Wittenbergae 1650; F.T. Moebius, *De transformatione hominum in bruta . . . sub praesidio J. Thomasii*, Leipzig 1667. In general, around the middle of the seventeenth century, the theme of werewolves became a great fashion in Germany: this is shown, for example, by *Cyllenes facundus, hoc est problema philosophicum de lycanthropis, an vere illi, ut fama est, luporum et aliarum bestiarum formis induantur? cum aliis quaestionibus hinc emanantibus. . . ?*, Spirae Nemetum 1647, which contains the titles of the speeches delivered by twelve professors and as many students in the gymnasium of Speier.

30. See the studies of O. Höfler, W. E. Peuckert, L. Kretzenbacher, etc., cited in n. 3.

31. See W. Deonna, 'Croyances funéraires. La soif des morts. . .', *Revue de l'histoire des religions*, t. CXIX (1939), pp. 53–77.

32. See above, p. 100.

To Combat in Ecstasy

33. Cf. *The Night Battles*, p. 197, and the isolated mention in Peucer (above, p. 134).
34. Cf. the passage of Wittgenstein cited in the Introduction, p. 15.
35. Cf. for all that follows M. Bošković-Stulli, 'Kresnik-Krsnik, ein Wesen aus der kroatischen und slovenischen Volksüberlieferung', *Fabula*, III (1959–60), pp. 275–98 (a revised version is now translated in *Metodi e ricerche*, n.s. VII, 1988, pp. 32–50). Knowledge of this excellent essay would have permitted me to treat adequately the juxtaposition *benandanti-kresniki*, which was dealt with too hastily in *The Night Battles*, p. 142. On the enduring vitality of these phenomena, see P. Del Bello, *Spiegazione della sventura e terapia simbolica. Un caso istriano* (thesis defended at the University of Trieste during the academic year 1986–7; the sponsor, G. P. Gri, kindly sent me the most relevant sections).
36. The text was published for the first time in 1837; here I take account of corrections proposed by Bošković-Stulli (p. 279 n. 11) and, independently, by G. Trebbi, 'La Chiesa e le campagne dell'Istria negli scritti di G. F. Tommasini', *Quaderni giuliani di storia*, I (1980), p. 43.
37. Bošković-Stulli maintains that the *kresniki* can be both men and women (art. cit., p. 278): in fact, all the cases cited except one (p. 281) involve men.
38. See D. Burkhart, 'Vampirglaube und Vampirsage auf dem Balkan', *Beiträge zur Südösteuropa-Forschung...*, 1966, pp. 211–52 (a very useful essay, although occasionally flawed by over-insistence on such outdated categories as animism or preanimism).
39. Cf. *The Night Battles*, pp. 59–60.
40. For linguistic reasons, the bibliography in Hungarian has remained inaccessible to me. See, however, on the analogy between *benandanti* and *táltos*, the excellent essay by G. Klaniczay, 'Shamanistic Elements in Central European Witchcraft, and (more generally), M. Hoppál, 'Traces of Shamanism in Hungarian Folk Beliefs', in *Shamanism in Eurasia*, pp. 404–22, 430–46 – both overlooked by A. M. Losonczy, 'Le chamane-cheval et la sage-femme ferrée. Chamanisme et metaphore équestre dans la pensée populaire hongroise', *L'Ethnographie*, 127 (1986), nn. 98–99, pp. 51–70. These studies complement the bibliographic review by J. Fazekas, 'Hungarian Shamanism. Material and History of Research', in *Studies in Shamanism*, C.-D. Edsman ed, Stockholm 1967, pp. 97–119. In Italian cf., besides M. Hoppál, 'Mitologie uraliche', *Conoscenza religiosa*, 4 (1978), pp. 367–95, the booklet by A. Steiner, *Sciamanesimo e folklore*, Parma 1980. Still fundamental, although contentious in part and outdated, are G. Róheim, 'Hungarian Shamanism', *Psychoanalysis and the Social Sciences*, III (1951), pp. 131–69, and V. Diószegi, 'Die Ueberreste des Schamanismus in der ungarischen Volkskultur', *Acta Ethnographica Academiae Scientiarum Hungaricae*, VII (1958), pp. 97–134, which summarizes longer works that appeared in Hungarian in 1926 and in 1958, respectively. On the ethnographic researches of Diószegi, see T. Dömötör in *Temenos*, 9 (1973), pp. 151–5; E. Lot-Falck, in *L'homme*, XIII (1973), n. 4. pp. 135–41; J. Kodolányi and M. Varga, in *Shamanism in Eurasia* pp. XIII-XXI. For other indications, see M. Sozan, *The History of Hungarian Ethnography*, Washington 1979, pp. 230–45 (on Róheim), pp. 327–30 (on Diószegi). On the etymology of *táltos*, cf. B. Gunda,'Totemistische Spuren in der ungarischen "táltos"-Ueberlieferung', in *Glaubenswelt und Folklore der sibirischen Völker*, V. Diószegi ed, Budapest 1963, p. 46, which recalls (in the wake of a study by D. Pais) the Turkish *taltis-taltus* – i.e., 'he who hits', 'he who clubs until the loss of the senses' – seeing in this an allusion to ecstasy (or perhaps to battles?). Another etymology, from the Finnish *tietaja* (wise man, sorcerer), has been proposed by Róheim, art. cit., p. 146. On Hungarian witchcraft, one can also consult with profit V. Klein, 'Der ungarische Hexenglaubem', *Zeitschrift für Ethnologie*, 66 (1934), pp. 374–402.

Ecstasies

41. The passage from the trial has been translated by G. Ortutay in *Kleine ungarische Volkskunde*, Budapest 1963, pp. 120–21. Cf. also T. Dömötör, 'The Problem of the Hungarian Female *Táltos*', in *Shamanism in Eurasia*, pp. 423–9, especially p. 425.
42. Ibid., p. 427.
43. Cf. Klaniczay, art. cit. It should be noted that Diószegi, art. cit., pp. 125 ff., dwells on the theme of the struggle among the *táltos*, but not on its objectives – the fertility of the fields: cf. instead Róheim, art. cit., pp. 140, 142. Mention, albeit quite insufficient, is made of the military organization that emerges from the Hungarian witchcraft trials in *The Night Battles*, p. 184 n. 73. The wealth of details on this point has led T. Körner ('Die ungarischen Hexenorganisationen', *Ethnographia*, 80, 1969, p. 211 – a summary of an essay which appeared in Hungarian) to suppose that towards the middle of the sixteenth century Hungarian peasants accused of witchcraft had created a real sect, organized militarily. The hypothesis, which is explicitly counterposed to that of Murray on the survival of a prehistoric religious sect, is, however, equally lacking in documentary evidence. But on the question of the possible correspondences between these myths and specific rituals, see below, pp. 191 ff.
44. The connection between *táltos* and *kresniki* had already been grasped by Róheim, art. cit., pp. 146–7. In Bošković-Stulli's essay a comparison with the Hungarian phenomena is absent – as was pointed out by T. Dömötör, 'Ungarischer Volksglauben und ungarische Volksbräuche zwischen Ost und West', in *Europa and Hungaria*, G. Ortutay and T. Bodrogi eds, Budapest 1965, p. 315 (the same criticism applies to *The Night Battles*: see n. 43).
45. See J. Klaproth, *Voyage au Mont Caucase et en Géorgie*, 2 vols, Paris 1823 (on the Ossetians, cf. II, pp. 223 ff.)
46. Cf. H. Hübschmann, 'Sage und Glaube der Osseten', *Zeitschrift der deutschen Morgenländischen Gesellschaft*, 41 (1887), p. 533.
47. Cf. Klaproth, op. cit., II, pp. 254–5. This passage is not mentioned in the studies cited in the note that follows.
48. Cf. on all this the research of B. Gatiev (1876) and of V. Miller (1882), already singled out and used by Georges Dumézil, *Le problème des Centaures*, Paris 1929, pp. 92–3. They have been made accessible to me thanks to the help of Aleksándr Gorfunkel (who supplied me with a copy) and of Marussa Ginzburg (who translated it for me). To both my gratitude.
49. Cf. Evliyâ Celebi, *Seyahâtnâme*, VII, Istanbul 1928, pp. 733–7. Peter Brown, besides telling me about this testimony, sent me an English translation of it: I thank him warmly.
50. It should be noted that (if one excepts the broom) domestic utensils rarely appear among the vehicles used by European witches to go to the Sabbath. Among the exceptions were the witches of Mirandola who sat astride benches and stools: cf. G. F. Pico, *Strix sive de ludificatione daemonum*, Bononiae 1523 c. Dvr.
51. See *The Night Battles*, pp. 75 ff.
52. Cf. *Il libro degli Eroi. Leggende sui Narti*, Georges Dumézil ed, It. trans., Milan 1979, pp. 107–31: Soslan in the country of the dead (the commentary does not consider the analogy with the ecstasy of the *burkudzäutä*). Cf. also Georges Dumézil, *Légendes sur les Nartes suivies de cinq notes mythologiques*, Paris 1930, pp. 103 ff.
53. See above, pp. 107 ff.
54. Cf. Georges Dumézil, *Storie degli Sciti*, It. trans., Milan 1980, p. 12; J. H. Grisward, 'Le motif de l'épée jetée au lac: la mort d'Artur et la mort de Badraz', *Romania*, 90 (1969), pp. 289–340, 473–514.
55. On the very brief states of loss of consciousness that precede the vocation and

transformation into animals of the *táltos*, cf. Diószegi, art. cit., pp. 122 ff.; of a different opinion is Róheim, art. cit., p. 147.

56. See above, p. 162.

57. Cf. V. Foix, 'Glossaire de la sorcellerie landaise', ' *Revue de Gascogne*, 1903, pp. 368–9, 450 (I thank Daniel Fabre for having informed me of this essay and sending me a copy).

58. Among the *benandanti*, one (Menichino from Latisana) mentioned only three dates – St. Matthew, Corpus Domini, St. John: cf. *The Night Battles*, p. 75. Among the *táltos*, the only precise date indicated is the night of St. George, in the area of Debrecen: see Róheim, art. cit., p. 120.

59. It is obvious that each of these elements, taken by itself, delimits a much vaster space, unusable, in fact, for the purposes of this research. For confirmation see E. Arbman, *Ecstasy or Religious Trance*, 3 vols, Uppsala 1963–70, which, assuming I have perused it accurately, does not even mention the phenomena analyzed here.

60. The reference is to Ludwig Wittgenstein's celebrated pages, *Philosophical Investigations*, para. 65 ff. It is known that the notion of 'family resemblance' (p. 47, para. 67) was suggested by an experiment of Francis Galton. I have not seen any acknowledgement (but someone will certainly have made it) of the likely conduit between Wittgenstein and Galton's work, namely, Freud's *Interpretation of Dreams*, where 'family resemblances' are introduced, in a slightly different sense, to illustrate the phenomena of dream condensation. On the theme in general and its implications, see Needham's fundamental 'Polythetic Classification', *Man*, n. s. 10 (1975), pp. 349–69.

61. For all this see Eliade, 'Some Observations on European Witchcraft', pp. 158–9. *History of Religions*, 14 (1975). In general see also H. A. Senn, *Were-Wolf and Vampire in Rumania*, New York 1982.

62. On all this see the acute essay by G. Ravis-Giordani, 'Signes, figures et conduites de l'entre-vie-et-mort; finzione, mazzeri et streie corses', *Études Corses*, 12–13 (1979), pp. 360 ff. (courteously sent to me by the author), which discusses the analogies with the *benandanti*. Useful ethnographic material can be found in D. Carrington and P. Lamotte, 'Les "mazzeri"', ibid., n. 15–16 (1957), pp. 81–91; D. Carrington, *Granite Island*, London 1971, pp. 51–61. In a very superficial book (*Le folklore magique de la Corse*, Nice 1982), R. Multedo mentions (p. 248), without further indications, shamans (or are these *mazzeri*?) who in their ecstatic journey use a bench covered by a horse's skin.

63. See *The Night Battles*, p. 63.

64. Ibid., pp. 73 ff. On being born feet-first, see Belmont, op. cit., pp. 129 ff.

65. Cf. Bošković-Stulli, art. cit., p. 277.

66. On its diffusion in various parts of Europe, see E. F. Knuchel, *Die Umwandlung in Kult, Magie und Rechtsbrauch*, Basel 1919.

67. Cf. L. Allacci, *De templis Graecorum recentioribus . . . De Narthece ecclesiae veteris . . . nec non de Graecorum hodie quorundam opinionibus. . . .*, Coloniae Agrippinae 1645, pp. 140 ff. Babies born between Christmas day and St. Basil's day, and therefore suspected of being able to become vampires (*vrikolakes*), had their feet placed in a hot oven: see G. Drettas, 'Questions de vampirisme', *Études rurales*, 97–98 (1985), p. 216 n. 4. In Hungary they pretend to throw into the fireplace babies suspected of having been switched by the midwife or to put them in a pot: cf. Losonczy, art. cit., p. 62. For instances of interrogation similar to that reported by Allacci, see Knuchel, op. cit., p. 7; *The Night Battles*, p. 88.

68. Already noted by C. Lawson, *Modern Greek Folklore and Ancient Greek Religion*, Cambridge 1910, p. 210 (there exists an anastatic reprint of this still indispensable book – New York 1964 – with a preface by A. N. Oikonomides).

69. I warmly thank Nikolaos Kontizas and Gianni Ricci for their information on this point.
70. On all this see Lawson, op. cit., pp. 190–255.
71. See, respectively, F. Boll, 'Griechische Gespenster', *Archiv für Religionswissenschaft*, 12 (1909), pp. 149–51, which rejects the derivation, proposed by B. Schmidt, from the Turkish 'Kara-Kondjolos' (vampire); G. A. Megas, *Greek Calendar Customs*, Athens 1958, pp. 33–37. There is nothing new on the *kallikantzaroi*, apart from a superficial attempt at psychological explanation, in R. and E. Blum, *The Dangerous Hour*, New York 1970, pp. 119–22, 232 and 331.
72. Cf. Needham, art. cit.
73. See Introduction, pp. 14–15.
74. For the first, see *The Night Battles*, pp. XXI, 32; Eliade, art. cit., pp. 153 ff. For the *táltos* after the studies of G. Róheim and V. Diószegi, see now Klaniczay, art. cit., which extends the parallel with the shamans to the *kresniki*. For the werewolves, see G. H. von Schubert, *Die Geschichte der Seele*, Tübingen 1839, pp. 394 ff., resumed by R. Leubuscher, *Ueber die Wehrwölfe und Thierverwandlungen im Mittelalter. Ein Beitrag zur Geschichte der Psychologie*, Berlin 1850, pp. 39–40 in note. Despite a reference by Roscher to the passage in Leubuscher (art. cit., p. 21 n. 52) the link between shamans and werewolves has been largely ignored by the subsequent literature: see, however, G. Vernadsky, 'The Eurasian Nomads and their Art in the History of Civilization', *Saeculum*, I (1950), p. 81; and now, Å. Hultkrantz, 'Means and Ends in Lapp Shamanism', in *Studies in Lapp Shamanism* p. 57; R. Grambo, 'Shamanism in Norwegian Popular Legends', in *Shamanism in Eurasia*, p. 396. The traces of shamanistic motifs in Russian *byline*, where, it will be remembered, there also appear references to werewolves, have been highlighted by Meriggi (op. cit., pp. 12, 21 ff., etc.); cf. also Jakobson, p. 134. On, the *burkudzäutä* see the rapid but relevant mention in É. Benveniste, *Études sur la langue ossète*, Paris 1959, pp. 139–40. For the *mazzeri*, cf. Ravis-Giordani, art. cit., pp. 369 ff., which criticizes the analogy with the shamans proposed by R. Multedo, *Le 'mazzerisme' et le folklore magique de la Corse*, Cervione 1975 (which I have not seen).
75. This is the assumption of M. Eliade, *Shamanism, Archaic Techniques of Ecstasy*, Princeton (N.J.) 1974 (with an extensive bibliography, brought up to date till 1964), which, however, ends up considering phenomena not characterized by ecstasies in the strict sense shamanistic: see the criticisms advanced by D. Schroeder, *Anthropos*, 48 (1953), pp. 671–78, and by Lot-Falck, art. cit. L. Vajda, 'Zur phaseologischen Stellung des Schamanismus', *Ural-Altaische Jahrbücher*, 31 (1959), pp. 456–85, concurs in considering the ecstasy one of the distinctive traits of Siberian shamanism. At the same time, he emphasizes that none of these traits (on which see below, p. 165–6) can be considered exclusively shamanistic: what constitutes the originality of shamanism is their simultaneous presence. A select bibliography precedes the excellent collection edited by U. Marazzi, *Testi dello sciamanesimo siberiano e centroasiatico* (Turin 1984).
76. Cf. Peucer, op. cit., p. 143r: '*horis viginti quatuor elapsis, revertente spiritu ceu e profundo somno cum gemitu expergiscitur exanime corpus, quasi revocetur in vitam ex morte qui conciderat'*.
77. Cf. *The Night Battles*, p. 69.
78. Ibid., p. 19: in Friuli in the second half of the sixteenth century the time granted to the spirit to return into the body was twenty-four hours. In Lapland, according to information gathered in 1922, it was rather three days and three nights: see T.I. Itkonen, 'Der "Zweikampf" der lappischen Zauberer (Noai'di) um eine Wild-rentierherde', *Journal de la Société finno-ougrienne*, 62 (1960), no. 3, p. 4, n. 3.

79. Cf. V. Diószegi, 'Le combat sous forme d'animal des chamans', *Acta Orientalia Academiae Scientiarum Hungaricae*, II (1952), p. 315–16 (summary of a long essay in Russian). A hint in this direction can already be found in Harva (Holmberg), *Les représentations religieuses des peuples altaïques*, Paris 1959, p. 326, which mentions the *fylgia* of Scandinavia (on which see below p. 264). The distinction between 'white' shamans and 'black' shamans met with especially among the Buryats probably possesses another significance, as Vajda observes, art. cit., pp. 471–3, which identifies the battles fought in ecstasy as one of the distinctive traits of shamanism. But see also L. Krader, 'Buryat Religions and Society', in *Gods and Rituals*, J. Middleton ed, Austin and London 1967, pp. 117 ff.

80. Cf. *Monumenta historica Norvegiae latine conscripta*, G. Storm ed, Kristiania 1880, pp. 85–97. See also Hultkrantz, art. cit., p. 54; R. Grambo, 'Shamanism in Norwegian Popular Legends', in *Shamanism in Eurasia* cit., pp. 391 ff.; R. Boyer, *Le monde du double*, Paris 1986, pp. 65–6.

81. Cf. the important essay by Itkonen, art. cit., pp. 1 ff. And see L. Bäckman, 'Types of Shaman: Comparative Perspectives', in *Studies in Lapp Shamanism*, p. 77.

82. Klaniczay rightly insists on this point, art. cit., p. 414.

83. They agree substantially with the traits isolated by Vajda, art. cit. (which I read only after having written these pages). Some of the discrepancies are of minor significance (for example, on p. 465 Vajda mentions the physical peculiarities of future shamans without isolating them as a distinctive trait). The most notable is the absence of cosmological implications in the phenomena analyzed here: cf. Vajda, pp. 470–1, on the Siberian shamans.

84. See T. Lehtisalo, *Entwurf einer Mythologie der Jurak-Samojeden*, Helsinki 1924, p. 114. And see below, pp. 263 ff.

85. Cf. Lot-Falck, art. cit., p. 6.

86. See A. Ohlmarks, *Studien zum Problem des Schamanismus*, Lund 1939; R.T. Christiansen, 'Ecstasy and Arctic Religion', *Studia septentrionalia*, IV (1953), pp. 19–92; Å. Hultkrantz, 'Type of Religion in the Arctic Cultures. A Religio-Ecological Approach', in *Hunting and Fishing...*, H. Hvarfner ed, Luleå 1965, pp 264–318 (especially p. 310, which reasserts, in a more nuanced form, Å. Ohlmarks' old theses). For a more profound perspective see E. De Martino, *Il mondo magico*, Turin 1948, pp. 91 ff.; Vajda, art. cit., pp. 260–1; E. Lot-Falck, 'Psycopathes et chamanes yakoutes', in *Échanges et communications. Mélanges offerts a Cl. Lévi-Strauss*, J. Pouillon and P. Maranda eds, The Hague and Paris 1970, I, pp. 115–29; idem, 'Le Chamanisme', pp. 4 ff.

87. *The Night Battles*, pp. 39, 84.

88. Cf. Olaus Magnus, op. cit., pp. 115–16.

89. See D. Strömbäck, 'The Realm of the Dead on the Lappish Magic Drum,' *Arctica. Studia Ethnographica Upsaliensia*, XI (1956), pp. 216–20.

90. They have been published by K. R. Hagenbach in *Die Basler Hexenprozesse in dem 16ten und 17ten Jahrhundert*, Basel [1840?], which insists several times on the exceptional character of the trial. An equally distorted echo of similar themes is possibly encountered in some witchcraft trials held in Szged (Hungary) in 1728; cf. T. Dömötör, *Hungarian Folk Beliefs*, Bloomington (Indiana) 1982, pp. 70–1.

91. See Z. Kovács, 'Die Hexen in Russland', *Acta Ethnographica Academiae Scientiarum Hungaricae*, 22 (1973), pp. 51–85, especially 82–3; the author points out the analogy with the trials of Hungarian witches. Kovács' essay seems to have escaped R. Zguta, 'Witchcraft Trials in Seventeenth-Century Russia', *The American Historical Review*, 82 (1977), pp. 1187–207.

4

Disguised as Animals

1. Under the pressure of bishops, preachers and inquisitors, beliefs about the cohorts of the dead, previously considered more or less innocuous superstitions, were forcibly assimilated to the stereotype of the Sabbath. The diabolical aura that surrounded them began to disappear after the middle of the seventeenth century, as the persecution of witchcraft diminished. Only then did those beliefs begin to be considered with detachment, in a historical perspective. At the end of his dissertation *De Exercitu Furioso* (1688), the Lutheran pastor P.C. Hilscher observed that the oldest evidence on the procession of souls dated back to the times in which Christianity, by now widespread in Thuringia, Franconia and Swabia, had begun to be corrupted by the errors introduced by the Roman Church.[1] The superstition had continued throughout the sixteenth century; according to an anonymous informant of Hilscher's – probably the pastor of Erfurt – the apparitions had for some time been much more infrequent. At this point Hilscher referred to a custom extant in Frankfurt (we do not know for how long). Every year a number of youths were paid to take a large cart covered with leaves from door to door, to the accompaniment of songs and predictions which, to prevent errors, they had been taught by experienced people. The populace (Hilscher concluded) asserts that in this way the memory of Eckhard's army is celebrated.[2]

2. So then, the spectators recognized in the Frankfurt ceremony a representation of the 'furious army' – the cohorts of the dead, at whose head alternated various mythical figures, among whom, we may remember, there featured old Eckhard. Their reaction allows us to identify a ritual in this ceremony. Naturally, the youths who for a fee impersonated the procession of the dead on the basis of other people's instructions, remind us of professional actors, rather than followers of secret youthful associations possessed by demonic fury.[3] But what for some was a canvas on which to sketch a kind of theatrical representation, was for others part of a core of memories that could be reactivated and transmitted.

This early example of rediscovery or reinvention of a tradition proves once

182

more that popular culture (especially urban) in pre-industrial Europe was anything but static.[4] But it also suggests some more general reflections. All rituals (including those born from a revolutionary break) search for their legitimacy in a real or imaginary past.[5] Since the invention of a ritual always presents itself as a reinvention, the apparent artificiality of the situation described by Hilscher is by no means exceptional. The establishment of a ritual – a profoundly contradictory occurrence insofar as the ritual is by definition untouched by the flow of time – presupposes the conflict between those who hark back to a tradition, usually presented as immemorial, and those to whom it is alien.

Unfortunately, Hilscher does not tell us when the Frankfurt ceremony was instituted, or at what time of year it took place, or who imparted the instructions to the youth who celebrated it. Were they perhaps old people, harking back to a remote lived experience, who resuscitated customs by now fallen into disuse? Or were they scholars who, on the basis of literary competence, sought to resuscitate ancient rituals, true or imaginary?

3. The latter hypothesis cannot be dismissed out of hand. During this period the relationship between Christmas or carnival customs and Greek and Roman festivities had elicited the curiosity of the German antiquarians. Almost simultaneously with Praetorius' *Saturnalia* in 1670 there had been published in Leipzig a scholarly work by M. Lipen (Lipenius), entitled *Integra strenarum civilium historia*. Among the numerous testimonies discussed therein was a sermon against the January calends delivered on the day of the Epiphany in the year 400 by Asterius, Bishop of Amasea in Cappadocia. Besides condemning the tradition, also customary in Rome, of exchanging gifts at the beginning of the year, Asterius denounced certain rituals widespread in his diocese. Charlatans, conjurors, and some of the populace (*demotai*) divided into groups and ran from door to door: amid shouts and applause they wished prosperity on the inhabitants of the house and demanded money from them; the siege was lifted only when, out of weariness, the requests of the importunate were met. The begging went on until late in the evening; children also took part in it, distributing apples for double the sum of money they were worth. On the same occasion, on a cart like those one sees in a theatre, among soldiers disguised as women, a fictitious sovereign was enthroned who was derided and mocked.[6] That the troops stationed in lower Moesia and Cappadocia were in the habit of nominating a king during the period of the January calends is attested by a document on the life of St Dasius, a Christian soldier martyred in 303 at Durostorum on the Black Sea (today Silistria in Bulgaria) for having refused to perform the role.[7] Groups of youths who once a year (we do not know when) went from door to door in the evening, singing songs and making predictions: the meagre details that have come to us from Hilscher allow us to discern a possible resemblance to some of the Cappadocian rituals condemned by Asterius. Might not the cart bedecked with leaves be an

allusion to that which transported the ephemeral King of the Saturnalia? And might not the ceremony in Frankfurt be an erudite commemoration inspired by some antiquarian less inclined than Lipenius moralistically to condemn pagan ceremonies?[8] What leads us to discard this hypothesis is the reaction of the spectators. If, as Hilscher observes, the populace (Asterius had spoken of *demotai*) was able to decipher the full significance of the ceremony, it could not be based on a series of erudite references. The cart that accompanied the throng of youths was most likely that of Holda, which also appears in a sixteenth-century description of the Nuremberg carnival.[9]

4.   At this point the vague analogy we have glimpsed with the rituals described by Asterius might appear relevant. But the matter is more complex. Unlike the traditions linked to the temporary enthronement of the King of the Saturnalia, the alms-collecting rounds continued well beyond the fifth century. Up until quite recent decades, over a very large area, comprising part of Europe, Asia Minor and central Asia, during the twelve days between Christmas and Epiphany (less frequently halfway through Lent), hordes of children and young boys used to go from house to house, often disguised as horses or other animals, singing ditties, begging for sweets and small sums of money. The insults and curses incurred by refusal preserved the ancient aggressive connotation of the alms-seeking rounds, already noted by Asterius. Generally, however, the alms were granted: the collectors greeted them with songs of greeting addressed to the inhabitants of the house. In some cases the custom has survived to our day.[10]

In the hordes of masked children and adolescents who scurried through the villages there has been recognized a representation of the cohorts of the dead, who traditionally appeared with especial frequency during the twelve days.[11] The forays of children in the English-speaking countries on both sides of the Atlantic during the night of Halloween (31 October) constitute a living example of an analogous custom. The apparently playful ritual of the begging rounds would seem to have induced ambivalent feelings – fear, guilt, the wish to obtain favours through penance – connected with the ambivalent image of the dead.[12] These psychological implications are conjectural; however, the identification of the collectors with the dead seems undeniable.[13] Yet it leaves in the shadows a decisive question: whether the meaning of the ritual was always explicitly shared by actors and spectators. In the Frankfurt case the consciousness of the latter is incontrovertible: the youths – we do not know if they were collectors – who made the rounds from house to house singing greeting songs (*non sine cantionibus et vaticiniis*, Hilscher wrote) were explicitly identified by the populace with the cohorts of the dead.

5.   The ceremony was repeated in Frankfurt annually; that it took place during the period of the twelve days is merely a conjecture. But this evidence, however summary, is precious. The reactions of the populace offer us a basis

for the reconstruction of the correlative rituals of the myths explored up to this point. Myths and rituals, however, refer to different levels of reality; their relationship, although intimate, is never specular. We may consider them heterogeneous languages which reciprocally translate each other, without utterly coinciding. Rather than of coincidences, we shall speak of more or less partial isomorphisms.

Since the early centuries of the Christian era the feast of the January calends was accompanied by hitherto unattested ceremonies. In Cappadocia, as we can see from the sermon delivered by Asterius in the year 400, soldiers disguised themselves as women. Analogous disguises, on the same occasion, were alluded to, albeit vaguely, by Massimo da Torino around 420; and, in more precise fashion (again in connection with soldiers), a century later by Cesarius of Arles. But this is an isolated convergence: on the whole, evidence about the rituals practised during the January calends, though invariably referring to an atmosphere of festive unruliness, reveals substantial divergences. In the West, and more precisely in the Celtic-Germanic sphere, we find the custom of disguising oneself as an animal and leaving behind nocturnal offerings of food on tables intended for invisible female beings. In the East, we find the begging rounds of children and youngsters and, among the soldiers, the enthronement of the ephemeral King of the Saturnalia.[14]

This schematic summary does not throw much light on the meaning, or meanings, of these rituals. But let us try to examine them closely. According to Cesarius of Arles, during the night of the calends, tables laden with food were set out so as to ensure a prosperous year. The custom was certainly long-lived: five hundred years later Burchard of Worms still felt obliged to condemn it, specifying that the table was laid with three knives meant for the *Parcae*. We have seen that the latter were none other than the Celtic *Matronae*, long worshipped as good mistresses (*bonnes dames, bonae dominae*). Together with the goddess of prosperity and the dead who led them – Habonde, Satia, Richella – these figures, associated with nocturnal ecstasies, received from their male (or female) followers offerings of food and drink.[15] Thus, between the rituals performed during the calends of January and the ecstatic cult which we have attempted to reconstruct, there is a link, which it seems legitimate to extend to another custom, widespread during the same period. No reasonable person would believe this – once again it is Cesarius of Arles speaking – but there are mentally healthy individuals who disguise themselves as stags (*cervulum facientes*); others don the skins of sheep or goats; yet others disguise themselves with animal-like masks (*alii vestiuntur pellibus pecudum, alii assumunt capita bestiarum*), exultant because, having assumed a bestial appearance, they no longer seem to be men (*gaudentes et exsultantes, si taliter se in feriunas species transformaverint, ut homines non esse videantur*). As early as the mid-fourth century we find prohibitions of this kind, which, along with the stag, usually mention the heifer (*vetula*) and, in one instance, possibly the mare (*hinnicula*).[16] We propose to treat these animal disguises as a ritual

185

correlative of the animal metamorphosis experienced during ecstasy, or of the ecstatic cavalcades astride animals which constitute a variant thereof. If we accept this hypothesis, the majority of the rituals performed both in the West and East during the January calends slot into place in a coherent picture. Child alms-collectors, tables laid for the nocturnal divinities, and animal disguises represented different ways of making contact with the dead – the ambiguous dispensers of prosperity during the crucial period when the old year ends and the new begins.[17]

6.   We have reached this conclusion, as yet provisional, by deciphering texts which are precocious, full of lacunae, or stereotyped (in any case enigmatic) through much later testimonies. To reject this option would be to preclude any possibility of ordering non-synchronous documents in homogeneous series – and thus all possibility of interpreting the past.[18] It has been objected, however, that the animals evoked in the masquerades – the stag, the heifer, and perhaps the mare – are not mentioned in the evidence about the ecstatic journeys in the retinue of the nocturnal divinities. But this discrepancy is a superficial datum: the variety of mounts associated with the ecstasy (or, alternatively, of animals involved in the metamorphosis) conceals substantially homogeneous myths.[19] Greater difficulty arises with the expansion of the geographical frame as a result of the comparison with the child-begging at the beginning of the year accompanied by animal masquerades. The oldest testimony originates in Cappadocia; the recent or very recent covers, as we have seen, a vast and diverse area, running from France to central Asia, passing by the Greek, Armenian and Turkish communities of Asia Minor. How can we reconcile this distribution with the strictly Celtic or Celto-Germanic milieu which supplies the evidence about animal disguises of the early Middle Ages? That the convergences are merely vague must, it seems, be excluded. Masquerades with goat skins staged on the Balkan peninsula (Albania, Thessaly, Macedonia and Bulgaria) at the beginning of January, on the occasion of pantomimes with an erotic and clownish flavour, recall the custom, condemned by Cesarius of Arles, of wearing sheep or goat skins (*alii vestiuntur pellibus pecudum*) during the same period.[20] The 'obscene deformities' of the animal masquerades – probably a phallic allusion – which Cesarius characterized as shameful and deplorable (*in quibus quidem sunt quae primum pudenda, aut potius dolenda sunt*), were possibly in the West, and perhaps as early as the sixth century, also the pretext for ritual pantomimes. All this invites us to pursue the analysis, extending the comparison to Central and Eastern Europe.

7.   From the Balkan peninsula to the Ukraine, the ceremonies that attend the end and beginning of the year are celebrated by juvenile or youthful groups of an initiatory type, invariably composed of males, and designated by different names according to the region: *ceăta* in the Carpathians; *eskari* in Bulgarian Macedonia; *surovaskari* in eastern Bulgaria; *coledari* (from

calendae) in Serbia and western Bulgaria; *regös* in Hungary; *koljadanti* in the Ukraine; and so on.[21] The *coledari*, for instance, are generally unmarried or newly wed; sometimes they are accepted in the group only until the birth of their first child. They assemble a few weeks before Christmas in the presence of a leader: on Christmas Eve they roam through the village streets, masked, singing special songs (*colinde*). They foretell wealth, prosperity for the livestock; before the houses where someone has died during the year they intone funeral chants and bring news from the departed. They are rewarded with food and sometimes with money. The *koljadanti* make requests in a threatening tone; the *eskari*, it appears, levy actual tributes. Sometimes they do a little filching, but no one takes any notice. The sizes of these groups vary a great deal; the *surovaskari* can be as many as forty or fifty; the *koljadanti* are no more than three or five. All wear masks; the *surovaskari* have huge wings and head coverings two metres tall. The processions almost always include an animal (said to be a goat or horse), usually represented by several people who walk in a file under a mantle.

These winter rituals are sometimes echoed by spring-time rituals. Here too we have centuries-old traditions: a testimony from 1230 informs us that in Macedonian Bulgaria, during the Pentecost, groups of young people ran through the villages singing, staging obscene shows and extorting gifts.[22] Among the Rumanians of Macedonia, the *cǎlusari* are active between the first of January and Epiphany; in Rumania, on the occasion of Pentecost (*rusaliile*). Underlying this fluctuation we can discern a probable correspondence between the two different calendars, solar and lunar.[23] It is underscored by the funerary connotations which the spring festival of blooming roses had already assumed in pagan times. Like the twelve days, the Pentecost – the Christian reincarnation of the ancient *Rosalia* – is a period consecrated to the dead.[24] As in the case of the *coledari*, all these figures can be defined as personifications of the dead.[25] In the light of the documentation with which we commenced, we must specify: personifications of the dead and, at the same time, mediators with the beyond. Not unlike the *benandanti*, for example, the *coledari* or the *regös* offer news of the departed. All this reinforces the conclusion provisionally advanced: at least some of the customs linked to the January calends or to the Pentecost expressed, in the language of ritual, myths relived by the men and women who, in ecstasy, periodically visited the realm of the dead.

8.   A dense web of convergent data confirms this isomorphism. At Driskoli in Thessaly, the masked figures who perform pantomimes between the first of January and Epiphany were named *karkantzaroi* – one of the many synonyms by which the *kallikantzaroi* were referred to.[26] In this instance the correspondence between everyday life (the children born during the twelve days), myth (beings that roam about during the twelve days) and ritual (youths charged with impersonating the errant beings during the twelve days) seems perfect, although distributed over a span of three centuries (between the

187

beginning of the seventeenth and twentieth centuries), and over a rather vast area (the island of Chios, the Peloponnese and Thessaly). But, as we are bound to remember, inclusion of the *kallikantzaroi* in the ranks of mediators with the beyond has not been conclusively demonstrated. We must look for corroboration. It is furnished us by a series of Rumanian testimonies.

In the middle of the seventeenth century Friar Marco Bandini, Archbishop of Marcianoplis (and lower Mesia) and of Durostorum and Tomis (on the Black Sea), described in detail the extraordinary feats of the enchanters and enchantresses of Moldavia.[27] People consult them to learn the future, to be cured of the illnesses that afflict them, or to find stolen objects. Once they have chosen an appropriate site, they begin to whisper, twist their heads, roll their eyes and contort their mouths, grimace and shake all over; then they fall to the ground with hands and feet spread eagled and remain motionless, as if dead, for an hour (sometimes for three or four). When they come to, they present a horrendous spectacle to onlookers: at first they rear on trembling limbs as though agitated by infernal furies; then, awakening, they reveal their dreams, as if they were oracles. We do not know whether this description was based on direct observation: in any event, the isolated reference to the classical furies does not impair its ethnographic value.[28] What is being described is, undoubtedly, a ritual: a public ceremony that occurred in a specific place (*certo . . . loci spatio*) and possibly at a specified time, with men and women as actors. However, Rumanian testimonies closer to us indicate a predominantly female propensity to ecstasy.

In certain villages there were women who habitually fell into ecstasy during the Pentecost (*rusaliile*): when they came to, they said they had spoken with God, with the saints, with the living and the dead. It was said of one of them, who prescribed medicaments without asking to be paid, that she had become *rusalie* (or, alternatively, a witch) from the time she was a little girl. Now, the *rusalii* are the spirits of the dead (identified in the Slavic context with female aquatic divinities).[29] Beyond the divergences in the calendar (in the Friuli, for instance, the ecstasies took place during the Ember weeks), we again encounter phenomena by now familiar to us. The Rumanian counterparts of the *benandanti* women, having achieved a state of temporary death through ecstasy, likewise brought their clients news from beyond, earning the reputation of practitioners of witchcraft in consequence. The same occurred until a few decades ago in a Macedonian village, Velvendos, where a group of women who called themselves *angeloudia* or *angeloudes* (angels) supplied information about the community's dead, maintaining that they had received it while in a state of ecstasy from the angels. In this case the gatherings took place in secret, generally at night.[30] At Duboka, a mountain village in eastern Serbia near the border with Rumania, by contrast, the ecstasies were (and perhaps still are) public, like those described by Bandini three centuries ago. During the Pentecost, young and old women fall into catalepsy while surrounded by a group of men who perform a frenetic dance; their leader, who holds in his hand a knife adorned with garlic, camomile and other medicinal plants, sprays river water mixed with the juice of chopped herbs onto the faces of the inanimate women to awaken them.[31] The ritual is closely connected with the dead: people who have recently died are evoked indirectly by this display of gifts intended for them, or by playing their favourite tunes.[32]

Together with the three *kraljevi*, three *kralijce*, that is, 'queens', participate in the Duboka ritual: a female group present in eastern Serbia and in the Serbian Banat.[33] It alternates with an analogous male group, which is more properly Rumanian: the *călușari*, whose rituals have been compared to those of Duboka.[34] Of all the Balkan juvenile associations the *călușari* group is the only one that permits us to ascertain through something other than conjecture the beliefs underlying the seasonal rituals. The manifold activities of the *călușari* – dances, pantomimes, healings, processions, sword and flag parades – take place under the protection of a mythical empress to whom they render homage. She is sometimes called Irodeasa or Arada, sometimes Doamna Zînelor, the mistress of the fairies (*zîne*). They are synonyms for the names used by the authors of the penitential books of the early Middle Ages, followed by bishops and inquisitors, to designate the nocturnal divinity who led the cohorts of the dead in the West: Herodias and Diana.[35] That identical formulae, elaborated by the culture of the clerics, circulated for centuries in much of Europe, is obvious enough. Less obvious is the profound unity of the behavioural patterns and beliefs which those formulae sought to interpret. The elusive connection between rowdy seasonal rituals and myths experienced in the immobility of ecstasy has left an irrefutable trace in the Rumanian documentary record.

9. The kinship between Irodeasa, Arada, Doamna, Zînelor and the nocturnal goddesses traced in Celtified Europe would appear self-evident. Those terms indicate that the twofold translation, scriptural and pagan, suggested by the clergy, ended up being introjected by laymen to the extent of erasing the name(s) of the local divinity. She is hypothetically identified with an indigenous Daco – Getan divinity,[36] but the data collected to date leads us to suspect a more remote provenance. At all events, the assimilation of a lexical covering imposed from without should not deceive us: the offensive of the Easton Orthodox Church against superstitions was weaker than that launched in the West by the Roman Church.[37] In all likelihood this explains the longevity of rituals that are elsewhere erased or introjected into the solitude of a private ecstasy.

From Moldavia where, it will be remembered, Friar Marco Bandini had recorded the presence in the mid-seventeenth century of enchanters and enchantresses capable of falling into ecstasies, comes the first and almost contemporaneous evidence about the *călușari*. Describing the region, Prince Cantemir spoke of those he called *caluczenii*, of their rites, of the beliefs surrounding them. They would gather in groups of seven, nine, eleven; they disguised themselves as women, feigning a female voice; they wrapped their faces in white bandages; leapt as if flying, with drawn swords; healed the sick; if they killed anyone, they were not punished.[38] As we have seen, an identical impunity, restricted to small thefts, is guaranteed to this day to the groups of youths in whom we have identified a ritual transposition of the wandering dead: simultaneously hostile and beneficent entities, bearers of prosperity and misfortune. We have here a revealing analogy. According to Cantemir, the _caluczenii_ were expected to perform the ritual tasks entrusted to them for nine years: otherwise they were persecuted by the spirits (_frumosi_). Later documents speak instead of mythical female beings (_rusalii_), who roam at night during Pentecost (_rusaliile_) to defend against the _călușari_, who wander about the village during the same period bearing garlic and absinthe. But anyone struck by the _rusalii_ begins to jump and shout like the _călușari_. Contraposition and identification mingle in an ambiguous relationship.[39] In northern Bulgaria groups analogous to the _călușari_ are without further ado called _russalzi_.[40] Now, the _rusalii_ were, as we said, souls of the dead; the _frumosaele_, the female version of the _frumosi_, have been compared to mortuary figures such as the _bonae res_ or Celtic fairies.[41] The goddess who presides over the rituals of the _călușari_ – Irodeasa, Arada, Doamna Zînelor – was, like her Western counterparts, certainly a goddess of the dead.

10.   In the texts of Celtic origin about the animal masquerades of the January calends women are never mentioned: a silence which, in this instance, has the status of proof, for their participation would have underscored in the eyes of clerical observers the scandalous nature of those customs. On the other hand, we do not know whether organized groups of youth analogous to those who appear in the Balkan and Slav seasonal rituals participated in them. We are invariably dealing with groups of men, at most disguised as women, like the _caluczenii_ of Moldavia. The Serbo-Croat _kralijce_ – evenly numbered groups of women disguised as men, armed with swords, associated with the Pentecost (like the _călușari_, whose features they seem to reproduce in a symmetrical and inverse form) – appear, by contrast, to be a totally exceptional manifestation.[42] It is impossible to say whether it takes us back to a more ancient stage in which men and women alike participated in the public sphere of the ritual, each symbolically denying his or her own sexual identity.

In the private experience of ecstasy we have seen a tendential sexual specialization delineated: on the one hand, the predominantly female escorts of the nocturnal divinities; on the other, the generally male groups engaged in the battles for fertility. This last feature is occasionally present among the _călușari_: but a comparison with the male _benandanti_ brings to the surface a series of partial but clear correspondences.[43] Both appear as specialized healers of the evil spells cast, respectively, by _rusalii_ and witches. For a specified though variable number of years, generally coinciding with the period of their youth, both are forced to participate (the former materially, the latter 'in spirit') in the collective rituals enveloped in silence. The society (ritual and mythical, respectively) of which they become part is in both cases an association of an initiatory kind organized in military fashion and led by a chief, replete with flags, musical instruments, vegetable weapons – garlic and absinthe for the *căluşari*, fennel bundles for the *benandanti*. The animal disguises of the *căluşari* (i.e., 'little horses') feature equine manes or a stick adorned with a horse's head; long before this they were accompanied by a dancer masked as a stag or wolf.[44] The extraordinary leaps that punctuate their dances imitate both the flight of the *rusalii* and the jumping of horses. The society of the *căluşari* is in fact patterned after the mythical one constituted by the *sântoaderi*, knights equipped with equine tails and hooves who, during carnival week, on the occasion of the feast of St Theodore (a saint associated with the dead), wander menacingly through the village streets at night, dragging chains behind them and beating a drum.[45] A subterranean homology links the *rusalii* and the *sântoaderi*: it is said that during another feast of St Theodore, twenty-four days after Easter, their squads meet, play together and at the end exchange a bunch of wood balm (*todoruse*).[46] *Căluşari* and *benandanti* – the former to protect themselves from the *rusalii* or the *sântoaderi*; the latter to ward off male and female witches – tried, through the divergent paths of ritual and myth (animal disguises, animal metamorphosis), to identify with their adversaries by transforming themselves into spirits, becoming temporarily dead. We reached the same conclusion, it will be remembered, when analyzing other cases of mythical sectarian groups – werewolves, *táltos* – based on periodic animal metamorphosis, destined to be repeated over a definite though variable number of years. In all these cases, what renders the identification with the dead possible is an initiation, real or symbolic; because initiation is always, symbolically, a death.

11.   The presence of an initiative dimension probably explains the mortuary air that surrounds the behaviour of groups of youth in disparate societies, who are sometimes associated in forms of ritual violence, at other times bound together in warring organizations. The oldest testimony on a ritual such as the *charivari*, intended to control the customs (especially sexual) of a village, identified the tumultuous squad of masked youths with the cohorts of the dead, led by mythical beings like Hellequin.[47] In the eyes of actors and spectators, the excesses of the youthful 'consortia' must have long preserved these symbolic connotations.[48] In all probability they explain the right to theft tacitly accorded, in the Swiss Löschental, to the *Schurtendiebe* ('thieves in short skirts') who, during carnival, descend from the woods to the village to loot, their faces masked, their bodies in sheepskin, their waists adorned with cowbells.[49] Similar phenomena occurred in ancient societies. We have only to think of the tests (thefts, murders of helots casually encountered) required of members of groups of an initiatory character like the Spartan *krypteia*, after a period of isolation spent in the wild on the outskirts of the city.[50]

191

The Phoceans who (according to Herodotus and Pausanias) marched at night against the Thessalians, with their faces and their weapons coated with chalk; the Harii, whom Tacitus compared to an army of the dead (*exercitus feralis*) because they went into battle with their shields and faces blackened in order to terrify the enemy, have been compared to initiatory groups.[51] The state of bellicose fury and the metamorphoses into ferocious animals described by the Icelandic sagas made the *Berserkir* (literally, 'bear sheath") a living incarnation of the cohorts of the dead guided by their leader Odin.[52] In all these cases we recognize an aggressive attitude associated with identification with the cohorts of the dead. We are seemingly far from the playful violence of the childish beggars, but the mythical matrix is the same.

12.   We have seen that the ceremonies of the *călușari* lack precise echoes of the dramatic struggle waged by the *benandanti* in a state of ecstasy. Certainly, the atmosphere of violence – not always (or not merely) ludic – in which the rituals of these groups of youths occurred, contained vaguely ritualistic aspects. Above all, the Slovenian *koledari* and the *eskari* of Macedonian Bulgaria were animated by very strong hostility to their counterparts from neighbouring villages. When the two groups of *eskari* met, bloody, sometimes deadly brawls erupted which, if they took place on 1 January, were covered by a total immunity not unlike that which to this day applies to minor or minimal infractions, such as thefts or malicious practical jokes committed by bands of young questers.[53] But unlike those lived in a state of ecstasy or dream by the Dalmatian *kresniki*, these forms of territorial hostility never proved to be symbolically associated with the enhancement of the community's material well-being.

13.   This, however, was the declared purpose of a ritual practised at the beginning of the sixteenth century – we do not know exactly when it began – in a number of Alpine valleys. In a brief historical and geographical work about the Grisons (*Die uralt warhafftig Alpisch Rhetia*), which appeared in 1538 in Basel, the Swiss scholar Gilg Tschudi included a description of a ceremony that was celebrated every year, in localities such as Ilanz and Lugnitz: groups of masked men called *Stopfer* (literally, 'piercers'), armed with big clubs, went from village to village, leaping high into the air and colliding violently. The reformer Durich Chiampel, who had attended the same ceremony at Surselva, a few years later reworked Tschudi's remarks, specifying that the *punchiadurs* (this is what they were called in Romancio, a dialect form of Ladino) would gather, because of an 'almost hereditary' custom, above all during religious feasts (*in bacchanalibus quae vocantur sacris*). The two testimonies concurred on the purpose of the ceremony: to obtain a more abundant harvest of wheat. A superstition, Tschudi commented: pagan nonsense, Chiampel echoed. Their concordant testimony leaves no room for doubt: we have here a fertility ritual, identified as such by the direct accounts of actors and spectators. The perfectly recognizable gap between their

interpretation, and that of the hostile observers who recorded it, excludes any possibility of distortion. The followers of the insolent cult of the *punchiadurs*, Chiampel observes, said in all seriousness (*omnino serio asserentes*) that at the end of the ceremony there was always one participant who was missing. For Chiampel, this invisible participant was a demon.[54]

Protestant pastors and Catholic parish priests tried to eradicate these peasant fertility rituals. In the case of the *punchiadurs*, the disappearance was complete.[55] Other, more or less similar rituals were transformed into innocuous festivities. Along the entire Alpine arc seasonal ceremonies celebrated by groups of masked men have continued to this day. The cowbells which, according to Chiampel's report, hung from the backs of the *punchiadurs*, still adorn the costumes of those who participate in Swiss and Tyrolean masquerades.[56] Up until the last century in a number of localities in Austria and Bavaria, groups of 'beautiful' and 'ugly' Perchtas confronted each other during carnival; later, only the 'beautiful' remained. Their name preserves the trace of an ancient cult: Perchta (whom canonists and inquisitors identified with Diana or Herodias) was one of the names of the nocturnal divinity, harbinger of prosperity, to whom the ecstatic women paid homage. In the Tyrol the belief that the passing by of the Perchta procures abundance endured for a long time.[57] In Rumania, as we have seen, Irodeasa and Doamna Zînelor still live in the ceremonies of the *căluşari*.

It is this mythical background that enables us to interpret the meagre data on the *punchiadurs*. In many localities along the Alpine arc, often linked to places of sanctuary or pilgrimage, the custom of celebrating particular festivities with ludic clashes between groups of youths persists: but these ritual battles (because that is what they undoubtedly are) usually take place after the harvest – not before, to propitiate its outcome.[58] A specific analogy with the fertility ritual practised by the *punchiadurs* must be sought elsewhere, in the battles for fertility fought in a state of ecstasy during the same years by the *benandanti* of the Friuli, on the opposite slope of the Alps.[59] But a comparison restricted to the Alpine arc would unquestionably be insufficient: the *benandanti* draw behind them the Balkan *kresniki*, the Hungarian *táltos*, the Baltic werewolves, the *burkudzäutä* of the Iranian Caucasus.[60]

14.   Among the populations of the Caucasus the isomorphism of the two versions (competitive or otherwise) of the myths and rituals analyzed hitherto, emerges with particular clarity. In Georgia actual struggles between opposing groups occur, at times corresponding to two sections of the town or village. Depending on the locality, on varying occasions – sometimes during carnival, sometimes in spring, sometimes at the beginning of January – the contenders enter the field covered with animal skins, their faces blackened with soot, performing erotic pantomimes. Wrestling and boxing matches follow (in a village near Tbilisi metal weapons are explicitly forbidden), often preceded by dances and parades of maskers. The people think that the winners will have a good harvest.[61] Among the Ossetians, we may remember,

the *burkudzäutä* say that they fight on the meadows of the beyond to wrest the shoots of wheat from the dead. But in Georgia we also find the *mesultane* (from *suli*, soul): women, or girls over the age of nine, who possess the faculty of visiting the beyond in spirit. After plunging into a lethargy broken by mutterings, they awaken and describe their journey and communicate the requests of the dead to particular individuals or to the community: from this they derive honours and prestige.[62] In parallel (and inversely), among the Ossetians, the Pschavi, the Chevsuri, groups of questers, in some instances with their faces covered with a cloth mask, go from house to house at the beginning of January, threatening to break down the door of anyone who does not give them the gifts requested; at night they slip in unobserved, drink a little liquor, and munch a few small pieces of meat. Very little: to take more would be shameful. Sometimes the owners of the house wake by themselves, at other times they are awakened. The thieves receive food and drink; when day arrives the inhabitants of the village playfully beat them.[63]

15. In these symbolic nocturnal thieves we must certainly have recognized the ritual counterpart of the dead of the Ariège, of the *benandanti* in the Friuli, the sorcerers of the Valais. Their thirst, their incursions 'in spirit' into the cellars led us through the double labyrinth of the myths about the cohorts of the souls and the battles for fertility. Around these we have sought to construct a morphologically compact documentary series, without worrying about justifying it in historical terms. The wholly provisional disjunction of morphology and history had the purely heuristic purpose of outlining, via a series of probes, the contours of an elusive object. A bizarre detail, an apparently negligible convergence has gradually brought to the surface a myriad of disparate phenomena, scattered in time and space. The offers of food and drink to the *Matronae*, the presence of Irodeasa at the head of the Căluşari, the Alpine and Caucasian battles for fertility – these have furnished the proofs of an isomorphism between myths relived in ecstasy and rituals usually connected with the cycle of the twelve days or the Pentecost. Behind the stories, roaming questers, brawls and disguises, we have deciphered a common content: the symbolic identification with the dead, in the immobility of ecstasy or the frenzy of ritual.

16. In the case of the *benandanti*, *táltos*, and so on, the comparison with Eurasian shamans, suggested by the presence of a series of specific analogies, clashed with the absence of public ecstasies of a ritual character. However, we have seen that, halfway through the seventeenth century, such ecstasies as described by Marco Bandini were practised by the enchanters and enchant-resses in Moldavia, who sought to speak with the dead or to recover lost objects – exactly like the Lapland or Siberian shamans. It has been supposed that Bandini was alluding to practices common among not a Rumanian, but rather a Magyar population, ethnically and culturally tied to the Asian steppes – the Tchangö of the Moldavian Carpathians.[64] But this hypothesis is far

194

from being taken for granted. As we have already mentioned, as late as just a few decades ago, in the Serbian village of Duboka, groups of women publicly fell into ecstasy at Pentecost. Although rare, this kind of phenomenon seems to bear the perdurable trace of typically shamanic rituals in a European setting.[65]

It seems difficult, however, to extend this conclusion to ceremonies like those of the *căluşari*.[66] More generally, the suggestion that the dances and seasonal ceremonies should be seen as a derivation from shamanistic rituals, on the basis of elements like the use of the stick with the horse's head (hobby horse), seems insufficiently founded.[67] Here we do not find men or women marked by a precise ecstatic vocation, announced from birth by peculiarities, physical or otherwise, but rather predominantly male groups composed of boys or youths (older evidence refers to heterogeneous crowds from which women seem to be excluded).[68] In the first case the symbolic relationship with the realm of the dead was delegated to specialists; in the second, to the members of an age group.

17. But the two alternatives are not incompatible, as is shown, for example, by descriptions of the great Chinese Ta No festival: a seasonal ritual celebrated in January between the end of the old year and the fifteenth day of the new, during a period consecrated to the spirits of the dead. A person clothed in red and black, wrapped in a bear skin with four eyes of yellow metal, led 120 children between the ages of ten and twelve, with a red cap on their heads and a half-red, half-black tunic. They shot hawthorn arrows from peachwood bows to expel the plagues of the old year from the walls of the imperial palace. The pestilences were represented by twelve animal masks which corresponded to the twelve months of the year; other animal masks (among them the tiger) figured in the opposing ranks. Male and female witches participated in the ceremony, armed with rush brooms. The shamanistic physiognomy of the person disguised as a bear at the head of the cohort of children has been emphasized several times, as has the affinity between exorcizers and exorcized.[69] One is tempted to align this Chinese ceremony with the rituals, ecstatic or not, which – from the Friuli to the Caucasus – feature cohorts, contrasting but profoundly similar, in the fight for fertility: *benandanti* against witch doctors, *kresniki* against *kresniki*, 'beautiful' Perchtas against 'ugly' Perchtas, *burkudzäutä* against the dead, and so on.

18. Earlier we cautiously hinted at the possibility that the presence of analogous mythical forms in heterogeneous cultural contexts might be the result of semi-erased historical relationships. In particular, we supposed that the ecstasies from which we had set out were a specifically (though perhaps not exclusively) Eurasian phenomenon. This hypothesis now seems to be confirmed by the identification of a number of likely corresponding rituals – but at the same time inserted in a much wider sphere of research. The

masked processions symbolizing the souls of the dead, the ritual battles and the expulsion of demons have been compared to other customs (initiations, sexual orgies) which in traditional societies accompany the beginning of the year, solar or lunar. From the Near East to Japan these rituals, modelled on meta-historical archetypes, would seem to symbolize, with the overthrow of the existing order, the periodic irruption of a primordial chaos, followed by a temporal regeneration or a new cosmic beginning.[70] The spatial dispersion of evidence has led to the conjecture that this recurrent ritual erasing of history dates back to an extremely archaic, indeed prehistoric period; their cultural physiognomy, on the other hand, has led to the supposition that this is a very recent phenomenon arising in the context of grain-producing societies.[71] But both hypotheses run the risk of dissolving the specific web of myths and rituals from which we set out. For example, it is not easy in the mass of documentation to isolate the ritual battles aimed at procuring fertility, distinguishing them from generic fertility rituals and vague ritual battles. The annual ceremony during which, according to two Hittite inscriptions that go back to 1200 BC, a band armed with bronze weapons and a band provided with weapons made of cane commemorated a certain historical event – the Hatti's victory over the Masa – this too was probably a religious ritual, given that, or so it would appear, its conclusion was a human sacrifice. But that it was, as has been supposed, a ritual linked to vegetation is far from certain, though one of the inscriptions states that it occurred in the spring.[72] On these, or even more tenuous grounds, the scattered traces of ritual battles in the ancient world have often been compared, in passing, to the seasonal ceremonies of modern folklore, such as the chasing of winter or the bonfire of the old woman. However, we do not know why on specific – but (to us) unknown – calendrical occasions groups of persons belonging to the same city or even to the same family (brothers, fathers and sons) ferociously fought each other, flinging stones for whole days, seeking, as St. Augustine tells us, to kill each other.[73] This was certainly a ritual combat (*sollemniter dimicabant*) like that in Rome, in the middle of October, which saw bands (*catervae*) belonging to the Via Sacra and the Suburra oppose each other in the attempt to conquer the head of a sacrificial horse. In this instance, probably, the ceremony was not intended to ensure the prosperity of the harvests.[74] Fertility was, however, the declared purpose of another Roman feast, that of the Lupercalia, which was celebrated every year on 15 February. Two bands of youths, called Luperci (*Quinctiales* and *Fabiani*) raced against each other around the Palatine, striking the married women with strips made of ram skin to make them fertile. Even though many details are indecipherable for us, it seems significant that the ceremony should have taken place during the nine days (13–21 February) in which, according to the Roman calendar, the dead wandered about, eating the food that the living had prepared for them.[75] Might the affinity between the two bands of the Luperci be compared to that between the Baltic werewolves (or the *benandanti*, the *burkudzäutä*) and the sorcerer-dead who were their adversaries?

19. Our morphological itinerary has taken us to societies, times, and spaces ever more distant from the cultural milieu in which the Sabbath crystallized. Perhaps this could have been foreseen. Unforeseen, however, is the contrast between the heterogeneity of the contexts and the morphological homogeneity of the data. This poses questions that it is impossible to evade.[76] But in order to arrive at an answer it will be necessary to assay a hitherto unexamined possibility: namely, that these formal convergences may be due to connections of an historical character.

Notes

1. On Hilscher, see above, p. 138.
2. Cf. Hilscher, *De exercitu furioso*, cit., c. '*Dv. Consuetudine receptum fuerunt Francofurti, ut quotannis iuvenes pretio allecti currum multis vestitum frondibus visoque conspicuum vesperi conducant ostiatim non sine cantionibus et vaticinis, quae tamen, ne fallant, abs consciis earum rerum, de quibus rogandi sunt, edocti fuerunt. Memoriam exercitus illius Ekkartini ita celebrari vulgus ait* (there follows a reference in a note to Praetorius' *Blockes-Berges Verrichtung* – on which see above, p. 138).
3. Thus supposed O. Höfler and other scholars influenced by him: cf. above p. 173 n.2.
4. See Peter Burke, *Popular Culture in Early Modern Europe*, London 1978; *The Invention of Tradition*, E. J. Hobsbawm and T. Ranger eds, London 1984.
5. Cf. M. Ozouf, *La fête révolutionnaire* (1789–1799), Paris 1976.
6. There now exists a critical edition of the text (already available in Migne), *Patrologia Graeca*, XI, coll. 22–26): Asterius of Amasea, *Homilies I-XIV*, C. Datema ed, Leiden 1970 (the sermon against the Calends is the fourth). For the date and circumstances, cf. ibid., pp. XVIII and 228 ff. Besides an allusion of M. Lipenius, *Integra strenarum civilium historia...*, Lipsiae 1670, p. 94, see the comment of Nilsson, *Studien...*, in *Opuscula Selecta*, Lund 1951, I, pp. 228 and 247 ff.
7. Cf. ibid., p. 247 ff. for a discussion of the hypotheses proposed by F. Cumont (who discovered and published the documents on the life of St. Dasius) and by others. Frazer sees in this text a confirmation of his theories on the ritual killing of the king: but see the observations of G. Brugnoli, 'Il carnevale e i Saturnalia', *La ricerca folklorica*, 110 (October 1984), pp. 49–54. See now R. Pillinger, *Das Martyrium des Heiligen Dasius*, ('Oesterreichische Akademie der Wissenschaften, phil.-hist. Klasse, Sitzungsberichte, 517. Band'), Wien 1988.
8. See the characteristic comment with respect to an attempt to trace the origin of the carnival in the festival of the calends of January: '*Hoc vero est primam istam strenarum diabolicarum insaniem in vitam revocare*' (Lipenius, op. cit., p. 121)
9. See above, pp. 114, n. 43.
10. Cf. K. Meuli, 'Bettelumzüge im Totenkultus, Opferritual und Volksbrauch' (which does not however, mention Asterius's text): the essay, originally published in 1927–8, has been reprinted with additions in *Gesammelte Schriften*, T. Gelzer ed, I, Basel-Stuttgart 1975, pp. 33 ff. Mueli's conclusions largely coincide with those reached almost contemporaneously by Dumézil, *Le problème des Centaures*, Paris 1929, pp. 3 ff. (this book, later disowned by its author because overly influenced by Frazer, still seems very much alive). Copious material on France can be found in A. van Gennep, *Manuel de folklore français contemporain*, I, VII, Part I, Paris 1958, p. 2874–981. On Asia Minor, cf. Nilsson, op.cit., p. 257. On central Asia, cf. R. Bleichsteiner,

'Masken- und Fastnachtsbräuche bei den Völkern des Kaukasus', *Osterreichische Zeitschrift für Volkskunde* 55 (1952), pp. 3–76, especially pp.18–19 and 43 ff. M. Meslin, *La fête des Kalendes de janvier dans l'empire romain. Étude d'un rituel de Nouveau An*, Brussels 1970, p. 78, conjectures a connection between the rites described by Asterius and the young men's masquerades. There are other references in J. Bremmer and N. M. Horsfall, *Roman Myth* (op. cit.) pp. 82–83, in which one may also find a refutation of Meuli's interpretation.

11. Cf. Dumézil, op. cit., pp. 44 ff. According to Meuli, art. cit. (and see also *Gesammelte Schriften* pp. 211, 296 ff. and *passim*) the dead should be identified with the ancestors. But the rites and myths which we are analyzing seem to refer rather to the dead as a distinct group: an age class among those who constitute the community of the village (cf. A. Varagnac, *Civilisation traditionelle et genres de vie*, Paris 1948, p. 244.) Along the same lines, see Claude Lévi-Strauss, 'Le Père Noël supplicié' *Les Temps Modernes*, 7 (1952) pp. 1573 ff., especially p. 1586. This essay, although written in a seemingly jocose tone, poses in a very compressed form various decisive questions, some of which (if I am not mistaken) have not been taken up in Lévi-Strauss's subsequent work.

12. See Meuli, art. cit.

13. Bremmer (*The Early Greek Concept of the Soul*, Princeton 1983, p. 116 n. 128) rejects Meuli's interpretation as based on 'reductive hypotheses' of an evolutionistic type, adapted from ethnological documentation. It should be noted, however, that the, as it were, parallel researches conducted by Dumézil (and not discussed by Bremmer) are based on testimonies drawn from European folklore. Meuli himself represented the conclusions of 'Bettelumzüge' in the most solid form in essays like 'Die deutschen Maskeen' and 'Schweizer Masken und Masken-bräuche', based on a limited comparison (cf. *Gesammelte Schriften*, pp. 69–152 and 177–250). On Meuli's *Gesammelte Schriften*, cf. J. Stagl, *Anthropos*, 72 (1977), pp. 309 ff., and F. Graf in *Gnomon*, 51 (1979), pp. 209–16, in particular pp. 213–14.

14. On this whole question the researches of M. P. Nilsson (op. cit., pp. 214 ff.) remain fundamental, even if certain conclusions must, as we shall see, be corrected. Little new is added by Meslin, op. cit. For the attribution to Cesarius of Arles of the sermon on the calends traditionally attributed to St. Augustine, see the bibliography cited by E. K. Chambers, *The Medieval Stage*, II, Oxford 1903, p. 297.

15. Cf. Nilsson, op. cit., pp. 298 ff. (and see above, p. 130).

16. Cf., ibid., pp. 234 ff.; on *vetula* (which does not mean 'old woman', as Usener thought) and *hinnicula* (perhaps in relation to Epona), cf. ibid., pp. 240–1. Cf. also R. Arbesmann, 'The 'cervuli' and 'anniculae' in Caesarius of Arles', *Traditio*, 35 (1979), pp. 89–119, which follows the variant proposed by Rohlfs (*anicula*), but not his interpretation ('vecchia', old woman): the term would signify, generally, 'young female animal'.

17. This conclusion is explicitly rejected by a scholar of positivist formation like Nilsson: see his polemical reference to chthonic interpretations fashionable among German scholars (op. cit., p. 293, note 124). But the criticism addressed immediately after to E. Mogk, in regard to the connection between 'Modranicht' and the return of the dead within twelve days – those who passed away are male ancestors (i.e., fathers) while the mothers refer, in all religions, to a completely different sphere of representations (*ganz anderen Vorstellungskreis*) – is aprioristic (see above, n. 11). It should be noted that, when republishing his studies on the calends with biblio-graphical additions, Nilsson did not cite the studies of Meuli and Dumézil which had appeared in the meantime. Their conclusions, as has been said, indisputably reinforce, from different points of view, the chthonian or funerary hypotheses.

18. Cf. Introduction, pp. 14–15.
19. The interpretation of the animal disguises as an exclusively Celtic (or Celto-Germanic) phenomenon proposed by Nilsson (op. cit., p. 296) is contradicted by the researches of Meuli and Dumézil. Besides the latter's criticisms of Nilsson, see his observations on the interchangeability of the animals in the modern masquerades (op. cit., p. 31 ff. and 25). The lack of an examination of the animal masquerades vitiates the conclusions of the essay by J. -C. Schmitt, otherwise rich in subtle observations, 'Le maschere, il diavolo, i morti nell'Occidente medievale' (in *Religione* cit., pp. 206–38).
20. 'Pecudum' can refer to both sheep and goats. On the Balkan ceremonies, besides the bibliography cited by Nilsson (op. cit., pp. 252–53) cf. A. J. B. Wace, 'More Mumming Plays in the Southern Balkans', *Annual of the British School at Athens*, XIX (1912–13), pp. 248–65, which shows how in some cases the Eastern Orthodox Church succeeded in transferring these pantomimes from the beginning of the year to a date close to carnival.
21. Cf. R. Wolfram, 'Altersklassen und Männerbünde in Rumänien', *Mitteilungen der anthropologischen Gesellschaft in Wein*, LXIV (1934), p. 112; G. Fochsa, 'Le village roumain pendant les fêtes religieuses d'hiver', *Zalmoxis*, III (1940–42), pp. 61–102; R. Katzarova, 'Surovaskari. Mascherate invernali del territorio di Pernik, Breznik e Radomir', in *Atti del convegno internazionale di linguistica e tradizioni popolari*, Udine 1969, pp. 217–27; S. Zečević, '"Lesnik" – The Forest-Spirit of Leskova in South Siberia', Serbia, *Ethnologia*, I (1969), pp. 171 ff.; E. Gasparini, 'L'antagonismo dei "koledari"', in *Alpes Orientales* cit., I, pp. 107–204; K. Viski, *Volksbrauch der Ungarn*, Budapest 1932, pp. 15 ff. (on the *regös*); V. J. Propp, *Feste agrarie russe*, It. trans., Bari 1978 (but the text dates from 1963), pp. 77 ff. and 197 ff. These are very uneven studies: debatable but rich in ideas, the best is Gasparini's. For a general picture, cf. Meuli, art. cit. and Dumézil, op. cit., pp. 3 ff.
22. Cf. G. Kligman, *Căluş. Symbolic Transformation in Rumanian Ritual*, Chicago 1981, p. 47.
23. Cf. a reference by Wolfram, art. cit., p. 119 and, more extensively, O. Buhociu, *Die rumänische Volkskultur und ihre Mythologie*, Wiesbaden 1974, pp. 46 ff.
24. Cf. Nilsson, 'Das Rosenfest', in *Opuscula selecta*, I, pp. 311–29; K. Ranke, *Rosengarten, Recht und Totenkult*, Hamburg s. a. pp. 18 ff.
25. Cf. Gasparini, art. cit., p. 11. Dumézil, op. cit., pp. 36 ff., arrived at the same conclusion. This allows us to grasp the symbolic inversion which is at the centre of a story by Noël du Fail (*Les propos rustiques*, 1547: I quote from the Paris edition of 1878, edited by H. de la Borderie, pp. 75–84): Mistoudin, a Breton peasant who fell victim to a particularly violent round of begging, takes over the booty of his assailants by disguising himself as a dead man. (Cf. also N. Z. Davis, *Fiction in the Archives*, Stanford (Cal.) 1987, pp. 69–70.
26. Cf. Wace, art. cit., pp. 249 and 264–65.
27. I do not assign any importance to the fact that it was actually at Durostorum that the martyrdom of St Dasius took place.
28. Of a different opinion M. Eliade, '"Chamanisme" chez les Roumains?' *Societas Academica Dacoromana. Acta historica*, VIII (1968), pp. 147 ff. (now in idem, *De Zalmoxis à Gengis Khan*, Paris 1970, pp. 186–97, with the addition of a brief appendix). Bandini's text has been edited by V. A. Urechia, *Codex Bandinus. . . .*, *Analele Academiei Romane*, XVI (1893–94), *Memoriile sectiunii istorice*; the passage in question is on p. 328.
29. Cf. Nilsson, 'Das Rosenfest' pp. 327 ff. Contemporary Greek material is discussed by F. K. Litsas, 'Rousalia: The Ritual Worship of the Dead', in *The Realm of the*

Ecstasies

Extra-Human Agents and Audiences, A. Bharati ed, The Hague and Paris 1976, pp. 447–65.

30. See L. Rushton, 'The Angels. A Woman's Religious Organisation in Northern Greece', in *Cultural Dominance in the Mediterranean Area*, A. Blok and H. Driessen eds, Nijmegen 1984, pp. 55–81.

31. See G. A. Küppers, 'Rosalienfest und Trancetänze in Duboka. Pfingstbräuche im osterbischen Bergland', *Zeitschrift für Ethnologie*, 79 (1954), pp. 212 ff., based on an inquiry conducted in 1938–9; to the bibliography add M. E. Durham, 'Trances at Duboka', *Folk-Lore*, 43 (1932), pp. 225–38.

32. Cf. ibid., p. 233, where – without clarifying it – the connection between ecstasy and attention for the dead is registered.

33. Cf. ibid., and Kligman, op. cit., pp. 58 ff. (which, however, overlooks the sometimes divergent data gathered by M. E. Durham and G. A. Küppers). Kligman also touches, but in very superficial terms, on the possibility of an interpretation of the Duboka rituals in a psychoanalytical register.

34. See R. Vuia, 'The Rumanian Hobby-Horse, the Căluşari' (1935), *Studii de etnografie si folclor*, Bucharest 1975, pp. 141–51, in particular p. 146.

35. On the *căluşari* see Kligman, op. cit., which almost exclusively examines the ritual aspects of the phenomenon. On the mythical aspects, besides Vuia, art. cit., very useful is the unpublished thesis of O. Buhociu, *Le folklore roumain de printemps*, Université de Paris, Faculté de Lettres, 1957, partially utilized by Eliade in art. cit. On Irodeasa cf. Wolfram, art. cit., p. 121; Buhociu, op. cit., p. 240; M. Eliade, 'Notes on the Căluşari' *The Journal of the Ancient Near Eastern Society of Columbia University*, 5 (1973), p. 115; idem, art. cit., p. 159, where the more than sheerly terminological identity between these Romanian figures and their Western counterparts is finally recognized. The *zîna-Diana* linkage had already been brought to light by Lesourd, 'Diane et les sorciers', *Anagrom*, 1972, p. 72. In a text of semi-scholarly origin circulating in Tuscany towards the end of the nineteenth century Aradia had assumed anti-Christian and rebellious tendencies: see C. G. Leland, *Aradia: The Gospel of the Witches*, London 1974 (1st edn. 1899) – on which cf. E. Rose, *A Razor for a Goat*, Toronto 1962, pp. 213–18.

36. Cf. Eliade, art. cit., pp. 159–60; see also idem. op. cit., p. 173.

37. Cf. Eliade, art. cit., p. 158.

38. See D. Cantemir, *Descriptio Moldaviae*, Bucharest 1872, p. 130. Eliade, 'Notes on the Căluşari', p. 117, distorts the passage, speaking of "masks" and of "change of voice so as not to be recognized".

39. See Vuia, art. cit.; on the same lines Eliade, 'Notes on the Căluşari', p. 117.

40. See Wolfram, art. cit., p. 119.

41. Cf. Wesselofsky, 'Alichino e Aredodesa', *Giornale storico della letteratura italiana*, XI (1888), p. 330 n. 5.

42. Cf. Kligman, op. cit., pp. 59 ff; N. Kuret, 'Frauenbünde und maskierte Frauen', in *Festschrift für Robert Wildhaber*, Basel 1973, pp. 334–47, in particular pp. 342 ff. See also R. Wolfram, 'Weiberbünde', *Zeitschrift für Volkskunde*, N. F., IV (1932), pp. 137–46 (influenced by O. Höfler); W. Puchner, 'Spuren frauenbündischer Organisationsformen im neugriechischen Jahreslaufbrauchtum', *Schweizerisches Archiv für Volkskunde* 72 (1976), pp. 146–70. The presence of boys and girls among the Ukrainian *koljadanti* (cf. Propp, op. cit., p. 75) appears unusual: but cf. A. van Gennep, *Le Folklore des Hautes-Alpes*, I, Paris 1946, pp. 263–4 (Château-Ville-Vielle).

43. They have been identified and partially discussed by Eliade, 'Some Observations', pp. 158 ff. References to fertility occur in a pantomime of the Slobozia *căluşari*

described by A. Helm, in the appendix to A. Brody, *The English Mummers and their Plays*, Philadelphia 1970, pp. 165–6.

44. See Buhociu, *Le folklore*, p. 250.

45. Cf. the rich analysis in ibid., pp. 159–234. On the connection between St. Theodore and horses, see also T. A. Koleva, 'Parallèles balkano-caucasiens dans certains rites et coutumes', *Ethnologia Slavica*, III (1971), pp. 194 ff.

46. Cf. Eliade, 'Notes on the Căluşari', p. 121. In the orthodox calendar the festivals associated with the name of St. Theodore are three in number, attached to three different saints.

47. See the present author's 'Charivari, associations juvéniles, chasse sauvage', in *Le Charivari*, by J. Le Goff and J.-C. Schmitt eds, Paris and La Haye 1981, pp. 131–40. In criticizing my interpretation, H. Bausinger has remarked that it basically repeats that of O. Höfler ('Traditionale Welten, Kontinuität und Wandel in der Volkskultur', *Zeitschrift für Volkskunde*, 81, 1985, pp. 178–9). I should have stressed – together with the fact that Höfler in turn was preceded by Meuli ('Die deutschen Masken', pp. 96 ff.). J. -C. Schmitt (*Religione* cit., pp. 206–37) reaches partly different conclusions.

48. See the texts cited by A. Kuhn, 'Wodan', *Zeitschrift für deutsches Altertum*, XV (1845), pp. 472–94 (which identified Robin Hood with Wodan) and by R. Wolfram, 'Robin Hood und Hobby Horse', *Wiener Prähistorische Zeitschrift*, XIX (1932), pp. 357–74 (which dissents in part from the conclusions of the preceding essay). The mythical implications are neglected in the otherwise excellent essays devoted to the *charivari* by N. Z. Davis ('The Reasons of Misrule', in *Society and Culture in Early Modern France*, Stanford 1975, pp. 97–123) and E. P. Thompson ('Rough Music': le Charivari Anglais', *Annales ESC*, XXVII, 1972, pp. 285–312). On the latter, see also my 'Charivari, associations juvéniles'. On Robin Hood see now P. R. Coss, 'Aspects of Cultural Diffusion in Medieval England: the Early Romances, Local Society and Robin Hood', *Past and Present*, 108 (August 1985), pp. 35–79.

49. Cf. Meuli, *Bettelumzüge*, pp. 57–8 and idem, 'Schweizer Masken', pp. 179–80; in general see also E. Hoffmann-Krayer, 'Knabenschaften und Volksjustiz in der Schweiz', *Schweizerisches Archiv für Volkskunde*, VIII (1904), pp. 81–89, 161–78; G. Caduff, *Die Knabenschaften Graubündens*, Chur 1929.

50. H. Jeanmaire, in a well-known essay ('La cryptie lacédémonienne', *Revue des études grecques*, 26, 1913, pp. 121–50) first suggested a comparison with the ethnological data on the initiation of the young men. See the same author's *Couroi et Couretes*, Lille-Paris 1939, pp. 540 ff.; J. Ducat, 'Le mépris des Hilotes', *Annales E.S.C.*, 29 (1974), pp. 145–64; Pierre Vidal-Naquet, *Les chasseur noir. Formes de pensée et formes de société dans le monde grec*, Paris 1981, pp. 151 ff. Bremmer, 'The "suodales" of Poplios Valesios', *Zeitschrift für Papyrologie und Epigraphik*, 47 (1982), pp. 133–47 Bremmer and Horsfall, *Roman Myth*, op. cit. On a more general level, see Lévi-Strauss, art. cit.

51. Cf. on both of these L. Weniger, 'Feralis exercitus', *Archiv für Religionswissenschaft*, 9 (1906), pp. 201–47 (on p. 223 an anti-French war-mongering digression). On the initiatory value of colouring one's face with chalk (like the Kouretes in the Cretan myth on the infancy of Zeus), see J. Harrison, *Prolegomena to the Study of Greek Religion* (1903, 1907) London 1980, pp. 491 ff.; idem, *Themis* (1911), London 1977, pp. 1–29. On the Phoceans, see A. Brelich, *Guerre, agoni e culti nella Grecia arcaica*, Bonn 1961, pp. 46–52; from a different point of view, P. Ellinger, 'Le Gypse et la Boue: I. Sur les mythes de la guerre d'anéantissement', *Quaderni urbinati di cultura classica*, 29 (1978), pp. 7–35.

52. Cf. H. Güntert, *Ueber altisländische Berserkergeschichten*, Beilage zum Jahresbericht des Heidelberger Gymnasiums 1912, Heidelberg 1912; Weiser, *Altgermanische*

Junglingsweihien, Baden 1927, pp. 47–82; W. Müller-Bergström, 'Zur Berserker-frage', in *Niederdeutsche Zeitschrift für Volkskunde*, 12 (1934), pp. 241–44; G. Sieg, 'Die Zweikämpfe der Isländersagas', *Zeitschrift für deutsches Altertum und deutsche Literatur*, 95, (1966) pp. 1–27; Dumézil, *Heur et malheur du guerrier*, Paris 1985, pp. 208 ff.

53. See Gasparini, art. cit., p. 111 and *passim*, which suggests a connection (not documented) with village exogamy, in its turn linked to hypothetical matriarchal structures. See the same author's *Il matriarcato slavo*, Florence 1973, in particular pp. 434 ff.

54. On all this see the essay (inspired by Meuli) by H. Dietschy, 'Der Umzug der Stopfer, ein alter Maskenbrauch der Bündner Oberlandes', *Archives Suisses des traditions populaires*, XXXVII (1939), pp. 25–43; Meuli, 'Schweizer Masken', pp. 183–5. In re-editing his *Rhaetiae Alpestris Topographica Descriptio* (published only in 1884), D. Chiampel (Ulricus Chiampellus) at various points followed the Latin translation of Tschudi's pamphlet published by Sebastian Münster in 1538: but the additional details are obviously the result of direct observation.

55. Tschudi, harking back in 1571 (*Gallia Comata*, published two centuries later) to the page on the *Stopfer*, observed that the custom had been abandoned some years ago; at Surselva, however, it was still practised (cf. Dietschy, art. cit.).

56. Cf. W. Hein, 'Das Huttlerlaufen', *Zeitschrift des Vereins für Volkskunde*, 9 (1899), pp. 109–23 and, in general, Meuli, *Schweizer Masken*.

57. Cf. Meuli, 'Bettelumzüge', p. 58; Dönner, *Tiroler Fasnacht*, Wien 1949, pp. 137–84.

58. Cf. the extensive comparative picture delineated by G. Gugitz, 'Die alpenländischen Kampfspiele und ihre kultische Bedeutung', *Oesterreichische Zeitschrift für Volks-kunde*, 55 (1952), pp. 101 ff. (it lacks, however, any reference to the *punchiadurs*).

59. The analogy with the Perchten, already proposed by Caduff (op. cit., pp. 99–100), is developed by Dietschy, art. cit., pp. 34 ff. Meuli has queried whether the *punchiadurs* were armed dances or actual ritual battles ('Schweizer Masken', p. 184): the Friulian documentation suggests the second alternative.

60. Dietschy recalls the stories of old Thiess (art. cit., p. 37 n. 1), apparently interpreting them, as Meuli had, in the ritual rather than the mythical sense. For his part Meuli ('Schweizer Masken' p. 185) supposes that the rituals of the *punchiadurs* were of German origin.

61. On all this see the very rich essay by R. Bleichsteiner, art. cit. On the author – a person of original and secluded scholarship – see the obituary and bibliography edited by L. Schmidt, in *Archiv für Völkerkunde*, IX (1954), pp. 1–17.

62. See G. Charachidzé, *Le système religieux de la Géorgie païenne*, Paris 1968, pp. 266 ff.

63. Cf. Bleichsteiner, art. cit., pp. 11 ff. and 42 ff.

64. Cf. Eliade, 'Chamanisme': this is a conjecture by V. Diószegi, adopted in the essay's conclusion as a certain fact, which would prove the non-existence in the Rumanian sphere of forms of 'shamanism' (see below, however, n. 66).

65. See the documentation collected by W. Müster, *Der Schamanismus und seine Spuren in der Saga, im deutschen Märchen und Glauben*, Diss. Graz 1957 (which I have been able to consult thanks to the courtesy of Dr. Pietro Marsilli), and especially the useful review of A. Closs, 'Der Schamanismus bei den Indoeuropäern' *Innsbrucker Beiträge zur Kulturwissenschaft*, 14 (1968), pp. 289 ff. The same Closs (cf. 'Der Ekstase des Schamanen', *Ethnos*, 34, 1969, pp. 70–89, 77) traces the rituals connected to Perchten back to a 'religious, more or less shamanistic complex', despite the absence of ecstasies or trances.

66. In "Chamanisme" chez les Roumains?' (1968) Eliade limits himself to a rapid mention of the *căluşari*. In 'Notes on the Căluşari' (1973) he discusses them at length,

calling their dances 'para-shamanistic' and excluding them, due to the absence of references to ecstasy, from 'shamanism' in the real sense. In 'Some Observations on European Witchcraft' (1975) he compares the *căluşari* with the *benandanti*, accepting in the latter case the analogy with shamanistic ecstasy proposed by the present writer. Over the years Eliade has continued to see in ecstasy the distinctive feature of shamanism: but the identification of ecstatic characteristics in the Rumanian *strigoi* (ibid., p. 159) has implicitly modified the panorama drawn in the 1968 essay.

67. Cf. E. T. Kirby, 'The origin of the Mummers' Play', *Journal of American Folklore*, 84, (1971), pp. 275–88. On the danger of unduly extending the notion of shamanistic ecstasy, cf. H. Motzki, *Schamanismus als Problem religionswissenschaftlicher Terminologie*, Köln 1977 (which on p. 17 cites an injunction to prudence formulated by Van Gennep in 1903).

68. On children (non-initiated) as representatives of the dead (super-initiated), cf. Lévi-Strauss, art. cit., p. 1586.

69. See the very well-known pages of M. Granet, *Danses et légendes de la Chine ancienne*, Paris 1926, I, pp. 298 ff.; see besides D. Bodde, *Festivals in Classical China*, Princeton 1975, pp. 75–138; J. Levi, *Aspects du mythe du tigre dans la Chine ancienne. Le représentations de la sauvagerie dans les mythes et le rituel chinois*, thesis of the 3rd cycle (typewritten), pp. 133 ff. The figure covered with a bear skin with four eyes of yellow metal is compared by Lévi-Strauss to the multiple masks of the Eskimos and Kwakiutl (*Structural Anthropology*, Harmondsworth, p. 288): cf. also R. Mathieu, 'La patte de l'ours', *L'homme*, XXIV (1984), p. 23, which (referring back to C. Hentze) records in this the power to see everything that the Ugrian inhabitants of the Ob region attribute to the bear.

70. See M. Eliade, *Le mythe de l'éternel retour*, Paris 1969, especially pp. 83 ff. It should be remembered that in the preface to a reprint of the English translation (*Cosmos and History. The Myth of the Eternal Return*, New York 1959, pp. VIII-IX) Eliade tried to redefine the word 'archetype' in ontological and not psychological terms, disassociating himself from Jung. In this book (by far his most original) Eliade repeated a number of elements already isolated by Frazer (cf., for example, *The Golden Bough*, IX: *The Scapegoat*, New York 1935, p. 328), combining them with mortuary themes that emerged from the research of Dumézil (*Le problème des Centaures*), Höfler (*Kultische Geheimbünde*) and one of the latter's followers, A. Slawik. The pathos of defeat inspired Eliade, who had behind him a Fascist and anti-Semitic experience. (see F. Jesi, *Cultura di destra*, Milan 1979, pp. 38 ff.), to construct a theory of the flight from history. Though starting out from a partly analogous reflection on the theme of crises and a new beginning, the opposite conclusions were reached by E. De Martino in *Il mondo magico* (1948).

71. Cf., respectively, Eliade, *Le mythe*, p. 87, which resumes the conclusions of A. Slawik (but at the same time declares that it is not concerned with the genesis of mythico-ritual forms); and V. Lanternari, *La grande festa*, Bari 1976, pp. 538 ff. (where Eliade's ahistorical and quasi-mystical perspective is criticized).

72. Cf. H. Ehelolf, 'Wettlauf und szenisches Spiel im hethitischen Ritual', *Sitzungsberichte der preussischen Akademie der Wissenschaften*, XXI (1925), pp. 267–72; W. Schubart, 'Aus der Keilschrift-Tafeln von Boghazköi', *Gnomon*, 2 (1926), p. 63 (proposes a somewhat different translation from the preceding one); A. Lesky, 'Ein ritueller Scheinkampf bei den Hethitern', *Archiv für Religionswissenschaft*, 24 (1926–27), pp. 73 ff. (supposes that this is a matter of a vegetation ritual that is no longer intelligible and therefore related to an historic event; p. 77 refers back to a passage of G. Tschudi on the *Stopfer*); A. Götze, 'Kulturgeschichte des alten Orients', in *Handbuch der Altertumswissenschaft*, III, 3, Munich 1933, p. 152 (denies that this is a ritual).

73. See H. Usener, *Heilige Handlung*, Part II: *Caterva*, in *Kleine Schriften*, IV, Leipzig and Berlin 1913, pp. 435–47 (as usual full of very acute insights). Cf. also van Gennep, *Le Folklore des Hautes-Alpes*, I, p. 62.

74. Against this interpretation, advanced more than once, see Dumézil, *La religione romana arcaica*, It. trans. Milan 1977, pp. 197 ff.; and idem, *Fêtes romaines d'été et d'automne*, Paris 1975, pp. 181 ff. (particularly convincing is the demonstration on pp. 204–10 of the retrospective, not optative, significance of the words of Festus, *ob frugum eventum*).

75. See Dumézil, *Le religione romana*, pp. 206 ff. (with bibliography) and 322–3. W. H. Roscher ('Das von der "Kynanthropie"') strongly underscores this point; cf. also E. Rohde, *Kleine Schriften*, Tübingen and Leipzig 1901, II, pp. 222–3.

76. Years ago, having counterposed symbolists (Frazer, Freud, and Cassirer in his first period) and functionalists (Durkheim and his followers, J. Harrison, Malinowski, Cassirer in his second phase), Edmund Leach resolutely took his stand with the second group, stating that whilst many of the comparisons proposed by Frazer were genuinely significant, since their context was systematically ignored, functionalist doctrine dictated that one ignore their implications ('Lévi-Strauss in the Garden of Eden: An Examination of Some Recent Developments in the Analysis of Myth', *Transactions of the New York Academy of Sciences*, s. II, vol. 23, 1961, p. 387). But to violate Leach's injunction does not necessarily mean to return to Frazer. Certain questions formulated by Frazer can be asked again without accepting his replies (my Frazer had read Wittgenstein).

PART THREE

I

Eurasian Conjectures

1. Two bearded men confront each other with shields held high, brandishing daggers. One wears a helmet, the other is bare-headed. They wear tunics gathered at the waist by a belt and wide embroidered trousers. Between them a man on horseback, his chest covered by a cuirass made of scales, holds a short spear, turning it against one of the two men on foot. He too wears a pair of trousers, but they are tighter fitting. On the ground a horse lies on its back. The beards, the hair, the scales of the cuirass, the embroidery of the garments, the muscular bodies of the dead and live horse gleam in a uniform golden light. Five minuscule crouching lions support the comba-tants. From the pedestal on which the lions rest ray out the long parallel teeth of a comb. Both the lions and the teeth of the comb are gold (fig.13).

   Three centuries before Christ a Greek craftsman, who probably lived in a city on the shores of the Black Sea, carved and poured this comb for the wife, concubine or daughter of some Scythian chieftain. The details of the scene depicted on the comb's edge (just over five centimetres high) are carved to obtain a sharper finish. But the overall effect, despite the minuscule size, is majestic. Here the language of Greek monumental sculpture has been applied to represent foreign realities.[1] Perhaps the battle scene that adorns the comb alluded to a Scythian legend suggested to the artist by the anonymous person who commissioned him. The trousers worn by the three warriors certainly have nothing Greek about them.

2. The Greeks called 'Scythians' a conglomeration of nomadic and semi-nomadic populations with whom they had come into contact in the Black Sea area. The Scythians did not know how to write. What we know about them comes from the excavations of the archaeologists and the descriptions of outside observers, first among them Herodotus. In the mass of objects found in tombs, Scythian artifacts (studs, cart ornaments, cups) lie side by side with those of Greek manufacture. Among the latter we find the golden comb with the battle scene. The contrast between the stylistic code and the reality represented immediately brings to mind the accounts and descriptions contained in Herodotus' fourth book, devoted precisely to the Scythians.[2]

207

That all descriptions are culturally conditioned, and therefore not neutral, is (or should be) obvious. Herodotus' voracious curiosity in collecting and relaying information and news was guided by powerful (and potentially distorting), albeit often unconscious, patterns and categories. It would be naive to ignore this element; but to deduce from it the impossibility of going beyond the horizon of Herodotus' text would be simply absurd. For instance, precious fragments of knowledge have emerged from a comparison between the descriptions contained in Herodotus' fourth book and other documentary series, selected fortuitously or on the basis of cultural and mental patterns different from his: on the one hand, archaeological finds; on the other hand, traditions deriving from a population with an Iranic language like the Ossetians, descendants of the Alans and the Roxolans, in their turn descendants of the Scythians. Here, as elsewhere, the objectivity of the reconstruction is guaranteed by the intersection, not always convergent, of different testimonies.

3. Herodotus tells us (IV. 73–5) that the Scythians, having buried their dead, purify themselves like this: they hoist three poles and lean them toward one another, cover them with felt cloths and sit beneath them, around a basin filled with red hot stones onto which they throw hemp seeds. The aromatic smoke released by the hemp makes them moan with pleasure. A comparison between this passage and the descriptions of similar Siberian ceremonies composed by travellers and ethnographers has led us to suppose the existence of shamanistic practices aimed at producing ecstasy among the Scythians who lived in the region to the north of the Black Sea. To bolster this hypothesis one can cite an exceptional archaeological document. At Pazyryk, in the mountains of the eastern Altai, a number of tumulus-shaped graves have been uncovered, dating back to two or three centuries before Christ and preserved under ice. Besides a horse disguised with reindeer antlers, a number of hemp seeds have been found in them, of the *cannabis sativa* (i.e., marijuana) variety, as well as of *cannabis ruderalis Janisch*. Some were preserved in a leather flask, others were roasted among the stones contained in a small cone-shaped bronze basin with handles wrapped in birch bark. In the same grave were found a drum and string instrument, similar to those used two thousand years later by the Siberian shamans.[5]

4. From the eighth century BC nomadic populations originating in central Asia began to make incursions to the west, along the borders of the Iranian highlands, and to the east, into the strip of land between Mongolia and China. It is not clear what caused this twofold, opposite migratory wave across the Eurasian continent – the first such wave documented with certainty in a series destined to be repeated at regular intervals for about two thousand years.[6] It has been assumed that around the year 1000 BC a period of prolonged drought led people over much of Central Asia to abandon less fertile cultivated land, bringing about the emergence of a regime of nomadic shepherds which until then was only latent.[7]

The Scythians, who between the years 800 and 700 BC established their domination over the Iranian highlands, belonged to these nomad populations. Later, the ascent of the empire of the Medes drove them toward the Caucasus and the Black Sea. The Greeks bought gold, amber and furs from them. It may be (but it is not certain) that among the Scythians there were also groups of Mongolian ancestry.[8] In any case, the shamanistic elements that have been traced in the religion of the Scythians and also that of Zoroaster (but here the opinion is very controversial) would, according to one suggestion, derive from contacts with the culture of the steppes of Central Asia.[9] We know that there were specialized soothsayers among the Scythians who predicted the future with willow tree rods or with the bark from linden trees. These soothsayers, Herodotus says (IV. 67; 1. 105) were called *Enares*, that is, non-men, women-men: an appellation which led people to think of the trans-sexualism and transvestism frequent among Siberian shamans.[10] A greater wealth of information, though doubly indirect, has been transmitted by the legend surrounding a Greek of the Hellespont, Aristeas of Proconnesus (a small island in the sea of Marmara), who possibly lived in the seventh century BC. In a poem, the *Arimaspian Songs*, of which only a few verses survive, he told how, possessed by Apollo, he had wandered north among the anthropophagous Issedones, from whom he had received information about creatures living even further north: the one-eyed Arimaspians, the griffons, who guard the treasures, and the Hyperboreans. Herodotus (IV. 13–16), who presents the journey as real, attributes to Aristeas miraculous traits, such as his death in a washerman's shop , the subsequent mysterious reappearance of his corpse before a double resurrection – six years later at Proconnesus, and no less than 240 years later at Metapontum. Here Aristeas had a statue erected to himself alongside that of Apollo, whom he was in the habit of accompanying in the shape of a raven. In later traditions these magical characteristics were further elaborated. According to Maximus of Tyre (second century AD), Aristeas' soul had temporarily left his inanimate body to fly across the skies like a bird: the land, rivers and populations seen from on high had later become the subject of his poem. Pliny (*Naturalis Historia*, VII. 174) mentions a statue that portrayed Aristeas in the act of making his soul issue from his mouth in the shape of a raven. According to other witnesses, Aristeas was capable of falling into catalepsy at will; upon returning from these ecstatic journeys, he predicted plagues, earthquakes and floods.[11] All this shows that the Greek colonies, established as early as the seventh century BC on the shores of the Black Sea, had absorbed several shamanistic traits found in Scythian culture.[12]

We have seen that even at the end of the last century among the Ossetians, distant descendants of the Scythians, there existed individuals (the *burkudzäutä*) who periodically plunged into ecstasies, visiting the realm of the dead in spirit.[13] The beyond entered by Soslan, one of the protagonists of the Ossetian legends of the Narti, bears a striking resemblance to that described in the legends of the Altaian peoples (Tatars, Buryats). In both cycles the hero or heroine sees a series of persons engaged in incomprehensible activities, later deciphered as penances or rewards for their actions on earth. Sometimes details coincide: for example, the married couple who live in discord fight over a cover made of an ox's skin; happy couples rest serenely on the skins of hares.[14] Such precise convergences, though derived from very late records, confirm that the Scythians, before undertaking their migration toward the West (eighth century BC), had lived for a long time in close contact with the nomadic populations of Central Asia. In the culture of these shepherds, as in that of the hunters stationed further north in the Siberian *taigá* covered with fir and birch trees, shamanistic practices occupied an important place.[15]

5.   To reconstruct the folkloric roots of the witches' Sabbath we set out from the evidence on the ecstatic cult of the nocturnal goddess. Its geographic distribution seemed at first to delimit a Celtic phenomenon. But this interpretation collapsed when confronted by a series of eccentric testimonies of Mediterranean origin. New hypotheses then emerged. Anomalous details, such as the resurrection of bones, suggested the possibility that in the physiognomy of the nocturnal goddess, and more generally in the multiform stratum of beliefs that merged in the stereotype of the Sabbath, were encrusted much more ancient elements, originating with the nomadic populations of Central Asia, in their turn linked to the cultures of the hunters located in the extreme northern regions. The distribution of phenomena such as the battles fought for the prosperity of the community or the seasonal rituals which hinged on animal masquerades likewise transcended the confines of the Indo-European linguistic space. Areas of contact emerged – Lapland, Hungary – which did not seem at all sufficient to explain the precocious and dispersed presence of shamanistic traits on the European continent.

As the scope of the research broadened to include distinctly heterogeneous times, places and cultures, the possibility of adopting an historical perspective seemed to become more remote. Limiting ourselves to a rigorously morphological analysis seemed the only possible path. Now the connection between Scythians and the nomadic populations of Central Asia at last allows us to glimpse the possibility of inserting the data gathered up to this point into an historical context which is plausible, even if only known in a fragmentary manner.

6.   At the beginning of the sixth century BC small groups of Scythians left the shores of the Black Sea, pushing West. After crossing the Dniester and the Danube they established themselves permanently in Dobrugia. The Thracians, who lived there, recognized the Scythians' supremacy. The region – a plain partially covered by swamps – was accordingly called 'Little Scythia'. Here, at the beginning of the fourth century BC, flowed Celtic populations, swept up by an expansionist drive which, having overrun part of

the Balkan peninsula, ended with the foundation of Galatian colonies in Asia Minor. We might ask whether the confluence of Thracians (or Thraco-Getas), Scythians and Celts in the area of the lower Danube – extreme limit of the immense steppe corridor that joins Asia to Europe – does not furnish us with a key to decipher the physiognomy of the goddess followed by cohorts of souls, on the one hand, and, on the other, the geographical distribution of her ecstatic cult.[16]

In the multiform image of the nocturnal divinity we identified a complex cultural stratification. Behind Diana and Herodias, mentioned in the penitential books of the High Middle Ages, emerged the protagonists of a series of local cults – Bensozia, Oriente, Richella, and so on – which echoed Celtic divinities like Epona, the *Matres*, Artio. But the representations of Epona, the Celtic goddess on horseback, remind us of the Thracian goddess Bendis – probably the 'queen' goddess whom Herodotus assimilated to Artemis. Bendis was worshipped in Athens together with a Thraco-Phrygian goddess, Adrasteia, namesake of one of Zeus' Cretan nurses, whom Diodorus Siculus identified with the Mother goddesses of Engyon. The latter have been set alongside the nymphs of Celtic physiognomy worshipped in the Thracian sanctuary of Saladinovo.[17] It has been supposed that Brauron, the sanctuary where Artemis was venerated by young girls disguised as female bears, was a Thracian name.[18] Artemis Agrotera (i.e., wild) inherited several features of a female divinity, a 'great goddess' worshipped in prehistoric times on the northern shores of the Black Sea: this cult had been appropriated by the Cimmerians who, at the beginning of the Iron Age, had invaded the region.[19] The Scythians, who around 700 BC in their turn chased the Cimmerians out of southern Russia, pushing them westward, worshipped a goddess, half-woman, half-serpent, surrounded by pairs of serpents: an image which can immediately be assimilated to those of the so-called 'mistress of the animals', which is Artemis' epithet in the *Iliad*.[20] This web of resemblances, of identical names and hybridizations, would seem to reinforce the hypothesis, already cautiously advanced, that the very ancient physiognomy of Artemis, expressed in the Homeric appellation, 'mistress of the animals', is of Eurasian derivation.[21] The Middle Eastern and Mediterranean portrayals of an often semi-bestial divinity invariably surrounded by pairs of horses, birds, fishes and snakes, have been compared to the 'mother of the animals' which some Siberian populations (Yakuts, Tungus) worship in the shape of a bird, elk or fawn, considering her the progenitrix of shamans.[22]

In the nocturnal goddess, semi-bestial or surrounded by animals, at the centre of an ecstatic cult of the shamanistic variety, identified with Diana by canonists and inquisitors, we recognized a very remote heir of the Eurasian divinities, protectors of the hunt and the forest.[23] This alignment, which in one leap covers two thousand years and thousands of kilometres of *taigá* and steppes (steppes which, as we have said, do not divide but join), was formulated on purely morphological bases. Now we discern the possibility of

211

translating this into a historical sequence: nomads of the steppes – Scythians – Thracians – Celts. We have seen that the shamanistic themes, such as ecstasy, the magic flight, animal metamorphosis, were present in the Scythian as well as in the Celtic context. Even the raven that abandoned the body of the Scottish witches fallen into 'extaseis and transis', could be aligned with the raven that represented the soul of Aristeas.[24] Certainly, the raven was an animal sacred to Apollo, the divinity with which Aristeas proves to be closely associated.[25] But the kingdom of the elves described in the Scottish witch trials bears also an indisputably Celtic stamp. The presence of variants or re-elaborations tied to specific cultural contexts does not contradict the hypothesis of a common pattern: the ecstatic journey into the realm of the dead usually accomplished in animal shape.

7.   Individuals able to transform themselves into birds were mentioned, with ostentatious incredulity, by Ovid (*Met.* XV. 356 ff.), who located them against the background of a composite northern landscape, in which the Chalcidican peninsula (Pallene) reminded him of Thrace (Lake Triton) and Scythia:

> in Hyperborean Pallene there live men who, after having plunged twice in Lake Triton, are covered with downy feathers. I don't believe it: but it is said that Scythian women are able to do the same, by covering their limbs with magic ointments.[26]

The immersion in a Thracian lake, most likely ritual and repeated nine times, reminds us of the equally ritualistic immersion performed by werewolves in an Arcadian pond, assuming animal shape for nine years. For the rest, the Neuroi, to whom (as we know from Herodotus' sceptical mention) was traditionally attributed the ability periodically to transform themselves into wolves, were perhaps a Thracian population.[27]

From the plains of Thrace these beliefs of a shamanistic character could well have been propagated to the west and north. It is known for certain that the Scythians went all the way to the Baltic Sea, crossing Rumania, Hungary, Silesia, Moravia and Galicia – which still preserves in its name the traces of the Gallic, that is, Celtic, colonization, which occurred in the third century BC.[28] To the contact between Scythians and Celts in the region of the lower Danube and in Central Europe, we might perhaps trace back phenomena otherwise not readily explained, such as the massive presence in Ireland of legends linked to werewolves, the surfacing of shamanistic elements in certain Celtic sagas, the convergences of Ossetian epics with Arthurian romances.[29] Against this backdrop the analogy between the battles for fertility fought in ecstasy by, respectively, the Ossetian *burkudzäutä* and Livonian werewolves, likewise appears less inexplicable.

8.   We arrived at a hypothesis of a Eurasian continuum comprising, alongside Tungus shamans, Laplandic *no' aidi* and Hungarian *táltos*, figures

1. Roofing tile from Roussas, in the Dauphiné, from the end of the fourth or beginning of the fifth century AD. A veiled figure, roughly drawn, grapples with an animal (perhaps a deer or a peacock, but more probably an imaginary animal). The words that accompany the figure reveal its identity: it is Hera, 'the cruel Hera'. The cult of this funerary divinity thrived in various parts of Europe for more than a millennium. (From F. Benoit, *L'heroisation equestre*, Gap 1954, table I, 2).

2. Epona, the Celtic goddess, here represented with a horse. Paris, Louvre. (From K. H. Linduff, *Epona, a Celt Among the Romans,* in 'Latomus', 38, 1979).

3. Bas-relief representing the *Matres* or *Matronae,* divinities venerated over a large area of Celtic Europe. Often, as in this image, they are represented in groups of three; more rarely singly. The caps that adorn the heads of the figures at the sides probably recall some local hair-style. Bonn, Rheinisches Landesmuseum.

MATRONIS
AVFANIABVS
QVETTIVS·SEVERVS
QVAESTOR·C·C·A·A
VOTVM·SOLVIT·L·M
MACRINO·ET·CELSO·COS

4. Detail of the mosaic pavement in the Cathedral at Otranto, built by the priest Pantaleone in 1163–65. The character represented is, as the script indicates, the mythical king Artú, who, it was popularly believed, led a band of wandering animals. (Photo: Scala Archive, Florence).

GRATIA PROPOSTA DAL
REVERENDO PADRE INQVISITORE DI
FERRARA MODONA REGGIO, &c.

A tutti li fideli Chriftiani cadduti in Herefia, che fono fotto la fua Giurifditione.

FRATE Camillo Campeggio da 'Pauia dell'Ordine de 'Predicatori nelle Città di Ferrara di Modona, di Reggio & nelle loro Diocesi Inquisitore, & in tutto lo stato dell'Illustrissimo & Eccellentissimo Sig. il Signor Don ALFONSO Quinto Duca di Ferrara &c. Contra gli Heretici & altri numici della santa fede, dalla Apostolica Sede Commissario specialmente deputato, a tutti li fideli christiani in qual si voglia modo pertinenti alle sudette Città, o loro diocesi salute gratia, & pace, in Christo Giesu nostro Sig. e 'Padre. Hauendo io sempre desiderato che le anime smarrite, con la verga di pietà si riducchino al ouile del gran pastore nostro Giesu Christo, persuadendomi che molti sconchiosamente dormino ne gli errori, non curandosi di uscire dalle prigioni del Demonio, per la vergogna, o confusione che pare loro di riceuere ogni volta che col mezzo de l'abiuratione o penitentia publica venghino alla riconciliatione della santa Chiesa. Cosa però che non doueria punto ritenergli, essendo l'errore o vitio de l'Heresia tanto graue, enorme, & in disgratia a N. S. Dio, che per alcun tempo fia stato in tal peccato doueria ricusare o temere qual si voglia sorte o modo di penitentia anchora che vituperosa, o asprissima fosse, accostandomi alla pietà di questa nostra santa Madre, che accetta, & raccoglie tutti pur che di cuore tornino a penitentia, baciando questa compassione alla misera, & fracida conditione humana. Con l'autorità apostolica a me in questa parte commessa, ho deliberato di assignare vn termine di gratia fra il quale ciascheduno che circa la Fede o Dottrina della santa Chiesa Romana, in qual si voglia modo hauesse errato troui la via piu piana, e piu facile di saluarsi, ritornando alla concordia, & vnione della sudetta madre. La onde per questa presente qual sarà in loco di publico editto e grida. Si commonisce, si inuita, si esorta ogni fidele che si troui fuori della vera strada di salute, seguendo la via sinistra de gli heretici a riceuere questa gratia che io con tanta pietà e cortesia gli porgo.

SI fa dunque intendere che chi per suggestione di Sathana padre della bugia e nemico della verità, fosse caduto in false opinioni, o in qual si voglia modo si fosse accostato alla Dottrina di qualche Lutherano o altro heretico, o hauesse tenuto o letto libri heretici, o hauesse fatto qualche altra sorte d'incanti o superstitione, la quale manifestamente contenghi la deformità de l'heresia.

Chi hauesse altramente creduto circa li Sacramenti o loro ministerio di quel che tiene e crede la santa Romana Chiesa Catholica, ouero hauesse vsato le cose Sacramentali in maleficij.

Chi hauesse inuocato, o pregato li demoni per sapere da loro le cose occulte, o che hauno a venire, o datogli honore riuerenze, incensi, profumi, o sacrificij, ouero chi hauesse fatto qualche altra sorte d'incanti o superstitione, la quale manifestamente contenghi la deformità de l'heresia.

Chi hauesse rinegata la santa fede christiana, conuertendosi al giudaismo e circoncisosi, o al paganesimo, o a qualche altra setta o sorte d'infidelità.

Chi hauesse sprezzato le leggi, ordini, decreti, statuti, constitutioni, consuetudini, officij, messe, cerimonie, censure, scommuniche, o pene fatte, instituite, & assignate dalla santa Romana chiesa con credere o dire che non legitimo, o oblighino il christiano ad osseruargli, o vbidirgli.

Chi hauesse negata la potestà del summo Pontefice, o della santa Romana chiesa.

Et in somma chi fosse caduto in qualche altra maniera di errori pertinenti al giudicio della santa Inquisitione purche non sia publico o notorio ma secreto, et che non sia relapso, s'inquisito, o denontiato, o altrimente notisiato appresso il santo officio in questo dominio, o altroue, o se ne venghi nel termine di quindeci giorni dopo la notificatione di questa, ben penito ad accusare o confessare sincera, & interiamente tutti gli errori e complici suoi da me, ouero in mia absentia da miei Vicarij e Locotenenti, o dà me a questo officio specialmente eletti sarà admesso e riceuuto alla abiuratione e penitentia secreta per gratia singolare.

Auertendo poi ciascheduno di qual si voglia stato, grado, ordine, & conditione, che passato il detto termine delli quindeci giorni si procederà poi al castigo di quelli che sarà no per heretici o sospetti di heresia denontiati al santo officio della Inquisitione.

Astringendo, & obligando ogni fidel Christiano sotto pena di escommunicatione, che sappi alcuno tenere, o credere, o sparlare delle sudette cose, o tenghi o legga libri probibiti in termine di quindeci giorni da che lo hara saputo manifestarlo giuridicamente al santo officio nostro, assicurandogli che tutti li denontiatori saranno tenuti secreti.

E perche il vitio della heresia è grauissimo, e si come merita grandissima pena, così non è da imputare così leggiermente. Però ogn'vno auertita a non dare false imputationi al prossimo per appetito di vendetta, o per qualche altra passione, ma tutti si armino di giustitia, e di verità, e di zelo christiano, e cerchino di dare a Christo, quello che è di Christo, & a Cesare quello che è di Cesare. 'Ponendosi il timore di N. S. Dio innanzi a gli occhi, la salute del prossimo, e la gloria di Giesu Christo qual priego vi instradi, e guidi tutti al suo santo Regno, in cui si viue ne i secoli delli secoli Amen. Data in Ferrara nel officio della santa Inquisitione. Alli 2. di Genaro 1564. nell'anno Quinto del Pontificato del Santissimo in Christo 'Padre e Signor nostro. Il Signor Pio 'Pappa Quarto.

Frate Camillo Campeggio Inquifitore e Comiffario.

Rainaldus de Hectore Santiffimę
Inquifitionis de mandato.

LO Illuftrifimo, & Eccellentifimo Sig. il Sig. Duca di Ferrara fa intendere ad ogn'vno come Principe veramente Chriftiano Catholico e pio, che accioche le fuderte cofe fiano offeruate, & adempire, promette di dare a miniftri della Santa Inquifitione ogni braccio, & fauore, non folamente nelle cofe qui efplicate, ma in altre occafioni fecondo che alla giornata auerranno. Di Ferrara 2. di Genaio. M. D. LXIIII.

Gio. Batt. Pigna.

Stampata in Ferrara per Francefco di Rossi da Valenza. 1564.

5. Proclamation of the Inquisitor Brother Camillo Campeggi, dated January 2, 1564. Moderna State Archive, *San Uffizio* b.1 (Photo: Modena State Archive).

6. Detail of the preceding figure. The woman in the chariot is the mysterious goddess who appears at nocturnal gatherings; the old woman in front of them is a witch. The capital letter derives in all probability from *A Pleasing Dialogue* (now lost) written by the philosopher Vincenzo Maggi of Brescia, professor at the University of Ferrara, in which the goddess of the night was called 'Fantasima'. (Photo: Modena State Archive).

7. Bas-relief discovered at Camaro, near Messina. The three figures are assumed to represent the mother goddesses: there was a sanctuary dedicated to them near the city of Engyon. (Photo: Soprintendenza ai Beni Culturali e Ambientali, Syracuse).

8. Votive group in bronze representing the goddess Artio, second to third century AD. A recent restoration has shown that the female figure was a later addition. (Photo: Historisches Museum, Berne).

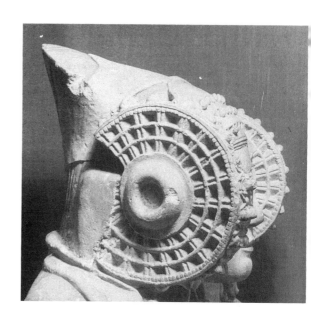

9. Female bust – here seen in profile – found at the end of the nineteenth century at Elche, the ancient *Ilici*, an area on the Spanish coast opposite Ibiza. It was known as the *Woman of Elche*. It probably belongs to the fourth or fifth century BC. It may be a fragment of a standing figure. Madrid, Archaeological Museum.

10. *Woman of Elche*, seen from the front.

11. Wooden sculpture from Ch'angsha, China, from the third or fourth century BC. Now in the British Museum, London. (From A. Salmony, *Corna e Lingua*, Milan 1968).

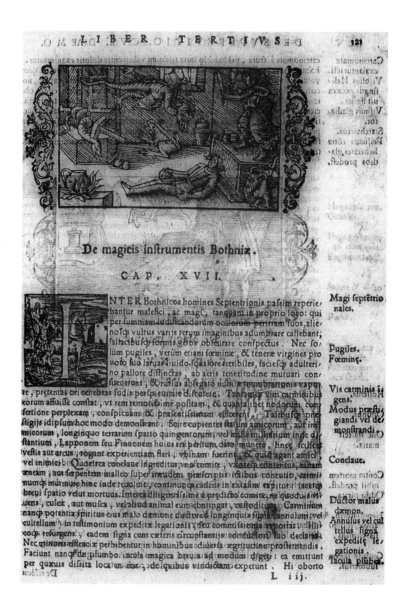

De magicis inſtrumentis Bothniæ.

CAP. XVII.

NTER Bothnicos homines Septentrionis paſsim reperie／
bantur malefici , ac magi , tanquam in proprio loco: qui
per ſummam ludificandorum oculorum peritiam ſuos, alie／
noſ̃ vultus varijs rerum imaginibus adumbrare callebant,
fallacibuſ̃ formis veros obſcurare conſpectus . Nec ſo／
lùm pugiles , verùm etiam fœminæ , & tenerę virgines pro
voto ſuo larvas liuido ſ̃ualore terribiles , facieſ̃ adulteri／
no pallore diſtinctas , ab aëris teneritudine mutuari con／
ſueuerunt , & ruſſus abſtegato nubila ſ̃ inumbrationis vapo／
re , prętentas ori tenebras ſudia perſpicuitate diſcutere . Tantamq̃ vim carminibus
eorum affuiſſe conſtat , vt rem remotiſsimè poſitam , & quantaliber nodorum con／
fertione perplexam , conſpicuam & præſentiſsimam efficerent . Talibuſ̃ prę／
ſtigijs idipſum hoc modo demonſtrant . Scire cupientes ſtatum amicorum , aut in／
micorum , longinquo terrarum ſpatio quingentorum , vel mille milliarium inde di／
ſtantium , Lapponem ſeu Finnonem huius rei peritum , dato munere , ſineꝗ ſcilicet
veſtis aut arcus , rogant experientiam, fieri vbinam fuerint , & quid agant amici
vel inimici . Quòritea conclaue ingreditur vnoſ̃ comite , vxoreꝗ contentus , ranam
æneam , aut ſerpentem malleo ſuper incudem præſcriptis ictibus coharcit , carmi／
numꝗ murmure hinc inde reuoluit , continuoꝗ cadens in extaſim rapitur , iacetꝗ
breui ſpatio velut mortuus . Interea diligentiſsimè à prędicto comite , ne quoduis in／
uens , culex , aut muſca , vel aliud animal eum contingat , cuſtoditur . Carminum
nanꝗ potentia ſpiritus eius malo dæmone ductore à longinquo ſigna, annulum, vel
cultellum , in teſtimonium expeditæ legationis ſeu commiſsionis reportat vt illi
coꝗ reſurgens , eadem ſigna cum cæteris circumſtantijs odmduction ſuo declarat .
Nec minoris efficaciæ perhibentur in hominibus diuerſa ægritudines proſternendis .
Faciunt nanꝗ de plumbo , iacula magica breuia ad modum digiti : ea emittunt
per quæuis diſsita loca vniuerſos, de quibus vindictam expetunt . Hi oborto

L iij.

12.   Lapp shamans in ecstasy. (From Olaus Magnus, *Historia de gentibus septentrionalis*, Rome 1555).

13. Golden comb from the tumulus of Solocha, Melitopol, Ukraine. It probably dates from the fourth century BC and was engraved by a Greek artisan for some Scythian woman; the people represented are Scythians, as their dress shows. Leningrad, Hermitage Museum.

14. Visigothic buckles found at Badajoz, Spain, dated at about 550–600 AD. From the John Walters Museum, Baltimore.

15. Scythian buckle, seventh or eighth century BC. Los Angeles, Los Angeles County Museum.

16–17.   Statue of a young woman being initiated into the Eleusinian cult, first century AD, and detail. (Roman copy of a Greek original of the fifth century BC). Rome, Palazzo dei Conservatori. (Photo: Vasari, Rome).

18. Urs Graf, *Crippled Devil*, engraving, 1512. Basle, Kunstsammlung. (From S. Sas, *Der Hinkende als Symbol*, Zurich 1964).

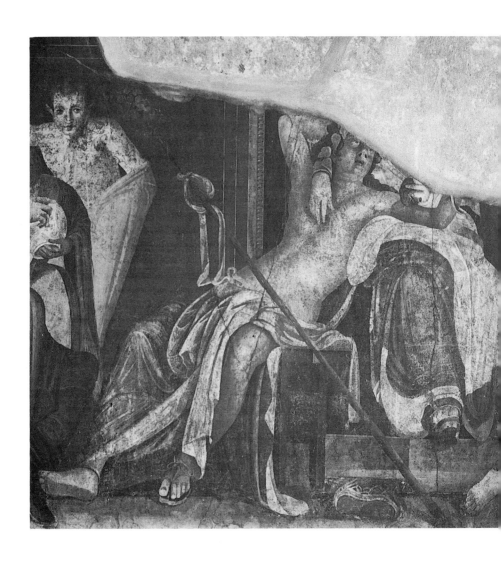

19. Detail from a fresco in the Villa dei Misteri at Pompeii, first century BC, showing an initiation rite. (Photo: Fabbri Archive, Milan).

originating in the Indo-European cultural milieu, such as *kresniki, benandanti*, women followers of the nocturnal goddess, and so on, via a purely morphological itinerary. The series has been reconstructed by means of comparisons, the selection of a set of traits such as ecstasies, battles for fertility, mediation with the world of the dead, the conviction that there existed individuals endowed with special powers since birth. None of these traits was specific: specific was their combination (sometimes only partial). Analogous forms of classification have already been proposed in the linguistic context.[30] Now, the sequence Siberian nomads – Scythians – Thracians – Celts introduces not only temporal, but also genetic elements into a presentation that has hitherto remained deliberately achronic.[31] Given cultural convergences of the amplitude that we have described, the theoretically possible explanations are three: (a) diffusion; (b) derivation from a common source; (c) derivation from structural characteristics of the human mind.[32] The one we have offered fits into category (a): the presence of shamanistic beliefs in the European milieu is traced back to a process of diffusion. Is this an acceptable explanation?

9. Before answering, it is necessary to say something about the nature of the documentation. As we have seen, to classify beliefs or practices in folkloric culture, known via indirect, casual, often stereotyped testimonies interspersed by hiatuses and silences, is difficult. But to translate these classifications into historical terms appears in many cases to be impossible. For example, a series of convergences between the folkloric culture of the Romanian Carpathians and that of the Caucasus has led us to suppose that the relationships between the two regions had in the past been very intense: but when? At the beginning of the century, when the shepherds of the Carpathians owned large numbers of flocks in the Crimea? Or at a much more distant period, through indirect contacts? And if this is the case, who were the intermediaries? The Alans, some of whom abandoned the steppes in the thirteenth century to migrate westward?[33] Uncertainties of such importance are anything but exceptional. It is true, of course, that linguistic evidence sometimes allows us to reach more precise conclusions. Here too we shall restrict ourselves to one example. The presence in Hungarian of borrowings from the Ossetian presupposes that the two linguistic communities, today separate, were in the past geographically contiguous. We do not know when this happened. But on the basis of the characteristics of the borrowings, it has been maintained that the contact was with a population that spoke a language similar to one of the Ossetian dialects, *digor*: that is, the Alans.[34] The function of cultural intermediaries which they performed appears, in this instance, quite well founded. It may be that linguistic traces might also offer a more solid basis for the attempt to reconstruct the diffusion of beliefs of a shamanistic kind. As we have seen, they were shared by populations that spoke Indo-European as well as Uralic languages. The example of Hungarian and Ossetian indicates that this did not preclude

213

linguistic exchanges. In conjunction with the words, beliefs, rituals and customs could circulate.[35] And, naturally, things.

10. Indeed, a way of circumventing the obstacle represented by the scarcity of dated information (or information that can be dated with certainty) on, or about, shamanistic beliefs or practices is offered us by things. More precisely, by the products of the "animal style" art or art of the steppes. These terms conventionally indicate objects, often adorned with zoomorphic decorations, that derive from a geographical ambit situated between China and the Scandinavian peninsula, between approximately 1000 BC and 1000 AD.[36] Chinese amulets of the Chou period, ornaments on ceremonial staffs in Inner Mongolia, golden bracelets from central Asia or Siberia, Iranian broaches, Thraco-Getan silver vases, Celtic disks (*phalerae*), Visigoth and Lombard fibulas (fig. 14), display – beyond the particularities that distinguish them – a disconcerting family resemblance, from a stylistic as well iconographic angle.[37]

From mediaeval Europe we are once again driven back to the boundless Eurasian steppe, traversed by nomads on horseback. We see an interminable saga of intricate cultural exchanges take shape: but beginning when, and where? The debate on the origin of the "animal style" is still extremely lively: but the bridging function between Asia and Europe performed by Scythians in this instance too is indubitable.[38] Their contacts with Middle Eastern, especially Iranian, art, are obvious. More controversial, but credible, is the hypothesis that they also utilized figurative themes and patterns from the steppes of central Asia, or perhaps actually from the forests of northern Siberia.[39] Through the direct or indirect mediation of the Scythians, elements of the art of the steppes probably transmigrated into Sarmatian, Scandinavian and Celtic art.[40] Among these contacts, the one joining Thracian culture (or the culture that crystallized on the plains of Thrace) and Celtic culture appears particularly close. It is significant that the place of origin of the celebrated Gundestrup cauldron (second–first century BC) has been sought, alternately, in Thrace and in northern Gaul.[41]

Siberian hunters, nomadic shepherds of the steppes of Central Asia, Scythians, Thracians and Celts: the chain we have postulated in order to explain the diffusion of shamanistic beliefs from Asia to Europe, from the steppes to the Atlantic, was proposed (amid not a few objections) to explain the diffusion of the themes and forms of "zoomorphic art". Here too we have a reconstruction, in part conjectural, which seeks to justify a series of formal resemblances in historical terms. Without a doubt the sum of two hypotheses – even two converging hypotheses, suggested by different documentary series – does not yet constitute proof. Yet it must be noted that unlike the evidence on shamanistic belief, the products of the so-called "animal style" are a direct, first-hand source, not filtered through foreign eyes or cultural schemes (except ours, of course). They confirm that the historical trans-mission we conjectured is, if not certain, at least likely. But there is more. It may be that the link between the two circuits (that of the objects and that of the beliefs) was even closer. Indeed it has been proposed that in the struggles between animals, real or imaginary (bears, wolves, stags and griffons), portrayed by the art of the nomadic peoples, we should recognize a representation of the struggle between souls, transformed into animals, fought by the Eurasian shamans (alongside whom we might place, in the European sphere, the Hungarian *táltos* or the Balkan *kresniki*). With a good dose of simplification the attempt has been made to trace "animal style" back to a shamanistic ideology.[42]

11.   We have reached a first conclusion: the series we have constructed on purely morphological grounds is compatible with a documented web of historical relationships. The hypothesis of borrowings would seem to be confirmed. But 'compatible' does not mean 'connected in fact'. In the case of phenomena such as those of which we are speaking the relationship between existing evidence, possible evidence and the realities attested to, is supremely uncertain. Eloquent in this respect is the extraordinary success of an iconographic motif: the so-called 'flying gallop', which depicts a horse belly to the ground, almost flattened against it. Objects of the most diverse provenance and physiognomy are adorned with this motif: a Mycenean gold-covered wooden box (sixteenth century BC); a Scythian buckle (eighth–seventh century BC) (fig. 15); a golden Siberian plaque (sixth–fourth century BC); a cameo from Sassanid Persia (third century AD); a Chinese vase of the Ming period (1500 AD); and so on. We know with certainty that the motif of the 'flying gallop' returned to the West toward the middle of the eighteenth century thanks to Giuseppe Castiglione – a Genoese painter, a Jesuit who derived it from Chinese art and passed it on to Stubbs and Géricault.[43] By contrast, we do not know where and when the 'flying gallop' had its origins, or how it was propagated. Naturally, we cannot exclude the possibility that the motif was independently invented in different civilizations. But what has led us to suppose the contrary is its conventionality: it is a formula at once extremely effective and without any referent in reality.[44] The basic analogy with the questions posed by the myths and rituals that we have examined (did they arise independently? did they spread from a particular place and at a particular time?) is evident. But another, more specific analogy exists, tied to the presence of the 'flying gallop' motif in "animal style". That the diffusion – if diffusion there was – occurred from West to East, from Crete and Mycenae to Asia, as has been supposed, appears most unlikely.[45] The dates of the evidence we possess have a relative value: more ancient objects, especially if made of easily perishable materials like those used by the nomads (wood, leather, felt), may have been destroyed. Might not the populations that settled in Greece during the Bronze Age, having come from the East, have brought with them objects similar to those of the art of the steppes, and equally fragile?[46] An eventuality of this kind would imply an inversion – from East to West, rather than from West to East – of the

'flying gallop's' diffusion. In any case, it re-tables a much more general hypothesis: the possibility that the tenacious and elusive cultures of the nomads of the steppes have left a profound trace, albeit one hard to document, on other cultures closer to us, beginning with the Greek. Perhaps the circulation of images and beliefs that we have outlined was made possible by a prior sedimentation.

12.   By dint of regressing to an ever more remote past, one is apt to slip unconsciously from an explanation in terms of borrowings or diffusion (a) to an explanation in terms of derivation from a common source (b). This second proposition is anything but new. An Indo-Uralic linguistic stratum has been postulated, purely hypothetically, to explain a series of concordances between Indo-European and Uralic languages.[47] Quite independently, the presence of shamanistic traits analogous to the Siberian traits in Vedic poems has been attributed, once again hypothetically, to an extremely remote phase of cultural contact that supposedly involved populations which spoke proto-Uralic and proto-Indo-European languages, in a region situated in all probability in the steppes north of the Black Sea, between the Dnieper and the Caucasus.[48] A partially similar hypothesis has been suggested by the comparison between Greek myths concerning the figure of Prometheus and Caucasian myths about another hero punished for defiance of the divinity: Amirani. The analogies (and differences) between the two series have been traced back to the enduring relationship that must have been established, in a period before the second millennium BC, between Indo-European linguistic communities, which also included the ancestors of the Greeks, and linguistic communities of an altogether different type, which also included progenitors of the current inhabitants of the southern Caucasus.[49] We might observe that a linguistically heterogeneous area like the Caucasus seems to be the only one in which the three groups of substantially isomorphic phenomena under investigation are present simultaneously (see map 3).[50] Ecstatic experiences, predominantly female, tied to the processions of the dead; ecstatic experiences, predominantly male, tied to nocturnal battles for the fertility of the fields; male rituals, tied both to the processions of the dead and the battles for fertility – might not all these be re-elaborations that derive from a common nucleus?

Underlying a hypothesis of this kind, as with those we have already mentioned, we recognize the fascination and perils of a model which is Romantic even before it is positivist: that of the genealogical tree. Having occasioned the successes of Indo-European comparative linguistics, the illusion of being able to attain realities most proximate to the original language, ended up fuelling its excesses. It was thought that by classifying linguistic phenomena on the basis of discrete entities (the languages) linked by genealogical relationships of a vertical kind, it was possible to regress toward ever more ancient and less documented strata. But as one gradually moved away from documented realities (the branches of the tree), the

216

reconstruction tended to fade into utterly conjectural proto-languages. It has been observed that the majority of attempts to reconstruct cultural and religious phenomena belonging to an extremely remote or only indirectly documented past, have explicitly or implicitly followed this model, which has been repeatedly criticized for over a century.[51] But to postulate, in a totally hypothetical manner, the existence of specific historical relationships based on existing documentation, would seem a very different procedure.[52] Within these limits, a cautious recourse to chronological regression appears inevitable for the phenomena with which we are dealing.

13. As we can see, all explanations in terms of diffusion, as well as those in terms of common derivation, run into very serious difficulties. We should add that they share a tendency to mistake description of phenomena of one type or the other for an explanation of the largely unexplored processes of cultural assimilation. But diffusion is a fact, not an explanation.[53] This analytical flaw seems particularly serious when, as in the cases under consideration, the propagated trait (a belief, a ritual, a figurative formula) proves to be both preserved for very long periods (centuries, indeed millennia) and disseminated in extremely heterogeneous contexts (societies of hunters, nomadic shepherds and peasants).

To understand the reasons for this twofold characteristic – persistence in time, dispersion in space – it seems necessary to follow a different route: the third (c) of those indicated earlier. But there is no reason to suppose that these perspectives are mutually exclusive. We shall therefore seek to integrate in the analysis the external historical data and the internal structural characteristics of the transmitted phenomenon.[54] We shall do this on a reduced scale, isolating a specific element – a small detail – from the set of phenomena we have been examining.

Notes

1. See M. Artamonow, *Goldschatz der Skythen in der Ermitage*, Prague 1970, p. 46 and plates 147, 148 and 150; *L'oro degli Sciti*, Venice 1975, chart at fig. 26.
2. Cf. in this sense P. Jacobsthal, *Early Celtic Art*, Oxford 1944 (new edn. 1969), p. 161.
3. In *Le miroir d'Hérodote*, Paris 1980, F. Hartog inspired by Roland Barthes and especially Michel de Certeau, more than by Rostovtzev or Dumézil (pp. 24–5), proposes to analyze not the Scythians, but 'Herodotus' Scythians' in relation to the 'shared knowledge' (*savoir partagé*) of fifth-century Greeks (p. 27; the notion recalls that of 'horizon of expectation' elaborated by H. R. Jauss, cited on p. 14). This programme was clearly incapable of sustaining the weight of the book's subtitle (*Essai sur la représentation de l'autre*): hence the comparison, casual but inevitable, between passages from Herodotus and other documentary material (pp. 98 ff. on the cult of Dionysos in the area of the Black Sea; pp. 130 ff. on the ritual of taking an oath; pp. 141 ff. on divination); cf. also Georges Dumézil, *Le courtisane et les seigneurs colorés*, Paris 1983, p. 129. On the general questions mentioned here, see the present

author's 'Prove e possibilità', in an appendix to N. Z. Davis, *The Return of Martin Guerre*, It. trans., Turin 1984, pp. 143–5.

4. See the fundamental essay by K. Meuli, 'Scythica' (1935), reprinted with corrections and additions in *Gesammelte Schriften*, Basel-Stuttgart 1975, pp. 817–79. Further, in part contentious, developments can be found in E. R. Dodds, *The Greeks and the Irrational* (see also A. Momigliano's introduction to the Italian edition, *I Greci el'irrazionale* Florence 1959, p. XI). Meuli's hypothesis on the shamanistic roots of Greek epic poetry is restated, with less caution, by A. T. Hatto, 'Shamanism and Epic Poetry in Northern Asia', in *Essays on Medieval German and Other Poetry*, Cambridge 1980, pp. 117–38. For refutations (in my opinion not convincing) of Meuli, cf. K. Dowden, 'Deux notes sur les Scythes et le Arimaspes', *Revue des études grecques*, 93 (1980), pp. 486–92, and J. Bremmer, *The Early Greek Concept of the Soul*, Princeton 1983, pp. 25 ff. It should be noted that at the beginning of the nineteenth century J. Potocki had already linked the Siberian shamans to the Scythian soothsayers described by Herodotus (*Voyage dans les steps d'Asrakhan et du Caucase. Histoire primitive des peuples qui ont habité anciennement ces contrées . . .* Paris 1829, p. 171). And the core of Meuli's essay (also here in regard to Herodotus IV. 75) had already been anticipated by B. Niebuhr: cf. 'Untersuchungen über die Geschichte der Skythen, Geten, und Sarmaten (Nach einem 1811 vorgelesenen Aufsatz neu gearbeitet 1828), in *Kleine historische und philologische Schriften*, Bonn 1828)', I, pp. 352–98, in particular pp. 361–2. But all this does not diminish the originality of Meuli's essay.

5. Cf. M. P. Griaznov, 'The Pazirik Burial of Altai', *American Journal of Archaeology*, 37 (1933), pp. 30–45 (Meuli missed it); more extensively in S. I. Rudenko, *Frozen Tombs of Siberia*. Berkeley and Los Angeles 1970, pp. 284–5 (which does not cite Meuli). In general see G. Azarpay, 'Some Classical and Near Eastern Motifs in the Art of Pazyryk' *Artibus Asiae*, 22 (1959), pp. 313–39. See also F. Hancăr, 'The Eurasian Animal Style and the Altai Complex', ibid. 15 (1952), pp. 180 ff.; Balázs, *Ueber die Ekstase . . .*', in *Glaubenswelt*, cit. 71 ff.; G. M. Bongard-Levin and E. A. Grantovskij, *De la Scythie a l'Inde*, Fr. trans., Paris 1981, p. 91. The slabs of stone in the form of rams discovered in Siberia and Central Asia (cf. the beautiful essay by A. Tallgren, 'Some North-Eurasian Sculptures', *Eurasia Septentrionalis Antiqua*, XII, 1938, pp. 109 ff.) were possibly portable altars used to burn hemp seeds: cf. K. Jettmar, 'The Slab with a Ram's Head in the Rietberg Museum', *Artibus Asiae*, 27 (1964–65), pp. 291–300, in particular p. 295.

6. Cf. W. Watson, *Cultural Frontiers in Ancient East Asia*, Edinburgh 1971, pp. 96 ff. See also R. Heine-Geldern, 'Das Tocharerproblem und die Pontische Wanderung', *Saeculum*, II (1951), pp. 225 ff.; H. Kothe, 'Die Herkunft der kimmerischen Reiter', *Klio*, 41 (1963), pp. 5 ff. (in polemic with the preceding essay); G. Vernadsky, 'The Eurasian Nomads and Their Impact on Medieval Europe', *Studi medievali*, 3ª s., IV (1963), pp. 401–35, in particular p. 403; K. Jettmar, 'Die Entstehung der Reiternomaden', *Saeculum*, 17 (1966), pp. 1–11. On the hypothesis (today largely disputed) of migrations of nomadic populations from central Asia towards the West in the second millennium BC, see A. M. Tallgren, 'La Pontide pré-scythique après l'introduction des métaux', *Eurasia Septentrionalis Antiqua*, II (1926), pp. 214 ff.; J. Wiesner, *Fahren und Reiten in Alteuropa und im alten Orient*, Leipzig 1938 ('Der alte Orient', 38, Heft 2.–4.), pp. 46 ff.; S. Gallus -T. Horváth, *Un peuple cavalier préscythique en Hongrie*, Budapest 1939 ('Dissertationes Pannonicae', s. II, 9); W. Borgeaud, *Les Illyriens en Grèce et en Italie*, Geneva 1943, pp. 66, which attributes to putative eastern nomads a culture permeated by shamanistic elements. The important studies of A. Alföldi (on which see pp. 289, n. 207) set out from partially similar hypotheses.

7. Cf. A. M. Khazanov, *Nomads and the Outside World*, Cambridge 1986, pp. 85 ff.

8. These theses were first formulated by Niebuhr (art. cit. pp. 352 ff.) The subsequent discussion has often been impaired by patent ethnocentric and racist prejudices, not to mention the inability to distinguish between language (in the case of the Scythians, certainly of Iranian stock) and ethnic affiliation. On this whole question see E. H. Minns, *Scythians and Greeks*, Cambridge 1913 (off-set reprint, New York 1965), pp. 85, 97 ff. Subsequently, Minns ended by denying the presence of populations of Mongolian stock among the Scythians (see E. D. Phillips, 'In memoriam Ellis Howell Minns', *Artibus Asiae*, 17, 1954, p. 172), while asserting with ever greater conviction the Siberian origin of Scythian art: cf. O. Maenchen-Helfen, cited by K. Jettmar, 'In den Jahren 1955 bis 1962 ershienene Werke zur frühen Nomadenkunst der Asiatischen Steppen', *Kunstgeschichtliche Anzeigen*, V (1961–1962), p. 194. The discussion continues: cf. M. Gimbutas, *Bronze Age Cultures in Central and Eastern Europe*, The Hague 1965, pp. 528 ff., in particular pp. 576–7 (in favour of the thesis of the Asian provenance of the Scythians); H. Kothe, 'Pseudo-Skythen', *Klio*, 48 (1967), pp. 61–79 (opposed to it).

9. See H. S. Nyberg, *Die Religionen des alten Iran*, Germ. trans., Leipzig 1938, pp. 167 ff. (p. 177 repeats Herodotus' interpretation in Book IV. 75, as given by Meuli), criticized by W. B. Henning, *Zoroaster, Politician or Witch-Doctor?* Oxford 1951. On this discussion, see A. Closs, 'Iranistik und Völkerkunde', *Acta Iranica*, 4 (1975), pp. 111–12. A more profound discussion of Nyberg's thesis can be found in P. Gignoux, 'Corps osseux et âme osseuse': essai sur le chamanisme dans l'Iran ancien', *Journal asiatique*, 267 (1979), pp. 41–79. And see W. Nölle, 'Iranisch-nordostasiatische Beziehungen im Schamanismus', *Jahrbuch des Museums für Völkerkunde zu Leipzig*, XII (1953), pp. 86–90.

10. Cf. Meuli, 'Scythica', pp. 824 ff.; Georges Dumézil, 'Les énarées scythiques et la grossesse de Narte Hamyc', *Latomus*, 5 (1946), pp. 249–55. See in addition W. R. Halliday, in *The Annual of the British School at Athens*, XVII (1910–11), pp. 95–102.

11. In all this I follow Meuli, 'Scythica', pp. 853 ff.; see also W. Burkert, *Weisheit und Wissenschaft Studien zu Pythagoras, Philolaos und Platon*, Nürnberg 1962, pp. 124–5. The objections raised by J. D. P. Bolton (*Aristeas of Proconnesus*, Oxford 1962) and by Bremmer (op. cit., pp. 24 ff.) do not seem convincing to me. On Bolton see also Eliade, *De Zalmoxis à Gengis Khan*, Paris 1970, p. 45 n. 44. An attempt to identify the peoples mentioned by Aristeas can be found in E. D. Phillips, 'The Legend of Aristeas: Fact and Fancy in Early Greek Notions of East Russia, Siberia and Inner Asia', *Artibus Asiae*, 18 (1955), pp. 161–77; idem, 'A Further Note on Aristeas', ibid. pp. 159–62. See also Bongard-Levin and Grantovskij, op. cit., pp. 28 ff.

12. On the Greek colonization of the Black Sea, see A. H. Graham, 'The Date of the Greek Penetration of the Black Sea', *Bulletin of the Institute of Classical Studies of the University of London*, 5 (1958), pp. 25–42; R. Drews, 'The Earliest Greek Settlements on the Black Sea', *Journal of Hellenic Studies*, 96 (1976), pp. 18–31. For the proposal to push back the inception of Greek commercial penetration to the eleventh century, see G. Charachidzé, *Prométhée ou le Caucase*, Paris 1986, pp. 326 ff.

13. Cf. above, p. 162–3

14. See Harva (Holmberg), *Les représentations religieuses des peuples altaïques*, Paris 1959, pp. 247–51, which, however, neglects the probable provenance from central Asia of the distant ancestors of the Ossetians: the Scythians. It would therefore be quite difficult for the convergence, to prove, as Harva maintains, the 'international character' of the themes he has indicated. A comparison with the legend of Soslan in the country of the dead shows that what is involved is rather a quite specific link: cf. Dumézil ed, *Il libro degli Eroi*, Milan 1979, pp. 107–31. But it should be noted that here (as elsewhere) Dumézil tends to consider the culture of the Ossetians in an

exclusively Indo-European perspective. It is significant that Meuli's essay ('Scythica', 1935) has been registered by Dumézil, with a good forty years delay and, what is more, in rather reductive terms: cf. *Storie degli Sciti*, (1978) It. tr. Milan, p. 214 n. 6. But an indirect echo of Meuli's research is noticeable on another, almost contemporaneous page of Dumézil's:

> Marcel Granet, who liked spectacular syntheses, said that from the coast of Ireland to the coast of Manchuria there existed but one civilization. With these words he expressed the idea that after prehistory no natural obstacle had impeded communications, eruptive or osmotic, from one end to the other of the long plain of northern Eurasia, which is interrupted only by the chain of the Urals – and they can be easily scaled. As for the Indo-Europeans, it is a fact that the northern branches of the family present more original features compared to the southern branches, as has been recorded and observed from the Finno-Ugrics to the Tungus. One is especially struck by the importance assumed by more or less pure forms of shamanism. . . .

With such statements (which should be quoted in full) Dumézil implicitly reviewed specific judgments formulated in the past, such as the denial of shamanistic traits in the figure of Odin (see above, p. 151–2 n. 109). More generally, the hypothesis of a 'north Eurasian continuum', characterized by the presence (but Dumézil speaks of 'intrusion') of shamanistic forms, conflicts with the thesis of Indo-European cultural and religious specificity, repeated – but without arguments – in the discussion with Abaev on the tri-functional ideology (see below, p. 291 n. 228). The attempt to restrict to northern Europe the traces of this Eurasian continuum is, as I try to prove in this book, not sustainable. As for the Caucasus, see the research of G. Charachidzé (op. cit.; and see below pp. 254 ff.) In the figurative sphere the existence of a Eurasian continuum has been demonstrated by Leroi-Gourhan, *Documents pour l'art comparé de l'Eurasie Septentrionale*, Paris 1943.

15. Cf. Harva (Holmberg), op. cit., pp. 13 ff.
16. Strabo repeatedly mentions this, VII. 3.2; VII. 4.5; VII. 5.1. Posidonius speaks of a 'Scythian-Celtic zone' separated from the 'Ethiopian zone' by an 'intermediate zone' (ibid., II. 3.2). In general, see R. F. Hoddinott, *The Thracians*, London 1981, pp. 89 ff.
17. See above, p. 125.
18. See I. Chirassi-Colombo, 'The Role of Thrace in Greek Religion', in *Thracia II*, Serdicae 1974, pp. 71 ff., especially pp. 77–8.
19. Cf. M. Rostovtzeff, 'Le culte de la Grande Déesse dans la Russie méridionale', *Revue des études grecques*, XXXII (1914), pp. 462–81.
20. Cf. the image portrayed on a headband of a bridle preserved at the Hermitage (this too is a work in gold commissioned by Scythians from Greek artisans): *L'oro degli Sciti*, fig. 24. Cf. Dumézil, *La Courtisane*, pp. 90–6, which does not, however, discuss these parallels.
21. In a series of manuscript notes, written, two years before he died, in the margin of his own essay, 'Die Baumbestattung und die Ursprünge der griechischen Göttin Artemis' (*Gesammelte Schriften*, pp. 1083 ff.), Meuli wrote that tracking down the intermediate historic links (*historischen Zwischenglieder*) between the Greek Artemis and the (possibly prehistoric) 'mistress of the animals' postulated by the ethnologists, was a 'task for the future' (p. 1116). W. Burkert has attempted it, in 'Heracles and the Master of the Animals', in *Structure and History in Greek Mythology and Ritual*, Berkeley 1979, pp. 78–98 and 176–87. On the 'mistress of the animals' in the ethnological sphere, see the bibliography cited in Bremmer, op. cit., p. 129, to which

should be added Brelich, *Paides e Parthenoi*, I, Rome 1969, p. 132 n. 49. On the level of imagery, see B. Goldman, 'Some Aspects of the Animal Deity: Luristan, Tibet and Italy', *Ars orientalis*, 4 (1961), pp. 171–86, already anticipated by Leroi-Gourhan, op. cit., pp. 82–4: in particular, cf. Leroi-Gourhan fig. 335 (Caucasus bronze) and Goldman fig. 9 (Etruscan bronze). The fortune of a similar theme in the Christian milieu has been studied by W. Deonna, 'Daniel, le "maître des fauves"....', *Artibus Asiae*, 12 (1949), pp. 119–40 and 347–74.

22. See R. Bleichsteiner, 'Zum eurasiatischen Tierstil. Verbindungen zwischen West und Ost', *Asien Arbeitskreises*, Heft 2, June 1939, pp. 9–63, in particular pp. 36 and 25.

23. A connection of this kind is implicitly suggested, vis-à-vis the Eurasian shamans, by J. Haekel, 'Idolkult und Dualsystem bei den Ugriern (zum Problem des eurasiatischen Totemismus)', *Archiv für Volkerkunde*, I (1946), pp. 95–163, in particular p. 156, which develops the hypothesis of Bleichsteiner cited in the previous note, assuming a cultural diffusion from the West to the East.

24. See above, p. 100.

25. Cf. Bremmer, op. cit., p. 35.

26. '*Esse viros fama est in Hyperborea Pallene / Qui soleant levibus velari copora plumis / Cum Tritoniacam noviens subiere paludem. / Haud equidem credo: sparsae quoque membra veneno/ Exercere artes Scythides memorantur easdem*' (Met. XV. 356 ff.). In this connection Georg Sabinus cites, besides the passage in Herodotus on the Neuroi, the very recent case of a so-called werewolf captured by a group of peasants and imprisoned by the Duke of Prussia (Ovid, *Metamorphoseon libri XV . . . quibus nunc demum accessit Georgii Sabini interpretatio*, II, Lipsiae 1621, pp. 353). A reference to werewolves also occurs in F. Taeger, *Charisma*, II, Stuttgart 1957, p. 170 n. 228. In general see the comment of F. Bömer on Books XIV-XV of the *Metamorphoses*, Heidelberg 1986, pp. 346–8.

27. See Hoddinott, op. cit., p. 96.

28. See Vernadsky, art. cit., pp. 82 ff.

29. On werewolves in Ireland see above, p. 157. On shamanistic elements in the Celtic sagas, cf. Beneš, 'Spuren von Schamanismus in der Sage "Buile Suibhne"', *Zeitschrift für celtische Philologie*, 28 (1961), pp. 309–34. On the convergences between Arthurian romances and the Ossetian epic cf. Grisward, 'Le motif de l'épée jetée au lac: la mort d'Artur et la mort de Badraz', *Romania*, 90 (1969), pp. 476–7, which attributes scant importance to the establishment of groups of Alans (descendants of the Scythians) in Armorica in the fifth and sixth centuries BC: on this matter, see B. Bachrach, 'The Alans in Gaul', *Traditio*, 23 (1967), pp. 476–89; idem, *A History of the Alans in the West*, Minneapolis 1973, pp. 110 ff. On the basis of the convergences a derivation of the Arthurian epic from Ossetian traditions has been suggested, which would have been introduced into Britain around 175 BC by troops of Sarmatian origin: see C. Scott Littleton and A. C. Thomas, 'The Sarmatian Connection. New Light on the Origin of the Arthurian and Holy Grail Legend', *Journal of American Folklore*, 91 (1978), pp. 513–27; C. Scott Littleton, 'The Cauldron of Annwyn and the Nartyamonga. A Further Note on the Sarmatian Connection', ibid. 92 (1979), pp. 326–33; idem, 'From Swords in the Earth to the Sword in the Stone', in *Homage to Georges Dumézil*, E. C. Polomé ed, *Journal of Indo-European Studies Monographs*, n. 3, s.l. 1982, pp. 53–67. The inconsistency of the hypothesis has been demonstrated by R. Wadge, 'King Arthur: A British or Sarmatian Tradition?', *Folklore*, 98 (1987), pp. 204–15.

30. Cf. the famous essay (revised in 1936) by N. S. Trubetzkoy, 'Gedanken über das Indogermanenproblem', in *Acta Linguistica*, I (1939), pp. 81 ff. Alluding to the

contemporary racist distortions, Trubetzkoy defined as true conceptual absurdities such expressions as 'Indo-European peoples', 'native homeland of the Indo-Europeans', and so on (warnings which are indeed still necessary). The convergence between these pages of Trubetzkoy and the morphological reflections contained in Wittgenstein's almost contemporary annotations on Frazer (see Introduction, p. 15) seems to me significant: I do not know whether they are due to direct or indirect contacts.

31. Cf. U. Drobin, 'Indogermanische Religion und Kultur?', extract from *Temenos*, 16 (1980), p. 10, which detects in the essay by Trubetzkoy, alongside the polemic against the excesses of the genealogical method, the aim (in truth not clearly manifested) of saving the legitimacy of the genetic perspective. However, the distinction between genealogy and genesis is formulated explicitly by E. Pulgram, 'Proto-Indo-European Reality and Reconstruction', *Language*, 35 (1959), pp. 421–6 (it too mentioned by Drobin), which distances itself to some extent from Trubetzkoy.

32. In the conclusion to his important book *Prométhée ou le Caucase*, which, in a different sphere and perspective, faces problems partly analogous to those discussed here, G. Charachidzé lists four possibilities to explain a series of convergences between Greek and Caucasian myths: '(1) common heredity; (2) elaboration on the basis of a model extraneous to both; (3) contingent or typological convergence; (4) borrowing, in one direction or another' (p. 322). In my opinion (2) can be considered a particular case of (1), on the condition that 'derivation' is substituted for 'heredity' – an ambiguous term because both biological and cultural; 'structural characteristics of the human mind' is an expression preferable to 'typological convergence' – an expression that Charachidzé considers not very clear (p. 323).

33. See O. Bohociu, 'Thèmes mythiques carpato-caucasiens et des régions riveraines de la Mer Noire', *Ogam-Tradition celtique*, VIII (1956), pp. 259–78. It has been suggested that the *kralijce* (on which see above, p. 189) came from the Pontic-Iranian cultural milieu: cf. M. Gušic, cited by N. Kuret, '*Frauenbünde* und maskierte Frauen', in *Festschrift für Robert Wildhaber*, Basel 1973, p. 344.

34. See B. Munkácsi, 'Alanische Sprachdenkmäler im ungarischen Wortschatze', *Keleti Szemle*, 5 (1904), pp. 304–29; H. Sköld, *Die ossetischen Lehnwörter im Ungarischen*, Lund and Leipizig 1924 (which I have not seen); idem, 'Woher stammen die ossetischen Lehnwörter im Ungarischen?', *Zeitschrift für Indologie und Iranistik*, 3 (1925), pp. 179–86; J. Harmatta, *Studies in the History and Language of the Sarmatians*, Szeged 1970, p. 62, which makes reference to the studies of V. Miller and V. I. Abaev.

35. See, for example, the relations between the Alans' religious conceptions and those of a population of the Caucasian language like the Svani, analyzed by G. Charachidzé in *La mémoire indo-européene du Caucase*, Paris 1987.

36. For a first orientation, see the article 'Steppe, culture', edited by M. Bussagli, in the *Enciclopedia Universale dell'Arte*, XII, Venice and Rome 1964. Specific studies will be cited as we proceed.

37. The examples are taken from E. C. Bunker, C. B. Chatwin and A. R. Farkas, '*Animal Style': Art from East to West*, New York 1970, figs 69, 89, 40, 11, 139, 142, 143, 144 and related entries. Although surpassed by subsequent research, the picture drawn by M. I. Rostovtzev in *The Animal Style in South Russia and China*, Princeton 1929, remains extraordinarily suggestive.

38. This confirms the lexicological hypotheses of V. Brøndal, 'Mots "scythes" en nordique primitif', *Acta Philologica Scandinavica*, III (1928), pp. 1 ff.

39. The origin of "animal style" in northern Siberia was hypothesized by G. Borovka, *Scythian Art*, London 1928, pp. 30 ff., which actually speaks of a 'Scytho-Siberian

animalistic style' (p. 40). The same conclusions were reached by E. H. Minns, 'The Art of the Northern Nomads', in *Proceedings of the British Academy*, 1942, pp. 47–93; see also Hančar, art. cit. and, on the basis of stylistic arguments, O. Sudzuki, 'Eastern Origin of Scythian Art', Orient, 4 (1967), pp. 1–22. See now E. Jacobson, 'Siberian Roots of the Scythian Stag Image', *Journal of Asian History*, 17 (1983), pp. 68–120. K. Jettmar, who had previously supported the mid-Eastern hypothesis (cf. 'Ausbreitungsweg und sozialer Hintergrund des eurasiatischen Tierstils', *Mitteilungen der anthropologischen Gesellschaft Wien*, XVII, 1962, pp. 176–91) has, on the basis of the results of recent digs, declared in favour of an origin in central Asia: cf. also E. C. Bunker, in idem et al., op. cit., p. 13. The question is still open.

40. The importance of the Scythian-Celt connection (already referred to by N. Kondakov, J. Tolstoï and S. Reinach, *Antiquités de la Russie méridionale*, Paris 1891, pp. 330–1, and M. Rostovtzev, op. cit., p. 65) is insisted upon by Minns, art. cit., pp. 79 ff. P. Jacobsthal calls the genesis of Celtic art an 'enigma', pointing to some inexplicable similarities, not so much with what might properly be called Scythian art, as with the art of the Altai, of Siberia and China (op. cit., p. 158; see also pp. 51, 156 ff. and 162). On Jacobsthal's dissatisfaction with the way in which he had treated the problem, see the testimony of C. Hawkes in *Celtic Art in Ancient Europe. Five Protohistoric Centuries. Proceedings of the Colloquy held in 1972...*, P.-M. Duval and C. Hawkes eds, London, New York and San Francisco 1976, pp. 58–9. Cf. also Bunker et al., op. cit., pp. 153–5.

41. Cf. respectively T. G. E. Powell, 'From Urartu to Gundestrup: the Agency of Thracian Metal-Work', in *The European Community in Later Prehistory. Studies in Honour of C. F. C. Hawkes*, J. Boardman, M. A. Brown and T. G. E. Powell eds, London 1971, pp. 183–210; G. S. Olmsted, *The Gundestrup Cauldron*, Brussels 1979, which tries to connect the iconography of the scenes represented on the cauldron with Celtic legends.

42. See A. Alföldi, 'Die theriomorphe Weltbetrachtung in den hochasiatischen Kulturen', *Jahrbuch des deutschen archäologischen Instituts*, 46 (1931), 393–418, in particular 400 ff. The symbolic value of these representations had been mentioned already by F. Fettich, 'Die Tierkampfszene in der Nomadenkunst', in *Recueil d'études dediées à la mémoire de N. P. Kondakov*, Prague 1926, pp. 81–92, in particular p. 84. The link between shamanistic and animalistic art is reviewed, in inadequately critical manner, by C. B. Chatwin, 'The Nomadic Alternative', in *'Animal Style'*, pp. 176–83; but see the sober remarks of E. C. Bunker, in ibid., pp. 13–15.

43. See the very fine essay by S. Reinach, *La représentation du galop dans l'art ancien et moderne*, Paris 1925 (which appeared originally in *Revue archéologique*, 1900–1901); E. C. Bunker, 'The Anecdotal Plaques of the Eastern Steppe Regions', in *Arts of the Eurasian Steppelands*, E. Denwood ed, London 1977, pp. 121–42, above all p. 123; I. B. Jaffe (with G. Colombardo), 'The Flying Gallop: East and West', *The Art Bulletin*, LXV (1983), pp. 183–200 (with new elements, above all on the return of the motif in the West).

44. This feature, demonstrated by comparison with the photographic researches of E. Muybridge (*Animal Locomotion*, Philadelphia 1872–87), is strongly emphasized by Reinach.

45. See Reinach, op. cit., pp. 82–3, on the presence of Mycenean motifs in the art of the Cimmerian Bosphorus. But see Charachidzé, *Prométhée*, pp. 334–5, on the linguistic features that have led to the supposition of homogeneity between the 'Aegean' substratum and Caucasian culture.

46. See M. J. Mellink, 'Postscript on Nomadic Art', in *Dark Ages and Nomads c. 1000 B.C. Studies in Iranian and Anatolian Archaeology*, M. J. Mellink ed, Istanbul 1964, pp. 63–70, in particular pp. 67–8 (but the entire volume is important).

47. In a series of studies conducted with great prudence B. Collinder tried to demonstrate, including by recourse to the laws of probability, that the affinity between the Indo-European languages and the Uralic languages is not due to chance, and that consequently – on an exclusively linguistic plane – it is legitimate to introduce an 'Indo-Uralic' hypothesis: cf. *Indo-Uralisches Sprachgut. Die Urverwandschaft zwischen der Indoeuropäischen und der Uralischen (Finnishchugrish-Samojedischen) Sprachfamilie*, Uppsala 1934; idem, *Sprachverwandschaft und Wahrscheinlichkeit*, B. Wickman ed, Uppsala 1964. On the history of the question, cf. A. J. Joki, *Uralier und Indogermanen. Die älteren Berührungen zwischen den uralischen und indogermanischen Sprachen*, Helsinki 1973, pp. 373–4, which, however, ends by going beyond the linguistic terrain, formulating on lexical grounds which seem rather fragile hypotheses about the relations between populations speaking Uralic and Indo-European languages. From a not altogether different perspective, cf. P. Aalto, 'The Tripartite Ideology and the "Kalevala"', in *Studies in Finno-Ugric Linguistics in Honor of Alo Raun*, D. Sinor ed, Bloomington (Indiana) 1977, pp. 9–23.

48. Cf. Bongard-Levin and Grantovskij, op. cit., which formulates in a different and less adventurous manner a thesis proposed at the beginning of the century by Bâl Gangâdhar Tilak (see pp. 12–14). Besides involving himself deeply in the struggle for Indian national independence (for a favourable biography, cf. D. V. Athalye, *The Life of Lokamanya Tilak*, Poona 1921), Tilak wrote two books which (a) pushed back by two millennia (to 4500 B.C.) the date commonly accepted for the composition of the *Veda*, on the basis of the astronomic indications contained in them; (b) maintained that the ancient Arii came from a region situated close to the Arctic Circle, which they had inhabited in the Interglacial period (*The Arctic Home in the Vedas, Being Also a New Key to the Interpretation of Many Vedic Texts and Legends*, Poona and Bombay 1903, preceded by *Orion, or Researches into the Antiquity of the Vedas*, 1893, which I have not seen). A similar hypothesis had already been formulated, in a vaguer fashion, by J. Rhŷs, *Lectures on the Origin and Growth of Religion. . .* , London 1898. This re-elaborated the other, much more astounding hypothesis of W. F. Warren (*Paradise Found. The Cradle of the Human Race at the North Pole*, London 1885; reprinted several times), according to which the polar regions in the blessed interglacial age had been the cradle of the entire human race. Contra Darwin, Warren sought to reconcile the Old Testament and science – in particular the botanic researches (inspired by those of O. Heer) which located the Arctic regions as the origin of all the plants that exist on the terrestrial globe. Interventions on this question lasted for several years, as is shown by the pamphlet (based on Tilak's) by G. Biedenkapp, *Der Nordpol als Völkerheimat*, Jena 1906. Subsequently, the theory of the boreal origin of the Indo-Europeans was taken up in Nazi circles. It has recently been revived by J. Haudry, *Les Indo-Européens*, Paris 1981, pp. 119–21 (who cites Tilak) – on which see the severe judgment of B. Sargent, 'Penser – et mal penser – les Indo-Européens', *Annales E. S. C.*, 37 (1982), pp. 669–681, especially p. 675. In any event, the idea that the origin of civilization must be localized in the North – that is, that the Indians and the Greeks (initially only the Greeks) had inherited their cultural patrimony from a highly civilized people who in the remotest times had inhabited central or northern Asia, is very old. On its eighteenth century versions (F. Bailly, C. Dupuis, etc.), see C. Dionisotti, 'Preistoria del pastore errante', in *Appunti sui moderni*, Bologna 1988, pp. 157–77. In his turn Bailly (cf. *Histoire de l'astronomie ancienne. . .* , Paris 1775, pp. 323 ff.) utilized for different ends the impressive documentation gathered by O. Rudbeck (*Atlantica*, 4 vols, Uppsala 1679–1702) to prove that Atlantis was situated in Sweden, indeed at Uppsala (cf. J. Svenbro, 'L'ideologie "gothisante" et l'"Atlantica" d'Olof Rudbeck' *Quaderni di Storia*, 11, 1980, pp. 121–56). An echo of

Rudbeck resurfaces in Rhŷs, op. cit., p. 637. The entire discussion can be considered a branch of the one on Atlantis: cf. P. Vidal-Naquet, 'L'Atlantide et les nations', in *Représentations de l'origine, Cahiers CRLH-CIRAOI*, 4 (1987), pp. 9–28.

49. Cf. Charachidzé, *Promethée*, pp. 323 ff.; on p. 340 n. 1 it is noted that his hypothesis is reinforced by the linguistic research of T. Gamkrelidze and V. Ivanov (1984). It should be noted that V. Brφndal had posited the existence of a 'global crossroad' through which flowed cultural and linguistic elements from central Asia and the Aegean, that were then diffused among the Ugro-Finnic populations and the peoples of northern and central Europe (art. cit., p. 22).

50. See above, p. 193–4 (naturally, this is a provisional conclusion, which could be disproved by further research).

51. See the acute essay by Drobin, art. cit., which connects to the theories of J. Schleicher on the genealogical tree the conceptual grounds on which the research of Dumézil, among others, is based (cf. on p. 3).

52. See the studies of B. Collinder cited in n. 47.

53. Cf. C. Renfrew, *Before Civilisation*, London 1979; idem, 'The Great Tradition versus the Great Divide: Archaeology as Anthropology?', *American Journal of Archaeology*, 84 (1980), pp. 287–98, in particular p. 239. These subtly argued pages are to be preferred to the rather trivial fits of impatience elsewhere, such as the adjective 'meaningless' applied to the concept of 'diffusion' (*Approaches to Social Anthropology*, Cambridge (Mass.) 1984, p. 114).

54. See in this regard the lucid observations of Claude Lévi-Strauss, 'Split representation in the art of Asia and America', in *Structural Anthropology*, Harmondsworth 1977, pp. 245–68, in particular p. 258:

> Even if the most ambitious reconstructions of the diffusionist school were to be confirmed, we should still be faced with an essential problem which has nothing to do with history. Why should a cultural trait that has been borrowed or diffused through a long historical period remain intact? Stability is no less mysterious than change. . . . External connections can explain transmission, but only internal connections can account for persistence. Two entirely different kinds of problems are involved here, and the attempt to explain one in no way prejudges the solution that must be given to the other.

On the question tackled by Lévi-Strauss in this essay (the analogies between archaic Chinese art and the art of the north-western American coast) M. Badner and R. Heine-Geldern ('Two Studies of Art in the Pacific Area', *Weiner Beiträge zur Kulturgeschichte und Linguistik*, XII, 1966) have successively intervened, from a diffusionist perspective. The latter refers to an unpublished report of Lévi-Strauss' at the 29th Congress of the Americanists (1949), where, strangely, he does not cite 'Split Representation' (which appeared in 1944–5).

2

BONES AND SKIN

1. A French anthropologist who is writing a huge tetralogy on American Indian myths realizes, almost half-way through the work, that he has been guilty of an oversight.[1] In the preceding volume, among innumerable other myths, he had reported and analyzed one about an Indian population of Amazonia (the Tereno) omitting, however, a detail whose importance he suddenly grasps. (The myth had reached him through a triple filter, less indirect as it progressed: a German ethnographer who wrote in Portuguese; a native interpreter who spoke Portuguese and Tereno; a native informant who spoke only Tereno).[2] What is at stake is a 'minimal' detail: as a result of certain spells cast by his wife, the protagonist of the myth about the origin of tobacco becomes lame. The anthropologist notices that lameness also appears in a Tereno ritual, but not only there: it features in a great number of myths, and especially documented rituals, in the Americas, China, continental Europe and the Mediterranean. They are all connected – it seems to him – with the passage of the seasons. A trans-cultural connection that covers so boundless an area evidently cannot be traced back to particular explanatory causes. Assuming one does not wish to trace the ritual of the lame dance to the Paleolithic (that, the anthropologist observes, would explain its geographical distribution but not its survival), one must, at least by way of hypothesis, seek for an explanation of a structural order.[3] The anthropologist hazards one – though he is fully aware of the meagreness of the American documentation. If the problem posed by these rituals is that of shortening (*écourter*) one season in favour of another, by accelerating its passage, the lame dance offers a correlation or, rather, a perfect diagram of the desired imbalance. Had not Montaigne, in his famous essay on the lame, set out precisely from the calendar reform by which Pope Gregory XIII shortened the year?[4]

2. To explain a phenomenon recorded from the Mediterranean to the Americas with the help of a quotation from Montaigne represents taking a liberty which risks discrediting the validity of the method – the anthropologist observes, not without coquettishness. But if his argument appears obviously inadequate, the question which provoked it (why do myths and rituals hinging

226

on lameness recur in such different cultures?) is real enough. The search for a more satisfying answer to such a question once again means running into a series of difficulties which, in the course of our investigation, have remained unsolved. Themes we have previously encountered will suddenly appear to us in a new light.

3.   The anthropologist who noticed the trans-cultural importance of mythical and ritualistic lameness had not considered it opportune to bring up the myth of Oedipus in this regard. And yet, although he was not the first, he had certainly emphasized with particular vigour the importance of the allusion to a defect in walking contained in the myth of Oedipus (as in the name of his grandfather, Labdacus, 'the lame one').[5]

A prophecy states that the son of Laius, King of Thebes, will kill his father and wed his mother. To ward off this dreadful fate, the boy is abandoned immediately after his birth: first, however, his ankles are pierced. Hence the name Oedipus, that is, swollen foot.[6] This is an explanation advanced since antiquity. But even then someone did not consider it sufficient. Why had a new-born obviously incapable of escaping been treated so ferociously? The author of a gloss on Sophocles' *Oedipus Rex* supposed that the child had been disfigured so that no one would think of taking him home.[7] This is a rationalistic conjecture, undoubtedly alien to the spirit of the myth. Even less admissible, is the hypothesis that the incomprehensible detail of the mutilated feet might be a later addition, suggested by the name 'Oedipus'.[8]

A singular name, no doubt; not very suitable for a hero or a god. It has been compared to that of Melampus, 'black foot', a soothsayer and healer of Thessaly. A myth tells us that immediately after his birth he had been exposed in a forest; the sun had burnt his bare feet – hence the epithet.[9] In the figure of Oedipus and that of Melampus a link with the subterranean divinities has been identified; in the deformities that mark them, euphemistic allusions to the black and swollen body of the most typical of the chthonic animals, the serpent. This last conjecture is patently absurd.[10] But there is no doubt that Oedipus and Melampus, besides both being soothsayers, share a malformation of the feet brought about by exposure. These convergences, as we shall see, are not fortuitous.[11]

Let us for a moment leave Melampus and return to Oedipus. His name and his function as the unconscious instrument of his parents' misfortune have been interpreted as the residues of a semi-erased fairy-tale nucleus.[12] It has been identified with an elementary plot, typical of fables dealing with magic: after performing a difficult task by extraordinary means, the hero marries the princess (sometimes after having killed the old king). In the version of the myth that has reached us, the killing of the king, Laius, precedes the difficult task: the solution of the riddle posed by the sphinx.[13] Furthermore, the foundling hero, instead of arriving in a foreign kingdom, returns to his own home – which implies the parricide and the incest. This last variation, in which we today recognize the properly 'Oedipal' nucleus, is supposedly a late graft which, in the elaboration of the tragic poets, ended up profoundly transforming the more ancient fabular plot.[14]

The attempt to distinguish different strata within a myth is almost inevitably conjectural. It must, however, be emphasized that 'more ancient' does not mean 'more authentic' (since the myth is always accepted en bloc by the culture that adopts it); nor does it mean 'original' (since the origin of a myth is by definition inaccessible).[15] But if we accept that in principle a distinction between the various strata is possible, Oedipus' mutilated feet seem to belong to the fabular nucleus, not to subsequent superimpositions. Although widespread in many cultures, the riddle of the Sphinx ('what animal walks on four legs in the morning, on two at noon, on three in the evening?'), whilst referring to humanity in general, acquired a particular significance when posed to an individual like Oedipus, whose feet were disfigured and who was fated, as an old man, to lean on a blind man's cane.[16] But in Sophocles' *Oedipus Rex* the mutilation is most often evoked in an indirect manner: it is of marginal importance to the gradual unveiling of the protagonist's true identity.[17] Perhaps this slow and enveloping dramatic strategy was inspired, not solely by artistic choice, but also by the difficulty of explaining a detail which had been inherited from mythical tradition, but had by now become incomprehensible.

It has been suggested that it echoed a remote initiatory ritual, which subjected the novice first to symbolic wounds, then to a period of segregation: two stages that in the case of Oedipus would correspond to the pierced feet and the childhood spent among the shepherds.[18] In Greece there remained only faint and indirect traces of such customs.[19] But their diffusion in the most varied cultures has left behind an indelible trace in fables about magic. In them a recurrent structure has been deciphered: the hero, after journeying to the world of the dead – the mythical equivalent of initiation rites – returned to earth to wed the queen. We may suppose that in the most ancient version of the myth of Oedipus (identified, as we have indicated, with a fable about magic) the wound to the feet, the exposure, the period spent on the margins of the world of the *polis* on the wild heights of Mount Cithaeron, the struggle with the Sphinx – later mitigated by the solution of the riddle – marked the stages of an initiatory journey to the beyond.[20] This interpretation would confirm, by integrating and correcting it, the one already mentioned which sees in Oedipus a chthonic hero associated with infernal divinities like the Erinyes, ambiguous harbingers of prosperity and death.[21] Among the epithets that refer to the Erinyes, names ending in *pous* are especially frequent. It has been noted that in Euripides' *Phoenicians* (verses 1543–45), Oedipus – after having blinded himself – compares himself to a ghost, a dead man.[22] And the Sphinx is undoubtedly a mortuary animal.[23]

4. Yet these conjectures do not account for the particular form of mutilation inflicted on Oedipus prior to exposure.[24] Light is indirectly thrown upon it by another interpretation which, unlike the preceding one,

considers the myth in its totality, including, that is, the parricide and the incest.[25] The story of Oedipus is thus inserted into a set of myths and sagas that cover a vast geographical area: from Europe to south-eastern Asia, passing through North Africa, with branches that run from the Arctic Ocean to Madagascar.[26] They are based on a fundamentally analogous structure. An old king learns from an oracle that a young prince – whose father, grandfather, uncle, adoptive father or father-in-law he is – will kill him in order to succeed him. To elude the prophecy the young man is forced to leave his country: after various tests he returns, kills (voluntarily or involuntarily) the old king and succeeds to the throne, usually marrying his daughter or his wife. The Greek myths that wholly or partially follow this sequence can be divided into four groups, two of which can be further split into as many sub-groups:

I.a. (*voluntary parricide, although in diluted form*): Kronos (who castrates Uranus) and Zeus (who overthrows or castrates Kronos);

I.b. (*involuntary parricide*): Oedipus (who kills Laius); Theseus (who provokes the suicide of Aegeus); Telegonus (who kills Ulysses);

II.a. (*voluntary murder of the uncle*) Jason (who in the original version of the myth killed Pelias); Aegisthus (who kills Atreus, the brother of his father Thyestes); Telephus (who kills the brothers of his mother Auge); the sons of Tyro and of her uncle, Sisyphus (who kill Salmoneus, their father's brother and their mother's father);[27]

II.b. (*involuntary murder of uncle*): Perseus (who kills Acrisius, sometimes described as brother of his father, Proitos);

III. (*murder of grandfather*): once again Aegisthus (who kills Atreus, his mother Pelopia's father); and once again Perseus (who kills Acrisius, generally presented as the father of his mother, Danae);

IV. (*murder of future father-in-law*): Pelops (who causes the death of Oenomaus, the father of Hippodameia); and once again Zeus (who, according to another conjectural version, overthrows Kronos after having lain with his own sister Rhea).

As we can see, the myths contained in this (incomplete) series are characterized by a similar structure, which is articulated in a series of substitutions, or rather attenuations, starting out from a radical hypothetical version, which anticipates voluntary parricide and voluntary incest with the mother.[28] The castration of celestial divinities (immortal by definition) or their loss of power, like the other alternatives we have listed, can in fact be considered attenuated variants of voluntary parricide. Similarly, Oedipus who unwittingly lies with Jocasta; Telephus who, at the last moment, avoids consummating the marriage with Auge; Telegonus, son of Circe, who marries his stepmother Penelope (while his double Telemachus, the son of Penelope, marries Circe) – all constitute progressively attenuated versions of voluntary incest with the mother.[29] These myths therefore appear to be

229

linked by a very dense web of resemblances of structural order, sometimes reinforced by convergences of a more specific character. A few examples will suffice. When Oedipus, by now blind, goes to Colonus, he is welcomed and protected by Theseus, who remembers the childhood they both spent in exile. But here too Sophocles' elaboration barely touches on the elements common to both myths. Their protagonists were born from the transgression of a prohibition on reproduction – absolute in the case of Laius, temporary in the case of Aegeus. In order to elude the prophecy, both have been expelled from the paternal home. Both have victoriously overcome their encounters with such monsters as the Sphinx and the Minotaur. Both have unintentionally caused the death of their respective fathers. Through their male descendants both prolong the curse that has struck them.[30] Further convergences have been recognized between the myth of Perseus and that of Telephus in the form of their mothers – segregated so as to thwart the usual prophecy, seduced (by Zeus and Heracles respectively), cast into the sea (in a sealed ark or a basket).[31] The animals (bees, bears and goats) who raise the baby Zeus in the caves of Crete, sheltering him from paternal anthropophagy, find a precise parallel in the doe that feeds Telephus, in the goat (*aix*) that feeds Aegisthus (*Aighisthos*). And so on.

5. Against this background of resemblances one in particular stands out, which until now has been mentioned only in an episodic and partial fashion: more than half of the protagonists of this mythical series are marked by peculiarities connected with walking.[32] Besides Oedipus of the pierced feet, we find Jason, who, fulfilling the prophecy, appears before his usurping uncle Pelias wearing only one sandal; Perseus, who, prior to fighting the Gorgon, receives from Hermes one of his sandals; Telephus, who, after killing the children of his uncle Aleus, is wounded in the left leg by Achilles; Theseus, who finds under a rock not only the sword, but also the gilded sandals of Aegeus which, upon his return home, will facilitate his recognition; Zeus, the sinews of whose hands and feet are severed by the monstrous Typhon, who hides them in a cave (where they will later be found).[33]

We therefore have figures distinguished (a) by malformations or wounds to the feet or legs; (b) by possession of a single sandal; (c) by possession of two sandals. The first characteristic, sometimes accompanied or replaced by other defects (absence of one eye, small stature, stuttering), was especially frequent among the Greek heroes: this observation already appears in a brief dramatic parody attributed to Lucian of Samosata, *Tragodopodagra*.[34] To the second characteristic we shall soon return. The last would at first sight seem to correspond to a normal situation against which possible deviations can be measured.

In reality, in the myth of Theseus the detail of the sandals has more complex implications. The lifting of the boulder by which Theseus comes into possession of the paternal sandals constitutes a veritable initiation rite that marks his entry into adulthood.[35] As has already been said, an initiatory

230

significance has also been attributed to Oedipus' pierced feet. Later, we shall see that the single sandal worn by Jason and Perseus has the same value. The stages of initiation identified in Oedipus' story – the symbolic wounds, his exile in a wild environment, the struggle with monsters – reappear, in a more or less modified form, in the other myths constitutive of the series.

In a number of them we also find the supreme test, of which only imperceptible traces have survived in the myth of Oedipus: the journey to the realm of the dead.[36] In fact, a fabular theme has been recognized in the sandals and sword left under the boulder by Aegeus: magical instruments that allow the hero to visit the beyond. Among the trials attributed by the mythical tradition to Theseus is his journey to Hades, in an attempt to retrieve Persephone, who has been carried off by the god of the dead.[37] After emerging from the Anauros River wearing only one sandal, Jason undertakes the expedition to Colchis in search of the golden fleece, in the course of which he descends to the nether world with the help of the sorceress Medea.[38] Perseus, who fights with the monstrous Gorgon wearing the magic sandal given him by Hermes (who was called 'monocrepid', i.e., one-sandalled), is also associated with the subterranean world.[39]

6. The triple connection between fated child, peculiarities linked with walking, and the world of the dead finds very clear confirmation in the figure of Achilles. One myth presents him as a fated child manqué: Zeus decided not to lie with Thetis because, according to the prophecy, the son born to her would surpass his father.[40] The epithet that designated Thetis – 'silver foot' – referred to the mutilation inflicted on her by Hephaestus, the blacksmith-god with the crooked feet, who had flung a hammer at her as he pursued her intent upon rape.[41] This thickening of anomalies vis-à-vis gait prepares for the mutilation inflicted on Thetis' son Achilles, the 'quick-footed', immediately after his birth. His parents had rendered him partially invulnerable by immersing him in the waters of the Styx or (according to a different version) in fire: the heel burnt by the flames will be replaced by that of an extremely swift giant.[42]

The mortuary connotations suggested by the association with the Styx, the river of the nether world, are confirmed by other evidence. Behind the hero Achilles – who, according to a tradition unknown to Homer, was buried on the island of Leuca (today, Island of the Serpents) situated across from Olbia, on the northern shores of the Black Sea – another, more ancient Achilles, god of the dead, has been identified. Olbia was a Greek colony in a territory inhabited by Scythians. Alcaeus, at the end of the seventh century BC, in a poem of which we possess only a single verse, called Achilles the 'lord of the Scythians'. In the face of the wounded Patroclus, whom the painter Sosia portrayed on a famous cup beside Achilles, who is tending him, some have thought to recognize Scythian features.[43] In any event, Alcaeus' verse introduces a surprising note in the customary image of Achilles, the most typical of Greek heroes.

7. The immersion of the child Achilles in the fire has been set alongside two rituals: the first, described in the Homeric Hymn to Demeter (verses 231–55); the second, actually performed on the island of Chios at the beginning of the seventeenth century. Wishing to render the child Demophoön immortal, Demeter had repeatedly plunged him into fire, anointing him with ambrosia, food of the gods; but faced with his mother's fear, in an outburst of anger she had returned the child to his human state.[44] We have mentioned that, according to the scholar Leone Allacci, the inhabitants of Chios observed the custom of scorching the soles of the feet of children born between Christmas and Epiphany, to prevent them becoming *kallikantzaroi* – deformed spirits who, during the same period of the year, left the nether world to roam the earth.[45] If we accept the hypothesis that these figures of Greek folklore are derived from the ancient centaurs, the analogies with Achilles – son of a goddess with some equine characteristics like Thetis, raised by the centaur Chiron – become readily intelligible.[46] In the endeavour to ward off an unfortunate fate for the children of Chios, we can discern the reinterpretation of what must in the past have been a propitiatory ritual of an initiatory character, aimed at procuring a super-human condition for those who underwent it. Here too malformations or imbalances in gait differentiate beings (gods, men, spirits) suspended between the realm of the dead and that of the living.

8. That Jason, like Achilles, had been tutored by the centaur Chiron cannot at this point be considered a coincidence. The symbolic equivalence of swollen, deformed, scorched, or simply bare feet receives considerable confirmation outside the circle of myths within which we have been moving.

At the beginning of the nineteenth century, at Damascus, a small bronze statue was found representing a naked goddess with a sandal on one foot. A few decades later, she was identified with a funerary goddess, Aphrodite Nemesis: but the presence of a single sandal in other cults or myths was referred to solar mythology, as was then obligatory.[47] This iconographic singularity was subsequently forgotten. It re-emerged quite independently, in a different context, in the first years of this century. During the construction of the short tunnel to the Quirinale in Rome, an ancient statue representing a youth slightly smaller than lifesize was discovered. In the museum of the Palazzo dei Conservatori a poor quality copy was identified which dates back to the period of the Antonines. The youth holds in his arms a piglet (today removed because it was a subsequent addition, but a feature of similar sculptures). The presence of myrtle on the supporting trunk in the first instance, and of the piglet in the second (both sacred to Demeter), led to identification of the youth as an inititiate of the Eleusinian cults. But whereas in the statue discovered near the Quirinale the single preserved foot (the right one) is bare, in the copy at the Palazzo dei Conservatori one of the youth's feet (the right one) is bare and the other (the left) is shod in a sandal (figs. 16 and 17). It is thought that the custom of wearing a single sandal was connected with ritual situations in which, through more immediate contact with the ground, the attempt was made to achieve a relationship with the subterranean powers. This hypothesis seemed to be confirmed by some literary evidence. At the point of killing herself because she has been deserted by Aeneas, Dido takes off one of her sandals (*unum exuta pedem vinclis*, *Aeneid* IV. 517); and Medea does the same, in the act of evoking the goddess Hecate, associated with the nether world (*nuda pedem*, *Met*. VII. 182).[48] It is true that Servius, in commenting on the passage in Virgil, thought this to be a gesture of sympathetic magic: to tie and untie a sandal so as to bind and unbind another's will.[49] But the overall series suggests a funereal context. Initiation was a ritual death: in the initiatory scene frescoed in the Pompeian Villa of the Mysteries the figure of the lying Dionysos has a bare right foot (fig. 18).[50]

But other Mediterranean examples of monosandalism complicate the picture. Thucydides tells us (III. 22) that in the winter of 428 BC the Plataeans attacked the Spartans during a moonless night with only one foot (the left) shod. In a surviving fragment of Euripides' *Meleager* the heroes who gathered to hunt the Calydonian boar are listed: among them the sons of Thestius, wearing only one sandal on the right foot.[51] Virgil (*Aeneid* VII. 678 ff.) describes Caeculus, mythical founder of Praeneste, at the head of a phalanx of warriors with their left foot bare (while the right is shod in a crude boot). The obscurity of these passages is reinforced, rather than lessened, by the explanatory glosses introduced by the authors themselves or by their ancient commentators. Thucydides declared that, with their footwear, the Plataeans sought to 'proceed more surely through the mud': but in that case why hadn't they chosen to go barefoot altogether? According to Euripides, Thestius' sons followed a custom to give the leg greater agility common among the Aetolians: but Aristotle had already objected, in that case the shod foot should have been the left.[52] Servius, in his commentary on Virgil, observed that one enters battle left foot forward: unlike the right it is protected by the shield, and therefore, does not require footwear. Macrobius, in discussing these passages (*Saturn*. V. 18), proposed a different explanation, of an ethnic character: both the Aetolians described by Euripides and the Hernici, descendants of Caeculus, the founder of Praeneste, were of Pelasgian origin (he was unaware of Thucydides' passage on the Plataeans). In reality, Thestius' sons, Plessippus and Tosseus, were Kouretes, not Aetolians like their nephew and murderer, Meleager.[53] But the doubts, attempts at a rational explanation, or references to remote traditions evidently point to an inability to decipher a mythical and ritualistic content which, as early as the fifth century BC, seemed incomprehensible.

One content – or more. But the possibility that an analogous meaning is secreted in all of these cases cannot be excluded a priori. Attempts have been made to clarify the presumably ritual monosandalism of the Plataeans, aligning it with Jason's mythical version: both appear inspired by a model of ephebic behaviour, quite unlike that of adult soldiers, the hoplites (the shield bearers).[54] And yet this alignment, though convincing, only shifts the problem: why did the ephebe Jason wear only one sandal (the right one)?[55] We can search for an answer by inserting him in a larger series, including mythical figures characterized not only by a single sandal, but, more generally, by peculiarities linked to walking.[56] The symmetries between Jason and Philoctetes are immediately apparent.[57] After participating in the expedition of the Argonauts (led by Jason), Philoctetes had landed on the island of Lemnos: here, as he was approaching the altar (erected by Jason) to the goddess Chryse, he had been bitten in the foot by a snake. In the Sophoclean tragedy named after him, Philoctetes describes how his comrades, unable to endure the stench that emanates from his infected foot, have abandoned, indeed 'exposed', him, 'like a child abandoned by his nurse' (verses 5 and 702–3), on the deserted island of Lemnos. Ulysses disembarks there accompanied by Neoptolemus, the young son of Achilles, in order to gain possession by cunning of Philoctetes' bow, with which, according to the prophecy, the Greeks would be able to win the Trojan War. Philoctetes' borderline condition between life and death, between humanity and animality, has been compared to Neoptolemus' ephebic initiation; and the reintegration of the one into civil life has been compared to the attainment of adulthood by the other.[58]

Let us now proceed to Jason. In Pindar's fourth *Pythian Ode* (verses 108–16) he tells how, immediately after his birth, in order to protect him from the violence of his usurping uncle, his parents had pretended to weep over him as if he were dead: then, on the sly, they had entrusted him to the centaur Chiron. Emerging from the water of the Anaurus river with his left foot bare, the ephebe Jason leaves behind him a simulated death, followed by a childhood and early youth spent in a cave in the wilderness with a creature half-animal and half-human. Like Philoctetes' wounded foot, the single sandal worn by Jason refers to initiation and thus, symbolically, to death.

Caeculus was a god of the dead: Tertullian (*adv. nat.* 2. 15) says that his eyes were so dreadful that they deprived those who looked at him of their senses. The identity between this god and his namesake Caeculus, founder of Praeneste, is beyond doubt.[59] In the *Aeneid* the Hernici led by Caeculus wear on their heads tawny caps made of wolf fur, similar to the one worn, according to tradition, by Hades, the Etruscan god of the nether world.[60] The mention of the bare left foot that immediately follows would seem to seal the representation of a veritable cohort of the dead, comparable to the *exercitus feralis* that Tacitus will evoke vis-à-vis the Germanic tribe of the Harii.[61] The possibility that the bare foot of the Plataeans described by Thucydides had analogous implications should not be excluded.

9. The legends about the childhood of Caeculus tell us that he was a child who had been exposed, like Romulus – or like Oedipus. The first comparison is inevitable: the myths about Caeculus, son of a woman fertilized by a spark from the hearth (and therefore said to be the son of Vulcan), chief of a band of brigands and founder of a town (Praeneste), make him an obvious rival to

Romulus.[62] The other comparison, by contrast, may seem vague. But it is not.

The legends about the childhood of Caeculus, founder of Praeneste, closely resemble those surrounding the childhood of Cyrus, of Moses, of Romulus, in some ways of Jesus himself, and of many other founders of cities, empires and religions. The resemblances between these stories have been analyzed many times, from different, non-communicating points of view: psychoanalytical, mythological, historical and, finally, narratological.[63] Among the elements that recur most frequently in these biographies we find: a prophecy concerning the birth, presented as a misfortune for the reigning sovereign to whom the hero is sometimes tied by kinship; the preventive segregation of the mother referred to in the prophecy in closed or even consecrated places (so that the birth, which ensues despite everything, is often attributed to a god); the exposure or attempt to kill the new-born child, abandoned in wild or inhospitable places; the protective intervention of animals, shepherds, or both, who feed and raise the child; the return to the homeland, accompanied by extraordinary trials; the triumph, sudden irruption of an adverse destiny, finally death, followed in some instances by the disappearance of the hero's corpse. Myths like those of Oedipus, Theseus, Telephus, partly correspond to this patttern.[64] Such convergences could be utilized for propagandistic purposes. The analogies between Telephus and Romulus were accentuated during the period of friendship between Rome and Pergamon (third–second century BC).[65] Plutarch declared that the story of the origins of Rome presented by Fabius Pictor echoed, probably by way of a lost Greek historian (Diocles of Peparethos), a tragedy by Sophocles, *Tyro*, which was also lost. In it were recounted the vicissitudes of the sons of Tyro and the god Poseidon, the twins Neleus and Peleus: like Romulus and Remus, they had been entrusted to the waters of a river, until a bitch and a mare had adopted and raised them.[66] The birth of Jesus from a virgin, as the prophets had announced; Herod's anger against the infant destined to become King of the Jews; the slaughter of the innocents; the flight into Egypt – these are events that insert themselves into a narrative pattern widespread between the Iranian highlands and the Mediterranean.

10.   We have seen three sets emerge comprised of:

(a) Myths about the fatal son (or nephew or grand-child or or son-in-law);

(b) myths and rituals connected in some way with walking;

(c) myths and legends about the hero's birth.

Though only partially superimposable, these sets of myths are bound by a dense web of resemblances, which are probably due to the existence of a common thread: initiation understood as symbolic death.[67] Let us think of an example. Just as Oedipus ('swollen foot') liberates Thebes from the threat of the Sphinx, so Meleager frees Calydon from the threat of a monstrous boar. Like the one-sandalled Jason, and like Telephus, iater wounded in one leg, Meleager fulfils the prophecy by killing his uncle, while the division of the spoils of the stricken boar is under way. To avenge her murdered brothers, Althaea, Meleager's mother, casts into the fire an extinguished brand to which her son's life has been tied since birth – inverting, so to speak, the immersion in fire of Demophoön and Achilles, designed to obtain immortality for them. Euripides, Aristotle, and a scholium of Pindar (*Pyth*. IV. 75) concur in stating that the Aetolians customarily wear only one sandal. Meleager, the young son of the Aetolians' king, is therefore part of the series of heroes characterized by imbalances of gait or malformation of the feet.

In the legends about the childhood of the founders of empires or religions, these distinguishing marks occur very rarely.[68] But it does not seem fortuitous that from the nocturnal struggle on the banks of the stream Jabbok (*Gen*. 32. 23–33) with an unnamed being (Yahweh? an angel? a demon?) Jacob should issue limping, with his femur dislocated and a new name, Israel.[69] When we read that the followers of Caeculus (and, by extension, Caeculus himself) marched with one bare foot, this apparently negligible detail acquires an unexpected salience in the light of the configuration that we have seen gradually take shape. A hero with a single boot and weak eyes (as his name Caeculus indicates) can be considered a diluted counterpart of a lame and blind hero: Oedipus.[70]

11. Before taking possession of the kingdom, Cyrus – Strabo tells us – had lived among bandits (*kardakes*); Romulus, whom an analogous tradition portrays as surrounded by outlaws and criminals (*latrones*), is described by Eutropius (I. 1.2) as a cattle thief. This convergence (one of the many) between the two legendary cycles has been considered proof of the importance that male associations had assumed in the Iranian highlands and in Latium.[71] Perhaps: at any rate, it is a detail linked to a common narrative pattern, as is demonstrated by Euripides' reference (*Phoenicians*, 32 ff.) to the theft of Laius' horses by Oedipus.[72] In the legendary biography of the young hero, the theft of livestock carried out in league with their contemporaries was an obligatory stage, virtually an initiation ritual. It repeated a very ancient mythical model, amply documented in the Indo-European cultural milieu: the journey to the beyond to steal the livestock of a monstrous being.[73]

It has been suggested that this myth should be seen as a re-elaboration of the ecstatic journeys to the realm of the dead made by shamans to procure game for the community.[74] We reached a similar conclusion when analyzing the nocturnal feats of the *burkudzäutä*, the Baltic werewolves, and the Friulian *benandanti*, which aimed at wresting from the dead and sorcerers shoots of wheat or an abundant harvest. A mythical structure, presumably generated in a society of hunters, was adopted (and partially modified) by very different societies based on sheep farming or agriculture. The links in this cultural transmission elude us. But it is perhaps not irrelevant that Heracles, the principal protagonist of this cycle of myths on Greek soil, proves to be connected with the Scythian world in various ways. According to a myth reported by Herodotus (IV. 8–10), Heracles, after having seized Geryon's cattle, arrived in the then deserted Scythia, copulated with a local divinity, half-woman half-serpent, and begat the Scythians. His teacher, the archer Teutaros (Heracles was originally armed with a bow and not a club), is sometimes portrayed in Scythian garb. The presence in China of a mythical hero to whom feats analogous to those of Hercules are attributed, has been tentatively ascribed to Scythian mediation.[75]

12. The recovery of Iphicles' cattle by Melampus (*Od.* XI. 287–98); XV. 225 ff.) has also been compared to the myth revolving around the theft of cattle in the beyond.[76] Melampus, taken prisoner by Iphicles, manages to escape from the collapsing jail by detecting, with his very acute hearing, the sound of the woodworm gnawing at the beams. This is one of the many fabular elements that characterize Melampus. For example, it was said of him that two snakes cleaned his ears with their tongues: this is how he was able to understand the idiom of birds. The same faculty was possessed by Tiresias, the blind seer who was transformed into a woman for seven years because he had witnessed the copulation of two snakes.

We saw what analogies tied 'swollen foot' Oedipus to 'black foot' Melampus. The analogies between Melampus and Tiresias, between Tiresias and Oedipus (three soothsayers), are equally evident. In a famous scene of Sophocles' *Oedipus Rex*, Oedipus recoils, horrified, at learning from Tiresias the hitherto concealed identity of the person whose guilt has visited the plague upon Thebes. The dialogue between the two is dominated by a juxtaposition that harbours an imminent symmetry. On the one hand, we have the blind seer who knows; on the other, we have the unknowing culprit, destined to issue from the metaphorical darkness of ignorance and plunge into the real darkness of blindness. The halting step with which (according to Tiresias' prophecy) Oedipus will depart for foreign lands as an exile and beggar, supported by a cane, recalls that of Tiresias himself, leaning on the seer's staff given him by Athena.[77]

Tiresias, and a fortiori Melampus, are the mythical prototypes of the iatric Greeks – healers, soothsayers, magicians, ecstatics – who have been compared to the shamans of Central and Northern Asia.[78] Amongst them we find figures who really existed, but who are enveloped in a legendary aura: Pythagoras of the golden thigh, Empedocles who vanished into Mount Etna, leaving behind a single trace – a bronze sandal, flung up from the bottom of the crater.[79] Apparently negligible details which, touched by the magic wand of comparison, suddenly reveal their secret physiognomy.[80]

13. In Greece unbalanced gait was associated in a very particular way with one divinity: Dionysos, whose cult, according to Herodotus (II. 49), had been

introduced by Melampus.[81] It was said that Dionysos was born from the thigh of Zeus.[82] In the sanctuary of Delphi a Dionysos *Sphaleotas* ('who makes one totter') was worshipped. A myth illustrated this epithet. En route to Troy the Greek fleet had landed in Mysia by mistake. During a battle Achilles had clashed with the sovereign of the region, Telephus. Dionysos, angered because he had not been received with sufficient honour in Mysia, had contrived for Telephus to get entangled in a vine, stumble and fall: Achilles had wounded him in a leg. The hero of the vulnerable heel; the hero of the wounded leg; the god that makes one totter or stumble: in the physiognomy of the myth's three protagonists we perceive the same symbolic feature refracted in different forms. We are acquainted with a ritualistic equivalent of it: the *askôliasmos*, a game (played during the festivities in honour of Lenaean Dionysos) which consisted in hopping while balanced on one foot.[83]

The term *askôliazein* was used to describe the cranes' habit of standing on only one leg.[84] And in this instance too there were ritualistic implications. A 'dance of the crane' was performed at night in Delos and Crete; in the second century AD, Plutarch spoke of it as an extant custom. According to tradition, the dance, in which both boys and girls participated, imitated the winding paths of the labyrinth from which, after killing the minotaur, Theseus had issued thanks to Ariadne's artfulness. It has been suggested that the name of the dance underscored the analogy between individual dancers and the manner in which cranes walk.[85] Such a ritual seems compatible with what has already been said about the initiatory character of Theseus' exploits. That the labyrinth symbolized the realm of the dead and that Ariadne, mistress of the labyrinth, was a funerary goddess, are more than probable conjectures.[86] In Athens the marriage of Dionysos and Ariadne was celebrated every year on the second day of the Anthesteria: an ancient springtime festival that coincided with the periodic return to the earth of the souls of the dead, ambiguous harbingers of well-being and harmful influences, who were placated with offerings of water and boiled cereals.[87] We know that in Delos the dance of the crane was performed around the temple of Apollo, the god to whom Dionysos was intimately related, sometimes symmetrically, sometimes antithetically.[88] Precisely at Delos, around 300 BC, a certain Karystios dedicated to Dionysos a marble stele representing a crane overshadowed by a phallus.[89]

The connection between Dionysos and the dance of the cranes is only hypothetical. Yet it does not seem overly audacious to connect the stumbling or hopping to the subterranean and funereal aspect of Dionysos' figure. 'Hades and Dionysos are one and the same thing,' Heraclitus had said.[90]

14. In the China of the fourth century BC, during the age of the Warring Kingdoms, the Taoist philosopher Ko Hong described in great detail in a treatise the so-called 'step of Yu': a dance that consisted in advancing now with the left, now with the right, dragging along the other leg in such a way as

to impart to the body a hopping gait. The mythical hero from whom the dance took its name, Yu the Great, a minister and the founder of a dynasty, was half-paralyzed. Powers of a shamanic kind were attributed to him, such as changing into a bear or controlling floods. Until quite recently there existed in some parts of China female shamans who, their face covered by a handkerchief, would dance the step of Yu until they fell into a trance.[91] Originally, it was part of an animal dance (possibly connected with the monkey), comparable to the equally asymmetrical dances that took their names from mythical birds with a single leg: the Pi-fang, genius of fire; the Chang-yang, genius of rain; and the pheasant with the human face in which a sort of symbolic counterpart of Yu has been recognized.[92]

We do not know whether the ancient Chinese dance named 'of the white cranes' had this asymmetrical character. A legend tells us that the daughter of Ho-lu, King of Wu (514–495 BC), offended by a father who offered her a fish after eating half of it, had killed herself. Ho-lu had the daughter buried in a tomb which was entered through a subterranean passage. At the end of the dance of the white cranes he had ordered dancers and spectators to enter the subterranean passage and had buried them alive.[93] Here too, as in the Cretan myth, the dance of the cranes is associated with a subterranean corridor and a human sacrifice: insufficient, perhaps, to claim that two such distant phenomena derive from one another, or to postulate a common genesis for them.[94] Isolated identities can be the fruit of coincidences. Multiple parallelisms rooted in a profound isomorphism pose more disquieting questions. The step of Yu has been set beside the two coloured garments, half-black and half-red, worn by the participants in the ceremony with which the new year opened, during a period consecrated to the spirits of the dead: the expulsion of the Twelve Animals that symbolized demons and illnesses.[95] In both cases the imbalance in gait seems to be associated with communication with the realm of the dead. Now, in Europe too it was believed that the souls of the dead roamed among the living, especially between the end of the old year and the beginning of the new, during the twelve nights between Christmas and Epiphany.[96] As we have seen it was precisely then that the forays of the Greek *kallikantzaroi* and of the Livonian werewolf occurred. One group was led by a lame 'great *Kallikantzaros*'; the other, by a lame boy.[97]

15. At first sight the calendar circumstances by which these Chinese, Greek, Baltic phenomena are linked offer evidence for the hypothesis – advanced in a contentious manner – that mythic-ritualistic lameness is a trans-cultural phenomenon connected with the passage of the seasons. In other rituals of European folklore this connection seems absolutely clear: for example, in the Brandenburg region, the individual who impersonates the winter that is coming to an end pretends to limp; in Macedonia, bands of children celebrate the arrival of March by hurling invective at 'lame February'.[98] But an explanation of this kind can be accepted only if we isolate

one object (mythical and ritualistic lameness) on the basis of immediate and hence superficial characteristics.[99] The search for deep isomorphisms has led us to broaden the picture, juxtaposing apparently different phenomena linked by the real or symbolic reference to imbalance of gait: limping, dragging a wounded leg, having a vulnerable heel, walking with one foot unshod, stumbling, hopping on one foot. This redefinition of the formal characteristics of the *explanandum* has in most instances rendered the old interpretative hypothesis unsustainable. To connect the set of myths analyzed hitherto – beginning with that of Oedipus – with the passing of the seasons would be patently absurd.[100]

In the physical imbalance that characterizes divinities like Hermes or Dionysos, or heroes like Jason or Perseus, we have deciphered the symbol of a more radical transition – a permanent or temporary connection with the realm of the dead.[101] This is confirmed by the funereal connotations of the twelve nights during which werewolves and *kallikantzaroi* roamed through countrysides and villages. But this observation is inadequate on its own. How is it possible for similar myths and rituals to re-emerge, with such insistence, in such extremely heterogeneous cultural environments – from Greece to China?

16.   There is of course a ready answer. An archetype has been discovered in mythic-ritualistic lameness: an elementary symbol that would appear to be part of humanity's unconscious psychological patrimony.[102] Similar conclusions have been reached by another attempt to identify, through the dispersion of ethnographic evidence, a limited group of phenomena which can be defined as cultural universals. For example, the myth, documented in the most varied contexts, of the unilateral or half-man, provided with only one leg, one arm, one eye and so on, would be an archetype arising from an unconscious psychological propensity of our species.[103] To this small archetypal procession might be added those who wore one sandal or hopped on one foot. Obviously, a proliferation of this kind would nullify the theoretical ambitions inherent in the notion of the archetype. Fashioned to grasp some basic constants of the human psyche, the idea seems to be threatened by two opposing tendencies: to crumble into units which are too limited, as in the proposals just described; or, to evaporate in broad categories of the Great Mother type, inspired by an ethnocentric psychology.[104] In both cases this notion presupposes the existence of self-evident, universal symbols – the archetypes, in fact – whose significance can be grasped intuitively.

The presuppositions of the research we are conducting are altogether different. Its object is not given, but must be reconstructed via formal affinities; its significance is not transparent, but must be deciphered via examination of the context, or, better, of the pertinent contexts. It is of course true that different methods can sometimes arrive at results that are partially similar (if not equally cogent). The psychological approach to the putative archetype of lameness has shed light on its initiatory component. Anthropological inquiry into the half-man has discussed the possibility that in an area encompassing continental Asia, Borneo and Canada, this supposed archetype basically expresses the mediation between the world of human beings and that of the spirits and gods. But in the end this interpretative hypothesis has been rejected, on the grounds that neither an in-depth analysis of specific cases, nor a more extended comparison, would result in a unitary interpretation of the mythic-ritualistic complex hinging on the half-man.[105] An archetype, in short, is an archetype: what is identified in an almost intuitive fashion cannot be subjected to a more thorough analysis.

In reality, comparison permits us to go beyond so tautological a conclusion. Among the Ibo of Africa, the Miwok of California, the Bororo of Amazonia, those who participate in a ritual with the body painted vertically, half-black and half-white, impersonate the spirits. In northern Borneo the cultural hero who, having risen to heaven, discovers the rice plant, is a half-man. Among the Siberian Yakuts there is talk of halved shamans.[106] Again, in Siberia, the hero of an extraordinary Samoyed fable, killed four times by a mysterious antagonist, is resuscitated four times by an old man who has only one leg, one hand, one eye, and knows the path leading into a subterranean place inhabited by skeletons and silent monsters: here an old woman restores life to the dead by sleeping on their bones, which are reduced to ashes.[107] The overall tendency is therefore clear. And with it we revert to evidence originating in a cultural tradition much closer to us: Arthurian romance. The man with one leg, made completely of silver and encrusted with gold and precious stones, whom Gauvain encounters – one of the two protagonists of Chrétien de Troyes' *Perceval* – sits silently on the threshold of a castle surrounded by flames in which are believed to be persons who died long ago.[108] From Africa to Siberia, via medieval Ile-de-France, the half-man – like the lame, the one-sandalled, and so on – appears to be an intermediary figure between the world of the living and that of the dead or the spirits. One is tempted to say that constriction of a formal kind shapes the most disparate cultural materials, casting them in a relatively small number of pre-existing moulds.

According to a myth about the origins of the human species collected from the island of Ceram (Molucca), the stone wanted men to have only one arm, one leg, one eye, and be immortal; the banana tree wanted them to have two arms, two legs, two eyes and to be able to procreate. The banana tree won the dispute: but the stone insisted that men be subject to death. The myth invites us to recognize symmetry as a characteristic of human beings.[109] If we add to this a more specifically, though not exclusively, human characteristic, erect posture – we have before us a bipedal, symmetrical human being.[110] The trans-cultural diffusion of myths and rituals revolving around physiological asymmetry most probably sinks its psychological roots in this minimal, elementary perception that the human species has of itself – of its bodily image. Anything that modifies this image on a literary or metaphorical plane therefore seems particularly suited to express an experience that exceeds the limits of what is human: the journey into the realm of the dead, accomplished through ecstasy or initiation rituals. Recognition of the isomorphism of these features does not mean uniform interpretation of so disparate a complex of myths and rituals. It does, however, involve conjecturing the existence of predictable connections. For example, when we read that Soslan, one of the heroes of the Ossetian epic, visits the beyond while alive, we may anticipate that his body, grasped at birth by the tongs of the blacksmith of the Narts, was rendered invulnerable with one unfortunate exception: the knee (or the hip).[111]

17. The notion of archetype is thereby reformulated radically, because it is solidly anchored to the body[112] – more precisely, to its self-representation. We can conjecture that it operates as a schema, as a mediating instance of a formal kind, which is able to re-elaborate experiences bound up with the physical characteristics of the human species, translating them into potentially universal symbolic configurations.[113] By posing the problem in these terms we will avoid the mistake habitually made, as we have seen, by those who search for archetypes: that of isolating more or less widespread specific symbols, mistaking them for 'cultural universals'. The inquiry we are conducting has demonstrated that the universal element is not represented by single units (the lame, half-men, men wearing only one sandal), but by the series – open, by definition – which includes them. More precisely: not by the concreteness of the symbol, but by the categorial activity which, as we shall see, re-elaborates concrete (corporeal) experiences. Among the latter we must also – indeed, above all – include the corporeal experience degree zero: death.[114]

18. The definition must be taken literally. One cannot speak of death on the basis of direct experience: where death is, we are not, and vice versa.[115] But for thousands of years the journey into the beyond has inspired myths, poems, ecstasies and rituals.[116] A narrative form that spread throughout the Eurasian continent, with branches in the Americas, has crystallized around this theme. In fact, it has been established that the fundamental structure of magic fables, hinging on the hero's peregrinations, re-elaborates the theme of the journey (of the soul, of initiates, of shamans) to the world of the dead.[117] This is the same mythical nucleus that we uncovered in the ecstatic procession following the nocturnal goddess; in the battles fought in ecstasy for fertility; in the ritual parades and battles; in the myths and rituals concerning lame, one-sandalled and halved men. All the routes we have negotiated to clarify the folkloric dimension of the Sabbath converge on one point: the journey into the realm of the dead.

19. The statement that there exists a resemblance between fables about magic and the confessions of the men and women accused of being male and female witches seems at first sight only too obvious. Usually, this resemblance is attributed to conscious imitation. Goaded by torture or by the

psychological pressures of the judges, the defendants supposedly strung together a series of commonplaces drawn from fables learned in childhood and tales heard around the hearth, etc. Plausible in some instances, this hypothesis does not hold up when the resemblances go deeper. In analyzing the myths or rituals pertaining to folklore which eventually fused in the witches' Sabbath, we have seen the emergence of a fundamental distinction between the agonistic version (battles with sorcerers, the dead, and so on) and a non-agonistic version (bands of roaming dead). An analogous bifurcation, within a common structure, has been indicated between magic fables that include the function 'struggle with an opponent' and fables that exclude it.[118] To attribute isomorphisms of this kind to impromptu and superficial contamination would be manifestly absurd. We discern a more profound affinity between the magical fable and the folkloric nucleus of the witches' Sabbath. Might one illuminate the other?

20.   Almost a century ago the universal characteristics of the fable or fairy tale, and of a number of myths replete with fabular elements (foremost among them the journey to the beyond), were traced back to the equally universal experience of the splitting of body and soul induced by dream.[119] We are tempted to reformulate this rather simplistic thesis by hypothesizing a middle term between dream and fable: the shamanistic ecstasy.[120] But the resemblance of fables the world over remains to this day a decisive – and unresolved – question,[121] repeating in an exasperated form the dilemma encountered in our research.

All that remains is for us to accept the challenge, by analyzing a specific fairy tale: the story of *Cinderella*. Because of its characteristics and its extraordinary diffusion (see map 4) this option is almost inevitable.[122]

21.   In the best-known European version, Cinderella, the abused step-daughter, cannot attend the prince's ball because her stepmother has forbidden it (prohibition); she receives a dress, slippers, etc. (gift of magical instruments from an assistant); she goes to the prince's palace (defiance of the prohibition); she flees, losing a slipper, which at the prince's request she is later able to put on (difficult task leading to the recognition of heroine), while the step-sisters vainly try to do the same (the false hero or heroine stakes unfounded claims); she unmasks the step-sisters, who are her antagonists; and marries the prince. The plot, as we can see, rehearses the scheme that we have identified in the magical fables. One of its functions – the mark impressed on the hero's or the heroine's body – is easily recognizable in the crucial detail of the lost slipper.[123] Cinderella's monosandalism is a distinguishing sign of those who have visited the realm of the dead (the prince's palace).[124]

Up to this point we have considered Cinderella as a compact unit, neglecting the numerous variants. Let us examine those which refer to the figure of the magical assistant from whom the heroine receives the gifts that

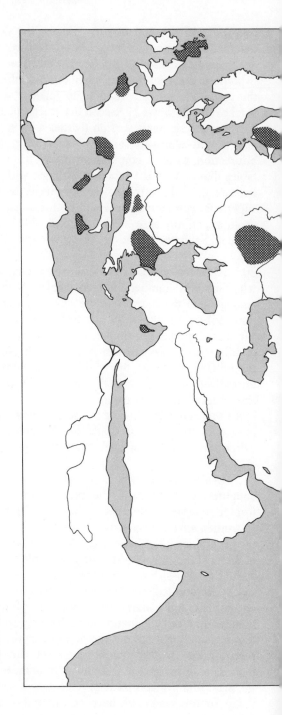

Map 4

Cinderella. Versions in which the magic helper (mother, godmother, animal) arises after the gathering and burial of the bones.
The map is merely indicative.

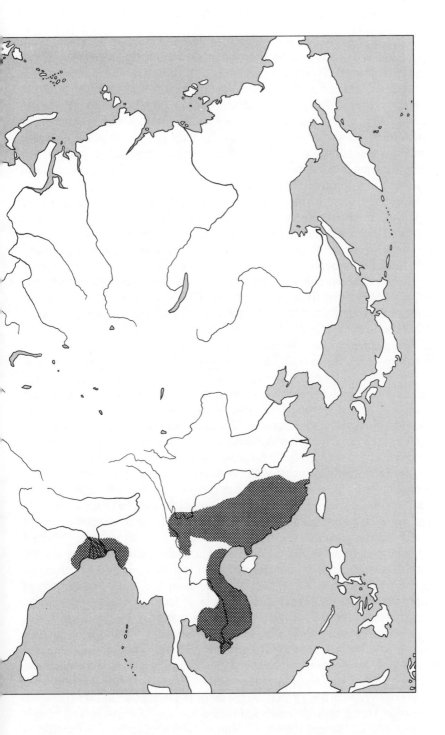

allow her to go to the ball at the palace. In Perrault's version the assistant is a fairy, Cinderella's godmother. More often, the same tasks are performed by a plant or by an animal – a cow, a sheep, a goat, a bull, a fish – whom the heroine protects. For this reason the animal is killed by the stepmother or at her command. Before dying, it entrusts its bones to the heroine, begging her to gather, bury, and water them. In some cases the bones are magically transformed into gifts; in others the heroine finds gifts on the grave, on which a tree has sometimes grown.[125] In three versions the animal assistant – a sheep or a lamb in Scotland, a cow or a fish in India – rises from the bones and consigns the magical gifts to the heroine.[126]

As we have seen, myths and rituals wherein bones wrapped in skins are used to obtain the resurrection of slaughtered animals have been traced over a vast and heterogeneous geographical ambit. This encompasses a great part of Europe (from the British Isles to the Alps); of Asia (the sub-Arctic band from Lapland to the Bering Strait, the Caucasus and the Iranian highland); North America; equatorial Africa.[127] In general, because of the importance attributed to the dissolution of the corpse, this complex of myths and rituals connects up with the custom of double burial found over an even vaster area, which also includes the Pacific Ocean.[128] More specifically, the gathering of the bones is tied to the legendary, chiefly Eurasian theme of the magic tree that blossoms on the grave.[129] In the fairy tale of *Cinderella*, as we have seen, the two elements (bones and magic tree) alternate. Versions containing the gathering of the bones are documented in China, Vietnam, India, Russia, Bulgaria, Cyprus, Serbia, Dalmatia, Sicily, Sardinia, Provence, Brittany, Lorraine, Scotland and Finland.[130] So immense and varied a distribution precludes the possibility that the presence of this theme in the fable's plot is the result of a casual graft.[131] A further hypothesis is permissible: namely, that the version which includes the resurrection of the killed animal is the more complete one, even though it has survived in only three instances.

It is no doubt a very ancient version. Toward the middle of the eighteenth century, as we have noted, the Lapp shamans (*no'aidi*) explained to the Danish missionaries that the bones of sacrificed animals must be collected and arranged with the maximum care: Horagalles, the god to whom the sacrifice is offered, will then restore them to life even stronger than before. As we should remember, Horagalles was identified as a Lapp counterpart of Thor, the Celto-Germanic god who, in a famous page of the *Edda*, resuscitates a number of slaughtered billy goats by having their bones collected and striking them with his magic hammer.[132] But one of the billy goats (the *Edda* tale continues) limps on one leg: Thor notices this and reproaches the peasants, accusing them of having carelessly broken the animal's thigh bone. The same story recurs in various Alpine legends, from the Western Alps to the Tyrol (only the name of the miracle worker changes). Alongside them, though more indirectly, we may set myths and rituals documented in the most diverse cultures, which describe the expedients employed to ensure the more or less perfect resurrection of animals and human beings. In the Semitic sphere the prohibition on breaking the bones of the paschal lamb (*Exodus*. 12. 46), repeated vis-à vis the crucified Christ (*John*. 19.36), is undoubtedly linked to these beliefs.[133] In a completely different context, in Lombardy around the end of the fourteenth century, the followers of Oriente replaced the missing bones of the oxen whose meat they had devoured during their nocturnal banquets with pieces of elder wood. In a Tyrolean saga, a girl, first quartered and then resuscitated by using a piece of alder branch to replace one of her ribs, is called the 'alder wood witch'. The Abkhaz of the Caucasus say that if Adagwa, the god of the forest, realizes he has swallowed a bone while eating game, he replaces it with a small piece of wood. The Loparians of Siberia replace the missing bones of the slaughtered game with those of the dog who has eaten them. The Ainu, who inhabit the northern islands of the Japanese archipelago, will tell you that if a bear eats a man, the leader of the bears will force it to resuscitate him by licking his bones; but if the bear has eaten the bone of the man's little finger, he must replace it with a twig.[134] In this culturally heterogeneous, but morphologically coherent series we must include the two Scottish versions of the fairy tale of Cinderella, which include the gathering of the bones and the subsequent resurrection. In both the resuscitated animal (a sheep and a lamb, respectively) limps: in the first case, the heroine has forgotten to collect the hooves; in the second, the hind shin bone is missing.

The analogy with Thor's billy goat is obvious.[135] But the Celtic variant of the limping animal, as we have seen, fits into a much larger mythical and ritualistic context. It allows us to generalize the belief, recorded at the beginning of the thirteenth century by Gervase of Tilbury, according to which if one paw of a werewolf was severed, he immediately reassumed human form.[136] Anyone who goes to or returns from the nether world – man, animal, or a mixture of the two – is marked by an asymmetry. The series that we have reconstructed allows us to grasp the symbolic equivalence between the lameness of the resuscitated animal and Cinderella's subsequent loss of the slipper. Between the one who offers assistance – animal, fairy godmother, or, indeed, mother – and the one who receives it, there exists a hidden homology.[137] Cinderella (like Thor, St Germanus, Oriente) can be thought of as a reincarnation of the 'mistress of the animals'.[138] Her gestures of piety for the bones (burying them, watering them) have an effect similar to the magical touch of Thor's hammer or Oriente's wand. In a version of the fables collected in Split, which presents the theme of resurrection in a diluted form, the resemblance is even stronger: the youngest daughter touches the kerchief that contains the killed mother's bones with a wand, restoring voice to them.[139]

The exaltation of the female foot's daintiness, around which the plot of *Cinderella* revolves, has been related to the custom, practised by the upper classes in China, of binding women's feet from childhood. This is a plausible conjecture.[140] On the other hand, we know that the most ancient version of the Cinderella story available was written down by an erudite functionary, Tuang Ch'eng-Shih (800–63), who had heard it told by one of his servants, born in Southern China. By gathering the bones of a miraculous fish, which has been killed by her stepmother, the protagonist – Sheh-Hsien – receives a pair of golden sandals and a dress made of kingfisher feathers which she wears to the feast where she will meet the king. It has been noted that the sandals, probably not very common among the aboriginal population of Southern China, were rather a typical component of the shaman's outfit. It has also been suggested that the epithet 'as beautiful as a celestial being' applied both to the protagonist and the dress of kingfisher feathers worn by her at the feast in the grotto, alludes to a tale with a shamanic basis – that of the swan-girls – originating, in all probability, in northern Asia.[141] These cautious hypotheses appear even more convincing when set beside the magical nucleus that we have identified. Certainly, the relationships between the heroine and her mother, her stepmother, her step-sisters, her future husband, remain outside this analysis. But perhaps we should extend to Cinderella's story the hypothesis formulated with an eye on the myth of Oedipus: namely, that the portrayal of tensions bound up with family relationships was already, even in the most remote periods, grafted onto the narrative trunk of a magic fable.[142] This juxtaposition is not altogether unjustified, as is shown by the similarities between the plot of *Cinderella* and that of *The Donkey's Skin*.[143] Both protagonists are forced to devote themselves to humble and fatiguing chores: the first because she is abused by her stepmother; the second because she is loved too much by her father, whose importunate requests for marriage compel her to flee home disguised as an animal. The affinity of the initial situation in the two fables can become a partial superimposition: in a Russian version of *The Donkey's Skin* the heroine removes the animal pelt (in this instance a pig's skin) that covers her, goes to the prince's palace where she forgets her slipper, etc.[144] But the initial situation in *The Donkey's Skin* reproduces, in an inverted form, that of Oedipus: instead of a son who inadvertently marries his mother, we have a father who deliberately tries to marry his daughter. The latter theme returns in a diluted form in another plot, morphologically connected with *The Donkey's Skin* as well as *Cinderella*: the father imposes a contest on his daughters to find out which of them loves him most (this is the fabular nucleus of *King Lear*).[145]

22.   From Oedipus' lameness to Cinderella's slipper: a tortuous itinerary, full of advances and retreats, guided by a formal analogy. By reconstructing the profound affinity uniting myths and rituals originating in the most diverse contexts, we have been able to construe apparently inexplicable or marginal details encountered in the course of our research: a lame child at the head of a band of Livonian werewolves, the animal resuscitated by Oriente. But if we begin to introduce some geographical distinctions into this complex of myths and rituals, however broad, we begin to see the outline of a contrast. Themes

248

like the half-man, or the collection of the bones to achieve the resurrection of animals, appear in Eurasia, North America and continental Africa. But the variant represented by the missing bone – eventually replaced by pieces of wood or other bones – seems to be completely absent in continental Africa.[146] An analysis of the distribution of *Cinderella* yields the same conclusion. The innumerable variants of this tale cover an area that stretches from the British Isles to China, with a significant appendix along the southern coasts of the Mediterranean, in Egypt and Morocco (Marakesh); they maybe reach North America; but they do not touch continental Africa, where the very rare exceptions are attributable, in all probability, to recent contacts with European culture.[147] The exclusion of continental Africa also applies to another phenomenon which we have not as yet mentioned: scapulimancy – that is, divination or soothsaying based on the scapular bone of sacrificed animals (above all, rams). It appears to be present in an area circumscribed by the Bering Strait to the east: by the British Isles to the west; and by North Africa to the south.[148]

A fairy tale (*Cinderella*), a myth (the missing bone), a ritual (scapulimancy). In the last case a central Asian, possibly Mongolian, origin has been suggested.[149] An analogous, perhaps more northern, origin is likely for the other two. But the absence from continental Africa of such common and intimately linked cultural traits cannot be accidental. We propose to relate it to the absence in the same area of shamanistic phenomena analogous to those found in Eurasia and, in more diluted forms, in North America. In fact, in continental Africa we find phenomena of possession: not the ecstasy followed by the journey of the shaman's soul into the beyond. The shaman rules the spirits; the possessed person is at the mercy of the spirits and is ruled by them.[150] Behind this sharp contrast we perceive a presumably very ancient cultural differentiation.

23. Although also present in cultural areas free of shamanistic phenomena in the strict sense, myths and rituals involving collection of the bones of the killed animal seem to retrace the anguished inner itinerary via which the shaman recognizes his vocation: the experience of being cut to pieces, of contemplating his own skeleton, of being reborn to a new life.[151] In the Eurasian milieu this sequence includes a further element, which presents a demonstrably (though not exclusively) shamanistic physiognomy: the return from the beyond, expressed by the missing bone or the lost slipper. This is a trace of the contacts between the Greeks and the cultures of Central Asia, through the mediation of the Scythians. Alcaeus' enigmatic reference to Achilles as 'master of the Scythians' must be seen in this light.[152] Another example is offered us, together with the association with scapulimancy and the resurrection of the bones, by another myth: that of Pelops.[153]

Pelops had been killed by his father Tantalus, who had cut him into pieces, which he then boiled in a cauldron and offered to the gods to eat to test their omniscience. Only Demeter fell into the trap and she ate one of the boy's shoulders. Pelops' body was recomposed and brought back to life: his shoulder, however, was replaced by a piece of ivory. The analogy with Eurasian myths and rituals, in which the missing bone is replaced by pieces of wood or (more rarely) by other bones, is self-evident.[154]

Every year, in a complicated ritual, a black ram was sacrificed in Pelops' honour. The ritual was performed at Olympia on the occasion of the chariot race. In fact, another myth recounts that Pelops had been able to marry Hippodameia by defeating her father, Oenomaus, during a chariot race and causing his death. It will be remembered that this murder of the future father-in-law, forecast by an oracle, suggested the insertion of Pelops in the series of Oedipus' counterparts.[155] His figure is only apparently lacking in the kind of anomalies that characterize other fatal heroes such as Oedipus, Jason or Perseus. There exists in fact a mythical situation in which the absence of the scapular bone implies lameness: when the victim of the mutilation is a quadruped. There is a clear relation of equivalence between Pelops and the ram sacrificed at Olympia in his honour.[156]

24. The Greeks knew two similar myths: that of Tantalus and that of Lycaon. In both by subterfuge a man offers the gods the flesh of his son, on its own or mixed with that of animals; in both myths the gods discover the deceit, punish the culprit and restore life to the dismembered human victim. The sharing of a meal by men and gods, as well as the anthropophagy, evoke by contrast a third myth: Prometheus' institution of bloody sacrifice.[157] Here too, as Hesiod's *Theogony* (verses 535–61) informs us, there is an attempt at deception, only seemingly crowned by success. Prometheus divides the large sacrificial ox into two parts: the meat and the offal, intended for men, and the bones, destined to burn on the altar for the gods. Upon seeing the bones presented to him smothered in appetizing lard, Zeus pretends to be taken in. The contest continues with the episode of the fire, which Prometheus steals in order to give to man; with the revenge of Zeus, who sends Pandora, a most beautiful and fateful gift, to earth; and, finally, with the punishment of Prometheus, chained to a rock in the Caucasus, prey to the eagle that tears at his liver (only Hercules will, with Zeus' consent, free him from this torment).[158]

The possibility that the sacrificial division proposed to Zeus by Prometheus historically derives from Laplandian, Siberian or Caucasian rituals, in which the bones of the killed animals were offered to the gods so that they could restore them to life, was suggested long ago.[159] It is now rendered more plausible by the demonstration of the relationship between the Greek myths about Prometheus and the chiefly Georgian myths about Amirani. On this basis, as we have already said, a series of contacts has been postulated, two thousand years before Christ, between populations speaking Indo-European languages and populations speaking Caucasian languages.[160] But these hypothetical contacts were in all probability reactivated during a period much closer to us. A copious archaeological record demonstrates that between the seventh and fourth centuries BC the Scythians penetrated into trans-Caucasia: into western and central Georgia, into the region inhabited by the Abkhaz, and into the region where the Ossetians who speak Iranian are established even today.[161] If the comparison between the legends of the hero Amirani (handed down in precisely these areas) and the Promethean cycle were extended to the myth about the institution of blood-letting sacrifice, the cultural intertwining between Caucasian populations, Scythians and Greeks, would probably prove to be even closer – and the originality of the Greek re-elaboration even more significant.[162]

Something, however, can be glimpsed in Hesiod's account. It is usually taken for granted that the struggle between Prometheus and Zeus described in *Theogony* definitely refers to the Greek ritual of the blood-letting sacrifice. And yet the correspondence between myth and ritualistic practices is anything but perfect. Hesiod counterposes bones and meat, without mentioning the viscera (*splanchna*), which played an important part in the sacrifice.[163] What is more, the gesture of Prometheus, who places 'meat and innards (*enkata*) rich in fat . . . inside a skin', after having hidden them 'in the ox's belly',[164] has no counterpart in the ritual of the sacrifice – at least not in Greek sacrifice. But if we take the Scythian sacrifice as a term of comparison, we witness an unexpected convergence. The Scythians, Herodotus tells us (IV. 61), 'encase all the meats in the belly' of the ox (or some other animal); then, after mixing them with water, they boiled them.[165] This is a further proof of the close cultural contiguity between the Scythians and the nomadic shepherds of Central Asia. In fact, the Buryats also follow the custom of cooking the animals wrapped in their skin, after having filled it with water and red-hot stones.[166]

Two very different texts: Hesiod's tells the story of the foundation of the Greek sacrificial ritual in a mythical key; Herodotus' describes, from a perspective that we would today call ethnographic, the sacrificial ritual performed by a foreign, indeed nomadic population. In the second as in the first, the Greek sacrifice is continually present as a sometimes conscious, sometimes unconscious term of comparison. From the gamut of possible victims Herodotus chooses the one most obvious for him – the ox – precisely in order to give greater prominence to the singularity of the Scythian practice. But the method used by them to handle the meat of the victims cannot be attributed to a projection of Herodotus, since in the Greek sacrificial context nothing of the kind is to be found.[168] On the other hand, Hesiod's narrative aims do not qualify (nor do they explain) the punctual convergence with Herodotus' description.[169] The conclusion is unavoidable. The tradition bequeathed to Hesiod preserves the memory of Scythian sacrifice: it is, however, inserted in a mythical re-elaboration designed to illustrate, by means of the contest between Prometheus and Zeus, the decisive novelty of the Greek sacrifice.

25. Blood sacrifice established a clearcut and irreversible separation between men and gods, on the one hand, and between men and beasts, on the other. The religion of the city, whose centrepiece lay in sacrifice, now found that it had to confront a double challenge on both sides of this division, represented by the forms of radical religiosity upheld, respectively, by the followers of Pythagoras and the followers of Dionysos. The former condemned – more or less resolutely – the consumption of meat as an obstacle en route to a perfection designed to bring men closer to the gods. The latter tended to abolish the distance between men and animals through the bloody ritual of eating raw meat, in which the animals were dissected and devoured still uncooked – almost still alive.[170] In the foundation myth of the blood sacrifice, equivalent to an option for cooked meat (Prometheus is also the one who gives men the gift of fire), we have recognized traces of the sacrificial customs of the nomads of central Asia, even though inserted in a totally different context. An analogous re-elaboration is perhaps also present in the partially converging positions of those who opposed the traditional sacrifice, either by refusing the first term (meat), or by refusing the second (cooking).

The convergence of these two positions can be explained, on the one hand, by the documented presence of Orpheus in the Dionysiac rituals; on the other hand, by the prominent position allotted Dionysos in the so-called Orphic books. An Orphic sect never existed: rather, from the fourth century BC there appeared a series of pseudo-epigraphic poems written by different persons (among whom, it would seem, was Pythagoras himself), who hid behind the name and authority of Orpheus.[171] In one of these poems a myth was recounted which we know mostly through the late testimonies of Christian authors, Greek (Clement of Alexandria) as well as Latin (Firmicus Maternus, Arnobius). The subject of the myth was the murder of the child Dionysos (sometimes identified with Zagreus, the mythical Cretan hunter) by the Titans. Their faces covered with chalk, the Titans kill Dionysos after diverting him with tops, dice, a mirror and other toys; then they cut him into pieces, boil him in a cauldron, roast him on a spit, until they are struck by Zeus' lightning bolt. Some versions add that Dionysos is devoured by the Titans; others that he comes back to life: resurrected from the heart which had been taken from the executioners by Athena, or from the limbs which had been recomposed by Demeter or by Rhea.[172]

Dismemberment, followed by immersion in a cauldron of boiling water, is used by the witch Medea to rejuvenate Jason and to kill his uncle, the usurper Pelias, by a trick.[173] Dismemberment, boiling, recomposition of the limbs and resurrection follow one another, as we certainly remember, in Pelops' story; Demophoön and Achilles had been unsuccessfully subjected to immersion in fire as a means of ensuring immortality. The resemblances between these myths and that concerning the killing of Dionysos have been traced back to a common initiatory element.[174] It has been objected that this interpretation neglects the sacrificial connotations of a myth containing (as already noted in a pseudo-Aristotelian problem) an explicit reference to the traditional Greek sacrifice, whose sequence it inverts. In fact, Dionysos is first boiled and then roasted, whereas during the sacrifice one first ate the victim's viscera, cooked on the spit, and then the boiled meat.[175] But these two interpretations are not necessarily incompatible: in the case of Dionysos the blood sacrifice could very well symbolize an initiatory trajectory, since it was followed by a resurrection. In some versions of the myth, as we have said, it was achieved by removing the victim's heart, in others by recomposing his limbs.[176] In this last case the allusion to the collection and recomposition of bones is implicit, given that, in the myth, the corpse of Dionysos is not only dismembered, but cooked twice and (in certain versions) even devoured.[177]

That the Orphic myth of Dionysos, in the sequence killing-dismemberment-boiling-roasting-recomposition of the bones-resurrection, re-elaborated Eurasian myths and rituals is only a hypothesis: more accurately, the fruit of several hypotheses. We do, however, know that a sanctuary of Dionysos existed as early as the sixth century BC in Olbia, the Greek colony situated on the shores of the Black Sea, adjacent to the territory inhabited by the Scythians. Herodotus (IV. 78–80) tells a story which well illustrates the attraction and repulsion provoked by this geographical and cultural proximity. Scyles, the king of a tribe of nomadic Scythians, but born of a Greek-speaking mother, used to disappear for long periods of time during which he secretly adopted the garb and cults of the Greeks. At a certain point he decided that he wanted to be initiated into the mysteries of Dionysos. When the Scythians, warned by an informer, saw their king walk through the streets of Olbia, mingling with the band of the followers of the Bacchic Dionysos, possessed by the god, they were indignant and revolted against him: 'It is absurd, they say, to imagine a god who drives men to madness.'[178] The cult that fascinated Scyles is not completely unknown to us. Among the archaeological evidence found in the area of Dionysos' sanctuary in Olbia, as well as in the surrounding country, there are numerous rectangular bone tables, sometimes polished on one side, sometimes on both, approximately the size of the palm of a hand. Occasionally, they are accompanied by inscriptions. On one of these tables, which dates back to the fifth century BC we read: 'Life-death-life. Truth/A/Dio(nysos)-Orpheans (two signs shaped as zigzags)-/Dio(nysos)- Orpheans'.[179] We may presume that an object of this kind had a ritualistic function. We do not know exactly what: but it does not seem too daring to assume the existence of a relationship with the Orphic myth of Dionysos, the god killed and then reborn from his own collected and recomposed bones.

26.   The pseudo-Aristotelian problem in which the matter of precedence between boiled and roast meats in the sacrifice is discussed also mentions the title of the poem, attributed to Orpheus, in which the myth of Dionysos' murder was told: *Ritual (or: Rituals) of Initiation (Teletē, Teletai)*.[180] The presence of an initiatory nucleus in this myth is beyond doubt.[181] The followers of Pythagoras or of Dionysos set before the initiate models of

individual asceticism, which were undoubtedly very different, but had in common their lack of connection with the exclusively public dimension of the city's religion. During the Hellenistic age interest in such forms of religious experience, as well as the impulse to reinterpret them allegorically, intensified. Plutarch wrote that the myth of Dionysos' murder by the Titans was a 'myth that referred to rebirth (*eis tèn palinghenesian*)', to inner renewal.[182] In short, the myth, and the ritual probably tied to it, offered the followers of Dionysos the possibility of identifying with the death and resurrection of their god.

It has been supposed that this mythical-ritualistic complex echoed shamanistic initiation: a phenomenon which the Greeks had encountered at Olbia, or, more generally, through their relations with the Scythians.[183] The possibility that the myth of Dionysos' re-birth re-elaborated the Eurasian ritual of the gathering of the bones reinforces such an hypothesis. Certainly, they were difficult relations. The indignation of the subjects of Scyles, the king who had tried to be initiated into the Dionysian mysteries, sprang from a Scythian attitude of intolerance toward foreign customs (further examples of this are known).[184] Moreover, the condemnation reported by Herodotus – 'It is absurd, they say, to imagine a god who drives men to madness' – gives us a sense of the distance between Dionysian possession and shamanic ecstasy, which the Scythians in all likelihood knew.[185] But a figure like Aristeas of Proconnesus makes it clear that phenomena of Graeco-Scythian religious hybridization were possible, despite everything.[186]

More often these shamanistic figures originated in remote regions like the land of the Hyperboreans, or half-wild regions like Thrace. Nevertheless, it is precisely Orpheus, the Thracian bard who knew the language of the animals and the path to the beyond, who shows how shamanistic figures and themes, once transplanted onto Greek soil, assumed a completely different physiognomy.[187] In Plato's time, itinerant priests and seers knocked at the doors of the rich spreading books attributed to Orpheus, in which it was explained how sacrifices were to be performed. The written word was breaking into a milieu traditionally given over to the oral tradition, entrusted, what is more, to the priestly caste.[188]

27. The religious movements and the philosophical-religious sects which emerged in the course of the sixth century offered their followers models of asceticism or of mystical exaltation, depending on the case. The significance assumed by a god as ancient as Dionysos, in close contact with the nether world, contradicted the denial of death expressed by the Homeric gods. This profound transformation was possibly also elicited by the encounter with cultures containing the figure of a professional mediator with the beyond.[189] But the traces of these contacts are few and elusive. The presence of reworked, shamanistic elements in Greek civilization will have to be sought in less obvious phenomena, including physical asymmetry in myth and ritual. It is significant that it should characterize the protagonists of the Greek myths

that concern the foundation of the blood sacrifice – or the refusal of it, formulated, from opposite viewpoints, in the name of a god 'who totters' (Dionysos *Sphaleotas*) or a sorcerer-philosopher to whom tradition attributed a golden thigh (Pythagoras).[190]

But Prometheus, responsible, according to the myth, for the blood sacrifice, does not totter, does not have a golden thigh, is not even lame. True enough. It should, however, be noted that the relations between Hephaestus, the blacksmith god of the crooked feet, and Prometheus, the god of fire, are so close as to render them almost interchangeable. It has been suggested that Hephaestus established himself on Olympus, supplanting Prometheus (but the reverse hypothesis too has been formulated).[191] Might Hephaestus' physical asymmetry have made explicit a trait obliterated or latent in the figure of Prometheus? In favour of this prima facie specious hypothesis one can adduce an unexpected comparison.

A legend recorded half a century ago among the Svani of the Caucasus presents a partially anomalous version of the feats of Amirani (which, as has already been mentioned, display notable affinities with those of Prometheus). At a certain point Amirani is left without fire. He discovers that the only ones to have it, within a radius of many miles, are a family of subterranean demons, the Devs: nine brothers, one of whom is lame. Amirani enters their house, assaults all of them except the lame one, takes possession of the fire, and leaves. The rarity of lame figures in Caucasian mythology suggests a comparison with the myth in which Prometheus steals fire from the forge of Hephaestus, the limping god. So punctual and concrete a convergence – it has been said – contrasts with the level of abstraction generally characteristic of the relations between the Caucasian Amirani cycle and the Greek Prometheus cycle. Therefore: (a) the lameness of the two victims of theft is undoubtedly due to a borrowing; (b) the direction of the borrowing necessarily went from Greece to the Caucasus.[192]

Both conclusions appear debatable. When we learn that the protagonist of a Georgian myth is a shaman with crooked legs, or that the myths about the nine Devs (one of whom is lame) are revealed by shamans in a state of trance, we are led to think that in the mythologies of the Caucasian populations lameness possesses an importance and significance not dissimilar from its salience in those we have reconstructed.[193] If we include lameness in the wider series of asymmetries, we discover that Amirani also fits into it. The legend recorded among the Svani says that, immediately after the theft of the fire, he is swallowed by a dragon, who sinks deep into the earth; he manages to come out of the dragon's viscera; after various adventures he encounters an eagle which, in exchange for twelve pairs of oxen and a corresponding quantity of bread, agrees to carry him to the surface. The eagle rises in a spiral, eating meat and bread at the end of each circle. There are only two circles to go when Amirani realizes that the supplies are exhausted. At that

> he cuts a piece of his own flesh and puts it in the eagle's beak, the eagle finds it much more tasty than the previous morsels and arrives on earth without stopping

again. Amirani alights and the eagle gives him a piece of its wing, telling him to rub it on the wound. The wound heals immediately.[194]

The Caucasian legend does not provide us with any further details about Amirani's self-inflicted mutilation. To find out more about it we must turn to a Mantuan fable recorded less than twenty years ago: *Sbadilon*.[195]

Sbadilon (big shovel) is a labourer who wanders through the world, together with two companions, with a shovel on his shoulder. After various adventures they come to a country where the princess has been abducted. In a meadow they see a stone: Sbadilon lifts it with two fingers, sees a big hole, lets himself down on a rope. When he arrives underground he kills five sorcerers with blows of his shovel and finds the princess, who as a token of her gratitude promises to marry him. Sbadilon gets his two companions to pull her up: but as soon as he tries to climb up, his companions cut the rope and leave with the princess.

> He Sbadilon poor fellow, when he found himself down there, opened another door, and out flew an eagle: 'Oh, Giovanni, what are you doing here?' and so he tells it that he had saved the princess and he says: 'How am I going to climb up there now?' The eagle says, 'Listen, if you've got any meat I'll take you up there too.' 'Oh, there's plenty of it! Do you like sorcerer's meat?' 'Yes', says the eagle. And so he puts two or three sorcerers on his shoulders and he puts himself on the eagle's back. 'And now when I tell you: give me a piece of meat, you'll give me a piece of meat.' And sure enough, 'give me a piece of meat, give me a piece of meat', but when they had gotten almost to the top there are no sorcerers left, and so when the eagle (tells him): 'give me a piece of meat' instead of maybe saying: 'there isn't any more' he cut off a piece of his heel and so they managed to get all the way up in time. When they were up he says: 'oh god, how this foot stings'. And so the eagle says: 'Quiet, I've got a little bottle here that makes heels grow back'. And sure enough the eagle emptied – these are real fables you know?! – emptied that little vial of stuff there and his heel grew back and then they said goodbye, he and the eagle. . . .[196]

28. 'These are real fables you know?!': as the narrator of Cesole near Mantua says, standing back for a moment from the prodigious event she is recounting.[197] How could she know that almost forty years earlier another narrator had told us the same feat, in virtually identical words, at a distance of thousands of kilometres, in the mountains of the Caucasus, following a pattern that is probably more than a thousand years old? But precisely because they are fables, narrative underpinned by a peculiar but iron logic, we can fill the lacuna represented by Amirani's unspecified mutilation with Sbadilon's severed heel.[197 bis]

The substantial identity of the two episodes is all the more astonishing inasmuch as it does not involve Prometheus' mediation. The existence of a myth in which Prometheus, having plunged underground, returns to the surface on the back of an eagle, feeding it with his heel, is a priori improbable, since in the Greek cycle the eagle always has a negative function (whereas in the Caucasian cycle the contrary is the case).[198] The series of story-tellers between the Caucasus and the Po Valley who for generation after generation have told the same story in innumerable languages – or rather, the same episode inserted into innumerable different stories – did not know the myth of Prometheus; or if they did, they did not take it into account. But if we abandon the plane of identity for that of isomorphism, our conclusion alters. It is very likely (not – note – certain) that Prometheus was marked by a physical asymmetry which, purely fortuitously, does not appear in the evidence we possess. Rather than a severed heel, Prometheus could have crooked feet like Hephaestus; or a wolf's knee-cap like Amirani, who uses it to break into a crystal tower, in which a dead giant lies.[199] The severed heels of Amirani and Sbadilon are clearly the distinguishing mark of those who have accomplished the subterranean journey into the world of the dead (which, in the Mantuan fable, one enters by lifting a stone slab). It has been pointed out that Amirani has several shamanic traits.[200] In Prometheus – a god who acts as a mediator between Zeus and men – they are almost obliterated. But it is prudent to specify: in the Prometheus we know.

We started out from the symmetry between the episode of the Caucasian legend in which Amirani gains possession of the fire without harming a hair on the head of the lame Dev, and a myth in which Prometheus steals the fire from limping Hephaestus. What we actually have here is a twofold symmetry, that involves not only the victims, but also the perpetrators of the theft: both seem bound by a relation that is indeed specular.[201] To put it simply, we might say that we have four variants, grouped in twos, of the same character. Three of them are distinguished by a different ambulatory asymmetry: knee with a wolf's cap (Amirani); lameness (Dev); crooked leg (Hephaestus). As for Prometheus, we must restrict ourselves to conjectures. But it is clear by now that the lame and, more generally, characters distinguished by asymmetries of gait cannot be considered a superficial element and hence attributable only to a borrowing.[202]

29.   While investigating the folkloric roots of the Sabbath, we witnessed the emergence of a series of testimonies that spoke of men and women who in a state of ecstasy underwent experiences similar to those of the Siberian shamans: the magical flight and animal metamorphosis. Apart from cases in Lapland and Hungary (where the cultural and ethnic connection with Central Asia was obvious) in order to explain the presence of these phenomena on European soil two suppositions were possible. The first was that the connection was created by a population which – save for language – had cultural affinities with the nomads of the steppes, such as the Scythians with whom first the Greeks (from the seventh century BC) and then the Celts (from the fourth century BC) had commercial links along the shores of the Black Sea. The second was that contact with the Scythians had reactivated, in the Greek as well as the Celtic case, cultural elements which were latent but which had existed as a sedimentary deposit for a very long time – centuries, perhaps thousands of years. Unlike the first hypothesis, the latter rests on a

documentary void. What leads us to resume it, in the form of a postulate (and as such undemonstrable), is the difficulty of tracing back to the contact with the Scythians (basically limited) the astonishing dissemination of shamanistic traits across the European continent, which were later forcibly merged into the stereotype of the Sabbath. The hypothesis of a long period of contiguity, before the second millennium BC and in a region situated perhaps between the Black Sea and the Caspian Sea, of populations speaking Indo-European languages and populations speaking Caucasian languages, has replaced that – fashionable some time ago – of one or more invasions of shamanistic horsemen from central Asia.[203] But in both cases we are dealing with conjecture.

Well-documented, by contrast, is the subterranean layer of unitary Eurasian mythology that has emerged from the analysis of myths and rituals hinging on ambulatory asymmetry. We could continue the inquiry, concentrating on medieval Europe, to show how the goose foot of the mythical Queen Pédauque, the disproportionately large foot of 'big foot Bertha' (a variant of Perchta), the webbed or donkey foot of the Queen of Sheba (a reversed Oedipus, who sets riddles for Solomon), the bone leg of the Russian baba-jaga, and so on, have been replaced by devil's goose foot, equine hoof, or lameness (fig. 18).[204] In the multiple variants of an apparently marginal detail are enclosed a thousand-year-old history.

30.   Guided by this detail, down a side road we have again encountered the nocturnal goddess who resuscitates animals (Part Two, chapters 1 and 2). An equally peripheral route will permit us to view such phenomena as the night battles and the ritualistic masquerade from a different perspective (Part Two, chapters 3 and 4). Hitherto we have analyzed a mythical and ritualistic feature in extremely heterogeneous contexts, demonstrating that a persistence of form was matched by a substantial continuity of meaning. Let us now examine the reverse situation, in which different contents correspond to an almost identical form. Why has the form survived?

The Vogul-Ostyak, who are today settled in western Siberia, until the thirteenth century occupied a vast region around Perm, on the far slope of the Urals. A myth tells us that a long time ago, upon their return from the forest, some hunters were preparing something to eat. Suddenly, they saw a hostile band approaching. Some of the hunters fled, clutching the still raw meat. The others remained and began to cook the meat in the cauldrons: but before it was cooked they had to deal with an attack by their enemies and came out of it with broken noses. The descendants of the raw meat-eaters, called *Mos-chum* (i.e., men similar to the gods), are considered intelligent, civil and good; the descendants of the half-cooked meat-eaters, called *Por-chum*, are considered stupid, coarse, wicked. Each group has its own cult site and its own ceremonies; animals and vegetables are classified, depending on the case, as *Mos* (for instance, the goose or birch tree) or as *Por* (for example, the bear or larch). *Mos* and *Por* constitute two exogamous phratries: it is only permissible to marry members of the other group. The myth also speaks of a pair of heroic brothers who are related to this dualistic system.[205]

On the shores of the Mediterranean a similar story is told (Ovid, *Fasti*, 2. 361 ff.). Here the two brothers, Romulus and Remus, are the protagonists. In keeping with the ritual, a number of goats are sacrificed to the god Faunus. While the priests are preparing the sacrificial offerings, skewered on willow sticks, Romulus and Remus take off their clothes and compete with other young men. Suddenly, a shepherd sounds the alarm: some brigands are making off with the calves. Without bothering to take their weapons, the young men dash off in pursuit. Remus comes back with the booty, removes the frying pieces of meat from the skewers and eats them, sharing them with the Fabii: 'The victor is certainly entitled to these.' Then Romulus arrives disappointed, sees the bare bones (*ossaque nuda*) and begins to laugh, regretting the victory of Remus and the Fabii, and the defeat of his Quintilii. Every year, to commemorate this distant event, on 15 February the feast of *Lupercalia* was celebrated in Rome: *luperci Quinctiales* and *luperci Fabiani* competed by running naked around the Palatine.

Several legends about the earliest history of Rome tell of a sacrifice interrupted by a battle. Even closer are the analogies between Ovid's story and the myth of Cacus, the brigand. Cacus steals a herd of oxen; Hercules retrieves them, kills Cacus and institutes a cult at the *Ara Maxima*, entrusting the celebration of the sacrifice to the representatives of two noble families, the Potitii and Pinarii; Pinarius arrives late, when the offerings have already been eaten and, together with his descendants, he is expelled from the cult.[206] But none of this illuminates the truly disconcerting analogies between the myth of the Vogul-Ostyak and that recorded almost two thousand years previously, about the origin of the *Lupercalia*.[207] That the two stories about the meal (or sacrifice) interrupted by the arrival of the cattle thieves might be the result of an independent convergence seems most unlikely. We are left with two hypotheses: derivation from a common model; or a borrowing.[208] Both imply that this narrative schema has endured practically intact for a very long time – centuries and centuries, if not millennia. Analysis of the respective contexts should allow us to see how this has been possible. On the one hand, we have an area, basically coinciding with central Asia, in which (a) there are many cases of dual monarchy or dual power; (b) it is customary to classify kinship ties on the basis of two broad categories, respectively identified with the 'bone' (the paternal line) and the 'meat' (the maternal line); and (c) the matrimonial system frequently involves generalized exchange which, as preferred option, implies marriage between matrilateral cross-bred cousins (the son of the sister marries the daughter of the brother).[209] On the other hand, there is Latium, where (a) is present in the form of traces, whereas (b) and (c) are completely absent.[210] In the two myths exogamous classes and the meat/bone juxtaposition are separated: in the myth of the Vogul-Ostyak we find only the first, while in the myth reported by Ovid there is only the second. Naturally, it would be absurd to see in this lack of connection proof that in Latium too there must have existed, in a proto-historical age, a system based on exogamous classes. It is more reasonable to suppose that the two myths interpreted the dualistic elements which were present, to a very different degree, in the two societies. In the Old Testament the hostility between the twins Esau and Jacob anticipates and justifies that between their respective descendants, Idumaeian and Israelites. And in this case too Jacob's supremacy is accompanied by a renunciation of food: the lentil soup given to Esau in exchange for the primogeniture (*Gen.* 25. 29–34).

31.   A great number of dualistic societies have been found in Asia, the Americas and Australia (they are much rarer in Africa). Among the characteristics they share we find various elements that also appear in the founding myth of the Vogul-Ostyak: presence of exogamic halves, linked by not only matrimonial, but also economic or ceremonial exchanges; descendants often matrilineal; a prominent position accorded in the mythology to a pair of brothers or twins; in many instances the sharing of power between two chiefs, with different functions; classification of beings and things by juxtaposed pairs; games and contests in which the relationship between exogamic halves – simultaneously one of rivalry and solidarity – is expressed.[211] The dispersion of societies with such common characteristics has been interpreted in various ways: supporters of the historical thesis lean towards diffusion from a specific point; supporters of the structural thesis postulate the independent action of an innate human tendency. For these reasons the origin of dualistic societies has been considered a crucial case study in the discussion of the relationship between history and structure.[212] Once again we encounter the theme that runs through this entire inquiry. But the results we have already obtained point to a solution. Even if it were possible to demonstrate that dualist societies spread out from a particular point in Central Asia (this is a fictitious example), the reasons for their distribution and persistence would still remain unexplained. Here considerations of a structural order come into play, concerning the potential – and not the actual – existence of dualist societies. The dichotomous physiognomy of these societies (so it has been said) is the result of reciprocity, of a complementary relationship that involves an exchange of women, of economic services, of funerary and other sorts of ceremonies. In its turn, the exchange springs from the formulation of a series of oppositions. And the capacity to express biological relations in the form of systems of oppositions is the specific characteristic of what we call culture.[213]

As we can see, the elementary characteristics of dualist societies have prompted reflections of a very general nature. But it is still possible to go down part of the road in this direction.

32.   The most ancient phases of human history are traditionally distinguished on the basis of the materials used to make tools: stone (chipped or

polished), iron, and bronze. This is a conventional classification based on external elements. But it has been observed that the use of tools, although decisive, is not the *differentia specifica* of the human species. Albeit to a very limited degree, it is shared by other animal species. By contrast, only the human species is in the habit of collecting, producing, hoarding or destroying (as the case may be) objects which have a single function – that of signifying: offerings to the gods or to the dead; funerary wares buried in tombs; relics; works of art; or natural curiosities preserved in museums or collections. Unlike *things*, these objects, bearers of signification, or *semiophores* (as they have been called) enjoy the prerogative of establishing communication between the visible and invisible – that is, with events or persons distant in space or in time, if not with beings placed outside of both – the dead, ancestors, divinities. After all, the ability to transcend the sphere of immediate sense experience is the trait that distinguishes language and, more generally, human culture.[214] It is born from the elaboration of absence.

In the intellectual development of the human being this elaboration begins during earliest childhood, during the process of the construction of a world of objects, and continues via the activity of symbolic formation.[215] One might be tempted to restate the old thesis that ontogenesis recapitulates phylogenesis, that in his or her growth the individual retraces the stages traversed by the species. Observation of the present would thus permit us to grasp an otherwise unobtainable past. The gesture of the eighteen-month-old infant, who (perhaps) relives the reactions aroused by the mother's absence and return by flinging away a spool of thread, only joyfully to retrieve it immediately afterwards, has been recognized as a model of controlled, uncoerced symbolic repetition of the past. But is it permissible to search for the roots of mythical-ritualistic symbolism in infant psychology?[216]

So let us say that the child uses the spool as a semiophore; that the spool designates the mother, *is* the mother. One example will suffice to illustrate the potentialities and limitations of the analogy between individual and species. The custom of collecting the bones of slaughtered animals in order to resuscitate them is certainly very ancient, as we can see from the geographical distribution (Eurasia, Africa and the Americas) of mythical and ritualistic evidence. Let us try to suppose (a) an animal species that (b) draws a good part of its sustenance from the killing of (c) other species of animals, who are (d) vertebrate and (e) found in limited quantities. There are strong probabilities that this species will sooner or later end up using the bones of the animals as semiophores.[217] However, a further decisive condition must be added to those already mentioned: the species in question must already dispose of those symbolic capacities that we attribute exclusively to the species *homo sapiens*. Herewith the circle is closed. The origin is by definition precluded.[218]

Besides, it isn't even certain that a ritual of this kind was (as has been supposed) practised during the Paleolithic age.[219] But whoever the hunters were who first collected the bones of a dead animal so that it would be reborn, the meaning of their act seems clear: to establish communication between the visible and invisible, between the world of sense experience, governed by scarcity, and the world beyond the horizon, populated with animals. The perpetuation of the species beyond the death of the single individual (the single prey) proved the efficacy of the magical ritual based upon the gathering of the bones. Every animal that appeared on the horizon was a resurrected animal. Hence the profound identification of animals with the dead: two expressions of otherness. Initially, the beyond was literally elsewhere.[220] Death can be considered a particular instance of absence.

33.   These considerations (inevitably more mythopoeic than mythological) shed light on the distribution and persistence of dualistic societies. In the relationship between initiates and non-initiates, indeed in all situations in which society divides into two groups, has been recognized the expression of the supreme opposition – that between the dead and the living.[221] An assertion of such general scope may seem imprudent. But our research into ecstatic phenomena in the European sphere has led us to identical conclusions. Underlying the descriptions of battles fought in ecstasy or in dream by *benandanti*, *burkudzäutä*, werewolves, *táltos*, *kresniki* and *mazzeri*, we discerned a subterranean affinity between these protagonists and their adversaries. On the one hand, the living assimilated to the dead through ecstasy; on the other, depending on the particular case, the dead, sorcerers, other members of the same initiatory group. Among the possible ritualistic equivalents of these ecstatic battles we cited the *Lupercalia*: a feast that occurred at a time of year consecrated to the dead and which involved a competition between two homologous initiatory groups which had the explicit purpose of procuring fertility.[222] Homologous but not symmetrical, as the interrupted sacrifice that describes the origin of the *Lupercalia* in Ovid's *Fasti* reminds us. The less appetizing or inedible foods – raw meat or bones, respectively – fall to the hierarchically superior beings: among the Vogul-Ostyak, to the *Mos-chum*, the men like gods; in the Latium, to Romulus, the future king deified after his death as Quirinus.[223] We have already noted that Jacob, the future chosen one of God, renounces his lentil soup; and that the sacrifice of Prometheus allots meat and viscera to men, bones to the gods.

34.   We have defined animals and the dead as 'two expressions of otherness'. Here too the somewhat hasty formula sends us back to results already obtained. On the funerary connotation of divinities, semi-bestial like Richella or surrounded by beasts like Oriente – distant heirs of the very ancient 'mistress of the animals' – there is no need for us to insist. The followers of Diana, of Perchta and Holda traverse the skies astride unspecified beasts; during their catalepsies, the *benandanti* let the spirit issue from the inanimate body in the shape of a mouse or a butterfly; the *táltos* assume the appearance of stallions or bulls, the werewolves of wolves; male

and female witches join the Sabbath mounted on billy goats or transformed into cats, wolves and hares; those participating in the rites of the calends disguise themselves as stags or heifers; shamans dressed in feathers in preparation for their long ecstatic journey; the hero of magic tales, using mounts of all kinds, set off for mysterious and remote kingdoms – or, quite simply, as in a Siberian tale, leapt over a tree trunk and transformed himself into a bear, entering the realm of the dead.[224] Metamorphoses, cavalcades, ecstasies, followed by the egress of the soul in the shape of an animal – these are different paths to a single goal. Between animals and souls, animals and the dead, animals and the beyond, there exists a profound connection.[225]

35. In his poem *The Argonautica* (c. 250 BC) Apollonius of Rhodes describes the landing of Jason's companions on a beach of Colchis called Circea (III. 200–9). Here grow abundant tamarisks and willow trees. Corpses are tied to the treetops. Even today, Apollonius explains, when a male inhabitant of Colchis dies, they hang him from a tree outside the town, wrapped in an untanned ox's skin; the women, by contrast are buried. In the Caucasus (where ancient Colchis was located), and in particular among the Ossetians, these funerary practices were still widespread up until a few decades ago. Several eighteenth-century travellers recorded them, by now on the wane, among the Yakut of Central Asia.[226]

The custom of burying the dead by placing them on an elevated platform, or hanging them from trees, is found over an immense area that includes a large part of Central and Northern Asia, as well as part of Africa.[227] But to wrap or sew the dead (males) inside animal skins is a much more specific custom. The parallel with the Eurasian resurrection ritual, based on the collection of the bones wrapped in the skin of dead animals, is evident. It allows us to decipher an otherwise incomprehensible detail which features in a group of Caucasian legends. Among the Ossetians it is said that Soslan succeeds in conquering a city by having himself enclosed in the skin of an ox killed for the purpose and pretending that he is dead. This last detail is perhaps a dilution. In the Circassian variant of the same legend Soslan is brutally mocked as though he were truly dead: 'Hey, you magician with the crooked legs, the worms are swarming all over you!' Soslan, whose knees are vulnerable as a result of a failed attempt to guarantee his immortality when he was a child, is in fact a sorcerer, a sort of shaman, a man capable of venturing into the beyond and returning from it. Thus he can be resuscitated from the ox skin in which he is wrapped.[228]

But the analogy with the ritual based on the collection of the bones is insufficient. To decipher the meaning of this animal skin we must employ a more indirect and encircling strategy, similar to the one followed vis-à-vis the lame.

36. In the *Islendigabók* ('Book of the Icelanders'), written by Ari the Wise around 1130, it is said that the law-giver Thorgeir decided to convert to

Christianity together with his compatriots after having lain a day and a night, without uttering a word, covered by his mantle: an act that has been identified as a shamanistic ritual.[229] We rediscover it, in conjunction with many other such features, in the sagas composed in Iceland between twelfth and the fourteenth centuries.[230] In the *Hávardar Saga*, for example, a warrior who is part of a group of men expert in magical art is overcome, shortly before the battle, by a sudden drowsiness which forces him to lie down on the ground and cover his head with his cape. At the very same instant one of his enemies begins to stir in his sleep and sigh loudly. A duel takes place between the souls of the two warriors, plunged into catalepsy, which ends with the victory of the first.[231] The scene of the duel between shamans, generally transformed into animals, is undoubtedly Laplandic.[232] But in Lapland ecstasy is sought by incessantly beating the shamanic drum, rather than, as in Iceland, by recourse to inner concentration, protected by a cloth of skin.[233] In other Arctic regions the two techniques were combined. On 1 January 1565, the English merchant Richard Johnson, who during his explorations had reached the Samoyeds beyond the Arctic Circle, witnessed a magical ritual on the banks of the Pečora river. Some time later he described it in a report: the sorcerer (the shaman) beat a large drum similar to a sieve with a hammer, emitting savage cries with his face entirely covered by a cloth adorned with animal bones and teeth; all of a sudden he fainted and remained motionless, as if dead, for some time; then he came to, gave instructions for the sacrifice and began to sing.[234] Covering the face, falling into lethargy, performing inspired acts: this is the same sequence that we find in the Icelandic sagas. Why cover one's face?

In Iceland (as in the islands of northern Frisia) those born with a caul were considered to be people gifted with second sight.[235] They were the only ones who could see the battles which, according to the Icelandic sagas, were fought 'in spirit' by the *fylgia*, the external soul that abandoned the body in the shape of an invisible animal.[236] Tied in certain respects to the notion of *fylgia* is the parallel notion of *hamingja*, the vital force: a term possibly derived from the more ancient *hamgengja* (ability to metamorphose into an animal) and in any event related to *hamr*, envelope, in the twofold sense of the form of the soul – generally that of an animal (wolf, bull, bear, eagle) – and the envelope surrounding the foetus, namely, the placenta.[237] *Berserkir* – i.e., 'bear sheath' – was the name of the warriors who (the sagas tells us) were periodically overcome by fits of bestial fury.[238] This web of meanings is not so remote from the belief, common among the Samoyeds, according to which the person who is born clothed (i.e., enveloped in a membrane) becomes a shaman (i.e., capable of assuming a second skin, turning into an animal).[239]

We are moving in an immense, but from the cultural viewpoint a relatively homogeneous, ambit: the regions of the extreme north, from Iceland to Siberia. But as we recall, credence in the shamanistic virtues of those born with a caul is much more widespread. In Russia they become werewolves; in the Friuli, *benandanti*; in Dalmatia, *kresniki*. In the southern regions of

Sweden, a pregnant woman who, naked, tramples the amnion of a foal, avoids the pains of childbirth but delivers a werewolf or (if she has a daughter) a *mara*, that is, a creature capable of assuming a second shape, animal or human.[240] These figures, who through ecstasy temporarily enter the realm of the dead, seem to confirm the parallelism between the amniotic rag and the shroud suggested in 1578 by the French physician, Laurent Joubert.[241]

To cover the face of the dead seems – but is not – a natural act. The act of Socrates, Pompeius and Caesar, who veiled their heads before dying has (perhaps rather simplistically) been attributed to the need symbolically to separate the sacred and the profane.[242] Veiled, because assimilated to the dead, were those who, according to the ancient Italic custom called *Ver sacrum* (sacred spring), were sent to found a colony, fulfilling a vow made at their birth twenty years previously.[243] In ancient Icelandic law anyone who did not perform the duty of covering a dead person's face with a cloth was banished.[244] In Greek as well as Germanic mythology, we hear of skin or fur hats, helmets or mantles, that assure those who wear them – Hades, Perseus, Odin-Wotan – the invisibility typical of spirits.[245] We see the emergence of two series of symbolic equivalences: (a) amniotic rag or caul/animal skin/ mantle or cap or veil that hides the face; (b) *benandanti* or *kresniki*/ werewolves/shamans/the dead. 'You must come with me because you have something of mine', had ordered 'a certain invisible thing . . . that resembled a man', which appeared 'in a dream' to the *benandante* Battista Moduco. The 'something of mine' was the caul in which Battista had been born, and which he wore around his neck.[246] The amnion is an object that belongs to the world of the dead – or that of the non-born.[247] An ambiguous, borderline object that marks borderline figures.

Not only animal coverings, then, but more generally, in disparate cultures, whatever encloses or enfolds is in some way connected to death. This has been demonstrated at a linguistic level, setting out from the name of Calypso, the goddess loved by Ulysses: 'she who covers', 'she who veils'.[248] We can relate her to the mysterious woman who, according to Saxus Grammaticus, the Danish King Hadingus sees crouching near the hearth, with a bundle of fresh hemlocks: when Hadingus, astonished – it is winter – asks her where she found them, the woman wraps him up in her cape (*proprio obvolutum amiculo*), carrying him alive underground into the world of the dead.[249] (It goes without saying that Hadingus is lame and, what's more, has a ring sewn into one of his legs.)[250] Outside the Indo-European milieu we also find the same connection, attested to by the relation between the Hungarian *rejt* (to hide) and the ancient Hungarian *rüt, röt, röjt* (to faint, to fall into ecstasy): the *regös* were groups of youths (numbering anything from two or three to twenty or thirty) who, during the twelve days between Christmas and Epiphany, roamed through the villages making a din, bringing news from the beyond and communicating the wishes of the dead.[251] Further confirmation is offered by the well-nigh universal association between masks and the spirits of the dead. The Latin *larva* designates both; in the Middle Ages *larvatus* is the person who wears a mask or is possessed by demons. *Masca*, a term used in the edict of Rotari (643 AD) and which later passed into the dialects of northern Italy, means witch.[252]

37. In the myths and rituals that refer to death the idea of coming back to life, of being reborn, recurs insistently. Terms such as to envelop or conceal express annihilation via uterine metaphors. At the end of the series that we have seen gradually emerging – to be wrapped in the amnion, enveloped in a mantle, sewn into an ox skin, masked, veiled, and so on – we again find, as in the case of lameness, a primary experience of a corporeal character.

It is probable that this characteristic, potentially trans-cultural because elementarily human, is not irrelevant to the extraordinary communicability of this family of myths and rituals. A conclusion of this kind nevertheless immediately raises a difficulty. It is conceivable that in the sphere of the individual unconscious very early, or even prenatal, experiences occupy a privileged position by a kind of biological imprinting.[253] If we extend this hypothesis to myths and rituals, we apparently come to a fork in the road: we must either deny myths and rituals the character of social phenomena, or postulate the existence of a collective unconscious.[254] But the results obtained up to this point allow us to avoid the dual trap. As we have seen, the mythical and ritualistic isomorphisms from which we started refer us back to a series of exchanges, contacts and filiations between different cultures. These historical relations constitute a necessary condition for the occurrence of isomorphic phenomena, but they are insufficient for their diffusion and preservation. Diffusion and preservation also depend on elements of a formal character which ensure the solidarity of the myths and rituals. The constant re-elaborations to which they are subjected clearly illustrate this inter-mingling of history and morphology. The inventiveness of the social actors whom we discern behind sequences of variants such as lame – one-sandalled – hoppers on one foot, etc., encounters very precise limits within the inner form of the myth or ritual. Its transmission, like that of the deep structures of language, is unwitting – although this does not imply the presence of a collective unconscious. The myth or ritual transmitted through historical channels implicitly contains the formal rules of its own re-elaboration.[255] Among the unconscious categories regulating symbolic activities, metaphor occupies a prominent position. The relations between dying and being enveloped are of a metaphorical character, as are those between the single variants of the two series: lame – one-sandalled – hoppers. . . ; amnion – skin – mantle – mask. . . . Now, among rhetorical figures, metaphor occupies a special position, which explains the intolerance of it manifested by all rationalistic poetics. By assimilating phenomena that pertain to different spheres of experience and different codes, metaphor (which is by definition reversible) subverts the orderly and hierarchical world of reason. We can consider it the equivalent, on the rhetorical plane, of the 'symmetrizing' principle which constitutes an irruption of the unconscious system's logic into the sphere of normal logic. From the prevalence of metaphor is born the intimate kinship between dream and myth, poetry and myth.[256]

The documentation we have accumulated proves beyond all reasonable doubt the existence of an underlying Eurasian mythological unity, the fruit of cultural relations sedimented over millennia. We are inevitably led to ask ourselves whether, and to what extent, the inner forms that we have identified are capable of generating isomorphic rituals and myths within cultures that are not historically connected. Unfortunately, this last condition (the absence of any form of historical connection whatsoever between two cultures) is, by definition, undemonstrable.[257] We know and always will know too little about human history. In the absence of proof to the contrary, we can only postulate, behind the phenomena of cultural convergence that we have investigated, an intermingling of morphology and history – a reformulation, or a variant, of the ancient contrast between what exists in nature and what exists by convention.

Notes

1. Cf. Claude Lévi-Strauss, *Du miel aux cendres* (*Mythologiques*, II), Paris 1966, pp. 395 ff.
2. Cf. H. Baldus, 'Lendas dos Indios Tereno', in *Revista do Museu Paulista*, n.s., IV (1950), pp. 217 ff., in particular pp. 220–21 (Ger. trans. in idem, *Die Jaguarzwillinge*, Kassel 1985, pp. 132-35); Lévi-Strauss, *Il crudo et il cotto* cit., pp. 139–40.
3. Idem, Claude Lévi-Strauss, *Du miel* cit., p. 400, which repeats almost word for word a passage written twenty years before (see above, p. 225, note 54).
4. Cf. Michel de Montaigne, *Essais*, A. Thibaudet, ed, Paris 1950, pp. 1150 ff. (*Des boyteux*, III, II)
5. Cf. Claude Lévi-Strauss, 'La structure des mythes', in *Anthropologie Structurale*, cit. pp. 227–55, in particular p. 236 (where it is suggested that the same element recurs in the name of Laius, 'left-handed': but see further on). For Lévi-Strauss' other discussions on the same theme which also relate to myths of the 'Perceval' type, see 'The Scope of Anthropology' (1960), in *Structural Anthropology 2*, Harmondsworth 1978, pp. 3–32; 'Le Graal en Amérique' (1973– 74), in *Paroles données*, Paris 1984, pp. 129 ff.; most recently, in an almost paradoxical key, *La vasaia gelosa*, It. trans., Turin 1987, pp. 180 ff. The first of the cited essays ('La structure des mythes') has had a lasting echo: but the interpretation of the myth of Oedipus as an attempt to resolve the contradiction between autochthony and sexual generation has been unanimously rejected. M. Delcourt had already insisted, from a different standpoint, on the deambulatory difficulties of the Labdacidies: M. Delcourt, *Oedipe ou la légende du conquérant*, Liège 1944, pp. 16 ff. (recalled by Lévi-Strauss); and see C. Robert, *Oidipus*, I, Berlin 1915, p. 59. Finally, see Jean-Pierre Vernant, 'From Oedipus to Peryander: Lameness, Tyranny, Incest in Legend and History, *Arethusa*, 15, 1982, pp. 19–38; M. Bettini, 'Edipo lo zoppo', in *Edipo. Il teatro greco e la cultura europea*, Rome 1986, pp. 215 ff.
6. On this etymology there is broad agreement: cf. O. Höfer, 'Oidipus', in W.H. Roscher ed, *Ausführliches Lexikon der griechischen und römischen Mythologie*, III, I,

Hildesheim 1965 (reprint of 1897–1902 edition), 700–46, in particular 740–43. The same goes for Labdacs='lame'. Laius ('left handed') which is suggested rather doubtfully by Lévi-Strauss is, however, unacceptable: Höfer (art. cit., col. 742) compares 'Laius' ('public') to one of Hades' nicknames, 'Agesilaus' ('he who gathers together many people').

7. Ibid., coll. 741–42.
8. Cf. instead, in this sense, L. Edmunds, 'The Cults and Legends of Oedipus', in *Harvard Studies in Classical Philology*', 85 (1981) pp. 221–38, in particular p. 233.
9. Cf. D. Comparetti, *Edipo e la mitologia comparata*, Pisa 1867, pp. 81–82, who points out that Oedipus and Melampus are both intelligent heroes. Delcourt, op. cit., pp. 166–67, considers the analogy between the two names 'bien obscure'. Edmunds, art. cit., pp. 230–31, regards the two etymologies as unlikely, but does not pursue the question further. On Melampus: cf. Wilamowitz-Moellendorff, 'Isyllos von Epidauros' *Philologische Untersuchungen*, 9(1886), pp. 177 ff., note 33; K. Hanell, *Megarische Studien*, Lund 1934, pp. 101–5; Nilsson, *Geschichte der griechischen Religion*, I, München 1967, p. 613, note 2; J. Schwartz, *Pseudo- Hesiodeia*, Leyden 1960, pp. 369–77 and 546; J. Löffler, *Die Melampodie*, Meisenheim am Glau 1963, pp. 30 ff.; P. Walcot, 'Cattle Raiding, Heroic Tradition and Ritual; the Greek Evidence', *History of Religions*, 18 (1979), pp. 326–51, in particular pp. 342–43.
10. Cf. P. Kretschmer, *Die griechischen Vaseninschriften. . .*, Gütersloh 1894, p. 191, note 3; Idem, 'Oidipus und Melampus', in *Glotta*, XII (1923), pp. 59–61, followed by Höfer, art. cit., coll. 741 ff.; opposed by L. R. Farnell, *Greek Hero Cults and Ideas of Immortality*, Oxford 1921, p. 332 (note). The chthonic interpretation of Oedipus had been suggested by C. Robert.
11. F. Wehrli, 'Oidipus', in *Museum Helveticum*, 14 (1957), p. 112, suggests a comparison between Oedipus, the solver of riddles, and the contest between the two diviners Calchas and Mopsus, described in the lost poem *Melampodia*. It should be noted that both names (*Melam-pous*, *Oidi-pous*) allude to a single foot. An analogous asymmetry seems implied by epithets such as *argyropeza* (from 'foot of silver') attached to Thetis (see further on, note 41). On the comparison of Oedipus with Melampus see Bettini, art. cit., p. 231 (Bettini begins with a problem similar to the one presented in these pages but arrives at different conclusions).
12. The first to notice this was Comparetti, op. cit., pp. 63 ff. It was not recorded by Nilsson, 'Der Oidipusmythos' in *Opuscula selecta*, Lund 1951, I, pp. 335–48 (as is observed by Edmunds, 'The Sphinx in the Oedipus Legend', in *Oedipus: a Folklore Casebook*, L. Edmunds and A. Dundes, editors, New York and London 1981, p. 149). In his introduction to Tesauro's *Edipo* (Padua 1987, pp. 13–14), C. Ossola speaks of Comparetti as the anticipator of Propp.
13. Sometimes Oedipus is portrayed killing the Sphinx (see Höfer, art. cit., coll. 715 ff.). In an essay which is contradictory, yet rich in insight, L. Edmunds (art. cit.) maintains that the Sphinx is a later addition – suggesting on the contrary, that it is a fusion of the monster which is defeated by the hero, and the queen who is promised as a bride (and who, in fables of the 'Turandot' type, poses riddles to her suitors).
14. Cf. Vladimir Propp, *Edipo alla luce del folclore* (1944), in the homonymous Italian volume (Turin 1975), pp. 85 ff. (but see, in the same sense, Comparetti, op. cit., and Nilsson, art. cit.). Here I am overlooking the weakest part of Propp's essay, namely, the attempt, strongly influenced by Frazer, to link the theme of parricide to presumed ancient customs that supposedly regulated the succession to the throne.
15. These distinctions are ignored by the rigorously synchronic perspective adopted by

Lévi-Strauss, who considers all versions of a myth on the same plane, rejecting *a priori* any attempt to distinguish one particular version as 'authentic or primitive' (*Anthropologie Structurale*, p. 240).

16. Jean-Pierre Vernant strenuously insists on the first point: 'Ambiguità e rovesciamento. Sulla struttura enigmatica dell "Edipo re."' in Vernant and P. Vidal-Naquet, *Mito e tragedia nell' antica Grecia*, It. trans., Turin 1976, pp. 100–1; cf. also Edmunds, art. cit., pp. 18–19. Riddles similar to those of the Sphinx are extremely widespread: see A. Aarne, *Vergleichende Rätselforschungen*, II, Helsinki 1919 (FF Communications No. 27), pp. 1 ff.

17. Cf. Vernant, art. cit., p. 101. See also P.G. Maxwell-Stuart, 'Interpretations of the Name Oedipus', in *Maia*, 27 (1975), pp. 37–43.

18. Cf. Propp, op. cit., pp. 103–4, which rejects Robert's thesis that Oedipus' pierced feet had been invented to explain his recognition.

19. Cf. Brelich, *Paides e Parthenoi*, I, Rome, 1969, on which see Calame, *Philologie et anthropologie structurale* in *Quaderni Urbinati*, II (1971), and the very critical review by Sourvinou-Inwood in *The Journal of Hellenic Studies*, XCI (1971), pp. 172-78. In general L. Gernet, *Anthropologie de la Grèce antique*, Paris 1968, pp. 188–90 and *passim*.

20. I make use of Vladimir Propp, *Le radici storiche delle fiabe di magia* to round out the conclusions (which are, strangely, left unfinished) of the essay on Oedipus which appeared two years previously. In his research, Propp focused on a group of Russian fables drawn from Afanasjev's collection: but both the interpretive context and the conclusions had much broader, indeed universal, dimensions.

21. According to A. L. Brown, 'Eumenides in Greek Tragedy', in *The Classical Quarterly*, 34 (1984), pp. 260 ff., the Eumenides of *Oedipus at Colonus* should not be identified with the Erinyes, nor be associated with the nether world.

22. Cf. Edmunds, art. cit., pp. 229 ff.

23. Cf. Delcourt, op. cit., pp. 108–9 and 119 ff. , which refers back to L. Malten, 'Das Pferd im Totenglauben,' in *Jahrbuch des deutschen archäologischen Insituts*, XX1X (1914), pp. 179–255.

24. This is also emphasized by Edmunds, art. cit., p. 22, but, as we shall see, he proposes a substantially different solution.

25. In relation to the following see the splendid essay by S. Luria, ' "Ton sou huion phrixōn" ' (Die Oidipussage und Verwandtes)', in *Raccolta di scritti in onore di Felice Ramorino*, Milan 1927, pp. 289–314 (but the crucial importance of the 'fatal infant' theme had already been grasped by Comparetti, op. cit.). On Luria, see. A. Momigliano, *Terzo contributo alla storia degli studi classici e del mondo antico*, II, Rome 1966, pp. 797 ff. Although often cited, Luria's essay has had only a very limited influence (cf. Edmunds, art. cit., pp. 22–23). It is argued from a rigorously morphological perspective, which is similar – for example in its brand of formalized notation – to the one adopted by Vladimir Propp in *Morfologia della fiaba* which was published a year later after a long gestation (see the introduction, dated July 15, 1927). Furthermore Luria, inspired like Propp by Goethe, tried to reconstruct at least the substance of the original written version of the myth (*Urform*, *Urredaktion*), attributing it to the earliest period (*Urzeit*) of the history of humanity. But recourse to ethnology, to the history of religion and to psychoanalysis is rejected from the start: the only path immune to the vicious circle is, according to Luria, that offered by internal historico-mythical categories. In this declaration we hear the echo of formalism (the 'purely literary') and perhaps also the presence of Husserl, mediated by his pupil Gustav Špet, in the Russian culture of that time: cf. P.

Steiner, *Russian Formalism*, Ithaca, New York 1984, p. 18, and E. Holenstein, 'Jakobson and Husserl: A Contribution to the Genealogy of Structuralism', in *The Human Context*, 7 (1975), pp. 62–63. It should be noted that Vernant has also spoken, independently, of a 'vicious circle' in regard to the Freudian interpretation of Oedipus the king: 'Edipo senza complesso', in Vernant and Vidal-Naquet, op. cit., pp. 65–66. In the essay on Oedipus (1944) (which appeared in a totally different political and cultural climate) Propp started from Luria's research, which he cited in a curiously incomplete fashion (cf. op. cit., p. 91): 'Luria has already noted that in folklore the prophecies are always realized', a sentence that refers implicitly to 'Ton sou huion' cit., p. 290. Another essay by Luria, 'La casa nel bosco', mentioned in (Propp) op. cit., note 42, is discussed in *Le radici storiche* cit., pp. 87–88.

26. Cf. Luria, art. cit., p. 292. The spread of Oedipal themes to Oceania has been maintained by W.A. Lessa, *Tales from Ulithi Atoll: A Comparative Study in Oceanic Folk-lore*, Berkeley and Los Angeles 1961, pp. 49–51 and 172–214 (and see Edmunds and Dundes eds, *Oedipus: a Folklore Casebook*, op. cit., pp. 56 ff.) : but see the objections of R.E. Mitchell, 'The Oedipus Myth and Complex in Oceania with Special Reference to Truk', in *Asian Folklore Studies*, 27 (1968), pp. 131–45. It should be noted that in the myth analyzed by Lessa the theme of the realized prophecy is missing.

27. This is completion of the myth reported in incomplete form (due to a gap in the manuscript tradition) by Hyginus (*Fabulae*, rec. H.J. Rose, Luguni Batavorum 1963, n. LX, p. 47; see also Roscher, op. cit., IV, col. 962).

28. Isolated analogies between this or that myth included in the series and the Oedipus myth had already been suggested before Luria (cf. Comparetti, op. cit., p. 75: Oedipus and Telephus), or independently of him, following the indications of C. Robert: cf. Delcourt, op. cit., p. 85 (Oedipus and Zeus); F. Dirlmeier, *Il mito di Edipo*, It. trans. Genoa 1987, pp. 15 ff. (Oedipus and Zeus, Oedipus and Kronos, Oedipus and Telegonus). Also the myth of Catreus, king of Crete, killed as the prophecy foresaw, by his own son Althaemenes, (Apollodorus, *La biblioteca*, III, 2, 1; Diodorus Siculus *Biblioteca storica*, V, 59, 1–4) has been compared with that of Oedipus (cf. C. Robert, *Die griech ische Heldensage*, I, Berlin 1920, pp. 371–72) and to that of Theseus (cf. C. Sourvinou-Inwood, *Theseus as Son and Stepson*, London 1979, pp. 14 ff.). On the myth of Meleager, see further on.

29. A Rumanian version of the myth of Oedipus concludes with a failed attempt at incest, as in the case of Telephus and his mother (cf. Vernant, 'Le Tyran boiteux: d'Oedipe à Périandre,' art. cit., pp. 79–86). Bettini speaks of Telephus as a 'weakened' Oedipus in art. cit., p. 219.

30. Cf. A. Green, 'Thésée et Oedipe. Une interprétation psychoanalytique de la Théseide', *Il mito greco* cit., pp. 137–89 (but the conclusions are gratuitous).

31. Cf. J. Schmidt, in Roscher, op. cit., V, col. 275.

32. Cf. O. Gruppe, *Griechische Mythologie und Religionsgeschichte*, Munich 1906, pp. 1332–3 and note 4. The negative cases are those of Kronos; of Telegonus, Aegisthus and the unnamed sons of Tyro and Sisyphus. But it should be noted that the Latin god Saturn, identified with Kronos, is often portrayed with a wooden leg: E. Panofsky, F. Saxl and R. Klibansky (*Saturn and Melancholy*, London 1964, pp. 206–7) suppose, without presenting evidence, that this is a detail derived from unspecified Eastern sources, in which an unconscious memory of the castration of Kronos would have surfaced. But perhaps it is not irrelevant that Kronos is described by Lucian (*Saturnalia*, 7) as an old gouty (*podagros*) man. Nothing is known about the sons of Tyro and Sisyphus. And very little about Telegonus. For

Pelops, see further on, p. 250. A hypertrophy of the extremities, and therefore in the last analysis a deambulatory anomaly, seems to be alluded to in the kick with which Althaemenes, the involuntary murderer of his own father, kills his sister Apemosyne, who has been raped by Hermes (Apollodorus, *La biblioteca*, II, 2,1; and see above, note 28).

33. Cf. Apollodorus, *La biblioteca*, I, 6, 3; but see Hesiod, *Theogony*, vv. 820 ff. (perhaps an old interpolation). These are re-elaborations of Hittite myths (in which, however, the god is deprived of heart and eyes) and Hurrite myths: cf. W. Porzig, 'Illujankas und Typhon', in *Kleinasiatischen Forschungen*, I (1930), pp. 379–86; P. Meriggi, 'I miti di Kumarpi, il Kronos currico', in *Athenaeum*, 31 (1953), pp. 101–57; F.Vian, 'Le mythe de Thypée et le problème de ses origines orientales', in *Éléments orientaux dans la religion grecque ancienne*, F.Vian ed., Paris 1960, pp. 17–37; and see also the remarks of C. Brillante in *Edipo. Il teatro greco*, pp. 231–32. The series in which the mutilation of Zeus is inserted, responds, if I am not mistaken, to the questions posed by M. Delcourt, *Héphaistos ou la légende du magicien*, Paris 1957, pp. 122 ff. and 136.

34. For this last observation cf. A. Brelich, *Gli eroi greci*, Rome 1958, pp. 243–48 and 287–290. Instead, with superficial anachronism Oedipus' lameness has been interpreted as the 'mark of a sacrificial victim' (Girard, *Il capro espiatorio*, cit., pp. 47, 54 etc.). The fact that in the Indo-European cultural ambit, as emphasized by J. Bremmer ('Medon, the Case of the Bodily Blemished King', in *Perennitas. Studi in onore di Angelo Brelich*, Rome 1980, pp. 67–76) the king must be immune to physical imperfections, questions again the significance of myths hinging on the contrary situation. The attribution of the *Tragodopodagara* to Lucian has been rejected by P. Maass, in *Deutsche Literaturzeitung*, 1909, coll. 2272–76; today the opposite thesis prevails. This was first formulated by G. Setti, 'La Tragodopodagra di Luciano', in *Rivista di filologia*, XXXVIII (1910), p. 161–200. It should be noted that, as in other myths of the group, we expect to see a Telegonus who is lame: on the contrary, in the list of the *Tragodopodagra* we find Odysseus (vv. 262 ff.) pierced through the foot by the sting of a skate. According to A. Roemer, 'Zur Kritik und Exegese von Homer etc.', in *Abhandlungen der philosophisch-philologischen Klasse der königlichen bayerischen Akademie der Wissenschaften*, 22 (1905), p. 639, note 1, in another myth Odysseus dies after being struck in the foot by Telegonus' arrow: but see A. Hartmann, *Untersuchungen über die Sagen vom Tod des Odysseus*, Munich 1917, pp. 161–62. For reasons which will be recounted, it is not surprising that Ulysses, who goes to the very threshold of Hades to call up the dead, should have a wound on his leg (cf. *Odyssey*, XIX, 386 ff.).

35. This interpretation does not contradict the pre-juridical element identified in Theseus' sandals by E. Cassin, *Le semblable et le différent*, Paris 1987, pp. 298 ff. (which refers to Gernet). On the initiatic implications of the Theseus cycle cf. Jeanmaire, *Couroi et Couretes* cit., pp. 227 ff., which also makes use of P. Saintyves (E. Nourry), *Les contes de Perrault et les récits parallèles* (taken up again by Propp, *Le radici storiche* cit., p. 86 and *passim*). 'Why does the initiate limp? Why are novitiates bound in iron shackles?' asks Riemschneider: but the simplistic identification of the foot with 'a veiled expression of fecundity' has led her to absurd conclusions (cf. *Miti pagani e miti cristiani*, It. tras. Milan 1973, pp. 99 ff.).

36. On Telephus and Pelops see further on. On the Sphinx as a mortuary animal cf. Delcourt, *Oedipe* cit., pp. 109 ff.

37. Cf. Gruppe, op. cit., p. 585.

38. Cf. ibid., pp. 1332–3, particularly note 4, and in general the studies on mono-sandalism cited further on, note 48.

39. Cf. J. H. Croon, 'The Mask of the Underworld-Daemon. Some Remarks on the Perseus-Gorgon Story', in *Journal of Hellenic Studies*, 75 (1955), pp. 9 ff., which develops an indication of F. Altheim, 'Persona', in *Archiv für Religionswissenschaft*, XXVII (1929), pp. 35 ff. On the mono-sandalled Mercury see. K. Schauenburg, *Perseus in der Kunst der Altertums*, Bonn 1960, p. 13; S. Reinach, *Catalogue illustré du Musée des Antiquités Nationales au Château de Saint-Germain-en-Laye*, II, Paris 1921, p. 168 (Gallo-Roman statuette found at St. Séverin, Nièvre).

40. Cf. B. K. Braswell, 'Mythological Innovation in the *Iliad*', in *The Classical Quarterly*, n.s. XXI (1971), p. 23. According to another prophecy (Hesiod, *Theogony*, 894–98) the son of Metis and Zeus had deposed the father; for this reason Zeus swallowed Metis.

41. The myth is recounted in a gloss to Lycophron's *Alexandra* (v. 175): cf. U. Pestalozza, *Religione mediterranea*, Milan 1970 (reprint), p. 96, note 30. The analogy with Achilles' heel (and with other myths, to which we shall return) is underlined by V. Pisani, '*Ellēnokeltika*' in *Revue des études anciennes*, XXXII (1935), pp. 145–48, who judges them 'not completely clear'.

42. Cf. Dumézil, *Le problème des Centaures*, Paris 1929, p. 185, note 3; and see also Cassin, op. cit., pp. 301–2, note 57.

43. Cf. B. Bravo, 'Une lettre sur plomb de Berezan. Colonisation et modes de contact dans le Pont', in *Dialogues d'histoire ancienne*, I (1974), pp. 111–87, in particular pp. 136–37 (on the verse of Alcaeus). In general see H. Hommel, 'Der Gott Achilleus', *Sitzungsberichte der Heidelberger Akademie der Wissenschaften*, 1980, I; additions in idem, *Sebasmata*, I, Tübingen 1983,p. 209; G. Ferrari Pinney, 'Achilles Lord of Scythia', in *Ancient Greek Art and Iconography*, Madison 1983, pp. 127–46. The mortuary characteristics of Achilles had already been brilliantly grasped, on purely etymological grounds, by P. Kretschmer, *Mythische Namen. I: Achill*, in *Glotta*, IV (1913), pp. 305–8.

44. Cf. Jeanmaire, *Couroi et courètes* cit., pp. 297. ff.; idem, *Dioniso*, It. trans. Turin 1972, pp. 385–86; *The Homeric Hymn to Demeter*, N. J. Richardson, ed, Oxford 1974, pp. 231 ff. It should be remembered that Apollonius of Rhodes (*Argonautica*, IV, 868 ff.) recounts the same myth, putting Achilles in the place of Demophoön, Thetis in the place of Demeter, Peleus in the place of Demophoön's mother.

45. Cf. W. R. Halliday, 'Note on the Homeric Hymn to Demeter, 239 ff', in *The Classical Review*, 25 (1911), pp. 8–11; Dumézil, cit., pp, 185–86; C.-M. Edsman, *Ignis divinus*, Lund 1949, pp. 224–29.

46. The hypothesis formulated by Lawson (see above, p. 169) is accepted among others by Dumézil, op. cit., p. 53 and by Gernet, op. cit., p. 170. It should be remembered here that the term *kentauros* is perhaps of Scythian origin, and that perhaps the myth of the centaurs re-elaborated the image of nomads on horseback coming from the steppes of central Asia: cf. J. Knobloch, 'Der Name der Kentauren', in *Serta Indogermanica. Festschrift für Günter Neumann zum 60. Geburtstag*, J. Tischler, ed., Innsbruck 1982, pp. 129–31.

47. Cf. L. Mercklin, *Aphrodite Nemesis mit der Sandale*, Dorpat 1854, eluded H. Usener, 'Kallone', in *Rheinisches Museum*, XXIII (1868), pp. 362–63. On the erotic-funerary polarity implicit in the symbol of a single sandal, see the superficial annotations of S. Eitrem, *Hermes und die Toten*, Christiania 1909, pp. 44–45; on the Persephone-Aphrodite connection see Zuntz, *Persephone*, Oxford 1971, pp. 174–75. But on this whole question see the fine essay by W. Fauth, 'Aphrodites Pantoffel und die Sandale der Hekate', in *Graz Beiträge*, 12–13 (1985–86), pp. 193–211.

48. For all this cf. W. Amelung, 'Di alcune sculture antiche e di un rito del culto delle

divinità sotterranee', in *Dissertazioni della Pontificia Accademia Romana di Archeologia*, II, IX (1907), pp. 115–35, which remains fundamental: cf. W. Helbig, *Führer durch die öffentlichen Sammlungen klassischer Altertümer in Rom*, II, Tübingen 1966, pp. 318–19. The essay by Amelung should be paired with that of Gruppe, op. cit., pp, 1332–33, above all note 4 (which appeared the year before). One should, however, correct the identification, proposed by Amelung, of the so-called 'Barberini suppliant' with Dido: it should be Callisto instead, as demonstrated by J.N. Svoronos ('Explication de la *suppliante* Barberini', in *Journal international d'archéologie et numismatique*, XVI, 1914, pp. 255–78). The chthonic interpretation proposed by Amelung (who, however, had not succeeded in explaining the detail of a single sandal) is supported by W. Deonna, 'Essai sur la genèse des monstres dans l'art', in *Revue des études grecques*, 28 (1915), pp. 288 ff.; idem, 'Monokrēpides', in *Revue de l'histoire de religions*, 112 (1935), pp.50–72 (amplified version of the preceding essay) in polemic with the superficial note of J. Brunel, 'Jason monokrēpis' in *Revue archéologique*, II (1934), pp. 34 ff. see also O. Weinrich, in *Archiv für Religionswissenschaft*, XXIII (1925), p. 70; W. Kroll, '*Unum exuta pedem –* ein volkskundliches Seitensprung', in *Glotta*, XXV (1937), pp. 152-58, at first favourable to Amelung's interpretation, then later opposed to it. Further information in the comment of A. S. Pease on the fourth book of the *Aeneid*, Cambridge, Mass, 1935, pp. 432-33. Important observations in A. Brelich, 'Les monosandales', *La nouvelle Clio*, VII-IX (1955–57), pp. 469–84; see also P.Vidal-Naquet and P. Lévêque, 'Epaminondas pythagoricien ou le problème tactique de la droite et de la gauche', in *Le Chasseur noir. Formes de pensée et formes de société dans le monde grec*, Paris 1981, pp. 95 ff., in particular pp. 101–2 and 115 ff. A reconsideration of the question, with further bibliographic indications, in L. Edmunds, 'Thucydides on monosandalism (3. 22. 2)', in *Studies Presented to Sterling Dow on his Eightieth Birthday*, Durban (N.C.) 1984, pp. 71–75 (but the essay is, on the interpretative plane, inconclusive). On monosandalism in the Near East see Cassin, op. cit., pp. 67 ff. and 294 ff.

49. Cf. *Servii Grammatici qui feruntur in Vergilii carmina commentarii recensuerunt G. Thilo et H. Hagen*, II, rec. G. Thilo, Leipzig 1884, p. 183, taken up by Frazer (*The Golden Bough, III, Taboo and the Perils of the Soul*, London 1911, pp. 311 ff.) who in any case missed Amelung's essay.

50. Cf. L. Curtius, *Die Wandmalerei Pompeijs*, Darmstadt 1960 (reprint of the 1929 edition), p. 356, mentioned by Brelich (art. cit). Quite opportunely Edmunds (art. cit., p. 72, note 14) remembers that the protagonist of *War and Peace*, Pierre Bezukhov, also had to take off a shoe during the initiation ceremony to the Masonic lodge.

51. Cf. *Euripidis Tragoediae*, A. Nauck ed, III, Leipzig 1912, n. 534. On the murder of the sons of Thetis, see Ovid, *Met.* VIII, 434 ff.

52. Cf. *Aristotelis qui ferebantur librorum fragmenta*, collected by V. Rose, Leipzig 1886, n. 74.

53. This is not a secondary detail: the myth of Meleager hinges in fact on the contrast between horizontal ties (mother-brothers) and vertical ties (mother-children), expressed by the Kouretes' and Aetolians' rivalry. Brunel, art. cit., remembers a gloss to Pindar (*Pyth.* IV, 75) in which, in regard to Jason, it cites the Aetolians who 'all have a single sandal due to their bellicose nature'. Cf. also R. Goossens, 'Les Étoliens chaussés d'un seul pied', in *Revue belge de philologie et d'histoire*, 14 (1935), pp. 849-54, which remembers Thucydides' passage about the Plataeans, which eluded Brunel. If I have seen correctly monosandalism does not appear in the Roman sarcophaguses that portray the myth of Meleager (besides by G. Koch,

Die mythologischen Sarkophage, VI: *Meleager*, Berlin 1975, cf. G. Daltrop, *Die kalydonische Jagd in der Antike*, Hamburg-Berlin 1968).

54. Cf. Vidal-Naquet and Lévêque, art. cit., pp. 116–17 which recalls, in reference to Jason, 'Le chasseur noir et l'origine de l'éphébie athénienne', in op. cit., pp. 154–55. According to Edmunds, art. cit., the monosandalism of the Plataeans and that of the Hernici constitute a case apart.

55. Cf. Pindar, *Pythica*, IV, 97.

56. This approach to the question (not confined to the Greek ambit) had already been suggested by Brelich, art. cit., together with a sketch, not equally convincing, of the solution (the characters with a single sandal would represent the cosmos as opposed to chaos). For a less rigorous perspective see Deonna, op. cit., in particular p. 69. Brelich's invitation to a comparison of larger scope is proposed again by Vidal-Naquet and Lévêque, in op. cit., p. 102, note 31. Celtic parallels, tied more or less directly to the passage in otherworldly dimension, are cited by P. MacCana, 'The Topos of the Single Sandal in Irish Tradition', in *Celtica*, 10 (1973), pp. 160–66 (with further bibliography). I thank Enrica Melossi for pointing this essay out to me.

57. On the relations among Philoctetes, Telephus (on whom see above) and Jason, cf. Gruppe, op. cit., p. 635; L. Radermacher, 'Zur Philoktetsage', in *Mélanges H. Gregoire*, I, Paris 1949, pp. 503–9; C. Kerényi, *Gli dei e gli eroi della Grecia*, It. trans. II, Milan 1963, p. 320. Analyzing texts and documents of the Near East, Cassin has demonstrated the close connection between lameness and monosandalism (cf. op. cit., pp. 16 ff., 50 ff. and 294 ff.), emphasizing the ties with a more general notion of asymmetry (see above all p. 84). For an analogous conclusion see also, p. 223. Other symbolic implications of the footprint and the foot are indicated by W. Speyer, 'Die Segenskraft des 'göttlichen' Fusses', in *Romanitas et Christianitas. Studia Iano Henrico Waszink . . . oblata*, Amsterdam and London 1973, pp. 293–309.

58. Here I follow the fine essay by P. Vidal-Naquet, 'Il Filottete di Sofocle e l'efebia' (in Vernant and Vidal-Naquet, op. cit., pp. 145–69), combining it in part with other studies of the same author which are cited above, note 48. M. Massenzio, 'Anomalie della persona, segregazione e attitudini magiche. Appunti per una lettura del "Filottete" di Sofocle', in *Magia. Studi di storia delle religioni in memoria di Raffaela Garosi*, Rome 1976, pp. 177–95, emphasizes that the state of deep sleep – 'as that of someone who has reached Hades' (v. 861), – into which Philoctetes periodically falls, makes him comparable to a 'soothsayer'. Massenzio sends us back, however, (p. 185, note 2) to specific studies on shamanism.

59. The identity is denied by Wissowa (see the heading 'Caeculus' in Roscher, op. cit., I, col. 844). Cf. instead W. F. Otto, 'Römische 'Sondergötter', in *Rheinisches Museum*, 64 (1909), pp. 453–54, and above all, A. Brelich, *Tre variazioni romane sul tema delle origini*, Rome [1955], pp. 9–47, in particular pp. 34 ff. Other indications in A. Alföldi, *Die Struktur des voretruskischen Römerstaates*, Heidelberg 1976, pp. 184–85 and *passim;* idem, *Römische Frühgeschichte*, Heidelberg 1976, p. 25, where the relationship between Caeculus and Vulcan (the Etruscan *Velchanos*) is considered a proof of the prolonged domination of the Etruscans over Rome. See too the rich study by J. N. Bremmer and N.M. Horsfall, *Roman Myth*, op. cit., pp. 49–62.

60. '*Hunc (Caeculum) legio late comitatur agresti (. . .)/ Non illis omnibus arma/Nec clipei currusve sonant; pars maxima glandes/liventis plumbi spargit, pars spicula gestat/bina manu, fulvosque lupi de pelle galeros/tegmen habent capiti; vestigia nuda sinistri/instituere pedis, crudus tegit altera pero*'. Cf. K. Meuli, 'Altrömischer Maskenbrauch', in *Gesammelte Schriften*, T. Gelzer (ed), Basel-Stuttgart 1975, pp. 269–70, who,

however, insists only on the primitive character of the band led by Caeculus. The *galerus* was identical with the Greek *kuneē*. On Hades' head covering see above, p. 158.

61. See above, p. 192.

62. On all this see A. Brelich, op. cit. The identity of Caeculus with the bandit Cacus has been repeatedly discussed: bibliography in J. P. Small, *Cacus and Marsyas in Etrusco-Roman Legend*, Princeton (N.J.) 1982, p. 33, note 98 (which expresses a negative opinion).

63. Cf. above all O. Rank, *Il mito della nascita dell'eroe*, It. trans., Milan 1987 (the first edition appeared in 1909; reprinted several times with additions); Lord Raglan, *The Hero. A Study in Tradition, Myth and Drama*, London 1936; G. Binder, *Die Aussetzung des Königskindes. Kyros und Romulus*, Meisenheim am Glau 1964 (on Caeculus, pp. 30–31). On the first two studies, independent of each other, see the acute essay of A. Taylor, 'The Biographical Pattern in Traditional Narrative', *Journal of the Folklore Institute*, I (1964), pp. 114–29, which also introduces into the discussion Propp's *Morfologia della fiaba* (but ignores, for example, Luria's essay). Alternatively, D. Skeels is *very superficial* in his 'The Psychological Patterns Underlying the Morphologies of Propp and Dundes', in *Southern Folklore Quarterly*, 31 (1967) pp. 224–61. On all this see Bremmer and Horsfall, op. cit., pp. 27–30.

64. It was already noted by Lucian, who remembered in this connection the story of Cyrus raised by a bitch dog *(On Sacrifices*, 5). See also, more fully, Cl. Elianus, *Varia Historia* II, 42. On the Oedipus-Moses connection see the conjectures of S. Levin, 'Jocasta and Moses' Mother Jochebed', in *Teiresias*, suppl. 2 (1979), pp. 49–61; in general see M. Astour, *Hellenosemitica*, Leiden 1965, pp. 152–59 and 220–24.

65. Cf. I. Kertész, 'Der Telephus-Mythos und der Telephos-Fries', in *Oikumene*, 3 (1982), pp. 203–15, in particular pp. 208–9.

66. Cf. Apollodorus, *La biblioteca*, I. 9, 8; Binder, op. cit., pp. 78 ff.; based upon C. Trieber, 'Die Romulussage', in *Rheinisches Museum*, 43 (1888), pp. 569–82 (and cf. Momigliano, op. cit., I, p. 62) See also Pauly-Wissowa, *Real-Encyclopädie der classischen Altertumswissenschaft* art. 'Romulus', 1090.

67. On regal childhoods as the model for ephebes cf. Jeanmaire, *Couroi et Curetes* cit. pp. 371 ff. (to which P. Vidal-Naquet refers, art. cit., p. 157), On the connection between Oedipus' childhood and the myths concerning the childhood of the hero cf. Propp, *(Edipo)* cit., pp. 104–5 and 116. On the analogies between the story of Cyrus and that of Kypselos (in its turn related to that of Oedipus): cf. Vernant, art. cit. *(From Oedipus to Periander)*; cf. Wehrli. art. cit., pp. 113–14, which hypothesizes either the priority of the first, or the derivation of both from a a previous model.

68. A check on the extremely dispersed sources could perhaps integrate the rapid hints at physical defects in Rank, op. cit., p. 99, and Binder, op. cit., pp. 104–5 and 116. The latter observed that in the myths the children were exposed more often than happened in reality: in this connection see now W. V. Harris, 'The Theoretical Possibility of Extensive Infanticide in the Graeco-Roman World', in *Classical Quarterly*, 32 (1982), pp. 114–16, with further bibliography.

69. Superficial discussion in S. Sas, *Der Hinkende als Symbol*, Zurich 1964, pp. 117–20. On the episode's folkloric implications cf. E. Meyer, *Die Israeliten und ihre Nachbarstämme*, Halle a. S. 1906, pp. 51 ff. In the same sense see H. Gunkel, 'Jakob', in *Preussische Jahrbücher*, 176 (1919), pp. 339 ff., in particular, p. 349; idem, *Däs Märchen im Alten Testament*, Tübingen 1921, pp. 66 ff., which cites a Bosnian fable about a man who struggles for three hours with a vampire until the crow of the rooster, and then returns home ill. Aetiological implications (prohibition against eating the sciatic nerve: *Gen.* 32, 33) underlined by Gunkel

cannot fully explain the meaning of the story. On the comparison with I *Kings* 18, 26 (the hopping dance of the prophets of Baal) see W. Oesterley, *The Sacred Dance. A Study in Comparative Folklore*, New York 1923, pp. 113–114. Other studies stress the complex stratification of the text: see, for example. F. van Trigt, 'La signification de la lutte de Jacob près du Yabboq . . .', in *Oudtestamentische Studien*, XII (1958), pp. 280-309. Further bibliography in R. Martin-Achard, 'Un exégète devant 'Genèse', 32, 23–33, in *Analyse structurale et exégèse biblique*, Neuchâtel 1971, pp. 41–62. It is significant that in the same volume (pp. 27–39) Roland Barthes finds Propp's categories without difficulty in the Biblical story. I thank Stefano Levi Della Toree, who has made me privy to some of his thoughts on Jacob.

70. Servius (op. cit., p. 181) connects the name of Caeculus to the circumstances of his birth (*'quia oculis minoribus fuit: quam rem frequenter efficit fumus'*). On the structural connection between the blind hero (Horatius Cocles) and the hero whose hand is mutilated (Mucius Scaevola) see most recently G. Dumézil, ' "Le Borgne" and "Le Manchot"; The State of the Problem', in *Myth in Indo-European Antiquity*, G. J. Larson ed, Berkeley 1974, pp. 17-28. On the relationship between Caeculus and Cocles (who had a statue on the Volcanal, Vulcan's sanctuary) cf. Brelich, op. cit., pp. 34 ff. I do not believe that an affinity between Caeculus and Oedipus has ever been suggested.

71. Cf. A. Alföldi, 'Königsweihe und Männerbund bei den Achämeniden,' in *Heimat und Humanität: Festschrift für Karl Meuli zum 60. Geburtstag*, Basel 1951, pp. 11–16 (which refers to the studies on *Mannerbünde* by O. Höfler, L. Weiser-Aall etc., on which see above, p. 173, note 2), followed by Binder, op. cit., see besides Bremmer, art. cit., pp. 144–46 and *passim*; other useful indications in A. Napoli, 'I rapporti tra Bruzi e Lucani', in *Studi e materiali di storia delle religioni*, XXXVII (1966), p. 61 ff. (followed by D. Briquel, 'Trois études sur Romulus', in *Recherches sur les religion de l'antiquité classique*, R. Bloch ed., Geneva 1980, p. 289).

72. The detail, which also recurs in Nicolaus of Damascus, alludes implicitly to the *Odyssey* XI, 287 ff. on which see W. Pötscher, 'Die Oidipus-Gestalt', in *Eranos*, 71 (1973), pp. 23–25. The perplexity expressed by J. Rudhardt, 'Oedipe et les chevaux', *Museum Helveticum*, 40 (1983), pp. 131–39, seems therefore out of place.

73. Cf. Gernet, op. cit., pp. 154–71, on the nocturnal expedition of Dolon in the Greek camp (canto X of the *Iliad*): but it will be good to keep in mind the observations of A. Schnapp-Gourbeillon, *Lions, héros, masques*, Paris 1981, pp. 112 ff. In addition see H. J. Rose, 'Chthonian Cattle', in *Numen*, I (1954), pp. 13–27; C. Gallini, 'Animali e al di là,' *Studi e materiali di storia delle religioni*, XXX (1959), pp. 65 ff., in particular p. 81; B. Lincoln, 'The Indo-European Cattle-Raiding Myth', *History of Religions*, 16 (1976), pp. 42–65; Walcot, art. cit.; B. Bravo, 'Sulan', in *Annali della Scuola Normale Superiore di Pisa*, Classe di lettere, etc., III, 10 (1980), pp. 954–58; F. Bader, 'Rhapsodies homériques et irlandaises', *Recherches sur les religions*, cit. Bloch ed, pp. 9–83.

74. Cf. Burkert, 'Heracles and the Master of Animals' in *Structure and History in Greek Mythology and Ritual*, Berkeley 1979, pp. 78 ff.

75. Cf. O. Maenchen-Helfen, 'Herakles in China', in *Archiv Orientalní*, 7 (1935), pp. 29–34.

76. Cf. Burkert, art. cit., pp. 86–87.

77. Cf. *Oedipus the King*, vv. 300–462. On Tiresias' staff cf. Kerényi, op. cit., II, p. 102.

78. On Melampus cf. Nilsson, op. cit., pp. 615. On the possibility of speaking of Greek shamanism, cf. Meuli, 'Scythica' in op. cit.; E. R. Dodds, *The Greeks and the Irrational*, 1951 California. More cautiously Burkert, 'GOES. Zum griechischen

Schamanismus', in *Rheinisches Museum*, 105 (1962), pp. 36–55; idem, *Weisheit und Wissenschaft*, Nürnberg 1962. p. 123 ff. Bremmer is sharply critical, *The Early Greek Concept of the Soul*, Princeton 1983. In an intermediate position, close to that of Burkert, is I. P. Couliano, *Esperienze dell'estasi dell' Ellenismo al Medioevo*, It. trans., Bari 1986, pp. 19 ff. It is worth remembering here that Lévi-Strauss' Oedipus has been called 'a limping shaman' by G. Steiner (*After Babel*, Oxford 1975 p. 29).

79. Cf. Diogenes Laertius, *Life of the Philosophers*, VIII, 11 and VIII, 69. The interpretation delineated here develops that proposed, in regard to Pythagoras, by Burkert (cf. op. cit., p. 134, which supposes a connection with the birth of Dionysos from Zeus' thigh: see further on, note 82); idem, 'Das Proömium des Parmenides und die Katabasis des Pythagoras', in *Phronesis*, XIV (1969), pp. 1–30, where it is shown that the wound to the thigh, frequently associated with the Phrygian-Anatolian Great Mother, had an initiatic value like the symbolic dismemberment of the shamans. On the shamanistic components in the figure of Empedocles, see the contrasting opinions of Dodds, op. cit., pp. 182 ff. and C. H. Kahn, 'Religion and Natural Philosophy in Empedocles' Doctrine of the Soul', in *Archiv für Geschichte der Philosophie*, 42 (1960), pp. 30–35. See also Couliano, op. cit., pp. 26–27.

80. M. Bloch, 'Pour une histoire comparée des sociétés européennes' in *Mélanges historiques*, I, Paris 1963, p. 22, likened this comparison to the 'fork of a water diviner'.

81. On this point I am chiefly using the documentation gathered, from a different perspective, by M. Detienne, *Dioniso a cielo aperto*, It. trans., Bari 1987, pp. 63–81. See besides Jean-Pierre Vernant, 'Le Dionysos masqué des "Bacchantes' d'Euripide" in *L'homme*, XXV (1985), pp. 31–58.

82. Cf. Burkert, op. cit., p. 134, note 245, where it is hypothesized that an initiatic significance exists which is analogous to Pythagoras' golden thigh. The interpretation is repeated in Burkert's *Greek Religion* cit. above, p. 165. In the *Dionysiaca* (IX, vv. 18–22) Nonnus interprets the name Dionysos as 'lame Zeus', observing that in the dialect of Syracuse *nysos* means lame (I thank Gabriel Sala for this information).

83. Cf. K. Latte, 'Askoliasmos' in *Hermes*, 85 (1957), pp. 385–91 (also used by M. Detienne). Cf. also W. Deonna, *Un divertissement de table 'à cloche-pied'*, Brussels 1959, pp. 25–29 and 36–39.

84. Cf. Latte, art. cit., pp. 38–86 (who cites Elianus, *De natura animalium*, 3, 13).

85. This hypothesis is mentioned by H. Diels, 'Das Labyrinth', *Festgabe von Fachgenossen und Freunden A. von Harnack zum siebzigsten Geburtstag . . .*, Tübingen 1921, pp. 61–72, in particular p. 67, note 2. See also U. Wilamowitz-Moellendorff, *Griechische Verskunst*, Berlin 1921, p. 29, followed by K. Friis Johansen, *Thésée et la danse à Delos*, København 1945, p. 12; P. Bruneau, *Recherches sur les cultes de Délos*, Paris 1970, p. 29 ff., in particular p. 31. Cf. also H. von Petrikovits, 'Troiaritt und Geranostanz', in *Beiträge zur älteren europäischen Kulturgeschichte, Festschrift für Rudolf Egger*, I, Klagenfurt 1952, pp. 126–43. A great deal of material, gathered with scant critical sense, in H. Lucas, *Der Tanz der Kraniche*, Emsdetten 1971. Not persuasive the over-all interpretation of M. Detienne, 'La grue et le labyrinthe', in *Mélanges de l'école Française de Rome, Antiquité*, 95 (1983), pp. 541–53.

86. Cf. D. C. Fox, 'Labyrinth und Totenreich', in *Paideuma*, I (1940), pp. 381–94. Much material, which is chiefly iconographic, can be found in H. Kern, *Labirinti*, Milan 1981.

87. Cf. Jeanmaire, op. cit. *Dioniso*, pp. 46–54; Bremmer, op. cit., pp. 108–23; Burkert, op. cit. (*Greek Religion*), pp. 237–40.

88. On the presence of Dionysos in the sanctuary of Delphi, and in general on the relations between the two divinities, cf. Jeanmaire, op. cit., pp. 187–98.

89. Cf. Lucas, *Der Tanz* cit., p. 6 and plate 1.
90. Cf. *I presocratici*, A. Pasquinelli ed, Turin 1958, pp. 189-90: see Jeanmaire, op. cit., pp. 46–54. On stumbling as a presage of death in Scandinavian culture cf. B. Almqvist, 'The Death Forebodings of Saint Oláfr, King of Norway, and Rögnvaldr Brúsason, Earl of Orkney', in *Béaloideas*, 42–44 (1974–76), pp. 1-40 (poor in quality). Completely independently, Claude Lévi-Strauss sees in the act of stumbling the symbol of a defect in communication ('Mythe et oubli', in *Le régard éloigné*, Paris 1983, pp. 253 ff., in particular p. 259).
91. Cf. M. Granet, 'Remarques sur le Taoïsme ancien', in *Asia Major*, 2 (1925), pp. 146–51; idem, *Danses et légendes de la Chine ancienne*, Paris 1926, II, pp. 466 ff. and 549 ff.; M. Kaltenmark, 'Ling-Pao: Note sur un terme du Taoïsme ancien', in *Mélanges publiés par l'Institut des Hautes Études Chinoises*, II, Paris 1960, pp. 559–88, in particular pp. 572–73; idem, 'Les danses sacrées en Chine', in *Les danses sacrées*, Paris 1963, p. 444; W. Eberhard, *The Local Cultures of South and East China*, 2nd ed. (revised), Leiden 1968, pp. 72–80, in particular pp. 74–75. On the custom of covering one's head during the shamanistic ritual see also, pp. 264 ff.
92. Cf. Granet, op. cit., II, pp. 550, note 3, 552 ff. and 575–76; Eberhard, op. cit., p. 74.
93. Cf. Granet, op. cit., I, pp. 221–22.
94. Heine-Geldern, 'Das Tocharerproblem und die Pontische Wanderung', *Saeculum*, II (1951) p. 252 has explored in depth a diffusionistic hypothesis that had been formulated superficially by E. A. Armstrong, 'The Crane Dance in East and West', in *Antiquity*, 17 (1943), pp. 71–76. Recently Lévi-Strauss, to explain some analogies between Greek myths and Japanese legends (that of Midas, for example), has suggested the likelihood of a common genesis in central Asia.
95. Cf. Granet, op. cit., I, 326, note 1, and Kaltenmark, art. cit., p. 578; on the ceremony of the Twelve Animals see above, pp. 175–76.
96. Cf. J. G. Frazer, *The Golden Bough*, IX: *The Scapegoat*, New York 1935, pp. 324 ff. (with bibliography), which adheres to the theory that the twelve days are a period interpolated between the lunar year and the solar year. A. van Gennep, *Manuel de folklore français contemporain*, I, VII, 1: *Cycle de Douze Jours*, Paris 1958, pp. 2856 ff., in particular pp. 2861–62, discusses the various interpretations, judging those which hinge on funereal elements as unilateral, because they fail to explain the festive rather than sad character of the 12 days cycle. So superficial an evaluation, which seems to deliberately ignore the contradictory characteristics usually attributed to the dead, as bearers of both fertility and misfortune, is probably explained by distrust (common in Van Gennep) when confronted by the notion of ambivalence.
97. See above, pp. 157 and 169. The analogy between the two phenomena had not escaped B. Schmidt, *Das Volksleben der Neugriechen und das hellenische Alterthum*, I, Leipzig 1871, p. 154, note 1.
98. Cf. the facts accumulated in a disorderly fashion by F. Sokoliček, 'Der Hinkende in brauchtümlichen Spiel', in *Festgabe für Otto Höfler zum 65. Geburtstag*, II, Vienna 1968, pp. 423–32. Further material in R. Stumpfl, *Kultspiele der Germanen als Ursprung des mittelalterlichen Dramas*, Berlin 1936, pp. 325 ff., which derives strictly from the research of O. Höfler. Cf. also D. Strömbäck, 'Cult Remnants in Icelandic Dramatic Dances', in *Arv*, 4 (1948), pp. 139–40 (dance of the lame horse, documented between the end of the seventeenth and the beginning of the eighteenth centuries).
99. One might say that Lévi-Strauss' fault in formulating the problem of mythic and ritual lameness has, paradoxically, that of being inspired more by Frazer than by himself.

100. The interpretation of Oedipus as the 'annual god' (*Jahresgott*), formulated by C. Robert, was promptly refuted by Nilsson, art. cit.

101. It is significant that the category of the rite of passage had been discovered by R. Hertz through the analysis of burial rites.

102. Cf. Sas, op. cit. (inspired explicitly by Jung's analytical psychology). From an analogous point of view, but independently, T. Giani Gallino, *La ferita e il re. Gli archetipi femminili della cultura maschile*, Milan 1986, pp. 37–46 compares mythical lameness to menstruation, using quite debatable arguments (see for example p. 43).

103. Cf. R. Needham, 'Unilateral Figures', in *Reconnaissances*, Toronto 1980, pp. 17–40, which develops considerations presented in *Primordial Characters*, Charlottesville 1978 (on pp. 45–46 a rather unconvincing attempt to circumscribe the partial divergences in regard to a postulation of Jung's).

104. Cf. E. Neumann, *Die grosse Mutter*, Zürich 1956. A criticism of the empirical basis for this notion in P. Y. Ucko, *Anthropomorphic Figurines of Predynastic Egypt and Neolithic Crete . . .*, London 1968.

105. Cf. Needham, art. cit., pp. 34 ff.

106. Ibid. Among the studies cited by Needham I have seen: D. Zahan, 'Colors and Body-Painting in Black Africa: The Problem of the "Half-Man"', in *Diogenes*, 90 (1975), pp. 100–19; A. Szabó, 'Der halbe Mensch und der Biblische Sündenfall', in *Paideuma*', 2 (1941–43), pp. 95–100; A. E. Jensen, *Die mythische Vorstellung vom halben Menschen*, ivi, 5 (1950–54), pp. 23–43. The first two are superficial, the second and third are deformed by a Euro-centric metaphysic. Further material in D. J. Ray, *Eskimo Masks*, 1967, pp. 16 and 187–88.

107. Cf. A. Castrén, *Nordische Reisen und Forschungen*, Ger. trans. IV, St. Petersburg 1857, pp. 157–64 (Needham cites it by way of G. Hatt, *Asiatic Influences in American Folklore*, København 1949, pp. 87–89). The possibility that in specific cultures the image of the unilateral man might have a different significance, can certainly not be excluded. But a psychoanalytical interpretation such as that proposed by J. Galinier, 'L'homme sans pied. Metaphores de la castration et imaginaire en Mésoamérique', in *L'homme*, XXIV, 1984, pp. 41–58) gives little prominence, for example, to the fact that for a Mexican population like the Otomi, those who deprive themselves temporarily of a leg, before transforming themselves into women and flying away in the form of birds (pp. 45–46), are in fact shamans.

108. Cf. C. Foulon, 'Un personnage mystérieux du roman de *Perceval le Gallois*: l'"eschacier" dans la seconde partie du *Perceval*,' in *The Legend of Arthur in the Middle Ages. Studies Presented to A.H. Diverres*, P. B. Grout et al, eds., Cambridge 1983, pp. 66–75, which effectively responds to the conjecture of R. S. Loomis, *Arthurian Tradition and Chrétien de Troyes*, New York 1949, pp. 443–47, according to which *eschacier* (man with only one leg) would be a misapprehension, introduced by Chrétien or copied from his source, of an original *eschaquier* (chess board). In reality, this last term constitutes a *lectio facilior*, as is shown by its presence (which Loomis interprets differently) in three manuscripts of *Perceval le Gallois*. Loomis' conjecture is followed by Riemschneider, op. cit., pp. 34–35. It should be noted that the man with only one leg is a Celtic motif: cf. S. M. Finn, 'The Eschacier in Chrétien's *Perceval* in the Light of Medieval Art', in *The Modern Language Review*, XLVII (1952), pp. 52–55; P. MacCana, *Branwen*, Cardiff 1958, pp. 39 ff; J. Le Goff, *Il meraviglioso* cit., p. 126, note 73. H. Wagner, 'Studies in the Origins of Early Celtic Civilization', in *Zeitschrift für celtische Philologie*, 31 (1970), p. 26, note 32, proposes to decipher the aerial battle between the gods and the deformed *Fomorians*, described in the poem *Mag Tured*, on the basis of a Samoyed myth (described by T. Lehtisalo) in which the bull of the north, which brings the rain,

fights amid the clouds against the demons with only one hand, one leg and one eye, thus bringing on the drought (see on this point the Samoyed fable mentioned above, note 107). The shamanistic implications of the man with a silver leg are heavily emphasized by C. Corradi Musi, 'Sciamanesimo ugrofinnico e magia europea', in *Quaderni di Filologia Germanica della Facoltà di Lettere e filosofia dell' Università di Bologna*, III (1984), p. 60. On the theme of the journey into the other world in the Arthurian romance, see above, pp. 107–8.

109. A. Szabó proposes an utterly misleading juxtaposition (art. cit., p. 97) with the myth recounted by Plato in the *Symposium*, in which love is described as the joining together of two divided individuals.

110. Hence the ambiguous reactions aroused in humans by other species capable of erect posture, such as monkeys and bears. The crucial importance of erect posture in the evolution of the human species has been illustrated by A. Leroi-Gourhan, *Le geste et la parole, Technique et language* Paris 1964.

111. Cf. G. Dumézil, *Storie degli Sciti*, It trans., Milan 1980. p. 94. The corresponding figure to Soslan among the Circassians – a kind of shaman, capable of every sort of transformation – is sarcastically called the 'magician with the crooked legs'.

112. It should be remembered that Benjamin, in a letter to Scholem on August 5, 1937, said that he considered Jung's psychology 'the devil's work through and through, which should be attacked with white magic'. (W. Benjamin and Gershom Scholem, *Correspondence 1932–1940*, New York 1989, p. 203.)

113. Useful elements of reflection on all this in J. Fédry, 'L'expérience du corps comme structure du language. Essai sur la langue sàr (Tchad)', in *L'homme*, XVI (1976), pp. 64–107. In general cf. R. Cardona, *I sei lati del mondo*, Bari 1985.

114. Cf. R. Jakobson, 'Signe Zero', in *Selected Writings*, II, The Hague–Paris 1971, pp. 211–19.

115. The extraordinary verses of Lucretius, *De rerum natura*, III, vv. 830 ff. should be remembered.

116. On the link between the fable and the epic theme of the hero's journey into the beyond cf. L. Radermacher, *Das Jenseits im Mythos der Hellenen*, Bonn 1903, pp. 28– 29, note 2 and *passim*, and above all K. Meuli, *Odyssee und Argonautika. Untersuchungen zur griechischen Sagengeschichte und zum Epos*, 1921 (reprint, Utrecht 1974) in particular pp. 22–23, which through A. Heusler ('Altnordische Dichtung und Prosa von jung Sigurd', in *Sitzungsberichte der preussischen Akademie der Wissenschaften*, phil.-hist., Klasse, 1919, I, p. 163) draws indirectly on the essay of F. von der Leyen, cited further on, note 119. On the relationship between magical fable and myth cf., besides the observations of Propp, *Morfologia* cit., pp. 96, 106–7, the illuminating thoughts of W. Benjamin, 'The Story Teller. Reflections on the Works of Nikolai Leskov,' in *Illuminations*, New York 1968, pp. 83–109.

117. The hypothesis, formulated by Propp in *Morfologia* cit., pp. 112–13, of an historical connection between the structure of magical fairy tale and beliefs in the peregrinations of the soul in the beyond, were developed in *Le radici storiche delle fiabe di magia* cit., accentuating the relationship with the ritual context. This change of perspective should perhaps be attributed at least in part to the political climate in which the book was published. In any case the two works, though so different, form part of a unified project, as is shown also by the retrospective observations in the appendix to *Morfologia della fiaba* (which originally was to be entitled *Morfologia della fiaba di magia*) cit., pp. 208–10. On Propp cf. R. Breymayer, 'Vladimir Jakovlevič Propp (1895–1970), Leben, Wirken und Bedeutsamkeit', in *Linguistica Biblica*, 15–16 (April 1972), pp. 36–77; I. Levin, 'Vladimir Propp: an Evaluation on His

Seventieth Birthday', in *Journal of the Folklore Institute*, 4 (1967), pp. 32–49; A. Liberman, introd. to Vladimir Propp, *Theory and History of Folklore*, Minneapolis 1984. The presence of initiatic themes in some fables, amply discussed in *Radici storiche*, had already been suggested (in a perspective influenced by a solar mythology that had by then already gone out of fashion) by P. Saintyves [É. Nourry], *Les contes de Perrault et les récits parallèles. . .*, Paris 1923, pp. XX, 245 ff. (Tom Thumb), 374 ff. (Blue Beard), etc. But Propp, who read and quoted this book, apparently ignored the much more important one by H. Siuts, *Jenseitsmotive in deutschen Volksmärchen*, Leipzig 1911, which develops in an original manner some observations of von der Leyen, 'Zur Entsstehung des Marchens', *Archiv für das Studium der neuren Sprachen und Literaturen*, 113, (1904).

118. Cf. Propp, *Morfologia* cit., pp. 107–10, where he does not exclude the possibility (obviously not demonstrable) that the two types were originally historically distinct.

119. This is a thesis of E. B. Tylor, presented again with the support of a great deal of documentation by von der Leyen, art. cit. (appeared in *Archiv für das Studium der neueren Sprachen und Literatur*, 113 (1903); pp. 249–69; 114 (1904), pp. 1–24; 115 (1905), pp. 1–21 and 273–89; 116 (1906), pp. 1–24 and 289–300). In this essay, as in a preceding, very brief version ('Traum und Märchen', in *Der Lotse*, 1901, pp. 382 ff., which I have not seen) the author mentions *The Interpretation of Dreams* by Freud, with whom he had a correspondence: see *The Complete Letters of Sigmund Freud to Wilhelm Fliess*, J. Moussaieff Masson, ed, Harvard (Mass.) 1985, pp. 444–46 (letter of July 4, 1901). Von der Leyen's thesis, prompted by ideas expressed by E. Rohde (*Psyche*, Berlin 1893) and before that by L. Laistner (*Das Rätsel der Sphinx*, 2 vols., Berlin 1889) is based in part on material discussed also in this book, beginning with the saga of King Guntram (on whom see above, p. 138). The interpretation is often reductive: the image of the soul as a mouse, for example, is traced back (art. cit., 1904, p. 6) to the etymology of the word 'muscle' (from *mus*, mouse) .

120. Cf. R. Mathieu, 'Le songe de Zhao Jianzi. Étude sur les rêves d'ascension céleste et les rêves d'esprit dans la Chine ancienne', in *Asiatische Studien – Études asiatiques*, XXXVII (1983) pp. 119–38.

121. Cf. Propp, *Morfologia* cit., pp. 23–24.

122. For a bibliographic review see the heading 'Cinderella', in *Enzyklopädie des Märchens*, Berlin & New York, 1977, coll. 39–57 (R. Wehse, ed). An indispensable starting point is still M. R. Cox, *Cinderella. Three-hundred and Forty-five Variants*, London 1893 (with an introduction by A. Lang), to be combined with A. B. Rooth, *The Cinderella Cycle*, Lund 1951. Very useful is the collection *Cinderella, A Casebook*, A. Dundes, ed, New York 1982: see above all the cartographic review by A. B. Rooth, *Tradition Areas in Eurasia* (pp. 129–47) and the annotated bibliography of A. Taylor, *The Study of Cinderella Cycle*, pp. 115–28. Among specific contributions see E. Cosquin, 'Le "Cendrillon" masculin', in *Revue des Traditions Populaires*, XXXIII (1918), pp. 193–202; D. Kleinmann, 'Cendrillon et son pied', in *Cahiers de Littérature orale*, 4 (1978), pp. 56–88; B. Herrenstein Smith, 'Narrative Versions, Narrative Theories', in *Critical Inquiry*, 7 (1980), pp. 213–36.

123. Cf. Propp, *Morfologia* cit., pp. 31 ff. The mark corresponds to the function n. XVII (p. 57).

124. With extraordinary penetration H. Usener juxtaposes Cinderella to Aphrodite chosen for her beauty by Paris, underlining the funereal characteristics of the two figures (art. cit., pp. 362-63). O. Gruppe, following the path opened by Usener, included Cinderella in the series incorporating Perseus, Jason, etc. (op. cit., pp. 1332, note 4). In the same sense cf. also R. Eisler, *Weltenmantel und Himmelzeit*, I,

Munich 1910, p. 166, note 3. As far as I can make out, the successive studies of Cinderella have ignored this interpretative insight – with a single possible exception. In a very beautiful essay Freud recognized in Cordelia and Cinderella two incarnations of the goddess of death, with a connection to the funereal Aphrodite ('The Theme of the Three Caskets', in *Works*, vol XII, London 1958, pp. 291–301). An indirect echo of Usener's page could perhaps have reached Freud through the articles in Roscher's mythological dictionary (but this is a guess that requires verification. . .). In a letter to Ferenczi of July 7, 1913 Freud alluded to the autobiographical implications of his own essay (ibid., p. 205; Anna, his favourite, was the third child – the one who in the myth and fairy tale announced death).

125. If we assume the versions of the Cinderella fairy tale analyzed by Cox (distinguishing them from those typologically related) to be a valid, if unbalanced, sample it turns out that out of 319 one twentieth (16) present the theme of the gathering of the bones of the assistant.

126. Cf. J. G. Campbell, *Popular Tales of the West Highlands*, Edinburgh 1862, II, pp. 286 ff., K. Blind, 'A Fresh Scottish Ashpitel and Glass Shoe Tale', in *Archaeological Review*, III (1889), pp. 24–27; 'Aryan Folk-Lore', *The Calcutta Review*, LI (1870), pp. 119–21 (a summary of a much longer version, which appeared in *The Bombay Gazette*, but which I have been unable to obtain. The anonymous editor observes that in another version the cow, for religious reasons, had been supplanted by a fish; he emphasizes the analogy with the fairy tale published by Campbell). A. B. Rooth (op. cit., p. 57) affirms that in India the version in which the cow appeared was passed on to Indochina. This is a conjecture that has not been proven: in the Indo-Chinese versions, as in the Chinese, cow, bird and fish (the last appears in the oldest version) alternate: cf. W. Eberhard, *Typen chinesischen Volksmärchen* (FF Communications, n. 120), Helsinki 1937, pp. 52–54; A. Waley, 'The Chinese Cinderella Story', in *Folk-Lore*, 58 (1947), pp. 226–38; Nai-Tung Ting, *The Cinderella Cycle in China and Indo-China*, (FF Communications, n. 213), Helsinki 1974, pp. 47 ff.

127. The bibliography is very extensive. To the studies cited above (p. 148, note 78) add A. Friedrich, 'Die Forschung über das frühzeitliche Jägertum', *Paideuma*, 2 (1941–43), pp. 20–43; idem, 'Knochen und Skelett in der Vorstellungswelt Nordasiens' *Weiner Beiträge zur Kulturgeschichte und Linguistik'*, 5 (1943), pp. 189-247; H. Nachtigall, 'Die kulturhistorische Wurzel des Schamanenskelettier-ung', in *Zeitschrift für Ethnologie*, 77 (1952) pp. 188–97; Gignoux, '"Corps osseux et âme osseuse": essai sur le chamanisme dans L'Iran ancien', in *Journal asiatique*, 267 (1979), pp. 41–79. On North America cf. a reference of Hertz, op. cit., p. 79, Friedrich, art. cit., p. 28, cites two studies on African phenomena, which have remained inaccessible to me.

128. Cf. Hertz, op. cit. The connection with the theme of the gathering of the bones is pointed out by Lévi-Strauss, 'L'art de déchiffer les symboles', in *Diogène*, n.5 (1954), pp. 128–35 (apropos Rooth's book).

129. Cf. Propp, 'L'albero magico sulla tomba. A proposito dell' origine delle fiabe di magia' (1934), in *Edipo* op. cit., pp. 3-39, which also alludes to the presence of this theme in *Cinderella*.

130. For China, cf. Waley, art. cit. The references that follow, taken from Cox, op. cit., have been checked. Vietnam: A. Landes, *Contes et légendes annamites*, Saigon 1886, n. XXII, pp. 52–57; G. Dumoutier, 'Contes populaires Tonkinois. Une Cendrillon annamite', in *Archivio per lo studio delle tradizioni popolari*, XII (1893), pp. 386–91 (the story takes place at the time of the last Hung king, 4th century BC); India

(Calcutta): K. Blind, ('Aryan Folk-Lore') art. cit.; Russia: Aleksandr Afanasjev, *Russian Fairy Tales*, New York 1945 pp. 515–17 ('The Slovenly Mite'); Serbia: *Serbian Folklore*. W. Denton ed., London 1874, pp. 59–66; V. Karajich; Sicily: G. Pitré, *Fiabe, novelle e racconti popolari siciliani* I, Palermo 1870, pp. 366–67; Sardinia (Nuoro): P.E. Guarnerio, 'Primo saggio di novelle popolari sarde', in *Archivio per lo studio delle tradizioni popolari*, II (1883), pp. 31–34; Provence (Mentone): J. B. Andrews, *Contes ligures*, Paris 1892, pp. 3–7; Brittany: P. Sébillot, *Contes populaires de la Haute-Bretagne*, I, Paris 1880, pp. 15–22, where, however, the burial is not accompanied by the gathering of bones; cf. instead ibid., 'La petite brebiette blanche', pp. 331–32; Lorraine: E. Cosquin, *Contes populaires de Lorraine*, I, pp. 246–47 (which omits the episode of the lost slipper); Scotland (Glasgow): Blind, 'A Fresh Scottish Ashpite' (art. cit.); (West Highlands): Campbell, op. cit. See also Saintyves, op. cit., pp. 142–51.

131. By means of a different logic, A. B. Rooth (op. cit.) arrives at analogous conclusions. She distinguishes three plots: A: the stepmother starves the children, who are fed on the sly by the helpful animal assistant; when the animal is killed, the children gather the bones, burn them, and put the ashes in a vase from which grows a plant that nourishes them (in an alternative version, the children find precious objects in the animal's entrails); B: an object lost and found by chance (generally a slipper) puts the hero on the heroine's trail. The AB plot, which corresponds to the Cinderella fairy tale, is earlier than the two separate plots (this point is misunderstood by A. Dundes, op. cit., introduction). It should be emphasized that this relative chronology, reconstructed by a morphological approach, does not coincide with the absolute chronology of the testimonies: the oldest testimony of B (the story, reported by Strabo, of the eagle that flies from Naucratis to Memphis, flinging into the lap of the young King the slipper of the courtesan Rhodopis) precedes the older version of AB, written down by Tuang Ch'eng Shih (800-853) by about eight hundred years. This Chinese text, joined with the Cinderella fairy tale by the Japanese folklorist K. Minakata (1911), was translated for the first time into a Western language by R. D. Jameson, who explicitly denied the ritual implications of the gathering of the bones ('Cinderella in China'), in *Three Lectures on Chinese Folklore*, Peiping (Beijing) [1932] pp. 45–85, in particular p. 61, note). For a cartographic review of the diffusion of various motifs cf. Rooth, op. cit., (*Eurasia*) (in particular p. 137, series o, maps A and B).

132. See above p. 135.

133. Cf. J. Henninger, 'Zum Verbot des Knochenzerbrechens bei den Semiten', in *Studi orientalistici in onore di Giorgio Levi Della Vida*, in Rome 1956, I, pp. 448–58, reviewed and amplified in idem, 'Neuere Forschungen zum Verbot des Knochenzerbrechens', in *Studia Ethnographica et Folkloristica in Honorem Béla Gunda*, Debrecen 1971.

134. Cf. above all, on Siberian customs, Vladimir Propp, art. cit. (used also by Bertolotti, op. cit.) and U. Harva (Holmberg), *Les représentations religieuses des peoples altaïques*, Paris 1959, pp. 298–307. See also Mannhardt, *Germanische Mythen*, Berlin 1858, p. 58, which juxtaposes the Thor myth to a saga of the Vorarlberg; Röhrich, 'Le monde surnaturel dans les légendes alpines', *Le monde alpin et rhodanien*, 10 (1982), pp. 25 ff., texts n. 13 (Alpe de la Vallée), nn. 14–15 (Tyrol); Dirr, 'Der kaukasische Wild- und Jagdgott', *Anthropos*, 20 (1925), p. 140; K. Meuli, 'Griechische Opferbräuche', in op. cit., p. 235, note 5; Paproth, *Studien über das Bärenzeremoniell*, I, Uppsala 1976, p. 36 (on the Ainu). Of scant help R. Bilz, 'Tiertöter-Skrupulantismus. Betrachtungen über das Tier als Entelechial-Doppelgänger des Menschen', in *Jahrbuch für Psychologie und Psychoterapie*, 3 (1955), pp. 226–44.

135. This was pointed out by Campbell, op. cit.; more recently it has been mentioned again by L. Schmidt, 'Der "Herr der Tiere" in einigen Sagenlandschaften Europas und Eurasiens', in *Anthropos*, 47 (1952), p. 522. Cf. S. Thompson, *Motif-Index of Folk Literature*, Copenhagen 1955 ff.; E 32,3 ('dismembered pigs come alive again if only bones are preserved'); E3 ('Resuscitated eaten animals'); E 33 ('Resuscitation with missing member').

136. Cf. Gervaise of Tilbury, *Otia imperialia*, in *Scriptores rerum Brunsvicensium*, G.G. Leibniz, ed, I, Hanoverae 1707, p. 1003.

137. In some Balkan versions the miraculous bones are those of the heroine's mother killed by the sisters and devoured (in one instance, after having been transformed into a cow): cf. Cox, op. cit., nn. 31, 53, 54 and 124. The theme appears also in Greece: cf. M. Xanthakou, *Cendrillon et les soeurs cannibales*, Paris 1988 (very unsatisfactory).

138. Cf. Lévi-Strauss, op. cit. (*Anthropologie structurale*), p. 250.

139. Cf. Cox, op. cit., pp. 416 ff. Also the cow with the golden horn in the Sardinian fable asks the heroine to wrap her own bones in a handkerchief (Guarnerio, art. cit., p. 33).

140. This is suggested by P. B. Bourboulis, in A. Dundes, ed., op. cit., pp. 99 ff.

141. Cf. on all this Waley, art. cit. From a Chinese version (VIII century BC.) of the fable of the girl-swan, analyzed by Waley himself, derives the inspiration for the essay (which strongly emphasizes the shamanistic traits) by A. T. Hatto, 'The Swan-Maiden: a Folk-Tale of North-Eurasian Origin?' in *Essays in German and Other Medieval Poetry*, Cambridge 1980, pp. 267–97. The discovery of the resemblance between the Buryat version and the Chinese version of this fable goes back to U. Harva (Holmberg), op. cit., pp. 318–19.

142. See above, pp. 227–8. For an analysis, limited in fact to the Oedipal elements, of the Cinderella fairy tale, see the very superficial essay of D. Pace, 'Lévi-Strauss and the Analysis of Folktales', A. Dundes, ed, op. cit., pp. 246–58 (the reference to Lévi-Strauss is completely unwarranted).

143. They correspond respectively to the numbers 510 A and 510 B of Aarne-Thompson's classification (cf. Thompson, *The Types of the Folktale*, Helsinki 1961). Their typological affinity had already been pointed out by Cox, op. cit.

144. On the Russian version, collected by Afanasjev, of *The Donkey's Skin* cf. W. R. S. Ralston, 'Cinderella', in A. Dundes, ed, op. cit., pp. 44–45.

145. Cf. A. Dundes, ' "To Love My Father All": A Psychoanalytic Study of the Folklore Source of King Lear' in op. cit., pp. 230 ff.

146. Cf. Paproth, op. cit., pp. 25 ff. (p. 36, note 57 confutes, with the already cited example on the Ainu, Schmidt's assertion in art. cit., according to which the motif of the missing bone cannot be found in eastern or north eastern Asia).

147. Cf. besides Rooth, op. cit., *Tradition Areas*, p. 137, series o, maps A and B; W. Bascom, *Cinderella in Africa*, in Dundes, ed, op. cit., pp. 148–68; D. Paulme, 'Cendrillon en Afrique', *Critique*, 37 (1980) 288–302. The definition of Cinderella as an exclusively Indo-European fairy tale proposed by Propp (art. cit., p. 36) must of course be corrected on the basis of the essays cited above. Claude Lévi-Strauss (art. cit.) has criticized Rooth for not having included the North American versions (where Cinderella is a boy): but as is shown by the schema elaborated by him (op. cit., *Anthropologie Structurale*, pp. 250–51) they do not include the theme of the slipper.

148. Cf. R. Andree, 'Scapulimantia', in *Boas Anniversary Volume*, New York 1906, pp. 143–65; other material in the article entitled 'Spatulimantia' in *Handwörterbuch des deutschen Aberglaubens*, VIII, Berlin u. Leipzig 1936–37, coll. 125–40; and see also

R. Needham, introduction to A.M. Hocart, *Kings and Councillors*, Chicago 1970 (1st. ed. 1936), pp. LXXIII ff. An indirect reference to the importance attributed by the Jews to the shoulder in the distribution of the sacrificial food in *Gen.* 48, 22.

149. Cf. Andree, art. cit.

150. On this distinction L. de Heusch, 'Possession et chamanisme', in *Pourquoi l'éspouser? et autre essais*, Paris 1971, pp. 226–24, has effectively insisted; subsequently he has reformulated his view, accentuating, in a not always convincing manner, the continuity between the two phenomena ('La folie des dieux et la raison des hommes', in ibid., pp. 285–85.) The major difficulty, for anyone who perceives a sharp distinction, or indeed an antithesis, between shamanism and possession, is constituted by the phase of the 'dramatic trance' (which, in the shamanistic session, follows the 'cataleptic trance'), during which the shaman impersonates various animals, apparently losing his or her own identity to assume another (cf. Lot-Falck, 'Le chamanisme en Sibérie', *Asie du Sud-Est et Monde insulindien*, IV (1973), p. 8; see also Eliade, 'Chamanisme chez les Roumains', *Societas Academica Dacoromara*, VIII (1968), pp. 85, 93, 99 etc.) It should be said that in the phenomena analyzed before this – *benandanti, táltos*, etc. – the 'dramatic trance' is completely absent: therefore no relationship with forms of possession can be postulated.

151. For the connection with shamanism see Friedrich, 'Knochen', art. cit., pp. 207 ff., Nachtigall, art. cit.; K. Jettmar, 'Megalithsystem und Jagdritual bei den Dard-Völkern', in *Tribus*, 9 (1960), pp. 121–34; Gignoux, art. cit. More cautious Eliade, art. cit., pp. 160–65. Also Meuli, 'Die Baumbestattung' in op. cit., pp. 1112–13 speaks, as regards Pelops, of a 'typological link' with shamanism.

152. On the local implications of the cult of Achilles in the island of Leuca cf. M. Rostovzev, *Skythen und der Bosporus*, I, Berlin 1931, p. 4 (who, however, was thinking of Thracian culture).

153. Cf. Burkert, *Homo necans*, Turin 1981, pp. 80–85.

154. On the diffusion of these themes see the excellent essay by L. Schmidt, 'Pelops und die Haselhexe' in *Laos*, I (1951), pp. 67 ff.; idem, Der 'Herr der Tiere' cit., pp. 509– 38. More generic the reference of Burkert, *Homo necans* cit., p. 85.

155. See above, p. 229.

156. Burkert, *Homo necans*, op. cit., p. 84, comments on the 'strange' connection between Pelops and the ram whose throat is cut in his honour.

157. On Tantalus and Lycaon cf. Burkert, op. cit., pp. 73 ff., which mentions the hypothesis of a reciprocal influence between the two myths (on their relationship cf. H. D. Müller, *Mythologie der griechischen Stämme*, I, Göttingen 1857, pp. 110 ff.). On the sacrificial connotations of Lycaon's anthrophagy cf. Detienne, op. cit., pp. 159–60, note 38.

158. Cf. Jean-Pierre Vernant, 'Á la table des hommes. Mythe de fondation du sacrifice chez Hésiode', in Detienne and Vernant, *La cuisine du sacrifice en pays grec*, Paris 1979, pp. 37–132.

159. This line of research was initiated by A. Thomsen, 'Der Trug des Prometheus', in *Archiv für Religionswissenschaft*, XII (1909) (reworking of an essay that appeared in Danish in 1907). Important developments in Meuli's essay, *Griechische Opfer-bräuche*, in op. cit., pp. 907–1021. Other indications in A. Seppilli, *Alla ricerca del senso perduto*, Palermo 1986, pp. 61 ff. The attempt made by Meuli (and echoed by Burkert, op. cit.) to project the ritual of the gathering of the bones into prehistory seems more debatable: see further on, note 219. For other objections to Meuli, cf. Detienne (above, p. 17); P. Vidal-Naquet, 'Caccia e sacrificio nell' "Orestea"', in op. cit., p. 124; G. S. Kirk, 'Some Methodological Pitfalls in the Study of Ancient Greek sacrifice (in Particular)', in *Le sacrifice dans l'antiquité*, J. Rudhardt and O. Reverdin, eds, Geneva 1980, pp. 41 ff.

160. Cf. G. Charachidzé, *Prométhée ou le Caucase*, Paris 1986, pp. 333 ff.
161. Cf. M.N. Pogrebova, 'Les Scythes en Transcaucasie', in *Dialogues d'histoire ancienne*, 10 (1984), p. 269–84.
162. G. Charachidzé described (op. cit., p. 335, note 3) an essay – so far as I know not yet published – in which a passage of Apollonius of Rhodes' *Argonautica* (IV, 463–81) would be interpreted in the light of Georgian myths and Abkhazi rituals on the theme of dismemberment (the interpretative suggestions of M. Delcourt, 'Le partage du corps royal', in *Studi e materiali di storia delle religioni*, 34, 1963, pp. 3–25, and H. S. Versnel, 'A Note on the maschalismos of Apsyrtos', in *Mnemosyne*, 26, 1973, pp. 62–63, do not seem very persuasive). He does not however, foresee a discussion on the contest between Prometheus and Zeus in regard to the institution of sacrifice (a theme almost completely absent in Charachidzé's book). On the diffusion of the legends of Amirani cf. op. cit., pp. 14–16.
163. Cf. Vernant, art. cit., p. 45, note; and see a reference of J. Rudhart, 'Les myths grecs relatifs à l'instauration du sacrifice: les roles corrélatifs de Prométhée et de son fils Deucalion' in *Museum Helveticum*, 27 (1970), p. 5, note 13.
164. Hesiod, *Theogony*, vv. 528–39 (trans. G. Arrighetti, Milan 1984). Herodotus, *Histories*.
165. On Herodotus IV, 59–62, cf. F. Hartog, 'Le boeuf "autocuiseur" et les boissons d'Arés', in Detienne and Vernant, op. cit., pp. 251–69.
166. Cf. K. Neumann, *Die Hellenen im Skythenlande*, I, Berlin 1855, pp. 263–64, which cites a long passage from the account of a journey published in the middle of the eighteenth century by J. G. Gmelin. The importance of Neumann's book is not only to be found in the thesis of the Mongolian origin of the Scythians, which one can accept or reject (as Dumézil, *Légendes sur les Nartes suivies de cinq notes mythologiques*, Paris 1930, pp. 161–62, does implicitly in regard to another passage). The cultural linkages indicated by Neumann are an anticipation of Meuli (who apparently used his work very little).
167. Cf. Hartog, art. cit., p. 264.
168. For some culinary correspondences cf. the comment of M. L. West about *Theogony*, Oxford 1978, p. 319.
169. Cf. instead Hartog, art. cit., pp. 262–63: '*Sans doute Prométhée recouvre-t-il les chairs et les entrailles lourdes de graisse du ventre du boeuf, mais il s'agit d'une action de tromperie: donner à la part en fait la meilleur un aspect immangeable. . . .*' On the same interpretative line, but with a bit more caution, Vernant reasons: '*Décrivant les modalités du sacrifice chez les Scythes, Hérodote nous apporte des informations qui, plus encore peut-être que sur les moeurs de ce peuple, nous éclairent sur l'imaginaire grec concernant la gastér . . .*' (ibid., p. 93).
170. In reference to all of this I am following the introduction of Jean-Pierre Vernant to M. Detienne, 'Les jardins d'Adonis' (1972), now in *Myths and Society in Ancient Greece*, Brighton 1980, pp. 135–72, in particular pp. 166–69.
171. On all this see M. L. West, *The Orphic Poems*, Oxford 1983, pp. 1–26.
172. Cf. Jeanmaire, *Dioniso*, Italian ed., Tunn 1972, pp. 371–89; M. Detienne, 'Il Dioniso orfico e il bollito arrosto', in op. cit., pp. 123–64; West, op. cit., pp. 140–75, where among other matters he maintains (pp. 164–66) that the theme of the origin of the human race from the murderous Titans constitutes a late Neo-Platonic addition. According to Detienne, op. cit., pp. 143 ff., it is instead an integral part of the Orphic myth.
173. Cf. the testimonies presented by A.-F. Laurens, 'L'enfant entre l'épée et le chaudron. Contribution à une lecture iconographique', in *Dialogues d' histoire ancienne*, 10 (1984), pp. 203-52, in particular pp. 228 ff.

174. Cf. Jeanmaire, op. cit., pp. 385 ff. which mentions Demophoön and Achilles. On Pelias as Pelops' double cf. Gruppe, op. cit. I, p.145. On the comparison between Pelops and the child Dionysos cf. Gernet, op. cit., pp. 75–76.

175. On this point hinges the interpretation of Detienne, art. cit. (cf. in particular p. 139). On the question in general see also Burkert, op. cit., p. 237, note 29.

176. This last version, transmitted by Philodemus of Gadara and Diodorus, has been wilfully overlooked by M. Detienne (art. cit., p. 144). But see Jeanmaire, op. cit., p. 381.

177. In passing, one should remember that O. Rudbeck (on whom see above, p. 214, note 48) compared the resurrection of the billy goat by Thor and that of Dionysos by Demeter, in a list of Hyperborean myths spread among other populations: cf. *Atlantica*, Uppsala 1679–1702, 4 vols, II, p. 30.

178. Cf. Jeanmaire, op. cit., pp. 87–89; Hartog, *Le miroir d'Hérodote*, Paris 1980, p. 81 ff.

179. Cf. West, op. cit., pp. 17–19, idem, 'The Orphics of Olbia', *Zeitschrift für Papyrologie und Epigraphik*, 45 (1982), pp. 17–29, which analyzes three writing tablets. On the *recto* of the first (the one discussed above) one reads '*bios-thanatos-bios-alētheia-A-* [two signs in zigzag form] *-Dio[nysos]- orphikoi*'; on pp. 21–22, the reading of the last two letters of the word *orphikoi* is justified. On the *recto* of the second: '*eiréné-polemos-alētheia-pseudos- Dio(nysos)-* [a sign in the form of a zigzag] *– A*' (Peace-war-truth-deception-Dionysos-A). On the *recto* of the third: '*Dio(nisos)-alétheia-(. . .) ia- psychē-A*' (Dionusius-truth-?-soul-A). West reminds us that the person who wrote the first tablet made an effort to write these terms *bios-thanatos-bios* on the same line, without starting a new line, evidently in order to emphasize that it was a single sequence. The relationship between this triple sequence and the counterposed couples of the second tablet is not clear.

180. Cf. Detienne, art. cit., p. 131 and note 35.

181. Detienne (ibid., p. 139) is in disagreement with this opinion.

182. Plutarch, *De esu carnium*, I, 96.

183. Cf. West, op. cit., pp. 143–50. Jeanmaire, op. cit., has followed along this interpretative line; see also Gernet's review, op. cit., p. 89, which emphasizes the presence of shamanistic elements in the figure of Dionysos.

184. Cf. Dumézil, *Storie degli Sciti*, Milan 1980, pp. 348–54.

185. On this distinction, besides the essay of L. de Heusch cited above (note 150) see, more specifically, Dodds, *The Greeks and the Irrational*, p. 177; Couliano, op. cit., pp. 15–17; H. Jeanmaire senses the importance of the Scythian negative attitude towards Scyles (op. cit., p. 98), but does not go deeper into the question of Scythian shamanism. Also the pages of F. Hartog on the episode of Scyles (op. cit., pp. 82–102) are vitiated by the lack of a discussion on the interpretation of Herodotus, IV, 73–75 presented by Meuli (see above, p. 218, note 4).

186. See above, p. 208–10.

187. So far as I know, the first to juxtapose Orpheus' journey to the nether world and the ecstasies of the shamans (Laplanders, in this instance) was Rudbeck: cf. op. cit., III, p. 434.

188. Cf. Burkert, op. cit., p. 296 which speaks of 'revolution'.

189. I am developing a suggestion contained in a fine page of L. Gernet (op. cit., pp. 68–69). For a general picture cf. Burkert, op. cit., pp. 290 ff. Always precious, Dodds: op. cit.

190. Cf. above, p. 238.

191. On all this cf. Charachidzé, op. cit., pp. 238–40.

192. Ibid., pp. 249 ff.

193. Ibid., pp. 260 and 268–69. But see also the Ossetian Soslan (above, p. 242).

194. Ibid, pp. 251–52.
195. Cf. *Ventisette fiabe raccolte nel Mantovano*, G. Barozzi, ed, Milan 1976, pp. 466–73 (narrator: Alda Pezzini Ottoni, who on pp. 463–65 tells the story of her life). I thank Maurizio Bertolotti for having singled out the fable of Sbadilon in this fine volume.
196. Ibid., p. 473 (I have corrected a material oversight in the transcription.)
197. Ibid., p. 469; and see G. Barozzi, 'Esperienze di un ricercatore di fiabe', in ibid., p. 22 (which uses a slightly different transcription).
197. There exists, however, another possibility. According to a legend (Russian or
bis Vogul-Ostyakak) the bear-hero, when he has exhausted his reserves of food, feeds the eagle who is carrying him by cutting off his calf: cf. W. Bogoras, 'Le mythe de l'Animal-Dieux(!) mourant et ressuscitant', *Atti del XXII Congresso internazionake degli americanisti*, Rome 1928, p. 35 ff., in particular p. 38, which unfortunately does not give any precise geographical indications (this minimal but striking confirmation of Eurasian cultural unity has, once again, been pointed out to me, by Maurizio Bertolotti).
198. Cf. Charachidzé, op. cit., in particular the review on p. 287; in the Caucasian cycle one often finds a winged dog rather than an eagle. It should be noted that Sbadilon's exploits, like those of Amirani, are based exclusively on physical strength. Prometheus, 'he who foresees', has completely different characteristics.
199. Ibid., pp. 33–34 (where the initiatic nuance in the episode is rightly emphasized). Also Ambri, the giant who is neither alive nor dead, has an inert leg (pp. 50 ff.).
200. Ibid., pp. 46–47.
201. Here one touches on a profound mythical trait (to be juxtaposed to the isomorphism between the two bands that fight in the ecstatic battles for fertility: see above, p. 262.
202. Charachidzé takes the contrary view, op. cit., p. 269. Prometheus' deambulatory anomaly has been intuited (but argued in a more than debatable fashion) by C. A. P. Ruck, 'Mushrooms and Philosophers', in R. G. Wasson et al., *Persephone's Quest*, New Haven and London 1986, pp. 151–77, on the basis of Aristophanes' *The Birds*, 1553–64. On p. 174 Ruck has identified the shamanistic characteristic of lameness in the Greek ambit.
203. It has been supposed that this last hypothesis may have been influenced by the politico-ideological atmosphere of the 40s and 50s, the time during which they were formulated. The first hypothesis is mentioned also by S. Piggott, in the introduction to E. D. Phillips, *The Royal Hordes. Nomad Peoples of the Steppes*, London 1965, pointing to the pastoral elements present in the most ancient Celtic sagas.
204. On Baba-Yaga cf. Propp, *Le radici storiche* cit., pp. 323–29. The other figures merge in the folkloric tradition: cf. Lebeuf, 'Conjectures sur la "Reine" Pédauque', in *Histoire de l'Académie Royale des Inscriptions et Belles-Lettres*, XXIII (1756), pp. 227–35; K. Simrock, *Bertha die Spinnerin*, Frankfurt a. Main 1853; W. Hertz, 'Die Rätsel der Königin von Saba', in *Zeitschrift für deutsches Alterthum*, XXVII (1883), pp. 1–33, in particular pp. 23–24; in general A. Chastel, 'La légende de la reine de Saba', republished with additions of 'Fables, formes figures', Paris 1978, I, pp. 53 ff. (the punctual reference to Oedipus is on p. 79). On the persistence of the theme in the folkloric ambit cf. C. and D. Arbry, 'Des Parques aux fées et autres êtres sauvages . . .', in *Le monde alpin et rhodanien*, 10 (1982), p. 258. It should be noted that in the French medieval texts 'Berthe aux grands pieds' (identified with Charlemagne's mother) has two deformed feet: in the *Reali di Francia* (V,1) only one. This last detail comes from an unknown source, certainly closer to folkloric tradition (according to P. Rajna, *Ricerche intorno ai Reali di Francia*, Bologna 1872,

pp. 238–39, who, however, mistakenly casts doubt on the Berthe-Perchta resemblance). In addition, see the entry for 'Fuss' in *Handwörterbuch des deutschen Aberglaubens*, II, Berlin and Leipzig 1930–31, coll. 225–26.

205. Cf. J. Haekel, 'Idolkult und Dualsystem bei den Ugriern (zum Problem des eurasiatischen Totemismus)' in *Archiv für Völkerkunde*, I (1946), pp. 95–163, in particular pp. 123 ff., cited in part also by A. Alföldi, *Die Struktur des voretruskischen Römerstaates*, Heidelberg 1976, pp. 146–47, together with an essay by B. Munkácsi (which I have not seen).

206. Cf. Alföldi, *Die Struktur* op. cit., pp. 141–46; and see the comment of J. G. Frazer on *Fasti*, London, 1929, II, p. 365. See besides J. Hubaux, 'Comment Furius Camillus s'empara de Véius', in *Académie Royale de Belgique. Bulletin de la classe de lettres etc.*, 5ᵉ s., 38 (1952), pp. 610–22; and, by the same author, *Rome et Véies* Paris 1958, pp. 221 ff., in particular pp. 279 ff.

207. The first to see a resemblance between them was A. Alföldi (op. cit., pp. 141–46). In this singular book (dedicated to K. Meuli and M. Rostovzev) Alföldi re–elaborates, and more often juxtaposes research carried out over a fifty year span. Extremely acute insights are mixed up with antiquated, untenable ideas (as, for example, the connection between tripartite ideology and matriarchal society, bipartite ideology and patriarchal society). See the very harsh book review by A. Momigliano, who however, had called a preliminary draft a 'splendid study' (cf. *Sesto contributo alla storia degli studi classici e del mondo antico*, Rome 1980, II, pp. 682–85, concerning *Die Struktur: Quarto contributo...*, Rome 1969, pp. 629–31, and concerning A. Alföldi, *Die trojanischen Urahnen der Römer*, Basel 1957).

208. Alföldi, op. cit., p. 146, speaks rather vaguely of 'institutional analogies' which would emerge from the comparison of the two myths: this is evidently an allusion to the theme of the double monarchy (pp. 151–62). Further on he identifies a possible point of contact in the Indo-Iranian world between the Eurasian steppes and the Mediterranean (p. 161), while he barely mentions the Scythians; he frequently evokes the hypothesis of a common genesis, which would explain the resemblances between the society of central Asia and the society of ancient Rome. Such a hypothesis seems to depend implicitly on the migrations, themselves hypothetical, that would have been verified from East to West before the 1st millennium BC (cf. above, p. 218, note 6). It should be said that Alföldi, who refers in a general way to Lévi-Strauss' *Le cru et le cuit*, seems to ignore the discussions of the ethnologists on dualistic systems. See the critical observations of J. Poucet, 'Un héritage eurasien dans le Rome préétrusque?' in *L'Antiquité classique*, 44 (1975), pp. 645–51, and of R. Werner in *Gymnasium*, 83 (1976), pp. 228–38.

209. On the generalized exchange cf. Lévi-Strauss, *Les structures élémentaires de la parenté*, Paris 1949, pp. 486–87 and *passim*; on the counterposition between 'bone' and 'flesh' encountered in India, Tibet, China, Mongolia and Siberia, cf. pp. 459–502. It has been supposed that strong cultural ties must have existed among these countries in the past (ibid., pp. 462–63). Perhaps they extended much farther towards the West, since the Ossetians also distinguish between relations 'of the same bone' (*ju staeg*) and relations 'of the same blood' (*ju tug*): cf. Vernadsky, 'The Eurasian Nomads and their Art in the History of Civilisation', *Saeculum*, I (1950), p. 405, who, however, does not explain the significance of these terms. It should also be remembered that a practice like scapulimancy, which attributes to the bones a precise cultural significance, is especially widespread in central Asia (see above, note 148). Perhaps R. Needham's witticism 'if scapulimancy, why not prescriptive alliance?', which supposes an historical diffusion even in the second case (intro. to A. M. Hocart, op. cit., p. LXXXV) is less paradoxical than it seems.

210. On the absence of exogamy in Latium, against the opinion expressed by Alföldi, see Momigliano, op. cit., p. 684.

211. Cf. Lévi-Strauss, (*Les structures*) op. cit., pp. 87–88, which I am following almost literally here.

212. Cf. J. Needham, introduction to Hocart, op. cit., pp. LXXXIV-LXXXVIII. The structural thesis was formulated with exemplary clarity by Hocart (pp. 262–89).

213. Here I paraphrase (in reverse order) a very dense page of Lévi-Strauss (*Les structures*: op. cit., p. 175) in tense discussion with Frazer. The conclusion is echoed in a much more recent text (*L'homme nu*: op. cit., pp. 539–40). It should be noted that Hocart had already underlined the fact that the interaction explains the social dichotomy and not the other way round (op. cit., pp. 289–90). In *Paroles données*: op. cit., Lévi-Strauss has reviewed the discussion on dualist systems (pp. 262-67), referring to the 'already structuralist thought of Hocart' (p.263).

214. For that which precedes this see the very fine essay of K. Pomian, 'Collezione', in *Encyclopedia Einaudi*, 3, Turin 1978, pp. 330–64.

215. Cf. J. Piaget, *La construction du réel chez l'enfant*, Neuchâtel 1950, pp. 36 ff.; idem, *La formation du symbole chez l'enfant*, Neuchâtel 1945. A possible convergence between these results and the psychoanalytical perspective emerges, if I am not mistaken, from Freud's very dense pages entitled *The negation* (1925) where one reads among other things: 'The original pleasure-ego wants to introject into itself everything that is good and eject from itself everything that is bad. What is bad, what is alien to the ego and what is external are, to begin with, identical. (. . .) But it is evident that a precondition for the setting up of reality-testing is that objects shall have been lost which once brought real satisfaction' (I quote from the translation published in the *Complete Works*, London 1961, vol. XIX, pp. 237–238. On this passage see J. Hyppolite 'Commento parlato sulla "Verneinung" di Freud' in J. Lacan, *Scritti*, It. trans. Turin 1974, II, pp. 885–93.

216. The child was Freud's grandson: cf. 'Al di là del principio de piacere', in *Opere*, IX, It. trans. Turin 1977, pp. 200–3, where the episode is presented as an illustration of the compulsion to repeat a disagreeable situation. That the act had been born from 'an impulse for appropriation that is independent of the fact that the memory in itself was pleasurable or not', was, according to Freud, a less probable hypothesis. E. De Martino developed it, implicitly proposing a re-reading of the idea of the 'loss of the presence' previously formulated in *Il mondo magico* (cf. *Furore simbolo valore*, Milan 1962, pp. 20–22.)

217. The distinction between *things* and *semiophores* proposed by Pomian is certainly valid on the conceptual plane, but it does not exclude the existence of the intermediate cases: above all, in a phase that precedes the production of objects that have as their sole purpose that of signifying.

218. [J. Potocki], *Essai sur l'histoire universelle et recherches sur celle de la Sarmatie*, Warsaw 1789, p. 89: '*ainsi le polite qui sonde à des grandes profondeurs et voit sa corde filer jusqu'a la derniére brasse, n'en conclud point qu'il a trouvé le fond, mais qu'il ne doit point espérer de l'atteindre*'.

219. The prudence of A. Leroi-Gourhan, *Les religions de la préhistoire*, Paris 1976, pp. 15 ff. is echoed, on a more specific plane, by L. R. Binford, *Bones. Ancient Men and Modern Myths*, New York 1981, pp. 35 ff. (on the difficulty of demonstrating human intervention in the piles of broken animal bones that go back to the Paleolithic age). In general see H.-G. Bandi, 'Zur Frage eines Bären- oder Opferkultes im ausgehenden Altpaläolithikum der alpinen Zonen', in *Helvetia Antiqua (Festschrift Emil Vogt)*, Zurich 1966, pp. 1–8.

220. 'Animals came from over the horizon. They belonged *there* and *here*. Likewise they

were mortal and immortal. An animal's blood flowed like human blood, but its species was undying and each lion was Lion, each ox was Ox. This – maybe the first existential dualism – was reflected in the treatment of animals. They were subjected *and* worshipped, bred *and* sacrificed', J. Berger, *About Looking*, New York 1980, pp. 4–5; there follows a passage about the ambivalence of peasants towards their animals).

221. Cf. Lévi-Strauss, 'Le Pére Noël supplicie', art. cit.; and see above p. 198, note 11.
222. See above, p. 196.
223. Cf. G. Dumézil, (*La religione romana*) op. cit., pp. 224 ff. The untenable interpretation of R. Schilling, 'Romulus l'élu et Rémus le réprouvé', in *Revue des études latines*, 38 (1960), pp. 182–99, according to which Remus' behaviour would constitute a sacrilege which, in Ovid's intention, would put him in a bad light, hence justifying the murder.
224. Cf. L. Delaby, 'Mourir pour vivre avec les ours', in *L'Ours, l'Autre de l'homme. Études mongoles*, II (1980), pp. 17–45, in particular pp. 28 ff.
225. Cf. the observations of Propp, (*Le radici storiche*) op. cit., pp. 11 ff. and 120 ff. Further material is presented, in a comparative historical/religious perspective, by Gallini, art. cit.
226. Cf. M. Marconi, 'Usi funerari nella Colchide Circea', in *Rendiconti del R. Istituto Lombardo di scienze e lettere*, LXXXVI (1942–43), pp. 309 ff. To the bibliography cited add J. Jankó, in E. de Zichy, *Voyages au Caucase et en Asie centrale*, Budapest 1897, I, pp. 72–73, on the Ossetians' custom of hanging dead men sewn up in the pelts of oxen or buffalos. On the Yakuts cf. J.-P. Roux, *La mort chez les peuples altaïques anciens et médiévaux*, Paris 1963, p. 138. In his discussion with V.I. Abaev (cf. note 228) G. Dumézil also comments on the passage from Apollonius Rhodius, without, however, taking these studies into account (*Storie degli sciti*) op. cit., p. 274).
227. Cf. H. Nachtigall, 'Die erhöhte Bestattung in Nord- und Hockhasien', *Anthropos*, 48 (1953), pp. 44–70; see also Propp, (*Le radici storiche*) op. cit., pp. 363–69; Meuli, (*Die Baumbestattung*) op. cit.; Roux, op. cit., pp. 137 ff. A presentation of African data in P. M. Küsters, 'Das Grab der Afrikaner', in *Anthropos*, 16–17 (1921–22), pp. 927–33.
228. Cf. V. I. Abaev, 'Le cheval de Troie. Parallèles Caucasiens', in *Annales E.S.C.*, 18 (1963), pp. 1041 ff. who emphasizes the shamanistic element; Dumézil, op. cit., pp. 268–77, who denies it (a new intervention by Dumézil, 'Encore la peau de boeuf', in *La Courtisane et les seigneurs colorés*, Paris 1983, pp. 139–46, touches on a marginal point). The ritual of resurrection based on the gathering of bones, ignored by both scholars, from one perspective fully justifies Abaev, while from the other it gives prominence to the importance of the passage from Apollonius Rhodius (III, 200–9), remembered by Dumézil. More generic is Abaev's observation on the animal disguises worn by Eurasian hunters (on their emigration beyond the Bering Strait since the Paleolithic age cf. B. Anell, 'Animal Hunting Disguises among the North American Indians', in *Lapponica*, A. Furumark ed, Lund 1964, pp. 1–34). The use described by Apollonius aimed at the resurrection of the deceased had already been emphasized by S. Ferri, 'Kirke I Kirke II Kirke III. Mitologia lessicale o psicologia "medievale"?' in *Letterature comparate, problemi e metodo, Studi in onore di Ettore Paratore*, I, Bologna, 1981, pp. 57–66, in particular p. 60; see also idem, 'Problemi e documenti archeologici II (XI). Stele daunie – Una nuova figurazione di Erinni' in *Accademia dei Lincei. Rendiconti della classe di scienze morali*, s. VIII, XXVI (1971) fasc. 5–6, pp. 341 ff.
229. Cf. J. Hnefill Adalsteinsson, *Under the Cloak. The Acceptance of Christianity in*

Iceland. . ., Uppsala 1978, pp. 80–123 (only the second version of the *Islendigabók* has been preserved). The hypothesis, discussed by J. Lindow (*Ethnologia Scandinavica*, 1979, pp. 178–79) according to which the meditation under the cloak was nothing but a piece of play-acting, is hard to verify; in any case it does not impair the interpretation set forth above.

230. Cf. H. R. Ellis (later Ellis Davidson), *The Road to Hell*, Cambridge 1943, p. 126; P. Buchholz, *Shamanistische Züge in der altisländischen Überlieferung*, Bamberg 1968; H. R. Ellis Davidson, 'Hostile Magic in the Icelandic Sagas' in *The Witch Figure*, V. Newall, ed, London 1973, pp. 20–41.

231. Cf. Ellis Davidson, art. cit., p. 37; D. Strömbäck, 'The Concept of the Soul in the Nordic Tradition', in *Arv*, 31 (1975), pp. 5–22, which refers back to his fundamental study *Sejd* (1935); Hnefill Adalsteinsson, op. cit., pp. 119–21.

232. See above, p. 171.

233. Cf. Ellis Davidson, art. cit., p. 27, which refers back to E. Holtved, 'Eskimo Shamanism', in *Studies in Shamanism*, p. 26.

234. Cf. R. Hakluyt, *The Principal Navigations, Voyages, Traffiques and Discoveries of the English Nation* . . ., I, London 1599, pp. 157–58 is commented upon by J. Balázs, 'Über die Ekstase des ungarischen Schamanen', in *Glaubenswelt*, pp. 70 ff.

235. Cf. M. Bartels, 'Isländischer Brauch und Volksglaube in Bezug auf die Nachkommenschaft', in *Zeitschrift für Ethnologie*, 32 (1900), pp. 70–71.

236. Cf. Boyer, *Le monde du double*, Paris 1986, pp. 39 ff. Still useful M. Rieger, 'Über den nordischen Fylgienglauben', in *Zeitschrift für deutsches Altertum und deutsche Litteratur* 42 (1898), pp. 277–90; W. Henzen, *Über die Träume in der altnordischen Sagalitteratur*, Leipzig 1890, pp. 34 ff. Further bibliography in E. Mundal, *Fylgjemotiva i norrøn litteratur*, Oslo 1974. On sagas in general, see the useful review of J. L. Byock, 'Saga Form, Oral Prehistory, and the Icelandic Social Context', in *New Literary History*, XVI (1984), pp. 153–73. The *fylgia* has been regarded as the historical antecedent of the 'second sight' by W. -E. Peuckert, 'Der zweite Leib', in *Niederdeutsche Zeitschrift für Volkskunde*, 16 (1938), pp. 174–79, criticizing the exclusively psychological perspective of K. Schméing: of the latter see ' "Zweites Gesicht" und "Zweites Leib" ', ivi, 19 (1941), pp. 85–87 (while I have not seen *Das Zweite Gesicht in Niederdeutschland*, Leipzig 1937).

237. Cf. Belmont, *Les signes de la naissance*, Paris 1971, pp. 52 ff. and G. Chiesa Isnardi, 'Il lupo mannaro come superuomo' in *Il superuomo*, E. Zolla ed, III, Florence 1973, pp. 33 ff., which derives from de Vries, *Altgermanische Religionsgeschichte*, Berlin 1957, pp. 222 ff. (but see E. Mogk, *Germanische Mythologie*, Leipzig 1907, pp. 42–43). See now Boyer, op. cit., pp. 39 ff.

238. Cf. Güntert, 'Über altisländische Berserkergeschichten': Dumézil, *Heur et malheur du guerrier* cit.

239. Cf. Lehtisalo, *Entwurf einer Mythologie der Jurak-Samojeden*, Helsinki 1924, p. 114. Also among the Cuna of Panama the *nele* (seers) are those who are born with a caul (*kurkin*, 'hat'): cf. C. Severi, 'The invisible path. Ritual Representation of Suffering in Cuna Traditional Thought' in *RES, Anthropology and Aesthetics*, 14 (Autumn 1987), p. 71.

240. Cf. C. H. Tillhagen, 'The Conception of the Nightmare in Sweden', in *Humaniora. Essays in Literature – Folklore – Bibliography Honouring Archer Taylor on His Seventieth Birthday*, W. D. Hand and G. O. Arlt, eds., Locust Valley (N.Y.) 1960, pp. 316–29; see also Jakobson and Szeftel, 'The Vseslav Epos', *Memoirs of the American Folklore Society*, 42 (1947) p. 61, note 30.

241. The passage is cited at the beginning of N. Belmont's book (op. cit., p. 19) which, however, does not dwell on this point. A mention of the analogy between swaddling

clothes and the shroud occurs in W. Deonna, 'Les thèmes symboliques de la légende de Pero et de Micon' in *Latomus*, 15 (1956), p. 495.

242. Cf. S. Reinach, 'Le voile de l'oblation', in *Cultes, mythes et religions*, Paris 1922, I, p. 298 ff. And see in general H. Freier, *Caput velare*, Tübingen 1963.

243. Cf. J. Heurgon, 'Le "Ver sacrum" romain de 217', in *Latomus* 15 (1956), pp. 137–58. '*Perductos in adultam aetatem velabant atque ita extra fines suos exigebant*', can be read in a passage by Verrius Flaccus mentioned by Festus: cf. Ferri, op. cit., p. 59 (but the reference to Orphism seems gratuitous).

244. Cf. Bartels, art. cit., pp. 70–71; J. Hoops, 'Das Verhüllen des Haupts bei Toten, ein angelsächsisch-nordischer Brauch', in *Englische Studien*', 54 (1920), pp. 19–23.

245. Cf. Delcourt, op. cit., pp. 128–29, which develops a suggestion of H. Güntert, *Der arische Weltkönig und Heiland* (which I have not seen). On *pilleus, galerus* etc. and their implications see K. Meuli, 'Altrömischer Maskenbrauch' in op. cit., II, pp. 268–70. A reference to the importance of these themes in respect to being born in a caul can be found in Belmont, op. cit., p. 195. The case of Telesphorus, the small hooded figure, perhaps of Celtic origin, is controversial. He is often represented alongside Asclepius: on the various interpretations (phallic or funereal demon, genie who protects sleep) see W. Deonna, *De Télesphore au 'moine bourru'. Dieux, génies et démons encapuchonnés*, Brussels 1955.

246. Cf. *The Night Battles*, p. 160.

247. 'In the earthly world you cannot seize me because I live just as well among the dead as among the unborn' can be read on Paul Klee's gravestone (this is a passage from his *Diaries*): cf. F. Klee, *Vita e opera di Paul Klee*. It. trans. Turin 1971, p. 82. The hereafter is seen as the 'realm of the dead and embryos' by G. Lüling (*Die Wiederentdeckung des Propheten Muhammad*, Erlangen 1981, pp. 297 ff.) who, analyzing the symbolic significance of Mohammed's cloak (also compared to the amnion), arrives by different routes at conclusions that are similar to those formulated here (I thank D. Metzler very warmly for having told me about these pages). A comparison with shamanistic ecstasy is explicitly proposed by J. R. Porter, 'Muhammad's Journey to Heaven', in *Numen*, XXI (1974), pp. 64–80.

248. Cf. Güntert, *Kalypso* op. cit. (a very erudite and intelligent book).

249. Cf. Saxus Grammaticus, *Gesta Danorum*, J. Olrik and H. Raeder eds., I, Hauniae 1931, p. 30 (1,8,14): on the possible derivation of this page from Norwegian or Icelandic models, ibid., pp. XXIV -XXV (and see the comment of P. E. Müller, Haunia 1858, pp. 65–66). The presence of Odin-like themes in the description of the beyond, alongside remembrances of Latin authors (from Vergil to Martianus Capella) is underlined by P. Herrmann, *Die Heldensagen des Saxo Grammaticus*, II, Leipzig 1922, pp. 102–3; in the same sense see Dumézil, *Du mythe au roman*, Paris 1970, p. 107, note 1. The shamanistic implications of Hadingus' subterranean journey have been recognized by A. Closs, 'Die Religion des Semnonenstammes', in *Wiener Beiträge zur Kulturgeschichte und Linguistik*, IV (1936), p. 667.

250. Cf. Saxus Grammaticus, op. cit., I, 37; and see Riemschneider, op. cit., p. 47 (but her overall interpretation is untenable).

251. Cf. Balázs, art. cit., pp. 56 ff.; Viski, *Volksbrauch der Ungarn*, Budapest, 1932, pp. 15 ff. On the possibility of drawing upon a pre-Indo-European stratum in this ambit see in general Güntert, op. cit., pp. 44–54.

252. Cf. Meuli, 'Altrömischer Maskenbrauch' in op. cit., p. 268 (and in general 'Die deutschen Masken', in *Gesammelte Schriften* (op. cit), I, pp. 69 ff., and *Schweizer Masken und Maskenbräuche*, I, pp. 177 ff.); F. Altheim, *Terra Mater*, Giessen 1931, pp. 48-65; P. Toschi, *Le origini del teatro italiano*, Turin 1976, pp. 169–72; on *masca e talamasca*, L. Lazzerini, 'Arlecchino, le mosche, le streghe e le origini del

teatro popolare', in *Studi mediolatini e volgari*', XXV (1977), pp. 141–44 (but the entire essay is rich in insights and suggestions). In this context one should probably also insert the hood of the Harlequin's band, on which see Schmitt, op. cit., pp. 226–27. The thesis of a necessary connection between disguises and dualistic organizations is confuted by A. Kroeber and C. Holt, 'Masks and Moieties as a Culture Complex', in *Journal of the Royal Anthropological Institute*, 50 (1920), pp. 452–60: but a significant convergence between these phenomena (doubly significant in the light of the considerations expressed above) seems undeniable. In this case one must agree, in substance, with W. Schmidt (ibid., pp. 553 ff.)

253. Cf. I. Matte Blanco, *The Unconscious as Infinite Sets, An Essay in Bi-Logic*, London 1975 ... This book responds indirectly to the request, addressed by Jean-Pierre Vernant, 'to linguists, logicians, mathematicians' to furnish mythology with 'the instrument that it lacks: the structural model of a logic that is not the binary one of yes and no, of a logic diverse from the logic of the *logos*' ('Ragioni del mito', in op. cit., p. 250). An attempt at the application of Matte Blanco's research has been made by B. Bucher, 'Ensembles infinis et histoire-mythe. Inconscient structural et inconscient psycho-analytique', in *L'homme*, XXI (1981), pp. 526. Vernant's statement which is quoted above has been set as an epigraph to an essay by J. Derrida, 'Chôra', in *Poikilia*, pp. 265–96.

254. Cf. Lévi-Strauss, *La vasaia*, op. cit., pp. 169 ff.

255. Cf. idem, *L'homme nu* op. cit., pp. 581–82: '*s'il s'agit application particulière d'un procédé tout à la fois fondamental et archaïque, on peut concevoir qu'il se soit perpétué, non par l'observation consciente des règles, mais par conformisme inconscient à une structure* mythique *intuitivement perçue d'aprés des modèles antérieures élaborés dans les mêmes conditions*' (I have substituted *mythique* for *poétique*). Lévi-Strauss is speaking of a difficulty raised by F. de Saussure in regard to his own theory of the importance of anagrams in ancient poetry: the lack of explicit testimonies of theoreticians or poets on their use.

256. According to Matte Blanco, *The Unconscious*, pp. 44–45 and *passim*, there is a principle in operation in the unconscious system on the basis of which all relations are treated as symmetrical: for example, the father generates the son, therefore the son generates the father. In clinical observation, however, this principle is only applied to a limited degree: '*the principle of symmetry appears at a certain point and like a potent acid, dissolves all logic within reach that is, in the area where it is being applied. However the rest of the logical structure remains intact*' (p. 62, the italics are in the text; the observation could be extended to the myth). The analysis of the mode of being symmetrical (but Bucher proposes to speak of 'symmetricizing tendency': art. cit., p. 21) permits us to describe, even if in necessarily inadequate terms, the functioning of the unconscious system. On the metaphor, see R. Jakobson, 'Two Aspects of Language and Two Types of Aphasic Disturbances' in *Selected Writings*, II, The Hague 1971, pp. 239-259.) that rediscovers the counter position between the metaphoric pole and the metonymical pole (including synecdoche) also in dreams (referring to Freud). (p.44). In *The Interpretation of Dreams* Freud discusses at a certain point (It. trans. cit., p. 319) the example of a writer who, thinking in a half-wakeful state of correcting an awkward passage in his prose, sees himself in the act of planing down a piece of wood. Lévi-Strauss discusses this passage, remarking: 'the metaphor consists in a regressive operation carried out by the wild thought that annuls momentarily the synecdoche by means of which the domesticated thought operates' (op. cit., p. 177). The convergence with the passage from Matte Blanco cited above is perhaps involuntary, unless it was indirectly solicited by an essay of Bucher's that appeared in *L'homme* (art. cit.). In it,

Matte Blanco's theories are offered as a means of overcoming the opposition, formulated by Lévi-Strauss, between the unconscious expressed in mythical thought and the individual unconscious of psychoanalysis.

257. In the Palaeolithic age there could have been cultural exchanges which did not leave any documentary trace, as Lévi-Strauss has remarked several times when questions of this kind have been put to him: Cf. *(Paroles données)* op. cit., p. 134. The negative replies of history (cf. 'Le dédoublement', art. cit., p. 273: 'Si l'histoire, sollicitée sans trêve (et qu'il faut solliciter *d'abord*) répond non. . .') can never be absolute.

CONCLUSION

1. We started with an event: the emergence of the image of the witches' Sabbath in the Western Alps during the second half of the fourteenth century. The attempt to decipher its folkloric components has taken us very far in space and time. But only thus was it possible to show that an important part of our cultural patrimony originates – through channels that largely escape us – from the Siberian hunters, the shamans of Northern and Central Asia, and the nomads of the steppes.[1]

Without this slow sedimentation the image of the Sabbath could not have emerged. Beliefs and practices of a shamanistic flavour can also be found in the Alpine region. We have already spoken about the goddess resuscitator of animals, the ritualistic battles for fertility fought by the *punchiadurs* of the Grisons.[2] The testimony collected by folklorists over the last two centuries indicates that in the Wallensian valleys of the Piedmont – besides stories about werewolves, fairies and processions of the dead – there also circulated variants of the legend of King Guntram reported by Paul the Deacon. The insect (butterfly, bumble bee, horse fly) which enters the mouth of an inanimate person, bringing him back to life, is probably a very old shamanistic trait.[3]

The arrival, half way through the fourteenth century, of the plague bacillae – likewise from the steppes of Central Asia[4] – set off a series of chain reactions. Obsession with conspiracy, anti-heretical stereotypes and shamanistic traits fused, inducing the emergence of the image of the witch sect. But the transformation of the old beliefs in a diabolical direction occurred over decades along the entire Alpine arc. In 1438 at Morbegno in Valtellina, the Dominican Christoforo da Luino incarcerated persons suspected of practising magical arts and of entertaining relations with 'the good society, that is, with the devil'. In 1456 Baldassarre Pestalozzi, a wealthy physician from Chiavenna had to prove himself not guilty of the charge, brought against him twenty-four years earlier, of being 'sorcerer or attending, as the phrase goes, the good society'.[5] As late as 1480 two 'wicked' women of Valtellina, Domenega and Contessia, were condemned, in a deliberately laconic sentence, to a three-year banishment preceded by the pillory, for having worshipped the unnamed 'mistress of the game' (*domina ludi*).[6]

2.　For a long time the society of witches continued to be associated with the regions in which it had been first discovered. On 23 March 1440, during a public session of the council of Florence, Pope Eugene IV delivered an admonition against the anti-Pope Felix V (known to the world as Amedeo di Savoia), elected a few months earlier. In it it was insinuated that Amedeo had dared to rebel against the authority of the Church because he had been seduced by the enchantments of 'wicked men and little women who, having abandoned the Saviour, have turned to Satan, seduced by the delusions of the demons: little witches (*stregulae*), sorcerers or *Waudenses*, particularly widespread in his country of origin'.[7] The literal mould of the *Canon episcopi* (*retro post Sathanam conversi daemonum illusionibus seducuntur*) introduced a new reality, related to a specific situation, emphasized by the use of terms echoing the vernacular (*Waudenses*, and the diminutive *stregulae*, instead of *strigae*). But meanwhile the image of the new sect had begun to be known for a few years beyond the Alps. Johannes Nider had publicly read his *Formicarius* before the fathers gathered in Basel for the council.[8] Even before that there had been the indefatigible, sensational activity of a Minor Friar, Bernardino of Siena (sanctified soon thereafter). His itinerant preachings made a decisive contribution to the persecution of witchcraft.[9]

A reference to the *vetule re(n)cagante*, pug-nosed old women who say they travel *in cursio cum Heroyda in nocte Epiphanie*, can already be found in one of the sermons of the *De Seraphim* collection given by Bernardino in Padua in 1423.[10] Besides predicting misfortunes, these followers of Heroyda (i.e., Herodias) gave succour to bewitched children, women in labour, and the sick. Their accompaniment of Herodias during the night of Epiphany was not yet synonymous with joining in the Sabbath, although Bernardino, following in the footsteps of the *Canon episcopi* (*retro post Sathanam conversae*), considered them subjects of the devil. Two years later (1425), besides flinging occasional insults from the pulpit at the Sienese women who were listening to him ('and you bedevilled female who go to visit the enchantress at Travalle'), Bernardino devoted an entire sermon to sorceresses and enchanters.[11] But these were still isolated figures: mainly women. Shortly thereafter, at a crucial moment of Bernardino's life, something changed.

The devotion to the name of Jesus, which Bernardino had propagated with enormous success in his sermons, had provoked the charge of heresy against him from many sides. In the spring of 1427 Pope Martino V ordered Bernardino, who was at Gubbio, to suspend his preaching and come to Rome immediately. The journey, which probably occurred towards the end of April, was undertaken in an atmosphere of great tension. 'Some wanted me fried, some wanted me roasted,' Bernardino recalled ironically. His interrogation before the Pope and the theologians came to a favourable conclusion. He was cleared of all charges; he was again allowed to preach.

Yet the Pope, as we see from a small polemical treatise by the Augustinian Andrea Biglia (*Liber de institutis*), ordered Bernardino not to exhibit for the worship of the faithful the tablets in which the monogram of the name of Jesus was represented.[12] In short, the matter was anything but resolved. The situation was eased by the sermons that Bernardino delivered in Rome, in all likelihood between the beginning of May and the end of July 1427.[13] They have not come down to us: but we can partially reconstruct their contents thanks to the reference made to them by Bernardino himself while preaching in Siena on the Piazza del Campo from 15 August onwards. In Rome he had repeatedly attacked witches and sorcerers, arousing utter astonishment in his auditors: 'When I preached about these enchantments and witches and spells, what I said seemed to them that I was dreaming.' At first his exhortations to denounce suspects had no effect: but then 'I thought to say that any person who knew a man or woman who did such things, and did not report them, would himself be committing the same sin . . . And when I finished preaching, a multitude of witches and enchanters were accused.'[14] After a consultation with the Pope it had been decided to bring to trial only those who were suspected of the most serious crimes. Among these was Finicella, who was sent to the stake because (as we read in Stefano Intessura's chronicle), 'she diabolically killed many creatures and cast spells on many people, and all of Rome went to watch.'[15] She was probably the witch about whom Bernardino spoke in his Sienese sermons:

> One among the others (. . .) said and confessed without any torture that she had killed thirty children by sucking their blood; and she also said that she had liberated sixty of them (. . .) And furthermore she confessed that she had killed her own son, and turned him into dust, some of which she gave people for such purposes.[16]

Transformed from accused into the accuser of superstitious practices, Bernardino was able to turn a half-victory into triumph. The Augustinian humanist Andrea Biglia, writing immediately after the Roman sermons, observed that the devotion to the name of Jesus propagated by Bernardino entailed, not unlike the activity of wizards, soothsayers and enchanters, a sacrilegious exchange between symbol and the reality symbolized.[17] Twenty-five years later, Nicolas of Cusa, another and greater humanist, reminded the faithful of Bressanone that turning to Christ and the saints in order to obtain material advantages already signifies the commission of an act of idolatry.[18] The severe and difficult religion that can be glimpsed behind these sentences indirectly clarifies the reasons for Bernardino's success. He fought sorcerers and enchanters on their own ground, with weapons not too dissimilar from theirs. The 'game tables, songs, charms for amulets, lots, and hair' that he ordered to be burnt on the site of the Roman Campidoglio[19] were meant to clear the field for the tablet with the name of Jesus.

But the amazement of which Bernardino spoke ('what I said seemed to them that I was dreaming') cannot have been produced simply by what was, after all, the traditional polemic against witches and enchanters. From the

Sienese sermon of the summer of 1427 we know that Bernardino had received the latest information about the orgies and macabre rituals practised by an unknown sect:

> And there are some of these people here in Piedmont, and five inquisitors already went there to remove this curse, and they have been done to death by these evil people. And so no inquisitor can be found who wants to go there and take care of it. And do you know what these people are called? They are called people of the little keg. And they have this name because once a year they take a small child, and throw it from one to the other until he is dead. When he is dead, they grind him into the dust and put the dust into small kegs, and then give everyone to drink from this keg; and this they do because they say afterwards that nothing they do can be seen. We have a friar in our Order, who was one of them and has told me everything, that they also have the most dishonest ways that I think anyone could have . . .[20]

In this description we recognize the traits of one of the 'new sects and forbidden rituals' whose existence in the Western Alps had been reported as early as 1409 by another Minor Friar, the inquisitor Ponce Fougeyron.[21] The fantastic information about witches who, deceived by the devil, thought they metamorphosed into female cats after having covered their bodies with ointments, probably came from the same source.[22] For them, Bernardino warned, no mercy whatever was permissible: 'and therefore I tell you that wherever one can be found that is an enchantress or caster of spells, or enchanters or witches, make sure that they are exterminated in such a way that their seed will be lost. . . .'[23] In Bernardino's eyes witches and the sect of the little keg were still distinct realities. Shortly after, they definitely merged. In Todi on 20 March 1428, Matteuccia di Francesco, domiciled at Ripa Bianca near Deruta, was burnt as a witch. In the long sentence drawn up on the orders of Lorenzo de Surdis, the town captain, we find rhymed charms against the spirits (*Omne male percussiccio/omne male stravalcaticcio/omne male fantasmaticcio*, etc.); rhymed charms against the body's pain (*Lumbrica lumbricaia / che tieni core et anima / che tieni polmoncelli / che tieni fecatelli*, etc); spells to procure impotence or avoid pregnancy. All of a sudden, in the confessions of this country witch, there surfaces an extraneous fragment: after having covered herself with vulture fat, the blood of bats and suckling babes, Matteuccia invoked the demon Lucibello who appeared to her in the form of a billy goat, took her on his back transformed into a fly, and swift as lightning carried her to the walnut tree in Benevento where a very great number of witches and demons were gathered, captained by the great Lucifer.[24] Here the innocuously magical features of Diana's society have dissolved into the macabre and aggressive traits of the sect of the keg. The epithet 'the most cruel' (*crudelissimae*) which is used to characterize the followers of Diana in one of Bernardino's sermons, certainly delivered later than 1429, records this transformation.[25] It followed the pattern of the transformation that had already occurred in the Western Alps. During the same year as the trial in Todi (1428), the Lucerne chronicler Johann Fründ had introduced into his account a substantially analogous description of the

Sabbath, based on the witchcraft trials held in the valleys of Henniviers and Hérens.[26] But in the trial at Todi too we catch the echo of Bernardino's words. The sentence twice emphasizes that Matteuccia had cast her spells before Bernardino preached at Todi, in 1426.[27]

It is probable that Bernardino's sermons suggested to the judges the questions to ask those accused of witchcraft in the future. And probably after an initial bewilderment as in Rome, in Todi too there were those who, recalling the friar's injunctions, decided to denounce Matteuccia or to testify against her. The incitement to exterminate the witches took hold because it fell on favourable ground not only among the authorities.

3.   In the image of the Sabbath we distinguished two cultural currents, of diverse origin: on the one hand, as elaborated by inquisitors and lay judges, the theme of a conspiracy plotted by a sect or a hostile social group; on the other, elements of shamanistic origin which were by now rooted in folk culture, such as the magic flight and animal metamorphosis. But this juxtaposition is too schematic. The moment has come to acknowledge the fact that the fusion between the two lodes could only have been so firm and enduring in so far as there existed a substantial subterranean affinity between them.

In a society of the living – it has been said – the dead can only be impersonated by those who are imperfectly integrated into the social body.[28] This principle is perfectly illustrated by the Doghi funeral ritual, observed among the Xevsur of the Caucasus: in it the women and the dead are tacitly assimilated inasmuch as both are at once internal and external, participants and aliens in the clan.[29] But marginality, imperfect assimilation is also common to the figures who, in the arena of conspiracy and in that of shamanistic intermediaries, constitute the historical antecedents of witches and sorcerers. Rattles, coloured wheels, amniotic rags, an excessive number of teeth stigmatized lepers, Jews, heretics, *benandanti*, *táltos* and so on, as beings situated, depending on the case, on the border between social cohabitation and confinement, between true faith and false beliefs, between the world of the living and that of the dead. In 1321 the lepers had been accused of wanting to contaminate healthy people in order to repay them for their contempt. Two years before, the *armier* Arnaud Gélis had said that the dead, with whom he was in the habit of consorting, wanted all living men and women dead.[30] At the root of the image of conspiracy was a very ancient theme reworked in new terms: the hostility of the recently deceased person – the marginal being par excellence – for the society of the living.[31]

In many cultures the idea exists that specific animals – doves, owls, weasels, snakes, lizards, hares, and so on – sucked the milk of cows or goats (and occasionally of women). In Europe these animals are generally associated with witches or fairies. But behind the milk we discover blood; behind the witches or fairies, the dead. The convergence between the German name of the nightjar (*Hexe*, witch) and the conviction of the Tukana of South America that the souls of the dead, transformed into nightjars, suck the blood of the living, brings to the surface a profound datum.[32] We find it in Latin culture, where the hostility of the dead for the living, the thirst of the dead, the representation of the soul in the form of a bird (or a bee, or a butterfly) fused with the mythical image of the *strix*, the strident nocturnal bird thirsting for the blood of suckling babes.[33] But the term *strix* was also used with reference to women who, like the Scythian sorceresses mentioned by Ovid, could metamorphose into birds. [34] This semantic ambiguity reflected an idea with which we are by now familiar: to communicate with the dead one must, at least temporarily, become one of them. Scientific or religious concepts reworked (and complicated) the picture. At the beginning of the thirteenth century Gervaise of Tilbury spoke of the popular belief which identified the *lamiae* (or *mascae*, or *striae*) with women who went through the houses, stealing children from their cribs; he reported the contrary opinion of the physicians, according to whom the apparitions of the *lamiae* were sheer delusion; finally, he mentioned certain women from his neighbourhood who, while sleeping with their husbands, crossed the sea flying at an extraordinary speed in the procession of witches (*lamiae*). [35] A few decades later Stephen of Bourbon said the *strix* was a demon who, taking on the semblance of an old woman, wandered about at night astride a wolf, killing suckling babes.[36] As we have already said, this conception was supplanted by another, according to which witches were women of flesh and blood, knowing instruments of the devil. The accusation directed at the Jews, to the effect that they used the blood of infants for ritualistic purposes, probably also contributed to the assertion of such a thesis. The image of conspiracy proposed and diffused by lay and ecclesiastical authorities took root, at least in part, in the folk culture: to this too can be traced the reasons for its extraordinary success.

If we concede that burial is also a ritual *against* the dead, we can understand the value of purification attributed to the burning of witches and sorcerers, especially female witches, who, as we know, were far more frequent – even if the percentage of women among the defendants (or persons sentenced) in witchcraft trials varied a great deal, according to area.[37] To explain this phenomenon by the misogyny of the inquisitors would be simplistic: to explain it by a pervasive misogyny, already noticeable in the evidence and denunciations, would amount to being guilty of tautology. Certainly, it is not difficult to conceive that among those potentially accused of witchcraft, women (above all, when they were single and thus socially unprotected) should appear the most marginal of the marginal. But this marginality, besides being synonymous with weakness, perhaps also reflected in a more or less obscure manner the perception of a proximity between those who generate life and the formless world of the dead and the non-born.[38]

4. The endeavour forcibly to transplant the image of the witch sect, perfected by Bernardino of Siena in his Roman sermons, was repeated countless times, with more or less success, in and outside Europe. The hybridizations with

older beliefs, whose traces we have found in such heterogeneous and distant regions as the Friuli or Scotland, are, by comparison, much less frequent. Even rarer are the cases in which the Sabbath did not materialize even though all, or virtually all, the preconditions for it existed. In August 1492 Bartolomeo Pascali, canon of the Provostship at Oulx in Val di Susa (western Piedmont), put on trial two friars, both born in Umbria, who called themselves (as we see from the record of the interrogation) *barbae*, or itinerant Waldensian preachers. One of them, Pietro di Jacopo, explained that they wandered about the world preaching and listening to the confessions of members of the sect. Later, he listed the valleys of the Piedmont and those of the Dauphiné in which they were active: Val Chisone, Val Germanasca, Val Pellice, Val Fressinières, Val l'Argentière, and Val Pute. Of himself and his companions he said that they were called *charretani, alias fratres de grossa opinione, vel barlioti, adulatores, fraudatores et deceptores populi.* This was a list of offensive epithets: simulators of holiness (a behaviour then traditionally attributed to the inhabitants of Cerreto in Umbria); *Fraticelli* (little friars), but with a negative connotation (*de grossa opinone* rather than *de opinione*); friars of the *barlotto* or keg (from the infamous accusation hurled at the Fraticelli in 1466), flatterers, scoundrels and deceivers.[39] The reasons for this self-denigrating behaviour on the part of Pietro di Jacopo are not clear. In the subsequent interrogation he confirmed that in their jargon (*in eorum gergono*) they were called friars of the keg, vulgarly Waldensians, and in Italy friars *de opinione*, that is, *Fraticelli*. The interchangeability of these definitions seems to mirror a fluid situation in which, of the old sectarian distinctions, only the name had remained. By contrast, the description, perhaps manipulated by the judges, that Pietro di Jacopo and his companion gave of the sexual promiscuities practised in the assemblies or synagogues of the Waldensian sect was utterly traditional. The references to 'a certain idol called Bacco and Bacon' (*quoddam ydolum vocatum Bacum et Bacon*), which the members of the sect worshipped during their gatherings, seem to add a touch of quite incredible pastiche paganism. But the names that follow immediately after, almost separated by a beat – 'and also the Sibilla and the Fairies (*et etiam Sibillam et Fadas*)' – have a different flavour.[40] The reference to the Appennine Sibilla appears perfectly plausible in the mouth of someone who, like Pietro di Jacopo, was born in a village near Spoleto (Castel d'Albano). As for the fairies, their appearance in a heresy trial is totally absurd, and thus certainly authentic.[41] More than a century later, the same ingredients showed up which, precisely in that region, mingled for the first time with the image of the Sabbath: folkloric culture and heresies in a phase of decomposition, not very reliable confessions of sexual promiscuity and mythical female figures linked to the world of the dead. Elements in suspension, ready to recrystallize at the least jolt. But the contradictory stories of the friars of the keg caused not the slightest echo in the canon of Oulx.

5.   This anomalous trial reminds us of an only apparently banal truth: the

convergence between the readiness (sometimes spontaneous, more often elicited or imposed) of the defendant to confess, and the will of the judges to receive these confessions, was indispensable for the materialization of the Sabbath. To materialize, of course, as a creature of the imagination. But was this all the Sabbath was?

At the beginning of the fourteenth century the participants in the noisy processions of the *charivari* impersonated, in the eyes of the spectators, the bands of roaming dead led by Herlechinus. This is an example of the occasionally explicit, occasionally latent isomorphism linking myths and rituals that we have analyzed. The emergence, half a century later, of the demonic Sabbath distorted this symmetry to the point of rendering it unrecognizable. In the Sabbath the judges more and more frequently saw the accounts of real physical events. For a long time the only dissenting voices were those of the people who, referring back to the *Canon episcopi*, saw witches and sorcerers as the victims of demonic illusion. In the sixteenth century scientists like Cardano or Della Porta formulated a different opinion: animal metamorphoses, flights, apparitions of the devil were the effect of malnutrition or the use of hallucinogenic substances contained in vegetable concoctions or ointments. The suggestion offered by these explanations survives. [43] But no form of privation, no substance, no ecstatic technique can, by itself, cause the recurrence of such complex experiences. Against all biological determinism one must emphasize that the key to this codified repetition can only be cultural. Nevertheless, the deliberate use of psychotropic or hallucinogenic substances, while not explaining the ecstasies of the followers of the nocturnal goddess, the werewolf, and so on, would place them in a not exclusively mythical dimension. [44] Is it possible to demonstrate the existence of this ritualistic framework?

6.   Let us explore two hypotheses. The first is not new (only the attempt at demonstration is novel). It revolves around *claviceps purpurea*: a mushroom which, favouring rainy springs and summers, establishes itself on grains, in particular rye, covering them with blackish outgrowths called sclerotium. The ingestion of flour thus contaminated provokes real epidemics of ergotism (from ergot, the word that designates the mushroom in English and in French). Two varieties of this morbid condition are known. The first, recorded mainly in Western Europe, causes very serious forms of gangrene; in the Middle Ages it was known as 'St Anthony's fire'. The second, chiefly spread in Central and Northern Europe, provoked convulsions, extremely violent cramps, states similar to epilepsy, with a loss of consciousness lasting six to eight hours. Both forms, the gangrenous and convulsive, were very frequent due to the diffusion on the European continent of a grain-like rye, which is much hardier than wheat. In the course of the seventeenth century they often had lethal consequences, especially before their cause was discovered to be the *claviceps purpurea*. [45]

All of this leads us to think of victims of evil spells rather than of witches. [46]

But the picture drawn up until now is incomplete. In popular medicine ergot was widely used as an aborting agent. Adam Lonicer, who was the first to describe it in his *Krauterbuch* (1582), observed that women used it to bring about uterine pains, in doses of three sclerotiums, repeated several times.[47] In Thuringia, as J. Bauhinus noted almost a century later, the plant was used as an anti-hemorrhagic.[48] We know that midwives used to administer the outgrowths of *claviceps purpurea* (popularly called *Mutterkorn*, mother rye) to hasten birth pangs. In a few instances (as in Hanover in 1778) the authorities intervened to forbid this use: but by the beginning of the nineteenth century the efficacy of *pulvis parturiens* in the acceleration of labour was also recognized by official medicine.[49]

It is probable that ergot was part of popular, predominantly female medicine for a very long time. This means that some of its properties were known and checked on. Others emerge from descriptions of the symptoms of convulsive ergotism. For example, in a doctoral thesis in Wittenberg in 1723, J.G. Andreas spoke of the epidemic that had stricken Silesia a few years before. The manifestations of the illness varied greatly from patient to patient. Some were shaken by extremely painful contractions; others, 'like ecstatics fell into a deep sleep: when the seizure was over, they awoke and told of various visions.' A woman from Lignitz, a victim of the illness for over three years, was considered by the populace to be possessed; a nine-year-old child suffered seizures similar to those of epileptics, and came out of them telling about the visions he had had. People attributed all this to a supernatural cause.[50] Today we know that certain species of *claviceps purpurea* contain, in varying quantities, an alkaloid – ergonovine – from which lysergic acid diethylamide (LSD) was synthesized in 1943.[51]

Rye had been cultivated since ancient times in the Alps and in the greater part of central Europe; in other areas, for example in Greece, there grew other species of *claviceps* which contain alkaloids that could be used as substitutes.[52] But evidently the material accessibility of a potentially hallucinogenic substance does not prove that it was being consciously utilized.[53] More indicative are a number of terms popularly used to designate *claviceps purpurea*, such as the French *seigle ivre* (drunken rye) and the German *Tollkorn* (mad wheat), which seem to point to an ancient awareness of the potency of the plant.[54] Towards the middle of the nineteenth century, children in the German countryside were told about frightful beings such as the 'rye wolf' or 'rye dog' (*Roggenwolf, Roggenhund*). They were most likely mythical transfigurations of ergot, 'the rye mother' (*Roggenmutter*), also called 'wolf' (*Wolf*) or, because of its elongated form, 'Wolf's tooth' (*Wolfzahn*). In the stories told in certain regions the blackish excrescences of *claviceps purpurea* became iron breasts which the rye mother gave the children to suck so that they would die. Between the rye wolf (*Roggenwolf*) and the werewolf (*Werwolf*) there was a profound affinity. 'The werewolf sits amid the grain,' the people said.[55]

The hypothesis that ergot was used to obtain states of loss or alteration of consciousness is rendered plausible by this wealth of mythical associations.[56] It would be definitively confirmed were it possible to say that there existed a connection between a word of such obscure etymology as ergot and the German word *warg* (outlaw, but also werewolf): unfortunately, this is not demonstrable.[57]

7. A completely independent connection between werewolves and psychotropic substances has been hypothesized in an altogether different linguistic and cultural sphere. And with this we come to the second possibility. It has been supposed that the words *saka haumavarka*, which in Iranian texts designate a family from whom the Achaemenides descended, meant 'the people who change into werewolves by intoxicating themselves with *haoma*'. This would be an allusion to the state of belligerent frenzy that was considered a typical attribute of male secret societies. This interpretation, however, is anything but certain.[58] Moreover, we do not know exactly what *Haoma* was. In the *Avesta*, the sacred book of Zoroastrian religion, it is referred to as a plant which, at least in origin, was probably identical with *Soma*, from which a potion that the Vedic poems describe in exalted tones was extracted. After many fruitless attempts to decide to what plant *Soma* and *Haoma* corresponded – proposals, referring to one or the other or to both, include millet, grapevines, rhubarb, Indian hemp, etc. – a hypothesis has been advanced that seems to correspond perfectly to the indications contained in the texts. *Soma*, it would appear, is *amanita muscaria*: a mushroom that provokes a state similar to intoxication in those who eat it or drink its juice (sometimes possibly mixed with water), or drink the urine of a person who has eaten it (it seems that in the latter case the effect is particularly intense). The Siberian populations (with the exception of the Altaiche) make great use of this mushroom – especially the shamans, to attain ecstasy. In the region between Afghanistan and the valley of the Indus river, where the Aryan populations originating in northern Eurasia settled in the second millennium BC, it was less easy to procure the mushroom: *amanita muscaria* grows only near fir trees or birches. Perhaps the priests tried to replace it with surrogates. But the Vedic poems preserved a vivid memory of the ancient cult.[59]

The use of *amanita muscaria* to attain an ecstatic condition is certainly very ancient. Linguistic considerations lead us to believe that it dates back to at least four thousand years before Christ, when there still existed a common Uralic language. What is more, a group of words that designate *amanita muscaria*, mushroom in general, the loss of consciousness, the (shamanistic) drum in the Finno-Ugric and Samoyed languages, apparently derive from a single root, *poh*. It would seem that for reasons of taboo the Indo–Iranian populations substituted *Soma* and *Haoma* for words linked to this root.[60] But the replaced root possibly resurfaces in a Sanskrit word, apparently not of Aryan origin, tied to a Sanskrit hypothetical*paggala (mad, madness), from which various Indian dialectal terms would appear to derive. The Sanskrit word in question is *pangú*, which means 'lame, crippled'.[61]

The existence of a connection between the mushroom used by the shamans to attain ecstasy and lameness will at this point not seem inconceivable in principle. Furthermore, this convergence is not isolated. In a number of French regions gilled mushrooms (for example, *amanita muscaria*) have names like *bò* (Haute Saône) or *botet* (Loire) which immediately call to mind *bot* (cripple) and *bot* (toad). Here we see emerge the intersection of three elements: mushroom, toad and the ambulatory anomaly.[62] It has been maintained that the convergence between the adjective *bot*, 'crippled' (*pied bot*) and the noun *bot*, 'toad', is illusory, because the two words derive from different roots (**butt*, 'blunted', the first; **bot*, 'to swell', the second).[63] But the names that identify the toad with 'shoe', 'slipper', and so on, in the dialects of northern Italy would seem to indicate the presence of a semantic affinity, which certainly cannot be reduced to an external resemblance.[64] Equally unquestionable, although obscure, is the affinity between mushroom and toad. In China *amanita muscaria* is called 'toad mushroom', in France, *crapaudin* (from *crapaud*, 'toad').[65] 'Toad bread', *pin d'crapâ* is the name with which agaric mushrooms (including the *amanita)* are designated in Normandy.[66] In the Veneto, the *rospèr zalo* designates the *Amanita mappa*; in Treviso, in particular, the *jongo rospèr* is the *Amanita pantherina*.[67] Inedible mushrooms are called 'toad mushrooms' (*zabaci huby*), or 'similar to toads' (*zhabjachyi hryb*), in Slovakia (in the region of the Tatra mountains) and in the Ukraine, respectively.[68] Moreover, terms like 'toadstool', 'toad hat', and so on are used to designate these mushrooms in English, Irish, Welsh, Breton, Frisian, Danish, low German, Norwegian. It has been argued that such a close connection with an animal like the toad, considered ugly, disagreeable, or even diabolical, supposedly expresses a profoundly hostile attitude towards mushrooms, typical of Celtic culture.[69] But, as we have seen, the linguistic convergence of mushrooms and toads and, in particular, of *amanita muscaria* and toads is documented far beyond the confines of the Celtic world, even in China. If we eliminate the toad's negative connotations because they are belated and superficial, we see a different explanation emerge. From northern Italy to Germany, the Ukraine and Poland, the toad is designated 'fairy', 'witch' and 'sorcerer'.[70] It has been supposed on the basis of good arguments that the Italian *rospo* derives from the Latin *haruspex*, the sorcerer and soothsayer which the Latins had imported from Etruria.[71] In numerous cultures, apparently, the toad, like *amanita muscaria* and ambulatory anomalies, constituted a symbolic link with the invisible. It is difficult to say whether the psychotropic potentialities of bufotenina, a substance contained in the secretions of the toad's skin, contributed to this (opinions on the subject are controversial).[72]

We said that *amanita muscaria* is associated with trees like the fir and birch, which grow abundantly on European mountains. It is known that in the Alps, the Jura, and the Pyrenees witchcraft trials were particularly frequent. The confessions of the majority of defendants consciously or unconsciously echoed the models proposed by the inquisitors. But in the very few anomalous cases in which descriptions of a shamanistic type surface, *amanita muscaria* does not appear.[73] The connection with states of altered consciousness that would seem to be suggested by terms like *cocch matt, coco mato, ovol matt, bolé mat*, with which *amanita muscaria* is designated in the dialects of Lombardy, the Veneto and Emilia, is not confirmed in the trial records.[74] Only in some instances does it seem permissible to indicate a doubt at least. We have already said that during the trials of the Piedmontese heretics at the end of the fourteenth century there is mention at one point of the potion distributed by Billia la Castagna, a woman from Andezeno near Chieri, to those who participated in the ritual orgy.[75] The potion was made from the excrement of a large toad, which it would appear (*fama erat*) Billia kept under her bed, feeding it meat, bread and cheese. These repulsive or bizarre details may be partially due to a misunderstanding on the part of the inquisitors. From Europe to the Americas mushrooms are often referred to with names that evoke animal urine, faeces, or flatulence: 'dog piss', 'wolf fart', 'fox excrements' and 'puma excrements'.[76] Andezeno is not a mushroom region: but the author of the confession, Antonio Galosna, wandered as a preacher through the Piedmontese valleys. Might not the 'toad excrement' of Billia la Castagna be a distorted echo of terms connected with *crapaudin, pain de crapault* – 'toad mushrooms', which in France and elsewhere denote the *amanita muscaria*?

On the other side of the Alps, a few decades after Antonio Galosna's confessions, a young man told Peter von Greyerz, the judge from Berne (who in his turn spoke about it to Nider), of the macabre initiation ritual required of those who wished to become members of the witches' sect. The person who drank the macabre potion contained in a skin flask 'had all of a sudden the sensation of receiving and preserving within himself the image of our art, and the principal rituals of the sect'.[77] The possibility that these words may convey the distorted working of an ecstatic experience, induced by use of hallucinogenic substances, is very slight. Unlike the initiates of the sect we must admit that their rituals elude us. And in any case, it is not said that they ever existed.

8. Indubitable, by contrast, is the deep resemblance that binds the myths that later merged in the witches' Sabbath. All of them work a common theme: going into the beyond, returning from the beyond. This elementary narrative nucleus has accompanied humanity for thousands of years. The countless variations introduced by utterly different societies, based on hunting, on pasture and on agriculture, have not modified its basic structure. Why this permanence? The answer is possibly very simple. To narrate means to speak here and now with an authority that derives from having been (literally or metaphorically) there and then.[78] In participation in the world of the living and of the dead, in the sphere of the visible and of the invisible, we have already recognized a distinctive trait of the human species. What we have tried to analyze here is not one narrative among many, but the matrix of all possible narratives.

Notes

1. Cf. N. S. Troubetzkoy, *L'Europa e l'umanita*, It. trans., Turin 1982.
2. See above, pp. 134, 192–3 and *passim*.
3. Cf. M. Bonnet, 'Traditions orales des vallées vaudoises du Piemont', in *Revue des traditions populaires*', XXVII (1912), pp. 219–21; J. Jalla, *Légendes et traditions populaires des vallées vaudoises* (2nd ed. expanded), Torre Pellice 1926, pp. 38–39, where the wasp (*galabroun*) is called *masc*, 'witch' (both texts have been pointed out and sent to me by Daniele Tron, whom I thank warmly). On Guntram see above, p. 117. A comparison with shamanistic phenomena surfaces several times in R. Christinger and W. Borgeaud, *Mythologie de la Suisse ancienne*, Geneva 1963; in the preface E. Lot-Falck emphasizes (p.11) that Switzerland is a genuine crossroads of several civilizations.
4. This is a variety which was then called, by antonomasia, *Pasteurella pestis medievalis*: cf. Le Roy Ladurie, 'Un concept: l'unification microbienne du monde', in *Le territoire de l'historien*, II, Paris 1978, pp. 50 ff.
5. Cf. Giorgetta, 'Un Pestalozzi accusato di stregoneria', in *Clavenna*, 20 (1981).
6. Cf. idem, 'Documenti sull'Inquisizione a Morbegno nella prima meta del secolo XV', *Bollettino della società storica valtellinese*, XXXIII (1980), pp. 59–83, in particular pp. 81 ff.: the two women, '*malleficiatrices et in fide defficientes...*' had confessed spontaneously that '*a diabolo fore seductas et longo tempore in heretica pravitate extitisse et diabolicis suasionibus et serviciis obedivisse una cum certa mulierum quantitate eundo coram quadam appellata domina ludi, qui demon est, et cum ea certis nocturnis horis conversationem habuisse et in eius societate perseverasse, nonnulla committendo* que manifestam sapiunt heresim, que pro presenti non veniunt publicanda...*' (my emphasis).
7. Cf. *Monumenta conciliorum generalium saeculi decimi quinti Concilium Basileense*, III, 1, Vindobonae 1886, p. 483. See also J. Gill, *Il concilio di Firenze*, It. trans., Florence 1967, pp. 377–78.
8. P. Paravy rightly insists on this point: cf. 'Faire croire. Quelques hypothesès de recherche basées sur l'étude des procès de sorcellerie en Dauphiné au XVe siècle', in *Faire croire*, Rome 1981, p. 124.
9. Bibliographical information under the heading 'Albizzeschi, Bernardino degli' in *Dizionario biografico degli italiani* (R. Manselli, ed). Among recent publications see particularly *Bernardino predicatore nella società del suo tempo* (Convegni del Centro di studi sulla spiritualita medievale, XVI), Todi 1976.
10. Cf. Lazzerini, 'Arlecchino, le mosche, le streghe e le origini del teatro popolare', *Studi mediolatini e volgari*, XXX (1977) p. 100 (this is a Latin translation of the transcription of a listener, the Paduan Daniele de Purziliis). The expression '*andare in corso*' can already be found in Boccaccio, *Decameron*, Day VIII, story 9): cf. Bonomo, *Caccia alle streghe,*, Palermo 1959, pp. 59 ff.
11. Cf. san Bernardino of Siena, *Le prediche volgari. Predicazione del 1425 in Siena*, C. Cannarozzi, ed. I, Florence 1958, pp. 3, 5 and 55–66.
12. Cf. B. de Gaiffier, 'Le mémorie d'André Biglia sur la prédication de Saint Bernardin de Sienne', in '*Analecta bollandiana*, LIII (1935), pp. 308–58. That Bernardino's interrogation took place in 1427 and not 1426 has been proven in a persuasive manner by E. Longpré, 'S. Bernardin de Sienne et le nom de Jésus', in *Archivum Franciscanum Historicum*, XXVIII (1935), pp. 460 ff. But the entire essay is important: cf. ibid., pp. 443–76; XXIX (1936), pp. 142–68 and 443–77; XXX (1937), pp. 170–92. Yet it is still true that, on the basis of the deposition given by Leonardo Benvoglienti in one of Bernardino's trials of canonization, this event

should be put back to the preceding year, (1426): cf. D. Pacetti, 'La predicazione di San Bernardino in Toscana...' in *Archivum Franciscanum Historicum* XXXIII (1940), pp. 299–300, and, with more decisiveness, C. Piana, 'I processi di canonizzaione...,' ivi, XLIV (1951), pp. 397–8, notes 3 and 4, and p. 420, note 2; in the same sense see the unsatisfactory *Enciclopedia Bernardiniana*, IV, L'Aquila 1985, p. XVIII (M. Bertagna, ed.). But Benvoglienti (who spoke in 1448 of events going back to twenty years earlier) simply spoke of having attended the Roman sermons of 1426 (that are also known from another source: cf. Longpré, art. cit., 1935, p. 460. The reasons advanced by Longpré to situate Bernardino's interrogation in 1427 rather than 1426 are not in the least disproven by Benvoglienti's testimony, because his reference in it to 'some witches' (*nonnullas sortilegas*) who were burnt at the stake by Bernardino in Rome and Perugia certainly points, at least in the first case (the reference to Perugia cannot be checked) to 1427: see additionally, note 15.

13. Cf. Longpré, art. cit., 1936, pp. 148–49, note 6: Bernardino preached in St. Peter's for eighty days.
14. Cf. San Bernardino of Siena, *Le prediche volgari*, P. Bargellini, ed, Rome 1936, pp. 784 ff. (the volume reproduces the text of Sienese sermons in the summer of 1427 according to the edition of L. Banchi, 1884). The importance of this and other passages of the same sermon has been emphasized by Miccoli, 'La storia religiosa,' in *Storia d'Italia*, II, Turin 1984, pp. 814–15.
15. Cf. S. Infessura, *Diario della città di Roma*, O. Tommasini ed., Rome 1890, p. 25, which places the event on 8th July (perhaps it should be altered to 28 July) 1424. The manuscript on which L. A. Muratori based his edition of the *Diario* indicates another date, 28 June: but on those days, as Longpré notes (art. cit., 1935, pp. 460–61, note 5) Bernardino was in Siena. In any event, the reference to the year 1424 is in all probability the result of a chronological error – one of the many that stud the *Diario* (cf. O. Tommasini, 'Il diario di Stefano Infessura...' in *Archivio della Società Romana di Storia Patria*, XI, 1888, pp. 541 ff.) The witch Finicella is in fact identified with one of the two anonymous Roman witches mentioned by Bernardino in a sermon of the summer of 1427, in the course of an abrupt digression which is not preceded by temporal qualifications ('I want to tell you what we did at Rome...' :cf. San Bernardino, op. cit., p. 784) and is therefore quite likely relating to very recent events. It seems logical to correct the date from 1424 to 1427; 1426 also seems to be excluded because between June and July of that year Bernardino, who had preached in Rome since the beginning of April, went on to Montefalco and Spoleto (cf. Longpré, art. cit., pp. 460–61, note 5). It should be noted that Miglio, after having (rightly) praised Longpré's essay, follows the chronology proposed by Piana, correcting, without any explanation, the Infessura date from 1424 to 1426: but then, in contradiction to this he cites a passage from the Sienese sermons of the summer of 1427, declaring that they were delivered 'some months after' the Roman event. For coherence's sake he should have written 'a year after' ('Il pontificato e S. Bernardino', in *Atti del convegno storico Bernardiniano...*, Teramo 1982, pp. 237–49, in particular pp. 238–39).
16. Cf. San Bernardino, op. cit., p. 785.
17. Cf. de Gaiffier, art. cit., p. 318: '*Aut unde magos, ariolos, praestigiatores reprehendimus et dampnamus, nisi quod quibusdam caracteribus fide adhibità, demonum responsa atque auxilia eliciunt? Totumque hoc genus sacrilegii est, pro rebus figuras amplecti*'. Cf. R. Fubini, 'Poggio Bracciolini e S. Bernardino...' in *Atti del convegno*, p. 157, in regard to Miccoli, 'Bernardino pedicatore...' in the volume with the same name (cit. above), note 9. On the date of the small treatise by Biglia I follow Longpré, art. cit., 1936, pp. 147–48.

18. See above, p. 72.
19. Cf. Infessura, op. cit., p. 25 (under the date 21 July; in other mss., 21 June).
20. Cf. San Bernardino op. cit., pp. 607–8 (on pp. 1140–4 notes 33 and 35, Bargellini repeats the mistaken interpretation suggested by Banchi, the previous editor, which interprets 'keg' as a synonymn of 'dumb', suggesting a hybridization, also unfounded, with the Valdensian 'barbetti'). The text is also singled out by Cohn, *Europe's Inner Demons*, 1975, pp. 49–50, who, however, does not emphasize the references to the area in which the witches' Sabbath emerged. Further on, Cohn proposes (pp. 50–54), convincingly, that it had been Bernardino who told Giovanni da Capestrano, the ferocious persecutor of heretics and Jews (who was later canonized), the stories about the rituals of the keg, later extorted from the Fraticelli in 1466 in Rome (or even earlier in 1449 at Fabriano).
21. See above, pp. 68–70.
22. Cf. San Bernardino. op. cit., pp. 758 ff.: 'And they were saying that they covered themselves with them [jars of ointments], and when they were fully smeared in it, they seemed to be cats, but this was not true; for their bodies did not change into any other shape, but they thought that they had.' Here I am following (p.786) a reference to the *Canon episcopi*.
23. Ibid, p. 788.
24. The sentence has been published several times: see most recently D. Mammoli, *Processo alla strega Matteuccia di Francesco, 20 marzo 1428*, Todi 1983 (in particular pp. 16, 18, 20, 30 and 32).
25. Cf. Lazzerini, 'Arlecchino, le mosche, le streghe e le origini del teatro popolare', in *Studi mediolatini e volgari*, XXV (1977), p. 101, which refers to Saint Bernardino of Siena, *Opera omnia*, I, ad Claras Aquas, Florentiae 1950, p. 117: for the date – between 1429 and 1436 – cf. pp. XVIII-XIX.
26. See above, p. 73.
27. Besides Mammoli, op. cit., cf. Longpré, art. cit., 1935, p. 458.
28. Cf. Lévi-Strauss, 'Le Pére Noël supplicié', in *Les Temps modernes*, p. 1586.
29. Cf. Charachidzé, *Le systéme religieux de la Géorgie païenne*, Paris 1968, pp. 369 ff., in particular pp. 398–99.
30. Cf. Duvernoy, *Le registre de Jacques Fournier*, I, Paris 1965, I, p. 135: '*Dixit etiam quod mortui, prout audivit ab aliquibus ex eis, vellent quod omnes homines et mulieres viventes esse mortui*'. See also above, p. 41.
31. Cf. Hertz, *Sulle rappresentazioni collettive* cit.
32. Cf. R. Riegler, 'Caprimulgus und Verwandtes', in *Wörter und Sachen*, VII (1912), pp. 136–43, which grasps the general implications of the theme very well, but stops short of the identification of the witch-like stratum. Claude Lévi-Strauss makes a passing reference to the funereal connotations of the nightjar in Europe, concentrating later on those (in part analogous) that it has in South America (*La vasaia* cit., pp. 33–35) and in North America (ibid., pp. 55 ff.) On the 'animal-dead' connection (on which see above, p. 262–3) cf. in general R. Riegler, 'Lo zoomorfismo nelle tradizioni popolari', in *Quaderni di semantica*, (1981), pp. 305 ff. See also M. Alinei, *Barbagianni, "zio Giovanni" e altri animali-parenti: origine totemica degli zoonimi parentelari*', ivi, pp. 363–85, in particular p. 371 (rich in material and observations, even if the rigidly totemistic position leaves one feeling rather dubious).
33. On the soul as a bird, butterfly and so on, the bibliography is extensive. I limit myself to a select group of titles: G. Weicker, *Der Seelenvogel in der alten Litteratur und Kunst*, Leipzig 1902; O. Tobler, *Die Epiphanie der Seele in deutscher Volkssage*, Kiel 1911; O. Waser, 'Über die äussere Erscheinung der Seele in den Vorstellungen der Völker, zumal der alten Griechen', in *Archiv für Religionswissenschaft*, 16 (1913), pp. 336–88;

Güntert, *Kalypso. Bedeutungsgeschichtliche Untersuchungen auf dem Gebiet der indoger-manischen Sprachen*, Halle a. S 1919, pp. 215 ff.; M. Haavio, 'Der Seelenvogel', in *Essais folkoriques, Studia fennica*, 8 (1959), pp. 61–81; M. Bettini, *Antropologia e cultura romana*, Rome 1986, pp. 205 ff. On the impossibility of identifying in the *strix* a specific nocturnal bird cf. F. Capponi, 'Avifauna e magia', in *Latomus*, XL (1981), pp. 301–4. Less convincing S. G. Oliphant, 'The Story of the Strix: Ancient', in *Transactions and Proceedings of the American Philological Association*, XLIV (1913), pp. 133–49; idem, 'The Story of the Strix: Isidorus and the Glossographers', ivi, XLV (1914), pp. 44–63, who leans towards the bat. For other suggestions see A. Scobie, 'Strigiform Witches in Roman and Other Cultures', in *Fabula*, 19 (1978), pp. 74–101; Alinei, op. cit., p. 212.

34. Cf. above, p. 192. Of Ovid see also *Ars amatoria*, I, 8, 13 ff.; I, 14, 40 (on the pimp Dipsas who transforms herself into a bird); *Fasti*, 6, 131 ff. In this last passage F. Bömer (*Metamorfoses*, Heidelberg 1986, II, pp, 344–45) sees Ovid's yielding to popular beliefs.

35. Cf. Gervase of Tilbury, *Otia imperialia*, pp. 987 ff. A fragment of John of Damascus (VII-VIII sec.) in *Opera Omnia*, M. Lequien, ed, Parisiis 1712, I, p. 473, cited by Tartarotti, *Apologia del congresso notturna delle lammie*, Venice 1751, p. 160, spoke of women (called *stryngaio* or *gheloudes*) who, according to popular beliefs, fly around houses, enter through the barred doors and disembowel newborn babies in their cradles.

36. Cf. A. Lecoq de la Marche, *Anecdotes historiques. . .tirés du recueil inédit d'Étienne de Bourbon*, Paris 1877, pp. 319 ff. And see Schmitt, 'Les traditions folkoriques dans la culture médiévale. Quelques refléxions de méthode', *Archives de sciences sociales des religions*, 52 (1981), pp. 212–13.

37. Iceland is probably a completely anomalous case. If the facts contained in an old study (O. Davidsson, 'Islandische Zauberzeichen und Zauberbücher', in *Zeitschrift des Vereins für Volkskunde*, 13, 1903, p. 151) are precise, witchcraft trials were held between 1554 and 1720: only nine of the accused were women. The panorama that emerges from the records of the Friulian Holy Office is very different: in the span of two centuries (1596–1785) the number of men and women accused of practising magical arts is almost equal (386 and 391); see the chart devised by E. W. Monter and J. Tedeschi, 'Toward a Statistical Profile of the Italian Inquisition, Sixteenth and Seventeenth Centuries', in *The Inquisition in Early Modern Europe*, G. Henningsen and J. Tedeschi, eds., Dekalb (Ill.) 1986, p. 135. Disparities also emerge if one examines those condemned to death for witchcraft. In the Pays de Vaud, in the period 1581 to 1620 there were 970: 325 (equal to 34.2 %) were men; 624 (equal to 65.8%) women (in 21 cases the facts are lacking) (cf. P. Kamper, 'La chasse aux sorciers et aux sorcières dans le Pays de Vaud', in *Revue historique vaudoise*, 1982, pp. 21–33). In south-western Germany the episodes of massive persecution of witchcraft led, between 1561 and 1684, to the sentencing to death of 1050 women and 238 men (cf. Midelfort, *Witch-Hunting in Southwestern Germany, 1562–1584*, Stanford 1972 pp. 180–81); but from the Würzburg trials (1627–29) there emerges a more complex picture (ibid., pp. 172 ff.). To annul these contrasts (chosen almost at random) in order to attempt generalizations on a European scale does not seem very useful.

38. See above, p. 293, note 247.

39. On the 'charretani' cf. P. Migliorini, 'I cerretani e Cerreto', in *Romance Philology*, 7 (1953–54), pp. 60–64, which records the diverse significance of the 15th century attestations (the first is from 1477, just before the trial we are analyzing) in respect of those of the following century, when the term took on the meaning of 'quack doctor' or 'charlatan'.

40. Cambridge University Library, ms Dd. 3. 26 (H6), c. IX: '*et eorum lege consueverunt adorare [canc.: quandam ydolam] quoddam ydolum vocatum Bacum et Bacon [canc: et fade consueverunt facere] et etiam Sibillam et Fadas. Et quod illi Bacon et fade consueverunt facere dictas congregationes in quibus nullus habetur respectus de filia ad patrem nec de commatre prout tamen habetur extra dictam sinagogam. . . .*' On these trials see Cohn, op. cit., pp. 40–41, who dwells only on the presence of Bacchus, confirming the fact that this is a matter of confessions which were completely extorted or falsified by the judges. E. Cameron, *The Reformation of the Heretics. The Waldenses of the Alps (1480–1580)*, Oxford 1984, after having emphasized, perhaps too heavily, that the defendants were Fraticelli and not Waldensians (p.15) also lists the other idols, speaking of 'perplexing admissions' (p. 112; and see also the index, at the heading 'Jacopo, Pietro di'); he does not dwell on the self-denigrating elements. The hypothesis that these interrogations had been manipulated by the judges was previously formulated by M. Vulson, *De la puissance du Pape*, Geneva 1635, p. 207 (and see E. Cameron, op. cit., p. 236).

41. On the Sibilla see above, pp. 108–9 ff.

42. The trial against the *benandante* Olivo Caldo (*The Night Battles* pp. 138–41) shows in an exemplary manner the effects of the judges' sceptical attitude towards confessions about the Sabbath.

43. Cf. P. Camporesi, *Il pane selvaggio*, Bologna 1980, pp. 123 ff. Other indications in Duerr, *Traumzeit*, Frankfurt am Main, 1978, pp. 165–73.

44. Here I am developing a point of view formulated in *The Night Battles*, op. cit., pp. 16–18.

45. Cf. G. Barger, *Ergot and Ergotism*, London 1931. The link between gangrenous ergotism and rye sclerotium, identified for the first time in 1630, gained ground slowly. See K. Brunner's account, 'De granis secalis degeneribus venenatis', in *Miscellanea curiosa sive ephemeridum medico physicarum Germanicarum Academiae Caesareo – Leopoldinae naturae curiosorum decuriae III*, II, Lipsiae 1695, pp. 348–49: finding himself in the Black Forest he ran into a case of gangrenous ergotism but failed to identify the cause, which, nevertheless, appeared obvious to the local surgeon. It is not clear to what the difference between gangrenous ergotism and convulsive ergotism can be attributed: cf. V.A. Bauer, *Das Antonius-Feuer im Kunst und Medizin*, Basel 1973 (with a preface by A. Hofmann).

46. L. R. Caporael has hypothesized that the morbid phenomena witnessed at Salem in 1692, and interpreted then as cases of diabolic possession, were in reality episodes of convulsive ergotism: 'Ergotism: The Satan Loosed in Salem?' in *Science*, vol. 192, n. 4234, April 2, 1976)., N. P. Spanos and J. Gottlieb are of the opposite opinion, and offer persuasive arguments ('Ergotism and the Salem Village Witch Trials', *Science*, vol. 194, n. 4272, December 24, 1976). Caporael's hypothesis has been reformulated in a European context by Naama Zahavi in a Master's thesis (discussed at the Hebrew University of Jersusalem, sponsor Prof. Michael Heyd). I thank Dr. Zahavi for letting me read a full summary of his work, which has indirectly influenced the thrust of my argument.

47. Cf. Barger, op. cit., p. 7, who observes that the dose, equivalent to about 0.5 grams repeated several times, is the same as that still in use.

48. Cf. J. Bauhinus – J.H. Cherlerus, *Historia plantarum universalis*, II, Ebroduni 1641, p. 417.

49. Cf. Barger, op. cit., p. 10, note; A. Hofmann, *Die Mutterkorn-Alkaloide*, Stuttgart 1964, p. 11; Mannhardt, op. cit., pp. 314-15.

50. Cf. *De morbo spasmodico populari hactenus in patria sua grassante . . . praeside . . . Christiano Vatero . . . exponet Joannes Gotofredus Andreas*, Wittenberg 1723, pp. 6, 8 and 26.

51. It is the same scientist, A. Hofmann, who appears in R. G. Wasson *et al, The Road to Eleusis*, New York and London 1978, pp. 25 ff. Hofmann tested the hallucinogenic effects of lysergic acid on himself.

52. A. Hofmann (ibid., pp. 33 ff.) mentions, for example, the *claviceps paspali* that grows on the grass *Paspalum distichum*. Rye is one of the most recent cereals cultivated by man: in the protohistoric age it was unknown in China, Japan and Egypt; it was cultivated by the Slavs, Germans and Celts (cf. O. Janicke, *Die Bezeichnungen des Roggens in den romanischen Sprachen*, Tübingen 1967, p. 7).

53. I. P. Couliano is of the contrary opinion, *Eros e magia nel Rinascimento*, It.trans. Milan 1987, p. 380. The chemist, A. Hofmann, demonstrates, in the observation cited below, a greater historical sensitivity.

54. Cf. A. Hofmann, in Wasson, op. cit., p. 26. Other examples in Camporesi, op. cit., p. 120 ff.

55. Cf. W. Mannhardt, *Roggenwolf und Roggenhund. Beitrag zur germanischen Sittenkunde*, Danzig 1866, pp. 23–24, 43 and *passim*. According to the myth, the Harpies also offered the breast to nurslings to poison them. The identification between the 'wolf of the rye' and rye sclerotium is proposed, on the basis of the data collected by Mannhardt, by M. R. Gerstein, 'Germanic Warg: The Outlaw as Werewolf', in *Myth in Indo-European Antiquity* pp. 131-56, in particular pp. 147–48 (to be added to the texts cited above, pp. 176, note 26). A rich collection of material has been presented under the heading 'Korndämonen', in *Handwörterbuch des deutschen Aberglaubens*, V, Berlin und Leipzig 1932–1933, coll. 249–314.

56. Curiously, H. P. Duerr waves them aside as banal (op. cit., p. 173, note 25)

57. The proposal has been set forth by Gerstein, art. cit., pp. 150–55. The author seems to ignore the possible extra-linguistic connection constituted by the hallucinogenic potentiality of ergot: yet she realizes that the demonstration on the linguistic plane is not attained ('whatever the exact linguistic relationships may be', p. 155). Prof. Riccardo Ambrosini has reached the same conclusion – while not excluding the possibility of a connection cancelled by an undemonstrable linguistic taboo – expressing this opinion in some letters of October 1982. I thank him warmly for the patience with which he has replied to my questions.

58. Cf. S. Wikander, *Der arische Männerbund. Studien zur indoiranischen Sprach- und Religionsgeschichte*, Lund 1938, pp. 64 ff., which refers also to the research of O. Höfler cited above (p. 152, note 2). See also M. Eliade, 'Les Daces-loups', in *Numen*, 6 (1959), p. 22. But see H. Kothe, 'Der Skythen-begriff bei Herodot', in *Klio*, 51 (1969), pp. 77 ff.

59. On all this see R. G. Wasson, *Soma, Divine Mushroom of Immortality*, s.l.n.d. (Verona 1968); on p. 95–147 an essay by W. Doniger O'Flaherty, 'The Post-Vedic History of the Soma Plant'. The identification between Soma and *amanita muscaria* has been rejected, among others, by the Sanskrit scholar J. Brough: but his discussion with Wasson deals with themes extraneous to this book. In general see Claude Lévi-Strauss, 'Les champignons dans la culture', in *L'homme*, X (1970), pp. 5–16 (very favourable).

60. Cf. Wasson, op. cit., p. 164 ff. (this part is based on the research of B. Munkácsi, T. Lehtisalo, J. Bálázs, partially translated in the appendix, p. 305 ff.)

61. Cf. R. L. Turner, *A Comparative Dictionary of the Indo-Aryan Languages*, Oxford 1966, nn. 7643 and 7647, mentioned by Wasson, *Soma* op. cit., p. 169, (note), which adds as a conjecture, the possible connection with the root 'po'. See also Joki, *Uralier und Indogermanen. Die älteren Berührungen zwischen den uralischen und indogermanischen Sprachen*, Helsinki 1973, pp. 300–1.

62. Cf. Wasson, op. cit., p. 189, and, with greater emphasis, in *Persephone's Quest*, New Haven and London 1986, pp. 80–81.

63. Cf. J. Hubschmid, 'Romanisch–germanische Wortprobleme: franz. bouter und it. buttare', in *Zeitschrift für romanische Philologie*, 78 (1962), pp. 111–26, in particular pp. 122 ff.

64. Criterion 'futile because it always succeeds ... This conception should be supplanted with the idea of "cultural pertinence"': M. Alinei, 'Rospo arusplice, rospo antenato', in *Quaderni di semantica*, VIII (1987), pp. 265–96, in particular p. 294. In the same essay iconographic evidence of the toad as 'foot' or 'clog' is presented. On 'toad-slipper' and so on, see H. Plomteaux, 'Les dénominations des batraciens anoures en Italie: le crapaud', in *Quaderni di semantica*, III (1982), pp. 203–300, in particular pp. 245–53.

65. Wasson, op. cit., p. 189, observes that the devil is *le bot* (the lamed one) by antonomasia. However, he does not mention the Sanskrit *pangú* (on which cf. above, note 61). For *crapaudin* cf. ibid., pp. 10, 35 etc.

66. Cf. C. Joret, *Essai sur le patois normand du Bessin* . . ., Paris 1881, p. 75. In the France of the sixteenth century *pain de crapault* was a generic expression to indicate wild mushrooms: cf. Wasson, op. cit., pp. 186–87.

67. Cf. O. Penzig, *Flora popolare italiana*, I, Genoa 1924, pp. 231 and 467 (this and other indications have been courteously communicated to me by Prof. Tullio Telmon).

68. Wasson, op. cit., p. 193.

69. Ibid., pp. 185 ff.

70. Cf. Plomteaux, art. cit., pp. 287–90 (*fada* at Mantua etc.); Alinei, art. cit., p. 289.

71. Cf. ibid., pp. 265 ff., which refers, for the shamanistic implications of the toad in a specific culture, to the rather confused essay by A. B. Kennedy, 'Ecce Bufo: the Toad in Nature and in Olmec Iconography', in *Current Anthropology*, 23 (1982), pp. 273–90.

72. Cf. Duerr, op. cit., p. 166; Kennedy, art. cit., pp. 250 ff.

73. Its absence in the trials of European witchcraft is underlined by Wasson, op. cit., p. 176.

74. Cf. Penzig, op. cit., p. 27.

75. Cf. above, p. 77.

76. Cf. Lèvi-Strauss, art. cit., p. 15.

77. Cf. *Malleorum* cit., I, p. 718: *'Postremo de utre bibit supradicto: quo facto, statim se in interioribus sentit imaginem nostrae artis concipere et retinere, ac principales ritus hujus sectae'*.

78. Cf. Benjamin, 'The Storyteller' cit., p. 94. 'He [the storyteller] has borrowed his authority from death' (but see the entire essay. I believe that this essay also inspired G. Swift, *Waterland*, London 1983, p. 47, which I read after having written these pages).

Index

Aalto, P., 224
Aarne, A., 269, 284
Aaron (prophet), 46
Aaron, 48
Abaev, V. I., 220, 222, 291
Aberdeen, 113
Abdon, 45
Abrahamse, D. de F., 84
Abry, C., 288
Abry, D., 288
Abundia (Satia), 6, 94, 101, 104, 105, 185
Abkhaz, 134, 163, 247, 251, 286
Achemenidi, 305
Achilles, 17, 230, 231, 232, 234, 236, 238, 249, 252, 272, 285, 287
Acre, Xavier, 146
Acrisius, 229
Adagwa, 247
Adeline, Guillaume, 79, 86
Adhemar de Chabannes, 75, 84
Adrasteia, 128, 211
Aegean, 223
Aegeus, 229, 230, 231
Aegisthus, 229, 230, 270
Aeneas, 233
Aetolians, 233, 236, 273
Afanasjev, A.N., 269, 283, 284
Africa, 4, 8, 74, 134, 154, 229, 241, 246, 249, 260, 261, 263, 282
Agassa, Bernard, 60
Agassa, Guillaume, 41, 42, 43, 47, 52, 53, 56, 57, 60, 61, 67, 73, 74, 80
Agde, Council of, 90
Agen, 39
Agimet, 67
Agnesina, 146
Agyrion, 124
Ainu, 134, 247, 283, 284
Akrotiri, 127

Alani, the, 162, 208, 213, 221, 222
Alasia de Garzo, 77
Albania, 186
Albertos, M. L., 144
Albe, E., 56, 61
Albi, 39, 55
Alcaeus, 231, 249, 272
Aldrada, 148
Aleus, 230
Alexander V, Pope, see Filargis, Pietro
Alexandria, 74
Alfayti, Yaco, 50
Alföldi, A., 144, 218, 223, 274, 276, 289, 290
Alföldi, G., 118
Alinei, M., 310, 311, 314
Allan, 125, 142
Allacci, Leone, 168, 169, 179, 232
Almqvist, B., 278
Alphandéry, P., 54, 61
Alps, 77, 89, 96, 103, 130, 131, 134, 192, 193, 194, 246, 296, 297, 304, 306, 307
Alsace, 111
Altai, 208, 209, 223, 305
Althaea, 236
Althaemenes, 270, 271
Altheim, F., 272, 293
Alvino, A., 176
Aly, W., 142
Amasea, 183
Amadeus VI of Savoy, 67
Amalricus Auger, 53
Amaltheia, 126
Amati, G., 85, 86
Amazonia, 226, 241
Ambri, 288
Ambrosini, Riccardo, 313
Amelung, W., 272, 273
America, 49, 154, 225, 226, 242, 246, 249, 260, 261, 282, 284, 300, 307, 310

315

Amicedich, King, *see* Jerusalem, King of
Amiens, 49
Amilhati, Bartholomeus, 56
Amirani, 216, 250, 251, 255, 256, 257, 286, 288
Anatolia, 277
Anaurus river, 231, 234
Anchel, R., 59
Anchra, Council of, 90, 116
Andezeno, 77, 307
Andreas, J. G., 304
Andree, R., 174, 284, 285
Andrews, J. B., 283
Anell, B., 291
Angiolillo, S., 143
Anglo, S., 151
Anjou, 45, 57
Anjou, Count of, *see* Philippe de Valois
Ankarloo, A., 140
Annibaletto, L., 286
Anthi, 157
Antonio da Settimo, 78
Antoniou, A., 143
Aosta, 68
Apollo, 124, 127, 209, 212, 238
Apemosyne, 271
Aphrodite, 232, 272, 281, 282
Apollodorus, 270, 271, 275
Apollonius of Rhodes, 126, 263, 272, 286, 291
Apostolics, 77
Apulia, 67
Aquitaine, 36, 37
Aquileia, 167, 168
Aragon, King of, 50
Aratus, 126
Arbesmann, R., 198
Arbman, E., 179
Arcas, 126, 127
Arcadia, 126, 127, 136, 156
Arctic, 134, 135, 224, 229, 246, 264
Ari the Wise, 263
Ariadne, 238
Arias, P. E., 141
Ariège, 91
Arii, 224
Arimaspians, 209
Aristaeus, 143
Aristophanes, 127
Aristotle, 233, 236, 252, 253
Aristeas of Proconnesus, 209, 212, 219, 254
Arlt, G. O., 292
Armenia, 47, 75, 186

Armstrong, E. A., 278
Armorica, 106, 221
Arnaud de Pomeriis, 113
Arnobius, 252
Arrighetti, G., 286
Arrigoni, Giampiera, 143, 144, 145
Artamanow, M., 217
Artemidorus, 133
Artemis, 100, 104, 116, 126, 127, 128, 129, 130, 131, 136, 143, 144, 145, 149, 211, 220
Arthur, King (Arthurian legends) 101, 107, 108, 110, 119, 121, 123, 139, 140, 165, 212, 221, 241, 280
Arthus, 101
Artio, 128, 129, 130, 144, 211
Artois, 59
Aryans, 305
Asclepius, 293
Ashanti, 27
Asia, 16, 17, 154, 184, 186, 194, 197, 208, 209, 210, 211, 214, 215, 223, 229, 241, 246, 248, 249, 251, 252, 257, 258, 259, 263, 272, 284, 289, 296
Asia Minor, 74, 84, 125, 128, 184, 186, 197, 211, 251, 252, 257, 258, 259, 263, 272, 284, 289, 296
Assia, 114
'Assassins', sect, 51
(Asterius), Bishop of Amasea, 183, 184, 185, 197, 198
Astour, M., 275
Astruc, C., 84
Athalye, D. V., 224
Athena, 146, 237, 252
Athens, 127, 128, 149, 211, 238
Atlantic, 184, 214
Atlantis, 224
Atreus, 229
Attimis, Troiano de, 89
Aubrey, J., 113
Aucher, J-B, 84
Audisio, G., 85
Auge, 229
Augé, Marc, 27
Auger, Bishop, 110
Augustinian order, 298
Auldern, 96, 113
Aura, Pierre de, 48
Austria, 193
Australia, 260
Avalle, D. S., 29, 114
Aveneris, François de, 48
Avienus, 142

Avignon, 45, 57, 58, 63, 65, 67, 68, 69
Ay, 46
Aymeric, viscount, Lord of Narbonne, 64
Azande, 3, 4
Azarpay, G., 218
Azor, 45

Baba-Yaga, 258, 288
Babylon, Sultan of, 42, 43, 44, 51, 52
Bacchus, 253, 312
Bachofen, J. J., 144
Bachrach, B., 221
Bäckmann, L., 149, 150, 181
Bader, F., 276
Badner, M., 148, 225
Baer, F., 61
Baetke, W., 115
Bailly, F., 224
Bakhtin, M. M., 27
Balavigny, surgeon, 67, 74
Balázs, J., 218, 292, 293, 313
Baldinger, K., 140
Baldus, H., 267
Baltic, 23, 154, 157, 158, 159, 193, 196,
    212, 236, 239
Balkans, 141, 164, 186, 189, 190, 193,
    199, 211, 215, 284
Baluze, E., 53, 54, 55
Bananias, 45, 46, 47, 52, 57
Banat, 189
Banchi, L., 310
Bandi, H-G., 290
Bandini, Fr Marco., 188, 189, 194, 199
Banti, L., 144
Barber, M., 54, 55, 57, 58, 61
Barberino, Andrea da, 109
Barclay, R. S., 113
Barcelona, 63
Bardinet, L., 57, 58
Bargellini, P., 309, 310
Baron, F., 175
Baron, S. W., 58, 59, 61, 81
Barger, G., 312
Baroggi, G., 288
Barruel, Abbot, 12
Bartels, M., 111, 292, 293
Bartha, András, 161
Barthes, Roland, 217, 276
Bartolomea del Papo, 132
Baruch, 54
Baruffaldi, Girolamo, jr., 115
Bascom, W., 284
Basili, Florida, 167
Basle, 68, 69, 172, 192, 297

Basques, 25, 26, 137
Bauer, V. A., 312
Bauhinus, J., 304, 312
Bausinger, H., 201
Bautier, R. H., 84
Bavaria, 193
Baza, 133
Bazin, H., 149
Bech, Giovannie, 77, 85
Beck, A. C. M., 117
Becker, J., 141
Bede, Venerable, 105
Beguines, heretical sect, 43
Beitl, K., 149
Belmont, N., 174, 179, 292, 293
Beltramino da Cernuscullo, Fr., 91, 92, 93
Bendis, 128, 144, 211
Benedict XII, Pope, *see* Fournier, Jacques
Benedictine Order, 75
Beneš, B., 152, 221
Benevento, 299
Benezeit, André, 64, 65
Benjamin, Walter, 280, 314
Bennett, E. L., 145
Benoît. F., 116
Bensozia, 91, 100, 211
Benveniste, Émile, 19, 23, 30, 180
Benvoglienti, Leonardo, 308, 309
Berchta, 114
Berchtholda, 102, 114
Berecinzia, 116
Beriac, F., 54
Berger, J., 291
Bering Strait, 246, 249, 291
Bernardino of Siena, 23, 297, 298, 299,
    300, 301. 308, 309, 310
Bernardo da Como, 83, 96, 112
Berne, 78, 128, 307
Bernese Simmenthal, 69, 70, 71
Bertagna, M., 309
Berthiaume, G., 127
Bertolotti, M., 27, 30, 112, 147, 149, 283,
    288
Bertrand, J-B, 82, 83
Beschi, L., 143
Bettini, M., 267, 268, 311
Bever, E. W. M., 121
Bezukhov, Pierre, 273
Bharati, A., 200
Bickel, E., 142
Bickermann, E., 83
Bieberstein, J. R. von, 27
Biedenkapp, G., 224
Biedermann, F. von, 140, 150

Biel Bruell, 108
Biget, J-L., 57
Biglia, Andrea, 298, 309
Billia la Castagna, 77, 307
Bilz, R., 283
Binder, G., 275, 276
Binford, L. R., 290
Binz, C., 112, 145, 174, 175
Biraben, J-N., 80, 81
Birkhan, H., 119, 173
Bitburg, 128
Black, F., 174
Black Sea, 183, 188, 207, 208, 209, 210,
    211, 216, 217, 231, 253, 257, 258
Blanco Freijeiro, A., 147
Blankenburg, 67, 83
Blazy, L., 60
Bleichsteiner, R., 15, 111, 197, 202, 221
Blind, K., 282, 283
Bloch, Marc, 12, 27, 61, 277
Bloch, R., 276
Blocksberg, 137, 138
Blois, Count of, 35
Blok, A., 200
Blum, E., 180
Blum, R., 180
Blumenkranz, B., 54, 59, 62
Boardman, J.,
Boccaccio, G., 308
Bodde, D., 203
Bodin, J., 151, 175
Bodrogi, T., 178
Boeckh, A., 141
Boeotia, 133
Bogatyrev, P. G., 29
Bogomils, 77, 84
Bogoras, W., 288
Bohemia, 56
Boi, 106
Bois, Guy, 55
Boislisle, A. de, 58
Boissonade, Fr, 84
Boissieu, A. de, 141
Boll, F., 180
Bolton, J. D. P., 219
Bömer, F., 221
Bongard-Levin, G. M., 218, 219, 224
Bona Socia, *see* Bensozia
Boner, F., 311
Bonfante, G., 145
Bonnet, M., 308
Bonomo, G., 110, 111, 113, 117, 120, 140,
    151
Borborians, 74, 84

Bordeaux, 42, 43
Borderie, H. de la, 199
Boreau, A., 56
Borgeaud, P., 142, 143
Borgeaud, W., 218, 308
Borneo, 241
Bororo, 241
Borovka, G., 222
Borst, A., 82
Bosnia, 77, 160, 275
Bosphorus, 223
Bourboulis, P. B., 284
Bouquet, Dom M., 53, 54, 61
Bourgeois, A., 59
Bourgin, G., 85
Bošković-Stulli, M., 177, 178, 179
Botheler, *see* Gélis, Arnaud
Bovet, R., 115
Boyer, R., 181, 292
Brabant, 134, 147
Brachat, P., 86
Brandenburg, 78, 239
Braque, 28
Braswell, B.K., 272
Bravo, B., 29, 272, 276
Brauron, 127, 128, 129, 211
Brescia, 115
Brelich, A., 17, 29, 141, 201, 221, 269,
    271, 273, 274, 275
Bremmer, Jan, 113, 142, 152, 176, 198,
    201, 218, 219, 220, 221, 271, 274, 275,
    277
Breslau, 68, 130
Breslavia, 56
Bressanone, 94, 112, 129, 130, 298
Breymayer, R., 280
Briançon, 73, 80
Briggs, K. M., 113
Brillante, C., 271
Briquel, D., 276
Britannia, 105, 106, 107, 134
British Isles, 246, 249
Brittany, 38, 106, 107, 108, 118, 123, 140,
    246, 283
Brittia, 106
Brody, S. N., 62, 201
Brogsitter, K. O., 120
Brøndal, V., 222, 225
Brough, J., 313
Brown, A. C. L., 119
Brown, A. L., 269
Brown, E. A. R., 56, 57
Brown, M. A., 223
Brown, Peter, 178

Brouwer, H. H., 113
Brugger, E., 118
Brugnoli, G., 197
Bruiningk, H. von, 173, 175
Bruneau, P., 277
Brunel, J., 273
Brunner, K., 312
Bucher, B., 294
Buchhold, P., 292
Bühler, T., 176
Buhociu, O., 199, 200, 201, 222
Bukharin, N., 57
Bulgaria, 183, 186, 187, 192, 246
Buni, Caterina, 122
Bunker, E. C., 222, 223
Burgundy, 59, 138
Burkert, W., 17, 28, 142, 145, 149, 174,
    219, 220, 276, 299, 285, 287
Burkhardt, Bishop of Worms, 90, 105, 157,
    175, 185
Burkhart, D., 177
Burn, A. R., 118
Burton, George, 116
Bury, J. B., 118
Buryats, 136, 181, 209, 251, 284
Bussagli, M., 222
Buvignier, C., 59
Buxton, R., 175
Byock, J. L., 292

Cacus, 259, 275
Caduff, G., 201, 202
Caeculus, 233, 234, 235, 236, 274, 275,
    276
Caen, 39
Caesar, Julius, 265
Cahors, 39, 56
Calabria, 67
Calame, C., 29, 269
Caldo, Olivo, 312
Calidonius, 233
California, 241
Callate, Agnes, 172
Callimachus, 126
Callisto, 126, 127, 128, 129, 142, 143, 273
Calogierà, A., 111
Caluwé, J., de 120
Calvino, Italo, 24
Calypso, 265
Calydon, 236
Camàro, 125
Cameron, A., 119
Cameron, E., 312
Campbell, J. G., 282, 283, 284

Campeggio, Camillo, 115
Camporesi, P., 312, 313
Canada, 241
Canvoese, 96
Cantemir, Prince D., 189, 190, 200
Capocratians, 74,
Cappadocia, 183, 185, 186
Capponi, F., 311
Caporael, L. R., 312
Carano, 132
Carcassonne, 36, 37, 38, 39, 41, 49, 50, 53,
    59, 60, 64, 65, 68
Cardano, G., 150, 303
Cardini, F., 173
Cardona, C. R., 280
Caro Baroja, J., 25
Carpathians, 186, 194, 213
Carrington, D., 179
Carthage, 74, 123
Castel d'Albano, 302
Caspian Sea, 258
Cassin, E., 271, 272, 273, 274
Cassirer, E., 204
Castellar, 133
Castelnau de Montmirail, 39
Castiglione, Giuseppe, 215
Castrén, A., 279
Catiline, 74
Catalonia, 63, 64
Cataphrygans, 74, 84
Caterina della Libra, 132
Caucasus, 23, 134, 162, 165, 193, 194, 195,
    209, 213, 216, 220, 222, 223, 246, 247,
    250, 251, 255, 256, 257, 258, 263, 288,
    300
Celestinian Order, 78
Çelebi, Evliyâ, 163, 164, 168, 178
Celts, 103, 104, 105, 106, 107, 109, 110,
    116, 117, 118, 119, 120, 122, 123, 125,
    128, 129, 134, 135, 138, 139, 147, 150,
    157, 159, 165, 185, 186, 189, 190, 199,
    210, 211, 212, 213, 214, 221, 223, 246,
    247, 257, 274, 279, 288, 293, 306, 313
Ceram, 241
Cerreto, 302
Cerro de los Santos, 133
Certeau, Michel de, 217
Cerutti, Simona, 24
Cesarius of Arles, 185, 186, 198
Cesole, 256
Chabrand, J-A., 86
Chadwick, N. K., 119
Chalcidican, 212
Chalon-sur-Saône, monastery of, 59

Chambers, E. K., 198
Chambéry, 67, 72
Chambry, E., 140
Ch'angsha, 135, 149
Chantraine, P., 142, 145, 149
Charachidzé, G., 202, 219, 220, 222, 223, 225, 236, 287, 288, 310
Charles, the Fourth (the Handsome), 34, 49
Chartres, 75
Chastel, Andre, 24, 288
Chatwin, C. B., 222, 223
Chavanon, J., 84
Cherlerus, J. H., 312
Cherniss, H., 118
Chevalier, J., 83
Chevsurs, 194
Chiampel, Durich, 192, 193, 202
Chieri, 77, 307
Chiesa Isnardi, G., 292
China, 135, 149, 195, 208, 214, 215, 223, 225, 226, 237, 238, 239, 240, 246, 248, 249, 282, 284,289, 306, 313
Chinon, 36, 44, 54
Chios, 168, 169, 188, 232
(Chirassi-Colombo) I., 116, 140, 144, 220
Chiron, 232, 234
Chrétien, H., 57, 58, 60
Chrétien de Troyes, 30, 241, 279
Christiansen, R. T., 181
Christidis, T., 145
Christinger, R., 308
Christou, C., 144, 146
Christ, *see* Jesus
Christsonday, 97
Cicero, 124
Cinderella, 17, 243, 246, 247, 248, 249, 281, 282, 283, 284
Cimbrans, 118
Circassians, 163, 164, 170, 263, 280
Circe, 229
Circea, 263
Cistercians, 59
Cisalpine, Gaul, 104, 117
Cithaeron, Mount, 228
Cividale, 89
Clairvaux, 79
Clark, S., 25
Claudia Savaria, 105–6
Claudian , 106, 118
Claus, A., 143, 144, 149
Clemen, O., 175
Clement, VI, Pope, 67, 82
Clement of Alexandria, 252

Clifford, J., 122
Closs, A., 202, 219, 293
Coddians, 84
Cohn, Norman, 7, 8, 10, 25, 26, 27, 60, 83, 84, 85, 86, 112, 310, 312
Colchis, 231, 263
Collinder, B., 224, 225
Cologne, 101, 105
Colombardo, G., 223
Colonus, 230
Comaschi, Lella, 56
Comparetti, D., 118, 268, 269, 270
Compayré, C., 55
Como, 71, 78, 93, 96
Concordia, 167, 168
Condom, 33
Conserans, Council of, 91, 100
Conserans, 103, 110
Constantinople, 63
Contessia of Valtellina, 296
Conway, R. S., 145
Copernicus, 28
Cordelia, 282
Cornwall, 118
Corominas, J., 86
Corradi Musi, C., 120, 280
Corsica, 166, 170
Cosquin, E., 281, 283
Coss, P. R., 201
Costa de Beauregard, C.A.M., 81, 82, 83
Couliano, I. P., 277, 287, 313
Cox, M. R., 281, 282, 284
Cozzando, L., 115
Craveri, M., 118
Crémieux, A., 81
Crete, 124, 125, 126, 127, 129, 169, 201, 211, 215, 230, 238, 239, 252, 270
Creteia, 126
Crise, 234
Croatia, 160, 190
Croon, J. H., 272
Cumont, F., 197
Cuna, 292
Curetes, 233, 273
Curtius, L., 273
Cusa, Nicholas of 94, 95, 96, 104, 112, 129, 130, 132, 298
Cybele, 103, 115, 116, 124, 141
Cyrus, 235, 236, 275
Cyprus, 47, 125, 126, 246
Cyzicus, 126
Czaplicka, M. Z., 150

Dalyell, J.G., 113

Dalmatia, 23, 160, 161, 173, 192, 246, 264
Dama of Baza, 133
Dama of Elche, 133, 146
Danae, 229
Damascus, John of, 311
Damascus, 232
Daneau, L., 24
Danube river, 210, 211, 212
Daremberg, C., 176
Darwin, Charles, 224
Datema, C., 197
Dauphiné, the, 7, 65, 67, 68, 71, 72, 73, 77, 80, 82, 104, 109, 125, 302
David, King, 46
Davidson, O., 311
Davis, Natalie, 86
Davis, N. Z., 199, 201, 218
Debrecen, 161
Delabi, L., 291
Del Bello, P., 177
Delcourt, M., 267, 268, 269, 270, 271, 286, 293
Delisle, L., 54
Della Porta, G. B., 137, 150, 151, 303
Delos, 238
Delphi, 238, 277
Del Rio, M., 25
De Martino, E., 28, 181, 203, 290
Demeter, 129, 136, 143, 232, 249, 252, 272, 287
Demophoön, 232, 236, 252, 272, 287
Denmark, 137, 246, 265
Denwood, E., 223
Deonna, W., 113, 146, 176, 221, 273, 274, 293
Derrida, J., 294
Deruta, 299
De Simone, C., 145
Despoina, 136, 149
Detienne, Marcel, 17, 18, 19, 28, 29, 30, 149, 277, 285, 286
Devic, C., 55
Devs, 255, 257
Diacono, Paolo, 138, 296
Diana, 6, 7, 9, 10, 13, 14, 90, 91, 92, 93, 94, 96, 100, 101, 102, 103, 104, 109, 110, 114, 117, 130, 135, 137, 138, 139, 148, 159, 189, 193, 211, 262, 299
Dido, 233, 273
Diels, H., 277
Dietrich, B. C., 149
Dietrich von Bern, 101, 114
Dietschy, H., 202
Di Gesaro, P., 146

Digne, 63
Digor, 163
Dillon, M., 119, 120
Dilthey, K., 116
Dimock, J. F., 175
Diocles of Pepareto, 235
Diocletian, 142
Diodorus Siculus, 124, 125, 126, 140, 141, 142, 211, 270, 287
Diogenes Laertius, 277
Dionisotti, C., 224
Dionysos, 217, 233, 237, 238, 240, 252, 253, 254, 255, 277, 287
Diószegi, V., 177, 178, 179, 180, 181, 202
Dirlmeier, F., 270
Dirr, A., 148, 283
Dnepropetrovsk, 133
Dnieper river, 216
Dniester river, 210
Doamna Zînelor, 103, 117, 189, 190, 193
Dobrugia, 210
Dobrusky, V., 141
Dodds, E. R., 218, 276, 277, 289
Doghi, 300
Dölger, F. J., 83, 84, 116
Döllinger, von, 85
Dognon, P., 60, 61
Domenatta, Caterina, 168
Domenega of Valtellina, 296
Dominican order, 33, 43, 69, 101, 296
Dömötör, T., 177, 178, 181
Doniger O'Flaherty, W., 313
Dönner, A., 111, 115, 202
Dorians, 129
Dottin, G., 119
Douglas, Mary, 56
Dowden, K., 218
Drettas, G., 179
Drever, Jonet, 113
Drews, R., 219
Dreyfus, Captain, 60
Driessen, H., 200
Driskoli, 187
Drobin, U., 222, 225
Duboka, 188, 189, 195, 200
Dubrovnik, 161
Duby, Georges, 120
Du Cange, 110, 116
Ducat, J., 201
Duerr, H. P., 27, 312, 313, 314
Duerrholder, G., 58
Dugi Otok, 161
Dumoutier, G., 282

321

Dumézil, Georges, 19, 29, 151, 173, 178, 197, 198, 199, 202, 203, 204, 217, 219, 220, 225, 272, 276, 280, 286, 287, 291, 292, 293
Duncan, T., 30
Dundes, A., 268, 270, 283, 284
Duplés-Augier, H., 54
Dupront, A., 54
Dupuis, C., 224
Duraffour, A., 86
Durand, J-L., 149
Durand, U, 111
Durham, M. E., 200
Durkheim, E., 204
Durostorum, 183, 188, 199
Duval, P-M., 223
Duvernoy, J., 54, 56, 61, 110, 113, 121, 310

Eberhard, W., 278. 282
Ebermann, O., 111
Ebert, M., 118
Eckhart, 108, 137, 182
Edholm, Erik of, 173
Edinburgh, 103
Edmunds, L., 268, 269, 270, 273, 274
Edsman, C-M., 177, 272
Egger, E., 116
Egypt, 8, 38, 235, 249, 313
Ehelolf, H., 203
Ehrismann, G., 119, 120
Ehrle, F., 85
Eisler, R., 174, 175, 281
Eitrem, S., 272
Elche, 133
Elders of Zion, 3
Eliade, M., 14, 18, 27, 28, 179, 180, 199, 200, 201, 202, 203, 219, 313
Elias, 47
Eliano, C., 275, 277
Elijah, 45, 162, 163
Elkana, Yehuda, 24
Ellis (later Ellis Davidson) H.R., 292
Ellinger, P., 201
Emilia, 307
Empedocles, 237, 277
Enders, C., 141
Endter, A., 114, 115
England, 4, 5, 6, 12, 35, 101, 105, 146, 184
Enodia, 116
Elwert, W. T., 115
Enoch, 45
Engyon, 124, 125, 126, 127, 129, 211
Epona, 104, 105, 108, 116, 117, 198, 211

Ephesus, 94, 104, 130, 131, 146
Ephraïm, M., 82
Epiphanius of Salamins, 84
Erfurt, 68, 182
Eric, 108
Erinyes, 228, 269
Erler, A., 176
Eruli, 118
Esau, 260
Eskimos, 203
Espérandieu, E., 142
Essen, L. van der, 147
Essex, 3, 4
Estremadura
Esterhazy, M., 60
Etna, Mount, 123, 237
Etruscans, 158, 234, 274, 306
Euboea, 169
Eulenberg, 56
Eurasia, 14, 19, 135, 136, 159, 170, 171, 172, 194, 195, 208, 211, 212, 214, 215, 220, 242, 246, 249, 250, 253, 254, 258, 261, 263, 267, 288, 289, 291, 305
Euripides, 128, 228, 233, 236
Europe, 1, 2, 3, 4, 6, 7, 8, 10, 12, 13, 14, 23, 34, 38, 39, 63, 73, 80, 96, 97, 101, 106, 122, 136, 138, 171, 172, 178, 184, 186, 189, 195, 198, 210, 211, 212, 213, 214, 215, 226, 229, 239, 243, 246, 249, 258, 262, 300, 301, 303, 304, 306, 307, 310
Eutropius, 236
Eugene IV, Pope, 297
Evans-Pritchard, E. E., 3
Evian, 69, 70

Fabii, 259
Fabius Pictor, 235
Fabre, Daniel, 117
Fabriano, 310
Fail, Noël du, 199
Farkas, A. R., 220
Farnell, L. R., 268
Fatos, Simuel, 50, 51
Faider-Feytmans, G., 117, 144
Fairy-Boy, 116
Fata Morgana, *see* Morgan La Fay
Faunus, 259
Faure, P., 143
Fauth, W., 140, 272
Fay, H. M., 56
Fazekas, J., 177
Febvre, Lucien, 21, 30
Fédry, J., 280
Felix V, anti-Pope, *see* Amadeus VI of Savoy (67)

Ferenczi, S., 282
Ferrara, 96, 131, 146
Ferrari Pinney, G., 272
Ferri, S., 147, 291, 293
Festus, 293
Fettich, F., 223
Fié allo Scilliar, 132
Filargis, Pietro, Archbishop of Milan, Pope Alexander V, 68, 72, 82
Finicella, 298, 303
Finley, M. I., 29, 141, 145
Finland, 177, 246
Finn, S. M., 279
Firmicus Maternus, 252
Flacelière, R., 140
Flanders, 36, 134
Flavius Josephus, 38, 55
Fleck, J., 151
Fleischer, R., 149
Florence, 47, 77, 297
Fochsa, G., 199
Foix, V., 179
Forcalquier, 63
Fortune, 94
Foucault, Michel, 54
Fougeyron, Ponce, 68, 69, 71, 82, 299
Foulon, C., 279
Fournier, Jacques, Bishop of Pamiers (Pope Benedict XII), 41, 42, 43, 49, 54, 60, 61, 80, 89
Fournier, P-F., 24, 110
Fox, D. C., 277
Frank, 118
France, 12, 34, 35, 36, 37, 39, 41, 44, 46, 49, 50, 51, 52, 53, 57, 65, 67, 69, 71, 76, 101, 103, 105, 123, 186, 226, 304, 306, 307, 314
Francescato, G., 118
Francis of Assisi, 39
Franciscan order, 68, 77
Franconia, 56, 104, 182
Franks, 106
Frankfurt, 68, 182, 183
Franz, A., 111
Franz, R., 142
Fraticelli, 75, 76, 302, 310, 312
Fraw Berthe, 101
Fraw Helt, 101
Frazer, J. G., 8, 15, 27, 197, 203, 204, 222, 273, 278, 289, 290
Freibourg, 79, 86
Freier, H., 293
Freixas, A., 118
Freud, Anna, 282

Freud, Sigmund, 27, 179, 204, 270, 281, 282, 290, 294
Freymond, E., 121
Fridrich, S., 150
Friedberg, E., 110, 116
Friedrich, A., 282, 285
Friedrich, J., 86
Friis Johansen, K., 277
Frisia, 119, 264
Fritzner, J., 150
Friuli, 9, 10, 13, 14, 16, 19, 23, 89, 97, 100, 102, 103, 107, 109, 113, 119, 139, 155, 158, 159, 160, 161, 168, 171, 173, 180, 188, 193, 194, 195, 202, 236, 264, 302, 311
Frund, Johann, 73, 299
Fubini, R., 309
Furumark, A., 291

Gaidoz, H., 116, 147
Gaiffier, B. de 308, 309
Gaillac, 39
Galand, Jean, 60
Galatians, 211
Galicia, 212
Galinier, J., 279
Gallini, C., 276, 291
Gallus, S., 218
Galosna, Antonio, 77, 78, 79, 307
Galton, Francis, 179
Gamkrelidze, T., 225
Gand, 134, 148
Garcia y Bellido, A., 147
Gasparini, E., 199, 202
Gasparo, 172
Gatiev, B., 178
Gaufridus de Dimegneyo, 59
Gauls, 212, 214
Gautier, P., 84
Gawain, 241
Geertz, H., 5, 25
Gélis, Arnaud, 89, 100, 101, 109, 300
Gellner, Ernest, 55
Gelzer, T., 144, 197, 274
Geneva, 68
Génicot, F., 114
Gennep, A van, 56, 197, 200, 203, 204, 278
Genoa, 63, 215
Gerona, 64
Gentili, B., 28
Georgia, 193, 194, 250, 251, 255, 286
Georgiev, V. J., 142
Gérard-Rousseau, M., 145

Geraud, Hugues, Bishop of Cahors 52, 54
Géricault, T., 215
Germany, 68, 101, 102, 128, 137, 153, 154,
   157, 158, 162, 173, 183, 185, 186, 199,
   202, 226, 234, 300, 304, 313
Gernet, L., 176, 269, 271, 272, 276, 287
Gersoian, N., 84
Gerstein, M. R., 313
Gervaise of Tilbury, 140, 247, 284, 301,
   311
Geryon, 237
Ghibbellines, 47
Giani Gallino, T., 279
Gignoux, P., 219, 282, 285
Gill, J., 308
Gimbutas, M., 175, 219
Ginzburg, Marussa, 178
Giorgetta, G., 111, 308
Giovanni da Capestrano, 310
Giraldus Cambrensis, 157, 175
Girard, René, 82, 271
Girard de Frachet, 35, 54
Giuliano Verdena, 131
Giulio d'Assisi, Fr, 89
Glaserin, Dilge, 172
Gmelin, J. G., 286
Gočeva, Z., 144
Goethe, Johann von, 28, 138, 140, 269
Golamina, N., 147
Goldman, B., 221
Gonnet, G., 85
Goossens, R., 273
Gorfunkel, Aleksándr, 178
Gorgon, 131, 230, 231
Gothia, 137
Gottlieb, J., 312
Götze, A., 203
Goulliard, J., 84
Gowdie, Isabel, 96, 97, 112
Graf, A., 118, 140
Graf, F., 198
Graham, A. H., 219
Grambo, R., 151, 176, 180, 181
Granada, King of, 35, 36, 42, 43, 44, 45,
   46, 47, 48, 52, 59, 60
Granet, M., 203, 220, 278
Granfield, P., 83
Grantovskij, E. A., 218, 219, 224
Grass, N., 112
Grasse, 64
Gratch, N., 147
Graumann, C. F., 27
Graus, F., 82
Grayzel, S., 58, 59

Gratzian, 91
Greece, ancient, 19, 104, 123, 126, 128,
   129, 131, 133, 136, 157, 169, 183, 186,
   207, 209, 215, 216, 220, 222, 228, 229,
   230, 231, 232, 234, 237, 238, 239, 240,
   249, 250, 251, 253, 254, 255, 256, 257,
   265, 288
Greece, country, 133, 169, 170, 284, 304
Green, A., 270
Gregorius Magnus, 70
Gregory XIII, Pope, 226
Gregory of Tours, 104, 116
Grenoble, 65
Greyerz, Peter von, 69, 70, 71, 78, 83, 307
Gri, G. P., 177
Griaznov, M. P., 218
Grimm, Jakob, 9, 15, 86, 116, 117, 119,
   121, 138, 139, 148, 151, 152, 173
Grisons, 192, 296
Grisward, J. H., 178, 221
Gross, H., 54
Grout, P. B., 119, 120, 279
Gruppe, O., 17, 270, 271, 273, 274, 281,
   287
Guarnerio, P. E., 283, 284
Gubbio, 297
Guenée, B., 59
Guérard, B. E. C, 84
Guerchberg, S., 81
Guerreau-Jalabert, A., 120
Guerrini, P., 115
Gugitz, G., 202
Gui, Bernard, 33, 36, 44, 54, 57
Guibert, L., 56
Guibert of Nogent, 76, 85
Guichard, Bishop of Troyes, 52
Guillaume de Lorris, 113, 152
Guillaume de Machaut, 82
Guillaume de Nangis, 35, 36, 52, 54
Gunda, B., 177
Gunkel, H., 275
Güntert, H., 117, 201, 292
Guntram, King, 138, 151, 152, 281, 296,
   208
Gurevič, A.J., 110, 111, 114
Gušic, M., 222
Guthrie, W. K. C., 143

Haavio, M., 311
Habonde, 96, 100, 115, 117, 136, 152, 185
Hades, 158, 234, 238, 265, 268, 275
Hadingus, King, 265, 293
Haekel, J., 289
Haerecura, *see* Hera

Hagenbach, K. R., 181
Hakluyt, R., 292
Hahl, L., 140
Hallauer, Hermann, 112
Halle, A. S., 275
Halliday, W. R., 219, 272
Hallowell, A. I., 148
Hamayon, R., 150
Hančar, F., 218, 223
Hand, W.D., 292
Hanell, K., 268
Hanika, J., 111, 146, 173
Hanover 304
Hansen, J., 24, 83, 86
Harf-Lancner, L., 117, 174
Harlequin, 294
Harmatta, J., 222
Harrians, 192
Harris, W. V., 275
Harrison, J., 201, 204
Hartmann, A., 271
Hartog, F., 26, 217, 286, 287
Harva (Holmberg), U., 150, 181
Haselriederin, Katherina, 146
Hatt, G., 279
Hatti, 196, 234
Hatto, A. T., 218, 284
Haudry, J., 224
Haug, E., 119
Hauser, Hans, 121
Haverkamp, A., 82, 83
Hawkes, C., 223
Hazlitt, W. C., 113
Hebron, 45
Hecate, 100, 113, 131
Heddernheim, 128
Heer, O., 224
Heidelberg, 156
Heiligendorff, W., 117
Heine, Heinrich, 119, 151
Heine, W., 202
Heine-Geldern, R., 148, 149, 218, 225, 278
Helbig, W., 273
Helgoland, 106
Helike, 126
Hellenism, 19, 23
Hellequin, 191
Hellespont, 209
Hellot, A., 54
Helm, K., 111, 112, 201
Henig, M., 117
Henning, W. B., 219
Henninger, J., 148, 283

Henningsen, G., 25, 26, 27, 140, 311
Henniviers, 73, 300
Hentze, C., 203
Henzen, W., 292
Hephaestus, 231, 255, 257
Hera, 104, 117
Heracles, 230, 237
Heraclitus, 238
Hercules, 250, 259
Hérens, 73, 300
Herenstein Smith, B., 281
Herlechinus, 101, 303
Hermes, 230, 231, 240, 271
Hernici, 233, 234, 274
Herod, 53, 62, 235
Herodias, 10, 90, 91, 92, 93, 94, 100, 104, 108, 130, 132, 148, 189, 190, 193, 194, 200, 211, 212, 297
Herodotus, 30, 128, 154, 157, 175, 192, 207, 208, 209, 211, 217, 218, 219, 221, 237, 251, 253, 254, 287
Herolt, Johannes, 101, 102, 103, 114
Herrmann, P., 293
Hertz, Robert, 56, 175, 297
Hertz, W., 146, 174, 288, 310
Herzegovina, 160
Hesiod, 119, 250, 251, 271, 272, 282, 286
Hesse, 109
Heubeck, A., 145
Heurgon, J., 293
Heusch, L. de, 285, 287
Heusler, A., 280
Hibschmann, H., 178
Hill, D. L., 30
Hilscher, P. C., 138, 151, 182, 183, 184, 197
Hippodameia, 250
Hippodamus, 229
Hittites, 196, 271
Hnefill Aðalsteinsson, J., 291, 292
Hobsbawm, E. J., 197
Hocart, A. M., 285, 289, 290
Hoddinott, R. F., 141, 220, 221
Hoeniger, R., 81, 82
Hoepffner, E., 82
Höfer, O., 268
Hoffman-Krayer, E., 201
Hofmann, A., 312, 313
Höfler, O., 114, 115, 173, 174, 176, 197, 200, 201, 203, 276, 278, 313
Holda, 6, 7, 10, 91, 94, 101, 109, 111, 114, 115, 138, 148, 184, 262
Holenstein, E., 270

Holland, 103
Ho-lu, King, 239
Holt, C., 294
Holtved, E., 292
Homer, 19, 104, 118, 211, 231, 232
Homnel, H., 272
Honnorat, S. J., 24
Hoops, J., 293
Hoppál, M., 150, 177
Horagalles, 135, 246
Horsfall, H. M., 176, 198, 201, 274, 275
Horváth, T., 28
Hosea, 46
Hubaux, J., 289
Hubert, H., 116
Hubschmid, J., 314
Huerta, 128
Hulde, Hulden, *see* Holda
Hultkrantz, Å., 149, 150, 180, 181
Hunan, 135
Hungary, 23, 51, 161, 162, 164, 173, 179, 181, 187, 193, 210, 212, 213, 215, 257, 265
Hurrites, 271
Husserl, 269
Hvarfner, H., 181
Hyperboraens, 209, 212, 254, 287
Hyères, 63
Hyppolite, J., 290

Ibo, 244
Iceland, 192, 264, 265, 293, 311
Ida, Mount, 126
Ihm, M., 117, 140, 142
Ilanz, 192
Ile-de-France, 241
Ilion, 146
Ilos, 146
India 246, 282, 289
Indochina, 282
Indus river, 305
Intessura, Stefano, 298, 309, 310
Iphigenia, 128
Iran, 162, 193, 208, 214, 219, 235, 236, 246, 305,
Ireland, 100, 108, 109, 113, 134, 137, 157, 158, 175, 212, 220, 221
Iron, 163
Islands of the Blessed, 107
Isle-sur-Tarn, 39
Israel,, 45
Istria, 104, 160, 168
Italy, 47, 76, 101, 103, 105, 161, 265, 266, 306

Itkonen, T. I., 174, 180, 181
Ivanov, V., 29, 225

Jabbok river, 236
Jacob, 236, 260, 262, 276
Jacobson, E., 223
Jacobsthal, P., 147, 217, 223
Jacoby, M., 176
Jacopo da Varazze, 94, 100, 134
Jaffe, I. B., 223
Jakobson, Roman, 20, 28, 29, 174, 180, 280, 292, 294
Jalla, J., 308
James, R. O., 175
Jameson, R. D., 283
Janicke, O., 313
Janko, J., 291
Japan, 134, 135, 196, 247, 283, 313
Jason, 229, 230, 231, 232, 233, 234, 236, 240, 250, 252, 263, 273, 274, 281
Jauss, H. R., 217
Jean d'Outremeuse, 35, 36, 54
Jean de St Victor, 35, 37, 54, 55
Jeanmaire, H., 201, 271, 272, 275, 277, 278, 286, 287
Jensen, A. E., 279
Jericho, 45, 46
Jerusalem, 45, 46
Jerusalem, King of, 45, 47, 52
Jesi, F., 203
Jessen, E. J., 148, 149
Jesus, 70, 71, 93, 95, 97, 149, 235, 247, 297, 298
Jettmar, K., 218, 219, 223, 285
Joan of Arc, 97
Joan, Queen of Navarre, 52, 64
Jobstin, Anna, 146
Jocasta, 229
Jodab of Abdon and Semeren, 45
Jodogne, O., 120
Johansons, A., 173
John XXII, Pope, 45, 47, 52, 57, 58, 62
John of Ojun, 75, 76, 84, 85
Johnson, Richard, 264
Johnson, S. E., 145
Joki, A. J., 224, 313
Jolles, A., 28
Jordan river, 132
Joret, C., 314
Josafat, 165
Jost, M., 149
Joubert, Laurent, 265
Jourdain, 42, 43
Jukagir, 134

Jung, Carl, 17, 18, 28, 203, 279
Jungmann, J. A., 83
Jupiter, 81
Jura, 306
Jurgensburg, 153
Justin, 74
Justinian, 118
Jutland, 106

Kahil, L. G., 143, 144, 149
Kamper, P., 311
Kahn, C. N., 277
Kalleničenko, Semyon, 172
Kaltenmark, M., 278
Karajich, V., 283
Karsten, R., 149
Kaufmann, F., 111
Karystios, 238
Katzarova, R., 199
Kempter, Martina, 110
Kennedy, A. B., 314
Kerényi, C., 274, 276
Kern, H., 277
Kershaw, J., 55
Kertész, I., 275
Keysler, J. G., 117, 138, 151
Khazanov, A. M., 218
Kieckhefer, R., 6, 25, 27
Kiev, 155, 172
Kimmerians, 118
King, A., 117
King of the Fairies, 96
Kingdon, R. M., 26
Kirby, E. T., 203
Kirk, G. S., 28, 285
Kirk, R., 113
Klaniczay, G., 177, 178, 180, 181
Klapper, J., 111, 114, 121, 145
Klaproth, Julius, 162
Klee, F., 293
Klee, Paul, 293
Klein, V., 177
Kleinmann, D., 281
Klenke, M. A., 119
Klibansky, R., 270
Kligman, G., 199, 200
Knirk,' J. E., 176
Knossos, 126
Knobloch, J., 272
Knuchel, E. F., 179
Ko Hong, 238
Koch, F., 140
Koch, G., 273
Koch, J., 112

Kodolányi, J., 177
Köhler, E., 120
Kohn, R,. 59
Kolendo, J., 113
Koleva, T. A., 201
Kondakov, N., 223
Königshofen, Justinger von, 73
Konigshoven, Jacob Twinges von, 82
Kontizas, Nikolaos, 180
Koppers, W., 148
Kore, 125, 136
Korner, T., 178
Kornmann, Heinrich, 109
Kothe, H., 218, 219, 313
Kovács, Z., 181
Krader, L., 181
Krahe, H., 145
Kral, Giovanni, 83, 120, 146
Krappe, A. H., 111, 114, 140
Kraust, 116, 146
Kretschmar, F., 176
Kretschmer, P., 145, 149, 268, 272
Kretzenbacher, L., 174, 176
Kriegel, M., 56
Krk, 161
Kroeber, A., 294
Kroll, W., 273
Kronos, 107, 229, 270
Krüger, E., 116
Kügler, H., 173
Kuhn, A., 201
Kukahn, K, 147
Küppers, G. A., 200
Kuret, N., 111, 200, 222
Kurze, D., 85, 86
Kusters, P. M., 291
KwaKiutl, 203
Kynosura, 126, 127
Kypselos, 275

Laager, J., 142
La Baume, 63
Labdacus, 227, 268
Labourd, the, 137, 139
Lacan, J., 290
Laconia, 169
Laistner, L., 281
Laius, 227, 229, 230, 236, 267, 268
Lambert, M., 84, 85
Lamothe-Langon, E. L., 86
Lamotte, P., 179
Lancelot, 108
Lancre, Pierre de, 136, 137, 139, 150, 151
Landes, A., 282
Landucci Gattinoni, F., 117, 118

Lang, A, 281
Langlois, C. V., 57, 58, 59
Langlotz, E., 147
Langmuir, G. I., 55, 59
Lanhers, Y., 113
Lanternari, V., 203
Lapps, 23, 135, 150
Lapland, 23, 134, 135, 136, 137, 138, 139, 170, 171, 172, 174, 180, 194, 210, 212, 246, 250, 257, 264, 287
Larson, G. J., 276
Larchevêque, Jean, Lord of Parthenay, 35, 44, 49, 57
Larenaudie, M-J., 55
Larner, C., 11, 13, 26, 27, 112
La Tene, 109
Latham, M. W., 113
Latium, 236, 259, 260, 262, 290
Lateran Council (1215), 38
Latte, K., 277
Laurens, A-F., 286
Lausanne, 49, 70
Lavergne, G., 54, 56
Lawson, C., 179, 180, 272
Lazard, 6, 57
Lazzari, F., 114
Lazzerini, L., 293, 308, 310
Leach, Edmund, 56, 204
Lear, King, 248
Le Beuf, J., 288
Lecoq de la Marche, A., 311
Le Braz, A., 119
Leem, K., 148
Lefebvre, 61
Leglay, M., 117
Le Goff, Jacques, 24, 27, 56, 61, 114, 120, 140, 201, 279,
Lehtisalo, T., 181, 279, 292, 313
Lehugeur, P., 57
Leibniz, G. G., 284
Leibundgut, A., 144
Leith, 103, 116
Leipzig, 137, 138, 158, 183
Leland, C. G., 200
Leman, Lake, 67, 71, 110
Lemnos, 234
Leontini, 124
Leo, 46
Le Provost, A., 53
Lepschy, G. C., 29
Lequien, M., 311
'Lercheimer, Augustine' (*pseud.*), *see* Witekind, Hermann
Leroi-Gourhan, A., 28, 220, 221, 280, 290

Le Roux, F., 118
Le Roy Ladurie, Emmanuel, 24, 26, 30, 61, 81, 110, 113, 152, 308
Lesky, A., 203
Lessa, W. A., 270
Lestang, 41
Leubuscher, R., 180
Leuca, 285
Lévêque, P., 142, 143, 273, 274
Levi della Torre, Stefano, 24
Levi, Giovanni, 24
Lévi, Jean, 24
Lévi-Strauss, Claude, 17, 19, 20, 21, 22, 28, 29, 30, 149, 198, 201, 203, 204, 225, 267, 268, 269, 277, 278, 282, 284, 289, 290, 291, 294, 295, 310, 313, 314
Levin, S., 275
Levin, I., 280
Lévy, E., 150
Lesourd, D., 117, 200
Leyden, F. von der, 146, 152, 280, 281
Liberman, A., 28
Liborio, M., 30
Liebenau, T. von, 83
Liermann, H., 112
Lignitz, 304
Limoges, 39, 41, 49, 52
Limors, 108
Lincoln, B., 118
Lindskog, B., 174
Lindow, J., 292
Linduff, K., 116
Lipen (Lipenius), M., 183, 184, 197
Litsas, F. K., 199
Lithuania, 27, 158
Little, L. K., 55, 56
Livonia, 13, 14, 19, 27, 97, 137
'Livonus, Hermannus', (pseud.), *see* Witekind, Hermann
Lixfeld, H., 151
Lloyd-Jones, Hugh, 143
Loeb, I., 82
Loeb, J., 58
Löffler, J., 268
Lohmann, 121
Lollianos, 74
Lombardy, 77, 109, 247, 307
Lombardo de Fraguliati, 92
Longobards, 214
Longpré, E., 308, 309, 310
Lonicer, Adam, 304
Loomis, L. Hibbard, 119, 152
Loomis, R. S., 119, 120, 140, 279

Loparians, 247
Lopes de Meneses, A., 81
Lormea, Lorenzo, 79
Lorraine, 246, 283
Losonczy, A. M., 177, 179
Lot, F., 119
Loth, J., 118
Lot-Falck, E., 150, 177, 180, 181, 285, 308
Lotman, J. M. 20, 29
Lötschental, 191
Louis IX, 39
Lovecy, I., 120
Lucifer, 299
Luard, H. R., 61
Lucas, H., 277, 278
Lucerne, 72, 299
Lucian, 270, 271, 275
Lucian of Samosata, 230
Lucibello, 299
Lucifello, 93, 96
Luciferians (nt), 78
Lucretius, 280
Ludwig, Lord of the Pays de Vand, 67
Lugnitz 272
Lüling, G, 293
Luria, S., 15, 17, 269, 270, 275
Lycaon, 126, 127, 156, 157, 250, 285
Lycophron, 272
Lykosura, 149
Lyons, 69, 74, 77

Maass, F., 117
Maass, P., 272
MacCana, P., 274, 279
MacCulloch, E., 176
Macculloch, J. A., 112
Macedonia, 186, 187, 188, 192, 239
Macfarlane, Alan, 3, 4, 8, 14, 25, 27
Mâcon, 48, 49, 52, 60
Macrobius, 113, 233
Madagascar, 229
Madonna Oriente, 6, 7, 14, 19, 92, 93, 96, 100, 101, 102, 114, 123, 131, 134, 135, 136, 247, 248, 262
Maenchen-Helfen, O., 219, 276
Maggi, Vincenzo, 115
Maggiulli, G., 142
Magnen, R., 116
Magyars, 194
Mahlen, L., 269
Maiolati, Francesco, 85
Majorel, Pierre, 48
Malet, C., 55, 56, 81

Malinowski, B., 204
Malitz, J., 140
Mamson, 67
Man, Andrew, 97
Manetho, 38
Manchuria, 220
Manicheans, 75, 78
Mann, J., 148
Mannhardt, W., 114, 147, 283, 312, 313
Mannheim, 68
Manosque, 63
Manselli, R., 62, 308
Mansi, G. D., 57
Mansionario, G., 111
Manteyer, G. de, 56, 62
Mantua, 131, 132, 256
Maranda, P., 181
Marakesh, 249
Marazzi, U., 180
Marcadé, J., 150
Marcellus, 124
Marciac, Council, of (1330), 38
Marcianopli, 188
Marcionites, 74
Marconi, M., 140, 291
Marcus, G. F., 112
Margherita called the Vanzina, 132
Margherita called Tessadrella, 132
Margherita dell 'Agnola called Tommasina, 132
Marinatos, S., 143
Marmai, Ippolito, 146
Marmora, Sea of, 126, 209; *see also Propontis*
Marocco, Jacopo, 89
Mars, 81
Marténe, E., 54, 111
Martianus Capella, 293
Martin, Jacques, 111, 141
Martin-Achard, R., 276
Martin V, Pope, 297
Martino da Presbitero, 77, 78
Marx, Karl, 21, 30
Masa, 196
Masonic Order, 12
Massenzio, M., 274
Massilli, Pietro, 202
Massimo da Torino, 185
Mathesius, J., 114
Mathieu, R., 203, 281
Matocyiis, Giovanni de, 94
Matronae, see 'Mothers'
Matte Blanco, I, 294, 295
Matteuccia di Francesco, 229, 300
Maximian, 142

Maximus of Tyre, 209
Maxwell-Stuart, P.G., 269
May, W. H., 62
McCartney, E. S., 146
McGowan, M. M., 151
Medea, 231, 233, 252
Medes, 209
Mediterranean, 123
Megas, G. A., 180
Meillet, Antoine, 144, 145
Meisen, K., 114, 115, 151
Melampus, 227, 237, 238, 268, 276
Melanchton, Philip, 157, 175
Meleager, 223, 236, 270, 273
Mellink, M. J., 223, 224
Melossi, Enrica, 274
Mengarde de Pomeriis, 113
Menichino da Latisana, 164, 165, 179
Menicis, G. de, 141
Menochio, J., 146
Mercklin, L., 272
Mercury, 272
Mercutio, 105
Meriggi, B., 174, 180, 271
Merker, P., 119
Merlingen, W., 142
Meriones, 124
Merlo, G. G., 85, 86
Meslin, M., 198
Messina, 63, 123, 125
Metapontum, 209
Metis, 272
Metz, 59
Metzler, D., 293
Meuli, K., 15, 17, 173, 197, 198, 199, 201,
   202, 218, 219, 220, 274, 276, 280, 283,
   285, 286, 287, 289, 291, 293
Meun, Jean de, 152
Meyer, E., 275
Meyer, E. H., 116
Meyer-Matheis, E., 152
Mexico, 279
Miccoli, G., 54, 309
Michel, F., 55
Michelet, J. 59, 151
Michels, A. K., 116
Middle East, 211, 214
Middleton, J., 181
Midelfort, H. C. E., 10, 25, 26, 27, 311
Miglio, M., 309
Migliorini, P., 311
Migne, 84, 110, 175, 197
Milan, 6, 91, 96, 102, 103, 131, 133
Miller, V., 178, 222

Minakata, K., 283
Minns, E. H., 219, 223
Minoa, 127
Minor order, 297, 299
Minotaur, 230
Minucius Felix, 74
Mirandola, 178
'Mistress of the animals', 132, 136, 211,
   220
Mitchell, R. E., 270
Miwok, 241
Möbius, H., 144
Mócsy, A., 117
Modena, 25, 96
Modica, 123, 125
Modron, 108
Moduco, Battista, 89, 265
Moebius, F. T., 176
Moesia, 183, 188
Mogk, E., 198, 292
Mohammed, 293
Moldavia, 188, 189, 190, 194
Molinier, A., 55, 60, 61
Mollat, G., 53, 58, 61
Molucca, 241
Momiano, 168
Momigliano, Arnaldo, 24, 25, 28, 55, 141,
   218, 269, 275, 289, 290
Moncenisio, 77
Monfalcone, 168, 170
Monginevro, 77
Mongolia, 208, 209, 214, 219, 249, 286,
   289
Montaigne, Michel de, 226, 267
Montauban, 39
Montefalco, 309
Montenegro, 160, 161
Montepaone, C., 143
Monter, E. W., 24, 311
Montfaucon, B. de, 59, 110
Montreux, 67
Moon, W. G., 143
Moore, R. I., 55, 56, 61
Morard, N., 59
Moravia, 212
Morbegno, 296
Morgan le Fay, 108, 123, 125
Morocco, 249
Morrigan, 108, 123
Moray Firth, 96
Moses, 46, 235
Moscovici, S., 27
'Mothers', the (*Matronae*) 124, 125, 126,
   127, 129, 136, 141, 142, 157, 185, 194,
   211

Motzki, H., 203
Moulinas, R., 58
Mounin, Georges, 29
Moussaief Mason, J., 281
Mücke, G., 119, 151
Mühl, M., 140
Mulinen, W-F. de 82
Müller, H. D., 285
Müller, P. E., 293
Muller-Bergstom, W., 202
Multedo, R., 179, 180
Mundal, E., 292
Munich, 78
Munkácsi, B., 222, 289, 313
Münster, Sebastian, 202
Munzer, F., 140
Muraro, L., 26, 111, 115
Muratori, L. A., 138, 309
Muri, 128, 144, 145
Murray, M. A., 3, 4, 7, 8, 9, 26, 112, 113, 178
Musès, C., 121
Müster, W., 202
Musti, D., 143
Mutzenbecher, A., 116
Muybridge, E., 223
Mycenae, 126, 127, 129, 215, 223
Mysia, 238

Nachtigall, H., 282, 285, 291
Nai-Tung Ting, 282
Napoli, A., 276
Narbonne, 64, 65
Narses, 118
Narti, 165, 209, 242
Nauck, A., 273
Near East, 196, 273, 274
Needham, Rodney, 17, 28, 179, 180, 279, 285, 289, 290
Neleus, 235
Nemesis, 232
Nennius, 134
Neoptolemus, 234
Neuchâtel, Lake, 109
Neumann, E., 279
Neumann, K., 286
Neuroi, 157, 212, 221
Neustadt, E., 142, 143, 144
Niccoli, Ottavia, 111, 114
Nicias, 124, 125, 126
Nicola of Damascus, 276
Nicolini, G., 146, 147
Nider, Johannes, 69, 70, 71, 72, 78, 79, 82, 83, 94, 154, 297, 307

Niebuhr, B. G. 218, 219
Niger, 125
Nilsson, M. P., 15, 117, 118, 142, 143, 144, 150, 197, 198, 199, 268, 276, 279
Niolo, 167
Nivardus, 148
Nogaret, Council of (1290), 38
Noll, R., 118
Nölle, W., 219
Nolting-Hauff, I., 120
Nonnus, 277
Nora, P., 60
Norcia, 108
Nordmann, A., 82
Normanh, Guillaume, 41, 43
Normandy, 49, 123, 306
Norway, 137, 293
Nosovki, 172
Nourry, E., 271, 281
Novae, 100
Novara, 105
Nuremberg, 184
Nyberg, H. S., 219

Oaks, L. S., 116
Ob, 203
Obelkevich, J., 25
Odin, 101, 118, 139, 151, 152, 192, 220, 265, 293
Oedipus, 17, 227, 228, 229, 230, 231, 235, 236, 237, 240, 248, 250, 258, 267, 268, 269, 270, 271, 275, 276, 277, 279, 284, 288
Oenomaus, 229, 250
Oesterley, W., 276
Ohlmarks, A., 181
Oikonomides, A. N., 179
Olaus Magnus, 137, 139, 152, 158, 172, 176, 181
Olbia, 231, 253, 254
'Old Man of the Mountain', 51, 52
Oliphant, S. G., 311
Olender, M., 60
Olmsted, G. S., 223
Olrik, A., 149, 293
Olympus, Mount, 126, 255
Olympia, 250
Oppolzer, T. von, 57
Orderico, Vitalie, 53
Orient, 161
Oriente, see Madonna Oriente
Orpheus, 252, 253, 254, 286
Orkney, 113

Orléans, 49, 75, 78, 84
Oron, Pierre d', 59
Ortutay, G., 178
Orvieto, 158
Ossolani, The, 162
Ossory, 157
Otomi, 279
Otranto, 107, 140
Otto, W. F., 274
Oulx, 302
Oyotte, J. Y., 55
Ozouf, M., 197

Pace, D., 284
Pacetti, D., 309
Pacific Ocean, 246
Padua, 297
Pais, D., 177
Paione, G., 28
Palatinate, 104, 128
Palatine, 196, 259
Palazzolo Acreide, 141
Pales-Gobilliard, A., 55
Pallene, 131, 212
Palmer, L. R., 142
Pamiers, 41, 47, 53, 54, 80, 89
Pamiers, Bishops of, *see* Fournier, Jacques
Panama, 292
Panciroli, G., 28
Pandora, 250
Panfilo, F., 85
Panizza, A., 120, 146
Panofsky, E., 270
Panzona, Maria, 100, 155
Paolino Veneto, 55
Paproth, H. J., 148, 283, 284
Paravy, P., 83, 308
Parcae, The, 105, 157, 185
Paris, 36, 37, 44, 46, 48, 49, 57, 59
Paris, 281
Paris, G., 119
Paris Matthew, 51, 52, 61
Parrot, R., 113
Parthenay, Lord of, *see* Larchevêque, Jean
Pascal, C. B., 116, 117
Pascali, Bartolomeo, 302
Pasquinelli, A., 279
Patlagaen, Evelyne, 84
Patroclus, 231
Patzig, H., 119
Paul of Samosata, 75
Paul de Saint-Père de Chartres, 75, 84
Paulicans 75, 76, 84
Paulme, D., 284

Pauly-Wissowa, 141, 142, 143, 149, 158, 175, 192
Pazyrik, 208
Pearl, J. L., 27
Pease, A. S., 273
Pedora River, 264
Pédaque, Queen, 258
Pegna, Francesco, 83, 112
Pelasgians, 127
Pelias, 229, 230, 252, 287
Peleus, 235, 272
Pelopia, 229
Peloponnese, 126, 129, 169
Pelops, 136
Penelope, 229
Penzig, O., 314
Perchta, 6, 7, 91, 101, 102, 115, 146, 193, 195, 258, 262, 289
Percival, 108, 267
Perez, Diego, 50, 51
Pergamon, 285
Perigord, 36
Perigueux, 39
Perm, 258
Pernier, L., 144
Perrault, 246
Persephone, 231, 272
Perseus, 229, 230, 231, 240, 250, 265, 281
Persia, 215
Perugia, 77, 309
Pestalozza, U., 272
Pestalozza, Baldassarre, 296
Peter III, King, 64
Peter of Berne, 94
Petronius, 158, 175
Pettazzoni, R., 144
Pettersson, O., 149
Peucer, Caspar, 137, 139, 150, 152, 156, 157, 170, 175, 177, 180
Pezzini Ottoni Alda, 288
Pfeffeingen, 172
Phigalia, 143
Philadelpheus, A., 143, 144
Philip the Fifth (the Long One), 34, 35, 37, 45, 48, 49, 54, 58, 59, 61
Philip the Sixth *see* Phillipe de Valois
Phillipe V, *see* Philip the Fifth
Phillips, E. D., 219, 288
Phillippe de Valois, Count of Anjou (later Philip the Sixth), 45, 46, 47, 49, 57
Philippson, E. A., 117, 118, 173
Philoctetes, 234, 274
Philodemus of Gadara, 287
Phocians, 192, 201

Phoenix, 126
Phylacus, 237
Piaget, J., 290
Piana, C., 309
Picardy, 51
Piccaluga, 175
Pico, G. F., 178
Piedmont, 76, 77, 78, 79, 86, 109, 296, 299, 302, 307
Pierina de Bripio, 92, 93, 100, 102, 134
Pietro de Bripio, 92
Peter di Herenthals, 53
Pietro di Jacopo, 302
Piggott, S., 151, 152, 288
Pillinger, R., 197
Pinarii, 259
Pindar, 234, 236, 273, 274
Piniès, M. P., 110
Piotrovski, B., 147
Pisa, 68
Pisani, V., 145, 272
Pitcairn, R., 112, 113
Pitré, G., 140, 283
Plato, 254, 280
Plataeans, 233, 234, 273
Plessippus, 233
Pliny, 157, 158, 175, 209
Plomteaux, H., 314
Plutarch, 107, 118, 119, 124, 140, 146, 235, 238, 254, 287
Po Valley, 96, 103, 131, 257
Pócs, E., 141
Poggioli, R., 174
Pogrebova, M. N., 286
Poliakov, L., 27, 55, 81
Poitiers, 34, 44
Poitou, 49
Poland, 306
Polomé, E. C., 221
Pomerania, 78
Pomian, K., 290
Pompeii, 233
Pompey, 265
Pomorska, K., 29
Popov, D., 144
Porta Arnaud-Bernard, asylum of, 41
Porter, J. R., 293
Portuguese, 226
Porzig, W., 271
Poseidon, 235
Posidonius of Apamea, 124, 125, 140, 141
Posnansky, H., 144
Potitii, 259

Potocki, J., 218, 290
Pötscher, W., 276
Poucet, J., 289
Pouillon, J., 181
Powell, T. G. E., 223
Praeneste, 233, 234, 235
Praetorius, J., 137, 138, 151, 183, 197
Presedo Velo, F., 146, 147
Procopius of Cesarea, 106, 107, 118, 119
Prodinger, F., 111
Prometheus, 216, 250, 251, 252, 255, 256, 257, 262, 286, 288
Propontis, 126
Propp, Vladimir, 15, 16, 28, 120, 146, 152, 175, 199, 268, 269, 270, 271, 275, 276, 280
Prosperi, A., 30
Protagoras, 125
Proteus, 229
Prous Boneta, 53
Provence, 59, 63, 64, 65, 77, 123, 246, 283
Prudhomme, A., 58, 81, 82
Prüm, 104
Prussia, 158, 221
Pschavs, 194
Psello, Michelo, 75
Puchner, W., 200
Peuch, H-C., 84
Pugliese-Carratelli, G., 141
Pujols, 43
Pulgram, E., 222
Putorti, N., 141
Pylos, 126, 129
Pyrenees, 23, 26, 50, 64, 89, 137, 306
Pythagoras, 237, 252, 253, 255, 277

Queen, of the Fairies (Elves), 96, 97, 102, 122, 136
Queen Mab, 105
Quinoni, Dayas, 63
Quintilii, 259
Quirinus, 262

Rabb, A., 29
Radermacher, L., 152, 274, 280
Raeder, H., 293
Raglan, Lord, 275
Ragusa, 122
Rajna, P., 288
Ralston, W. R. S., 284
Ranger, T., 197
Ränk, G., 149
Rank, O., 275
Ranke, F., 173, 199

Raphaël, F., 111
Rapp, L., 146
Rasmus, Jonas, 118
Rategno, Bernardo, 71, 83
Ravazzoli, F., 280
Ravis-Giordani, G., 179, 180
Ray, D. J., 279
Raynaldus, O., 82
Regino of Prüm, 89, 94, 104, 130
Reinach, S., 116, 142, 144, 146, 147, 176, 223, 272, 293
Reinart, T., 116
Reiss, E., 121
Remedios, M. dos, 81
Remus, 259, 291
Renfrew, C., 225
Reverdin, O., 285
Reymond, M., 86
Rhea, 124, 126, 229, 252
Rhine river, 68
Rhineland, 103, 105, 117, 128
Rhodes, 133
Rhŷs, J., 224, 225
Ricci, Gianni, 180
Ricci, S. de, 118
Richardson, N. J., 272
Richella, 94, 95, 96, 100, 104, 109, 129, 130, 131, 132, 136, 185, 211, 262
Rieger, M., 292
Riegler, R., 310
Riemschneider, M. 271, 279, 293
Riez, 63
Riga, 156
Ripa Bianca, 299
Rivel, Marc, 41
Rivière-Chalan, V. R., 55, 56, 58
Rivuhelos, 50
Robert, C., 149, 267, 268, 269, 270, 279
Robert, L., 116
Robert, U., 55, 56
Roberts, S. F., 56, 59
Robin Hood, 201
Rocco da Bedano, P., 83
Rochas, V. de, 55
Rochas d'Aiglun, A. de, 86
Rodez, 39, 56, 59
Rodi, 299
Roemer, A., 271
Rohde, E., 19, 175, 204, 281
Róheim, G., 177, 178, 179, 180
Rohlfs, G., 198
Romania, 27, 103, 159, 166, 187, 188, 189, 193, 194, 200, 202, 203, 212, 213, 270
Röhrich, L., 148, 151, 283

Rome, ancient, 104, 124, 183, 196, 235, 259, 274, 289, 301, 306
Rome, city, 23, 76, 77, 122, 232, 297, 298, 300, 301, 309
Romulus, 234, 235, 236, 259, 262
Rooth, A. B., 281, 282, 283, 284
Rosaldo, R., 112
Roscher, W. H., 15, 175, 176, 180, 204, 268, 270, 274, 282
Rose, E., 8, 200
Rose, H. J., 270, 276
Rose, V., 273
Rosenfeld, H., 174
Ross, A., 116
Ross, L., 141
Rossi, Francesco de', of Valenza, 115
Rossi, I., 29
Rossi, M. M., 113
Rossolans, 208
Rostovtzev (Rostovtzeff), M., 217, 220, 223, 285, 289
Rotari, 266
Rothberg, R. J., 29
Rouen, 97
Roussas, 104
Roux, J-P., 291
Ruck, C. A. P., 288
Rudbeck, O., 118, 224, 225, 287
Rudenko, S. I., 218
Rudhardt, J., 276, 285, 286
Rudolph, K., 115
Ruggero da Casale, Fr, 92, 93
Rupert, L., 57, 59
Rupp, H., 173
Rushton, L., 200
Russell, J. B., 10, 26, 85, 110
Russia, 149, 153, 155, 163, 211, 246, 248, 258, 264, 269, 270, 283, 284, 288
Ruto, 135
Růžičič, G., 174

Sabinus, Georg, 221
Sade, 114
Sadoch, 46
Saglio, E., 176
Saint-Denis, Chronicle of, 35, 51, 52, 54
Saintyves, P., 271, 281, 283
Sala, Gabriel, 277
Saladinovo, 125, 211
Sale, W., 142, 144
Salem, 312
Salimbeni, F., 119
Salmoneus, 229
Salmony, A., 148

Saluzzo, Antonio da, Archbishop of Milan, 92
Salvianus, 74
Samoyedi, 171, 241, 264, 279, 280
Samson, 47, 48
San Bernardo, 77
Sánchez Ruipérez, M., 145
Sandor, A. I., 119
Sandy, G. N., 84
Santaéra, Emanuela, 123, 140
Sappho, 143
Sardinia, 246, 283, 284
Sargent, B., 224
Sarmatians, 214, 221
Sartenais, 166
Sas, S., 275, 279
Satia, *see* Abundia
Satan, 90, 94, 137, 297
Saturn, 270
Saussure, Ferdinand de, 20, 21, 29, 30, 294
Sauval, H., 58, 59
Savardun, 43
Savoia, Amadeo di, 297
Savoy, 67, 71, 72, 73, 77, 79, 80, 121
Saxus Grammaticus, 265, 293
Saxl, F., 270
Sayers, W., 174
Sbadilon, 256, 257, 288
Scalera McClintock, G., 114, 146
Scandinavia, 101, 135, 175, 181, 214, 278
Scavius, 71
Schastel le mort, 108
Schauenburg, K., 272
Scheer, E., 118
Scheffer, J., 152
Schemëing, K., 292
Schenda, R., 174
Schieler, K., 82
Schiering, W., 144
Schilling, R., 291
Schleicher, J., 225
Schmidt, B., 180, 278
Schmidt, J., 270
Schmidt, L., 18, 147, 148, 202, 248, 285
Schmidt, W., 294
Schmitt, J-C., 29, 56, 62, 83, 115, 199, 201, 294, 311
Schnapp-Gourbeillon, A., 276
Scholem, Gershom, 174, 280
Schöne, A., 151
Schreckenberg, H., 55
Schreiber, H., 117
Schroeder, D., 180
Schubart, W., 203

Schubert, G. H. von, 180
Schulin, E., 82
Schulte, J., 28
Schwartz, J., 268
Sclavonia, 77
Scobie, A., 311
Scotland, 96, 100, 103, 108, 113, 121, 246, 247, 302
Scott Littleton, C., 221
Scylas, 253, 254, 287
Scythia, 133, 157, 162, 207, 208, 209, 210, 211, 212, 213, 214, 215, 217, 218, 219, 220, 221, 222, 223, 231, 237, 249, 251, 253, 254, 257, 258, 272, 286, 287, 289, 301
Sebillot, P., 283
Seiber, F., 114
Seligmann, S., 146
Semeren, 45
Semites, 247
Senn, H. A., 179
Seppilli, A., 285
Serbia, 77, 155, 187, 188, 189, 190, 195, 246, 283
Sergi, G., 85
(Servius), 233, 276
Setti, G., 271
Settis, Salvatore, 24
Settis Frugoni, C., 119
Severi, C., 292
Sfameni Gasparro, G., 141
Shakespeare, William, 117
Shatzmiller, J., 56, 81
Sheba, Queen of, 258
Sheh-Hsien, 248
Siberia, 134, 136, 149, 171, 180, 181, 194, 208, 210, 211, 213, 214, 215, 216, 218, 219, 222, 223, 289, 296, 305
Sibilla, 'Wise', 96, 108, 122, 132, 302
Sibillia de Fraguliati, 92, 93, 100, 102
Sicily, 63, 122, 123, 124, 125, 129, 133, 246, 283
Sieg, G., 202
Siena, 297, 299
Sigüenza, 128
Silesia, 212, 304
Silistria 183
Simpson, J., 150
Simrock, K., 288
Sinai valley, 46
Singer, S., 119, 120, 121, 145
Sinor, D., 224
Sion, 73
Siuts, H., 176, 281

Skeels, D., 275
Skeistan, 153
Sköld, H., 222
Slavs, 155, 157, 158, 160, 161, 171, 188, 190, 313
Slawik, A., 203
Slobozia, 200
Slovakia, 306
Smet, J-J. de, 81
Snorri Sturlusson, 134, 139
Soccia, 167
Socrates, 265
Söderhjelm, W., 121
Sokoliçek, F., 278
Solomon, King, 46, 258
Sophocles, 227, 228, 230, 234, 235, 237
Soslan, 165, 209, 219, 242, 263, 280, 287
Soubiran, J., 142
Sourvinou (later Sourvinou-Inwood), C., 143, 145, 269, 270
Spain, 101, 128, 133
Spanhol, Fertand, 41, 43
Spanos, N. P., 312
Sparta, 191, 233
Speier, 176
Špet, Gustav, 270
Speyer, W., 83, 84, 274
Sphinx, 228, 230, 236, 268, 269, 271
Spina, B., 146
Split, 247
Spoleto, 302, 309
St Augustine, 74, 84, 137, 196, 198
St Basil, 179
St Catherine *de monte Rotomagi*, monastery, 33, 62
St Ciliano, 104
St Dasius, 183, 197, 199
St George, 179
St Germaine, 247
St Germanus, 94, 100, 111, 134, 135
St John, 153, 179
St Lucy, 153
St Matthew, 179
St Mochua Cuanus, 147
St Moritz, 67
St Patrick, 109
St Pharaildis, 134, 147, 148
St Stephen of Condom, Monastery, 33
St Sylvester, 163
St Theodore, 190, 201
St Walpurgis, 137
Stammler, W., 119
Starobinski, Jean, 29
Staub, F., 85

Stephen of Bourbon, 301
Steinberg, A., 82
Steiner, A., 177
Steiner, G., 277
Steiner, P., 270
Stewart, C. T., 174
Stiglitz. R., 143, 150
Stinton, T. C. W., 143
Stockstadt, 128
Stone, Lawrence, 25
Storm, G., 181
Strabo, 133, 220, 236, 283
Strangfeld, G. J. 112
Strasbourg, 68, 72, 101
Straubergs, E., 175
Strauch, E., 176
Strömbäck, D., 151, 181, 278, 292
Stubbs, 215
Studer, E., 173
Stuessy, T. F., 30
Stumpfl, R., 278
Stussi, Alfredo, 24
Styria, 78
Styx river, 231
Suburra, 196
Sudzuki, 0., 223
Suisse Romande, 109
Surdis, Lorenzo de, 299
Surselva, 192, 202
Svani, 255
Svoronos, J. N., 273
Swabia, 182
Sweden, 137, 225, 265
Swift, G., 314
Switzerland, 104, 121, 191, 193, 308
Sydow, C. W. von, 147
Syracuse, 124, 277
Syrdon, 165
Szabó, A., 279, 280
Szentléleky, T., 118
Szeftel, M., 174, 292
Szged, 181
Szepessy, T., 83
Szombathely, *see* Claudia Savaria

Tabor, Mount, 45
Tacitus, 192, 234
Taeger, F., 221
Tallgren, A., 218
Tannhäuser legend, 108, 109
Tantalus, 249, 250, 285
Taranis, 147
Tarantasia, 68
Tarn, 59

Index

Tartarotti, Girolamo, 111, 138, 151, 311
Tartars, 209
Tatra mountains, 306
Taylor, A., 275, 281
Taylor, C. H., 57, 58
Tbilisi, 191
Tchango, 194
Tedeschi, J., 311
Telegonus, 229, 270, 271
Telemachus, 229
Telephus, 229, 230, 235, 236, 238, 270, 271, 274
Telesphorus, 293
Telmon, Tullio, 314
Templars, Order of the, 52
Tereno, 226
Tertullian, 74
Teruel, 50, 51, 52
Tesauro, 268
Thebes, 136, 227, 235, 237
Theseus, 229, 230, 231, 235, 238, 270, 271
Thessaly, 116, 186, 187, 188, 192, 227
Thestius, 233
Thetis, 231, 232, 272, 273
Thevenot, E., 116, 118
Thibaudet, A., 267
Thiess, 14, 153, 154, 155, 156, 157, 158, 159, 164, 165, 166, 171, 174, 202
Thrace, 125, 128, 210, 211, 212, 213, 214, 254, 285
Tholosan, Claude, 73, 83
Thomas, A. C., 221
Thomas, Keith, 2, 3, 4, 5, 6, 8, 14, 24, 25, 26, 27
Thomasius, 138
Thompson, E. P., 5, 25, 26, 201
Thomsen, A., 148
Thonon, 67
Thor, 134, 135, 147, 247, 283, 287
Thorgeir, 263
Thorstein, 150
Thucydides, 233, 234, 273
Thyestes, 229
Tibet, 289
Tilak, Bâl Gangâdhar, 224
Timaeus, 124, 125
Tiresias, 237, 276
Tissot, P., 113
Titans, 252, 254, 286
Tobler, L., 85
Tobler, O., 310
Todi, 299, 300
Tomis, 188
Tommasini, G. F., 160

Tommasini, O., 309
Tommaso de Cantimpré, 147
Toschi, P., 293
Tosseus, 233
Totenheer, 153
Toffolo di Buri, 170
Toulouse, 39, 41, 42, 43, 49, 86, 103
Toulouse, Archbishop of, 53
Touraine, 45
Tours, 36, 39, 44, 49, 57
Trachtenberg, J., 25, 55, 56, 57
Travalle, 297
Trebbi, G., 177
Trentino, 115, 120, 133
Trento, 97
Treviri, 104
Treviri, Council of, 91
Treviso, 306
Trevor-Roper, Hugh, 2, 3, 4, 25, 27
Trexler, Richard, 30
Trieber, C., 275
Trigt, F. van, 276
Triton, Lake, 212
Troiani, L., 55
Troina, 124
Tron, Daniele, 308
Troppau, 56
Troy, 238
Troyes, Chrétien de, *see* Chrétien de Troyes
Trubetzkoy (Troubeckoj), N.S., 221, 222, 308
Tshudi, Gilg, 192, 202, 203
Tuang Ch'eng-Shih, 248, 283
Tukana, 300
Tungusi, 171, 211, 212, 220
Tunis, King of, 47, 48, 52, 60
Turkey, 161, 162, 163, 168, 177, 186
Turner, R. L., 313
Turner, V., 56
Tuscany, 200
Tylor, E. B., 281
Typhon, 230
Tyro, 229, 235, 270
Tyre, 209
Tyrol, 117, 193, 246, 247
Tzetzes, 119

Uazilea, *see* Elijah
Ucko, P.Y., 279
Ugri, 203
Ukraine, 29, 173, 186, 187, 200, 306
Ulysses, 107, 118, 229, 234, 265, 271
Umbria, 108, 320
Unholde, *see* Holda

Unruh, G. C. von, 176
Unzent, 43
Uppsala, 158, 225
Urals, 220, 258
Uranus, 229
Urechia, V. A., 199
Ursa Major, 126
Ursa Minor, 126
Urso, 127
Usener, H., 141, 198, 204, 272, 281, 282
Usque, S., 81
Utley, F. L., 120
Uzerche, 41, 52

Vaillant, A., 84
Vaissete, Dom J., 55
Vajda, L., 180, 181
Valais, 72, 73, 77, 89, 101, 154, 159, 172, 194
Valbonnais, J-P., 81
Val Chisone, 302
Valdo (Valdes), 76
Val di Fassa, 94, 95, 96, 100, 108, 112, 129, 130, 132
Val di Fiemme, 96, 100, 108, 132, 133, 146
Val di Lanzo, 77
Val di Susa, 302
Val Fressinières, 302
Val Germanasca, 302
Vallentin du Cheylard, R., 142
Valois, N., 57, 58, 61
Val Pellice, 302
Val Pute, 302
Valtellina, 296
Varagnac, A., 198
Varga, M., 177
Varty, K., 119
Vassallo, Giovani, 140
Vasteenberghe, E., 122
Vaud, 56, 79, 86
Vaux-en-Bugey, 80
Velvendos, 188
Venaissin, 68
Veneto, 306, 307
Venturi, F., 151
Venus, 108, 109
Venus, Mount of, 108, 109
Verelde, 148; *see also* Holda
Verga, E., 111
Vernadsky, G., 180, 218, 221, 289
Vernant, Jean-Pierre, 17, 19, 20, 24, 28, 29, 30, 144, 149, 267, 269, 270, 274, 275, 277, 285, 286, 294
Verona, 94

Verrius Flaccus, 293
Versnel, H. S., 286
Veselovskij, A., *see* Wesselofsky, A
Vevey, 67
Via Sacra, 196
Vian, F., 271
Viard, J., 58, 61
Vicenza, 117
Vicomercato, 92
Vidal, J-M., 56, 57, 58, 60, 61, 62, 110
Vidal-Naquet, Pierre, 120, 201, 225, 269, 270, 273, 274, 275, 285
Vienna, 56
Vietnam, 246, 282
Villanueva, J., 81
Villeneuve, 67
Vincent, 61
Vincent of Beauvais, 51, 52, 70, 95, 100, 101
Virgil, 233, 293
Visigoths, 214
Viski, K., 199, 293
Vizille, 65
Vogel, C., 110
Vogul-Ostak, 258, 259, 262, 288
Voigt, 148
Volch Vseslav'evič, 155, 174
Volker, M., 120
de Vries, J., 114, 115, 116, 149, 151, 152, 292
Vseslav, Prince, 155
Vuia, R., 200
Vulcan, 234, 274, 276
Vulson, M., 312

Wace, A. J. B., 199
Wadding, 6, 82
Wadge, R., 221
Wagner, Richard, 30
Wagner, H., 279
Walbank, M. B., 143
Walcot, P., 268, 276
Waldensians, 7, 24, 75, 76, 77, 78, 79, 302, 312
Wales, 108
Waley, A., 282, 284
Walkyrie, 114
Walter, E., 115
Waltzing, J-P., 84
Warren, W. F., 224
Waser, O., 310
Wasserschleben, F. W. H., 110
Wasson, R. G., 288, 313, 314
Watson, W., 218

Webster, G., 117
Wehrli, F., 268, 275
Wehse, R., 281
Weicker, G., 310
Weiser, L. (also Weiser-Aall), 114, 150, 173, 176, 276
Welcker, F. G., 119, 141, 142
Wendel, C., 142
Weniger, L. 201
Werner, R., 289
Wesselofsky, A., 110, 114, 116, 148
West, M. L., 286, 287
Whatmough, J., 145
Wickersheimer, E., 81, 82
Wickman, B., 224
Wierschin, M., 119
Wiesner, J., 218
Wikander, S., 173, 313
Willets, R. F., 143
Wilamowitz-Moellendorff, U., 141, 142, 149, 268, 277
'Wilken', 174; *see also* Witekind, Hermann
William of Anvergne, 95, 100, 105, 117
William de Villers, 147
Winderkens, A. J. van, 145
Winkerlin, Juliane, 146
Winterthur, Chonrad Von, 68
Wissowa, G., 111, 274
Witekind, Hermann, 156, 157, 158, 175
Witkoswki, G., 151
Witte, H., 82
Wittgenstein, Ludwig, 15, 16, 27, 28, 177, 179, 204, 222
Wittenberg, 156, 157, 158, 304
Wolf, J. W., 147

Wolfram, R., 199, 200, 201
Wolfram, G., 82
Wolters, P., 150
Worms, 104
Wotan, 101, 102, 114, 201, 265
Wu, 239
Wunschilburg, Thomas 121
Würzburg, 311

Xanthakou, M., 284
Xevsur, 300

Yakuti, 211, 241, 263, 291
Yorak Samoyedi, *see* Samoyedi
Yo the Great, 239

Zabin, Sultan of Azar, 45
Zagreus, 252
Zahan, D., 279
Zahavi, Naama, 312
Zečivić, S., 199
Zeigeler, W., 112
Zeitler, J., 140
Zeus, 126, 127, 128, 156, 201, 211, 229, 230, 231, 238, 250, 251, 252, 257, 270, 271, 272, 277, 286
Zguta, R., 181
Zichy, E. de, 291
Ziletti, F., 146
Zolla, E., 292
Zoroaster, 209, 305
Zuan della piatte, 108, 109
Zuntz, G., 141, 272
Zupitza, E., 145
Zwicker, Peter, 78, 85

ABOUT THE AUTHOR

Carlo Ginzburg was born in Turin in 1939. He taught for many years at the University of Bologna, and has won world-wide acclaim for his scholarship in "microhistory"—the reconstruction of events or beliefs that have fallen outside the scope of major historical study. His previous books include *The Night Battles*, *The Enigma of Piero*, *The Cheese and the Worms*, and *Myths, Emblems, and Clues*. Ginzburg currently teaches history at the University of California in Los Angeles.

ABOUT THE TRANSLATOR

Raymond Rosenthal received the Present Tense Award for his translation of Primo Levi's *The Periodic Table* and has been nominated for two National Book Awards for translation. Among the other books he has translated from the Italian are Pietro Aretino's *Dialogues* and Primo Levi's *Other People's Trades*, *The Drowned and the Saved*, and *The Mirror Maker*.